THE WORLD IN THE GRIP OF AN IDEA

To T. G. Allen
To loosen the Grip —
Clarence B. Carson

Contents

Dedication

THIS WORK IS DEDICATED in sorrow to and with compassion for all the victims of the Idea.

It is dedicated to all who have been deprived in one way or another of liberty or property because of the Idea, to all who have been pressured, intimidated, coerced, beaten, or tortured because of it, and to all who have suffered deprivation as a result of efforts to put the Idea into effect.

But, above all, it is dedicated to those who have lost their lives in consequence of efforts to realize the Idea. None knows their exact number, except God, and attempts to arrive at a figure for them are fated to be no better than informed estimates. One thing we do know, the total number of the dead is an awesome and awful number. It is probable that more than 100 million souls have been dispatched by purges, murders, intolerable conditions of imprisonment and labor, famine, in transit to prisons, civil war, and such like. Numbers, however, are but abstractions; they can convey but little of the anguish, heartbreak, disorientation, fear, and misery that have surrounded all this. It is necessary, therefore, to picture the horrors of this century with as much concreteness as possible, horrors wrought by fixation upon the Idea.

To that end, this work is especially dedicated

To Czar Nicholas II, his immediate family, and household.

To all the victims on all sides, or none, of the civil war which raged in Russia, 1918-1921.

To all the landlords, businessmen, and entrepreneurs in the Soviet

Union who were scourged and denied their rights.

To the Kulaks who were driven from their farms to suffer and die during Stalin's forced collectivization of agriculture, and to all the peasants who suffered the bitter famine wrought by this effort in the early 1930's.

To the members of the Communist Party who were victims of Stalin's Purge in the mid-1930's. True, they had tied the nooses around their necks by being Party members, but compassion requires that we recognize them also as victims.

To ranking military men purged by Stalin just before World War II, and especially to all who suffered as a result of the lack of experienced leadership in the Soviet armies.

To those who have been interrogated by the Soviet secret police who have brought discredit to every combination of letters of the alphabet which have been attached to them, to those placed on the "conveyor" and tormented in session after session to wring confessions from them, to those who were beaten, isolated from human contact in tiny cells and made to endure unbearable tortures, and most especially to those who endured it or died rather than to betray others with false confessions.

To those who suffered ignominious death by being shot in the back of the head with a pistol.

To those who died in transit to remote slave labor camps.

To those of many religious faiths — Jews, Moslems, and Christians — who have suffered for their beliefs, and especialy to those evangelical Christians who have persevered against all odds to cling to their faith and to pass it on unsullied by the Idea.

To all those who have suffered and died in the camps of the Gulag Archipelago, and especially those consigned to the bitter cold to work in logging or mining camps in Siberia.

To the victims of Soviet aggression in Eastern Europe, and especially to the people of Poland who endured so much, first from the Nazis and then from the Communists. To the Polish officers shot down in the Katyn Forest by Soviet forces.

To all the victims of Nazi tyranny, and more particulary to those Jews who were deprived of property and status within Germany and subjected to humiliating discrimination, who were victims of a terror campaign against them, and especially to those Jews from all over Europe who were rounded up and shipped to concentration camps to suffer depersonalization and, in many cases, death; to those Jews who were herded into gas chambers to suffer the horrible death by asphyxiation, to have their pitiful attire stripped from their bodies, even the gold extracted from their teeth, and to have their bodies burned in ovens; to those wandering people, the Gypsies, for whom there was no place in Hitler's New Order but the concentration camps; to those other pariahs of nationalism, the Jehovah's Witnesses, who showed unexampled courage in their suffering at the hands of the Nazis.

To the victims of communism as it has spread around the world, and more particularly to refugees of many lands and to all people displaced by the ideological whims of the rulers of this century under the sway of the Idea; to the victims of terror and violence in all the countries of the earth as communism spreads; to those tormented by the Red Guard in China during the cultural revolution; to the Chinese on Taiwan who were driven from their homeland; to the Cambodians, Laotians, Vietnamese, Angolans, Letts, Finns, and all who have experienced the onslaught of communism.

And, to individuals everywhere (all of us) who have been beset by governments, dwarfed by organizations, and intimidated by numbers, and more particularly to the victims of inflation; to those who have seen their independence eroded away and management of their affairs taken from them; to all who have suffered as the assault upon custom, tradition, convention, norms, and civility, which is the underlying thrust of revolution in this age, has produced a wave of obscenity, vulgarity, and assorted atrocities on the mind and spirit of man.

May the evocation of the memories of the atrocities of our era raise such a gorge in the throats of all decent people that they will forever after be unable to swallow the Idea or any significant portion of it.

Preface

IF THE TWENTIETH CENTURY were a play, it would have long since driven the audience mad. The incongruity between the words spoken by the actors and the action on stage would be too great to be borne. The actors speak of peace, prosperity, progress, freedom, brotherly love, and a forthcoming end to the age-old ills of mankind. The action on stage has been world wars, dictatorships, slave labor camps, police states, totalitarianism, class and racial animosities, terrorism, and a more general coarsening of human behavior. The promises bespeak a beatific vision; the reality is a descending barbarism. We are continually led to believe that the barbarism is a temporary phenomenon, and that just beyond it lies the realization of the bright promise. Meanwhile, the terror and disorder continue to spread.

It is my contention that it is possible to grasp what has been happening in the twentieth century on a worldwide scale. To do so, it is necessary to ignore the promises, to keep our eyes firmly fixed on the action, and to attend to the ideas that are producing it. This work is an effort to do just this; it is, therefore, a new interpretation of twentieth century history, an interpretation in terms of ideas and their application in country after country. It has, of course, been necessary to focus most of the attention on a few countries. The plan of the book is, I hope, made sufficiently clear in the table of contents, so I will make no effort to describe it here. However, I should note that there is a historical pattern to the presentation. It begins in the nineteenth century, with the development of certain ideas, and proceeds to their application in the twentieth century. Since much of the account is made by taking up individual countries in different sections of the book, there is of necessity some going back and forth in time. Still, the central development in each section occurs later in time than the one in the section which precedes it. Thus, the Bolshevik Revolution precedes the Nazi revolution, and the triumph of the Labour Party in England follows both of these. And the Cold War, which is the concluding historical section of the book, follows what goes before, both logically and historically.

Despite the length of this work, it has been necessary to be rigorously selective in what is presented. For each anecdote told, a hundred had to be left out. For each fact presented, there were many others that might have been included. In many places, I have tried to make up for these necessary omissions with summary statements. It is my hope that my readers will supplement these with their own knowledge of concrete detail, for those who are able to do so will bring more vitality to the work than it possesses. This is my way of saying that I believe that the more evidence that is brought to bear on my thesis, the stronger it becomes. Had I known more than I do, it might have been possible to compress it in a shorter book, but the temptation would have been great to make it that much longer.

This work would not have been possible without the aid and encouragement I received from the Foundation for Economic Education. The central part of the work appeared serially and in somewhat different form in the foundation's publication, the *Freeman,* beginning with the January, 1977, issue and concluding with the one for September, 1979. In addition, the section on England was published in the same journal from December, 1968, through July, 1969. It has, of course, been revised to fit into the context of this book. I am especially grateful to Dr. Paul Poirot, editor of the *Freeman* over these years, for his encouragement, support, and enthusiasm for the project. He is without peer in promptness, and has few equals in decisiveness.

I am grateful to my family, too, for their endurance of what has to be considerable inconvenience — living with me when I am in the throes of writing. And I am especially grateful to my wife, who has been there when I needed her and has been thoughtful enough to stay out of the way when I didn't.

Credit for anything that is meritorious in the book must be shared with all who have helped in any way with it. However, the responsibility for any defects that may be discovered is mine alone. And I accept it, albeit with trepidation.

THE WORLD
IN THE
GRIP
OF AN
IDEA

Book I
The Idea

1
The Idea

SOMETIMES A PHRASE is concocted to say something that hardly needed saying before. These phrases should be of interest, for they frequently tell us something about what is new and different to our time. Such a phrase is "displaced person." It came into currency sometime around World War II. "DP's," they were called collectively just after World War II, people who could be seen wandering here and there across Europe, the remains of their pitiful possessions on their backs. They were Germans driven from their homes by the Czechoslovak government, Poles, Russians, Romanians, Letts, Ukrainians, brought thither to work for the Germans and now uncertain what to do or where to go. They were Jews now seeking some new homeland. War had caused these peoples to be transported hither and yon; now revolution was completing their displacement.

"Displaced" is a strange word to use in connection with persons. The most common word formed from "displace" is "displacement." It is used to describe what happens, for example, when a body is placed in water. A certain volume of water is "displaced," is moved from where it was to a new location. It is a mechanical operation in character. That is why it is unusual to use such a phrase to refer to people. They have wills; they may choose; they are not something to be "displaced," as if they were water. Yet, the phrase is apt. These people were as near to being displaced as people are likely to be. They had been taken, held, and moved against their wills. The human forces that swept over them had displaced them.

The phrase, "displaced person," has fallen into disuse. Many young

3

people may never have heard it. This is unfortunate, for it may be the best single phrase to describe much that has happened in the twentieth century. It could well be used to describe the Russian nobility who sought refuge elsewhere following or before the victory of the Red Army. Kaiser Wilhelm II became a displaced person when his government fell at the end of World War I. Many persons were displaced after that war as the boundaries in central and eastern Europe were redrawn. Most of the Jews in Germany and Poland were displaced in one way or another by the Nazis. Millions were displaced when India and Pakistan were divided into separate states. Arabs were displaced by the creation of the modern state of Israel. Millions of Chinese Nationalists were displaced by the victory of the Communists on the mainland of China. Many white residents were displaced from Africa when black rule was established in countries on that continent. Tens of thousands of Cubans have been displaced by the Castro regime. The same has now happened, or is happening, in South Vietnam.

I am aware, of course, that some of the peoples referred to above are not technically displaced persons; they are what is known as refugees. But they are, nonetheless, displaced persons. They have been displaced by revolutions and changes over which they had no control. They may have chosen to migrate, but they did not choose to lose their places which led them to migrate. Men are as surely displaced by revolutions as water is displaced when a ship is launched. This displacement, and the efforts to avoid displacement, are a major theme of this study.

If the idea of displacement is to serve adequately, however, it must be expanded. There is literal displacement and figurative displacement. In the figurative sense, it is possible to be displaced and yet never actually move from the original location. Partial and figurative displacement is widespread in the twentieth century. It is not as dramatic as the actual displacement but it is just as real in its own way.

Being in place for a person means being in familiar surroundings. One's sense of being in place grows out of familiarity with the customs, the traditions, the mores, and styles and either having adjusted to or being in accord with them. The sense of being in place, too, is bolstered by control of one's life and livelihood. Owning property actually provides a place for a person. (Our folk language recognizes this role for property by calling a homestead a "place" or, sometimes, a "home-place.") Place also has the connotation of position, as within a family, a community, an industry, or some organization. There is, too, man's place in the chain of being ("a little lower than the angels," it used to be held). Our sense of order, of security, and of well-being are connected with being in place. These, in turn, are essential to creativity and productivity.

The world is in the grip of an idea today. The thrust of the idea is to replace man, to remove the supports for him in the position that he occupies and to force him into a new place or configuration. The impact of the application of this idea is to displace people. The degree of the displacement is in some sort of proportion to the force exerted but in its subtler dimensions depends on the sensitivities of the persons involved.

Men resist this displacement in a variety of ways. But it is no easy matter to resist it. Resistance requires a place to stand. Any degree of displacement makes outright resistance difficult, and it becomes precarious or dangerous to resist by confrontation. As displacement becomes more pronounced, people tend to conform outwardly but to resist by evasion and by subtle attempts to manipulate power to their own advantage.

Literal displacement is easy enough to recognize. We may not be generally aware of the scale on which it has occurred in the twentieth century, but it does come to our attention from time to time in the midst of wars and revolutions as people flee from the advancing tyranny or are shoved out of their homelands. Figurative displacement, however, is not so readily discerned. After all, if people remain more or less where they have been, how could we tell that they have been displaced? The answer is this: we know it mainly by the way they behave toward the power over them. People who are being displaced in place, so to speak, attempt to thwart the displacing power by evasion and manipulation.

This sort of activity is by now well developed and deeply ingrained in the Soviet Union. Of course, millions have been displaced in that unhappy land over the years, the most dramatic displacement being that of those transported to slave labor camps. But those who never suffered such displacements have undergone a different kind of displacement. The reaction of these is discussed at length by Hedrick Smith in his recent book on *The Russians*. A recurring theme is that of how Russians make life tolerable for themselves within the repressive system by evasions, manipulations, connivings, and other imaginative ways. He describes it this way:

It fascinated me that there were such cunning devices for foiling the authorities and that Russians, of all people, supposedly being a nation of sheep, would resort to such expedients. For the notion of the totalitarian state, perhaps useful for political scientists as a bird's eye view of Soviet society, misses the

5

human quotient. It conjures up the picture of robots living a regimented existence. Most of the time, it is true, the vast majority of Russians go through the motions of publicly observing the rules. But privately, they are often exerting enormous efforts and practicing uncommon ingenuity to bend or slip through these rules for their own personal ends. "Slipping through is our national pastime," a woman lawyer smilingly commented to me.

These people, it appears, have no hope of altering the power over them, their only hope being to carve out as much of a place for themselves as they can in hidden niches. Smith describes their attitude this way:

> You also find an unbridgable chasm between the leaders and the led: between "Them" at the top and "us" at the bottom....
> For the common man, politics and the power of the leaders are like the natural elements. No ordinary mortal — worker, peasant, intellectual, Party member — dreams of doing anything about them. They are simply a given, a fact, irresistible and immutable... [1]

Something akin to this is happening in the United States. The thrust of the government is something alien to the American people, yet apparently beyond their power to alter. Americans strive to evade the impact of the government's thrust or to manipulate it to their advantage.

Many exert extensive efforts to keep as much of their income as possible. They pay lawyers, hire tax consultants, tailor their activities, arrange their accounts and investments so as to pay as little by way of taxes as possible. They seek out investments which will enable them to delay for the longest time the payment of taxes on whatever they have. They use whatever influence they can muster to get as large a tax write-off as possible in their particular undertakings. They ferret out just those investments which provide the best hedges against inflation.

Many businessmen have given up efforts to prevent government regulation of their activities. But they exert massive efforts to make these regulations work to their advantage. When there was talk of deregulation of the airline industry recently, several top executives in the industry spoke out against it. On the other hand, they do not spare expense in attempting to get advantages for their own companies, and sometimes for the whole industry. They collect reams of data, hire astute lawyers, propagandize, and otherwise seek to influence government policy in their behalf.

It is generally claimed that "white collar crimes" are on the increase in America. "White collar crimes," for any who do not know, are crimes committed by evasion, avoidance, and violation of government regulations, controls, and restrictions on economic activities. "Tokenism" has even entered our language as a word to signify not so much minimal compliance with regulations as making an appearance of complying by doing one or a few times what is generally required.

Americans in general often ignore or violate the rules and regulations they are supposed to observe. I had occasion recently to spend an hour or so in and about the lobby in a large hospital. There were signs all over the place: knock before entering, no smoking in this area, wear shoes and shirts for health reasons, exit here, enter there, go there, and return here, among others.

The state legislature had seen fit in its last session to make it a misdemeanor to smoke in public places where signs had been erected prohibiting it. Even so, I saw a hospital attendant dressed in white light a cigarette for a patient in such an area. Other people lighted up, too, oblivious to the law under which they might be punished. Although shoes were prescribed, a scantily clad young woman sitting in the row of chairs behind me hoisted her bare feet up on the back of the chair beside me. Other bare feet were in evidence. And, though shirts were prescribed, I had hardly gained entrance to the hospital before I saw a young man who had obviously just been treated walking down the hallway sans shirt.

There is considerable evidence that this practice of evasion has entered the legislative and executive branches of the government as well. Some members of Congress practice fairly open ways of evading the laws that they lay down for themselves. Nepotism on the staffs of Congressmen is now prohibited. Even so, Jack Anderson has reported a considerable number of instances where wives, children, and other relatives of Congressmen are employed by their colleagues or by Congressional committees. Undoubtedly such employment is a thinly disguised evasion of the rule against nepotism.

But the best example may well be that of behavior in the Executive branch connected with the Watergate Affair. The Nixon men behaved like displaced persons. Their actions were not what we would expect of men holding the reins of political power. They were for all the world like those out of power, like petty plotters in a "banana republic" seeking to spring themselves into power by some coup. They were not confidently exercising the full powers of government to consolidate their positions within it. They went outside the government to bring in men to violate the law. Then, they attempted to conceal from the government-at-large what they were doing. It was as if they were alien to the government.

There is an explanation for these developments, for the alienation from government, for the evasion and manipulation, for the displacement or efforts to displace which prompts it all. The explanation can be found in an idea. Ideas have consequences, the late Richard Weaver pointed out some years back in a powerful treatise on the subject. What we have been examining are consequences of an idea that efforts are being made to apply. The elective branches of the government in the United States have been in considerable degree displaced in the government by the bureaucracy and the judiciary. As the power and sway of government has grown, decision making has more and more shifted to the more permanent members and branches of government. As the grip of the idea increases, the displacement of all except those who wield power in the name of the idea becomes more pronounced.

What is the idea? Can it be named? That is not so easy to answer. There are names aplenty for the movements spawned by the idea. The most commonly used generic name for the movement is socialism. Some call it by the even more inclusive name of collectivism. The more virulent wing of the movement is known as communism. Another wing is called by such varied names as evolutionary socialism, gradualism, Fabianism, democratic socialism, and so on. At a deeper level, the broad general movement is called by the somewhat more obscure name, the new humanism.

These are useful terms, and anyone writing about the idea which has the world in its grip will surely find employment for them. But they do not name the idea, though the phrase — the new humanism — may come close to it. They actually name methods and emphases, not the idea which animates them. Even communists refer to socialism as the end and think of it as the idea, but it is not. It is a means, if it is anything. This does not mean that some people do not, as individuals, confuse these means with the end and the idea. Nothing is more likely than that they would, nor more certain than that they do. But these things named are offshoots of the idea, not the idea.

The animating idea has no name. It has no name because there is no name which its adherents accept. It is utopianism. But there is hardly a person to be found who will avow it as his belief. "Utopianism" is a contemptuous designation. In common usage, a utopian is one who is impractical and unrealistic. It has no name, probably, because to name a

8

thing is to risk trivializing it, to profane it, to circumscribe and limit it, and to vulgarize it.

The Second Commandment prescribes that God shall not be represented by any image. There is a deep insight behind this commandment. A god who can be represented by a statue is a god among other gods. He who cannot be represented in such a way is *the* God, the like of which there are no other gods. Whether some such insight has prevented the idea in question from being given a generally accepted name I do not know. It makes sense, however, that if the idea were named it would become an idea among ideas. It would become an idea to be examined, to be debated, possibly to be refuted, and certainly to be scrutinized.

Such treatment, the adherents of the idea apparently resist. They resist it by focusing upon the method for realizing it rather than the animating idea. The idea itself must be an unchallenged good. It must be the pearl beyond price, the holy grail, the Covenant borne in the Ark, and "The Lost Chord," all rolled into one. I have deliberately used religious terminology to evoke the character of the idea. For the animating idea is the root of a secular religion, the leading secular religion of our time. It catches up myriad vague longings set loose by the decline of religion, or, more precisely, it provides a faith with credible promises for those who no longer believe the promises of their traditional religions.

The idea is this: *To achieve human felicity on this earth by concerting all efforts toward its realization.* This is, on its face, a most attractive idea. A host of other ideas are clustered around it, too, adding to its glow, such ideas as: harmony, brotherhood, progress, peace, prosperity, comradeship, cooperation, equality, humanitarianism, solidarity, an end to the exploitation of man by man, fulfillment through sharing in a common effort, and so on. Who would deny that it would be good if we would all work together for the felicity of all? If this but animated us, would not all those barriers fall away which now separate man from man, group from group, race from race, and nation from nation? Think of the vast amount of energy expended on our contentions with one another. What if, instead, it were constructively employed for our mutual benefit and felicity? It is, indeed, an attractive idea, one to which men of good will are disposed to give their assent.

There is, however, a rather large fly in this ointment. In fact, there may be several, but let us focus on one. There is bountiful evidence that we are not in agreement as to what would constitute our felicity. One

9

man's felicity is often enough another's torment. One man's felicity entails climbing Mount Everest to stand at its crest amidst frigid howling winds. Another, probably most of us, would prefer to be at home watching the ascent on television, if that were possible. One man's felicity is a full stomach after a hearty meal, even if the eventual result is obesity. Another will deny himself perpetually in order to remain slim.

It is not that some of us do not share some of the same or similar preferences. It is rather that if we could be observed in the whole of our being and activity we would be seen to each have an individual pattern whose direction would be to maintain or achieve a sense of well-being or felicity. These patterns, in turn, give rise both to our achievements and to the conflicts and contests among us. Each of us appears to be determined to pursue his own well-being in his own way.

This individuality, these individual patterns, play hob with any concerted effort to achieve felicity. Utopians, or whatever they should be called, know this, of course. But they do not accept it as a permanent condition. If they did, they would have to give up their cause as hopeless at the outset. They do not conceive this individuality, this determination to pursue one's own interest in his own way, to be rooted in human nature and the conditions of life on this planet. Indeed, except as a figure of speech, they are not inclined to recognize that there is any such thing as human nature. It is just selfishness, they think, a selfishness that is culturally induced.

There are three prongs to the idea which has the world in its grip. The first has already been told: To achieve human felicity on this earth by concerting all efforts to its realization. The second is now before us, and can be stated in this way: *To root out, discredit, and discard all aspects of culture which cannot otherwise be altered to divest them of any role in inducing or supporting the individual's pursuit of his own self-interest.* The corollary of this is to develop an ethos which focuses attention on what is supposed to be the common good of humanity.

It is easy not to be aware of how radical socialism really is. For one thing, we have become acclimated to many ideas associated with it. For another, in lands where gradualism holds sway it is often not avowed as an ideology, and the whole pattern of activity associated with it is not perceived as stemming from it. Yet, it would probably not be possible to conceive a more radical idea than that of rooting out or altering everything in the culture that is individualistic.

Socialism is sometimes defined as the public ownership of the means of the production and distribution of goods. That is quite misleading. It is as if Christianity were defined as a belief in going to church on Sunday. The idea that has the world in its grip, an idea which may for practical purposes be called socialism, does not simply entail the alteration of ownership; it entails the alteration of the whole cultural environment.

How big an undertaking would this be? It is as big as, well, as big as all outdoors, or, perhaps, as big as all indoors, plus much that is outdoors as well. Man is to be transformed by the destruction or alteration of his culture. According to an old formulation, there is nature and nurture. Since nature is largely disallowed, there remains only nurture. What nurtures us, then, is the totality of the culture, as it is understood by those who hold these ideas. It is just about everything.

By what instrument is this transformation to be made? This brings us to the third prong of the idea. It is this: *Government is the instrument to be used to concert all efforts behind the realization of human felicity and the necessary destruction or alteration of culture.* Government was not the chosen instrument of those who forged this idea. It was quite often anathema to them. To use government to achieve human felicity would be akin to a notion such as that God should have used the Serpent as the means of redemption. The very attractiveness of the idea is that men must long to concert their efforts to achieve felicity. How could the use of force be introduced into the equation? Not by choice but out of necessity. The bent of men to pursue their own self-interest is so ingrained that only government could exorcise it. Force must be used to free men from the hold of selfishness. Hopefully, of course, government would be transformed in the process.

This, then, is a distillation of the idea that holds the world in its grip today. It is not only the idea underlying Soviet Communism or Chinese or Albanian Communism, but also the idea underlying the Fabianism of the British Labour Party, Swedish socialism, American liberalism, German Social Democracy, Canadian interventionism, and the thrust of government into people's lives on a consistent scale everywhere in the world today. There are particular articulations of the idea which are important and will be taken up, some of them, in their place. But the important point here is that they all arise from a certain root idea. They arise from a vision of the achievement of human felicity by a concerted effort by everyone to achieve it. All of them perceive the received culture as something to be destroyed or altered, depending on the exigencies of the situation. All of them use government in their attempts to get concerted efforts.

11

The proof of these assertions has not yet been introduced. It will be forthcoming, so much of it as can practically be adduced. But it is necessary to have this idea before us from the beginning. A great deal of energy has gone into confusing and obscuring the nature of socialism. In some countries, measures and activities are never linked to their socialist connection by their advocates. Thus, if the connections are to be shown, it must be understood from the beginning what is to be connected. The connection is between the root idea above and the great variety of socialist efforts going on in the world.

The idea that has the world in its grip is a totalitarian idea. It does not evince itself in that way in a good many lands as yet. It may never proceed to that point in some lands, but that does not keep it from being a totalitarian idea. The totalitarianism is implicit in the idea. If all constructive activity could be concerted to the end of achieving human felicity, everyone would be under the sway of the concerting force. It would be totalitarian whether the concerting force was some world-wide government, the people, or an idea. Whether it would produce felicity or not would be a moot question, for there would be no independent judgment to determine whether it was felicity or universal torment. It is the very condition of independence that one not be completely concerted. The advancement of the idea, then, is the advancement toward totalitairanism.

Even so, that is not the connection nor the impact that will occupy most of our attention. Nowhere has there been sufficient success in applying the idea that a people could be said to have concerted their efforts. What has happened, and is happening, is a struggle within lands where the efforts have been made to apply the idea. It is a struggle between men bent on pursuing their own self-interest and the rulers who are attempting to make them serve some other interest. It is the great undeclared war of our era, a war in which many of those most tenaciously defending themselves openly profess the social emphasis of the rulers. It is, in its deeper dimensions, the struggle of those being displaced against their displacers.

The impact which shall most occupy our attention is displacement. The attempt to remove the basis of individuality evinces itself as an assault upon the inherited culture. Indeed, all that has been inherited from the past becomes suspect to those under the sway of the idea, whether it should be called culture or not. The received social arrangements, the place of women in society, the place of men in society, the religious tradition, customs, habits, venerable modes of

12

address and ways of acting, everything which could conceivably give support to individuality comes under attack. The result is displacement.

Any man's actual as well as sense of place is culturally (as socialists use the word) derived. It is dependent upon the estimate of those among whom he lives and works. It relies upon continuity with the past. It is buttressed by family ties, duties, obligations, and achievements. His property, his savings, that which is owed to him and which he owes give solidity and backing to him. The teachings of his childhood have helped to form him. His religion may well provide him with transcendental support for his beliefs. A part of his definition as a being is that he is male or female with the meaning that has been packed into his understanding of the role of these. All the familiar adjuncts of his being — music, paintings, books, working instruments, language, furniture, and what not — are cultural artifacts which confirm and bolster his place.

The thrust of revolution in our time, and gradualism is piecemeal revolution, is not simply to divest us of ownership or control of our property. It is that, of course, but it is so much more. It is to divest us of our received culture. It is to break the ties that bind the members of family to one another. It is to sever religion from education. It is to interpenetrate every relationship with the power of the state, not in support of the individual but to have the relation determined by social imperatives. It is to so alter the familiar adjuncts to our being that they are no longer ours but belong to something beyond us. It is to blur the distinctions between male and female, to merge the concept of adult and child, to cut away the authority of culture, and to leave us naked.

The near perfect symbol of what is aimed at is public nudity. Clothes do serve some useful purposes: to keep us warm in some climes, to shield us from the burning rays of the sun in others, and pockets are convenient places to store odds and ends. Aside from that, though, clothes are emblems of all the received culture by which we maintain our privacy, define our status, and establish our independent realm. To be naked in public means to most of us to be exposed and helpless. Our last defenses are gone; we are at the mercy of all who behold us.

Those who claim that nudity would free us do not understand the matter well. To be disrobed in public no more frees us than to be plucked frees a chicken or to have the hair scraped off frees a hog. Just as the removal of their natural covering prepares animals to be consumed so the removal of the clothes of a person makes him available to be used by others. The removal of cultural protection is the prelude to tyranny.

13

Two nineteenth-century fantasies come to mind. The first was written by the beloved teller of fairy tales, Hans Christian Andersen, called "The Emperor's New Clothes." Men posing as clothiers appeared before the emperor and promised to make new clothes for him. But they warned that anyone who was not suited to his job would be unable to see them. The word spread both that the emperor was to get new clothes and that they would be invisible to those unsuited to their work. On the appointed day, an elaborate charade got underway. The non-clothes had been delivered to the palace. Yet neither those appointed to dress him nor the emperor himself would admit that there were no clothes; they went through the motions of dressing him and he of admiring his new haberdashery. The farce continued even when the emperor went before the public in a parade. At first, all pretended that the emperor was fully clothed, for none wished to admit the possibility that he alone could not see them because he was unsuited to his job. At last, however, a child, who would hardly be intimidated by this possibility, declared that the emperor had no clothes. That blew the cover, as we would say, or rather the lack of cover, and others could admit also that the emperor had no clothes.

The second fantasy is from *Sartor Resartus,* Thomas Carlyle's satirical treatise on clothes. First, Carlyle imagines the king bereft of his clothes in public:

"What would Majesty do, could such an accident befall in reality; should the buttons all simultaneously start, and the solid wool evaporate, in very Deed, as here in Dream? *Ach Gott!* How each skulks into the nearest hiding place; their high State Tragedy ... becomes a Pickleherring-Farce to weep at, which is the worst kind of Farce; *the tables* (according to Horace), and with them, the whole fabric of Government, Legislation, Property, Police, and Civilised Society, *are dissolved,* in wails and howls."

He continues with a vision of the House of Lords in a similar state:

Lives the man that can figure a naked Duke of Windlestraw addressing a naked House of Lords? Imagination ... recoils on itself, and will not forward with the picture. [2]

Neither of these fine writers lived to learn of the shocking denouement to their fantasies in the real life drama of twentieth-century revolution, a denouement, let it be said, which neither could have intended nor have wittingly contributed. Nonetheless, the brutal murder of Czar Nicholas II of Russia, his immediate family and their

14

attendants by their Communist captors is by extension a denouement to them. Here is a recent account of that horrendous event. As the account is taken up, the Czar, his family and their attendants have just been herded into a small basement room and told that they are to be shot:

Nicholas, his arm still around Alexis, began to rise from his chair to protect his wife and son. He had just time to say "What ...?" before Yurovsky pointed his revolver directly at the Tsar's head and fired. Nicholas died instantly. Alexandra had time only to raise her hand and make the sign of the cross before she too was killed by a single bullet. Olga, Tatiana and Marie, standing behind their mother, were hit and died quickly. Botkin, Kharitonov and Trupp also fell in the hail of bullets. Demidova, the maid, survived the first volley, and rather than reload, the executioners took rifles from the next room and pursued her, stabbing with bayonets. Screaming, running back and forth along the wall like a trapped animal, she tried to fend them off with the cushion. At last she fell, pierced by bayonets more than thirty times. Jimmy the spaniel was killed when his head was crushed by a rifle butt.

The room, filled with the smoke and stench of gunpowder, became suddenly quiet. Blood was running in streams from the bodies on the floor. Then there was a movement and a low groan. Alexis [heir to the throne, afflicted during his brief life with crippling hemophilia], lying on the floor still in the arms of the Tsar, feebly moved his hand to clutch his father's coat. Savagely, one of the executioners kicked the Tsarevich in the head with his heavy boot. Yurovsky stepped up and fired two shots into the boy's ear. Just at that moment, Anastasia, who had only fainted, regained consciousness and screamed. With bayonets and rifle butts, the entire band turned on her. In a moment, she too lay still. It was ended. [3]

Life was ended, but not the gruesome scenario. The bodies were wrapped in sheets, loaded on a truck, and taken to another location. There they were dismembered with saws and axes, burned, and their bones dissolved with acid. What remained was then thrown down a mine shaft. This ghoulish undertaking had taken the better part of three days. Though these murders had only been initially authorized by a local soviet's ruling body, their acts were subsequently approved by the Presidium of the Soviet Union.

It may be amusing to fantasize about emperors without their clothes. But there is nothing amusing about emperors, or, for that matter, kings, or members of the House of Lords, or chambermaids, or even cocker spaniels bereft of the cultural raiment which secures their places and provides protection. Without his cultural apparel, every man is exposed. He is a displaced person, even as the survivors of the Romanov family became displaced persons during and after the Bolshevik Revolution in Russia.

15

The idea that has the world in its grip tends to make displaced persons of everyone. It does so because it fuels the assault on culture, upon religion and morality, upon civilization itself. As these are taken away, or lose their vitality, men lose even the means by which they can defend themselves. In some lands, the displacement has been dramatic and drastic. Refugees from these lands now reside in new lands and seek to make places for themselves. In other lands, the displacement is more gradual and has not yet assumed the guise of direct brutality. The more thoroughly the idea is applied, however, the more the grip will tighten.

The world is not, however, simply in the grip of a general idea. It is in the grip of variations of the idea from land to land, as these have been shaped and applied by a variety of leaders from different backgrounds. We must turn now to particular developments of the idea.

2
Marxism: Revolutionary Socialism

Both for the production on a mass scale of this communist consciousness, and for the success of the cause itself, the alteration of men on a mass scale is necessary, an alteration which can only take place in a practical movement, a revolution; this revolution is necessary, therefore, not only because the ruling class cannot be overthrown in any other way, but also because the class overthrowing it can only in a revolution succeed in ridding itself of all the muck of ages and become fitted to found society anew. — KARL MARX

THE IDEA WHICH has the world in its grip has two poles. One pole is the revolutionary road to socialism; the other is the evolutionary road to socialism. The idea — to achieve human felicity on this earth by concerting all efforts toward its realization — is the same for both of them. Both poles, too, operate to root out and destroy the received culture and use government as the instrument that is supposed to move them toward the realization of their goal. The basic difference is one of tactics, then, though tactics are no small matter when they resolve into a question of whether persuasion or a shot in the back of the neck is at

17

issue, as it has sometimes been.

In any case, it is appropriate to begin the examination of particular approaches to socialism with Marxism. Indeed, there are compelling reasons for beginning with Marxism. One is that the world communist movement is traced to its source in Marxism. The other is that all modern socialism comes into focus better when seen from the angle of Marxism. It has been said that all of Western philosophy is a series of footnotes to Plato. It can be said with equal validity that modern socialism is a series of footnotes to Karl Marx.

Why this should be so is a baffling question. The facts of his life help hardly at all to explain it. Marx was certainly not a leader of men. He was repelled by most people, even if they were not by him. He championed the cause of the laborer (or industrial proletariat, as he chose to call him), yet he was himself an intellectual. He proclaimed the importance of action, yet he spent much of his life in libraries amidst the musty smell of books. His ghost hovers over the thrust toward planned economies for nations and empires, yet he was throughout his life incompetent to manage the financial affairs of a household. Even his literary output fell short of his aims and the expectations of those who provided financial aid. He is best known for *The Communist Manifesto,* a rather short pamphlet which was the joint effort of Marx and Friedrich Engels, and the one volume he completed of *Das Kapital.* Most of his other writing was done in spurts, and consisted mainly of critiques of other works at the time. There was much more of what was wrong with the thinking of others than there was of straightforward development of his own ideas.

The details of his life go further toward explaining why he may have held certain beliefs than they do to accounting for why others were attracted by the Marxian formulations. Marx was, for most of his adult life, a man without a country, if country be taken to mean not only a nation but also religion, culture, and sense of being a part of a received heritage. Marx's father and mother had been Jewish, but his father became a Protestant in a predominantly Catholic community, converted, it was said, to keep his government job. Karl Marx was baptized a Christian but in early manhood became a militant atheist.

He attended universities at Bonn and Berlin, but presented his doctoral thesis for his degree to the University of Jena, which he had never attended. He never had what could be called regular employment but earned such income as he did from writing and editorial work. Though he married and fathered several children, the family lived from

18

pillar to post, so to speak, as Marx sought refuge first here, then there. He was frequently in trouble with the political authorities for his revolutionary activity, seeking refuge in Paris, in Brussels, and finally in London. Such friends as he had were fellow revolutionaries, and, among revolutionaries, he got along only with those who agreed with his version of things. His country, if he had one, was in his mind, and that does help to explain his doctrines.

Even so, this alienated man, this man without a country, without traditional religious underpinnings, with few possessions, with only a boiling animosity toward his culture, who could be aroused to write only out of opposition, set forth the doctrines which are today used to hold more than a billion people under control. What brought this about? The answer is surely not to be found in the details of his life. The answer, if it can be had, is in the doctrines. It is in Marxism.

What is Marxism? One way to answer the question is to say that it is that body of doctrines which was formulated by Karl Marx in collaboration with Friedrich Engels in the course of both of their lives. (Engels outlived Marx by several years and continued to expand upon the work that Marx had done.) Or, it can be approached from the angle of its antecedents in German romanticism, Hegelianism, the materialism of Feuerbach, the socialism of Proudhon, the anarchism of Bakunin, and the whole complex of mid-nineteenth century radicalism which was nipping and yapping at European society. Or, it can be traced forward in time into Leninism, Stalinism, Titoism, Castroism, Maoism, and all the variants of it that have been shaped by men attempting to apply it or apply some variety of it.

But any or all of these approaches would take us away from rather than toward the core of Marxism. It is misleading, too, to treat Marxism as a system of thought, though at some point it has to be done. It is certainly not a system of thought by reason of fitting into the established categories for utilizing reason and experience. Marx did not proceed deductively from self-evident axioms. Nor did he proceed inductively to arrive at conclusions from the assembled evidence. But his is not a system of thought.

If it were a system of thought, it could be tested and found to be true or false. It could be held up against actuality and be refuted. Bertram D. Wolfe has noted that Marxism "cannot be shaken by mere rational or factual refutation of any number of its concrete propositions, even those that are central to its logical structure."[1] There may be several reasons for this, but a crucial one has not been much emphasized. Marx is not talking about actuality, or what we ordinarily call reality, in his basic propositions. It is difficult to refute from actuality what bears no demonstrable relation to actuality.

Marx's mode of arriving at conclusions needs to be illustrated by example to show that he was not operating in contact with actuality. This may be done best by his labor theory of value, which is the lynchpin of Marxism. Marx tells us, first, that the value of commodities is determined by the amount of labor used in making them. He put it this way: "The *relative values of commodities* are, therefore, determined by the *respective quantities or amounts of labour, worked up, realised, fixed in them.*"[2] But what is value? That was easy enough for Marx to answer. Price "is a peculiar form assumed by value." "*Price*, taken by itself, is nothing but the *monetary expression of value.*" He tells us, further, that, on the average, "the *market price* of a commodity coincides with its *value.*"[3]

The novice might suppose, then, that the value of labor equals the value of commodities produced by it. More, since price and value are, in effect, the same, the price of labor would be the price of commodities. But Marx would not have it as simple as that. He hastens to assure us that "there exists no such thing as the *Value of Labour* in the common acceptance of the word."[4] What the working man sells, he says, is not labor but *"Labouring Power."* "The *value* of the labouring power is determined by the quantity of labour necessary to maintain or reproduce it...."[5] There is another difficulty to be got out of the way, too. It might be supposed from Marx's initial formulation that the more work that went into a commodity the more it would be worth. Not at all, says Marx, it is not labor *per se* that determines value, but the amount of *"Social* labour" that goes into making the product.

It would be possible to follow Marx's analysis further, but perhaps it is not necessary here. Marx claims and may even appear to be talking about the actual world. He is not. Every key word and phrase he uses is loaded with his own special meaning. It is true that he uses market price in the common signification, but he makes clear that prices in the market are relative. All his certainty is reserved for those concepts he has given a special meaning. *Value* is not value — i.e., something which arises from our desires — ; it is the same thing as "natural price,"[6] an idea borrowed from the classical economists and dragged, one hopes, kicking and screaming into the discussion. *Labour* is not labor; it is *Labouring Power.* That amount of labor which determines the price of commodities is not just labor; it is *Social Labour.*

How do we know that the value, or price (as in his equation), of a commodity is determined by the amount of social labor in it? We know it, if we know it, only because Marx has told us. There are no calculations that can be performed to prove it. There is no way to add the amount of labor, set it beside the price, and demonstrate that the one is equal to the other. Moreover, even by his own formulation, that would not do it, for it is social labor, not labor that can be summed up in hours and minutes, that he says equals the value of commodities produced.

Is Marx's labor theory of value right or wrong? Let us put the difficulty of answering this way. Marx only appeared to be talking about the actual world; he was talking about his own vision of a world, a vision of a world that was, is, and will be, but could be conceived only by a willful negation of the world that *was* in 1865, when he spoke. The proof, if proof there would be, of Marx's assertion lay in the future, not in the past. If Marx's labor theory of value were a set of propositions about the actual world, it would be subject to refutation. It was not.

The labor theory of value belongs to Marx's special Revelation, a revelation vouchsafed to him and to all who have the will to believe it. The refutation of Marx is accomplished by disbelief or, most likely, a strongly held set of counter-beliefs, not by treating it as a coherent thought system.[7] This conclusion is buttressed by the tenacity of Marxists in the face of what appears to non-Marxists to be the most convincing demonstrations from reason and experience of its fallacies.

Marxism is an anti-religious religion. To see it in any other light is to miss its character and appeal. A lifelong student of Marxism describes it this way:

> In an age prepared for by nearly two thousand years of Christianity with its millennial expectations, when the faith of millions has grown dim, and the altar seems vacant of its image, Marxism has arisen to offer a fresh, antireligious religion, a new faith, passionate and demanding, a new vision of the Last Things, a new Apocalypse, and a new Paradise.[8]

It is commonly said that Marx stood the philosopher Hegel on his head. He did much more than that. He stood Christianity on its head. Marx held that Christianity was the perfecting of religion. It was, so to speak, the highest religion, as religion, possible. Its perfection would, as in everything else for Marx, result in its negation. Its negation was the flowing into Marxism of Christian imagery, hopes, and longings with everything reversed: eternity brought into time, spirit become matter, the Second Coming become Social Revolution, the Incarnation become

21

the proletariat, and communism become the hope of redemption. The appeal of Marxism, then, is not only that it is an anti-religious religion but also that it is an anti-Christian christianity.

Marxism is also an anti-philosophy philosophy. The reign of philosophy ended with Hegel, for whom philosophy became history as idea became actuality. Marx substituted matter for idea, which made philosophy even more a dead letter. Western philosophy has been dualistic following the insights of Plato. Marx propounded a dualism which would end finally in the destruction of one of the duo — the bourgeoisie — and with the triumph of communism an end to history as well. For Marxism, everything is finally being reduced to one. All the elements which have been developed and discerned will move finally to their resolution in one element.

Karl Marx was a poet and a prophet, a poor poet and false prophet, no doubt, but poet and prophet nonetheless. Not nearly enough has been made of the poetic flavor of Marx's writing. This is not surprising, for few undertakings are so remote from poetry as economics, particularly the ponderous variety of economics constructed by Marx. Yet, many of the Marxian formulations are best grasped as the work of a poet. Take the following, for example:

> The task of history, once the world beyond truth has disappeared, is to establish the truth of this world. The immediate task of philosophy which is at the service of history, once the saintly form of human self-alienation has been unmasked, is to unmask self-alienation in its unholy forms. Thus the criticism of heaven turns into the criticism of the earth, the criticism of religion into the criticism of right, and the criticism of theology into the criticism of politics.[9]

Whether this passage can be construed so as to make sense of it is a question that can be left to the side. My point is that if it could be it would have to be construed, much in the manner of an obscure poem. What is "the world beyond truth," or "the truth of this world," or "the saintly form of human self-alienation," or "the criticism of heaven"? Considered as prose, the whole passage is nonsense. Considered as poetry, what sense it contains can be discerned by consulting the Marxian framework. (Poetry has been traditionally construed by the knowledge of certain conventional allusions. Marx's phrases are construed by reference to his disillusions.)[10]

Marx was a prophet, too, not a prophet of God, of course, but a prophet of History. He was the John the Baptist of communism, traveling hither and yon to proclaim the imminent coming of the Revolution.

22

Marxism is foremost, and finally, an ideology. To Marx, an ideology was a complex of ideas and beliefs arising out of class arrangements which served as rationalization and justification for the ruling class. But those not under his sway have quite a different view of the matter. Ideology is understood today to mean any complex of ideas and beliefs in terms of which things are explained and understood. Marxism, as a phenomenon, gives added precision to the term.

Marxism is a self-contained set of notions which reduces reality to the dimensions of Marx's vision of history. It explains what has been, is, and will be by way of these propositions. It is a figment of the minds of Marx and his interpreters. All Marxian thought, so called, is an unraveling of propositions found in the ideology. Before Marx, thought was determined by material conditions, Marx thought; after Marx, such thought as is done is to be determined by and kept within the lineaments of the ideology. This last is not what Marx said, but it follows from the revealed nature of the ideology.

Everywhere Marx looked he saw paradox, contradiction, struggle, and eventual destruction. A vast and interlinked disharmony prevailed everywhere, a disharmony that was fated to continue and worsen until that should eventually occur which would bring an end to it and produce harmony and unity. The key concepts of the Marxian ideology are these: *alienation, class struggle, industrial proletariat, bourgeoisie, labor theory of value, capitalism, social revolution, socialism,* and *communism.*

There is a brilliance within Marxian ideology which what has been said thus far might not indicate. It should not be denied, however. Marx was an intellectual scavenger, taking in vast quantities of literature by his voluminous reading, opposing the particulars of almost every formulation he encountered, then subjecting all to his own particular turn of mind before he appeared in print with the result. He defined his position in opposition to what he read, but he also incorporated much of what he read into his position. Whether the brilliance comes mainly from what he incorporated or from what he originated is a question that here can be left open. That the brilliance is there should, however, be acknowledged. Unfortunately, he had a tendency to vulgarize.

This was so in the case of his theory of alienation. The Marxian theory of alienation was most fully developed in his earlier writings, and there is some tendency to discount it because some of these were not published until long after his death. Even so, it is crucial to his whole ideology. The theory can be stated in some such fashion as this. Man as we know him is not real, essential man. His reason is flawed. What he

23

experiences is distorted by ideology. He is not free but is rather imprisoned by circumstances and conditions over which he has no control.

The sources of this condition are what might be called mechanical conditions by which he is alienated. He is alienated from himself, first of all, by religion. Religion subjects him to the mediating powers of others. He is alienated from himself by private property. Property sets him at odds with others and alienates him from his social nature. He is alienated from himself by the state. The state is an artificial creature which arises from division into classes in society. It is an instrument of class rule. He is alienated from the product of his labor by its appropriation by the capitalist. This alienation is apparently exacerbated, too, by the division of labor.

This theory of alienation is usually known in its most vulgar form, i.e., in the alienation of the wage earner from the product of his labor. This is so, mainly, because Marx and Engels placed the greatest emphasis upon it by elaborating it so much. Here is a fairly typical expression of the alienation of the worker theory:

> The alienation of the worker in his object is expressed as follows in the laws of political economy: the more the worker produces the less he has to consume; the more value he creates the more worthless he becomes; the more refined his product the more crude and misshapen the worker; the more civilized the product the more barbarous the worker....[11]

The concept was vulgarized (vastly oversimplified, anyhow) by bringing it all to bear on the alienation of the worker.

In any case, it was alienation which made revolution necessary for Marx. Marx was certainly aware that during his lifetime governments were taking various measures intended to ameliorate the lot of the worker. Why might socialism not be achieved by gradual degrees in an evolutionary fashion? Marx sometimes wavered on the matter, but he returned again and again to the position that revolution will be necessary. It will be necessary because alienation is too broadly and deeply established. The Gordian knot of alienation must be broken, and revolution is the means by which he thought this could be accomplished. Revolution, presumably, would shatter the bonds forged by alienation.

What Marx meant by revolution, as what he meant by anything else in his special language, is colored by ideology, refracted through his special vision, and given a special meaning. One thing he meant was a

24

conflict in which the industrial proletariat should triumph over the bourgeoisie. Marx and Engels put it this way:

> The immediate aim of the Communists is the same as that of all the other proletarian parties: formation of the proletariat into a class, overthrow of the bourgeois supremacy, conquest of the political power by the proletariat.[12]

The revolution must proceed, however, to become a social revolution:

> But while a *social revolution* with a *political soul* is either a paraphrase or a meaningless expression, a *political revolution* with a *social soul* is a meaningful phrase. The *revolution in general* ... is a *political act....* However, *when the organizing activity* of socialism begins and when its *own aims,* its *soul* comes to the fore, socialism abandons its *political* cloak.[13]

The important thing here is that as a result of the revolution everything, *everything,* is to be altered and changed:

> The Communists disdain to conceal their views and aims. They openly declare that their ends can be attained only by the forcible overthrow of all existing social conditions.[14]

Everything is to be transformed:

> Communism is the positive abolition of private property and thus of human self-alienation and therefore the real appropriation of the human essence by and for man. This is communism as the complete and conscious return of man... . It is the genuine resolution of the antagonism between man and nature and between man and man. It is the true resolution of the struggle between existence and essence, between objectification and self-affirmation, between freedom and necessity, between individual and species....[15]

All existing relations must be abolished — destroyed — so that social man may emerge:

> Religion, family, state, law, morality, science and art are only particular forms of production and fall under its general law. The positive abolition of private property and the appropriation of human life is therefore the positive abolition of all alienation, thus the return of man out of religion, family, state, etc., into his human, i.e. social, being.[16]

Marx apparently realized that such a revolution would not be completed swiftly. He said that the working class "will have to pass through long struggles, through a series of historic processes, transforming circumstances and men."[17]

The remainder of the Marxian formulations have to do mainly with establishing "scientifically" that the revolution is inevitable. The labor theory of value was the lynchpin of this demonstration. If Marx was right in this theory, the laboring man was being robbed of the fruits of his labor. Moreover, he claimed that the more capital that was accumulated, invested, and concentrated, the more deplorable would be the plight of the industrial worker. More and more people would fall into this class; in numbers it would constitute the majority of people in a country. When the situation of the working class became sufficiently desperate, its numbers so overwhelming, it would revolt and throw over the ruling class. All of history had been a series of class struggles. The stage was being set, Marx proclaimed, for the final class struggle, the class struggle to end all class struggles, the class struggle between the proletariat and bourgeoisie.

It is often alleged that the tyranny of communism in practice is the result of some sort of aberration from Marxism, or from Leninism, or is the result of a historical residue of Oriental Despotism in certain lands, or whatever. On the contrary, the tyranny is implicit in the ideology. The tyranny of communism is so essentially a part of Marxism that if a committee of Albert Schweitzers were assembled to put it into operation in some land they could only proceed by becoming tyrants. A review of the essentials of Marxism should demonstrate why this is so.

The engine of Marxism is hatred, hatred for everything as it is, hatred of religion, hatred of the family, hatred of the division of labor, hatred of the state, hatred of capitalists, hatred of property, hatred of the "rural idiocy" (as Marx put it) of farmers, and, yes, hatred of industrial workers.[18] The proletariat who would triumph and be transformed into true man was not, of course, the industrial worker whom we actually encounter. He must be the class-conscious industrial worker, i.e., a worker become Marxist in his conceptions. Above all, Marxism is a hatred of the past, everything shaped out of it, everything drawn from it, which is to say, just about everything. Marxism is a hatred of all imperfection, and everything that is, is imperfect. In short, Marxism hates man as he is and has been.

The *modus operandi* of Marxism is destruction. That is the true meaning of Marxian revolution. It is no simple seizure of political power. It might better be conceived as a cataclysmic earthquake, followed by devastating tremor after devastating tremor until every relationship that was has been sundered. All the actuality that has been accumulated through the ages must be destroyed — property

26

relationships, religious belief, family ties, legal forms, the intellectual heritage, culture and civilization itself. How else, but by tyranny, can such a destruction be wrought?

Tyranny is embedded in the very framework of Marxism. What is history for Marx but a tyrant? The course of history is determined, according to him; it has a direction which is beyond our control. Such history is not guide, but dictator, so to speak. More, "History is the judge — its executioner, the proletarian."[19] Of course, the executioner and tyrant is not the whole body of the proletariat; it is to be carried out by the class-conscious wing. No clearer prescription for tyranny has been contrived.

On the other side of the divide, of course, Marx tells us that all this will end. The class struggle will end with the victory of the proletariat. With this victory, too, history will end. The state will be no more; it will wither away. The dictatorship of the proletariat will have ended because its work will be done. Man will no longer be separated from man; he will have become completely social. He will have become pure man, so to speak, with all his energies released and himself integrated. Even the rift between man and nature will be healed.

The appeal of Marxism lies in the fact that it justifies and sanctifies the release of the demonic urges in each of us. It justifies and sanctifies hate, envy, the love of power, the bent to destruction, the desire to set everything right (particularly, others), and all the vague and unfulfilled longings of man. It offers to the believer union with the forces of history, an end to his separateness, and the assurance of final victory which is inevitable. It offers, too, an end of struggle, that struggle which has been man's lot throughout history. Its deepest appeal has always been to intellectuals, to those men who sit on the fringes of society with their ideas. It holds out to them the hope and expectation that their ideas can at last become actuality.

The reality of communist practice proceeds directly from Marxian theory. The revolutionary road to socialism was staked out by Karl Marx and Friedrich Engels. The proof of this must be sought in the communist practice. But first, there is another road to socialism, the evolutionary road. That, too, draws sustenance from Marxism. Marx is even supposed to have suggested late in life that in some lands revolution might not be necessary. In the report of a speech in 1872, he is supposed to have said:

We know that one has to take into account the institutions, customs and

27

traditions of various countries, and we do not deny that there are certain countries, such as America and England, to which if I were better acquainted with your institutions, I would also add Holland, where the workers can attain their goal by peaceful means....[20]

But evolutionary socialism has its own ideology, and it needs to be examined on its own grounds.

3
Evolutionary Socialism

THE APPEAL OF Marxism to intellectuals has been oft noted. A part of
the reason for this is no particular mystery. Marxism holds out to the
intellectual the hope of escape from one of his most persistent
frustrations. An intellectual is, by definition, one who is devoted to
ideas, their formulation and exposition. But ideas are only completed or
fulfilled when they are put into practice. At least this is so for some
ideas, particularly those having to do with social change. Therein,
however, lies the source of frustration for modern intellectuals, as their
tribe has become more numerous and their ideas become so plentiful:
they are often denied any impact on society. Their ideas lie dormant;
they fill the pages of books but do not go into practice.

Karl Marx projected a vision of a dramatic ending of this state of
affairs. The history of ideas, to Marx, was really a history of ideologies.
These ideologies arose as rationalizations of class positions. The ideas
were necessarily disjoined from reality as the thinkers were alienated
from their own natures by class arrangements and conflicts. Come the
revolution, he claimed, the alienation would end, and ideas would
become actuality. With the destruction of classes, man's alienation from

his nature would end, and he could experience reality directly, no longer needing to view it through the distorted lenses of ideas. "Philosophy turns into the world of reality," he said.[1] The frustration of the intellectual would presumably end, for he would no longer have a conception of a world different from the world he would be experiencing.

Unfortunately, or, fortunately, if one prefers, the end of ideology with the revolution entails, logically, an end to the function of the intellectual, as Thomas Molnar has pointed out in *The Decline of the Intellectual*. When everyone perceives reality clearly and directly, there is no need for a special corps of interpreters. When idea has become actuality, there is no occasion for the contentions of intellectuals. Many intellectuals in communist lands neglected to figure this out, and some of them did not live to regret it.

There is a deeper reason for the appeal of Marxism to intellectuals; else, one suspects, it would never have gained the hold that it has had. It is that man needs an explanation of the world in which he lives. He wants to know where it came from and where it is going. Above all, he needs a purpose in life, a purpose which goes beyond himself but with which he can identify and find meaning. He needs, in a word, religion. But many intellectuals cut themselves loose from the traditional religions in the modern era. They either ignored religion or became agnostics or atheists, quite often of the most militant variety. Marxism supplied for them the place that religion has usually held for most men.

Marxism, as was earlier noted, is an anti-religious religion. It is an earthbound, materialistic, man centered, cataclysmic, prophetic, and dogmatic religion. Dialectical materialism is its revelation. History is its god. Marx is its prophet. Lenin is its incarnation. The revolution is its day of judgment. And communism is its paradise. Its claim to being scientific even satisfies the intellectual's desire to have a rational religion.

Of course, Marxism is not scientific; neither the economic analysis nor the historical prediction can pass muster as science. They are a compound of special pleading, wishful thinking, and carefully chosen abstractions. But it should not be supposed that the appeal of Marxism would be enhanced if it were a science. On the contrary, if it were a science, it would only be a dismal science. The appeal of Marxism lies in its paradoxes, its contradictions, in the very fact that to believe it requires an act of faith, as does any religion. The intellectual of the appropriate temperament finds in the Marxist religion hope for the

30

hopeless, meaning in history, the promised resolution of all conflict, and the expectation of union, even communion, with all men.

Marxism is, then, the religion of socialism. Many, many intellectuals have been, and are, attracted to this anti-religious religion called communism. Indeed, most socialists identify in some ways with it. Perhaps, they see in it the church to which they would belong had they only undergone the necessary experience of conversion. Most likely, they see in it a common undertaking like their own, only one which uses methods and tactics which they cannot approve. In any case, many of those attracted by it have not become communists. They have, for whatever reasons, turned to other varieties of socialism.

It might be more appropriate to say that they turned to the other *variety* of socialism, because for the purposes of this work all socialism is being classified as either revolutionary socialism or evolutionary socialism. It is tempting to deal with the other socialism as watered-down Marxism. There is some substance to this view. Certainly, when any other approach to socialism is compared with the revolutionary approach it pales beside it. More, the man who gave currency to the phrase, "evolutionary socialism," Eduard Bernstein, is usually classified as a revisionist Marxist.

It is, however, a temptation which should be resisted. Marxism is not the root of socialism; it is only the most virulent branch. Even German Social Democracy, in which both Marx and Bernstein can best be understood, was greatly influenced by Marx's contemporary, Ferdinand Lassalle. The English Fabians were probably as much influenced by Henry George, say, as by Marx. Guild socialism in France had yet other origins. In the United States, there were native Americans socialists who gave to American socialism its own national flavor. Indeed, one of the distinctions between Marxism and evolutionary socialism is that the latter is almost invariably national socialism while the former claims to be, and in certain senses is, international.

It may be most helpful to think of both socialisms as belonging to the same family but being different species. Undoubtedly, they share common traits as do members of a biological family. But they are sufficiently different from one another to be thought of as different species. The basic idea from which they spring is the same, but the articulation of it is distinctly different. It is so different that the two do not merge without becoming the one or the other. To be more exact, an evolutionary socialist may approve a revolution somewhere or other, but he does not thereby become himself a revolutionist. In like manner, a revolutionary socialist may approve, even work to bring about, some government intervention, but remain, all the while, a convinced revolutionist. Those of us who are not socialists may find such distinctions difficult to grasp, but, hopefully, they will become clearer with some exposition.

One major difference between the two is in the matter of religion. Marxism — revolutionary socialism — is a religion of sorts. Evolutionary socialism is not. That is not to say that there are not articles of faith and things which one believes if he is a socialist. There are. It is rather that they are only tinctured with religion. Nor should it be thought that socialist belief is less tenacious because it is not explicitly religious. My impression is that it may well be more so. The beliefs in evolutionary socialism are often acquired in the same manner as are customs, habits, and traditions. (All socialisms are anti-traditional in the deepest sense, of course, but it is the method of evolutionary socialism to operate within the inherited framework even as it is being altered.) They have the staying power of traditions once they are acquired.

There are three main elements in evolutionary socialist tactics. All three distinguish them from Marxism in theory, and at least two of them are real differences. They are: *gradualism, democracy or democratism,* and *statism.*

Gradualism has several meanings and functions within evolutionary socialism. At the most obvious level, it defines a difference between it and communism. Socialism is to be arrived at gradually, step by step, rather than as a transformation wrought by revolution. Another aspect of it is contained in the Fabian doctrine of permeation. As Sidney Webb described it, the policy of permeation was one of inculcating

socialist thought and socialist projects into the minds not merely of complete converts, but of those whom we found in disagreement with us — and we spared no pains in these propagandist efforts, not among political liberals or radicals only, but also among political conservatives; not only among trade unionists and co-operators, but also among employers and financiers....[2]

Gradualism was closely tied in with the theories of geological and biological evolution which were gaining currency at the same time as these socialist ideas. Marx had declared that the condition of the proletariat would continue to deteriorate, or, more precisely, that more and more people would be reduced to the proletarian condition. More and more wealth would be concentrated in fewer and fewer hands. This

32

would continue to the point at which it became intolerable. At this catastrophic point, the time would be ripe for revolution. The great change could only be effected by something like a revolutionary overthrow of the old system and the grasping of power by the proletariat. The theory of evolution was useful to Marx, too, for it could be used to support the idea that fundamental and basic changes could occur in human nature. But his revolutionary idea was tied to the notion of catastrophic rather than gradual change.

The gradualists, on the other hand, believed that conditions, particularly in advanced industrial countries, were already moving gradually toward a socialist conclusion. Bernstein put it this way:

> In all advanced countries we see the privileges of the capitalist bourgeoisie yielding step by step to democratic organisations. Under the influence of this, and driven by the movement of the working classes which is daily becoming stronger, a social reaction has set in against the exploiting tendencies of capital, a counteraction which, although it still proceeds timidly and feebly, yet does exist, and is always drawing more departments of economic life under its influence. Factory legislation, the democratising of local government, and the extension of its area of work, the freeing of trade unions and systems of co-operative trading from legal restrictions, the consideration of standard conditions of labour in the work undertaken by public authorities — all these characterise this phase of the evolution.[3]

The Fabians were given to emphasizing that the change taking place was not simply a result of changes in political power. It was, they claimed, inherent in the industrial system. One of the Fabian *Essays* described the process this way:

> The factory system, the machine industry, the world commerce, have abolished individualist production; and the completion of the co-operative form towards which the transition stage of individualist capitalism is hurrying us, will render a conformity with social ethics, a universal condition of tolerable existence for the individual.[4]

In short, the gradualists claimed that the direction of industrial, social, and political evolution was already toward their desired goal of socialism. How this differed from the Marxian view was well stated by Eduard Bernstein:

> The old vision of the social collapse which rises before us as a result of Marx's arguments ... is the picture of an army. It presses forward, through detours, over sticks and stones, but is constantly led downward in its march ahead. Finally it arrives at a great abyss. Beyond it there stands beckoning the desired goal — the

state of the future, which can be reached only through a sea; a *red* sea, as some have said. Now, this vision changes, and another takes its place.... *This* vision shows us the way of the working classes not only forward, but at the same time upward. Not only do the workers grow in numbers, but their economic, ethical, and political level rises as well.... [5]

The link was made, then, between the gradual movement toward socialism and the idea of evolutionary progress. One might say, following this junction, that socialism was the goal, gradualism the way, and evolutionary progress the engine to get there. It has certainly been a most useful propellant. The idea of progress has been mightily attractive in the last couple of centuries. Many have come to believe that great progress was actually taking place. If it was, why it had anything to do with socialism is an important question. But gradualists propounded it not as a proposition standing in need of proof but as the answer to the riddle of history. The notion that the movement toward socialism is progress has served them well. It has enabled them to claim that all acts moving in their direction were progressive, while those opposing them were retrogressive and reactionary.

When evolutionary socialists say that they are democratic it does not mean just what it appears to mean. To get in the vicinity of its meaning it is necessary to hark back to one of the issues that split German socialists in the middle of the nineteenth century. The issue was this: Should socialists run for and accept seats in legislatures? More broadly: Should socialists participate in bourgeois governments? To put it in present day jargon: Should socialists participate in the system? By participating in it would they not be giving tacit approval to it? Revolutionists tended to answer that they would. The state — and most emphatically, the bourgeois state — was the enemy. Those who took the other side were early called democratic socialists. They were also called parliamentarists, signifying their willingness to participate in the government.

Actually, evolutionary socialists are what is now often referred to as pragmatic. What this means in socialist terms is that they are not wedded to any particular means in the achievement of power and the enactment of their policies. Hence, democracy may mean for them majority rule when they have a majority. On the other hand, it may mean equality when they are pressing for the enfranchisement of someone or for the use of some other than a parliamentary device for the achievement of their ends. Even the form which socialism will eventually assume, indeed, whether it will have some *final* form, does

34

not much matter. Eduard Bernstein got in hot water with other socialists when he first tried to express this view. He had said that the "final aim" of socialism was of little account. Here is his further explanation of what he meant:

In this sense I wrote the sentence that the movement means everything for me and that what is usually called "the final aim of socialism" is nothing.... Even if the word "usually" had not shown that the proposition was only to be understood conditionally, it was obvious that it could not express indifference concerning the final carrying out of socialist principles, but only indifference — or, as it would be better expressed, carelessness — as to the form of the final arrangement of things.[6]

What was shocking about Bernstein's original statement was that he appeared to have got the matter wrong end to. What he should have said, one supposes, is that the means did not matter but that the end or final goal of socialism was everything. Yet, when pressed on it, he did not back off; he affirmed his devotion to principles, not to goals. Actually, he changed positions. He had said that "the movement means everything," not that principles do. His original meaning may have been closer to the core of evolutionary socialism. He was saying, if I understand him, that what the paradise of socialism is like does not matter so long as we are on the way there. It is in the concerting of effort to achieve it that the fruits of socialism are realized, not in some distant goal to be reached.

Despite any appearance to the contrary, what comes out of this is that methods do not matter so long as they are collectivist in principle. What he was arguing for was the necessity of political activity as the necessary immediate task of socialists. What he was arguing against was that to become embroiled in politics was the wrong way to achieve socialism, that the political means were not in accord with the final goal of socialism. He was arguing against those who were arguing from some blueprint of what socialism was going to be like. He had no such blueprint, he was saying, and he would not be turned away from using methods that were collectivist by some hypothetical final goal.

Does this mean that evolutionary socialists are democratic in principle? A biographer of Bernstein has summed up his mature position this way:

Social democracy fights for democracy in state, province, and community as a means of realizing political equality for all and as a lever for the socialization of the soil and of capitalist enterprises. It is not the workers' party in the sense that

35

it accepts only workers as members — everyone who subscribes to its principles may belong to it. But its chief appeal is to the workers, for the liberation of the workers must principally be the task of the workers themselves. The chief job of Social Democracy is to fill the working class with this idea and to organize it economically and politically for its historic fight.[7]

Sidney Webb described the connection between socialism and democracy in these words:

> So long ... as democracy in political administration continues to be the dominant principle, socialism may be quite safely predicted as its economic obverse, in spite of those freaks and aberrations of democracy which have already here and there thrown up a short-lived monarchy or a romantic dictatorship. Every increase in the political power of the proletariat will most surely be used by them for their economic and social protection....[8]

Actually, it would be more accurate to say that collectivism was the principle and democracy the means. Democracy offered the mode for collective decision making. More, it provided a means for thrusting toward enfranchising more and more of the population. With near universal suffrage, they hoped that socialist measures would be ever more likely to be enacted. Democracy became a mystique in the course of this effort, a mystique of the proper way to act and even a sort of mystical goal.

Evolutionary socialism is statist. It determinedly uses the power of government for its purposes. On the face of it, however, this does not distinguish evolutionary from revolutionary socialism. The difference, such as it is, is part theoretical and part the role that government is supposed to play and how it is to be done. In theory, Marxists are not statists. The State, according to Marx, was supposed to wither away under communism. This, however, depended upon a transformation of human beings and society which has not taken place. That aside, there are still differences between revolutionary and evolutionary socialism.

The evolutionists proposed to use the existing state and work within it. They would gradually transform the State even as men and society were being transformed. By contrast, revolutionists proposed that the old state structure would have to be destroyed and a new one erected in its place.

Evolutionary socialists have been *interventionists*. They proposed to work and accomplish their ends, in part at least, by intervening in the capitalist system, as they described it. They would eventually alter and transform the economic structure by their interventions. The revolu-

36

tionaries were holistic in their approach. They would take over the state apparatus, change it and redirect it so that it was no longer what it had been. They would use it not simply to alter the economy step by step but would destroy the old system and put another one in its place. Both are no doubt statist, at least to those who do not accept the mysteries of communist terminology, but there are differences in approaches.

There is no blinking the fact that evolutionary socialism differs somewhat and bears a different face from land to land. It has already been pointed out that by its nature it is nationalistic. It is even called by different names in different countries. In Germany, it is the Social Democratic Party today, though most political parties are apt to be to some extent under its sway. In England, the Labour Party has been the spearhead of evolutionary socialism. In some lands, it is the Christian Socialist parties. In the United States, its devotees are most often referred to as "liberals," but they have also been known by other names. The Democratic Party in more recent times has been at the forefront in pushing the gradualist type of reforms.

The tactics of socialists differ much from country to country. In those nations where socialism is avowed as a desirable goal, it is sometimes sufficient recommendation for measures that they are required by socialism. But in countries, such as the United States, where few of the actual advocates avow their socialism, and where it would hardly be considered a recommendation, measures are promoted on other grounds.

The amazing thing is the continuing impetus toward socialism and the remarkable consistency in what is sought from land to land. Despite even the most obvious failures, despite political setbacks from time to time, despite cultural differences from land to land, the impetus rises again and again and the same sorts of measures continue to be enacted.

The question must ever arise as to where and what is the source of this impetus and consistency. The impetus to and consistency of communism is not so difficult to explain. After all, communism is an international movement, supported by nations where communist parties are in power, such as the Soviet Union, the People's Republic of China, and Cuba. There is a party line controlled from Moscow, Peking, or wherever. Communism is spread, too, by military conquest. But the paraphernalia for this is missing largely from evolutionary socialism. There is no body with either the power or authority to promulgate a party line across the boundaries of nations. Even within countries, there is usually no authoritative body to enforce some party line. True, the

United States, or perchance other nations, may promote socialist measures through foreign aid programs, but these would hardly account for the continuing impetus toward socialism. The notion that it is done by some international cabal is appealing, but such organizations as exist lack the power and authority to promote socialism that thoroughly.

The answer, as we have explored it thus far, is this. The world is in the grip of an idea. The idea is to use government to achieve human felicity on this earth by concerting all efforts toward its realization and to root out and destroy all that stands in the way. The idea, in its Marxist articulation, is an anti-religious religion. The idea, in its gradualist posture is a secular faith. It is not proclaimed by the gradualists as being either secular or a faith. It is not a religion. It accepts votaries from every religion and none, lays claim to any good which it finds in these religions, and uses the elements of traditional religious belief which bear any resemblance to the idea to support it. Its faith is in progress, in collectivist democracy, in the possibility of changing human nature, and in eventually concerting all efforts behind the movement to achieve human felicity on this earth.

The Marxists offer to the intellectuals the hope that ideas will become actuality. The evolutionary socialists offer not just temporary employment to intellectuals but permanent positions. Since the evolution is an extremely long range affair, there is no probability that in the foreseeable future the need for ideas will end. To the have-nots, to the down-and-out, to any who conceive that they have not received their deserts (and the number of these is legion) both revolutionary and evolutionary socialism promise that all this will be changed. Both hold up a vision of perfection beside the realities of an imperfect world and proclaim that they know how to attain the perfection. If history is *for* them (either history whose process was supposedly scientifically discerned by Marx, or history discerned in progressive evolutionary patterns), who can be against them? These are the lineaments of a religion, on the one hand, and of a secular faith, on the other.

My main purpose in this work, however, is not to write about ideas. The emphasis is to be on the *grip*, not upon the idea. To show the grip, it is necessary to look at the actions of governments in some of the lands under the sway of the socialist ideas. There we shall discover not the beatific vision foretold by socialist prophets but the hard realities produced by the applications of force and violence.

The discussion of the ideas of revolutinary and evolutionary socialism has one main purpose here. It is to show the connection between the

38

ideas and the practices. Socialists of whatever persuasion focus attention upon and talk most about economic matters. They proclaim that the ills which beset us are economic in origin. But the task which they propose to undertake does not simply involve rearranging economies. An economy does not exist in lofty isolation from man, society, morality, religion, culture, habits, customs, and traditions.

Indeed, economy is what it is because man is what he is. This being so, anyone attempting to institute new and different economic arrangements must perforce also devise a new man, new society, new morality, and so on. It may be less painful to go about it gradually than in one fell swoop, but the damage must finally be done whichever way is taken. The damage must be done because the old man, the old society, the old morality, and so on, must be rooted out, altered, or destroyed. The evolutionary approach is much more subtle because much of this process is hidden beneath diversionary arguments and gradual methods. It is there, nonetheless.

The impact of the thrust toward socialism is to destroy the independence of the individual and leave him exposed to the power of government and the influence of whoever has it or will wield it. This is so because the thrust of socialism is to remove all the supports by which he may stand as an individual: the supports of a free society, or morality, or religion, of custom and tradition. The logic of this development is in the socialist idea.

We turn now to the exploration of this impact in several lands where it has been applied. Undoubtedly, the impact will vary from country to country. It will certainly vary depending upon whether it is revolutionary or evolutionary socialism at work. It will vary, too, depending upon the leaders from time to time and place to place. Each country has a different history, and each people different ways. But when all that has been said, there is but one definitive way to study the impact of an idea, and that is upon actual people in the situations which we find them.

Book II

The
Bolshevization
of Russia

4
Old Regime and New Revolutionaries

THE SOVIET RULE over the Russian Empire has been one of, if not *the*, most oppressive and tyrannical in all of history. It reached its nadir of arbitrary oppression under the dictatorship of Joseph Stalin, but it has been throughout its sixty-year domination a tyranny. There has been no shortage of efforts to explain this, or to explain it away, as the case may be. One of the most common explanations is that the Soviet government inherited an autocratic regime from Czarist Russia and continued it. Another explanation, one which goes even further afield, is that the dictatorship of the Soviet Union is out of some sort of mold of Oriental Despotism. Then, there are those explanations which focus on the personality of Stalin, largely ignoring the despotism of Lenin and of Stalin's successors. Thus, it is alleged that Stalin was paranoid and/or a megalomaniac. This focus on Stalin has been particularly popular since he was debunked by Nikita Khrushchev in 1956.

The major shortcoming of these and other such explanations is that they do not come to grips with the problem. They leave us with the need for an explanation of what has supposedly been explained. Why, we need to know, would the Bolsheviks or Communists (as they came to be known) have continued the autocracy from a regime which they hated and were pledged to displace root and branch? (This is not to deny that

43

there may have been some connections but rather to affirm the need for explaining these.) Why would European-oriented Communists have become Oriental despots? If Stalin was paranoid, how did it happen that he was able to come to power and rule for so long? Perhaps Stalin did have an inordinate love of power, but what enabled him to satisfy it? In short, why evade the issue?

There is an obvious explanation for the tyranny of communism. It is in Marxist ideology. An explanation begins to emerge when the matter is approached in the following way. Marxism has no political theory. It has a theory about politics but no political theory. Many critics of Marxism have focused on its misconceptions about economics. But at least Marx had a conception of economics, a conception derived from classical economics, however distorted it was in his formulation. By contrast, he abandoned political theory almost entirely.

The reason is not far to seek. No political theory was necessary because the state is unnecessary. Government, or the state, is an accident, in philosophical terms. It arose as an instrument for class rule. It is a figment, so to speak, of the class which controls the instruments of production and distribution of goods. Since, as Marx conceived the matter, this control always involved deep-seated and universal injustice, government, or the state, had been used to perpetuate the injustice and repress the dispossessed classes. Marx predicted that with the triumph of the proletariat the classless society would emerge and the state would wither away.

True, there would be an interval between the time of the initial triumph of the proletariat and the emergence of the classless society. During this interval, the proletariat, or the class-conscious arm of it, would take over the state apparatus and run it. This would be the period of the "dictatorship of the proletariat." But it would only be an interlude; the state would still be accidental and ephemeral; it would then wither and disappear. There was no need to trouble to devise polical arrangements for something which had no future. It would be like devising means for governing ghosts when all that would really be needed would be to exorcise them.

Marx had confused and, in effect, fused two distinct aspects of reality: government and economy. Out of his materialistic philosophy and under the deceptive lure of the potential perfection of economy as viewed from the angle of economic theory, he supposed the economic system to be essential and government to be accidental. Given a just economy, government, or the state, would have no reason for being. In

44

the real world, as contrasted with Marx's abstract poetic world, both government and economy are essential. Economy is essential to provide us with sustenance; government is essential to maintain the peace. Nor does the economic system determine the government; on the contrary, the character of the government determines, to considerable extent, the economic system. (This is not to deny reciprocal relations between the two but to emphasize the primary role of government by virtue of its monopoly of the use of force.)

Be that as it may, the important point is that communism has no general theory (or tradition) of government. In Marxist theory, government had been an accidental instrument of class rule; it will be only a temporary expedient for consolidating the position of the proletariat. There is no theory or tradition within it of what constitutes a legitimate government. There is no formalized requirement for the consent of the governed. There is no provision for the separation of powers, an independent judiciary, checks and balances, or any means for containing and restricting government. Indeed, since all conflict is supposed to disappear, and since all limitations presuppose conflict, Marxist theory cannot accommodate any of these ideas.

Marxism is a covert blueprint for unlimited, despotic, arbitrary, and tyrannical government. It is covert because the theory posits a potential harmony which nowhere exists and the absence of government when in fact government prevails everywhere. More, Marxists in power employ the full weight of political power in drastic efforts to transform human nature, power limited only by the imagination and lack of determination of those who wield it. If it were given a theory and tradition of government, it would no longer be Marxism. Marxism is committed to a vision of the future and an explanation of the past which does not accept the reality and permanency of government. Reality ignored does not, of course, go away; instead, it grows luxuriously and smothers all else. This is precisely what has happened in all communist lands.

In fact and in practice, communism is *rule by gangsters* who seek to give *legitimacy* to their governments and acts by *Marxism*. That they have been gangsters does not stem merely from the fact that they were outlaws and exiles before they seized power, though they were. Nor does it stem merely from the fact that they operate in a conspiratorial manner, though they do. It is more deeply a part of their mode of operations and reason for being than these things imply. They are gangsters, in the first place, because they are thieves. They take the property of others and use it for their own purposes. They are gangsters,

45

in the second place, because they operate by force and violence on those under their sway. They are gangsters, finally, because their rule is not legitimate, and the very ideology by which they would give legitimacy to their rule makes them gangsters.

But why call them gangsters? Why not despots? Or dictators? Or usurpers? These latter terms are, of course, to some extent appropriate, but they do not adequately describe the phenomenon with which we are dealing. There are despots and despots, dictators and dictators, usurpers and usurpers. They are relative terms. "Gangster," by contrast, is precise; it describes a possibility of a type of ruler for which the perversions implied by dictator, despot, and usurper do not prepare us.

Every communist regime appears capricious so long as we employ the usual terminology for the rulers. It is something to be accounted for by the peculiarities of a Stalin, or a Mao Tse-tung, or a Castro. But once they are conceived of as gangsters tied to Marxist ideology, any capriciousness becomes a secondary characteristic. There is a pattern to their behavior, a pattern that persists from Lenin to Stalin to Malenkov to Khrushchev to Brezhnev. It is a pattern of secrecy, terror, purges, rulers surrounded by henchmen, of expropriation (theft), of violence, and of fear. It is not that there are not variations from one set of rulers to another, nor that there are not peculiarities of individual rulers. Obviously, there are. It is rather that communist regimes must be explained by what persists, not by what changes from one to another. What persists is gangsterism tied to Marxism.

It is customary to write about communist regimes as if their main problem were economic. But their economic problems follow from the abuse of political power. To grasp the basic problem of communist regimes, it is necessary, first to imagine what the basic problem of gangsters would be if they were to gain control of the political apparatus. It should be obvious what that problem would be. It would be legitimacy.

If ordinary, non-ideological gangsters were to seize a government, the problem could probably be solved over a span of time. They would probably regularize procedures, as all governments tend to do. They would probably consolidate their regime by giving favors to influential individuals and groups. At some point, they would probably cease to be gangsters and become politicians, or something of the sort. Transformations similiar to this have occurred many times when armies composed of little better than bandits have seized power over a people.

The problem for communist regimes to establish legitimacy,

however, may well be insuperable. Marxism provides no handle to grasp with which to legitimize a regime. If it regularizes the government, it is on the way to making permanent what is supposed to be temporary. Marxism does not recognize the legitimacy of the motives of self-interest, the appeal to which would enable a regime to consolidate its power. Communist rulers are committed to erasing all those conflicts which make politicians necessary rather than becoming politicians.

A communist regime attempts to establish its legitimacy by its adherence to Marxism. The more gangster-like the rulers are the more fanatically they proclaim their Marxism. Indeed, theirs must be the only true, correct, and orthodox Marxism, else how can they justify the atrocities they commit? Marxism cannot legitimize their government, or any government, but it does legitimize, for them, their gangster-like rule. They may be completely cynical about the programs they advance, but they cannot tolerate the growth of any cynicism about the validity of Marxism, for if Marxism is invalid, they have no reason for being.

Gangsterism cannot, of course, be deduced from the verbiage of Marxism. Even the phrase, "dictatorship of the proletariat," does not presuppose the rule by gangsters. Gangsterism arises in the real world from the attempt to superimpose over it the visionary world of Marxism. In the real world, men are ordinarily devoted to the pursuit of their own interests as they conceive them. If they act in concert with others, in their ordinary employments, it is to advance their own interests as over against those of others.

In reality, governments encounter not harmony but conflicts of interest. Communism does not propose machinery for resolving these conflicts as they continually arise; instead, it proposes to dissolve them. Given the perpetuity of the conflicts, communism must be imposed from above downward. It must be imposed by those who connive to do so against the will of the populace. The attempt to do this requires determination and the will to use whatever measures are necessary to enforce it, i.e., the mentality and habits of gangsters.

Communist behavior does not, then, arise from the history and traditions of the lands over which its rule is imposed. On the contrary, it is implacably opposed to the history and traditions, and committed to their obliteration. It arises out of the inner necessities of the ideology. Nor is the communist conquest of power directly related to any oppression or tyranny which may have preceded it. Peoples seeking an outlet from tyranny would hardly turn to communism for that. This much needed to be got on the record before discussing the relation of the Czarist regime to the Bolshevik Revolution. It is often alleged that it was the oppression of the Czarist regime that set the stage for communism and contributed to its character in Russia. Whatever the degree of oppression under the Czars, it would not have justified communism; nor could it, except in tangential ways, have informed communism.

In fact, it was the deterioration and dissolution of Czarist rule which provided the opportunity for the Bolsheviks to come to power.

The end of the rule of the Czars came swiftly and ignominiously in the last days of February and early March of 1917. (If we follow the Julian calendar which was then in use in Russia. If not, it was in the middle of March, 1917.) This is usually referred to as the February Revolution in Russian history. On February 20, say, Nicholas II was the unchallenged Czar of the Russian Empire (except such of it as had fallen into the hands of the Central Powers). On March 2 (Julian calendar), Nicholas abdicated, and the rule of the Czars was effectively ended.

The events which signalled this sudden and swift dissolution could hardly have been predicted. For several days in late February there were massive demonstrations in the capital, Petrograd (lately, St. Petersburg, and before many years to be renamed Leningrad). Nicholas II had taken over the command of the armed forces and was away from the capital. When he heard of the disturbances, he ordered them to be stopped. To effect his order, soldiers were called out to end the demonstrations. They fired on the crowd, and some people were killed. Following this, some of the soldiers declared that they would not again fire upon their own people. A detail mutinied against its officers, and an officer was killed. The soldiers joined the city people and, spurred on by the Petrograd Soviet and leaders of the Duma (a sort of elective legislature), took over the City of Petrograd. When the Czar attempted to return by train to Petrograd he was unable to do so and wound up in Pskov instead. There, pressured by representatives from a provisional government and most of his generals, he abdicated in favor of his brother, Michael. Michael refused to accept the throne, and the three-hundred-year reign of the House of Romanov was over.

What had happened was the dissolution of the authority of the Czar. With the dissolving of that authority went virtually all the political authority in the empire. It was this dissolution of authority — not repression, not oppression, not backwardness, not progress, not even, in the final analysis, the potent solvents let loose by World War I — that set the stage for the Bolshevik Revolution later on in the year. There were would-be rulers aplenty, but mostly they had neither the determination nor the tradition to cement authority over an empire and conduct a major war simultaneously.

In retrospect, how the czars ever maintained authority over the empire may be more in need of explaining than why the authority dissolved. At the beginning of World War I, Nicholas II ruled over a vast empire which extended from Finland and Poland in the west to the Bering Sea in the east. This extensive land mass constituted the largest country in Europe and in Asia. It was truly an empire, for it contained not only the Russians but also Ukrainians, Finns, Poles, Georgians, Yakuts, Buryats, Letts, Germans, and so on.

The Russian Orthodox Church provided the official religion but there was also, among the Christians, the Old Believers, Baptists, Roman Catholics, Lutherans, and assortment of other sects. In addition to Christians and Jews, there were Moslems and Buddhists. Among all the peoples, however, the Russians were the most numerous and the dominant ones as well, which is why it is rightly referred to as the Russian Empire. In a similar fashion the Russian Orthodox Church was the dominant religion.

For several centuries, too, Russia had been pulled East and West. The East toward which Russia was drawn was not the Orient but the East of the Orthodox Church, the cultural East of Constantinople and the Eastern Roman Empire of the Middle Ages. The West was, of course, Western Europe and its culture and ways. There were Westernizers, and had been since Peter the Great, who wished to see Russia imitate and adapt to the culture of Western Europe. There were Russifiers who pushed for the Russification of the Empire. And, there was pan-Slavism, a movement, of sorts, to unite all the Slavic people under Mother Russia. There was a considerable contingent of Germans who wielded much intellectual influence. How anyone could rule over this polyglot assemblage is difficult to understand, yet rule over it the czars had done.

The czars ruled the Empire by the hold they had over the Russian people, by conquest of the outlying provinces, by repression, by tradition, and by concessions. The great bulwarks of the regime historically had been the Orthodox Church, the nobility, the bureaucracy and the landlords. The most repressive of czars in recent times had been Nicholas I (1825-55). The repression was abated by Alexander II (1855-81), under whom the serfs were freed, and the economic complexion began to change. Nicholas II (1894-1917) was almost certainly the least repressive of the czars of modern times, much less so than his father, Alexander III (1881-94). He granted major concessions in 1906 and further relaxed the repression thereafter.

In many ways, Nicholas II was an exemplary monarch. He loved the German princess, Alix of Hesse-Darmstadt, well, if not always wisely and was a beloved father and devoted to his four daughters and only son. He liked hunting especially, though he also appears to have enjoyed in general the trappings of royalty in the last halcyon days of royalty in the modern era. If he was not himself a man of great vision, he used two vigorous and far-seeing ministers, Sergei Witte and Piotr Stolypin, to good effect. Under the leadership of these men, Russia began to make considerable industrial progress, and Stolypin, before his assassination in 1911, did much to develop independent farming. (So heady was Stolypin's early success that some of the socialists began to despair of appealing effectively to the peasants.) The fact that some 15 million troops could be mustered, with little complaint, for World War I appeared to indicate widespread loyalty and acceptance of the regime.

But Nicholas II was hoist by his own petard, indeed, hoist by changes which had been made in the power structure, some of which went back to the time of Peter the Great in the early eighteenth century. Nicholas II was a proud and unrepentant autocrat, proclaimed his autocracy, and appears to have been determined to preserve and pass on his powers undiminished to his frail and sickly son. This was the case, even though the Constitution of 1906 indicated that he was to share his powers with the elected Duma. In fact, he proceeded through Stolypin to alter the constituency of the Duma to suit himself and to adjourn it or dismiss it when its actions became inconvenient.

Autocracy, in and of itself, did not cost him his throne. What did was that in solidifying their autocracy the czars had cut away the independent and responsible supports to monarchy. The Orthodox Church was surely a most important potential bulwark of monarchy. Yet Peter the Great had abolished the Patriarchate by which the church might have been independently and responsibly ruled. Some great cities still had Metropolitans, but their authority over the church in general was minimal to non-existent. In effect, the church had only a political director over it, a director who could hardly command the religious allegiance that was wanting.

Following the abolition of serfdom, the nobility and landlords lost much of their power. In general, there was an increasing tendency

50

throughout Russia to have local rule by committees. This not only violated the principle of monarchy but also of responsible government. The result was that when the authority of the czar was challenged, there were no responsible independent leaders to come forth to support it who carried the weight of traditional authority. Nicholas II's regime was isolated by its own autocracy. When challenged, the authority crumbled and dissolved.

Events in the years just prior to March, 1917, contributed much also to the dissolution of Nicholas II's authority. It is most difficult for an autocratic regime, indeed, any government, to survive military defeat. The more personal the power, the more dependent it is upon its effective exercise. Russia had been humiliatingly defeated by Japan in the war of 1904-05. Nor did matters improve in World War I; the Russian armies suffered crushing losses in major battles with millions of casualties. These defeats undoubtedly contributed to the deterioration of support for the regime.

On top of this, there was the bizarre affair of Grigori Rasputin. Rasputin was a gross, illiterate, and dissolute adventurer posing as a holy man who managed to worm his way into the confidence of Czarina Alexandra (as Alix was called after she married Nicholas II). His influence was gained because he was able to stop the bleeding, probably by hypnosis, of her only son, the Crown Prince Alexis. The boy suffered from hemophilia. The family lived in constant fear that the boy would bump or bruise himself so as to set off another bout with the affliction. It happened often enough, and the suffering was such that it was all the family could do to bear it. Physicians could do little but allow the affliction to run its course. Rasputin was able, on occasion, to attend the boy and reverse the course of the affliction. This earned for him the gratitude of the Czarina, gratitude which it pleased him to use to influence policy and appointments.

Rasputin was killed in 1916 — stabbed, shot, and finally drowned, so vigorous was the life in him — but the damage had already been done. The damage was done in this way. The Czarina exercised often decisive influence on the Czar's appointments in his last years. At a time when the regime needed strong and resolute ministers, and particularly prime ministers, ineffective and weak men occupied the posts. They were often the choice of Rasputin who may have had little more motive than rewarding the husbands of women with whom he was engaged in sexual dalliances. To be associated with such a man could hardly help the reputation of the Czarina either, for though they were ill-founded there

51

were rumors of illicit relations between Rasputin and Alexandra. This was the more devastating because the Czarina was German by birth, and Russia was at war with Germany. There is no reason now to question the loyalty of the Czarina to the Czar or to Russia, but the tales of machinations at court were sufficient at the time to damage greatly the prestige of the royal family.

There was yet another element in the erosion of the authority of the czars. There is no way of measuring such things, but it may have been the most important. Certainly, it was the most important for what lay in store for the Russian Empire in the future. It was the role of the intellectuals. Intellectuals have played an increasingly important role in the modern world, particularly in the spread of socialism.

Prior to the eighteenth century, most of what we now call intellectuals had church vocations of one sort or another. Following the Protestant Reformation, some of them were no longer under the strenuous discipline of a strong church and, at any rate, had the opportunity to follow and advocate their own particular views. With the spread of religious liberty, such activity by churchmen became common. But it has been with the decline of the power of churches in the last two centuries, coupled with the growth of secular education and a secular press, that intellectuals, many of them with a reformist bent, assumed such an important role.

The intellectuals owed their rise, too, to the spread of liberty and the much greater economic productivity which accompanied it. In the nineteenth century, they were most apt to subscribe to a liberalism in support of liberty. In Russia, however, such liberalism was mostly thwarted. The failure in 1825 of those of this inclination to wrest power from the hands of the czars turned them, according to some accounts, to more revolutionary inclinations. One writer describes the development this way:

In the early nineteenth century there was taking shape a group of men and women ... which called itself and was called by others the Russian intelligentsia.... The Russian intelligentsia was bound together not by class origin or wealth or economic function but by commitment to certain ideas.... The group may be defined as the politically-oriented portion of the educated class — that portion which was preoccupied with ideas concerning what state and society were like and what they ought to be like, in Russia as well as the rest of the world....

An air of dedication — which, carried to its logical extreme, would prompt Lenin to declare that he would not listen to Beethoven because it made him feel soft and weak — and a sense of risk pervaded the Russian intelligentsia.... The

52

Russian intelligentsia developed a fervor and fanaticism of their own, but applied them to the advancement of a stock of ideas which were largely imported from England, France, and Germany.[1]

It was of such people that Fyodor Dostoevsky wrote in his novel, *The Possessed.*

It was such intellectuals who formed the backbone of the revolutionary parties which sprouted and spread in Russia in the late nineteenth century. These revolutionists did not believe in or hope for peaceful and gradual change in Russia; they believed that there would have to be a drastic transformation. As one scholar puts it:

Until the very end of the tsarist regime the spokesmen for the radical opposition groups all belonged to the so-called intelligentsia. They were a motley assortment, consisting of "penitent nobles" and the sons of priests, merchants and peasants, who went among the people to preach their new doctrine, in which the main emphasis was placed on political and social revolution.[2]

These revolutionary parties were generally small before 1917, but they exercised influence far beyond their numbers. There was the Socialist Revolutionary Party which contained a considerable corps of anarchists, who were so active in the large number of assassinations and assassination attempts in the last decade or so of the nineteenth and the first decade of the twentieth centuries. A veritable reign of terror against government officials occurred in 1906-07. The Socialist Revolutionaries aimed their appeal toward the peasants as they settled down somewhat and were the prime moves for the nationalization and redistribution of the land.

There was the Russian Social Democratic Worker's Party, which was the Marxist party. It broke into two factions almost at the outset: the Mensheviks (minority) and the Bolsheviks (majority). The Bolshevik was the party of Lenin; it generally stood for an early proletarian revolution as opposed to the generally held Menshevik view that such a revolution must await the full development of capitalism.

There was a Labor Group Party which sought to advance the political role of industrial workers. There were also the Constitutional Democrats (Kadets) who may have been more liberal (in the old sense) than left, but they did advance the idea of some sort of land distribution.

The revolutionary parties had one thing in common: their determined and continued opposition to the government of the czar. They propagandized, campaigned (when they could), and attempted in whatever ways they could to undermine it. The central authority must go. The nationalities must become self-governing as must the peasant and the industrial workers. This campaign bore fruit. When the authority of the Czar dissolved in early 1917, there was no recognized authority to take its place. There was a multitude of factions and parties, each with its extensive program, attempting to gain or influence power. When Lenin arrived at the Finland Station in Petrograd in April, 1917, he found the situation ripening for him to grasp the power. The time was already nearly past when anyone but the most resolute and iron-willed could control events in the Russian Empire. Every change that was made was greeted by the revolutionaries with clamor for ever more radical change. Radical democracy had penetrated the armed forces with the enlisted men controlling their officers, had penetrated the factories, and was spread throughout the provinces. Czar Nicholas II and his family were in custody; the old regime was by now not even a very lively memory. The day of the new revolutionaries was at hand.

5
The Revolution Commences

WHAT WAS THE Bolshevik Revolution?

This became a momentous question as soon as the Bolsheviks seized power in Russia in the fall of 1917. It was at the outset a pressing question for those people within the Russian Empire who fell under the sway of the Bolsheviks (who proceeded shortly to change their name to Communist). The question has not diminished over the years but has rather gained in importance as communism has spread over the world. There are now at least 19 countries containing over a billion souls now under the power of communist parties. The revolutions going on in these lands are mostly patterned after the Bolshevik Revolution in Russia. To know the Bolshevik Revolution and its extended aftermath, then, would be to know much about communist revolution.

The Bolshevik Revolution — and all communist revolutions — must be examined at every stage from two different and often irreconcilable angles. One is the angle of ideology. This entails the Marxian mythology with its overlay of Leninism and whatever other interpretations may be involved. It contains its own peculiar language, its vision of history, its heroes and villains. The other angle is the reality of what is actually happening. The ideology can be understood, so long as it is kept in a separate compartment. So, too, we may suppose that we understand the reality apart from the ideology.

This latter point must be denied, however. This approach leads to continual misunderstanding of communism. Those who persist in viewing communism this way will interpret the acts of the leaders in such terms as the quest of power, expansionism, and other such historically familiar motives. It is not that communist leaders may not be moved by such aims; it is rather that their aims are clothed in and inseparable from the ideology. There is a continual interplay between ideology and actuality. The interplay is probably most often one of cause and effect; ideology is the cause usually, and the reality is the effect. To look at a communist revolution without taking into account the ideology is like surveying the damage done on Eniwetok Atoll without knowing that a hydrogen bomb was exploded there.

It is important, then, to grasp the pattern of the Bolshevik Revolution. It is equally important to make a running account of the interplay between ideology and actuality. Ideology was not only at work in the events in Russia from 1917 onward, but it was also being shaped and hardened by the particular turns of events. To put it another way, communist ideology today is largely Marxism plus the Russian experience as the latter has been ideologized. A topical approach is more appropriate to an account, then, than a strictly chronological one.

On October 25 (Julian calendar), 1917, the Bolsheviks gained control over the points of power in Petrograd, the capital city of the Russian Empire. The climactic event was the storming and taking of the Winter Palace by armed force on the evening of the 25th and the early morning of the 26th. The Winter Palace was the headquarters of the Provisional Government, and the cabinet was in session there even as Bolsheviks fought their way through the labyrinth of corridors and rooms to where they were. A guard entered the chamber where the cabinet was meeting.

Kishkin, the Governor-General, did not seem to know whether the Palace had actually been occupied. "It is taken," the cadet replied. "They have taken all the entrances. Everyone has surrendered. Only this room is being guarded. What does the Provisional Government order?"

"Tell them," said Kishkin, "that we don't want bloodshed, that we yield to force, that we surrender." [1]

So it was, with hardly a whimper, that the government fell.

In the next several weeks, the Bolsheviks consolidated their control. Prime Minister Aleksandr Kerensky escaped from Petrograd just as the revolt was coming to a head. He sought to gather an army to retake the capital, but he could muster only seven hundred soldiers from the once vast armies of Russia, and this force was turned back by Bolshevik forces only a few days after the storming of the Winter Palace. Moscow fell to the Bolsheviks with no greater struggle than had occured in Petrograd. Local soviets (councils) had for months held dominant positions throughout much of the empire. It was only necessary for Bolsheviks to dominate these in order to come to power, which they were usually able to do rather quickly.

The culminating act of the Bolshevik seizure of power came with the dissolution of the Constituent Assembly which met in January, 1918. Ever since the abdication of the Czar there had been talk of holding general elections, assembling a parliament, drawing up a constitution, and regularizing the government. The elections were held late in 1917. Even with freedom of campaigning curtailed and the Bolsheviks in power in many places, they still did not do well. The Bolshevik candidates received less than one-fourth of the total vote cast. The Socialist Revolutionary Party got a plurality of the votes and of deputies elected to the assembly.[2] The question then became whether or not the Bolsheviks would convene the assembly. The Bolshevik, Uritsky, put it this way: "Shall we convene the Constituent Assembly? Yes. Shall we disperse it? Perhaps; it depends on circumstances."[3] It was permitted to hold one meeting, but the Bolsheviks used force to prevent it when the Assembly tried to meet again. The Bolshevik Party held such reins of governmental power as existed in the Russian Empire.

How had the Bolsheviks been able to seize power? They were, after all, a minority party. The soviets, which brooked so large during 1917, were not even creations of the Bolsheviks for the most part. The party itself consisted of only a tiny portion of the vast population of Russia. The answer can be reduced to a single word — Violence! It was the willingness of the Bolsheviks to employ violence that offers the immediate explanation of how they came to power. It distinquished them from the Mensheviks. It distinguished them from the majority of the Socialist Revolutionaries. (A minority, called left S-R's, joined with the Bolsheviks.)

The Bolshevik use of violence may be sufficiently illustrated here by what happened when the Constituent Assembly met for its first and only session. On the day that it was to meet, the Bolsheviks called out large numbers of soldiers and sailors loyal to them to surround, guard, and control the Tauride Palace where the meeting was to be held. Even before the Assembly met, a crowd that had gathered outside was fired upon, and several were killed. The crowd dispersed, obviously intimidated by the killings. What then occurred has been described this way:

The Tauride Palace was an armed camp. All doors were closed except the main entrance. The entrance hall was crowded with armed soldiers and sailors, who examined the credentials of the deputies and amused themselves by commenting aloud on whether it was preferable to shoot, hang or bayonet the deputies. [4]

There was an attempt when the deputies had gathered in the hall to conduct the session according to Russian tradition. The custom was for the oldest member to preside during the organization. This task fell to a man by the name of Sergey Shvetsov, who was a Socialist Revolutionary. But the Bolsheviks would not have it so:

Suddenly there was an uproar. Everyone was shouting at once, the guards were hammering their rifle butts on the floor, the Bolshevik deputies were pounding their fists on the desks and stamping their feet, while Bolshevik soldiers in the public galleries coolly aimed their rifles at the unfortunate Shvetsov.... He had just time to say "I declare the Constituent Assembly open," and to ring his bell, when the bell was snatched from him. In place of the towering white-haried Shvetsov there was the small, dark, black-bearded Yakov Sverdlov, who announced amid cries of "Hangman!" and "Wash the blood off your hands!" that the Bolshevik Executive Committee ... had authorized him to declare the Constituent Assembly open. [5]

Some organization and activity was permitted, but the Bolsheviks finally grew weary and turned out the lights. Thus began and ended representative government in the Soviet Union.

Violence triumphed, and in its train came the Terror, but let that wait for now. Marx and Engels had envisioned the need for violent overturn of governments in order to bring about the revolution but for different reasons than prevailed in Russia. Indeed, Marx had not believed it possible that the first communist revolution would occur in Russia. The man who conceived the possibility, prodded it into being, contrived a theory for it, and led it was Vladimir Ilyich Ulyanov, known to the world as Nikolai Lenin, though he was also known as V. I. Lenin, and until his death was called "Ilyich" by those who knew him.

According to Marxian theory, Russia was not even close to being ripe for a communist revolution in 1917. It was, in the lingo of both progressivism and Marxism, a "backward" country. The population was preponderantly rural, and most people made their living by farming. The strides in industrialization before World War I had, it is true, increased the number of industrial workers in such centers as Petrograd and Moscow, but they were still only a small portion of the population. This situation did not fit into the Marxian theory of revolution. If a communist revolution was to be a proletarian revolution, and Marxism envisioned nothing else, Russia did not have the one ingredient essential to it — a proletarian majority.

To get around this difficulty, Lenin developed several strategems, mostly theoretical but tied in to some extent with the actual situation. By so doing, he wrenched Marxism off its supposed historical course and gave it a new direction. It was a fateful shift for the world, for it laid the groundwork for communist revolutions in industrially backward countries, which is where they have mostly occurred, and took Marx off the hook, so to speak, for the errors in his predictions about advanced countries. The doctrinal result is known as Leninism, though it is generally accepted by the communist faithful as orthodox Marxism.

Lenin attempted to patch over the gaping theoretical hole by proclaiming that the revolution in Russia was part and parcel of an imminent world-wide revolution. The time was right for that, he declared. Imperialism was the final stage of capitalism. World War I was the death agony of the last imperial thrust of moribund capitalism. In the midst of or in the wake of the war would come the inevitable communist revolution everywhere. The situation was ripening for revolution in Germany, and if Germany went, could the rest of the world resist? (It is easy to forget now how closely Marxian theory was tied to the German situation.) With the tide of history rolling shoreward to bring world revolution, what did it matter in the scheme of things if it rolled over Russia first? Except, it mattered a great deal to V. I. Lenin; it must come first in Russia. Why? There is an obvious answer. Lenin was Russian, and he was the chosen vessel to usher in the world revolution. No other will quite do.

Lenin was like a man possessed from the moment he arrived at the Finland Station in Petrograd in April of 1917. Indeed, he may have been obsessed for years, but the obsession appeared now to have him in its control. If an artist had been charged with the task of painting a portrait of a man possessed, he would have done well to choose Lenin as a model. Lenin looked the part with his wide forehead, large head, and penetrating eyes. He was cold, hard, determined, and often appeared to be devoid of ordinary human weaknesses. (After strenuous sessions when debates had gone on late into the night and sleep for most could hardly await a bed, Lenin could be found engrossed in reading or writing.) Time and again during the months from April to October, 1917, Lenin threatened defiance of all the party organs if he would not have his way. This childishness was a product, plausibly, of his obsession.

Now a case can be made, and has been, indeed, was made at the time, that Lenin was an agent of the German Imperial Government. It is fact that he and his entourage were shipped through Germany in a sealed train by the government. It is also known that the Bolshevik Party received money from the German government. [6] Moreover, Lenin's activities might have been little different from what they were had he been a paid German agent. From the moment he arrived in Russia he worked toward getting Russia out of the war. He labored also to undermine what remained of the morale in the army. Once the Bolsheviks seized power they acted as quickly as they could to end the war with Germany, which they accomplished with the Treaty of Brest-Litovsk in early 1918. Even those of less than average inclination to suspicion might suspect collusion from these circumstances.

But there is a better explanation than the German-agent theory, and it accounts for more of the facts. It is this. Lenin believed he had discerned the course of history, not the course of history in some general and theoretical way as Marx had, but its very unfolding before his eyes. The long-awaited revolution was ready to take place. Lenin believed himself to be riding the wave of history to its cresting, and when the moment came he must be at the helm to direct the course of the craft. The best evidence for this is his attitude and behavior in the weeks, days and hours just before October 25, 1917.

Lenin knew as well as anyone that the authority of the Provisional Government which had always been tenuous was deteriorating. It might have been toppled in July had the Bolsheviks directed the forces at their command during the demonstrations. General Kornilov attempted a "counter-revolution" in August, but it failed. Lenin had to go into hiding in August to keep from being arrested by the government. From that time on he became more and more insistent that the Bolsheviks must overturn the government. In early October, he wrote:

Comrades! Our revolution is passing through a highly critical time. This crisis coincides with the great crisis of a growing worldwide socialist revolution and of a struggle against world imperialism. The responsible leaders of our party are confronted with a gigantic task; if they do not carry it out, it will mean a total collapse of the internationalist proletarian movement. The situation is such that delay truly means death.[7]

He had become almost hysterical by October 24:

Comrades: As I write these lines on the evening of the 24th, the situation is impossibly critical. It is clearer than clear that now, in truth, a delay in the uprising is equivalent to death....
The bourgeois onslaught of the Kornilovists, the removal of Verkhovsky, show that we cannot wait. We must, no matter what, this evening, tonight, arrest the government, after we disarm the cadets....
We cannot wait! We may lose everything!![8]

Lenin was beside himself. Though he was repeatedly refused permission to come out of hiding and take up his work at Bolshevik headquarters, he finally ignored it and went there anyhow. From that moment, he took direct leadership of the revolution which he forged.

Whether there was a world revolution or not — there was not —, the fact remained that the Bolsheviks were a minority in Russia. They had promised land to the peasants and peace — withdrawal from the war — to everyone, particularly soldiers, but these promises did not secure a majority. The Bolsheviks still lacked a substantial "proletariat" as well as numerical majority.

Leninism entails making a revolution by imposing the will of a minority on the majority. Lenin, in fact, was contemptuous of majorities. Majorities, he declared, were simply means by which the "bourgeois" deceived the masses. The "important thing is not the number, but the correct expression of the ideas and policies of the really revolutionary proletariat."[9] In answer to the complaint of socialist opponents, he wrote:

They have not understood that a vote within the framework, the institutions, within the habits of bourgeois parliamentarism, is *part* of the bourgeois state apparatus, which must be smashed and broken up from top to bottom *in order* to realize the dictatorship of the proletariat, for the transition from bourgeois democracy to proletarian democracy.
They have not understood that *all* serious questions of politics are decided, not at all by votes, but by civil war, when history places the dictatorship of the proletariat as the order of the day.[10]

"Civil war" is the key to understanding communism, but how Lenin conducted it successfully with a minority needs to be grasped.

Lenin did not develop the theory of party rule simply as an expedient

61

when it turned out that the Bolsheviks were a minority in Russia. His task might have been easier had he had a majority in the Constituent Assembly, but it might not have. He should be believed when he says that majorities do not matter to communism (except for propaganda purposes), for communism must be imposed on the populace however elections turn out. The instrument for doing this would be the tightly knit, disciplined, and relatively small party. Lenin had for several years prior to 1917 been attempting to develop the core of such a party in Russia. He had also developed a justification of it within the outer bounds, at least, of Marxism. Alfred G. Meyer has summarized the theory this way:

The Leninist conception of the party is derived from this acknowledged superiority of socialist theory (consciousness) over the spontaneous movement of the working class. The party is conceived as the organization, incarnation, or institutionalization of class consciousness. In it, historical will and purposiveness are to acquire domination over unguided and irrational instinct and drift.... The task of the party is "to make the proletariat capable of fulfilling its great historical mission.... The party exists for the very purpose of going ahead of the masses and showing the masses the way."[11]

Even despite themselves, no doubt.

The manner in which the power of the party is exercised is a variation of the leverage principle. Whether the phrase has ever been used in connection with communism or not, it is a useful one for visualizing what is done. In financial circles, the leverage principle involves the use of a relatively small amount of money to control and profit from something much more expensive. For example, one might buy a $100 stock by putting up $20 in cash and borrowing the rest. Suppose that the next day the stock goes to $120; it might be sold, and the investor would have doubled his money. In communism, the leverage principle is the means by which a party composing a tiny minority controls and manipulates the whole populace.

The Bolsheviks showed themselves astute at using leverage from the outset. Even the adoption of the term, "bolshevik," was a leverage maneuver. The term means majority. Yet at the Social Democratic gathering where the followers of Lenin adopted the title many votes were taken and those who came to call themselves Bolsheviks won only one. Nonetheless, thereafter they claimed the prestige of being the majority. Bolsheviks maneuvered successfully to gain leverage in the soviets even before the revolution. They used the practice of having a political commissar in military units from the outset. They were not long in extending the practice of having such a person in factories, on collective farms, and so on. The secret police, which were reorganized as the Cheka by the Bolsheviks, were a prime example of leverage.

But what made the leverage principle work to enable a small party to control the whole? How, for example, could a single political commissar control a military unit? The answer is simple enough. The leverage was exerted by intimidation, violence, and terror. Intimidation, violence, and terror are not incidental to communism; they are central and essential. They are its *modus operandi*. There are those who believe that Lenin's insistence on attacking on October 25 arose not so much from its necessity in taking over the government, which might have capitulated anyhow, but from the desire to resort to violence. It is plausible enough. Only by letting loose violence would the party have the necessary means at its disposal.

And, in a land under the sway of violence, the man who is the most ruthless, determined, and arbitrary in employing it is king. Unrestrained use of intimidation and violence is, of course, the method of gangsters, but even gangsters must have a head or leader. The leader is the one who initiates the violence and thus dominates those around him. As indicated in an earlier article, communist rule is gangsterism plus ideology. Lenin was the ideologue personified; when he began to initiate violence he became also the leader of the gangsters.

Almost immediately following his death in 1924 Lenin was transformed into a virtual god by his followers (and even, it is said, by many who were not communists within Russia). The veneration of him went beyond all bounds. In death he became what he never was during his lifetime — all things to all men, the gentle persuader, the tolerant leader, the incarnation of a benign and beneficient communism. In fact, Lenin was the first dictator of the twentieth century, and he was a model of what made the term hated and despised. He was a dictator in practice, and developed a theoretical justification for it.

No sooner had the Bolsheviks seized power than Lenin began to rule by decree. It was the most personal and direct manner of rule. Much of it was done by telephone, for his desk was covered by the instruments. Examples of rule by decree abound, but one will have to suffice here. The following, issued in December, 1917, was supposed to remove all inequalities in the army:

1. To do away with all ranks and titles from the rank of corporal to that of general inclusive. The army of the Russian Republic is henceforth to be composed of free and equal citizens bearing the honorable title of "soldier of the revolutionary army";

2. To do away with all privileges and the external marks formerly connected with the different ranks and titles....[12]

Evidence that Lenin instituted terror survives in messages which he sent out. The following was sent in August, 1918:

Your telegram received. It is necessary to organize an intensive guard of picked reliable men to conduct a merciless mass terror against kulaks, priests and White Guards....

More explicitly, he wrote to the Soviet of Nizhni Novgorod in the same month:

An open uprising of White Guards is clearly in preparation in Nizhni Novgorod. You must mobilize all forces, establish a triumvirate of dictators, introduce immediately mass terror, shoot and deport hundreds of prostitutes who ply soldiers and officers with vodka. Do not hesitate for a moment. You must act promptly: mass searches for hidden arms; mass deportations of Mensheviks and security risks.[13]

Telegrams are given to being terse, but even after that is taken into account it is clear that Lenin did not ameliorate the severity of his death sentences by wishing that God might have mercy on the souls of the victims.

When two or three people are gathered together, even in the name of the Lord, one of them is likely to disagree with the others all too soon. Such disagreement is equally likely in secular affairs, and is certain where such an overweening concept is involved as concerting all activity to achieving felicity on earth. In short, the idea which holds the world in its grip is a subtle prescription for dictatorship, for only thus could all effort be concerted, if it could be done at all. Personal dictatorship is even more clearly required by communism. The violence and terror are supposed to be justified by the ends to be attained by the revolution. These, in turn, are certified by an orthodoxy of ideology. Such orthodoxy can only prevail when one man prescribes and all others accept or are beaten into submission.

Lenin put it somewhat differently, but the conclusion was about the same. He called his theory of dictatorship "Democratic Centralism." His meaning is fairly clear from this description of it:

The party is in a position in which the strictest centralism and the most stringent discipline are absolute necessities. All decisions of higher headquarters are absolutely binding for the lower.[14]

A scholar has characterized Lenin's views in this way: "We come closer to the real issue when we realize that all discussion was suspect to him, because it was a waste of time and because it might threaten the unity of the party in action."[15] When Lenin had wrought revolution, idea had become actuality, and those who differed were proposing to argue with reality. When the reality is a gun, the debate is closed. Lenin sent a telegram to Communists in Novgorod about something that they had done with which *he* disagreed. The message contained these words: "I warn you that I shall have the chairmen of the *guberniya* executive committees, the Cheka and the members of the executive committee arrested for this and see that they are shot."[16] Fortunately for them, he didn't go through with it.

Civil war is a part of the pattern by which ideology is linked to actuality in communism. There was a civil war in Russia from 1918 into 1921 between the Reds and the Whites, but that is not the civil war under discussion here, nor did Lenin refer to the conflict between the Reds and Whites in speaking about civil war in an earlier quotation. What is here being called civil war is what communists refer to as revolution. Revolution is too vague and general an appellation, whereas civil war calls attention to the true character of what was going on. It was a conflict between the Bolsheviks, or Communists, on the one hand, and the customs, institutions, and possessions of the people on the other.

J. P. Nettl emphasized the strangeness of these new rulers by the following description of them:

> A Bolshevik was ... anti-social in the normal sense of the word. He did not communicate readily, he did not seek friends, he did not attempt to make himself agreeable, he had no time for sociability or relaxation as such. Since he believed in a philosophy which was totally incomprehensible to non-Marxists, it was often difficult even to talk to him....
> The dichotomy between Party and society in the early days was thus reinforced by a clash of cultures and of language....[17]

Party against society, that was one dimension of the conflict, but there was also Party against the state, Party against the army, Party against religion, Party against the money supply, Party against the family, Party against property, Party against venerable custom and tradition, and Party against everything that had been Russian, Christian, or Western Civilization.

It may not have appeared this way to many people at first. True, there was a great wave of destruction that swept over Russia in the wake of the Bolshevik seizure of power, but many people accepted much of the destruction gladly. The remains of the old regime — the Duma, the Senate (supreme court), and local governments — were destroyed, but if their passing was mourned there is little record of it. The army was destroyed, but most soldiers hardly regretted that. As one historian notes: "The crumbling army was pushed to complete disintegration by decrees ordering election of officers … and abolishing all ranks and decorations. What units were left in being were speedily demobilized."[18]

The system of alliances with the rest of the world was discarded when the Bolsheviks made a separate peace with Germany. The Russian Empire was supposed to be dissolved, and the various nationalities were promised virtual independence. The workers were encouraged to take over the factories and run them. The peasants were bidden to take the land for their own. It looked at first as if the revolutionary promises might be fulfilled, as if a large portion of the populace was to be awarded the spoils of victory.

But the Bolsheviks gave, and the Bolsheviks took away, almost before the spoils could be grasped. The old state structure was destroyed, but in its stead a new state was built, more autocratic than the old, under the complete control of the Communist Party with no vestige of popular control, with a new secret police to impose its will. The old army was hardly demobilized before a new one was being built. Leon Trotsky forged this new army into fighting trim. Compulsory military training for workers and peasants was established, the death penalty for desertion restored (it having been abolished under the Provisional Government), election of officers ended, and many of the old officers brought back into service.

The only nationality ever to be granted independence was Finland; after that, under the leadership of Joseph Stalin the process of consolidation of the empire was renewed. There were no more foreign alliances, but in their stead the Communist International (Comintern) was set up to foment revolution around the world. The workers did not run the factories for long; the government nationalized the industries, brought back many of the old managers to run them, and commissars representing the Party kept a watchful eye over them. The peasants might own the land, but the government took the produce, or most of it, by simply confiscating it. Even peace was short-lived, for a real civil war between the Reds and the Whites broke out in 1918.

It is not possible to convey the full sweep of the revolutionary thrust of those first months and years. Perhaps the most symbolic event was the movement of the capital from Petrograd to Moscow. Peter the Great had moved it to what was then called St. Petersburg as a part of his program of the westernization of Russia. It was to be Russia's "window to Europe." Whatever the practical reasons for returning the capital to its ancient seat, the act was laden with symbolic meaning. The Kremlin, the walled city, was an ancient religious center. Its churches were some of the most magnificent of Eastern Christendom.

One might suppose that Moscow and the Kremlin were emblematic of all that the Bolsheviks hated and wished to destroy. So they undoubtedly were, but it never does to forget that the Communists were founding a new religion. What better way to do so than at the seat of the old, and what greater profanation of the old than to locate it in the Kremlin? Comintern and Party agents headquartered there could go forth to convert all nations even as Christian missionaries had done of old.

The Bolsheviks did not wait long to begin their assault on the family and religion. In a pamphlet on the family, Alexandra Kollontai, a leading Bolshevik, had this to say:

The family ceases to be necessary. It is not necessary to the state because domestic economy is no longer advantageous to the state, it needlessly distracts women workers from more useful productive labour. It is not necessary to members of the family themselves because the other task of the family — the bringing up of children — is gradually taken over by society.[19]

Lenin did not go so far. Instead, he acted to remove many supports to the stability of the family. A new marriage code required civil registration of marriages and made religious ceremonies of no account at law. Divorce was made possible on demand by either or both parties. Illegitimate children were accorded the same rights as legitimate children. Both sexes were declared to be equal. Abortion was legalized in 1920 "for so long as the moral survivals of the past and economic conditions of the present compel some women to resort to this operation."[20]

As to religion, the Party announced in 1919 that it was

guided by the conviction that the realization of planned order and consciousness ... can alone bring with it a complete dying out of religious prejudices. The party aims at a complete destruction of the link between the exploiting classes and the organization of religious propaganda by assisting the effective liberation of the toiling masses from religious prejudices and by organizing the broadest propaganda in favour of scientific enlightenment and against religion.[21]

67

But the attack on religion was hardly restricted to propaganda. Church and state were proclaimed to be separate. Church property was confiscated. Church activity in the schools was banned. And there was widespread persecution: some priests were killed, and churches were taken over for secular uses.

By 1921, the Russia that had been was virtually in ruins. The old order had been almost completely destroyed, but the bright utopia foretold by communist prophets had not emerged. Much damage had undoubtedly been done by participation in World War I and during the war between the Reds and Whites, but even more of the devastation should probably be charged to the revolutionary thrust. In 1921 industrial production was only about thirteen per cent of what it had been before World War I. Seventy-four million tons of grain had been harvested in 1916 compared with only 30 million tons in 1919, and production continued to decline. The Bolsheviks had almost destroyed the value of the money by drastic increases of the supply (inflation). Famine conditions existed in many areas.

The civil war was over, but new rebellions were already occurring. People were leaving the cities to seek sustenance in the countryside. The population of Moscow had been about 2 million in 1917, but it fell to 800,000 by 1920. The population of Leningrad had been 2,416,000 in 1916; it dropped to 722,000 by 1920. The situation was desperate.

That, then, was the Bolshevik Revolution and its outcome. The Russian people would suffer much more, and, in some ways, worse, as they were beset later by Permanent Revolution, to use Trotsky's phrase, but for the time being the revolutionary thrust was virtually ended. The Bolshevik Party had already become the Communist Party, and later revolutionary action would not be called or attributed directly to Bolshevism. Lenin restored some freedom of trade with his New Economic Policy (NEP) in 1921, and conditions began to improve somewhat.

Having intertwined ideology with developments in the account thus far, it is in order now to sort out the myth from the reality of communism.

6

The Communist Facade

THIS STORY IS said to have been told by a man who served as a tour guide in and around Detroit, Michigan. One day he was assigned to show Ford's River Rouge plant to a group of visiting Russian engineers. The guide noted that they were soon in a jovial mood, laughing, talking, and generally in a festive spirit. Just as they passed the huge parking lot filled with cars, they became even more animated than usual. The one who spoke the best English addressed this question to the guide:

"Do they prepare themselves like this to impress all their visitors? Or is it just for us?"

"What do you mean?" the guide asked.

"The impressive number of cars. It's a flattering illustration of Ford's capacity for production."

The guide pointed out that Ford would hardly have arranged such a display since the cars were used and some of them were old. Moreover, the visitors must have already observed that there were many cars in the United States. But his answer did not satisfy the Russian.

"Then to whom do they belong?"

"To the people who work at the plant and in the offices. Workers."

"You're kidding," he said, "so many cars?"

The guide explained that many of the Ford employees owned their own cars. The Russian declared that such a notion was typical propaganda. There was a way to prove it, the guide said. It would only be necessary to ask workers to whom they would talk on the assembly line whether they owned cars or not. But that would prove nothing, the Russian maintained.

"We know that old trick. The plant is well prepared for their visit. Every worker has learned by heart how to answer our questions. Unless he wants to be fired or arrested he'll have to give the proper answer."

All right, if asking them in the plant would not prove anything, why not wait until the shifts changed, and as a worker approached his car, ask him whose it was? But the Russian was only amused:

"What do you take me for," he asked, "an idiot? It's simple to stage such a show. I don't hold Americans for bunglers. If you do something, you do it well. You are a big nation, and you know how to deal with other nations."[1]

Nothing could convince the Russian that it was not a show staged for the benefit of the visiting engineers.

Variations on this story have been told a good many times. It is sometimes told to illustrate the disparity between the material condition of Soviet workers and those in the United States. That is undoubtedly an important point, but it is not the one to be emphasized here. It may also be told to call attention to the fact that tours in the Soviet Union have for many years had a carefully arranged itinerary through areas prepared in advance to provide a good impression to visitors. This brings us somewhat nearer the point, but does not begin to comprehend all that is involved in it.

What is involved is an attempt to grasp the impact of an idea which has had the Russian Empire in its grip for over sixty years. That impact is by no means easily understood. Our understanding of any complex development, or of anything, for that matter, is always partial and incomplete. In the best of circumstances, our vision is impaired by the limitations of the angle we are taking, by our inclination to put new wine into old bottles, i.e., to fit the new experience into the confines of what we already knew, and by the tendency to put the best or the worst face on a thing. But these usual obstacles to understanding are greatly augmented in the case of the Soviet Union by a massive propaganda effort and by a concerted deliberate effort to conceal the truth.

Communism has been deliberately hidden behind a facade, a more extensive facade than has ever been erected before, a facade of such dimensions that the parable with which this article begins may have actually occurred, either once or many times. That is, the Russian people are familiar with such an extensive facade that they could actually

70

imagine that Ford Motor Company would arrange an immense spectacle of automobiles to deceive a few obscure visiting engineers.

There are two common ways of misinterpreting the facade. One is the obvious mistaking of the facade for the reality of communism. The literature on Soviet Communism abounds with examples of people who returned from visits to Russia and wrote favorable accounts of what they saw, accounts whose credibility depended upon accepting the facade for the whole reality. The other misinterpretation comes from those who have grasped the dimensions of the facade and perceive the gigantic hypocrisy which has produced it. Such hypocrisy, they tend to conclude, can only mean that communism is only a sham, that Communists are hypocrites hiding their lust for power behind an ideological mask.

There is a goodly amount of literature, produced mainly in the last decade or so, which offers much inferential evidence in support of this interpretation. Nonetheless, those who draw this conclusion have got the matter wrong-end-to. They are looking at the effect and are mistaking it for the cause. The facade is an effect; so are the power opportunities. The love of power resides in every breast, dormant or active; the lust for power is an effect of opportunities to wield it without let or hindrance. Communist ideology is not a mask, it is a cause. It is *the* cause which has produced the above effects. Before explaining why, how, and in what ways the facade is an effect, however, it is in order to explore the dimensions of the facade in the Soviet Union.

The government of the Soviet Union is a facade. An elaborate governmental structure exists in the Soviet Union, a structure which bears no relation to decision making and very little to the exercise of power. In theory, the power of government is vested in the Supreme Soviet, which is composed of a Council of the Union and a Council of Nationalities. Members are elected by universal suffrage, and more than 90 per cent of those eligible usually vote. When the Supreme Soviet is not in session, which is most of the time, its legislative functions are supposed to be performed by an executive body, called a Presidium. What could be more democratic?

Except that the Supreme Soviet is only a facade, window dressing, so to speak. It merely approves the decisions that have already been made. There is usually only one candidate for office, and he (or she) has been selected by the powers that be. In reality, there is no impact upon the government from the populace. Actual power is supposed to be wielded by the Communist Party, whose membership over the years has ranged from, say, 2 million members upwards toward 10 million. There is an elaborate structure of party organization from bottom to top which parallels that of the formal government. But the Party is not a decision-making institution; it is a decision-executing institution. The way it works has been described by a historian thusly (He refers to the Stalin Era, but much the same could be said for the whole period of Communist rule.):

Huge as it was, the Communist party entrusted its authority to a Central Committee of some seventy or more. . . . Directing the labors of the Committee, and indeed of the mighty USSR as a whole, was the party *Politburo*, called the *Presidium* after 1952, usually of about sixteen men and women. This powerful, self-perpetuating institution responded in the final analysis to the will and whims of the arbitrary despot, Joseph Stalin.[2]

It should be clear, then, that the governmental structure involves not one facade but a series of facades in a row, as it were, each lower in visibility or height as it is looked at from front to back but greater in power. Popular elections are entirely facade, the most visible and the least substantial of the facades. The Supreme Soviet, the "parliament," is a front which exercises no real power. Its Presidium technically wields power, but it is actually a mechanism to be manipulated by those further behind the scenes. The Party, too, is a facade, in that it is a symbol of rather than the real source of power. Even the Politburo, or Party Presidium, has sometimes been mainly a facade, for its members have been subject to the will of the single man in charge.

Nonetheless, the Party is most important. He who can speak for the Party, i.e., lay down the Party line, rules the Soviet Union. The Party is not so much the base of power, though in periods when there is a contest for dominance within the Politburo it may sometimes have been, but it is always the ideological arm of power. As one man becomes dominant, his base of power becomes his control of all armed force, especially the secret police, for through them he controls all else. But all this hinges on control over the Party, which is a way of saying that it depends upon making the "correct" interpretation of ideology.

Lenin's greatest invention was of the *facade* of party rule. He did not, of course, invent party rule, for that had existed in England, say, before Karl Marx was even born. Party rule in England is a device for rule by majority, and the party claims its right to rule on the basis of popular election and ability to obtain majorities on key issues in the House of Commons.

Communists neither necessarily have nor do they claim to rule by majorities. The Communist Party is not a political party in the accepted or expected sense. It does not claim to be a *part;* it claims to be the *whole.* That is, it claims to act for all those who have any right to rule, i.e., the proletariat, the peasants, or whoever. It claims this right on the basis of ideology. It acts not by majorities but in unison and under strict discipline. The Party is a facade; the reality is ideology, and the personification of reality is the one man, and there can *only* be one man, who can set forth the correct interpretation of ideology. Every member of the Party must then accept this line or be subject to expulsion, or worse. Such party rule is now the norm in many parts of the world. It is rule by an idea.

Communism operates, too, behind a cover of words. It may be that the best place to examine this facade is in the Soviet constitutions. There have been several such documents. The first was promulgated in 1918, the second in 1924, and probably the most ambitious in 1936. They are in form constitutions, in content ideological, and, in fact, facades.

In form, a constitution sets forth the power of the government, who is to exercise the powers of government, may prescribe limitations on the power, and lays down the procedures by which the government is to operate. A constitution may affirm certain rights as belonging to the people as well as those that inhere in the limitations on the government. The Soviet constitutions appear to do most of these things. They describe a governmental structure, tell how it is to operate, and set forth certain rights belonging to approved classes, or to the people generally.

But all this is misleading. One writer attempts to get around this fact by ascribing a different purpose to the Soviet constitution than that of traditional ones. He says, "In the Soviet Union, the Constitution ... is regarded far more as a symbol or summary of the existing structure of government than as an immutable blueprint; it is descriptive rather than prescriptive...."[3] To which it must be replied that the constitutions are not very accurate as descriptions, either, but, if they were, we would still say that something which purports to be a constitution and is not prescriptive is not a constitution.

The Soviet constitutions are ideological in content. The first one was professedly a class document. "Members of the so-called exploiting classes — businessmen, monks and priests..., police agents of the old regime ... — were disfranchised and denied the right to hold office." More, "The Bill of Rights was restated in class terms. Freedom of

73

speech, of press, association, of assembly, and of access to education was to be reserved to the working class...."[4] They are ideological, too, in prescribing duties as well as rights. But they are ideological in the deepest sense in that they are neither faithful descriptions of the actual situation nor enforceable prescriptions of what should be; they are formal statements of the stages in history of the Communist Revolution in Russia at particular times.

The constitutions are facades. Neither the workers, nor any other class or group enjoy freedom of speech, press, association, or religion in the Soviet Union. There are no independent powers to contain or limit the exercise of power. The Constitution of 1924 declared that the member republics had an inalienable right to secede from the Soviet Union, but, as Stalin had said, "the demand for secession ... at the present stage of the revolution [has become] a profoundly conterrevolutionary one."[5] In short, secession was a right, but it could not be permitted. The first two constitutions did not even acknowledge the role of the Party in government. The Constitution of 1936 did ascribe a role to the Party, but it did not expose it fully. The nature of the facades erected by constitutions is well described in this summary by a scholar:

> The Soviet regime has demonstrated great skill in using the trappings of mass democracy to mask the entrenched position of the dictatorial elite which dominates Soviet society. Constitutional myths and symbols have been ingeniously adapted to contribute to the illusion of mass control. But the actual configurations of power in the system are difficult to conceal. The political realities of Soviet life speak the unmistakable language of one-party dictatorship in which ultimate power is deposited in a narrow ruling group in the Kremlin.[6]

Sometimes even traditional branches of the government are largely facade. So it is with the diplomatic and consular services. According to expert testimony, they serve mainly to provide intelligence information and promote espionage in foreign lands. *"Furthermore, the majority of personnel in Soviet embassies abroad are KGB* [the 'regular' secret police] *and GRU* [military secret police] *employees.* The proportion of KGB staff officers to the rest of Soviet embassy personnel is usually two men out of five. GRU staff officers number one man in five."[7] There is abundant testimony, too, that even cleaning women serve as spies, and that all personnel in an embassy are subject to the control of the secret police.

Perhaps the strangest facade of all is that of the Orthodox Church in the Soviet Union. It is strange because the Communist Party vowed

74

from the beginning to root out and destroy the remains of religion. The power of the government was vigorously used for many years, is still used, against religion. Party members may not be churchgoers; in general, those who have any position or status avoid the outward practice of religion. Churches, monasteries, and all sorts of religious establishment have been closed on a vast scale. Parents were forbidden to teach religion to their children. Priests and ministers have been persecuted. None of this succeeded in stifling religion in the Soviet Union. But the Communists have followed another tack, have done so more or less from the beginning. They have attempted to penetrate and subvert the churches, most notably the Orthodox Church, to use the churches, so far as possible, for their own ends.

One way the Church serves as a facade is by the hierarchy giving vocal support for the regime. Hedrick Smith says: "Patriarch Pimen and other Orthodox prelates make obligatory speeches praising Soviet policy at home and abroad. The Church donates millions of rubles to the Soviet Peace Committee and other Communist causes."[8] Another writer states the case more directly:

The Church is subject to the guidance of the State Council for Religious Affairs, which can overrule the Patriarch (the ruling bishop) or any Church authority on any issue, religious or secular. The council exacts huge "contributions" from the Church treasury for various ... causes, and compels Church elders to lend their presence to state occasions, particularly large receptions in the Kremlin to which foreigners are invited.[9]

Robert G. Kaiser gives examples of how high churchmen present a facade to newsmen to conceal the actual situation. These examples came out in a press conference. The Metropolitan declared to the assembled press that "The State does not interfere with the Church." In support of his view, he proclaimed that the Church was publishing many new Bibles. As it turned out, it had published 80,000 in 20 years, 4,000 per year for from 30 to 50 million believers. Those who attended the conference were each presented with a set of long-playing records which contained reproductions of the singing of much of the Church liturgy. "The state record monopoly made the album, but it has never been sold to the public. It is a special edition, made for the Church to hand out in occasions like this one."[10]

Considerable evidence has been accumulated that churchmen are often used as spies by the secret police, and that some of them may actually be members of the secret police. The Reverend Richard Wurmbrand testified in this fashion before a Congressional committee:

If you tell me that somebody is an official pastor in a Rumanian or a Russian church, I know that he is an informer of the Communist authorities. Without this, you can't be.

On Sunday you preach. On Monday you can be called to the so-called representative of the Government Council for the Affairs of the Religious Cults, and you are obliged to answer the questions: "Who has been in your church?" They don't care about these old ones. "What Youth has been in church?" "Who is a soulwinner?" If they have confessed something, "What have they confessed?" "Who is zealous in prayer?" "What are their political attitudes?"[11]

To the same effect, though much less dramatically, Kaiser says, "According to believers in Moscow, the hierarchy is riddled with agents and informers...."[12] In this manner, the Communists attempt to transform the churches into a facade.

Facades abound in Soviet Communism. Perhaps the most ubiquitous facade is equality. Women are supposed to be equal with men. It is supposed to be a land without special privilege, where even top Party officials receive only modest salaries. Inhabitants of rural areas are in theory equal to city dwellers. Though this facade is not well maintained, a good deal of energy goes into creating the appearance of equality. Politburo members often dress plainly and affect simple tastes. Yet, behind the scenes, privilege is the order of the day; indeed, there is such an intricate array of privileges that it requires considerable study to get to know them. Party members are, of course, privileged over the general citizenry. The secret police have their own special stores where they can buy goods not available to the general populace.

In one sense, women are equal to men, in the sense of working as hard as do men, or harder. One writer says that "there has appeared in the streets of Communist cities a strange creature whom people speak of as a 'working woman.' You can see her on cranes, in railroad yards, at the heaviest construction sites, in mines, on highway building jobs, etc."[13] But if she is married her "equality" surely adds to her burdens. "The chronically low level of the material sphere of life usually necessitates employment by both parties to the marriage, but the woman still has to care for her home and children. In such circumstances, the woman's life becomes in effect a kind of penal servitude of early rising, working in an office or factory from nine to five, standing in line for groceries..., doing the housecleaning..., preparing meals for her husband and children in moments of paralyzing exhaustion."[14] The facade of equality often masks a brutalizing inequality.

The special privileges of the leaders are at least partially hidden behind a variety of facades. Here is one brief description of how the system works:

License plates beginning with MOC belong to members and staff of the Party's Central Committee, and illegal left turns are one of the privileges that accrue to such citizens. They come to Granovskovo Street to collect more special privileges — food and clothing sold in a special store open only to them. The store is hidden behind a door marked BUREAU OF SPECIAL PASSES.... Granovskovo Street is usually lined with chauffeur-driven cars waiting for their official proprietors to come out of the store. Most of the customers emerge carrying nondescript packages wrapped in brown paper.[15]

Their special privileges are much more extensive, of course, but this one example exposes the character of the facade.

There is a great difference between life in the major cities and that in small cities and rural areas. A part of the communist facade is of a modernized, industrialized land with giant hydro-electric dams, huge steel and oil industries, large mechanized state farms, clean subway systems, and so on. Hedrick Smith reported this description by a Russian of actual conditions:

"On the stronger, larger state farms not far from Moscow or Leningrad, or those built for show..., conditions are better in every way — stone buildings, separate apartments for each working family, a sewage system, running water. This was the way it was on the first two state farms where I worked. They were each about an hour from Leningrad. But the third state farm was further out — about two hours. It was a weak farm. Wooden buildings. It lacked all conveniences. No central heating system. No sewage system. No running water. The greatest problem on all three was the lack of meat. There was almost none. As far as other food goes, the closer to Leningrad, the more the stores were selling. The further from Leningrad, the less they were selling. That was the rule. Apples you could get. But oranges, tangerines — only in Leningrad."[16]

Why all these, and other, facades? Why erect elaborate governmental structures that do not govern? Why the pretense of democracy? Why have extensive electoral campaigns when the results of the election are a foregone conclusion? Why bother to tally the votes when the electorate have no choice? Why have written constitutions when they neither inhibit those who rule nor assure any benefits to the ruled? Why would an atheist regime attempt to have a church serve as a facade? Why does the regime maintain a facade of equality when everywhere great inequities prevail? Why create model kindergartens, model state farms, model collective farms, and even model prisons, as the Soviet Union does? In short, why erect facade after facade at such tremendous effort and expense? Who are these supposed to impress?

It is widely believed that these facades, as they are being called here, are erected mainly to impress foreigners and conceal from them Soviet reality. Undoubtedly, this is one of the reasons for which some of the facade building takes place. For example the facade of freedom of religion presented by high churchmen is clearly for foreign consumption. Surely, too, the facade of a diplomatic service which conceals alien secret police is created for its effect on foreigners. Model farms, and such like, probably have as one of their reasons for being the impression of visitors to the Soviet Union.

It has always been important to the Soviet Union, too, to create a favorable impression on foreigners (though often enough they have not succeeded in this). The communist "experiment" was first undertaken on a large scale in Russia. A Communist International was organized by Lenin to spread communism around the world. The success of this movement would surely depend, to some extent, on at least the apparent success of communism in Russia. If communism was to be "the wave of the future," that future would surely need to look attractive if others were to be drawn to it.

But why facades? Why not present the actuality of the Soviet Union to the world? The answer to this question is so obvious, that it may have been unnecessary to pose it: The Soviet "achievement" has not been such as would be likely to favorably impress peoples from many parts of the world. The Soviet reality, at its nether reaches, is such that it repels decent people. The Soviet Union could only take a place among the governments of the world by creating a facade of democracy, of constitutionality, and of having something like a parliamentary system. If its gangster-like actions were not concealed by facades, it would be incumbent on people generally to recognize it for what it is.

But the facades are not just for the benefit of foreigners. They are for the inhabitants of the Soviet Union as well. How, it may be asked, can they be for the people who are unlikely to be fooled for long as to the nature of the regime and of conditions under which they live? It is possible, however, to be impressed by facades even if one is not misled by them. Millions of Americans have been thrilled, and horrified, by films about catastrophes even though they know they are not witnessing actual catastrophes. It is impressive that the Communist Party can garner an almost unanimous vote from the Russian electorate, even though the election is rigged, so to speak. The creation of such elaborate and extensive facades may be a more impressive demonstration of power than would the feeding of the poor, say.

But these explanations are surface explanations. Underlying them are deeper reasons which account for the continued, prolific, and pervasive facades. Communism is a deception. Efforts to impose it can only be maintained by erecting facade after facade. Facade is the natural fruit of deception. Communist ideology cannot produce the freedom that it proclaims, the democracy that it claims, the concerted effort that it seeks, nor the transformed man that it wills. Marxian ideology, on which it is based, is a kind of poetic vision of man, society, economics, and life which does not now, never did, and there is no reason to believe ever will, exist. All the efforts to bring it into being result in something quite different from what is sought. It is only possible to create illusions that it works; these illusions we can experience as facades.

Communism is not basically a social system, an economic system, or even a political system; it is basically a *conspiracy*. It evinces itself to the world as a conspiracy to gain, hold, and wield power to effect a great transformation. But in its inwards, so to speak, it is a conspiracy to deceive and an agreement to be deceived. It is, I say, a deception. Who does it deceive? The answer is this: *Communism is a conspiracy to deceive all who need to be deceived by it.* All who accept it, work to apply it, aid it in any way, or on whom it is being imposed, need to be deceived. Even those most deeply involved in creating the deception need to be deceived. Indeed, they have the greatest need to be deceived, because they have the greatest need to believe in it.

The members of the Politburo, or Presidium, have the greatest need to be deceived. They stand at the pinnacle of power in the Soviet Union because they are the ones charged with the task and who are supposed to know how to usher in communism. That it can be achieved is essential to their hold on power and position. They need to believe that they are concerting all effort toward achieving their goals. They need to believe that the workers, peasants, and intellectuals are solidly behind them. They need to believe that religion is dying out, that the young are committed to communism, and that communism is conferring great benefits on the people. They need to believe, above all, that socialism works and that they are approaching the final stage of communism.

A situation is created for the top men that enables them very nearly to believe all this. This is the role of the special privileges which they enjoy. They live in and around Moscow which has the best of everything

79

in Russia. And they have the best of the best: the finest cars, the most exclusive dachas, the choicest foods, the most sumptuous beach houses in the Crimea, and they fly in the most modern of jet planes. As Kaiser observes, "Privileges insulate those at the very top, a tiny group of perhaps only two or three dozen men, from all the harassments and discomforts of an ordinary citizen's life." "In sum," he says, "they live in a contrived environment. Even their vodka is better than the ordinary man's."[17]

But there is much more to their contrived environment than these special privileges. In a sense, most Russians are engaged in a giant conspiracy to prove that socialism, or communism, works. The quotas of production that are supposed to be filled are a part of that unwitting conspiracy. (Even prisoners in slave labor camps learned to exaggerate their output in order to survive.) The shoddy goods which are produced to fill quotas promote the conspiracy, for on the statistical sheets viewed by the Politburo they are not described as shoddy. The whole massive propaganda program enables those who will to believe in communism.

The need to be deceived spreads outward from the Politburo in concentric circles to reach finally to the whole world. The members of the Party in the Soviet Union need to be deceived, even as they are contriving to bring off the deception. Communist parties around the world need to be deceived. "Fellow-travelers" of the communist movement around the world need to be deceived. Indeed, all who wish to be need to be deceived, and all who will make sufficient effort can be. The whole paraphernalia of facades exists to assist them in the effort.

Whether or not the deceivers are actually deceived by their deceptions is somewhat beside the point. The point is that such a fabric of deception is created, entailing a vast conspiracy to bring it off, that reality is sufficiently distorted so as to make it difficult to determine what is real and what not. When the truth is sufficiently distorted and obscured, men may believe what they wish. The purpose of the deception is adequately achieved when those who need to believe are enabled to do so by it. There is a human tendency, communism aside, for men to believe what they want to believe. There is an even stronger tendency for men to believe what they have a strong need to believe.

Communists have built facade upon facade in the Soviet Union to assist any who will, and all who need to, to believe that communism works and is the wave of the future. Of course, one of the results of such widespread deception may be an equally widespread cynicism. The Soviet engineers, in the anecdote which opens this chapter, could not believe that the huge number of automobiles outside the Ford plant had not been assembled just to impress them. This meant also, of course, that they did not believe many of the spectacles created in the Soviet Union. But they pretend to believe them when they are at home, which may be almost as useful as actually believing. Such pretense undoubtedly degrades them, but degraded men are essential to corrupt systems. The success of the facades depends upon a conspiracy of degraded men.

Behind the facades, however, is a grim and brutal reality. It is the reality of terror on which the power of the rulers of the Soviet Union rests, a terror so extensive that for many years those who tried to tell the world of it were not believed.

The Reign of Terror

TERROR is Soviet Communism's substitute for law. It is not an accident that it is a substitute; it is not a whim of those who rule; it does not arise simply from the love of power. Terror is as essential to communism as oxygen is to fire. Its essentiality, its necessity, arises from the nature of things. The necessity for it is, if you will, ontological and metaphysical, lying at the core of how things are and the way they can be here on this earth. (*How much* terror is necessary is an entirely different matter; it is, in any case, a question for tyrants to debate.)

Karl Marx professed to believe that when private property was abolished the state would wither away. The available evidence indicates that Marx erred, that far from disappearing the state expands and grows luxuriously until it occupies every nook and cranny of the life of the people when private property is abolished. Marx's insight was off the mark. It is not the state which withers away when property is abolished, but law, and liberty, and private rights, and justice.

True, theorists of communism thought that the need for law would disappear as the revolution moved to its fruition. This would, however, occur simultaneously with the withering away of the state, or, at least, as a part of the same process. Law, according to Marxism, is a product of the class struggle. It is the means by which the ruling class imposes its will on all the rest. The state is the device which effects the imposition. The Bolshevik Revolution did indeed sunder ancient relationships between the state (and the government within it), property, law, and private rights. It sundered them sufficiently to reveal some connections which could have been known theretofore mainly by speculation. The Soviet experience should serve as a rich mine for political theory, but it can only do so by being separated from Marxian theory.

The major conclusion to be drawn from the Soviet experience is this: Law is neither essential to nor derived from the power of the state. On the contrary, law is an impediment to the exercise of governmental power. Government operates essentially by the use of force. The state is the territory within which a government has a monopoly of the use of force, at least within its jurisdiction. Law regularizes and *limits* the use of force by government. It limits it by prescribing how force shall be used, to what extent, and under what conditions. Law is no more necessary to governments than handcuffs would be to a boxer.

Law arises from and depends on property rights. All rights are extensions of property rights. This has been the case historically. Freedom of speech, of press, and of religion, for example, were only established after the foundation had been laid in rights to private property. This course of events was not accidental; it was essential. The law can protect only what it can define. Freedom of speech is a property right to one's utterances, depending for its use upon a place (property) from which to speak, and upon its defense for the means by which to enter into an adversary relationship with those (including government) who would deny it. Abolish private property, and you abolish all rights and liberties with it. Law can no more survive without these rights in property than can a building be suspended from sky hooks. Neither has any foundation.

Government requires neither private property nor law in order to function. They are inhibitions on its exercise of force. There is for government an alternative to law; it is terror. Government must act by law or by terror, or a combination of these two means. In the absence of private property and its corollary, law, government must act by terror. The exercise of force without the restraint of law is terror. No better definition can be given, and none is needed. It does not become terror because of the horrible character of the acts; every use of force is terroristic because it is arbitrary, unpredictable, and has no certain cause or explanation. None may know when force will be applied or when it will be halted, for there are no enforceable restraints.

The Soviet Union is a lawless nation at bottom. There is, of course, a facade of law. There are rules for the bureaucracy; there are statutes to apply to the populace; there is a constitution, have been several constitutions; and there is a system of courts. But these are all facade, because those who rule are unbound by them. They are unbound because the Russian people have no means for making them observe the law. They have no means because they have no private property, or so little that it is grossly insufficient for the task. They have no property because of communism. The lawlessness and terror derive from communism; they are its inevitable corollary. The extent of the terror depends upon the particular ruler; the necessity for terror, per se, arises from communism.

The history of the Soviet Union can be divided into episodes according to the degree, extent, and quality of terror by which it has been ruled. The first episode was that of War Communism from 1918 into 1921, a period of extensive terror and Draconian measures in behalf of revolutionary activity and the defeat of the White forces. The next episode was that of the New Economic Policy (NEP) which lasted from about 1921 to 1928. There is no doubt that the terror abated during this period. Much private economic activity was permitted; commercial laws were enacted; and some protections to private property were enforced.

The next episode properly encompasses the whole period of the personal rule of Joseph Stalin, 1928-1953, a period of 25 years of the most extensive and intensive reign of terror in all of history. The Stalinist terror can itself be broken into episodes — forced collectivization, forced industrialization, the Great Purge, and so on — but this would only involve distinctions based on the character of the victims not upon the extent of the terror.

Following Stalin's death, particularly during Nikita Khrushchev's middle period, so to speak, 1956 through the early 1960's, there was a dramatic abatement of the terror, a widescale freeing of political prisoners, and even some revelation of the extent of Stalin's terror. This does not mean Khrushchev's reign was lawful, only less terror-filled. The indications are that Leonid Brezhnev has restored much of the secretive atmosphere of Stalin as well as a modified terror.

One thing should be made clear: Every Communist regime in the Soviet Union has employed terror. All have used the secret police who were an instrument of the rule of terror, whose names have been changed over the years but not their character. All have been lawless in that none has been prevented from acting because it was against the law. No single instance has come to light of a member of the secret police being prosecuted for terrorist acts against the citizenry. Khrushchev reported some of the crimes of Stalin, but those who conspired with Stalin were not brought to justice.

The purpose of the terror in the Soviet Union is not primarily to maintain what in the United States is sometimes called law and order. This helps to explain the great variations in the degree, extent, and quality of the terror. If it were aimed at punishing or suppressing what is ordinarily called crime, there would be little reason to expect any great variation. After all, crimes against persons and property may increase or diminish over the years, but they do not ordinarily change much from one ruler to the next. In any case, ordinary crime — crimes against persons, such as assault, and theft of personal property — does not greatly excite the Soviet authorities. Most property belongs to the state, and theft or abuse of it is a political crime. "Political" crime is that against which the terror is waged. There is abundant testimony, even, that ordinary criminals are permitted, and probably intentionally used, to terrorize the political prisoners in prisons and slave labor camps.

Terror, then, is an ideological weapon. It is the main device used in the attempt to impose communism on the Russian people. A most important conclusion follows from this: The extent of the terror is in direct proportion to the effort being made to impose communism. The facts tend to support this conclusion. In the 1920's, under the New Economic Policy, there was an abatement of the terror. It is generally understood that the New Economic Policy was a conscious retreat, albeit temporary, from socialism or communism. Such restoration of private enterprise in trade, farming, and small manufactures as was made was admittedly a step backward.

Then, in 1928 Stalin began the "Great Leap Forward" with the initiation of his first Five Year Plan. Forced industrialization and forced collectivization were undertaken on an unprecedented scale. This was accompanied by such terrorism as had hardly been experienced before. Eugene Lyons has summarized the impact of this undertaking in the following manner:

The plan was launched like a war of conquest directed against the whole population....
In a mystic transport of "historic mission," the regime doomed millions to extinction, tens of millions to thinly disguised slavery, the whole nation to incredible suffering. Upon the alleged "completion" and "fulfillment" of the plan, half the country was caught in a fearful famine, the other half was on short rations, agriculture was wrecked, the forced-labor population in camps was nearing the ten-million mark....[1]

This particular interlude had many dimensions of terror, some of which would not be repeated, at least not on this scale. The most horrendous persecution was of the Kulaks (small farmers) and NEPmen (those engaged in private enterprise during the period of the New Economic Policy). These were disfranchised, deprived of their possessions, and, as Lyons says, "denied food rations and the right to schooling, driven from their homes, employed only as unskilled ... labor, or simply left to beg and starve and die."[2] This was clearly ideological, an attempt to wipe out all vestiges of private enterprise. Clearly, too, the efforts at industrialization and collectivization were in accord with communist ideology. (The debate about whether Stalin's methods were the best way to proceed are of interest only to those who believe that it can and ought somehow to be done.) The terror mounted as the attempt to impose the ideology was pursued.

It is important to grasp this point, because since the De-Stalinization of the late 1950's there has been a widespread effort to treat the Stalin terror as an aberration. Stalin was not, according to this view, a good communist. He reveled in the Personality Cult built around him, and terror was his device for concentration of all power in his hands.

Now it may well be that Stalin contrived a personality cult, and there can be no doubt that he consolidated all power in his hands, but it does not follow that he was not a good communist. On the contrary, if the analysis and facts here presented are accepted, Stalin stands out as the best communist ever to emerge in the Soviet Union. He applied terror more rigorously and thoroughly than has ever been done, before or since. He did so in accord with the logic of communist ideology. His crimes were not an aberration from communism: they were the product of his attempt to impose it.

The ideological purpose of terror is to produce conformity with the Communist Party line. More broadly, the purpose is to bring a whole people under the sway of the ideology, to make them instruments to be used in a common concerted effort. If this is to be accomplished, all dissent must be wiped out, and all individual resistance must be crushed. "You cannot make an omelet without breaking eggs," Khruschev said. Terror is the communist way to break eggs, and Stalin was its supreme exemplar.

At any rate, by the early 1930's the terror began to fall into a pattern. It would not be correct to say that it was regularized, for that would suggest that there were rules which limited and made it predictable. It was never predictable for it was too arbitrary for that. Nor was it ever ritualized. Amongst civilized peoples many acts are ritualized, and especially those that have to do with life and death and detention. Communism discourages all ritual and tends to leave all acts as blunt and unembellished as possible. But there was a pattern to the terror.

Ordinarily, the first step is the arrest. It can happen at any time and any place. Alexander Dolgun, an Amercian who spent about eight years in Soviet prison camps, was walking down a street in Moscow in the middle of the day when he was arrested. For others it came at home, in the middle of the night or whenever. Mothers of small children might be taken away with no provision made for looking after the children. There might be a search of the premises for papers or other incriminating evidence. Most likely, no charge would be made at the time of the arrest. The person might well be told that he was only being taken in for a little talk or questioning. The arresting officers would be men in plain clothes, members of the NKVD, MVD, MGB, KGB, or whatever name the secret police would be using at the time.

The second step is to be taken to a prison in the vicinity of where one is arrested. The terror begins there, if it had not already begun. This is no ordinary prison, if there is such a thing. It is a place of interrogation, and the facilities are designed to bring maximum psychological and physical pressure to break the prisoner and make him confess. The terror may begin in this prison, but it does not end there, unless it ends in death. The terror settles upon the prisoner, as it were, rending his soul and marking him for life. (Not everyone is as sensitive as Alexsandr Solzhenitsyn, but witness the Herculean effort he has made to tell the story to the world, in fictionalized accounts and in histories.)

Jail is bad enough in the best of times and places. The initial experience is one of helplessness, of loss of control over one's affairs, of being at the mercy of his captors. There are all sorts of things one knows he has to do, and yet his life is stopped, thrown into limbo , as it were. One may be buoyed at first by outraged innocence and the delusion that it is all a mistake. But in a Soviet prison all these must yield to something else, the necessity of clinging to sanity and the relics of selfness. All imprisonment involves loss of status and loss of respect of one's former fellows. Yes, even in the Soviet Union, the thought will not down that one must have done something to incur the wrath of the authorities, though for those who know better among endangered acquaintances or family there may be a sense of outrage that the person was so stupid as to get himself arrested.

As soon as the fact of one's being arrested and imprisoned becomes known, the terror, or fear, spreads to his family and acquaintances. The odds have now increased that they will suffer a similar fate. Alexander Dolgun's mother was arrested:

They had arrested her in 1950. For months she had pestered the MGB (it was still MGB then) for news of me. At first they told her I had been shot as a spy. She had a breakdown. Shortly after she recovered she got my triangle letter from Kuibyshev, in which I asked whether the American Embassy had given her my personal belongings. She went to the embassy to demand help. At the gates the MGB arrested her. She was still emotionally very fragile. They beat her with rubber truncheons, trying to get her to incriminate me. They pushed needles under her fingernails. Now her nails would never be straight again. After a very short period of this she went quite insane and, without sentencing her, they put her in a prison insane asylum in Ryazan. [3]

When she was released from the asylum, she could get no help from the authorities to get a place to live, reclaim her property or maintain herself because she had not been sentenced. Dolgun's father, too, had been imprisioned. Perhaps saddest of all, after Alexander Dolgun had been released and was living with his mother, the state of her mind was such that at times she believed him to be in the hire of the secret police and informing on her. There is no end to the terror.

The purpose of the initial imprisonment and interrogation is to extract a *satisfactory* confession from the prisoner. He will be interrogated for as short or as long a time as is needed to get the confession, or goes insane or dies from the tortures inflicted upon him. The usual method of getting a prisoner to confess is to put him on the conveyor, as it is called. The conveyor is a system of extended interrogation carried on by relays of interrogators, usually at night, broken by interludes of "rest" during the day in which the prisoner is not allowed to lie down or sleep. One careful student of the process describes it this way:

Interrogation usually took place at night and with the accused just roused — often only fifteen minutes after going to sleep. The glaring lights at the interrogation had a disorienting effect. There was a continual emphasis on the absolute powerlessness of the victim. The interrogators — or so it usually seemed — could go on indefinitely.

As one prisoner described the result:

After two or three weeks, I was in a semi-conscious state. After fifty or sixty interrogations with cold and hunger and almost no sleep, a man becomes like an automaton — his eyes are bright, his legs swollen, his hands trembling. In this state he is often even convinced he is guilty. 4

Most men, and women, probably crumble within a few days and provide the desired confession. If they do not, or cannot (for it is by no means easy to determine what to confess), they may be subjected to other tortures as well as or in addition to that of the conveyor. The tortures may be simple or exquisite; an interrogator may suddenly jump up and begin to beat the prisoner with his fists. They may be as simple as feeding a prisoner salt fish and allowing him no water for a day, or as exquisite as placing him in a room with water covering the floor and no place to sit. A present-day Soviet writer tells this poignant story of the torture of a woman (in a book that had to be published outside the Soviet Union):

Nestor Lakoba, poisoned by Beria and posthumously declared an "enemy of the people," left a wife who would not sign any false statements about him. A young and beautiful woman, rumored to be a Georgian princess, she was arrested and put in the Tbilisi prison soon after her husband's death. Nutsa Gogoberidze, the wife of Levan Gogoberidze, who shared a cell with Lakoba's wife, tells how this silent and calm woman was taken away every evening and was dragged back to the cell, bloody and unconscious. The women cried, asked for a doctor and revived her. When she came to, she told how they demanded that she sign an essay on the subject "How Lakoba sold Abkhazia to Turkey." Her reply was brief: "I will not defame the memory of my husband." She stood fast even when faced with the ultimate torture: her fourteen-year old son was shoved crying toward his mother, and she was told he would be killed if she did not sign. (And this threat ... was carried out.) But even then Lakoba's wife would not defame her husband. Finally, after a night of torture, she died in her cell. 5

Most people are not, of course, cut out of such an heroic mold, and the interrogator was not often denied the confession he sought.

What would be a satisfactory confession? Anyone innocent of knowledge of the Soviet secret police, and their masters, might suppose that what was wanted was a confession in accord with the facts. But this was usually unnecesary and unwanted. The aim of the interrogators was not facts at all in the accepted sense of something that has happened and can be verified by independent data. Facts belong to the real world of happenings and events. What they wanted belongs to a posited, an imaginary, a mentally constructed world in accord with communist ideology and the Party line.

The most grotesque facade of all in Soviet Communism was the facade erected from the tissue of these confessions. It was a facade compounded of assassination plots, of foreign-controlled spy networks, of domestic conspiracies, of industrial sabotage, of agricultural espionage, of fascist traitors, of "right wing deviationists," of "left wing deviationists," of Trotskyists, and so on. The picture that emerges from the confessions is a massive intertwined series of conspiracies and plots to undermine, thwart, and destroy communism in Russia. Millions of people were supposed to be involved, and many nations around the world were aiding and abetting it. All other conspiracy theories pale beside this one, for none other can produce millions of confessions to "prove" its case.

This facade of confessions constituted a huge "documented" rationale for Soviet actions and failures. The terror had the broad purpose of subduing the people and making them conform to the will of their rulers as well as the narrower purpose of producing confessions. But the confessions, we may believe, had a different purpose — to justify the regime to itself and to such others as were apprized of the "evidence." Was there a crop failure in some province? The explanation was at hand: saboteurs had provided rotten seed or the fertilizer had been tampered with. Did a factory fail to meet its quota? Saboteurs must have been at work there. In the Show Trials of the 1930's a man named Pyatakov made this confession:

In the Ukraine the work was carried on mainly in the coke industry by Loginov and a group of persons connected with him. Their work, in the main, consisted of starting coke ovens which were not really ready for operations, and of holding up the construction of very valuable and very important parts of the coke and chemical industry. . . .

The wrecking activities in the last period assumed new forms. Despite the fact that, after a delay of two or three years, the plant began to enter on its operation stage Maryasin created intolerable conditions, fomented intrigues, and in a word everything to obstruct operation. [6]

Even the terror itself might be "justified" by these conspiracies and plots. The government, it was made to appear, was vigilantly capturing and punishing its enemies. Indeed, the secret police could provide signed confessions of any sort of wrongdoing which the rulers ordered. The number of people who could be implicated was limited only by the number of secret policemen who could be assigned to get confessions.

Once a confession had been extracted, one along the desired lines, the next step was to sentence the prisoner. He could be sentenced in one of two ways: after a trial or by the "organs," i.e., the secret police. So far as the question of guilt or innocence was concerned, it did not matter which way was taken. In fact, there was never any question of guilt or innocence once a person had been arrested. He was guilty. The only question was, of what?

The trials that were held were farcical. Their lack of dignity was apparent during the Moscow Show Trials when Andrei Vyshinsky, the Chief Prosecutor, would howl to the court, "Shoot the dirty dog," or words to that effect. If a defense lawyer appeared, his effectiveness was sullied by the necessity for him to show his loyalty to the government. Even the sentences must have been prepared in advance of the trial. Robert Conquest points out that the trials of Evgenia Ginzburg took seven minutes. "The Court returned in two minutes with a 'verdict' which she estimates must have taken twenty minutes to type."[7]

The only real question to be answered by the sentencing was whether the prisoner was to be shot or sent for a number of years to a forced labor camp. True, the length of sentences varied, but whether it was for five, ten, or twenty-five years mattered less than it should have, for the "organs" could add an additional sentence when the first was completed if they saw fit. An important point to be grasped here is that once a prisoner had made, signed, and, if he was to be publicly tried, given, his confession, his purpose had been served. He became a nonperson, a thing, to be disposed of in whatever way the authorities might decide.

If he was to be shot, the sentence was usually carried out summarily. He was, according to lore, escorted to some dungeon room by secret police and shot in the back of the neck. No ceremony was involved; it was economical and effective. The price was the cost of a bullet, and a well-placed single shot severs the spinal column at the neck, bringing an end to sensation and probably instant death. Torture would have been superfluous at this point, since a confession had already been obtained, so the prisoner was simply dispatched in the most expeditious way.

Those sent to forced labor camps were almost certainly sentenced to a fate worse than death. It might be more accurate to say that in most cases they were sentenced to a fate worse than as well as death. The vast majority died, according to such testimony as we have, en route to or in the camps. What could happen en route to a camp was vividly told by a Pole, Andrey A. Stotski, who was a Soviet prisoner during World War II. There were 1,400 prisoners when they set on their journey to the far frozen north. A long portion of the journey was in the hold of a barge. They were fed, when and as they were, by bread and soup lowered into the hold on hooks. These same hooks were used to lift those who died to

91

the topside where they could be dumped into the sea. Let him take up the account:

The deaths were so frequent by this time that the guards left the hooks within our reach, so that all we had to do was fasten them into the body and jerk the ropes hard. Among the last victims was one from our number — one of the White Ruthenians. From our memories of a life that was now an eternity away, we recalled the prayers for the dead and commended to God this soul who had surely gone to Him. How we envied this man whose troubles were now over. And yet none of us could bring our will to the point of suicide. No, death would have to come when God pleased. [8]

Seven hundred twenty-seven of the 1,400 who had begun the journey survived this voyage. They then began the walk to the mines. On the way, they stopped for a while in a barracks, some fifty of their number were unable to continue the journey. "Before we were well away," he says, "the sound of pistol shots, at deliberately measured brief intervals, reached us." [9] They had been shot. About 400 eventually reached the camp.

The transfer from prison to forced labor camp was from torture to torment. There were at least two dimensions to this torment. One was psychological, and, if possible, it was the worst because of its impact on the human spirit.

The necessary environment to human dignity, even to humanness, is the sense that the individual has worth, that life has meaning, that each of us is important. The graces of culture and the outworks of civilization combine to support the belief that each individual is of great worth. The newborn baby is surrounded by attendants; the father has waited anxiously for the birth; relatives are eager to know its sex, weight, height, and who it looks like. The infant is given a name, staking out its individuality and uniqueness, as it were. Family and friends tend to provide the necessary warmth for nurturing human dignity. When a child becomes a man, he usually attains additional support from his job or position for his status as a valuable person. Even in death, the importance of the individual is celebrated by the commemorative services: the assembly of friends and loved ones, the expressions of grief and condolences, the rituals of burial, and the marking of the spot where the body has been placed. All this, of course, helps to reassure the living of the worth of the individual.

The forced labor camps stripped away every remnant of support to human dignity, except such as the most resolute could store in their hearts. "Life is meaningless," the forced labor camps seemed to say, "An individual is of no account." Solzhenitsyn has called the camps "Our Sewage Disposal System." This human garbage, these pitiful human beings, squeezed dry by torture and confession, were shipped off to remote areas to remove them from the sight and smell of others who were, relatively, alive and free. Everything in the camps confirmed that the prisoners were garbage: the language of the guards, the tattered rags the prisoners wore, the absence of amenities, and the cheapness of life. Tales abound of prisoners being shot merely because they stepped out of line in a formation or could not keep up.

Here is a story that reveals the assult on life in the camps. A prisoner made a dash for freedom. Other prisoners wanted to run after him and persuade him to return, but the guards would not permit it. Then, a guard by the name of Vanya took off across the ice and snow in a sleigh pulled by seven dogs in an effort to capture the man. The prisoner did not last long, for he was emaciated, and had fallen to the ground by the time Vanya reached him. He was tied to the sled and dragged back to camp. Though he was horribly torn and bleeding, he was still alive. Vanya unleashed a vicious dog named Nora, expecting that she would tear at and destroy the man:

Nora rose and slowly and cautiously approached the wretch on the ground, while all of us held our breath. The beast sniffed all around him and then opened wide her terrible mouth, and with her long, rough tongue began to lick Sasha's bleeding body. Finally she lay down by the remains of the man, pushing up close to him as if to protect him from the cold.

Vanya cursed and went off without a word. Somebody among the prisoners began to sob. Nora pushed still closer to what had once been a man. [10]

Brutes, of course, are incapable of evil, for they know no such distinction. Man, however, is, and the greatest evil is to attempt to deprive life of its meaning.

In these circumstances, men grasp for something that will supply meaning. The Reverend Richard Wurmbrand has told in one of his books how men greedily gathered around anyone who could remember and quote Scriptures, for they were indeed "Wonderful Words of Life." Alexander Dolgun relates how he survived in a cell dominated by regular criminals — the most brutal of all — by his ability to recall the plots to movies. We can surmise that what was of such importance to stories, aside from their value as entertainment, was that one could glean from them some glimmer of life with meaning.

93

A Polish woman prisoner in a Soviet camp tells how she was approached one day by one of the most vicious and cruel girls in the camp. This conversation ensued:

"Listen, you Polish lady, now that we are alone, tell me — " she hesitated, looking around to see that we were really alone. "I saw you, and I know you pray. Tell me, is there a God?"

My grip relaxed on the bucket. [She had been prepared to defend herself.] "There is."

"How do you know?"

Because I pray every day and God does take care of me...."

"Tell me," she began again. "Tell me, what is it like in your country? ... Is life in your country different from ours here? Is it true that people can really enjoy life there?"

"It is true, Katiushka," and I described to her what life was like in Poland. [This was Pre-Communist Poland.]

"You see," she sighed wearily when I stopped speaking, "I, too, would so like to have enjoyed life — to enjoy life!" [11]

The other source of torment in the camps was the work and accompanying hunger and debilitation. The economy of the forced labor camps was a grotesque parody of the dismal science, economics, as conceived by Malthus and Ricardo and revised by Marx. The natural price of labor, Ricardo had said, is the cost of subsistence. These prison camps went much further: they attempted to squeeze the maximum "surplus value" from these wretches by denying the necessities for subsistence to all except those who could meet the most unrealistic quotas of production. Thus, men endured cold, hunger, disease, lack of meaning, and faced eventual death in fruitless efforts to meet quotas. In some occupations, such as logging in the far frozen north, death came to most workers rather quickly. Those who survived the camps were apt to do so because they managed somehow to get the easiest jobs.

There is much to be learned from the experiences of men in such extreme conditions. One is the great value of private property. Prisoners had no private property, in the sense that the authorities could be depended on to protect it, but they did have a few pitiful possessions. These they treated as private property and protected by whatever means they could. Solzhenitsyn describes the watch over possessions in this way:

In the evening, when you lay down on the naked panel, you could take off your shoes. But take into consideration that your shoes would be swiped. Better sleep with shoes on. Better not scatter your clothes about either — they'd swipe them too. On going out to work in the morning you must not leave anything in the barracks; whatever the thieves did not bother to take the jailers would, announcing, *"It's forbidden!"* In the morning you would go out to work just as nomads depart from a camp site, leaving it even cleaner....

But you couldn't cart anything off to work with you either. You would gather up your chattels in the morning, stand in line at the storeroom for personal belongings, and hide them in a bag or a suitcase. You'd return from work and stand in line again at the storeroom and take with you what you could forsee you would want overnight.... [12]

Those who have never known such extremities have sometimes supposed that property rights are secondary to others. But when men are deprived of all except the relics of property, they cling to these as the last hope against total deprivation and death. Any property that one has is also a toehold on the way to reclaiming dignity, meaning, all other rights, legality, and liberty itself.

This, then, was the reign of terror. It is often said nowadays that the Soviet regime is a stable one. If it is, it is a testimonial to the effectiveness of terror in producing stability. We come much nearer to the truth, however, when we view it as a lawless regime ruled over by gangsters in the service of ideology. Stability means only that the people are subdued.

The impact of the terror on the prisoners has been examined. It is now in order to explore the effect on the population in general.

8

Impotent Populace and Massive State

THE ORDINARY METHODS and language of scholarship are inadequate for and inappropriate to the examination and assessment of Soviet communism. Some examples may illustrate the point. According to most accounts, the Soviet Union is now one of the leading industrial nations in the world. In fact, the Soviet Union has long been the leading exporter of communist ideology in the world. The few products it can sell on the world market are offered in support of the ideology. On the other hand, it must surely be the leading importer of scientific and technological information. It has had the most diligent crew of researchers and translators of scientific, medical, and technological journals from other lands of any country in the world. What is the balance of trade? Not even those trained in the new mathematics could compute the balance from the export of ideology and the import of scientific information.

A country which can only dispose of its shoddy merchandise by erecting barriers to keep other goods out and prevent its inhabitants from going elsewhere to shop should not be styled a leading industrial nation. (One of the considerable joys of those who can take a trip to Western Europe or America is the opportunity to go shopping. Those fortunate enough to be able to go abroad are usually besieged by friends to make purchases for them while they are there.) It should be called a leading jailer nation.

A nation which exports communist ideology and imports scientific information no more has a balance of trade than does a sprig of mistletoe attached to the limb of a tree. It is a parasite. The language of political science is only a hindrance in describing elections in which there is only one candidate, or constitutions whose guarantees of freedom of religion only serve the power of government in launching a massive campaign against religion. Such terms as "fraud," "deception," and "cruel joke" serve all too well. Legal scholars are superfluous to the study of trials in which the penalty has already been determined. The paraphernalia of scholarship, when applied to the Soviet Union, tends to conceal what is going on rather than expose it.

Zhores Medvedev, a Russian biologist, was seized by Soviet police in 1970 and locked up in a mental institution. The diagnosis described him as being unable to adjust to the social environment, as suffering from reformist delusions, and as having an exaggerated sense of his own importance. Medvedev suggests, in a book about his experience, that by the criteria applied to him certain important personages must have been in much worse condition than he was. While he prudently avoids naming them, since he was still in Russia, it is clear that he was talking about Stalin and Khrushchev. He says:

Take, for example, that outstanding figure [Stalin] whom we all remember so well as an economist, a military leader, philosopher, statesman and diplomat. And suddenly out of the blue he publishes his article on the problems of linguistics and personally begins to introduce tangerine and eucalyptus trees to the Crimea. Then there was that other great leader [Khrushchev], also wise politician, diplomat, economist, agricultural specialist and historian of the Party. Suddenly he begins to make decisions about the architecture of apartment houses, arbitrates in a disagreement between two schools of genetics . . . , forbids the private ownership of cattle in the countryside and teaches writers the secrets of their craft. And of each of them it was true to say that they were proud, expressed themselves dogmatically and were convinced of the supreme value and infallibility of their views. Of course eucalyptus trees never got accustomed to the Crimea and maize doesn't grow in the North, but the behavior of both of these men continued to be determined by the nature of their delusions without adapting to reality.

The behavior of one of them [Stalin] was further aggravated by persecution mania and sadism — which led him to spend a lot of time "discovering" imaginary conspiracies, introducing draconian laws, organizing mass arrests, executions and tortures, and he was completely isolated in a world of his own.[1]

It was not, I take it, Medvedev's point that either Stalin or

97

Khrushchev was insane, though he presents some strong evidence to that effect against Stalin. Rather, he wished to demonstrate that any delusions he might have were puny and dwarfed by the mammoth ones of these two leaders. (He might have added the delusions of Lenin and Brezhnev to the others, but he had risked enough already. Even though Stalin and Khrushchev are dead and in some ways discredited, it is not possible to know in what ways they may be safely attacked. But Lenin is a sort of god, and Brezhnev is alive and in command.) But by calling attention to their delusions he does provide an angle from which to begin the assessment of Soviet communism.

The delusions of Soviet leaders arise from communist ideology. Marxism is a fantasy. Karl Marx had the delusion that he had discovered the secret of history. His notion about the inevitable triumph of the proletariat is no more scientific than is the belief that the position of the planets controls our destiny. Yet his ideology provided the foundation for Lenin's delusion that the moment for the revolution had arrived in Russia, and from thence it should spread to the rest of the world. The delusion gave men the effrontery to attempt to impose the ideology on everyone within their power.

There is a crucial distinction between the delusions associated with insanity and those born of ideology. The insane person suffers from or is afflicted with his delusions. By contrast, it is those on whom ideological delusions are imposed that suffer. Marx did not suffer from his delusions, nor did Lenin, nor did Stalin, nor did Khrushchev, but a goodly portion of the peoples of the world have. Another distinction between ideological delusions and those of insanity is that the insane cannot function effectively in their environment. Ideologues, again, can function effectively, but they inhibit those on whom the ideology is imposed from acting very effectively.

The perverse effects of these delusions are to be accounted for by the assumptions and presumptions of the ideology. Karl Marx had what may best be described as a criminal mind. Not the mind of a petty thief, of course. Not even the mind of those who are ordinarily thought of as directing organized crime. He had a cosmic criminal mind.

The crime which Marx contemplated was theft, the theft of all property used in the production and distribution of goods. The method by which the property was to be taken he called Revolution. The cohorts who would assist in this enterprise — the proletariat — would be rewarded by receiving the fruits of production. Thus far, his scheme paralleled just about any plan for carrying out a robbery. But Marx added two dimensions to theft or crime which they do not ordinarily have. First, he declared that this act of universal robbery — the World Revolution — was inevitable. Second, he conceived an ideology which was supposed to justify this vast thievery. He wove the whole into the framework of an anti-religious religion.

The universal plunder which Marx prescribed was, of course, to be only a prelude, a necessary prelude to universal justice, peace, harmony, well-being, and freedom. Man was to be emancipated from all the constraints that had kept his true nature from emerging. He was to be transformed, following upon the transformation of the economy, and a new society would emerge. The eventual end would justify the plunderous means, though Marx held that the expropriation — plunder, thievery, robbery, or whatever it should be called — was also justified. Marx laid down no specifics for the emergence of this new society and new man. Presumably they would emerge naturally once the expropriation had been completed and the means of production were in the hands of the "workers."

If theft can be justified, then all other crimes are justified thereby: torture, slavery, extortion, compulsion, murder, fraud, threats, assault, and every species of restraint. If stealing is justified, nay, required, by the laws of history, then all resistance to theft must be met with whatever force is necessary to overcome it. The force to overcome the resistance to the robbery must be as great as, no, greater than, all the energy which men will put forth to cling to their possessions.

It is not simply that man has an affinity for property, though he has; it is even more the case that property has an affinity for man, so to speak. To put it more directly, property must be owned before it realizes its potential as property. Property without ownership is an abstraction, an abstraction waiting for an owner to appear to give it character and fulfillment. To divest man of this relationship and prevent him from forming it runs counter to a metaphysical chemistry between man and property. If it were justified, then so would every assault upon man which would achieve it.

Universalized theft, or nationalized theft, as it has been experienced thus far, requires universalized force. This accounts for the massive state that emerged with Soviet Communism. There is, however, yet another reason for this swollen condition. It, too, has its roots in the nature of property. Property requires attention if it is to be productive. Divesting individuals of private property does not remove this requirement; instead, it aggravates it. By and large, the property that

99

had been owned by individuals was taken over by the government in the Soviet Union. The management, or attempted management, of this property required a large number of bureaucrats. The combination of universalized force and bureaucratic management of property produced the massive state.

The delusions that accompany communist ideology are manifold. They are delusions such as are necessary to believe it and try to put it into practice. They are the delusions of the criminal mind writ large. Theft is a crime. So are all the acts done in support of theft. Marx conceived the most monstrous crime imaginable. Lenin and his followers carried out this crime within the Russian Empire and fostered its spread to the rest of the world. But it was necessary that they not think of it as a crime and desirable that people in general not think of it that way. To that end, the law which makes theft a crime must be held to be invalid; the moral code which supports the idea must be denied; the cultural inheritance which bolsters property and private rights must be negated; and the age-old conceptions of human nature must be put at naught. All that is left in support of communism is human will, the will to believe, and the force that resides in its monopoly by government. The more closely the prescriptions of communist ideology are fulfilled, the more nearly impotent the populace. The more massive the state the more helpless the populace.

Therein lies the dilemma of communism and, indeed, of all socialism. Communism could only succeed by engaging the efforts, the wills, the energies, and the initiative of the population behind it. But these are held in thrall by the massive state, by the ubiquitous police, by the swollen bureaucracy, and by the requirement of ideological conformity. The populace could only become effective by the reduction of the state and the restoration of freedom. Every step in that direction is a retreat from communism. The dilemma cannot be resolved; it is inherent in communism. The dilemma arose from the delusions of communism.

One of the primary delusions of communism is that human nature can be transformed so as to remove the pursuit of self-interest from human behavior. It should not be necessary to turn to experience and history to learn this. The contemplation of man and the condition in which he finds himself should be sufficient for discovering the essentiality of his pursuit of self-interest.

Human consciousness is such that only the individual concerned is aware of his needs and wants and what priorities they have. Life on this earth is of a character that requires that in many instances he must look after himself. He must look before he crosses the street lest he be run over. He must take care what he puts in his mouth lest he ingest some harmful substance. Even roses have thorns, and he who would pick them must be careful that he not be stuck by them.

The amounts of goods and services available are limited, but our desires for them are not. Hence, we contend or compete for them, and each does well to protect his own interest in the trades that take place. Indeed, it is difficult to grasp how any trade, sale, or purchase could be made if the individuals were not acting in their interest. A disinterested purchase would be one made without regard to what was wanted, the quantity and quality of the goods, or what priorities might exist about acquiring them.

A second delusion of communism is that removing the cultural supports to the individual would result in rooting out self-interest. On the contrary, the same culture which supports the individual acts to direct, limit, restrain, and civilize his pursuit of self-interest. Civilized people recognize and observe limits on their pursuit of self-interest. Good manners require that the individual take his place in line, that he defer to others in many cases, and that he respect the equal rights of others. A civilized culture even as it protects the individual in his pursuits inculcates the belief that there are occasions when the individual should deny himself in order to aid and care for others.

The family as a unit is especially dependent upon parental restraint in asserting their interests in order to provide for the children and those unable to take care of themselves. It is the duty of the parents as well to inhibit their children when they rambunctiously pursue their interests, in the interest of family harmony and peace in the community. Community, too, depends upon apparently selfless acts by its members in defense against aggressors and to rescue those who are endangered.

But none of this need be in derogation of the individual's pursuit of his own self-interest. One of the great missions of culture and civilization is to provide a peaceful and harmonious framework within which the individual can seek his own constructively. To destroy the culture because it supports the individual will not alter the individual's determination to pursue his self-interest; it will only remove the restraints upon it. The reason for this should be clear. Our pursuit of self-interest is not culturally induced; it arises from our nature and the nature of conditions within which we find ourselves. Communism delusively pits itself against culture when its true enemy is human nature.

101

A third delusion is that force, or government, can be used effectively to transform human nature and produce a peaceful and productive society. So far as we know, human nature cannot be changed, but human behavior can be, at least to some extent. But force is only a minor adjunct in successful efforts to change human behavior. It can be used to punish and inhibit wrongdoing, but it is the weakest of all means for producing rightdoing. Rightdoing proceeds from and engages the best efforts of the wills of individuals. Force can no doubt produce a modicum of obedience, but it will usually be minimal and will tend to be limited even further by its failure to engage the constructive ingenuity of the ones complying.

From these basic delusions follow the mass of delusions by which the Soviet Union has been misruled for over sixty years now.

It should not be necessary, as I say, to resort to historical evidence to validate the above observations. But if it is, the record of the Soviet Union provides a cornucopia of supporting evidence.

An early visitor to the Soviet Union proclaimed, in a burst of enthusiasm: "I have seen the future, and it works." Those who have examined the situation over a longer period of time and more thoroughly would be more likely to say: "I have seen the future of Communism, and not even the plumbing works." That is, however, but a poor joke and a half-truth. Surely, there are water closets in the Soviet Union that work, at least some of the time.

More important, if we should follow this lead it would take us away from, not toward, the greatest failures of Soviet communism. It would take us into the realm of that pseudo-science, macro-economics, where the greatest truth we would be able to discover is that statistics can be used to deceive. There is no comparison between goods produced by decree and those produced to supply wants registered in the market. Goods produced by decree are qualitatively inferior; they are orphans in the market place, seeking some kindhearted soul who will adopt them. Macro-economics can only deal with them by declaring them the equal of all other similar goods, for only thus can they be reduced to statistics. Since they are not, the result can only be a deception.

Even so, it needs to be affirmed that Soviet communism has had signal economic failures. The Soviet Union inherited one of the most productive grain-producing areas in the world and succeeded so well by collectivizing and introducing state farms that even by opening millions of acres of new land it became a grain-deficit land. Central planning of industrial activity is a recognized failure today, even by many Soviet economists. In fact, a multi-volumed encyclopedia on how not to produce goods could be compiled from the Soviet experience. A "successful" plant manager is one who can get a low quota of production, have a very large stockpile of parts he will need, and manage to produce a sufficient quantity of shoddy goods to exceed his quota.

One of the reasons for the failure of centralized planning coupled with an atmosphere of fear comes out in the story below. It was told by a man who had been a Soviet inspector.

As inspector I once arrived at a plant which was supposed to have delivered mining machines, but did not do it. When I entered the plant premises, I saw that the machines were piled up all over the place, but they were all unfinished. I asked what was going on. The director gave evasive answers. Finally, when the big crowd surrounding us had disappeared, he called me to his office.

There, the story came out. It seems that the specifications called for the machines to be painted with red oil-resistant varnish. But the only red varnish that he had was not oil-resistant. He had green oil-resistant varnish, but was afraid that if he used this in violation of instructions he would get eight years in prison. The inspector knew the machines were badly needed, was certain that whether they were painted red or green could make little difference, but he too feared a prison sentence should he authorize the change. He did cable the ministry hoping for a quick decision in favor of using the green varnish.

But it took unusually long. Apparently they did not want to take any chances at the ministry either, and they wanted to cover themselves. Finally I received permission. I put this cablegram from the ministry in my pocket and kept it for the rest of my life, and signed the note allowing the use of the green paint....[2]

The infelicities of Soviet production may be best summed up by this Russian joke related by John Gunther:

One Russian tells another that the Soviet authorities have perfected an intricate atomic bomb that will fit into a suitcase, and that this will one day be delivered to a target like New York. The second Russian replies, "Impossible. Where would anybody get a suitcase?"[3]

But the greatest failures of Soviet Communism have not been economic. Indeed, such successes as it has had, aside from the exportation of ideology, have been quantitative and economic. Large universities have been conceived and built, a modicum of education

103

made universally available to the young, numerous physicians trained, whole new cities brought into being, hydroelectric dams built, and so on.

Political power has been brought to bear so as to produce what was most wanted by those who ruled. The priorities of the political authorities have sooner or later been met, though it would be an error to conceive of this having been done economicaly. It has been done at horrendously excessive cost in lives, suffering, deprivation, and wasted natural resources. Indeed, in the absence of a free market, the Soviet rulers have no way of determining what it should cost to produce goods. Still, they have produced huge quantities of generally inferior goods.

The greatest failures of Soviet communism are social and spiritual. Many of these failures should be the occasion for rejoicing around the world. None can rejoice, of course, about the persecution, the terror, the suffering, and the hardships of the peoples of the Russian Empire. They have endured for many years now an occupation, as it were, by an alien force. That alien force has been animated by Communist ideology and includes all who have attempted to impose their will on the Russian people in its name.

That alien force launched the most massive assault upon the human spirit, upon individuality, upon religion, upon society, and upon the family that the world has ever known. This assault has been carried out by the assembled power of a totalitarian state, carried out by all the devices conceivable to a criminal mind: brutal murder, torture, propaganda, threats, exile, mass starvation, and incomparable terror. A gigantic effort has been made to wipe out the heritage of a people, to destroy the ancient bonds of community, and to break peoples under the wheel of the state. All who have any fellow feeling for others should view this action with sorrow and compassion for the peoples who thus suffer.

Nonetheless, there is occasion for rejoicing. Word comes to us from the Russian people that the human spirit has not been crushed. It is wondrously alive in the vibrant eyes and stern personality of Aleksandr Solzhenitsyn and, no doubt, in millions of others.

This is not to say that the unleashing of such might for such purposes against a people has not produced gaping wounds and ugly scars, so to speak. Surely it has. Many of the bonds of community have indeed been broken. The family has been sorely tried by informing, by the ease of divorce, by the necessity for women to do heavy work. Institutional religion has been made largely subservient to the state, where it has been permitted to survive. Society has lost control over all institutions by which it may function. Propaganda has taken a heavy toll upon mental development and understanding. Fear has driven frank conversation into nooks and crannies.

But human nature has survived and endured. The Soviet regime has not made a dent in the determination of the Russian people to pursue their self-interest. Farmers pursue their self-interest vigorously by avidly cultivating the little plots of land from which the government allows them to keep the produce. People are ever on the alert to hear of some scarce item available in the stores, and scurry out to purchase it when the word reaches them. The pursuit of self-interest by Party members is almost palpable, but they are distinguished from the general populace only in the corrupt methods available to them.

The Russian people have no intention of committing suicide, which is what the abandonment of self-interest entails. They may be hampered by the rules and regulations in their pursuit of it, but they seek it as certainly as an alcoholic sought booze in America during Prohibition. Those who value life, then, may rejoice that Russians are still pursuing their self-interest.

The wound is nowhere deeper and scars nowhere uglier than upon what for a better word we call society in the Soviet Union. In the vulgar language of today, all activity, life and relationships are divided into a public and a private sector. Where people are moderately free, there are actually several realms: the realm of government, the realm of society, and the realm of the individual that is personal and private. These are not exclusive spheres; they are rather complementary, interdependent, and interacting realms.

Society encompasses that realm of social relationships that are largely voluntary, the realm of manners, customs, traditions, morality, voluntary institutions, and ways by which individuals live fruitfully and peacefully with one another. The cultural heritage is activated and carried on largely by society. It is the arena of influence and persuasion rather than of force.

It may be correct to refer to a "public" and "private" sector in the Soviet Union, though the public sector has been elephantized and the private sector dwarfed. But society has been vitually destroyed. Society depends upon widespread trust, confidence, and general goodwill, as well as a considerable measure of freedom. These have been all but wiped out in the Soviet Union. Trust and goodwill can hardly survive the informing of children on parents, of neighbor upon neighbor, of husband upon wife; all of which has been fostered and encouraged, even

105

required, by the Soviet system. They can hardly survive, either, the constant surveillance, the hidden microphones, the keeping of extensive dossiers by the police, the listening in on telephone conversations, and the opening of mail: all common practice.

Society needs institutions which it largely controls: churches, clubs, libraries, markets, hospitals, and various sorts of voluntary associations. Where any of these have been permitted in the Soviet Union, they are under the thumb of the Party which, in turn, is an instrument of the state. The lines of communication on which society depends are clogged by a massive state.

Two developments have taken place in the absence of society. One is a crudeness of relationships in general. Clerks are usually rude and harsh of manner. Hedrick Smith notes that there is a Russian manner that comes across in "public as coarse indifference, passive fatalism, and pushy discourtesy. Western visitors have commented on the glum, shuttered faces of Russian street crowds, and the brusque, negative surliness of service people. In our early months, I remember nodding at Russians, or saying hello if their eyes met mine at close range in public but all I ever got in return was an impassive stare."[4]

This coarseness of social relations evinces itself in yet another way, in busybodiness, which has no doubt been promoted by communism. Leona Schechter, who spent several years in Moscow, gives several examples of it. Here is one. She had taken one of her children to school but had neglected to dress very warmly against the cold:

Just as we were about to go in the school door, a redhaired Russian lady ... stopped to harangue me about the way I dressed. I told her I didn't want to get Barney into the building late so she let me go, but she was waiting when I came out. She yelled at me that I was stupid to come out without boots. She warned that I would get very sick if I didn't dress properly. I stood listening to her lecture, freezing, wanting nothing so much as to run home and warm my feet. She believed she was doing her socialist duty.[5]

Socialist duty it might be, but sociable it was not.

The other development is the rudimentary rebuilding of society in tightly knit private circles. Friends gather in the kitchens — about the only possible meeting place — of private homes, reasonably safe from informers, from hidden microphones, and from the ubiquitous police. There, spontaneous and free communication can take place. The Russians are then quite different, according to Smith: "But in private,

106

within a trusted circle, usually the family and close friends but often embracing new acquaintances very quickly if some personal chord of empathy is touched, they are among the warmest, most cheerful, generous, emotional and overwhelmingly hospitable people on earth."[6]

There is some evidence that following the relaxation of the rigidity of Soviet regime in the 1960's these circles have expanded. Manuscripts of works that the regime will not permit to be published circulate in what are called *samzidat* editions (privately copied). Groups of people gather to view paintings that cannot get a showing in governmentally controlled museums. Concerts are even performed in what must be thought of as private. The account that Zhores and Roy Medvedev give of friends and colleagues who came to the aid of Zhores when he was locked up in a mental institution indicates that for some, at least, a considerable society is forming. The Communists have not succeeded, then, in destroying the old society and building a new one. Society has just gone underground, awaiting the opportunity, the freedom, to emerge once again in full flower.

Perhaps the most dramatic failure of the Soviet Communists, however, has been their inability to wipe out religion. Decades of atheistic propaganda, the widespread closing of churches, the denial of general access to means for study, worship, and religious training have failed to accomplish the sought-after result. Of course, the assault on religion has done great damage. Leona Schechter gives this foreboding account from one who had experienced it:

> But Pyotr with his sad, sensitive blue eyes and Christlike beard decried even the Revolution. For the first time we heard him speak from the depths of his spirit. He appealed for the return of the Christian values of the Russian Orthodox Church. "We were better off when we could appeal to human values, the values of the church. Our lives were richer and we had the excitement and mystery of holy days. We had a sense of man. Now all we have are empty slogans and corruption. The Revolution destroyed Christianity in Russia and it also destroyed the Russian spirit."[7]

It did not, of course, destroy Christianity or the Russian spirit. It did largely destroy the social and communal aspect of Christianity in Russia, driving it underground, and depriving public life of its redeeming values.

But religion is alive in Russia. An American correspondent was asked by a Russian acquaintance if he believed in God. He indicated that he did not. "Just wait," the Russian replied, "You have not lived in Russia long enough yet." That is hyperbole, to be sure, for not all Russians believe in God, but the point is well taken nonetheless. There is by most accounts the indication of a religious resurgence in Russia. The authorities long held that religion was dying out, that it was just a relic, and that only old women went to church. But an interesting phenomenon can now be reported: as one generation of old women dies out, another takes their place.

Those who attend church are mainly the ones who have no hope of gaining position or advantage from the Soviet powers, but even those who do have such hopes can practice their religion privately, and some do. Millions openly profess Christianity; an untold number of others await the day when they may do so.

The Schechters visited a museum in a remote province of the Soviet Union. It was next to the site of an ancient Christian church, destroyed by the Arabs in the tenth century. "Until recently no one knew what the original church looked like, but a traveler found a bas relief of it in Paris. Since then new buildings in the center of Yerevan have followed the lines of the church's architecture. Bits of colored mosaic and broken stone pieces left after the Arabs ... are sorted and waiting for the time when the church can be rebuilt."[8]

That is surely a parable of religion in Russia; it exists in carefully preserved bits and pieces awaiting the time when the church can be rebuilt.

Soviet Communism has failed; it has failed to provide people with goods and services economically and competitively; it has failed to root out self-interest; it has failed significantly to alter human nature; it has failed to build a new society; it has failed to crush religion. It has succeeded in erecting a massive state which has imposed an oppressive system on the Russian peoples. Undergirding this system is Communist ideology.

Herein lies a paradox. The Soviet system is underpinned by an ideology which none living under it may believe. True, the propaganda machine grinds out the same old phrases. Party members attend the interminable sessions on the ideology and the Party line. Those called upon to do so will mouth the correct words and sentences. But there is much speculation that no one believes what he is saying. Hedrick Smith reports this conversation:

"You have to go to these political meetings but nobody listens," said a plump Leningrad schoolteacher in her late thirties. ... "When the director of our school gives the lecture, he tries to make it interesting. He's a nice man — a Party member but a nice man. But everyone is bored and nobody believes it."

"What about the person giving the lecture?" Ann asked her.

"Even he doesn't believe what he's saying. The older generation really believed in Lenin and they felt this was the way to build a new society. But my generation doesn't believe it at all. We know it's false." [9]

Some even doubt that the members of the Politburo any longer believe in the ideology. [10]

Supposing this to be substantially true, what keeps Soviet Communism in power, then? Many things, no doubt, some obvious, some not so obvious. Soviet Communism has inertia going for it. Its leaders hold the power over a massive state that is well established. The populace is impotent, lacking either the means to contend with it or effective communication with those who may oppose it. Though the terror has abated in recent years, the Soviet state is still a fearful thing, and many still remember the harsh and prolonged terror of the Stalin years.

The Soviet Union has recognition from the ruling powers of the world. Two things more, at the least, sustain it. One is the idea that has the world in its grip. The Soviet Union represents the premier effort to concert all efforts behind the achievement of felicity on this earth. Those who are advancing what they believe to be a triumphant idea cannot, by and large, ever have it known or accepted that the idea has failed in Russia. The fall of communism in Russia would have a devastating impact on the idea; it must not be permitted to happen.

The other thing that keeps Soviet communism going is fear of the alternative. Communism has ever depended upon a hatred of those whom it denominates as its enemies. All its propaganda does not succeed in making communism loved, but it has much greater success in making enemies hated. "Capitalism" is, of course, the putative enemy of communism, but it invented an enemy which was the personification of all evil. The generic name of that enemy is "fascism." Fascism did, perhaps does, exist, of course, but not fascism as the Communist Party line would have it conceived, not the fascism which was the diametric opposite of communism. On the contrary, fascism was a species of socialism, revolutionary socialism even, bearing the closest resemblance of all to Marxism-Leninism.

For the examination of this supposed enemy of communism, we turn now for a look at Nazi Germany.

109

Book III

The
Nazification
of Germany

Ideology Contends for Power, 1918-1930

"By THEIR FRUITS ye shall know them," Scripture says. By contrast, ideologists contend that by their *intentions* you must distinguish among them. It is crucial to understand this mode of thinking as it is practiced, particularly by socialist ideologues. The idea that has the world in its grip gains adherents, spreads, and tightens its hold because of the alleged good intentions of its believers. The results of the idea are everywhere destructive, the degree of the destruction depending mainly on the extent of the application. But this is obscured so far as possible behind a smokescreen of good intentions.

If the methods of operation of Adolf Hitler in Nazi Germany and of Joseph Stalin (or Lenin or Malenkov) are compared, as they will be at a later point, it can be shown that their differences were insignificant alongside their similarities. They are differences such as there may be between the Communist penchant for the shot in the back of the neck or death by exposure in the frozen north and the Nazi preference for execution by poison gas. Yet Nazis and Communists are generally held to be quite different species, the Nazi behavior having been beyond the pale while we must learn to live with Communists. Their differences are supposed to be somehow decisive.

What are these differences? Let us go to what is supposed to be the nub of the matter at once. The Nazis, it is said, were racists, anti-Semitic, and sought to destroy the Jewish people. Grant the point, for the weight of the evidence is overwhelming that this was the case. But what of the Communists in the Soviet Union? Have they not persecuted and attempted to destroy the Jews in their own way? The point here is not so readily granted, for it is generally believed that some distinctions are in order, and perhaps they are. At any rate, let us make some.

In the first place, Jews have not been the only ones, or even the main ones, persecuted in the Soviet Union. A case could be made that Communists do not discriminate on the basis of race or nationality those whom they persecute, though examples could be given that would cast doubt on this proposition. But, for the sake of argument, let the statement stand, since members of every race, nationality, religion, or ethnic complexion have been persecuted by the Communists. More, some Jews have been able to survive within the Soviet Union. Some, who are technically called Jews, have even prospered, been members of the Party, and even sat in the councils of the government.

But at what price? In answering this we come closer to the crux of the matter. They had better not be Zionists. If they are to prosper, they must not practice the Hebrew religion, even if they have an opportunity to do so. More, their chances of succeeding would be greatly advanced if they could somehow divest themselves of every aspect of their culture which might distinguish them as Jews. In short, a Jew is likely to succeed in the Soviet Union to the extent that he is not a Jew.

It can be argued, of course, that Soviet persecution of Jews is not racial in origin. It is, instead, cultural. The Communists only wish to wipe out Jewish culture, or what might be called "Jewishness," not Jews. That is a most interesting distinction, one which would probably have appealed to the Medieval scholar, Duns Scotus (from whom we derive the word "dunce"), for he had an especial liking for subtle distinctions.

The difficulty lies in the fact that there is no such *thing* as "Jewishness." Hence, government cannot act on it. It cannot be arrested, locked up, interrogated, tortured, shot, or put in slave labor camps. That can only be done to real beings, and Communists have specialized in doing it to people, even Jews. Whether it would have comforted Zinoviev, Kamanev and Trotsky (Communist leaders of Jewish derivation put to death on orders from Stalin) or thousands of other Jews to learn that they were not put to death because they were Jews but because of the "Jewishness" we have no way of knowing.

Communists do not admit that they persecute Jews for their "Jewishness," but there is no doubt of the assault on the Hebrew religion, on Zionism, or on aspects of Jewish culture, and there is good reason to believe that Jews have suffered disproportionately for their heterodoxy in a land that requires orthodoxy. There comes a point when intentions matter not in the least; Zinoviev, Kamanev, and Trotsky are just as dead as they would have been had they died in a Nazi gas chamber. They died because they did not conform to some pattern in the mind of Stalin.

Communism and Nazism have common roots. The focus on Hitler's racism and the playing down of Soviet anti-"Jewishness" has helped to obscure this fact. These common roots are not only obscured but denied by the claim that communism belongs to the "left wing" and Nazism to the "right wing." According to this terminology, they belong to opposite ends of the political spectrum. Writer after writer in book after book employs these terms in this way as if they applied to some obvious actual state of affairs. What they are doing, however, is propagating an illusion, an illusion which in its day may have satisfied the Nazis well enough and still satisfies the Communists.

That Nazis and Communists were usually political opponents is true, but there is no reason to conclude from that fact that they belonged to opposite ends of the political spectrum. The rivalry between brothers in a family is often intense; it is not even something new, for Cain slew Abel. And communism and Nazism were brothers, or something of the sort, under the skin.

The full name of the Nazi Party was National *Socialist* German Workers' Party. But was Hitler a socialist? Clearly, opinions differ as to the correct answer to this question. According to the Communist Party line, he was not a socialist. The weight of opinion of avowed socialists, and their fellow travelers, around the world has been that he was not. Indeed, the gravamen of the claim that he belongs to the "right wing" is that he was not a socialist. Their desire to blame Hitler on something other than socialism is understandable (he's yours, not ours, they are saying), but that is hardly reason to accept their position.

Hitler claimed to be a *national* socialist, in contrast to *international* socialists. ("International," in Nazi ideology, would refer both to communism and to any socialism with which Jews might be associated.)

But if we look at the realities instead of the claims, this distinction tends to break down too. Hitler's Germany was hardly more nationalistic than Stalin's Russia, with its virtually uncrossable borders and chauvinistic appeals to the people. Indeed, every socialist regime is nationalistic in cutting its people off from trade and limiting intercourse with nonsocialist countries. Hitler's claim to being a socialist should be accepted, but since it is not generally, the demonstration of it will have to occupy a part of our attention.

The most direct way to determine in what corner of the political spectrum Nazism belongs may be to change the terminology. Instead of asking whether or not Hitler was a socialist, it will be much more fruitful to ask whether or not he was a *collectivist*. The answer to this can be made without equivocation: Hitler was a collectivist. The Nazi Party was collectivist. The purpose of so many of the practices, forms, and activities of the Nazis was collectivist — the mass meetings, the raised hand salute in unison, the cries of "Sieg Heil," the multitude of swastika-adorned flags, the jack-booted soldiers on parade with their exaggerated precision drills, and the highly emotional speeches of the leaders. These and other such activities were aimed at arousing a single emotion which all would share, the forging of a unity, a collective, through shared common experience. So, too, was the appeal to German nationality, to blood and soil, to the master race, to a common destiny. War was glorified by the Nazis precisely because more than any other activity it calls forth and sustains the unified effort which is the aim of collectivism. War is collectivism in action; the spirit of collectivism becomes flesh in battle.

Nazism was collectivist. Socialism is collectivist. Both of them are on the same side of the political spectrum. They belong to the "left wing," if such terms must be employed, though the present writer would be happy to see those phrases lumped together with a host of other journalistic argot which now corrupts the language, and consigned to the waste bin.

The kinship of these ideologies becomes apparent, too, when we recall the basic idea that has the world in its grip. The idea is: To achieve human felicity by concerting all efforts toward its realization, to root out and destroy the cultural supports to individualism and the pursuit of self-interest, and to use government to concert all efforts on behalf of a general felicity and destroy the cultural obstacles to it. All socialist ideologies, indeed all modern ideologies, if there are any that are not in some sense socialist, proceed by discovering some ill or ills that afflict

116

society (the apple in the Garden of Eden, so to speak) and set forth the means by which the ills are to be corrected. As the present writer noted some years ago:

The ideologue tends to fanaticism. Whatever it is that will set things right ... become for him a fixed idea. This fixed idea may be democracy, equality, the triumph of the proletariat, the coming of the kingdom, the single tax, or whatever his panacea happens to be. Come the proletarian revolution, one will say, and the good society will be ushered in. Employ creatively his abstraction, the "state," another will hold, and a great and productive social unity will emerge. Extend democratic participation into every area of life, and life will be glorious. Abolish property, abolish government, single tax the land, redistribute the wealth, maintain racial solidarity, organize interest groups, form a world government, develop an all-embracing commitment to the nation, use government to make men free, and so on through the ... enthusiasms which have animated those under the sway of some ideology or other.[1]

The content varies, but these ideologies come out of a similar mold of analysis and mode of operation.

The main ill besetting German society, Hitler claimed, was the Jews and their various intellectual offspring: cultural diversity, democracy, communism, artistic disintegration, finance capitalism, and so on. The Jews were a disruptive element preventing an organic unity of the German people. They were aliens within the society acting as a huge obstacle to its productive fruition. Root out, remove, and destroy this disruptive element and the Germanic or Aryan race could concert its efforts toward great ends. The Jews were to Nazism what the bourgeoisie (or capitalists) were to Marxism. The Jewish exploitation of Germans was to Nazism what capitalist exploitation of labor was to communism. The German race was to Nazis what the proletariat was to Communists. The parallels are even closer than this may suggest.

Hitler's most basic appeal was to German workers to rise up and throw off the exploitation of the Jews, though he did not always approach it in this way. The Nazis aimed, too, to root out and destroy every cultural artifact which was thought to be a product of Jewishness. A revolution was to be wrought in German life. Communism was one of the putative enemies, but a good case can be made that Nazism was an aberrant subspecies of communism. Its positions were paradigmatic; its methods were essentially the same.

Nazism was dipped from the simmering cauldron of ideologies contending for power in Germany in the 1920's. It may be, as some contend, that what is here being referred to as the idea which has the

117

world in its grip was born amidst the French Revolution in France, but the shaping of these ideologies was much more the work of Germans. In any case, Germans were mightily bent toward collectivism in the 1920's. Why this was so, and why Nazism emerged triumphant can be partialy explained by German history.

The three main ingredients of the German ideologies were nationalism, revolution, and social reform. It may well be that nationalism was the most important of these. Certainly, it has occupied the center stage for much of the time in the last hundred years or so of German history. In fact, strictly speaking, there is no German history prior to 1871. German was only a language, a language in search, it may be, of a state to encompass the area in which it was spoken. True, Germany had been united to some extent for a time in the Middle Ages as part of a larger empire. But it was not called Germany, and its boundaries were in no way restricted to what we now think of as Germany. At any rate, this empire broke up long before the modern era began. One writer describes the situation this way: "By the thirteenth century there were ninety-three ecclesiastical and fourteen lay princes. A century later there were forty-four lay princes, and their number continued to multiply as partitions took place between heirs. Many parts of the country were converted into tiny fragments."[2] The relics of empire were strengthened somewhat by strong Spanish monarchs in the sixteenth century, but their hold was severed by the Protestant Reformation and its aftermath.

German unification was finally accomplished in 1871 with the proclamation of a German Empire at the conclusion of the Franco-Prussian War. The architect of this unification was Otto von Bismarck. The king of Prussia was proclaimed as emperor (Kaiser) of Germany as well as retaining his old position as head of the leading German state. Princes and kings in other provinces retained their hereditary thrones, and provincial legislatures continued to share in governing the provinces.

The German Empire ruled over by Kaisers Wilhelm I (1871-1888) and II (1888-1918) was a federated empire. The symbol of its unity was the Kaiser himself, who also held the reins of power. Chancellors were not creatures of the legislature but of the Kaiser, though Bismarck gave distinction to the post. Although there was a German parliament composed of a Bundesrat, in which the state or provinces were represented, and a Reichstag, in which the populace was represented, the main instrument of unity was the Prussianized armed forces.

118

Although Austria, another German-speaking country, was not part of the German Empire, German unification had been virtually achieved.

In the closing days of World War I, this unity was shattered. The symbol of unity, Kaiser Wilhelm II, fled to Holland and abdicated, prompted by his prime minister and undeterred by the High Command. In short order, all the other German princes and kings abdicated as their power dissolved before them. The armed forces disintegrated both in consequence of the imminent military surrender and the thrust of soldiers and sailors organized into soviets or councils.

The stage appeared to be set for a repetition of the events that had taken place in Russia the year before. The parallels wth the February Revolution were very close. In Russia in February of 1917 and in Germany in November of 1918, the emperors abdicated, the armed forces refused to obey their commanders, and workers and soldiers organized into soviets or councils. Red flags were waving in the streets, and there were those ready to rush on immediately to a Bolshevik revolution in Germany. More, Friedrich Ebert, the leader of the Social Democratic Party, formed a provisional government and began preparations for having a constituent assembly.

But there were important differences between the German siuation and the Russian one, too. For one thing, the war was over in Europe, and the German provisional government did not have to wrestle with conducting a war. For another, the soldiers do not appear to have been as radicalized as they were in Russia. Even more crucial, the main Marxist party in Germany, the Social Democratic Party, had been largely won over to evolutionary or gradualist socialism. Its leadership could, and did, claim to be the party of the workers, thus defusing some of the revolutionary ardor, and Ebert used what armed forces he could assemble to suppress the incipient revolution.

The Communist Party was small — that was true in Russia too — and it was not under the discipline of leaders like Lenin and Trotsky. More, two of the communist leaders, Karl Liebknecht and Rosa Luxemburg, were put to death in the course of suppression of the revolution. Kurt Eisner, a socialist who had formed a republic in Bavaria, was shot down on the streets of Munich. Those determined to avert revolution used more muscle than those seeking to make one.

It is not too much to say, though, that Germany was waiting for the other shoe to drop, so to speak, in the 1920's. The first shoe had dropped, the first stage of revolution had occurred, in November of 1918. That is not to say that a revolution must go full cycle once it has begun. But once a government has been overturned an effective one, one which has authority over and has the respect or awe of the populace, must take its place sooner or later. Germany in the 1920's hung between continued disintegration and establishing an effective government. The bureaucracy, the police, the army, and local governments maintained authority when and where they would and could, but their attachment and loyalty to the government of the Weimar Republic was tentative and uncertain. The centripetal forces often gained on the centrifugal, opening the way again and again to revolution.

Germany was bent toward collectivism and collectivist nationalism by the Treaty of Versailles which was imposed on her after World War I. German leaders asked for and were granted an armistice. An armistice is what would most likely be called a cease-fire today, i.e., a stopping of hostilities in order to consider the terms of peace. It is not a surrender, and certainly not an unconditional surrender. Even so, the terms of the peace were not negotiated but imposed by the Allies on Germany.

Large areas mainly inhabited by Germans were separated from Germany or demilitarized or, in the case of the Ruhr, occupied by foreign troops for a time. Germany was supposed to have only a tiny army and only small ships in its navy. Most devastating of all, the German people were held to be collectively guilty for the war. Reparations were to be paid in huge amounts by the German government to the Allies. It did not matter that the German government of the Weimar Republic was not the government which had started and prosecuted the war. The German people were guilty, collectively guilty, the settlement proclaimed. Collective guilt, one suspects, can only be purged or renounced collectively.

The tendency of the Treaty of Versailles was to denationalize Germany, to make it a military nonentity, to make being German a shameful condition, and to penalize the status by reparation payments for several generations. Whether the treaty was just or not, it failed to produce the desired psychological effect on many Germans. Instead, it provoked the most virulent nationalist sentiments. Far from being ashamed that they were Germans, many found new virtue and pride in it, that special virtue attaching to those who are convinced they have been deeply wronged.

One of the most difficult tasks of the governments of the Weimar Republic was to send their foreign ministers, hat in hand, to seek concessions from the Allies. People who believe they have been wronged do not wish to go hat in hand for concessions; they are defiant, and wish to demand and force the righting of the wrong. To the more radical of the nationalists, anyone negotiating for concessions was a traitor.

But Germany was in much greater danger of falling apart in the 1920's than it was of unified or collective action. Indeed, a good case could be made that Germany had fallen apart at the end of World War I, and it was never drawn together in the 1920's. The method of election to the Reichstag prescribed by the Weimar Constitution, adopted in 1919, came close to guaranteeing this state of affairs.

The Constitution called for proportional representation of parties in the Reichstag according to the share of the vote which each party received in general elections. Many members of the legislature received their appointments from party lists. This assured party control over the members, gave impetus to having a multiplicity of parties, and fragmented German politics into ideological configurations. The dominance of party made it difficult for any leaders with popular following to emerge. The Reichstag hardly spoke or acted for Germany; it spoke and acted for the parties and their corporate ideological versions of what should be done.

The parties fell into three configurations generally. There were the socialist parties: the Social Democratic Party, the Independent Social Democratic Party, and the Communist Party. Then there were the center parties: the Democratic Party, the Catholic Centre Party, and, sometimes, the People's Party. The other grouping, usually described as "right wing," would have been made up of the Bavarian People's Party (though it might sometimes be centrist), the Nationalist Party, and the Nazis, among others.

From a parliamentary and, I believe, ideological point of view these classifications are drastically wrong in the cases of at least two of the parties. Neither the Communist nor the Nazi Party participated in any of the governments of the 1920's; they were purely opposition parties. Moreover, they usually opposed the same things. True, their spokesmen may have used their most vicious invective on one another, but if they are to be placed in any parliamentary bloc in the 1920's it is with one another. As to the ideological affinities of the Nazis, that is a point requiring further attention.

None of the parties ever gained a majority of the popular vote or had a majority of members in the Reichstag. This meant that every government organized had to be a coalition government, a coalition usually of at least three parties. The Social Democratic Party was the largest single party in the 1920's, but it infrequently participated in organizing a government, both because of its own finely honed principles and because non-socialists tended to shy away from any of the socialist parties.

The usual process for organizing a government was this. The President, Friedrich Ebert until 1925 and General von Hindenburg thereafter, would select some member of the Reichstag, usually a man with influence in his own party, to form a government. He would then begin negotiations with other party leaders to get their support for a government. The coalitions so formed were unstable, and one government followed another in dreary fashion throughout the twenties. Disaffection with the republic was always widespread, and the succession of compromise governments increased the frustration with the system.

One thing that this standoff of parties did do; it prevented any of the governments from taking very drastic or radical action. As one history notes, the Weimar Republic was largely the creation of the Social Democrats, but "it was remote from anything socialistic. No industries were nationalized. No property changed hands. No land laws or agrarian reforms were undertaken...; there was almost no confiscation ... of ... property...."[3]

It may be technically true that there was little confiscation of property, but there was, nonetheless, a massive and catastrophic redistribution of wealth. It came by way of the runaway inflation in 1922-23. The government flooded the country with paper money in ever-larger doses; the purpose, ostensibly, was to repudiate the reparations debt and resist French occupaton of the Ruhr. It failed on both counts, but it succeeded in wiping out domestic debt and virtually producing economic collapse. By November, 1923, it required over 2½ *trillion* marks to purchase a dollar. Shortly thereafter the inflation was ended, but such faith in the government as there had ever been was seriously eroded.

The conflict of ideologies was sharp and acrimonious in the Reichstag. When President Hindenburg entered the hall for his inauguration in 1925, the Communist members rose *en masse* and walked out. Nazis and Communists were generally considered to be pariahs to other members. Non-socialists generally resisted association with socialists. Votes were often dictated by parties on ideological grounds. Here is an example of such a vote. It concerned the building of an armored cruiser. The Social Democrats, who were militant antimilitarists, had campaigned against the building of such a cruiser. The Communists, not to be outdone, circulated a petition around the country to bar armored cruisers. These events then took place:

When the Reichstag reassembled..., the Social Democratic delegation moved that the construction of Cruiser A be halted. This move naturally evoked strong and angry reactions from the other ministers and their parties.... Such a step could well have had serious consequences for the entire government. All this could have been foreseen. But the dogmatists among the Social Democrats forced a resolution through the delegation, requiring that *all* party members, including the Social Democratic ministers, support the delegation's motion en bloc. Even the President's personal suggestion that the ministers be at least permitted to abstain found no mercy at the hands of the delegation's majority. Thus, on November 17, 1928, the German Reichstag witnessed the grotesque spectacle of chancellor Hermann Müller voting against a decision which a cabinet he had chosen had passed with him in the chair. [4]

The motion failed, but if it had passed the world might have been treated to the unusual spectacle of the fall of a government because its premier had voted with the majority!

But what went on in the Reichstag was generally peaceful and tame compared to what was happening around the country during much of the 1920's. The ideological conflict was hardly restricted to even the vigorous expression of ideas. Private armies, if not commonplace, were not unusual in the 1920's. A Red army existed for a time in 1920. It was organized in the wake of the Kapp Putsch in March of the same year.

A renegade brigade of the German army was used to drive the government out of Berlin and install Wolfgang Kapp at its head. A general strike paralyzed Berlin and much of the country, and Kapp capitulated. As the troops withdrew from the city, this startling incident occurred: "As they marched along the Unter den Linden, a boy in the crowd hooted at them. Some soldiers broke ranks, hurled themselves on the boy, clubbed him to death with their rifle butts and then stomped him with their hobnailed boots. The crowd shouted in horror, while the soldiers calmly returned to their column. Infuriated by the shouts of the crowd, an officer wheeled round and ordered his troops to shoot into it with rifles and machine guns. Then they marched out of Berlin, singing." [5]

The Nazi movement fed on the ideological conflicts and the violence which they engendered. Hitler began to gain his following with speeches in beer halls in Munich. Violence often served as a backdrop for his emotional tirades. Hitler's private army was probably organized

123

at first to protect him in these situations as well as to provide the violent setting. Here is an account of one of these conflicts:

A sudden shout from a Communist took him [Hitler] by surprise; he faltered when replying; and suddenly they were all standing up shouting and hurling beer mugs. There was a deafening chorus of "Freiheit!" Tables were being torn apart so the legs could be used as clubs. The storm troopers ... formed flying columns to wrestle with the Communists. One of the columns was led by Rudolf Hess who had already shown himself to be a formidable fighter. They used fists, chair legs, and beer mugs. ... When the battle was won, Hermann Esser jumped on a beer table and shouted: "The meeting continues. The speaker has the floor." [6]

Hitler then finished his speech.

Hitler did not wait long before trying to go on to bigger things. With the aid of General Ludendorf he attempted a *coup d'etat* in what is known as the Munich Putsch in 1923. It failed, and Hitler was subsequently arrested, tried and convicted of treason, and sentenced to prison. He served only a little more than eight months of the term before he was released, but while in prison he worked on his book, *Mein Kampf*. The book is an attempt not only to set forth his ideology and methods but also to give them a historical gloss by providing what purported to be the historical record of the Aryan race.

There were other private armies in the service of ideology in the 1920's. The largest of these was one organized by the Social Democratic Party, mainly in Saxony and Thuringia. It was called the Reichsbanner, and was founded in February, 1924. The Reichsbanner was supposed to defend the republic from its enemies, but that did not change the fact that it was a private army, composed mainly of Social Democrats. Within a short time, it had three million members. [7]

The German deterioration did not proceed on a straight line from bad to worse to revolution in the 1920's. If the Nazis, or the Communists, or whatever radical party, had brought off a revolution in late 1923 or early 1924 that would have been the case. The worst disorders — the initial revolt of the soldier's and worker's councils, the disintegration of the army, the Kapp Putsch, the assassinations of Eisner, Rathenau and Erzberger, the revolt of the Red army, the Munich Putsch, the runaway inflation — occured from 1918 through 1923.

The Weimar Republic weathered these and other disorders. Indeed, the political situation appeared to have stabilized during 1924-1929. A stable currency was introduced, the economy revived, the Allies began to grant concessions, foreign money began to pour into Germany, and the people enjoyed something approaching domestic tranquility for a few years. If Hindenburg's election to the presidency did not increase attachment to the republic, it at least reassured monarchists and nationalists that they were not without friends in high places. Even Hitler was more restrained for a time, as he concentrated his energies on developing a national following.

It was, of course, the calm before the storm.

The Weimar Republic survived for about fourteen years, more by luck than by design. It survived for want of a generally acceptable alternative — the socialists would not entertain the idea of restoration of the monarchy, and those who despised the republic could not unite behind a common banner — and, perhaps, because those who would make a revolution could not find a handle for bringing it off.

The French Republic survived the years from World War I to World War II without collapsing, and France had many political parties, revolving-door governments, sharp ideological conflicts, and a similar deterioration to that of Germany. But France had not suffered the German defeat, had not experienced a runaway inflation, and was not so clearly poised on the brink of revolution. Even so, it should be noted that the French Republic collapsed in less than five weeks in 1940 under pressure from German, then Italian armies. It required only a sufficient crisis to bring about collapse.

That crisis for Germany was the Great Depression. Many countries were hit by depression after 1929, but none harder than Germany. The foreign money which had poured into Germany after the adoption of the Dawes Plan was no longer available. Liquidity preference in Germany evinced itself in many instances in the transfer of bank accounts to other lands. Unemployment mounted. There were reparation payments to be made. Germany's unemployment insurance program placed a heavy burden upon the government and upon those who were working. By 1930, or in the course of the year, there was widespred agreement about the necessity of emergency measures.

Hitler was waiting in the wings, indeed, had been waiting for some time. The Nazi Party vote grew rapidly as the crisi deepened. It is not generally understood how cleverly Hilter had constructed the Nazi ideology, and never will be by those who insist on forcing it into a "left wing" or "right wing" mold. It is neither of these, if there are any such ideologies.

The Nazi ideology cut across the spectrum of German parties and ideologies. It was clearly designed to draw from all of them while being none of them. It claimed to be *national*, hence appealing to those concerned to establish national unity and military prowess. It claimed to be *socialist*, thus appealing to those for whom socialism was the elixir for modern man. It claimed to be *German*, which in its own freighted framework meant racist and anti-Semitic, and racism and anti-Semitism had much potential appeal in Germany, as elsewhere. And it was, it said, the party of *workers*.

There is no way of knowing how muh design went into the choice of words here. Hitler built his initial following on the base of a worker's party; hence the term might simply have been taken over without much thought. Whatever the case may be, he did seek to build his support on a broad base of manual workers. Beyond these, he proposed to go further than monarchy by establishing the leadership principle, i.e., personal dictatorship.

None of the existing parties could get a majority by their sectarian ideological appeals. He would draw from the several leading parties and ignore the established spectrum of parties. There were those, of course, from whom he would not attempt to draw. He was anti-Communist, anti-Semitic, anti-democratic, and anti-republican. These were the enemies: democrats were too ineffectual to merit anything more than his contempt, but Jews and Communists (quite often indistinquishable to Hitler) were powerful enemies to be overcome.

From the elements to which he would appeal Hitler intended to weld a powerful collective unity. Whether he could ever have got a majority in a free election is now a moot question. He came close enought to it to achieve his purpose of attaining power.

10
National Socialism in Power

IN THE presence of his prospective cabinet and before President Hindenburg of the Weimar Republic, Adolf Hitler intoned these words on the morning of January 30, 1933: "I will employ my strength for the welfare of the German people, protect the Constitution and laws of the German people, conscientiously discharge the duties imposed on me and conduct my affairs of office impartially and with justice to everyone." So saying, he was sworn as Chancellor of the Republic. The other members of the cabinet having taken their oaths, Hitler affirmed his good intentions to the President in a brief speech. Hindenburg, who had delayed asking Hitler to form a government for months, looked as if he were about to make reply but instead dismissed them with his favorite formula: "And now, gentlemen, forward with God!"[1]

Within months of this ceremony about the only relic of the Weimar Republic still standing was President Hindenburg, and he would not survive much longer. A Nazi revolution had taken place, was, as a matter of fact, still in process. This revolution was accompanied by the standard concomitants of modern revolution: suppression of liberty, confiscation of property, concentration camps, persecution of classes or categories of people, terror, and violence. The terror that gripped

Germany in the mid-1930's was soon extended beyond German boundaries and during World War II threatened much of the world, if not all of it.

Ever since, indeed, beginning while it was going on, a great deal of ink has been spilled in attempts to account for Hitler and Nazism. One main approach has been to try to explain the violence, brutality, and viciousness of Nazism by what may be called a biographical-psychological examination of the leaders. Thus, Hitler, Goering, Goebbels, Himmler, and others are studied in order to discover their frustrations, quirks, sexual inadequacies, deprivations, and other origins of their hatreds. For example, a psychological study of Hitler made during World War II speculated that his disorders might have begun with misguided toilet training due to the excessive neatness and cleanliness of his mother. Anyone familiar with the literature knows of the reputed homosexuality of Ernst Roehm (organizer of the ill-famed SA — "Storm Troopers") and of the drug taking of Hermann Goering, for example.

The major difficulty with the biographical approach, aside from the speculative nature of so much of it, is that while it may shed some light on the origins of the brutishness of Hitler and his henchmen it does not explain their success in gaining the support of so many Germans. For this, there is a supplementary explanation. It is to be accounted for by something in the German character.

Although the collective guilt of Germans for Nazi acts was officially rejected by the Nuremberg Trials after World War II, this did not keep it from being widely believed and frequently imputed to them by writers and commentators. The Germans have been accused of being especially drawn to authoritarian governments. This has been attributed by some to Martin Luther and the Lutheran Church. (But surely, it could be argued, if Luther was an authoritarian he was no more so than the Catholic Church. If this were once admitted, however, the specifically German character of this penchant would be refuted.) There are many variations on the Nazism-as-a-phenomenon-attributable-to-something-Germanic theme. Some focus on Prussian militarism, others on latent anti-Semitism, and so on.

Whatever the motives of those who advance the biographical-Germanic explanation (combined, usually, with the notion that Hitler belonged to the "right wing"), the impact is to disentangle and separate Nazism from what is crucially necessary to understanding it. The biographical-Germanic approach tends to make it *sui generis,* something peculiar to Germany. Those who add the supposed "right wing" attribute do attempt to universalize it but confine it to movements which either do not exist or have no common ground in the contemporary world.

A simple story may both show the fatuousness of some of these attempts at explanation and lead us toward an understanding of the character of Nazism. The story is about a scene which the present writer witnessed a good many years ago on the outskirts of the small German town Herzogenaurach. It is but a few miles from the seat of a well-known university at Erlangen but has no claim to fame or notice of its own. Another American soldier and I were walking along the road on a late summer afternoon. We heard a commotion up ahead and saw there were perhaps a dozen children involved in it. As we approached them, we made out what was going on. The children were chasing, taunting, and otherwise harassing a deformed person. Whether we broke it up or whether it was done by some older German escapes my memory, but it was broken up. The details have faded, but the shameful incident has stuck in my memory.

What is to be made of this incident, of this cruel attack by children, ganged up, on a deformed and helpless person? My first reaction, as I recall it, was quite conventional. What I had witnessed was the coming out of some loathesome trait in the German character. Or, the thought occurs to me now, perhaps the children should have been rounded up and taken to a psychiatrist in order to determine what it was in their earlier childhood that had bent them to participate in this particular cruel mischief. Mature reflection, however, convinces me that such approaches to an explanation are to be rejected.

What is misleading about this incident is that the person ganged up on and attacked was deformed. Once it is understood that this was incidental, what happened is all too commonplace. The person was not attacked because he (or she) was deformed but because he was *different*. It happens every day many times over. Children gang up to taunt and harass someone or other in their midst who is in some way different. The target often changes from day to day.

The present writer recalls having been beset by what seems to have been the whole female contingent of his eighth grade class when he announced that he was in favor of Wendell Willkie instead of Roosevelt for President. The community was pro-Roosevelt Democratic, and I was, for a moment, a threat to its solidarity. Such behavior is almost as natural to children as pecking to death one of their number which

129

develops an open sore is to barnyard fowls. Adults are not immune to it, though when they are trying to appear civilized they claim when they are picking on someone who is different that they are only teasing.

Nonetheless, herein lies the roots of collectivism. It is sometimes supposed that the wellspring of collectivism is envy. Undoubtedly, envy sometimes plays a role in collectivism, but it is not clear that it is essential. What is essential is the longing to be at one with some dominant group or order or class of people and to expel and, perhaps, destroy all who do not belong to it. It is, as H. L. Mencken once noted, the longing for the warm smell of the herd. It is powered much more by hatred than envy, hatred for the alien in the midst, the one who is different, and who thus disrupts the supposed unity. (This is mostly nonsense, of course, since such unity as exists arises from the focus on the alien. Expel the alien, and the differences among those in the "unified" group begin to stand out once again.)

None of us is immune to the collective urge. No doubt the Germans have it but so also do the French, the English, the Italians, the Russians, the Hottentots and the Bantu; the Jew and the Gentile, white and black, Protestant and Catholic, Oriental and Occidental. It may even be an urge which the human race shares with the lower animals. Nor is the collective urge necessarily and always productive of evil. When it is confined, restrained, limited, and civilized it enables us to enjoy the good fellowship and share in productive efforts with those of like mind and spirit. But when it is powered by hate, ideologized, and joined with the power of government — let loose to employ force — it is dangerous, wanton, and destructive. It becomes collectivism — the idea that has the world in its grip. The reason for including aspects of collectivism come out more clearly in it than elsewhere.

Adolf Hitler was a master of what for want of a better phrase may be called the Politics of Collectivism. The phrase has probably never had any currency because we do not ordinarily think of collectivism as having a politics. After all, politics has to do with persuasion, with compromise, with composing differences, and with gaining office or position. By contrast, collectivism has to do with concerting all energy behind a set of objectives, with the crushing of dissidence, and with the removal of offending elements. Politics entails the modes of behavior of those who would gain and hold favor when people are free to accept or reject them in ordinary usage.

Even so, there is what may be called a politics of collectivism. It entails the methods of operation by which total power is attained and imposed. It is the means by which a collectivist gets the weight of the populace behind him. When Lenin attempted it, he provoked civil war. Stalin achieved it, in so far as he did, by extensive and prolonged terror. Hitler used terror, too, but much more selective terror than Stalin, and it was coupled with other equally effective methods. His mastery of the politcs of collectivism can best be understood by exploring his methods.

Hitler's methods are revealed in Nazi ideology. Indeed, the ideology was itself a method of gaining and imposing power. There was always a tendency not to take Nazi ideology seriously, and for good reason. The intellectual level of it, in *Mein Kampf,* which is the major exposition of it, is very low. It is difficult to take a writer seriously who breaks into a historical discourse with statements about bowlegged Jews seducing young blonde German maidens, and that in the coarsest and most vulgar language. It is possible to laugh or cry at such hyperbole but hardly to take it seriously. Yet, as it turned out, Hitler was serious, perhaps even sincere, and Nazi ideology requires careful examination.

Nazi ideology, that is, Hitler's ideology, was not an intellectual system. It was not arrived at by deduction from self-evident truths (axiological) not by analysis (dialectics) nor built up from the facts (inductive). Probably the least important aspect of Nazi ideology, to Hitler, was whether it was true or false. He was not interested in improving people's mind but in attracting followers; his appeal was not to the intellect but to the feelings. If Hitler had been reliably informed that the incidence of bowleggedness among Jewish men was much less than that for the German populace as a whole, it is most doubtful that he would have revised *Mein Kampf* to accord with the new information.

Nazi ideology was a compound of what may be best characterized as beer hall or, in the American idiom, barroom exposition. The amount of alcohol that makes the generality of people convivial turns some people into public speakers. Such a person is likely enough to become a loud-mouthed expounder of ideas, taking for listeners any and all who are in the vicinity, though one will often serve as well as ten. He will expound at length on what is wrong with the world and how it can all be set right. Such a person may have a considerable fund of information, a good memory for striking detail, and be fairly well acquainted with popular ideas. However, he prefers monologue (his) to discussion, requires at most an occasional nod for encouragement, and will not brook disagreement with what he is saying. His ideas are to thought what Hollywood mock-ups are to buildings, imitations which could hardly bear close examination.

Hitler's main discovery was how to make such talk productive in getting followers. The beer hall, or barroom, habitue who becomes a public speaker under the influence does not attract followers; on the contrary, he is probably hard put to find drinking companions. We can surmise, if we think about it, why it is that he probably does not attract followers. It is not that he fails to take his ideas seriously or that many of those about him do not share his prejudices. It is rather that he does not take *himself* seriously. Everyone knows that regardless of how cogent his ideas, the talkative drinker is not going to do anything about them. Hitler learned how to make such talk attract followers. He learned how in the course of numerous meetings in beer halls in Munich in the early 1920's.

Hitler did take himself seriously. (There is no reason to suppose that he was one of those who become public speakers under the influence, for he cared little for drinking. His beverage was power, not alcohol.) The problem was how to get others to take him seriously and join forces with him. The way he discovered was to remove all doubt that he would act, all doubt that he meant business. Those who ventured to attend one of his meetings stood a good chance of witnessing the Nazi determination to act. Hitler did not hold seminars in Nazi doctrine; he arranged "happenings" as a backdrop to his fervent speeches. Any person or group which expressed their disagreement vocally was beaten up and thrown out of the meeting. He neither invited differences of opinion, nor did he tolerate them. The violent attacks on those who disagreed signified a determination and willingness to act. Those who did not take Hitler seriously in his meetings could suffer a broken head for the oversight.

There was more to it than this, of course. Hitler was an astute student of mass psychology. His meetings were a bizarre form of entertainment. He usually charged admission during the early years. The Storm Troopers would be in attendance, the threat of violence in the air, the beer hall the setting, and then the main fare, his speech. He scheduled speeches for the nighttime whenever possible, for, as he noted in *Mein Kampf,* people are more readily influenced at night. He usually spoke at great length, two or more hours. The critical powers of the mind decline as the posterior grows numb, and it is at this juncture that the demagogue can be most effective. Hitler could play on the vagrant prejudices which come to the fore as the mind ceases to discipline its contents; he could project feelings of discomfort onto the enemy of his choosing, thereby transforming discomfort into hatred.

132

All this would probably have been of no account without ideology. Hitler claims to have given considerable attention to various ideologies, particularly to Marxism both in its Communist and Social Democratic formulations, and to the various nationalist dogmas. He perceived, too, what must be their fatal error. They could not act decisively and forcefully. They tended to divisions among themselves which weakened them and made them irresolute. The solution to this that he hit upon was to have a single authoritative leader, though the idea may not have originated with him since Lenin had already exemplified it. But this would not solve the problem if the ideology divided the population drastically. It was in solving this problem that Hitler showed himself the consummate politician of collectivism.

Marxism as an ideology divides the people. With its focus upon and almost total reliance upon the proletariat, it alienates the rest of the population. Its atheism alienated Christians. Its internationalism, which Hitler ascribes to Marx's having been a Jew, failed to muster the national spirit of a people. Even so, Hitler gleaned much from Marxism. He believed Marxism to be right in destroying before making a revolution:

It indicates a lack of deep insight into historical developments when today people who call themselves folkish make a great point of assuring us over and over that they do not plan to engage in *negative criticism,* but only in *constructive work.... Marxism* also had a goal, and it, too, has a *constructive activity* ...; but previously, nevertheless, it *practiced criticism* for *seventy years,* annihilating, disintegrating criticism, and again criticism, which continued until the old state was undermined by this persistent corrosive acid and brought to collapse. Only then did its actual "construction" work begin. And that was self-evident, correct and logical.[2]

He denied that the success of the Marxists arose from the complicated Marxian literature. Instead:

What has won the millions of workers for Marxism is less the literary style of the Marxist church fathers than the indefatigable and truly enormous propaganda work of tens of thousands of untiring agitators, from the great agitator down to the small trade-union official and the shop steward and discussion speakers....[3]

Hitler described his ideology as the "folkish philosophy." He said:

The folkish philosophy is basically distinguished from the Marxist philosophy by the fact that it not only recognizes the value of race, but with it the importance of personality, which it therefore makes one of the pillars of its entire ediface. 4

What Hitler refers to as the "importance of personality" should be understood as the importance of leaders and the Führer principle. Actually, as Hitler noted, Communists have had to rely on "leaders." Hitler is quoted on this point, however, more to show that he was aware of or claimed similarity with the Marxists than for the acuteness of his distinction.

The major tactical difference between Nazism and communism was that Nazi ideology was not nearly so divisive. Hitler sought to forge an organic unity of the German people (excluding Jews and convicted Marxists, whom Hitler thought of as "ideologized Jews"). He would bind the Germans — industrialists, workers, military, and civil service — into a great productive and creative unity. To avoid dividing them, he steered clear of specific programs. As to what would be done economically, he said: "I had at that time and still possess today the unshakable conviction that it is dangerous to tie up a great politico-philosophical struggle with economic matters at too early a time."5 He inveighed, too, against those who would try to tie the Nazi Party to either a Protestant or Catholic base. This would only serve to divide rather than unite the people.

The way Hilter used the Christian religion deserves more space than it can be given here. While Hitler was almost certainly a pagan, he frequently spoke as if he were the leading defender of Christianity and conscientiously doing the will of God. Typically, he could effect being most pious when appealing for racial purity. Instead of preaching celibacy, he declares at one place, the Church ought to enjoin racial mixing, and by this "admonition finally to put an end to the constant and continuous original sin of racial poisoning, and to give the Almightly Creator beings such as He Himself created."6 Of course, Hitler did not derive this doctrine from Christianity at all; he was using phrases and ideas drawn from Chritianity to give a religious gloss to his own ideology.

Nazi ideology was concocted from German mythology, from the emanations of other contemporary ideologies, from anti-Semitism, and from pan-Germanism. Hitler intuited the ideological temper of the age and mixed a brew which would appeal to it. He was probably incapable of extended reasoning and he was certainly undisciplined to submitting conclusions to the test of evidence. He made contact with ideas at the point at which they have largely come loose from whatever gave rise to them. In this, he resembled the barroom talker. But, unlike our imaginary talker, he did not simply express them; he wove them into an ideology by repetition, by the skillful merging of images, by using his powerful will to hold them together. There was something demonic about his ability to express ideas that had a wide currency in Germany — that were popular and appeared to derive from the people — and yet to give every one of them his own context.

The Nazi ideology, though, should be thought of as a script to a play. People do not, by and large, read the script; they prefer to watch the performance, to see the words take on life, to see them entwined with the action. If anyone was ever won over to Nazism by reading *Mein Kampf* he has yet to be heard from. But many were drawn into the movement as the play began to unfold.

Hitler was a revolutionary, a revolutionary socialist mayhap, certainly a revolutionary collectivist. He made no secret of his revolutionary intent. *"National Socialism as a matter of principle,"* he said, *"must lay claim to the right to force its principles on the whole German nation.... It must determine and reorder the life of a people...."* [7] Its purpose was to be realized by "tearing down a world and building another in its place...." [8] Hitler did not, of course, specify much of what was to be torn down and he only promised that an organic unity would take its place.

Even though Hitler was a revolutionary, following his stint in prison in the mid-1920's he set upon a course of trying to come to power by popular support. There is no reason to suppose that his punishment had converted him to legality, but it may have helped him to see the futility of any attempted seizure of power. Germany was much more ready to fall apart than it was to be pulled together by revolution. Anyone who grabbed a particular power in Germany might well see it evaporate in his hand.

If the Reichstag were taken over, its powers might revert to the states. If the army chieftains submitted, the soldiers might refuse to fight. The unions could bring a revolution to naught, if it did not suit them, by a general strike. Control of Prussia was undoubtedly the key to the control of Germany (assuming that Catholic Germany did not then secede), but that was hardly easier for Hitler to achieve than control over all of Germany simultaneously. As much as he despised elections, they offered the most likely route to power.

The failure of the Munich *Putsch* in 1923 and the subsequent imprisonment of Hitler and other Nazis all but destroyed the Nazi Party. When Hitler got out of prison, the task of getting electoral support appeared almost insuperable. The Party had to be rebuilt, his own control of it reasserted, and if it were to be anything but a Bavarian party it would have to make a beginning along these lines. The leader of the Storm Troopers, Ernst Roehm, had left the country, and that branch of the movement would have to be rebuilt. Most of the German states prohibited Hitler from making speeches, thus stilling his most effective method of gaining followers. In the face of these difficulties, Hitler did manage to revive and rebuild the Party, and the restrictions were eventually removed. Even so, in the Reichstag elections of 1928 the Nazis only got a sufficient percentage of the vote to name 12 deputies, 12 out of 491!

As noted earlier, the Depression gave Hitler his opportunity. As unemployment rose in Germany, so did the Nazi vote. In the election held in September of 1930 the Nazi Party got the second largest number of delegates in the Reichstag, second only to the Social Democratic Party. But they still had only 107 of 577 total delegates. The crucial fact, however, was that with the growth in delegate strength of the Nazi and Communist parties, none of the three configurations of non-revolutionary parties which usually formed governments could muster a majority. If a grand coalition of parties of the center plus the Social Democrats could have been formed it would have commanded support from only about 250 delegates. The old center parties had only 107 delegates. The nationalists could probably not have mustered 90.

Heinrich Bruning was named Chancellor and formed a government which had representatives from parties with only 137 delegates. The Social Democratic Party did not participate in the government, but Bruning was only able to maintain power with its tacit support. He turned increasingly to rule by emergency decrees issued in conjunction with President Hindenburg in order to be able to function and still avoid votes in the Reichstag which would bring about the fall of the government. "In 1930 the Reichstag passed ninety-eight laws. In 1931 the number fell to thirty-four, while Hindenburg issued forty-two emergency decrees. In 1932 the Reichstag passed only five laws, while Hindenburg issued sixty decrees."[9]

The Reichstag elections held in 1932 help to explain this virtual parliamentary collapse. In the elections held in July of that year the Nazis became the leading party with 230 delegates in the Reichstag. The Communists had been gaining with each election and now had 89. Together the Nazis and Communists commanded 319 votes, a majority. There was, of course, no possibility that the two would form a

136

government and work together, but they could and would combine, by a vote of no confidence, to bring down at will any government named. It apparently meant, too, that the German voters had opted for revolution, though who should bring it about, whether Nazis or Communists, was not yet clear. It was ominous, too, that the vote for the more moderate parties had been steadily declining. The Democratic Party, such voice as nineteenth century liberalism had, elected only four delegates to the Reichstag. The German People's Party had only seven. Even the Social Democratic Party had been steadily declining in popularity.

Hindenburg had already tapped Franz von Papen to be Chancellor, and he formed a government from the center and nationalist parties. But he threw away whatever chance he might have had for tacit support from the Social Democratic Party (which would not have provided him with a majority in the Reichstag after the elections, in any case) by taking over the government of Prussia and driving the Social Democrats out. This was a fortuitous event for Hitler, for when he was made Chancellor he also took over the government of the largest state in Germany.

It may well have been that Papen's control of the government and the police in Prussia, which included the city of Berlin, prevented a Communist uprising, for Berlin was the center of Communist strength. The government ordered, too, the disbanding of the Nazi SA (Storm Troopers), but this order was shortly rescinded. Papen might govern without the Social Democrats but not without some sort of assent from the Nazis. In any case, Papen was dependent upon Hindenburg and his emergency decrees for the day-to-day governing of Germany.

The Reichstag had no sooner assembled after the election than the Communists proposed a no confidence vote in the Papen government. It carried by the whopping vote of 512 to 42. Hermann Goering, the Nazi President of the Reichstag, prevented Papen from filing a dissolution order from Hindenburg which would have forestalled the test. Hitler had already refused to come into the Papen government as Vice Chancellor, insisting that he must head any government in which the Nazis participated. Hindenburg could not accept that solution at this time. So, there was little to be done but call for a new election.

The Reichstag election held in November of 1932 hardly improved matters. The Nazis lost a few delegates; the Communists gained a few; the National Party gained a few, and the Social Democrats lost a few. The Nazis and Communists combined still commanded a majority of the delegates. For once, however, the Nazis allowed the Reichstag to

137

hold a few sessions without a crisis until it adjourned. Hindenburg called upon General Kurt von Schleicher to form a government. He maneuvered to try to get the support of enough parties to govern but in such a way that he lost whatever trust he had among party leaders. He tried to divide the Nazi Party by bringing Gregor Strasser into his cabinet. Strasser refused, and Hitler was furious with Schleicher. In like manner, he attempted to get support from the Social Democrats but succeeded only in irritating the leadership of that party. Meanwhile, Franz von Papen, who had earlier been a protege of Schleicher, began to maneuver behind his back.

With the January 31, 1933, meeting of the Reichstag facing him, Schleicher recognized that he could not govern. Most likely, he would have been subjected to a no-confidence vote as humiliating as that received earlier by Papen. There was one way, he thought, by which he could govern and Hitler could be prevented from coming to power. President Hindenburg should dissolve the Reichstag, grant him emergency powers to govern, and suppress the Nazis and Communists before any new elections were called, if any were called. Hindenburg would not agree to this course, and Schleicher resigned.

At this juncture, Hindenburg asked Hitler to become Chancellor of a new government. Historians, with perfect hindsight, have found fault with Hindenburg's decision ever since. He was, after all, 85 years old and almost certainly becoming senile. But if Hindenburg had been at the height of his intellectual powers, there is little reason to suppose he would have acted differently. He was on the horns of a dilemma. To follow Schleicher's proposal would be to make him, or someone else, dictator. It would almost certainly mean the end of constitutional government and the Weimar Republic as well. (Hindenburg's honor was involved here, for he had pledged himself to obey the Constitution and uphold the Republic.) Even then, there was no assurance that whoever he chose as dictator could govern, and Hindenburg did know this. Such a dictator would have to depend upon the regular army (the *Reichswehr*).

But could the army impose a dictator on Germany? Hindenburg doubted it, for good reason. The Treaty of Versailles, not Hindenburg, was to blame for this state of affairs. The army was restricted to 100,000 men, and the morale of those was an uncertain factor. Paramilitary forces vastly outnumbered the army, and many of them were armed and wore uniforms. Officers in the SA had been seen for some time swaggering about requiring regular army personnel to salute them. Any

138

attempt at suppressing the Communists might bring forth a general strike from the unions. What Schleicher proposed would, at the least, suspend the Constitution and most likely bring civil war. That was one horn of the dilemma.

The other horn was Hitler. For all his blustering, crudeness, and vulgarity — this was well known — he was still an unknown quantity in one sense. He had not yet had the authority or responsibility for governing. Might not responsiblity sober and tame him? Might not the necessity for getting a majority in the Reichstag restrain him? More, the cabinet might hold him in check. The Nazis were to have only two posts besides that of Chancellor. Papen was to serve as Vice Chancellor, and he was no wild man. Hugenburg, the head of the Nationalist Party, had a strong and tenacious personality; Hitler needed his party, and had him in the cabinet. Hindenburg detested Hitler, had delayed as long as he could raising him to power, but had finally to act. Reassured by his advisors, he made the fateful appointment.

Anyone dealt such a hand at cards as Hindenburg held, to change the figure of speech, should have asked for a new deal. Hindenburg already had, of course, but another election had left him holding the same cards, so to speak. Was there really any reason to hope that yet another election would bring about any great change? So, hoping for the best, Hindenburg listened to the cabinet being sworn and gave them his charge with his familiar parting words: "And now, gentlemen, forward with God!" Hitler was not a gentleman — far from it. Germany did not go forward with God; instead, it went down with Adolf Hitler. At last, Hitler had the opportunity to prove that he was serious.

He was serious. He meant every word he had written and spoken, and more.

11
The Promise and the Terror

To OUTWARD appearances Hitler came to power legally in January, 1933. The Nazi Party had received the largest percentage of the vote in the last two general elections and thus had the largest delegation in the Reichstag. President Hindenburg had appointed Hitler Chancellor, which was the method prescribed by law. Indeed, naming him to head the government could have presaged a return to substantial constitutional rule. Undoubtedly, Hindenburg hoped it would. Increasingly, for the past two years Germany had been governed by presidential decree because the Chancellors and their cabinets could not command a majority in the Reichstag. The naming of Hitler to head the government was supposed to be a step toward restoring parliamentary government by placing the head of the largest party at the focus of power.

But Hitler's rise to power was accomplished only apparently by legal means. The way is opened to seeing this when we realize that he was granted very little power on January 30, 1933. There were only three Nazis, including Hitler, in the eleven member Cabinet. The allegiance of the armed forces was to President Hindenburg, and he could assume command over them by declaring martial law. Most police powers were exercised by the states. President Hindenburg further circumscribed Hitler's powers by requiring that he obtain a parliamentary majority in order to retain his position. The Reichstag could, in theory, force his resignation at any time by a vote of no confidence. To all but Hitler, and probably a few others, he appeared to be boxed in.

Hitler had no intention of being boxed in or restrained, but it was crucial that he observe the forms of legality. Historians have continued to ponder over the years why the army did not put a stop to Hitler, why the labor unions did not go out on a general strike, and why this or that group (or even the German people) did not rise against him. There are a number of reasons for this, but the primary one is that he had been installed legally in his position. His legal hold on power tended to disarm his enemies and render them irresolute. One scholar has described Hitler's method of operation this way:

For Hitler's originality lay in his realization that effective revolutions, in modern conditions, are carried out with, and not against, the power of the State: the correct order of events was first to secure access to that power and then begin his revolution. Hitler never abandoned the cloak of legality; he recognized the enormous psychological value of having the law on his side.... [1]

He wore this cloak much more frequently during the first year and a half than he did thereafter.

Hitler was faced with political problems as soon as he was installed. The most pressing was to get a working majority in the Reichstag. Beyond that, he wanted to have passed an Enabling Act which would permit the cabinet to promulgate laws without Reichstag approval. This would allow him to bypass not only the Reichstag but also the President. There was a possibility that he could have got his working majority, but there was no possibility of getting an Enabling Act through the Reichstag with its present composition. The Social Democrats and Communists — the Marxist parties — almost certainly would combine to prevent that. As a matter of fact, the Social Democrats determined quickly after Hitler was installed as Chancellor that they would introduce the call for a no-confidence vote as soon as the Reichstag met.

The Cabinet considered three different approaches toward getting a working majority. Hugenberg, the Nationalist leader, wanted to expel the Communists from the Reichstag. Not only would this be illegal but it might also provoke the dreaded general strike. Hitler and the others rejected this approach.

141

Another, and legal, way would be to get the support of the Centre Party and possibly also the Bavarian People's Party, probably by bringing them into the government. Hitler did enter into negotiations with the leaders of these parties, but reported to the Cabinet that their demands were too great for any hope of agreement. There is a widely held belief that Hitler did not want to come to terms with these parties. That may well be, for he certainly would have been boxed in if he had accepted dependency on the Centre Party, say. Even a small party holding a balance of power would have great leverage.

In any case, Hitler adopted a third approach, one which he probably had planned from the outset: to ask President Hindenburg to dissolve the Reichstag and call for a new election. The election was set for March, 1933.

Hitler seemed to be taking a considerable gamble by holding new elections. This would be the third such election in less than a year, and the Nazi Party vote had been smaller in the second than in the first. If it should decline once again, Hitler's position would be less secure than it was. Of course, Hitler believed that as head of the government he would be able to employ fair means and foul to consolidate his position. The pretext for resorting to force, if he needed one, was provided by a fortuitous event: the Reichstag fire. On the night of February 27, 1933, the Reichstag building went up in flames.

While the building was still smoldering, Hitler concluded that the fire had been set by Communists, or more broadly, Marxists. It was a signal, he proclaimed, for a Bolshevik revolution in Germany. So far as has ever been determined, it was actually the work of a lone man, a Dutch ex-Communist who confessed to it and was executed. A great effort was made to prove that there was a Communist conspiracy; several Communists were arrested and tried. However, the court found them not guilty. It was widely held for a long time that the fire must have been set by Nazis, that it probably was directed by Hermann Goering, and some still believe this to have been the case. However, careful scholarly investigation since World War II has failed to turn up any solid evidence that the Nazis did it.[2]

In any case, the Nazis used the occasion to suspend liberties and step up the use of force. On the day after the fire President Hindenburg was induced to sign a decree permitting the government to place "Restrictions on personal liberty, on the right of free expression, including freedom of the press; on the rights of assembly and association ...," among other things.[3] Just prior to the election, "Some

142

four thousand Communist officials and a great many Social Democrats and liberal leaders were arrested, including members of the Reichstag, who, according to the law, were immune from arrest."

Truckloads of storm troopers roared through the streets all over Germany, breaking into homes, rounding up victims and carting them off to S.A. barracks, where they were tortured and beaten. The Communist press and political meetings were suppressed; the Social Democrat newspapers ... were suspended.... Only the Nazis and their Nationalist allies were permitted to campaign unmolested. [4]

The tenor of the campaign is revealed in these promises of Goering in a speech at Frankfurt two days before the election: "Certainly, I shall use the power of the State and the police to the utmost, my dear Communists, so don't draw any false conclusions; but the struggle to the death, in which my fist will grasp your necks, I shall lead with those down there — the Brown Shirts." [5]

Even with the power of an unrestrained government behind them, the Nazis failed to get the majority they sought; they received approximately 44 per cent of the total vote. However, it already had been decided that the Communist Party would not be permitted to seat any delegates in the Reichstag. Without them, the Nazis had their working majority. (It is generally believed that Hitler had only permitted the Communist Party on the ballot to forestall the shift of much of the vote of their followers to the Social Democrats.)

Hitler got his Enabling Act, too, when the Reichstag met. Only the Social Democrats, such of them as were not being held by the Nazis in prisons or concentration camps, voted against it. The scene on the day of the vote was reminiscent of that of the meeting of the Russian Constituent Assembly in January 1918. There were Storm Troopers all about, and the streets were filled with these uniformed forces, chanting for the passage of the bill. Only Otto Wels, the Social Democrat leader, got up enough courage to speak against it, and Hitler rose immediately after to denounce him. The final vote was 441 for and 84 against. The Reichstag had, in effect, voted itself into oblivion. Thereafter, "legality" hardly was distinguishable from the will of Hitler.

Even before the passage of the Enabling Act, Hitler had begun the process of subduing the potential of resistance of independent organizations in Germany. The main ones with such potential were: political parties, the states, labor unions, the churches, industrial and trade organizations, farmer groups, the regular army, professional associations, and, eventually, his own paramilitary organizations. With the Enabling Act in one hand, he could and did step up the pace of abolition, subversion, and subjection of these organizations.

Before describing this, however, the terroristic setting within which it occurred needs to be made clear. The main instrument of terror during the first year or so of Hitler's rule was the SA (Storm Troopers), though it was ably assisted by the SS, the Gestapo, and the regular police. The SA expanded rapidly after Hitler became Chancellor. It had, perhaps 400,000 members at the beginning of 1933; by the end of the year it had from 3 to 4 million members. Many Communists now came into the SA. "Between January and November, 1933..., the numerical strength of the Berlin SA rose from 60,000 to 110,000, and former Communists accounted for about 70 per cent of the increment."[6] In and around Berlin, Goering combined the SA with the police and loosed them against "anti-State organizations."

All the SA's basest instincts, all its pent-up social discontent, all that inflammatory orators and propagandists had been dinning into it for years, was given free rein — and Prussia turned into a terrorists' witches' cauldron. Mobile squads of SA swept through the streets of the towns, the worst thugs being in Berlin. Section 1c of SA headquarters ... drove so-called enemies of the State in front of it, dragged them into huts, shelters, cellars and out-of-the-way places, beat them up and tortured them. This state of affairs was not confined to Berlin; terror reigned in the provinces too....[7]

Rudolph Diels, who was able to use his position to get some of the prisoners released, described what happened to some of them: "The victims whom we found were half dead from starvation. In order to extort confessions from them, they had been kept standing for days in narrow cupboards. 'Interrogation' consisted simply of beating up, a dozen or so thugs being employed in fifteen-minute shifts to belabour their victims with iron bars, rubber truncheons and whips. When we entered, these living skeletons were lying in rows on filthy straw with festering wounds."[8]

The Nazis had no intention of tolerating political opposition, nor would they collaborate for long with other political parties which were independent of them. The Communist Party had been, in effect, proscribed since the Reichstag fire. In May, 1933, its assets and property were seized, and the Party ceased to exist. Shortly thereafter the property of the Social Democratic Party was taken, and it was officially dissolved in early July. Harassment of the other parties led their leaders

144

to dissolve them. Even the Nationalist Party, which had been most cooperative, was not permitted to survive. "On 21 June the police and S.A. occupied the Party's offices in a number of German towns, and a week later the leaders, bowing to the inevitable, dissolved the Party." To round it all off, Hitler promulgated this law on July 14, 1933:

Article I: The National Socialist German Workers' Party constitutes the only political Party in Germany.

Article II: Whoever undertakes to maintain the organizational structure of another political Party or to form a new political Party will be punished with penal servitude up to three years or with imprisonment up to three years, if the action is not subject to a greater penalty according to other regulations.[9]

The "other regulations" were probably the laws against treason. At any rate, there was now only one party in Germany.

The states were reduced to administrative units of the Reich government in a few months. That puts it too tamely: they were made into instruments of the will of Hitler and those immediately under him. Following the general elections in March of 1933 and the passage of the Enabling Act, the state legislatures were ordered reconstituted in accordance with the national elections. Even before that, however, the subjection of the states had begun. Papen, as Chancellor of the Reich, had gained control of the Prussian government in 1932. Under Hitler, Goering was given control over the police in Prussia, including Berlin. The government of Bavaria, the second largest German state, was seized by the Nazis, even before the last general election. Hitler eventually became "governor" of Prussia, and Goering its prime minister, thus consolidating the rule of Germany's largest state with that of Germany. A "Law for the Coordination of the States with the Reich" was set forth April 7, 1933:

This revolutionary statute deprives the States of independent authority and largely abolishes the federal system. It provides for the appointment of ... Governors appointed by, subject to, and directly representing the Reich government. They will take charge of the State governments and ensure that the latter observe "the political directions set forth by the Reich Chancellor"....
The ... Governors appointed during ensuing weeks are ... without exception Nazis, as a rule Nazi Gauleiters.[10]

The labor unions were supposed to be the most dangerous threat to the Nazis; a general strike could, in theory, paralyze the country. The Nazis moved stealthily and swiftly against them. The government declared May 1, 1933, a national holiday in celebration of labor. This "May Day" celebration was undoubtedly intended to quiet any fears the leaders might have that anything ominous was portending for them. Then, on May 2, the Nazis struck. The socialist unions were dissolved. "Early in the morning SA and SS men, aided by the police, occupy their offices, buildings and banks throughout the country. Their leading representatives ... are summarily arrested and incarcerated in prisons or concentration camps."[11] The Christian Trade Unions and such others as existed then "voluntarily" yielded up their independence to the Nazis. A German Labor Front controlled by the Nazis was set up to replace the independent unions. Workmen continued to pay their dues, but they no longer were able to take any action by way of the unions.

The churches, too, were subdued by the Nazis, but the approach to them was more subtle than to many other organizations. Hitler sought to use them as an instrument in forging German unity and to limit their impact when it would not be in that direction. The Roman Catholic Church posed the potentially greatest problem, since significant control over it was exercised from beyond the bounds of Germany. Hitler sent emissaries to the Vatican, and these eventually were able to work out a Concordat with the Pope. The effect of this was to tend to undermine any opposition from the Catholic clergy within Germany. So far as the Lutherans were concerned, Hitler managed to get Nazi sympathizers in positions of authority over many of them.

There can be little room for doubt, however, that the thrust of Christianity is in the opposite direction from National Socialism, that the unity and militancy of the Nazis ran counter to Christianity. Warfare is hardly a Christian ideal as it was an ideal for the Nazis. Undoubtedly, leading Nazis hoped eventually to replace Christianity with Hitler worship, but in the meanwhile they sought to subvert the churches, and they persecuted those who attempted to maintain the distinct mission and independence of Christianity.

Indeed, the brunt of Nazi terror was focused on carrying out religious persecution. The most dramatic, sustained, and, eventually, horrible instance of this was the persecution of the Jews. Hitler claimed, of course, that the assault upon the Jews was motivated by racial rather than religious considerations. Yet, if Jews were distinguishable from the rest of the population by anything other than a common religious background, Hitler never discovered it, for he required them to display the Star of David — surely a religious emblem — so that they would be recognized. Jews were subjected to discriminatory measures, to being

146

hounded out of the professions, to the loss of property, to harassment by the populace, to persecution in concentration camps, and encouraged to go elsewhere to live during the 1930's.

Jehovah's Witnesses were invariably persecuted because of their pacifist views. Of Catholic persecution, William L. Shirer says: "Thousands of Catholic priests, nuns and lay leaders were arrested, many of them on trumped-up charges of 'immorality' or of 'smuggling foreign currency.' Erich Kausener, leader of Catholic Action, was ... murdered.... Scores of Catholic publications were suppressed and even the sanctity of the confessional was violated by Gestapo agents."[12] Among Protestants, those who identified themselves as the "Confessional Church" were the most vigorously persecuted.

Neither industrialists, shopkeepers, nor farmers posed any great threat to the Nazi regime. They are, in any case, fundamentally engaged in peaceful pursuits, and such organizations as they possessed were used by the Nazis to direct and coordinate their activities. Much of German industry was already cartelized; it served Hitler's purposes for it to be even more so, for concentrated industry was much more readily controlled by the state.

The question often has been raised of why the Nazis did not meet greater opposition in Germany. Why, it has been asked, did the state leaders or political parties or labor unions not mount an effective opposition? Why did the churches not speak out strongly and unequivocally against Hitler? Why, even, did the Jews not serve as catalysts for a concerted opposition? Why did business leaders not resist the Nazi thrust to power? Why did the army not prevent the spread of terror and barbarism in Germany? Indeed, why was there such apparent widespread support among the German people for Hitler? What happened, it is well to ask, to journalists, writers, judges, lawyers, artists, and what may be thought of in general as the keepers of civility? Why did all these not raise such a storm of opposition that the Nazi tide would have been turned back from the beginning?

There are, of course, particular explanations to be made in answer to each of these questions, explanations which would account, in part, for the failure of particular groupings and organizations. But there is a broader explanation which includes all of them and is, hopefully, more complete than all the separate explanations would be. In the broadest sense, Germany did not rise in opposition to Hitler because it was deeply divided. It was divided into many different political parties, as has been shown, and most of these were locked in ideological conflict with one another. Many laborers were members of unions intent on gaining their own ends and in opposition to much of the rest of the populace. The army was imperiled by the paramilitary organizations. Many, many people were monarchist rather than republican in inclination.

What enabled Hitler to consolidate his power and subject the German people to his will was the Promise and the Terror. What Hitler promised was to end the divisions within Germany, to forge a national unity, to concert the energies of the people behind the building and expansion of a specifically German state. Hitler offered himself as the visible symbol, the Leader, of such a unity. He would lead Germany to the realization of its national greatness. Opposition to Hitler, in this context, became opposition to German unity, opposition to German greatness, opposition to the melding of the Germanic people into an organic whole.

Those who have contemplated Nazi Germany from a safe remove in time and place have imagined options which were not apparent to the German people. The alternative, if it could be called that, which Hitler offered was either to blend with and become a part of the organic unity or to be isolated and alone. In theory, no organization could exist which did not contribute toward the achievement of this unity and was not subordinate to it. Bishop Marahrens of Hanover had grasped the point when he made this public declaration in 1937: "The National Socialist conception of life is the national and political teaching which determines and characterizes German manhood. As such, it is obligatory upon German Christians also."[13] The Promise, to those who would so yield, was that they would realize their own potential by identification with the greatness of the nation.

Those who would not, or could not as in the case of the Jews and Gypsies, would be crushed. Underlying the Promise was the Terror. There was no real option of being left alone in Nazi Germany. Any who were not for Hitler were against him; all who were not of the collective were a menace to it. Just as a farmer insists on having all the pigs in the pen, so Hitler would have all broken to the mentality of his collective or destroyed. A stubborn pig will sometimes resist being penned, running hither and yon to escape his fate. He will, of course, be pursued, hounded, beaten about his tender nose, and otherwise tormented until he goes in or dies of exhaustion. There were object lessons aplenty in Nazi Germany for any who gave thought to resisting. Two examples may suffice.

The first usually is described as "The Night of the Long Knives." Most of the events associated with it took place June 30-July 1, 1934. During that time and in the succeeding days, the leaders of the SA were put to death, along with a goodly number of other peope whom Hitler feared or hated. "Put to death" may be too gentle a phrase; they were murdered, murdered in a manner that is usually associated with gangland massacres. Hitler personally went to Munich to oversee the round-up of victims there; the chief of these was Ernst Rohm, the commander of the SA. Himmler's SS carried out this purge, and it was the signal of the triumph of that organization over the SA. It is generally believed that several hundred were killed, but the exact number never has been determined.

The background, so far as it is known, is this. As already noted, the SA had expanded rapidly in the course of 1933 until it was far and away the largest organization in Germany with the potential of being a military force. The SA had been Hitler's main instrument of terror during his thrust to power in the early months of 1933. However, by the middle of the year Hitler was ready to declare, and did, that the political revolution had been accomplished and that henceforth change would be made gradually and by evolutionary means.

There were rumblings within the SA of the desirability of completing the "social revolution." But Hitler had no intention of allowing German industry to be destroyed by turning it over to the heavy handed and inept SA. Relations between Hitler and Rohm ranged from cool to cordial thereafter, but the impression prevailed that the SA leaders were champing at the bit to play some more vital role in the Reich. Rohm focused increasingly on one goal, to train and equip the SA as an army and have it become the bulwark of Germany's expanded and revitalized armed force.

The idea may have appealed to Hitler. His goal, of course, was a vastly expanded army following the repudiation of the Treaty of Versailles. In the SA he might have the potential for such an army already enlisted. But there clearly were drawbacks to such an approach. The Storm Troopers were street fighters, more like a mob than an army, and their loyalty — whether to Hitler or Rohm — was uncertain. More, the regular army leaders unalterably were opposed to being undercut by Rohm's amateurs. This was one area where President Hindenburg, a professional soldier himself, was adamant; the SA must be put in their place. Caught between these pressures, Hitler dallied, apparently reluctant to strike down an old comrade. But when he struck, he struck in his usual underhanded, masterful, and monstrous fashion. Rohm was sent on sick leave, and the SA was given a month's vacation in July with the promise that they would be reassembled at the end of that time. On the eve of their vacation, Hitler made his move.

It is doubtful that Hitler would have had several hundred people killed, and that illegally by all civilized standards, in order simply to downgrade the SA. Besides, a goodly number of those killed had no association with the SA. His sinister purpose may be revealed more clearly in the murder of two professional soldiers. "On the morning of June 30, a squad of S.S. men in mufti rang the doorbell at General von Schleicher's villa on the outskirts of Berlin. When the General opened the door he was shot dead in his tracks, and when his wife, whom he had married but eighteen months before ... stepped forward, she too was slain on the spot. General Kurt von Bredow, a close friend of Schleicher, met a similar fate the same evening."[14] The lesson hardly would be lost on military men. Their rank and status — Schleicher had been a Chancellor, too — would not protect them if they opposed Hitler. A man, even a professional soldier, is ever exposed and potentially alone, when he is subject to being shot down in his home on orders from the highest government officials. Hitler drove the point home in his speech to the Reichstag later that month: "And everyone must know for all future time that if he raises his hand to strike the State, then certain death is his lot."[15] And Hitler was the State.

The second example of the Terror shows also, but in a different way, the lot of the opponent, real or imagined, of the regime. It takes us into the concentration camps where the ultimate nature of revolutionary socialism is revealed. The concentration camp is as essential to revolutionary socialism as the garbage dump is to cleaning the modern city. Indeed, the functions of each are so similar that Solzhenitsyn has referred to the camps in Russia as a garbage disposal system, as already noted. The idea that has the world in its grip is that all human effort will be concerted toward achieving felicity. But there are those who will not be concerted or for one reason or another cannot be concerted. (Indeed, there may be no upper limit to the number who might be put in this category.) Something must be done with them, and the concentration camp is their most plausible destiny. They are, so to speak, the refuse of collectivism.

Nowadays, considerable effort is put into reclaiming for use the refuse of the cities: waste materials are recycled; sewage water goes through a purification process; even garbage might be reused in some way. In like manner, concentration camps have been used, to some extent, for "recycling" or "purifying" human beings and bringing them into accord with the collective. This "recycling process" entails separating them from society, isolating them from one another, cutting away every shred of their independence, and developing in them a longing to be identified with the collective, even their own jailers. Even if they cannot be finally repatriated, so to speak, collectivism finds its vindicaton and justification in their longing for it.

Bruno Bettelheim makes a particularly good witness about this aspect of the Terror and of concentration camps. An Austrian Jew, trained in psychology, Professor Bettelheim was confined in the Nazi concentration camps at Dachau and Buchenwald in the late 1930's, prior to the time when they became extermination camps. In contrast to many who have written about the camps, he concluded that the torments to which the prisoners were subjected ordinarily were not aimed at satisfying the sadistic whims of the SS guards. On the contrary, they were designed to bend and break the will of the prisoner in order not only to make him pliable but also to align him with the aims of the regime, or, at the least, make him useful in some way.

The first stage in this attempted transformation took place during the initial transportation to a camp. The prisoners were kicked, slapped, knifed, or wounded in other ways. They also were put in uncomfortable and unusual positions for long periods to produce extreme exhaustion. "The guards also forced prisoners to hit one another and to defile what the SS considered the prisoners' most cherished values. They were forced to curse their God, to accuse themselves and one another of vile actions and their wives of adultery and prostitution.... Until it was over, any failure to obey an order, such as slapping another prisoner, or any help given a tortured prisoner was viewed as mutiny and swifly punished by death." "The purpose of this massive initial abuse," says Bettelheim, "was to traumatize the prisoners and break their resistance...."[16] The purpose, too, was to cut the individual loose from the protection he usually received and confidence he had from being civil, moral, and decent. It began the process of severing him emotionally from society and isolating him from the protection of his fellows.

Although the attack on the personality was not so severe once they were in camp, it was much more prolonged. The way they were treated appeared to be designed to make them regress to a childlike condition. They were not permitted to address one another by their titles nor to use the formal modes of address. They were whipped for misbehavior, even as children sometimes are. Their attention was focused on bodily elimination, even as small children are, by allowing them insufficient time to take care of it and requiring them to obsequiously gain permission from the guards to seek relief. They were made to do meaningless work, sometimes were hitched to wagons like horses, and made to sing rollicking songs when they marched. They were being robbed of their status as adult human beings.[17]

Bettelheim experienced the next stage at Buchenwald; it was the merging of the individual into a mass, the group. This is how it was done:

Whenever possible the prisoners were punished as a group so that the whole group suffered for and with the person who brought about the punishment.... It was in the group's interest to prevent anyone from endangering the group. As already noted, the fear of punishment was more frequent than the reality, which meant that the group asserted its power over the individual more often and more effectively than the SS. In many respects group pressure was practically permanent. Moreover, each prisoner was unusually dependent for survival on group cooperation. This added further to a situation where the group was constantly controlling the individual.[18]

The final stage occurred when the prisoners had come to identify themselves with their captors, the SS, to imitate their behavior, and to treat other prisoners, and think of them, as did the SS. This was a stage reached only by "old prisoners," those who had been in the camps for years. How far this identification went is suggested by Bettelheim:

Old prisoners tended to identify with the SS not only in their goals and values, but even in appearance. They tried to arrogate to themselves old pieces of SS uniforms, and when that was not possible they tried to sew and mend their prison garb until it resembled the uniforms.... When asked why they did it, they said it was because they wanted to look smart. To them looking smart meant to look like their enemies.[19]

But, of course, the SS was no longer to them the enemy; the enemy had become anyone and everyone who by thought or deed resisted the rule by the SS. By extension, the enemy had become all who were not in accord with the collective will. The transformation of personality had taken place.

It might be supposed that once such a transformation had taken place the prisoner then would be released. The present writer has encountered no evidence that this happened generally. True, prisoners were released from concentration camps from time to time, but their release did not depend upon any stage of personality transformation, so far as we know. If one of the purposes of the camps was to terrify the general populace, and that must have been the case, the purpose probably would have been poorly served by sending back those who had so thoroughly adjusted to them. The camps are best understood as diabolical experiments in people control, not experiments whose results would be inmates reclaimed for society but experiments whose results could be used for controlling people more generally.

Legality is only an appearance when the idea that has the world in its grip has behind it the mechanisms of the state. It is an empty form whose substance has been drained away to be replaced by arbitrary power, force, and terror in the service, supposedly, of the collective will. The concentration camp is the "law school" of socialism.

12
Nazi-Soviet Parallels

ON AUGUST 21, 1939, a shocking announcement was made in Moscow: the Nazi government of Germany and the Communist government of the Soviet Union had reached an agreement. It was billed as a non-aggresion pact between the two countries and has been called by such various names as the Nazi-Soviet Pact, the von Ribbentrop-Molotov Pact, for the two foreign ministers who negotiated it, and the Moscow Pact. What was shocking was that these two avowed enemies should reach an accord; this, plus the dread implications it had for power alignments in the world. (There were dark rumors in those days of a Rome-Berlin-Moscow-Tokyo Axis against most of the rest of the world.) The Nazis were supposed to be on the "extreme right" and the Communists on the "extreme left" of the ideological spectrum. They had supported opposing sides in the Spanish Civil War, and Communists were proclaimed anti-Fascists (which included Nazis) while Nazis trumpeted their anti-Communism. The accord left many communists around the world facing in the wrong direction, so to speak.

The Nazi-Soviet Pact lasted for nearly two years. The portion that was made public appeared to be a non-aggression pact. But the secret protocols which accompanied it made it, in effect, a mutual aggression treaty. Eastern Europe was divided into spheres of influence between the Nazis and Communists. A few days after the signing of the pact, German forces invaded Poland, launching World War II. While Polish forces were more than occupied in the west, the Soviet armies invaded that hapless country from the east. The defeat of the Poles, which came with astonishing swiftness, was followed by the division of Poland between Germany and the Soviet Union.

When Hitler's armies invaded Poland, Britain and France declared war on Germany. When Stalin's armies invaded Poland, no action was taken against the Soviet Union. (Some history textbooks do not even mention the Soviet invasion; those that do, generally do not explore its significance. Less than a year later, when Italian armies invaded France following the Nazi incursion, President Franklin Roosevelt declared: "The hand that held the dagger has plunged it into the back of its neighbor." He might have made the same dramatic remark earlier about the Soviet Union, but he did not.)

During the ensuing fall and winter, while German and Allied forces were bogged down in a "phony war," the Germans safe behind the Siegfried Line and the French and British behind the Maginot Line, the Soviet Union continued its aggressions. Soviet forces occupied strategic locations in Latvia, Estonia, and Lithuania as a prelude to their annexation. Then, Soviet forces invaded tiny Finland. The Finns, in one of the more heroic episodes during World War II, held the Soviet armies at bay for most of the winter before they finally succumbed.

There was a more appropriate reaction in Western Europe and America to this act of aggression. The Soviet Union was expelled from the League of Nations, and the Allies offered military help to Finland but were unable to provide it because the other Baltic countries would not permit it to pass through their ports. Into the spring of 1940 the Soviet Union was running "neck and neck" with Germany for the lead as an aggressor nation. Thereafter, Germany forged ahead with the invasion of Norway, Denmark, Holland, and Belgium.

The point is this, however: for a brief interlude during the life of the Nazi-Soviet Pact the affinity of Nazis and Communists was displayed for all to see, even if many preferred to avert their eyes from the spectacle. This should not be taken to mean that there were not differences between Nazism and Communism. It is rather to say that such differences as there were, were accidental and inorganic. They were differences of focus, of intention, and of articulation. By contrast, the similarities were organic and essential.

Nazism and Communism are best understood as parallel systems spun from essentially the same ideological materials. That they were competitors for dominion over the peoples of the world there should be

155

no doubt, competitors whose eventual clash with one another may well have been inevitable. But competition arises from those offering essentially the same product or service, not from those at opposite ends of the spectrum. Their pact was a temporary agreement to divide up the territory over which they would hold sway, much as two giant cartels might agree to divide up the market until such time as one or the other would be strong enough to begin its incursion into the other's area.

The essential similarities of these parallel systems emerge from a comparison of them. Their modes of operation and political structure would hardly have been more nearly alike if they had come from the same mold.

In the first place, both Communists in Russia and Nazis in Germany seized power by the use of violence. True, the Nazis appeared to come to power legally, but actually Hitler only got into office legally, not to real power. As has been shown, the Nazis only attained a parliamentary majority by illegally denying seats to the Communist Party. In a similar fashion, Hitler got his Enabling Act by suppressing opponents and terrorizing his collaborators. There was nothing more than a semblance, if that, of legality in the suppression of political parties, the subjection of the states, and the subjugation of the labor unions. The murder of political opponents laid bare just how illegal had been Hitler's thrust to power. There was never any doubt, of course, that the Bolsheviks seized power in Russia.

Both Nazi and Communist rule was the imposition of the will of the minority on the majority. Both Nazis and Bolsheviks failed to get a majority in the last (relatively) free elections held before they consolidated their power and outlawed opposition parties. The Nazis tried to cover this over by holding plebiscites, elections in which the alternative was to be for whatever was being proposed or for nothing, i.e., against it. The Communists have tried over the years to provide an appearance of popular support for the regime by having elections in which there is only a single slate of candidates. The people are asked not to elect but to give approval to what already has been decided. Actually, since the parliament had no significant power in Nazi Germany and has none in the Soviet Union, the make-up of them came to be a matter of little importance.

Nazi Germany was and Soviet Russia is a one-party state. In both cases, once their leaders came to power, these parties ceased to be political parties, to the degree that they ever had been, and became instruments of the ruling elite. They were not originators of policy.

How could they be? It is only in opposition to other parties that party programs have any significance. They became, instead, tightly knit, fiercely loyal, and militant organizations to support the will of the rulers.

Nazi Germany had a personal dictatorship. In Nazi theory and practice all power and authority proceeded from the Fuhrer, the leader, Adolf Hitler. Hitler did not care at all for administrative detail and spent very little time on it. Some of the most momentous decisions he made, such as that of the extermination of the Jews, were not even recorded so far as has been determined. (He may not have wanted a record, of course, of the decision to exterminate the Jews.) Hitler's orders were often given out informally to associates and companions, more as wishes than commands. The method was more that of gangsters than what is ordinarily expected of prime ministers and heads of state (Hitler was both after the death of Hindenburg, though he wished to be addressed as "Mein Führer"). Many decisions apparently were handed down at the mid-afternoon dinners when Hitler was in Berlin. These frequently were attended by Goebbels, Himmler, Hess, and other leading figures, though rarely by Goering who preferred more sumptuous fare. Albert Speer, who often attended, put it this way:

Dining with Hitler regularly meant a considerable loss of time, for we sat at table until half past four in the afternoon....

Yet it was important for one's prestige to attend these dinners. Moreover, it was important to most of the guests to be kept abreast of Hitler's daily opinions. The round table was useful to Hitler himself as well, for in this way he could casually and effortlessly hand down a political line or slogan.[1]

The Soviet Union, too, has had a succession of personal dictators. The practice began with Lenin, reached its apogee with Stalin, and was continued with Malenkov, Khrushchev, and Brezhnev. Communists usually have made some effort to hide the personal character of the dictatorship behind a facade of "collective leadership," but the reality has surfaced too often for it to be generally believed. In his "Secret Speech to the Twentieth Party Congress," Khrushchev made clear the personal nature of Stalin's rule:

Stalin acted not through persuasion, explanation, and patient co-operation with people, but by imposing his concepts and demanding absolute submission to his opinion. Whoever opposed this concept or tried to prove his viewpoint, and the correctness of his position, was doomed to removal from the leading collective and to subsequent moral and physical annihilation....[2]

157

What Khrushchev's remarks may obscure, however, is that while there have been differences in degree of personal rule, it has been characteristic of communist goverments, whether in the Soviet Union or elsewhere.

There were even parallels in the style of living of Hitler and Stalin. Both men were "night owls," given to staying up to the wee hours of the morning and keeping their associates awake with them. They were both addicted to movies, Hitler's taste running to musicals while Stalin liked American westerns. Stalin had a screening room for films in the Kremlin, but Hitler had his own "theater" in his hideaway in Obersalzberg. Both men had warped senses of humor, preferring jokes at the expense of those around them. Stalin was, if anything, the cruder of the two. In late-night drinking sprees, he was apt to do such things as have Khrushchev, or others, perform a Russian folk dance in which they lacked all talent. Both were anti-Semites. Hitler, of course publicized his anti-Semitism, but Stalin was more circumspect in displaying his. Khrushchev gives these examples of Stalin's anti-Semitism:

When he happened to talk about a Jew, Stalin often imitated in a well-known exaggerated accent the way Jews talk. This is the same way that thick-headed, backward people who despise Jews talk when they mock the negative Jewish traits. Stalin also liked to put on this accent, and he was pretty good at it.

I remember when I was working in Moscow, some kind of trouble at the Thirtieth Aviation Factory was reported to Stalin through Party channels and by State Security. During a meeting with Stalin, while we were sitting around exchanging opinions, Stalin turned to me and said, "The good workers at the factory should be given clubs so they can beat the hell out of those Jews at the end of the working day." [3]

If Khrushchev is to be believed, he considered this a direct order from Stalin, but he did not carry it out.

Both Hitler and Stalin apparently were fearful of being alone, which was the main reason for keeping people around so late at night. Speer has said of the late nights with Hitler at Obersalzberg: "From one o'clock on some members of the company, in spite of all their efforts to control themselves, could no longer repress their yawns. But the social occasion dragged on in monotonous, wearing emptiness for another hour or more, until at last Eva Braun had a few words with Hitler and was permitted to go upstairs. Hitler would stand up about a quarter of an hour later, to bid his company goodnight." [4] Of Stalin, Khrushchev says: "He suffered terribly from loneliness. He needed people around him all the time. When he woke up in the morning, he would immediately summon us, either inviting us to the movies or starting some conversation.... He was depressed by loneliness and he feared it."[5]

There are many monstrous aspects to this immense concentration of power in one man but none more than their role in making war. According to Khrushchev, Stalin planned military operations on a globe! He never visited the front lines and could not be persuaded to consult detailed maps. Khrushchev told in detail the effects of this on one operation. It was in the Kharkov region in 1942. Stalin had ordered a massive encirclement operation. Those who were on the scene perceived the great danger of trying to carry it out. However, it was most difficult to reach Stalin on the matter, and when he finally was contacted he insisted that the operation must be carried forward as planned. "And what was the result of this? The worst that we had expected. The Germans surrounded our army concentrations and consequently we lost hundreds of thousands of our soldiers."[6]

Hitler believed himself to be a military genius, and many military men were greatly impressed with his early successes in directing military operations. Hitler was a master of the politics of collectivism, as already has been noted, and so long as he could conduct war in similar manner as his political moves, i.e., by surprise, by audacity, by swiftness, and by doing the unexpected, he was a master strategist. However, once his forces were on the defensive these tactics were of little use. Armies that are overpowered need to withdraw, to cut their losses, maintain discipline, shorten their lines and take up superior positions. Time and again Hitler refused to authorize tactical withdrawals, insisting that his units stand their ground or seize the initiative, only to have them overwhelmed or retreat in disarray. Although there is no satisfactory way to calculate such things, it is probable that the number of deaths attributed to Stalin and Hitler should be increased by several millions on account of their military blunders.

My main purpose here is neither to prove that Hitler and Stalin were dictators nor that dictatorship can have horrifying unwanted consequences. Those are points, of course, that are well taken, but they are generally, though not universally, accepted. The point is rather that collectivism entails dictatorship, entails the concentration of power in the hands of a single man, and that the ills that follow are a consequence of collectivism.

In short, dictatorship as we have come to know it in the twentieth century is an effect, not a cause. It is the necessary effect of the idea which has the world in its grip. If all effort is to be concerted to achieve an end, any end, that effort must be directed by a single man, else it will be dispersed due to the diversity of men. Communism was the cause of Stalin's dictatorship. Nazism was the cause of Hitler's dictatorship, even though it is conceivable that Hitler contrived the Nazi ideology in order to become dictator. Rule by one is the norm for the control and direction of all human organizations; rule by one is transformed into personal dictatorship by collectivism.

The key to understanding the effects produced by socialist or collectivist ideologies is their thrust to *concert* all efforts. These ideologies proclaim that man is not free and creative because he is not at one with those around him. He is not at one because there are those in his midst who have aims and purposes at odds with him. This external conflict internalizes itself in the individual as the drive to pursue his own self-interest, which, in turn, tends to set every man against every other man. Socialist ideologies propose a historical explanation for this condition. Marxists hold that the condition is a product of the class struggle, a struggle resulting from the control of the means of production of goods and services by some dominant class. In this latest age, capitalists constitute that dominant class, and they are the disrupters of the harmony and productivity of man. According to Nazi ideology, the historical conflict is basically racial. According to Hitler, what stood in the way of unity, harmony — at oneness — and freedom of the German or Nordic peoples was the presence in their midst of disruptive races, or, more specifically, the Jews.

What collectivist ideologies attempt to achieve, then, is at-one-ment. (This is the religious word "atonement," which socialists do not employ, but which captures the overtones of their meaning. The unity or at-one-ment they profess to seek, of course, is not with God but within society, which is the deepest reason for referring to them as socialists.) The basic device for achieving an at-one-ment within society is what is called by psychologists "projection." That is, they project upon some other group or class or race the blame for the ills or discontents that beset them. This is also known as "scapegoating." The Marxists blame the disruption upon the "exploiting classes," upon capitalists, imperialists, or whatever. The industrial worker is invited to project the blame for his condition upon the owners of factory and mine. The peasant is to lay the blame for his deprivation upon the landlord. Hitler, of course, projected the blame for the disharmony and disruption of the German people on the Jews.

160

Both Nazi and Marxist ideologues sometimes presented their cases very simplistically. To the Marxists, it would only be necessary for the proletariat to seize the means of production from the capitalists, and everything would be set right. To the Nazis, it would only be necessary to suppress and drive out the Jews, and the Germans would be freed from the incubus afflicting them. But, of course, it was never that simple. In both ideologies, society was supposed to be deeply infected; the sources of the disintegration of the individual and society lay deep.

To the Marxists, capitalist ideology was deeply imbedded in the whole cultural framework. This condition was described as the prevalence of bourgeois culture. Due to this prevalence, the pursuit of self-interest which occasioned the disharmony and produced the disruption in society had penetrated the arts, literature, the family, all social institutions, and was given the color of divine sanction by religion. Only the most advanced of an elite could be free from its sway at the outset.

The Jewish infection, as Hitler was given to calling it, was believed by the Nazis to have burrowed deeply into German culture, and into that of other peoples as well. There were, of course, many prominent Jews in literature, in music, in the other arts, and particularly in the field of publishing. The great carrier of the "Jewish infection," Hitler claimed, was international Marxism. But it takes no great insight to perceive that there was an even more pervasive source of "Jewish infection" in Germany, namely, the Christian churches. The roots of Christianity in Judaism, the fact that Jesus was born a Jew, were facts that Hitler might ignore publicly but which did not go away by being ignored. Some of the Nazis were as outspokenly anti-Christian as they dared to be. Heinrich Himmler and Martin Bormann were two of the more prominent. Speer says that Bormann carried on a continual verbal campaign against the churches with Hitler. Hitler's standard reply was, "Once I have settled my other problems..., I'll have my reckoning with the church. I'll have it reeling on the ropes."[7]

A part of the repression of Nazi and Soviet regimes was aimed at the "scapegoats," those on whom the blame for conditions was projected. Another part was aimed at rooting out and destroying any "infections" from these elements. The remainder of the repression, so far as it was ideological in origin, was aimed at concerting all efforts, i.e., producing action in conformity with the regime. Vladimir Yurasov, a defector from the Soviet Union, has summed up the impact of all this in a fictionalized account of his experiences. The following quotations in the

161

speech of one of his characters are supposed to be from General Serov, a real life head of military security:

We cannot permit our people to live as they please! Do you understand? People it seems have themselves too much in mind! But government deems that you should deny your own self, become the same sort of fanatic or else — off to a labor camp! Off to become a slave! Katia, *do you understand?*[8]

Hitler described the Nazi idea this way: "The underlying idea is to do away with egoism and to lead people into the collective egoism which is the nation."[9] Or again, "It is essential that the individual should slowly come to realize that his own ego is unimportant when compared with the existence of the whole people...."[10] He would, he declared, stamp "the Nazi *Weltanschauung* [world outlook] on the German people." For, "it is only the harshest principles and an iron resolution which can unite the nation into a single body...."[11]

In both the Nazi and Soviet systems, then, the individual could be of no importance. Only as he joined his efforts to those of the mass would they be of consequence. It follows that individual liberty would be dependent upon the will of the regime, that individual rights could hardly exist, that freedom of choice would be severely circumscribed, and that private property could exist in name only. So it is in the Soviet Union; so it was in Nazi Germany.

Neither freedom of speech, nor freedom of press, nor freedom of association could be tolerated. In the Soviet Union, individuals have been sentenced to years of servitude in forced labor camps for failing to report some anti-Communist remark or joke that they have overheard. A priest was sentenced to death in Nazi Germany for making an anti-Nazi joke in front of an electrician who was working at his rectory.[12] Joseph Goebbels, Propaganda Minister for the Nazis, was in charge of the news, among other things. He determined what should be reported and how it should be told. Daily press directives went out from the Propaganda Ministry to editors all over the country, directives which covered in minute detail how everything should be handled.[13] There are, of course, no private newspapers or television or radio stations in the Soviet Union; in consequence, all news is determined by political and ideological considerations. Crashes of Soviet airplanes are not reported, for instance, and the names of those killed are never published. There is good reason for this latter practice; no record is kept of passengers on airlines. So much for the individual!

Nazis held ceremonial book burnings at universities and other places. Not only were the works of Jews consigned to the flames but also many works of Gentiles that were considered dangerous. In general, modern art and modern music were proscribed in Germany. In the Soviet Union, all access to foreign materials is limited or restricted, and all publishing houses are government controlled. Much of the same sort of art and music that was prohibited in Nazi Germany is kept from view by the Communists. Both Communists and Nazis had ideological predilections toward "folk art," but in practice favored the classics.

Freedom of association may well be the most valuable of all freedoms. Certainly, without it all other freedoms are sterile and barren. It is the means by which voluntary cooperation takes place, by which men work together in groups to effect their ends, whether social, religious, charitable, business, or whatever. And, freedom of association is anathema to collectivism. Since all activity must be concerted, any voluntary association is suspect, or worse. It is a potential conspiracy against the state; hence, it must be broken up.

Association with an "enemy of the people" has long been proscribed in the Soviet Union. Penalties for it range from a few years in a camp to death. But it is not possible ordinarily to know who is an "enemy of the people" until he has been convicted or sentenced. Thus, all associations are fraught with danger, even with members of one's own family, for punishment ordinarily is retroactive for association with an "enemy of the people." There are, of course, many associations in the Soviet Union, but membership in them is hardly voluntary, and they are not free. There are associations of writers, of artists, of workers, of farmers, of clergymen, and so on. It is usually necessary to belong to the "association" in order to engage in the activity involved — to belong to the association of writers in order to get published, for example — but the association is under the direction and control of the state. It is an instrument of state, not of its members.

The restrictions on association were never as thorough and complete in Nazi Germany as in the Soviet Union, but it hardly could be said that the Germans had freedom of association. Only one political party was permitted so that there was no choice of political association. Only one labor union was allowed, and it was government controlled. In effect, there could be no private business associations or private farmer organizations. The government penetrated and controlled these. A dissident association of clergymen ended with many of its members in prisons and concentration camps.

163

The most strenuous restrictions on association were between other Germans and Jews. (Jews generally have insisted, and rightly, that they were Germans too.) The most rigorous restrictions were applied to marital and sexual relations between Gentiles and Jews, but they extended to other areas as well. Except for the aged, "German" women were not permitted to work in Jewish households. "Jewish pupils were excluded from the state-school system, and all Jews were debarred from public swimming-pools, sports grounds and parks.... A typical scene took place at a Berlin green-grocer's when a four-year old Jewish girl begged her mother for some cherries; when told that fruit was excluded from the Jewish ration she ran out of the shop crying."[14] It was precarious, of course, to associate with a Marxist, a pacifist, or anyone who might be anti-Hitler or anti-Nazi.

Private property is the necessary condition of individual rights. Without it, there is no place to stand against the state, and there are no means with which to protect oneself. It is well known that Russian Communists made a root and branch assault on private property. Such remnants of it as remain in the Soviet Union are privileges granted by the state, not rights belonging to the individual. The attack upon property was neither so direct nor so drastic in Nazi Germany as in the Soviet Union. The major exception was the property of Jews, much of which was confiscated. Indeed, the Nazi approach to property differed from that of revolutionary socialism. It was more nearly that of gradualist or evolutionary socialism. Hitler had declared in the middle of 1933 that henceforth he intended to follow an evolutionary road. This was generally so where private property was concerned.

Land titles and deeds generally were left undisturbed. Individual and family holdings were likely to remain technically in the same hands as before. "Technically" is the key word here, however, for property was treated as an adjunct of the state, something to be used and disposed of in the interest of the nation. The substance of private property was drained away while the form was left more or less intact. For example, from 1937 onward shareholders could no longer participate in determination of corporate policy. Many Nazis were placed on boards of directors, and control of companies was determined by a combination of managers, Nazi Party officials, and government policy. There was a movement toward a return to primogeniture and entail for rural property, which divested the owner of the power to dispose of the property. Agriculture was controlled by what was called the Food Estate. Some of its activities are described in the following:

164

The Food Estate maintained a dossier on each farm, in which it entered monthly reports on the state of crops and livestock, labour force and wages, delivery obligations and actual delivery data. Intent on its self-sufficiency drive, the regime also partly coerced and partly coaxed farmers into reducing the area under such crops as wheat, rye and — temporarily — hops in favour of beet, flax, rape and sunflowers.[15]

Coercion apparently extended also to farm animals, for the Food Estate prescribed that each hen should lay at least 65 eggs per year. It is unlikely, however, that Nazi Gauleiters came to the farms personally to wring the necks of non-conformist hens.

In brief, the Nazis controlled, or attempted to, the means of production and distribution of goods and services. All producers belonged to some sort of collective, one devised for the particular undertaking. These collectives, in turn, were interpenetrated and dominated by the government. Prices and wages were controlled; production quotas were set; and the unproductive were weeded out. Licensing for trades and crafts controlled the opening of new businesses. The socialist plank of the Nazi program was honored; even if it was not in the way prescribed by Marxists.

Repressive measures were not the only means used by Nazis or Soviet Communists to draw people into the collective effort. Both regimes sought to concert all efforts by "positive" measures. There were parallels here, too. Communists employ propaganda on a massive scale. Indeed, the language, the literature, the arts, and even the architecture is permeated with propaganda. Communists have long opposed the idea of "art for art's sake." The practical meaning of this is that art exists for ideological, political, and propagandic reasons. They are equally opposed to food for food's sake, tractors for tractors' sake, clothing for clothing's sake, sports for sports' sake, and so on. Everything that is produced and brought into being is for the glorification of communism: production is for the statistics of production (gross national product, as we would say); victories of Soviet athletes show the superiority of communism; tractors demonstrate the progress of Russia under communism. Foreign newsmen are apt to be accused of spying when they take pictures in the Soviet Union. Their offense, one suspects, is that they may get such pictures published without the propaganda gloss which is necessary to "understanding" them.

The Nazis used propaganda as vigorously and extensively as any regime ever has. Joseph Goebbels undertook to see that every medium of expression was used to glorify the Aryan race, the German people, the Nazis, and Hitler. Nazis probably were much more successful in drawing the people into and making them a part of the propaganda than communists have been. German might became visible by way of goose-stepping soldiers marching through the streets or massing at some rally. But millions of Germans who were not in the army wore uniforms. Eventually, nearly all children belonged to the Hitler Youth between the ages of 10 and 18. There was the SA and the elite corps of SS in their uniforms. The ideal German, German history, and German exploits were depicted in song, in story, in film, on canvas and, if it could be done, in architecture. The Third Reich was supposed to last for a thousand years, a millennium, according to Nazi propaganda, and its enduring foundation was being laid by Hitler.

There are too many parallels between the Nazis and Soviet Communists to be covered here. They parallel one another in such things as the Hitler Youth and Komsomol or Young Communists. Both attempted to use the schools for imbuing the young with their ideas. Both Nazi and Soviet leaders were gangsterlike in their operations. Both regimes relied on terror to consolidate and maintain their power. The list could be made longer, but surely the point emerges. The matter has been aptly summed up by Leopold Tyrmand in the opening paragraph of a chapter on "Communism and Nazism: a short comparative study":

Ruminating on this topic is generally regarded as vulgar, as something too unbecoming to be done. But why? No one really knows for sure. It is the terror of a convention. Too many people who later became respectable declared themselves Communists at some time in their lives. Those, however, who survived both Nazism and communism, without consenting to participate in either, are not versed in such subtleties. In Eastern Europe there are millions of such people, and the rule consecrated by intellectuals that communism and Hitlerism are *not* the same does not hold water with them. Because if one thinks about it unsqueamishly, pitilessly, and to the end, it is all too easy to establish their grisly similarity. [16]

The "grisly similarity" is a result of a similar cause: the commitment of both regimes to collectivism. The effort to produce human felicity in both cases produced widespread torment. Even grisly regimes, perhaps grisly regimes particularly, give rise to their own wry humor. Hitler was hardly a laughing matter to Jews, but their sense of humor, this last resort of the human spirit, did not entirely desert them. Here is a Jewish joke from Nazi Germany which might just as well have come from Soviet Russia:

Meeting the worried and abstracted Goldstein, Kohn tells him that Davidsohn has died. Goldstein shrugs his shoulders. "Well, if he got a chance to better himself...." [17]

13
World War II: A Socialist Conflagration

WAR IS FILLED with incongruities. On or about May 1, 1945, I watched a command performance of the Dresden Symphony Orchestra in a small town located along the border of Germany and Czechoslovakia. The command was probably issued by the commanding general of the First Infantry Division — the "Bloody Red One" — of the United States Army. The most obvious incongruity was that the United States and Germany were at war with one another, and here were American soldiers in battle dress being entertained by a German orchestra. Another incongruity was that amidst the incivility of war — as Patton's Third Army made its final thrust toward Prague — we paused for an hour or so to listen to one of the finest products of Western Civilization, glorious German music performed by a symphony orchestra.

The reason for Dresden's orchestra being quartered in this village adds to the incongruity of the situation. On February 13-14, 1945, Dresden had been subjected to a succession of air raids by British and American planes. Dresden had long been famed as a cultural center and was architecturally one of the most beautiful cities in Europe. It had little significance, almost none, as a military target and had until the above dates only two small raids.

Although Dresden was not an open city — though it was barely defended — there was a widely held belief that the Allies did not intend to bomb it. In consequence, refugees had poured into the city to double its population to 1,300,000 people. Allied intelligence had reported that German armor was passing through the city by rail, but this was apparently known to be false by air force commanders before the raids were sent out.

At any rate, these may well have been the most devastating raids in a brief period in all of history. The city was devastated, over 100,000 people killed according to some estimates, and 1,600 acres laid waste. In the midst of one of the British raids a fire storm broke out raising temperatures to over 1,000 degrees Fahrenheit and sucking high winds into the vortex of the fire. The American raid which followed was carried out in the daylight. The bombers were acompanied by fighter planes which added to the death-dealing destruction by strafing civilians. It was to find refuge from this destruction that the Dresden Symphony had moved to a small town.[1]

There may have been no particular malice behind the otherwise wanton bombing and strafing of Dresden. Certainly, the air force personnel involved in the raid were performing their assigned tasks as thoroughly as they could. Apparently malicious atrocities abounded, however, in World War II. Among the most horrifying of these followed in the wake of the assassination of SS leader Reinhardt Heydrich by Czech soldiers secreted into Czechoslovakia by the British in late 1941. In retaliation, the Germans immediately killed 1,500 Czechs. Three thousand Jews were shipped from Czechoslovakia to Poland to be put to death. A few days after Heydrich's death, the village of Lidice was apparently selected at random to become an object lesson to the Czechs. The whole village was sealed off by the SD. The next day the males were all killed in a massacre which took ten hours to complete. The females, excepting those who were pregnant, were sent to concentration camps. Pregnant women were sent to hospitals to be delivered when their time came. The newborn infants were put to death, and the mothers then sent to concentration camps.[2] The village of Lidice was physically destroyed as well.

Germans and Russians sometimes vied with one another in their cruelty to prisoners. The German admiral Canaris made this report from the Russian front in December, 1941:

169

Our own treatment of Russian prisoners is having awful consequences. In the retreat from Moscow we had to abandon German field hospitals as well. The Russians dragged out the sick and injured, hanged them upside down, poured gasoline over them, and set them on fire. Some uninjured German soldiers had to watch this torture, they were then kicked in the groin and sent back to the German lines with instructions to describe how the Bolsheviks were reacting to news of the mass executions and barbaric treatment meted out to their comrades in German captivity. On another occasion German prisoners were beheaded and their heads laid out to form the SS symbol.[3]

As the Russian armies swept into East Germany in early 1945, many of the inhabitants fled westward attempting to escape the terror. Here are two stories recounted by John Toland, from among many, many more:

One of these groups was entering the village of Nemmersdorf when Russian tanks abruptly appeared, bulldozing everything in their path. Dozens of carts were smashed, side-swiped, rolled over. Baggage spilled out, people were crushed. The tanks rolled ahead obliviously, but in a few minutes Dodge trucks appeared. Infantrymen jumped out and began pillaging and raping. At The White Mug restaurant four women were raped many times, dragged outside naked and nailed through the hands to a wagon. Not far away, at The Red Mug, another naked woman was nailed to a barn. When the Russians moved off, they left behind seventy-two dead civilians.

A few miles to the west, Russians were breaking into the village of Weitzdorf. A young woman, Lotte Keuch, watched in horror as her father-in-law and six male neighbors were shot. Next, a dozen French slave laborers at the manor were rounded up and their rings taken away — by slicing off their fingers. Then the Frenchmen were lined up, executed. And the raping began.[4]

Such barbarities — and their number is so great and the details so fulsome that the sensitivities are soon dulled and the mind numbed by accounts of them — require explanation. It is undoubtedly true that there have usually been atrocities in the midst of wars. War frequently musters and loosens passions which are not easily contained. It is not easy to prepare men for the business of killing without removing or lessening civilized restraints. The simplest approach is to get men to thinking of the enemy as less than human. This is advantageous, too, for then the soldier may commit acts against them while, hopefully, retaining his inhibitions against doing so against those on his side. At any rate, any historian should be able to call up stories of atrocities from many past conflicts, and he will usually have been aided in his task by those who have found advantage in picturing the enemy in the worst possible light.

170

Even so, the exigencies of war are not a sufficient explanation for the atrocities of World War II. Warfare may provide the setting for atrocities, but it also provides the setting for acts of bravery, restraint, and compassion. A conqueror may destroy all in his path or he may liberate and restore. The character of any particular war is a reflection of the state of civilization of the combatants. It is determined, too, by the aims and ideals of the participating countries. The events which comprise a war are not self-explanatory; they must be referred to the larger framework from which they arise. This is especially so when events conform to a pattern and when large numbers of people are involved in them.

The ferocity and brutality of World War II stands in special need of explanation. This is the case because the notion had been widely held that mankind was making great progress in the twentieth century. Barbarity was supposed to be diminishing as a result of the spread of civilization. President Woodrow Wilson had proclaimed that when democracy was in the ascendant wars would be no more. If universal suffrage and large-scale voting are sufficient evidence of it, democracy was in the ascendant between World War I and World War II. At the forefront of progress, according to socialist ideologues, was the spread and adoption of socialist ideas. These give added impetus to the need for explanation of atrocities and ferocity of World War II.

Despite the vast literature on the subject, there has been all too little effort to explain World War II by the ideologies that were involved or held sway. True, Nazi racist ideology is usually taken into account, but its explicit collectivism and tacit socialism are usually ignored. There have been ideological explanations aplenty, i.e., explanations by those under the sway of some ideology, but these have left socialism unindicted. Dictatorship or totalitarianism have been blamed often enough, but such explanations do not explain the rise of dictators or the advent of totalitarianism. The scribes of our era have hidden from the implications of the very ideas they hold dear.

World War II was the clash of socialist titans. It was ignited by revolutionary socialism and threatened for a time to consume the whole world in its fire. In the center ring of this struggle were Soviet Communism and National Socialist Germany. The main struggle was for dominance of central and eastern Europe, particularly eastern Europe. The English-speaking peoples were on the periphery of this contest though pride and confused alliances obscured the fact.

Everything conspired, it almost seems, to obscure and conceal ·he

171

nature of the main struggle in World War II. From August, 1939, into June, 1941, Germany and the Soviet Union had a non-agression and mutual assistance pact with one another. After the brief thrust into and conquest of Poland, the German effort for nearly two years was concentrated in western Europe: the Scandinavian countries, the low countries, France, and Britain. It was further confused by the push of Germany and Italy into southern Europe and North Africa. More, just as the nature of the struggle began to come into focus after the invasion of the Soviet Union by Germany in June, 1941, it was distorted once again by the Japanese assault on American possessions and the British Empire in the Pacific. With the conflict spread over half the world it is small wonder that many lost sight of its central stage, or even doubted that it had one.

A good deal of the confusion can be charged to Hitler's temperament and the adventures into which it led him. He was intuitive, opportunistic, and often governed by irrational prejudices. Ideology was apt to be sacrificed to whims or prejudices, particularly when he was frustrated by developments. Above all, much of the course of the war was beyond his control. His alliance with Mussolini was hardly founded in love for the Italian people. War against the British was almost certainly not to his liking, and he had little interest in North Africa or the Pacific. Expedient alliances and unwanted contestants led him to some strange places. He was given to blaming many of these misfortunes on the malign influence of world-wide Jewry.

Even so, World War II was mainly a contest for control over eastern Europe, and to a lesser extent all of continental Europe. This conclusion is supported from three different directions: the aims of the contestants, the arena of the major and protracted land battles, and the consequences of the war. It is tempting to describe it as a war between pan-Germanism and pan-Slavism, for that was certainly a major element in it, but that theme can here be subordinated to the contest between two brands of revolutionary socialism: National Socialism in Germany and Soviet Communism. This is so because revolutionary socialism provided the methods for the concentration of power for the expansive thrusts, whatever the ultimate motives of those who directed them.

World War II broke out as a result of the expansive efforts of Germany and the Soviet Union. Germany was expanding to the east: first Austria, then Czechoslovakia, and then the expansion into Poland which provoked the general war. The Soviet Union attacked westward: Poland, Finland, and annexed Latvia, Estonia, and Lithuania. The next most likely goal of both powers was the Balkan countries, although that

172

was delayed by Germany's war in the west. Germany and the Soviet Union were on a collision course with one another, though the fact was obscured for a time by the Nazi-Soviet Pact.

It brings some clarity to this confused situation to examine the aims of Germany and the Soviet Union, or, if that is too broad and ambitious, the aims of Hitler and Stalin. First, those of Hitler. A ponderous gloss was provided for Hitler's aims by the pseudoscience of geopolitics as advanced by Professor Karl Haushofer of Munich. Geopolitics is a way of looking at geography in terms of the interests and desires of a single nation without reference to the interests and possessions of others. It has been used by conquerors throughout history, but prior to the twentieth century none has attempted to give academic standing to the subject.

The key phrase drawn from geopolitics for Hitler's aims was *Lebensraum*. It can be literally translated as "living space," but it was freighted with the nationalistic aspirations of living space for and domination by Germany. It should be noted, too, that socialist regimes frequently suffer what might be called claustrophobia, a sense of being hemmed in and surrounded by enemies. This has been characteristic of the Soviet regime throughout its history. The reason for this is not difficult to grasp. The control over their own people is ever threatened by the existence of other countries independent of their will. The Nazis also used the term *Grossraum* which meant the "whole space" or area that they required. The term was applied in the following way:

Politically the New Order was simple. German hegemony was to be extended by German arms and accepted by everybody else. Nazi values were to be exported from their German centre and the pattern of Nazi revolution and Nazi life repeated in other lands. The first precondition of the New Order was conquest: the land had to be got. How much land was left vague. At the high tide of German successes the concept of the *Grossraum*, or Greater Germanic Estate, embraced Europe from the Atlantic to the Urals, although a little earlier it had seemed to make do with rather less of Russia. The determining features of the *Grossraum* were not its borders but its nature. Instead of finding where people lived and then drawing permanent or semi-permanent frontiers to fit the ethnic facts, the Nazis began by designating an area and then moved people around in order to make demography fit the facts of power. The *Grossraum* therefore might be any size and in 1942 one writer envisaged it as covering one sixth of the globe. It was not a fixed area but a biological habitat like a nature reserve. It was where the German family lived.[5]

More precisely, it was an area into which the German family might be moved and established after conquest.

One way to grasp what Hitler had in mind is to understand that he aimed to unify Europe under German hegemony. But it was not to be a unity of equals. Much of Europe, particularly eastern and southern Europe, was conceived as an area to be colonized. The closest thing he had by way of a model for what he had in mind was probably the English attitude toward and treatment of the North American Indians.

Hitler's racial theories were used to buttress the proposed conquest, domination, and uprooting of peoples. He held that many of the peoples of Europe were inferior, indeed all the others were inferior to the Germans. Other Nordic peoples were the next highest in the scale, and under German guidance they could probably be more or less self-governing. The Latin peoples would probably be next in line, though for expedient reasons — Germany was allied with Italy and hoped for alliances with Spain and France — their position in the ethnic scale was not carefully spelled out. Slavs were considered to be decidedly inferior, not worthy of being civilized, but good potential slaves. The Nazis heaped contempt on the Poles, spoke of them as being sub-human, but once his armies were in Russia, Hitler was equally contemptuous of the Russians. The level of education proposed for the Russians was described this way by Heinrich Himmler, head of the SS: "I can only repeat what the Führer has asked. It is enough if, firstly, the children are taught the traffic signs at school so that they won't run under our cars; secondly, they learn to count to twenty-five; and thirdly, they can write their names as well. No more is necessary."[6] At the bottom of the scale were the Jews.

What Hitler conceived was a Germano-centric Europe. Theretofore, Europe had been fragmented into many small countries, dependent upon one another and the rest of the world. Not only had Europe been fragmented but its focus had been "peripheralized." Russia had linked a considerable portion of the land mass of Europe, and some of the most fertile, to Asia. Italy's center was on the Mediterranean looking to Africa and the Near East. The countries fronting on the Atlantic had thrown themselves into colonizing in other portions of the world. Germany would become the heartland of a unified Europe, economically self-sufficient, and a power so formidable that the rest of the world would be at bay.

In the course of World War II enough of this program was carried out to indicate that Hitler was in earnest about it. Western and central Europe was virtually depopulated of Jews. There had been talk of resettling them on the island of Madagascar, but nothing ever came of this. They were shipped to the east, mainly to Poland, where a massive liquidation took place. Russian Jews were frequently killed on the spot. Poles were moved out of some areas of Poland and Germans resettled there. A vast displacement of persons took place as millions of Europeans were shifted about to work on German industries and farms. These peoples were segregated from the Germans as far as possible and constituted little more than slave labor.

Clearly, Nazi aims were in opposition to that of the Communists, but it needs to be made clear that the Soviet Union had aims of its own. Soviet expansion was (and is) fueled by three fairly distinct but interrelated aims. One of these aims is imperial in character. The Russian Empire was partially dismembered during and after World War I. Western portions were cut away to form nations, such as Estonia and Latvia. The thrust of the Soviet Union during the early months of World War II to reclaim this territory attests to the imperial aim. It is probable, too, that pan-Slavism still played some part in the quest to regain lost portions of the Russian Empire. The thrust of Germans eastward has long been matched by the Russian thrust westward. Russia has long been technologically backward and has looked toward the West in one way or other to make up this deficiency.

Another aim of Soviet expansion was strategic. Russia is very nearly landlocked to the west and south. Leningrad, the major western port before World War II, had access to the Baltic only through waters fronted by Finland, Latvia, Estonia, and Lithuania. Archangel lies far to the north in frigid waters. Russia has long sought, to no avail, a warm-water port in the south that would have access to the Mediterranean during time of war. More, there are no natural barriers of consequence separating central Europe from European Russia. Buffer states have provided such solution to this problem as has been offered, but when these have been unfriendly, as they generally were before World War II, they were unreliable buffers.

The other aim was ideological. Indeed, all other aims have generally been subsumed so as to be virtually a part of the ideological aims. When, for example, the Soviet Union established a Communist controlled government over Poland and made it a satellite state, the imperial, strategic, and ideological aims of the Soviet Union were satisfied in a single stroke.

The ideological aims of the Soviet Union pit that country against every non-Communist country in the world. In 1919 the Communist International, known for many years thereafter as the Comintern, was founded in Moscow. It purported to be a creature of Communist parties from around the world, but in fact control over it was monopolized by the Russians. Moscow became the center for the domination of communist parties founded in countries around the world. These parties were to foment revolution whenever and wherever they could. One of the points to which parties must concur was to this effect:

> In countries where a communist party is permitted by the laws to function legally it must nevertheless maintain, parallel with its legal organization, a "clandestine organisation capable at the decisive moment of fulfilling its duty towards the revolution."[7]

Moreover, all communist parties must have their ultimate allegiance to the Soviet Union:

> Communist parties must support unreservedly all soviet republics in their struggles with counter-revolution, urge workers to refuse to transport arms or equipment destined for the enemies of a soviet republic, and pursue propaganda by legal or illegal means among all troops sent to fight against a soviet republic.[8]

This last point shows the marks of having been formulated during the civil war in Russia, but in essence it still describes the relationship between the Soviet Union and any parties it controls in other lands.

This was a blueprint for the spread of communism around the world and domination by the Soviet Union. It did not necessarily entail conquest in the usual military sense but it did, in effect, envision the fruits of conquest for the Soviet Union. The great prize, historically, for communism was to be Germany. The writings of Marx were replete with references to the coming of revolution in Germany. The Communist Party in Germany was growing in appeal in the months before the Nazi takeover. Hitler set all that at naught.

The Nazis and Communists, then, were profound enemies. To Hitler, Communism was a Jewish conspiracy to dominate the world. To Stalin, Nazism, usually referred to as "Fascism," was the last virulent and aggressive stage of capitalism. It was the mortal enemy of communism come to life and moving on the world stage. To those not infected by either doctrine, communism and Nazism were profound enemies because they were different varieties of revolutionary socialism contesting for control over Europe, and perhaps the world.

Hitler considered asking Stalin for an armistice on several occasions. There was talk of making contacts by way of the Soviet embassy in

Sweden. Yet, each time he drew back. He is reported to have remarked that it would be of no use even if Stalin accorded an armistice. As soon as he was able Hitler would resume the assault on Russia. By most accounts, the conquest of Russia was Hitler's deepest and most abiding ambition, that and ridding Europe of Jews. Despite all their similarities, and in part because of them, Nazism and Communism were irreconcilable opponents at bottom.

The eastern front was the scene of the titanic struggle between these socialist powers. Most of the worst horrors and much of the ferocious fighting occurred there. (The major exception to this was the bombing and strafing of civilian populations by both sides in western Europe.) It was in the east that the liquidation of millions of Jews took place, first by massacres with shot and shell, and then in gas chambers. It was in the east that perhaps a half million Gypsies were slaughtered. It was on the eastern front that ideological murders took place, the killing of commissars whenever they could be taken and retaliation by Communists.

One way to measure the scale and ferocity of the fighting is the number of military personnel killed and otherwise lost in the war. The Soviet Union reported seven and a half million personnel as killed or missing. German military personnel killed or missing were reckoned at 2,850,000, though all of these were not lost on the eastern front. By contrast, the United States lost 292,100 in all theaters of operation, and the British Commonwealth somewhat over half a million.[9]

The scale of the war on the eastern front has probably never been matched in all of history. There have been greater concentrations of forces in smaller areas but not on such a far-flung front. The Germans invaded the Soviet Union in June of 1941 with 135 divisions of their own and 13 Finnish and 15 Rumanian divisions. The Russians brought to bear approximately 136 divisions of their own. At a later date in the war the Germans claimed to have identified 360 Soviet divisions fighting against them, and still later there was talk of the Russians having over 500 divisions. By contrast, the United States had 60 divisions on the western front in the spring of 1945. (The division was the largest standard sized unit employed in the war, but the size varied from country to country and from time to time.)

The war was fought on a front stretching for 2000 miles from Leningrad in the north to Rostov in the south. Leningrad was never taken by the Germans, but it was laid under siege for 900 days. "Without light or fuel, the inhabitants of the beleaguered city depended upon

177

supplies hauled across Lake Ladoga.... Enemy bombardment, starvation, and disease cut down a million citizens; the dead at times were heaped up in streets littered with refuse and excrement."[10] One of the reasons the Germans never took Leningrad was that Hitler did not want his armies bogged down in the house-to-house fighting of a large city. Even so, it happened in one of the decisive battles of the war, the battle for Stalingrad in the winter of 1942-43. Here is a brief description of the fighting there: "The closest and bloodiest battle of the war was fought among the stumps of buildings burnt or burning. From afar Stalingrad looked like a furnace and yet inside it men froze. Dogs rushed into the Volga to drown rather than to endure any longer the perils of the shore. The no less desperate men were reduced to automatons, obeying orders until it came their turn to die, human only in their suffering. The Germans were on half-rations from the end of November.... The final capitulation came on 2 February. Ninety-one thousand survivors, including a Field Marshal and twenty-four generals, were taken captive. The Russians had already taken 16,700 prisoners during the last weeks of the fighting. Some 70,000 Germans died during the siege, many of them from exposure or starvation, some by suicide."[11] The ferocity of Russian attacks gained force by the apparent unconcern of the leaders for casualties and lack of fear of death by the troops. A German specialist described their attitude this way:

"Soviet Russians reacted differently to battle from civilized city dwellers. They remained unaffected by high casualties ..., by close combat, by battles at night, in villages and in forests. They were used to misery, to lack of care, to absence of leave and of mail, to suffering cold and hunger. They faced death with fatalistic equanimity."[12]

This war on the eastern front was characterized by a ferocious assault not only on persons but also on property. As German armies moved into the Soviet Union they were followed by economic organizations bent on expropriating and using for their own efforts whatever they could take from the Russians. All state-owned property was simply confiscated. The Russians, on the other hand, destroyed whatever they could not take with them as they retreated. The horror of the war was augmented by the massive confiscation and destruction of property.

Much, indeed most of Europe — west, central, and east — was devastated in the course of World War II. Only three countries, each small in population and peripheral, escaped the destruction: Portugal, Sweden, and Switzerland. (True, Ireland and Spain were spared most of it, but Spain had experienced its own destruction in the civil war just preceding World War II.) European civilization, the most vibrant in all of history, was shattered. The greatest work of civilization is the city; indeed, "city" and "civilization" spring from the same etymological root and cities are the centers of civilization. The shattering of European civilization was visible during and immediately after World War II in the rubble of the cities.

The modern city is a marvelous tribute to man's imagination and ingenuity, a result of his aspirations to build, and a wondrous complex wrought from the cooperation of many men to bring it into being and operate its facilities. The network of highways and railroads which pour into and out of cities gives some indication of their centrality and economic vitality. The huge water mains that supply them, the maze of electric wires that light them, the subterranean sewers which drain them, and the vehicles that ply their numerous streets make it possible for hundreds of thousands of people to live in close proximity to one another in comfort and security.

War turned many of the cities of Europe into torture chambers for their inhabitants. Artillery bombardment, street fighting, and bombing broke water mains, cut off electricity, made movement precarious, and made rubble or shells of buildings. The desolation of such small cities as Aachen could only be overmatched by that of huge cities such as Berlin, Leningrad, or Hamburg.

It has sometimes happened in history that barbarians have conquered more civilized peoples and laid their cities waste. When the Germanic tribes conquered the remains of Roman Britain the technology of cities was beyond their abilities to operate and their needs to use. Those that were not destroyed must have been left to deteriorate and decay. So it was, too, for much of the western Roman Empire as Europe descended into the Dark Ages.

But Europe was not laid waste in World War II by barbarians who could not comprehend or utilize cities. On the contrary, every major power involved had large and complex cities of its own. The Germans who rained bombs on London and bombarded Leningrad into rubble had some of the finest cities in the world. The Americans and British who bombed Dresden and Hamburg and Berlin and Schweinfurt and many other cities were proud of their own great cities. Nor will it do to think of the Russians as constituting some uncivilized horde sweeping over Europe, tempting as it might be to do so. True, Russia has long been technologically backward compared to most other European

179

countries, but it was only relatively so in a common civilization.

The fury that gripped and laid Europe waste in World War II was of a different character. It was a fury born of ideology. It was a fury unleashed by people who had the trappings of civilization but whose civilized restraints had been weakened and cut away by ideology. Some account of this must now be made along with the story of further communist expansion and the reasons for the German defeat.

14

World War II: The Bitter Fruit of Ideology

THE IDEA THAT has the world in its grip is at its roots a simple, even a simplistic, idea. It is the notion that what ails us is the pursuit of self-interest by individuals, a pursuit which leads to the dispersal of energies, diversity, and competition, even conflict. The cure for this, so the proponents of the idea claim, is to forge a social unity in which all effort will be concerted toward the realization of common goals. Government is the means they employ toward this end. The method is to remove the legal, social, and cultural props which enable the individual to act in his own interest; removal of those props makes it necessary for him to act for common goals. Revolutionaries propose to bring this about by drastic and forceful measures. This articulation of the idea is commonly called revolutionary socialism.

World War II was a titanic struggle between opposing varieties of revolutionary socialism, between Soviet Communism and Nazi Germany. It was a struggle for dominance over Europe, particularly central and eastern Europe (and on the Japanese side for the dominance

181

of Asia and the Pacific). Hitler's variety of socialism was the more virulent of the two. Soviet Communism is inclined toward subversion, conspiracy, and the plodding pace of a projected historical development. Nazism was the vision of a single man, something to be realized in his lifetime. Hitler was the apotheosis of National Socialism, its personification and deification. Communism is supposed to be victorious in the world by the process of historical determinism. National Socialism's victory was supposed to be the destiny of a single man — and the German people.

Hitler grasped the rudiments of the idea that has the world in its grip; the subtleties eluded him, and he had no time for them. His socialism came to him by way of osmosis, something filtered into him from the intellectual climate of the time. He tacked his prejudices on the rudimentary idea, and the result was National Socialism. Whatever of intellectual gloss it had came from such fringe German thinkers as Houston Stewart Chamberlain, Oswald Spengler, Alfred Rosenberg, Karl Haushofer, Friedrich Nietzsche, and Richard Wagner. It should be noted that these were not socialist thinkers, as such, and most of those with a bent toward socialist ideology who entered the Nazi movement were either sloughed off or played minor roles in the government. Hitler's socialism was not Marxian socialism or Revisionist socialism or any other of the generally accepted varieties. It was Hitlerian socialism, i.e., National Socialism — Nazism. It was revolutionary, militant, anti-communist, racist, nationalist, and martial.

Left to his own devices, it is doubtful that Stalin would have gone to war against Nazi Germany. During their sixty-year span, Soviet Communists have gone to war against a major power only once voluntarily, and that was against Japan when it was apparent that the days of the Japanese Empire were already numbered. Soviet leaders have preferred to let "you and them" fight rather than to become embroiled in a major war. Communism is bent toward warfare, but it is civil war, not foreign wars in the usual sense. In the first place, communists make a kind of war against the people over whom they rule. In the second place, they foment strife in other countries which can break out as civil wars. The indications are that the leaders of the Soviet Union like very long odds in their favor when they go to war. The odds, if any, were on the side of Germany in 1941.

By contrast, Hitler sought war rather than avoided it, and major powers were the only ones really worthy of his steel, although he was quite willing to crush any small power standing in his path. Moreover,

Hitler frequently flouted world opinion and flaunted his obnoxious racial ideas before the world. His contempt for other peoples was hardly held in check. Yet, there were times when Hitler apparently longed to be not just the conqueror but the hero of the people of the world. Perhaps, he longed to be loved, as most men do, but was led by what he conceived to be his mission to do unlovely things. There is a vast amount of evidence to the effect that he had great personal magnetism and unusual leadership abilities. Time and again generals came to his headquarters discouraged and depressed, ready to give up, only to go forth from their session with Hitler inspired with a new zeal to fight on. It was not just sycophancy that led those around him to speak of his powers.

Anti-communism was his chosen route to world veneration. If the world would only see him as he wished to be seen it would see him as its savior from the menace of communism, or so he hoped. His assault upon Russia was to be a crusade against everything he hated: Bolshevism, international socialism, the Slavs, and the seat of what he conceived to be the Jewish conspiracy. In this struggle, he believed the rest of the world would join him if it only once understood what he was doing. Much of the world saw all too clearly what Hitler was doing in Europe, however, to hear what he was saying about Bolshevism. In any case, all that Hitler offered was a Germanic socialism to replace the "international" variety of communism.

World War II was, according to most savants, a total war. It was war waged not only between military forces but against civilians. It was a war in which vast resources on all sides were mustered behind the war effort. It was waged by propaganda, in battle, on land, on sea, in the air, and, above all, against cities. It was a war of conquest by the Axis powers and one which could only be ended by unconditional surrender, the Allies proclaimed. It derived its character from totalitarian ideologies and entailed the clash of socialist titans. How socialism gave the war its character needs now to be made clear.

Socialism attacks the foundations of civility at many different levels. Socialist analysis, whether Marxian, Bernsteinian, Hitlerian, or whatever, deals with society, and hence the people who compose it, as it were a machine. It speaks of classes or races, of industry and agriculture, of labor, of the proletariat, of the bourgeoisie, of nations, and so forth as if these were things mechanical in nature. It pits class against class, race against race, nation against nation, and group against group for dominance and control. It dehumanizes, reducing man to that accidental portion of himself by which he may be classified in some mechanical fashion. It decivilizes. (Statistics applied to man is the ultimate mental act of dehumanization, for it reduces man to a number. And it is hardly an accident that the use of statistics has grown with the spread of socialism, for they are a prime means of manipulation and directing change. Statistics ought to be used in public with the same restraint as profanity, for they profane man by reducing him to a virtual nullity.)

Another way that socialism attacks the foundations of civility is to weaken or destroy the inherited culture. Culture is society's way both of liberating and restraining man. Socialism, whether of the communist or Nazi variety, proceeds by undermining the received religion, morality, education, literature, and customs and either destroying or controlling and redirecting them for its purposes. The removal of civilized restraints was a major contributor to the ferocity, the extent, and the atrocities of World War II.

But it may be well to examine in some more depth the assault of socialism on the foundations of civility at a rudimentary level. The most basic and direct attack of socialism is upon private property. (That the Nazis gave other ideological grounds for their confiscation and control of private property did not alter the primacy of their assault on property.) This set the stage for much else that followed, including the atrocities of World War II and after.

A simple story may help illustrate the point. This is the story of a small atrocity, an atrocity so insignificant beside the monstrous ones of World War II that it would not appear to be worthwhile to tell it. Yet it is a poignant story and, if I mistake not, one pregnant with meaning. It happened in a village not far from Bonn, Germany on a raw overcast morning in March of 1945. The scene was the kitchen of a small house. In one corner of the room sat an old German couple, huddled in their winter clothes against the chill weather. In the center stood a couple of American soldiers, cooks for a mortar platoon of a heavy weapons company. I stood aside, watching. One of the soldiers was picking up china, piece by piece, dropping it to the floor and breaking it. The old couple cringed and mumbled to one another. The soldier silenced them with a menacing look and turned to us to say, "I've been in this war since North Africa, and the Germans are to blame." He proceeded to smash the rest of the china. It may not have been china that would have brought a great price in the market, but it was such as they had, and by the looks of them they could not easily replace the broken pieces. It was, as I said, only a small atrocity.

184

Whatever moved him to this destructive act, this callous soldier had grasped, however unwittingly, what lay at the root of the cause of World War II and was re-enacting it. I viewed his act at the time with a mixture of horror and disgust, but I was helpless to do anything about it, for I had no authority and was there only temporarily awaiting transportation to my platoon. What hurt me, of course, was his wanton disrespect for property, someone else's property at that!

I had been brought up to respect property, to use it with care, and to value it: mine, the family's, and that belonging to others. It was a lesson drilled into me as a child and reinforced on at least one occasion which I recall by a rare whipping from my father. One of my brothers and I had been throwing pieces of baked potatoes at one another. There were several violations going on, but I suspect that the most serious was the misuse of baked potatoes. They were intended to be eaten, not as missiles in fraternal conflict. I was taught respect for much else besides, but I now understood that undergirding and buttressing the rest was respect for property.

Socialism inculcates disrespect for property, not in the abstract, perhaps, but in the concrete. Socialists hold real property owners in contempt and particularly owners of productive equipment. When they are in power they confiscate property or take effective control over it. In theory, this might do no harm to the property, but in fact it is quite otherwise. One of the Catholic popes is supposed to have said something to the effect that property ownership may not be good for the individual but it is very good for the property. Whatever the merits of the first part of his proposition, the insight in the second part is sound: No better way has ever been found to have property cared for, protected, and used properly than private ownership of it. Property held in common is frequently abused and neglected, being protected mainly by such habits as have been formed in caring for private property. State-owned property can attract little more respect than the state that owns it; not much, one gathers, as the state becomes bloated with the tasks it takes on and poorly performs.

There is an essential nexus between property and man. It is the means of his livelihood, the base of his production, the goods with which he trades, and the foundation of his independence. Individual life depends upon it, and social life withers without it. Socialism breaks this connection between man and property. Socialists fulminate against property and the propertied, describe them as capitalists or "finance capitalists," as exploiters, and, by implication, hold property in contempt.

185

Property is a vital extension of the man who owns it. It is his lifeline to and from the world about him, a buffer from the outside and one of his most effective means of reaching out to others. In socialist theory, man's individual ownership and control over property is only an incident in his historical development. Property is, therefore, separable from the individual who owns it. So it is, of course, but if it is done against his will the effects are devastating. A man's heart is separable from the rest of his body, but if it is ripped out he must surely die. Man does not necessarily die when his property is taken away, though he may; but he is bereft of his main protection from, and means of contributing to, those about him.

My central concern here, however, is with the extended impact of the loss of respect for property and a general assault upon it. There is no way to launch an assault upon a man's property without at the same time assaulting him. To put it another way, lack of respect for property is part and parcel of lack of respect for the owner of it. Every property owner surely feels this; it tends to be one of his reasons for going to the defense of his property.

There is a shield, so to speak, which protects each of us from violation by others. Property is the outworks of the shield. It is the boundary line of our real property, the walls of our house, the enclosure of our vehicles, the door to our rooms, and the clothes that we wear. The innerworks of the shield are the awe in which we hold life and the respect for the individual and what is his. Loss of respect for property precedes or accompanies the destruction of the outworks of the shield. Respect for the individual and the awe with which life is held crumble as the outworks are breached. Of course, the assault upon religion, morality, and the received culture accompanies the assault upon property in socialist lands. This assault cuts away the respect for property, for the individual, and for life, too.

The ferocity and brutality of World War II, then, was a consequence of the erosion of respect for property, for the individual, and for life. It frequently occurred in that order, too. The trespass, confiscation, and alienation of control over property from the owner frequently preceded the assault upon the individual and the callous taking of lives. The Jews in Germany had generally lost the bulk of their property or control over it long before they were shipped to such places as Auschwitz to be exterminated. First, they lost control over department stores, publishing houses, and other types of businesses. Then they were denied employment in many areas. Only after they had lost whatever means

186

they had once possessed for protecting themselves were they subjected to the "final solution." Totalitarianism proceeded in Germany by divesting the people in general of the control of their property.

The serving up of Russian soldiers in vast numbers as cannon fodder had been preceded by the confiscation of their property and increasing control over their lives. The individual counts for nothing. Soviet propaganda had taught, and the leaders domonstrated the validity of the thesis using men as if they were nameless things in combat. A Russian detachment in retreat marched by the place where a Russian soldier was lying dead. Someone asked if they were not going to get his identification. "For what purpose?" asked the officer in charge. "So that you can notify his family," was the reply. "Oh, that's not necessary." the officer said, "when they don't hear from him after awhile they'll realize he is dead." Tens of thousands of German prisoners disappeared into the Soviet Union, never to be heard from again. The government of the Soviet Union proposed to plan every aspect of the economy for a huge empire, yet could not be bothered to perform the most basic task of government of notifying the next-of-kin of those who died in its charge.

Though we may not ordinarily think of it that way, much of the maiming and killing of war could not occur until property had been trespassed. This was certainly true for World War II. The millions of civilians that were wounded and killed by bombings and other sorts of bombardments were usually initially the victims of trespass first. Those under shelter were usually secure until the building around them had been struck, set fire, or demolished by shells or bombs.

Perhaps it can be visualized this way. One of my most vivid images from World War II is of rooms nakedly exposed to onlookers when the outer walls had been blasted away by bombs or shells. It sticks in my mind that I gazed upward once, though it may have occurred any number of times, into a delicately appointed bedroom indecently exposed for all to see. The three walls left standing were pink, the bed had one leg hanging over that portion of the floor that had been bombed away, and there was a dresser and table or stool. It was a room such as might have been lived in by a young girl. The trespass in such cases, and the violation of civilized rules and decorum, was virtually simultaneous with the maiming and killing.

This is not a brief against war as such. It is intended, however, to call attention to those ideologies which hold property, and hence life, in contempt, and by so doing turn war into a catastrophically destructive affair.

187

The boundaries of nations, too, serve as a shield protecting the lives and property of people within them. The trespass of these boundaries is, by extension, a trespass upon property. National boundaries were violated at will during World War II. Indeed, this was frequently done with callous disregard for the rules of relations among nations: without warning, without any declaration of war, and without restraint. German armies invaded Poland, Norway, Denmark, the Netherlands, Belgium, Luxemburg, and other lands in this fashion. Nor did the Soviet Union, Japan, and Italy observe civilized rules for beginning wars against nations. In consequence of such violations millions of persons were carted off to serve one or another nation as slave laborers for their war machines. The condition, once again, was the trespass of property.

One variety of socialism — Nazism or Fascism — went down to defeat at the end of World War II. That portion of the ideology which was racist and militaristic was as nearly discredited as such things ever are. Nazi Germany was thoroughly, completely, and ignominiously defeated. By the first of May, 1945, Allied armies had swept back the once proud German armies onto German soil and that was virtually all occupied. Hitler and his entourage were in an underground bunker in Berlin, a city shattered and devastated by repeated and prolonged bombings and now under siege by Soviet artillery. The roads out of the city were closed and no regular airports were available. In desperation, Adolf Hitler and his bride, Eva Braun Hitler, committed suicide. The SS detachment was hard put to get together enough gasoline to burn their bodies. Much of Germany was in ruins, and the power of the Nazis had evaporated. The rubble in the streets was the remains of Hitler's ambitious plans for architecturally redesigning such cities as Berlin.

The reasons for the defeat need some amplification. At its height, the Nazi empire had encompassed most of continental Europe from the Urals to the Atlantic with outposts in North Africa. That portion not occupied was under governments generally friendly to Germany, either neutral (Spain, Sweden, Vichy France, etc.) or allied with the Axis (Hungary, Bulgaria, Rumania, etc.) excepting mainly the Soviet Union. What had been European civilization, save the British Isles, was under German sway. Never before in history had continental Europe been so near to being under a single power.

Hitler had under his control many of the most highly developed lands in the world, a goodly portion of the most skilled peoples in the world, and experts of unsurpassed ability. German chemists were among the best in the world. (They probably could have made *ersatz* water if hydrogen and oxygen had been in short supply.) Only oil, among major natural resources, was not generally available in sufficient quantity to fuel his war machine. Even so, the potential was there for a Fortress Europe which would have been impervious to all outside power. Why that did not happen needs some explanations.

There were undoubtedly many contributing factors to the German defeat. Historical post mortems have already explored them, and they will not occupy our attention here. But the crucial fact is that Hitler never mustered most of the might of Europe behind him. Most of the peoples never identified with the Nazi cause. Such cooperation as they generally contributed to it was grudging at best and something less than half-hearted as a rule. Indeed, Hitler's only significant effort to get the willing support of the peoples of Europe was to picture his as an anti-Communist crusade. That was obviously a flawed position, however. He might have been able to overcome the implications of the Nazi-Soviet pact but not the fact that he was at war with Britain and the United States, among many other non-communist nations. Moreover, his own cruel regime was hardly an improvement over Soviet communism.

In the main, though, the Nazis did not even seek the willing aid of many of the peoples of Europe. On the contrary, the peoples were held in contempt, and the Nazis sought only to beat them into submission. This was in keeping with the ideology. Nazism was *national German* socialism, and all who were not predominantly Nordic or German were believed to be inferior peoples. The cruel treatment by the SS of the peoples in eastern Europe made the Nazis as feared and hated as the Communists had ever been.

Hitler refused on a number of occasions the importunings of his officers to be permitted to recruit an army from the Russian prisoners of war. Armies of other nations that fought with Germans enjoyed only a kind of honorary status as equals. Hitler generally held the Italian, Hungarian, and Bulgarian soldiers in contempt as inferior to the Germans. Not surprisingly, many of the Italian officers were eager to get out of the war, and the armies from central Europe were at best fair weather friends.

In short, the Nazis failed to muster the support of Europe because of their ideology. Their national racism could only be repugnant to all others. It appears that Hitler could only have mustered the willing support of Europe, if at all, by abandoning his ideology. At any rate, he did not get it, and without it his armies were overcome by forces from the outside even as they were weakened by resistance from within Europe.

Hitler had promised to build a "folkish state." He had promised to

189

augment the power of the individual by merging it with the collective, to elevate the German people by freeing them from their submission to the Treaty of Versailles. They would become masters by identification with him as the symbol and embodiment of themselves. There is no doubt, either, that many Germans felt the surge of power as they heard or saw Hitler speak, as they massed to participate in the performance of the Nazi rituals, as they looked on marching German soldiers and won their first great victories. The might of the German collective was palpable at the Nuremberg Party rallies, as hundred of flags waved above, as searchlights played upward in the skies, as thousands lifted their arms and shouted "Sieg Heil" in unison. For a few years, many, perhaps most, of the German people were caught up in the pomp, the pageantry, and the promises of a collective beatitude.

If so, their exaltation was shortlived. Hitler did not build a "folkish state." He built a state over which Nazi Gauleiters ruled and the "folk" were an instrument of state to be used as their rulers decided. The subjection of other peoples and the importation of forced labor may have hidden from Germans for a time the fact of their own subjugation. Collectivism augmented the powers of the rulers at the expense of those who were ruled. Much of the substance of Germany went into building the instruments for and fighting a war. The more the people built the less they had. However glorious the early victories, more and more of the young men were required to go to war. As the casualty lists lengthened many families came to know the ultimate cost of war. None could deny the curtailment of their lives as they spent more and more of their time in bomb shelters to escape the fury of the bombs. The Germans were not a master race, as Hitler had told them, they were only a mastered people.

Just when individual Germans realized this there is no way of knowing for a whole population. What we do know is that by the end of the war many Germans were glad indeed to have done with Hitler and his obsessive vision. In the last weeks of the war the armies of the Western Allies were often greeted by the Germans as heroes. As American tanks, trucks, and jeeps drove through many towns and cities people lined the sidewalks to wave and cheer. This would have been a smart thing to do in any case, but it had the look of spontaneity about it. At least at the moment of their arrival, the Western Allies were being treated as liberators.

In the east, a different kind of story was taking place. Germans, and others, were fleeing by the hundreds of thousands before the advance of the Red Army. Taking whatever they could with them, they fled toward the west seeking refuge from an army bent on plundering and pillaging and destroying what it would. Sometimes before, but certainly as soon as they could lay down their arms, German troops too sought to make their way west to surrender to the Western Allies. For several days after the end of the fighting, the relics of the German armies poured through the lines of the Western Allies making their way to places of internment. Men clung to the sides of whatever vehicle they could find that would enable them to evade the clutches of the Red Army.

The defeat of the Axis in World War II did not significantly loosen the grip of the idea that has the world in thrall, not for long anyway. True, the hold of the Nazi variety of revolutionary socialism was struck off from Western Europe, but in central Europe the grip of revolutionary socialism, communism, was established and tightened.

World War II had broken out in the wake of the German invasion of Poland. The British and French governments had declared war on Germany in an attempt to preserve the territorial integrity of Poland. When Hitler heard just before the end of the war that a Soviet sponsored puppet government was being set up in Poland he remarked the irony of it all. The British and French had gone to war against him to save Poland, and now the Poles were being turned over to Soviet tyranny. Indeed, any who would ponder the meaning of World War II, and the impact of the idea that has the world in its grip, could do not better than begin with Poland.

Poland has for several centuries been a bending and bent buffer between Russia and Western Europe. Time and again Poland has been the scene, or a part of it, of the clashes between European powers and the butt of the treaties by which they ended their conflicts. If ever a people deserved the compassion of men of good will it must surely be the unfortunate Poles. Shortly after the Nazi invasion of Poland the Soviet Union invaded from the east. The country was then partitioned. Part of the country was then "Nazified" while the remainder was being "Sovietized." The full fury of the SS was let loose in the Nazi "zone of occupation." Poland's relatively large number of Jews were subjected to a pogrom the like of which had never been seen before. Some of the most notorious Nazi concentration camps were located in Poland, and the most vicious extermination was carried out there. Thousands of Jews died in an heroic stand against the Nazis in the Warsaw Ghetto. The resisters were wiped out. Nor were Jews the only victims: numerous Poles were dislocated to allow Germans to move in;

191

intellectuals and potential leaders got vicious attention from the SS.

As the Red Army advanced upon Warsaw the Polish resistance movement made a determined effort to expel the Germans from the city. The Soviet armies halted their advance and waited, apparently with malice aforethought, for the Germans to wipe out the resistance. Roosevelt and Churchill appealed to Stalin at least to allow British and Americans to airlift aid to the resisters, but their appeal fell on deaf ears. On top of all this, thousands of Polish officers were shot down in cold blood by Soviet forces at the Katyn Forest Massacre. All that remained to be done to destroy Poland, it would seem, would be to sow the soil with salt.

At any rate, the Soviet Union had an eviscerated Poland upon which to impose its regime in 1945. The Soviet Union won the battle for central Europe, a main arena in the contest of World War II. Communist regimes were subsequently imposed on Hungary, Rumania, Bulgaria, Yugoslavia, Albania, and Czechoslovakia. Estonia, Latvia and Lithuania had already lost all semblance of independence by being incorporated into the Soviet Union. Part of Poland was incorporated into the Soviet Union, part of Germany into Poland, and a communist regime established in East Germany. Finland, too, lost territory to the Soviet Union.

Could it have been otherwise? Possibly. It was the style, in some circles anyhow, after World War II to blame the fall of these countries, particularly that of Poland, to communism, on decisions made at the Yalta Conference of Stalin, Roosevelt, and Churchill in early 1945. This is almost certainly a misreading of history. The concessions made to Stalin at that conference were largely in recognition of a *fait accompli*. The Red Army was already in or marching into these countries. It was the presence of the Red Army that made it possible to establish communist regimes generally.

The decision that sealed the fate of central and eastern Europe was almost certainly made in 1943. It was the decision to concentrate British and American forces in England for a cross-channel invasion of France in 1944. It was the decision for the English channel, so to speak, over the Adriatic and Aegean seas. The signal for the decision was given in December of 1943 when General Eisenhower was appointed Supreme Commander of Allied Forces and moved from Italy to England to prepare for the cross-channel invasion.

The Western Allies had already established a second front on continental Europe in 1943. It was in Italy. Winston Churchill favored an assult on the "soft under-belly of Europe," probably by way of the Adriatic. Militarily, the most strategic target in all of Europe was the Rumanian oil fields. Once the oil reaching German forces from Rumania and Hungary was cut off the days of the German air force, tank divisions, and guided missiles would be numbered. Politically, if the assault had been made in this way, much of southern and central Europe might have been spared the occupation by the Red Army, and the communist regimes. Instead, armed forces were concentrated in England, and in the course of 1944 much of the military force was withdrawn from Italy to attack westward in support of "Operation Overland," the cross-channel invasion. The die was cast many months before January of 1945.

The spread of communism greatly accelerated in the wake of World War II. The devastation of western Europe, the defeat and demilitarization of the Axis, left power vacuums in much of the world. Wherever these occurred, communists saw them as opportunities for expansion, either by way of joining coalition governments—and occupying key positions in them until one party emerged triumphant—or by fomenting civil wars. Not only had all of eastern, most of central, and much of southern Europe fallen to communism, but with Japan defeated and demilitarized, China became communist. As colonies were cut loose from demoralized European countries, these became prime targets for the spread of communism.

Communism was the only significant variety of revolutionary socialism in the world after World War II. But communism is not the only variety of socialism in the world. The idea that has the world in its grip has two faces: One is revolutionary socialsm; the other is evolutionary or gradualist socialism. It is appropriate now to turn our attention to some examination of the working of evolutionary socialism

Book IV

Gradualism in England

15

The Seeds of Rejection

IF IT CAN BE validly claimed that France during the French Revolution was the birthplace of the idea that has the world in its grip, then it can be held with equal validity that Germany was its spiritual home. Certainly, leadership in the development and spread of socialist ideas began to shift from France to Germany in the mid-nineteenth century. Marx and Bernstein were German. The Social Democratic Party made its first considerable impact in Germany and was the model for many other such parties in Europe. But while it was still only an idea, England became a kind of home-in-exile for it. Thither came Karl Marx to toil away in the British Museum collecting material for his magnum opus, *Das Kapital*. Thither came Eduard Bernstein, only a few years later, to make his major revision of Marxism in setting forth an evolutionary theory of socialism.

That there was considerable irony in this latter development has not escaped the notice of commentators. England in the latter part of the nineteenth century was the leader of what Marx called capitalism and the foremost exemplar of it. This leading capitalist country provided a refuge of freedom for its deadliest enemies, the proponents of the two most virulent species of socialism. England was, however, more than the home-in-exile of evolutionary socialism. A good case can be made that England was its birthplace. More than a decade before Bernstein published his revisions of Marxism in book form, a theory of gradualism was being shaped and propagated in England.

Be that as it may, there is no better place than England in which to study the development of evolutionary socialism from its inception to its eventual failure as a socialist regime. Not only was England a foremost exemplar of what is called capitalism but also a prime case of a country going down the evolutionary road to socialism. How the shift was made and impetus given to the newer movement will engage our attention as well as the impact of the idea as it gains power. For all these facets of the subject, England provides the classic materials for a case study.

There is a rough sort of chronology to this work, too, despite the necessity for going back and forth in time. The idea under consideration first provided the underpinnings for a regime in Russia in the 1920's. It underlay the Nazi regime in Germany in the 1930's. These two behemoths of revolutionary socialism engaged in a titanic struggle in the early 1940's. Socialism came to power in England in 1945. But it is necessary to go back to the Victorian era to pick up the beginning of a development which reached its fruition in the late 1940's. Indeed, it will be most helpful to take up the story at that point in time when England was at its height of influence and prosperity. For, strange as it may seem, it was just at this juncture that the seeds of rejection of the established ways were planted and the soil was prepared for socialism.

All indications were that in the middle of the nineteenth century the lot of most Englishmen was vastly improved over what it had been. Signs abounded that they were better paid, better fed, had more leisure, and could avail themselves of more of the things which adorn life rather than merely sustain it. Nor was there any reason for doubting that these benefits could be attributed, directly or indirectly, to Britain's stable and balanced government, to the security of persons and property, to the freedom of trade, to the moral code which prevailed, to hard work, to capital investment, and to technological innovations. Yet, in the midst of this spreading prosperity, these very things began to come under attack. A shorthand phrase for these conditions and means by which prosperity was achieved is "The Victorian Way." The Victorian Way came under assult during the Victorian period, though its repudiation would not be completed until early in the twentieth century.

The nagging, questioning, and doubting of the validity of the Victorian Way got underway in the midst of its triumph. At the outset, however, this challenge to the Victorian Way was made by a minority, most likely a tiny minority, whereas the vast majority accepted and prized it. Indeed, there were clergymen who pointed out the moral character of the Victorian Way, historians who wove it into its place in English history, statesmen who expounded and defended it, philosophers who claimed it within general theories of progress, and writers who advocted the expansion of it. This story should be alluded to before attending to the critics.

Though Frederick Harrison was exaggerating when he wrote the following in 1882, and obviously more than a little piqued by it all, his words do indicate that there were many who saw virtue in the developments which brought England to greatness:

> Surely no century in all human history was ever so much praised to its face for its wonderful achievements, its wealth and its power, its unparalleled ingenuity and its miraculous capacity for making itself comfortable and generally enjoying life. British Associations, and all sorts of associations, economic, scientific, and mechanical, are perpetually executing cantatas in honour of the age of progress.... The journals perform the part of orchestra, banging big drums and blowing trumpets....[1]

Thomas Babington Macaulay, the historian, is usually credited, or blamed, for being the leading apoligist for the Victorian Way. He was the man who first made what is usually called the Whig interpretation of history. He did so in his *History of England* which made its appearance in the middle of the nineteenth century. It sold unusually well for a history, or for anything else. When the first two volumes appeared, 13,000 copies were sold in four months. The next two volumes sold 26,500 copies in ten weeks.[2] Macaulay certainly was not one to hide his light under a bushel; whatever views he held, he held firmly and expressed forthrightly. One gets a sense of the measure of the man in this reference to a work by Robert Southey, Poet Laureate of England:

> It would be scarcely possible for a man of Mr. Southey's talents and acquirements to write two volumes so large as these before us, which should be wholly destitute of information and amusement.... We have, for some time past, observed with great regret the strange infatuation which leads the Poet Laureate to abondon those departments of literature in which he might excel, and to lecture the public on sciences of which he has still the very alphabet to learn. He has now, we think, done his worst.[3]

It is not surprising that his own works have come in for strong criticism. Be that as it may, his work pointed out the improvements that had occurred in England since the Glorious Revolution and ascribed these to the security of liberty and property and stable government, among other things. He opened his *History* by declaring that "the general effect of this chequered narrative will be to excite thankfulness in all religious minds and hope in the breasts of all patriots. For the history of our country during the last hundred and sixty years is eminently the history of physical, of moral, and of intellectual improvements."[4] In short, he maintained that "the history of England is emphatically the history of progress."[5] In explaining the difference between England and France — the France of the July (1830) Revolution — Macaulay ascribed it to the political institutions of liberty:

To what are we to attribute the unparralleled moderation and humanity which the English people have displayed at this great conjuncture? The answer is plain. This moderation, this humanity are the fruits of a hundred and fifty years of liberty.... For many generations we have had the trial by jury, the Habeas Corpus Act, the freedom of the press, the right of meeting to discuss public affairs, the right of petitioning the legislature. The vast portion of the population has long been accustomed to the exercise of political functions.... Thus our institutions had been so good that they had educated us into a capacity for better institutions.[6]

In like manner, W. E. H. Lecky, who published his prodigious *History of Rationalism* at the age of 27, was unstinting in his admiration for and praise of English leadership and economic development. He pointed out that England has been the leader in the development of political economy as a science as well as in mechanical inventions. "It is not surprising," he said, "that a land which has attained this double supremacy, and which possesses at the same time almost unlimited coal-mines, an unrivaled navy, and a goverment that can never long resist the natural tendency of affairs, should be pre-eminently the land of manufacturers."[7] Lecky was an enthusiastic follower and expounder of developments in political economy from Smith through Say, and ascribed the peace of his times to the applications of these doctrines, particularly to the freeing of trade. He declared that an understanding and applicaiton of political economy is the corrective to the evil of war. Political economy denies, he said, that one nation's gain in trade is another's loss. Instead,

It teaches ... that each nation has a direct interest in the prosperity of that with which it trades, just as a shopman has an interest in wealth of his

200

customers. It teaches too that the different markets of the world are so closely connected, that it is quite impossible for a serious derangement to take place in any one of them without its evil effects vibrating through all.... Each successive development of political economy has brought these truths into clearer relief.... Every fresh commercial enterprise is therefore an additional guarantee of peace.[8]

The "scheme of progress which political economy reveals" goes something like this, according to Lecky. Men form habits of thrift and self-restraint in order to improve their material condition. As that improves, they develop the gentler ways of civilization.

And the same principle that creates civilisation creates liberty, and regulates and sustains morals. The poorer classes, as wealth, and consequently the demand for their labour, have increased, cease to be the helpless tools of their masters. Slavery, condemned by political economy, gradually disappears. The stigma that attached to labour is removed. War is repressed as a folly and despotism as an invasion of the rights of property. The sense of common interests unites the different sections of mankind, and the conviction that each nation should direct its energies to that form of produce for which it is naturally most suited, effects a division of labour which renders each dependent upon the others. Under the influence of industrial occupations, passions are repressed, the old warlike habits are destroyed, a respect for law, a consideration for the interests of others, a sobriety and perseverance of character are inculcated.[9]

In such fashion, the Victorian Way became a part of the historical perspective for many.

Men in other walks of life affirmed the Victorian Way also. Prince Albert, consort to Queen Victoria, declared in 1851:

"We are living at a period of most wonderful transition, which tends rapidly to accomplish that great end to which indeed all history points — the realization of the unity of mankind."[10]

In a speech before Parliament, Lord Palmerston said:

"We have shown the example of a nation, in which every class of society accepts with cheerfulness the lot which Providence has assigned to it; while at the same time every individual of each class is constantly striving to raise himself in the social scale — not by injustice and wrong, not by violence and illegality, but by preserving good conduct, and by the steady and energetic execution of the moral and intellectual faculties with which his creator has endowed him."[11]

Speaking from the pulpit, the Reverend Charles Kingsley proclaimed

201

the reasons why Englishmen should give thanks to God. He tells how others have been beset by wars and destructions,

and yet here we are, going about our business in peace and safety in a land which we and our forefathers have found, now for many a year, that just laws make a quiet and prosperous people; that the effect of righteousness is peace, and the fruit of righteousness, quietness and assurance for ever; — a land in which the good are not terrified, the industrious hampered, and the greedy and lawless made eager and restless by expectation of change in government; but every man can boldly and hopefully work in his calling, and "whatsoever his hand finds to do, do it with all his might." in fair hope that the money which he earns in his manhood he will be able to enjoy quietly in his old age, and hand it down safely to his children, and his children's children.... Oh, my friends, who made us to differ from others, or what have we that we did not receive? Not to ourselves do we owe our blessings.... We owe it to our wise Constitution and to our wise Church, the principle of which is that God is Judge and Christ is King....[12]

Herbert Spencer rendered at least a part of the Victorian Way into a philosophical framework. There was probably much about mid-Victorian England that Spencer did not approve, but he approved the general trend toward establishing greater freedom, and mainly wanted the principle expanded until it bcame universal. His statements on free trade illustrate this penchant in his works:

Fortunately it is now needless to enforce the doctrine of commercial freedom by any considerations of policy. After making continual attempts to improve upon the laws of trade, from the time of Solon downwards, men are at length beginning to see that such attempts are worse than useless. Political economy has shown us in this matter — what indeed it is its chief mission to show — that our wisest plan is to let things take their own course. We have here learned, what our forefathers learned in some cases, and what, alas! we have yet to learn in many more, that nothing but evil can arise from inequitable regulations. The necessity of respecting the principles of abstract rectitude — this it is that we have had another lesson upon. Look at it rightly and we shall find that all the Anti-Corn-Law League did, with its lectures, its newspapers, its bazaars, its monster meetings, and its tons of tracts, was to teach people — what should have been very clear to them without any such teaching — that no good can come of violating men's rights. By bitter experience and a world of talk we have at length been made partially to believe as much. Be it true or not in other cases, we are now quite certain that it is true in trade. In respect to this at least we have declared that, for the future, we will obey the law of equal freedom.[13]

Spencer was optimistic in thinking that the British had learned their lesson about trade once and for all, but this was the one thing that libertarians managed to get almost all parties to agree to as a cardinal principle for so long.

This examination can be closed by referring to the man who has often been singled out as the stereotype of the apologists for the Victorian Way, Samuel Smiles. Samuel Smiles was a popular writer in the latter part of the nineteenth century who did indeed approve the Victorian Way, and who devoted his pen to elucidating its virtues. The titles of his works show what he considered some of those virtues to be: *Self-Help, Thrift, Character,* and *Duty.* He placed great emphasis upon work, saving, honesty, perseverance, charity, and self-help. *Self-Help* made its appearance in 1859 and sold 20,000 copies that year. In addition, some 130,000 copies were sold in the next thirty years. But the reference here will be to another work, in which he discusses saving, capital, and labor:

The men who economize by means of labor become the owners of capital which sets other labor in motion. Capital accumulates in their hands, and they employ other laborers to work for them. Thus trade and commerce begin.

The thrifty build houses, warehouses, and mills. They fit manufactories with tools and machines. They build ships and send them to various parts of the world. They put their capital together, and build railroads, harbors, and docks. They open up mines of coal, iron, and copper; and erect pumping-engines to keep them clear of water. They employ laborers to work the mines, and thus give rise to an immense amount of employment.

All this is the result of thrift. It is the result of economizing money, and employing it for beneficial purposes....[14]

This was surely an abstract of the English experience, put into language that every man could understand.

The Victorian Way was not without its exponents, apologists, and defenders, then. Indeed, numbered among them were some, or most, of the illustrious names of the century. But they were matched, and eventually overmatched, by a rising chorus of critics in the course of the nineteenth and early twentieth century. In the wake of this mounting criticism, the work of many of the most able exponents fell into disrepute, in many circles anyhow. It happened to Macaulay, to Spencer, and of course, to Smiles. More importantly, the ideas, principles, and practices which were at the heart of the Victorian Way became suspect, and were eventually rejected.

To understand the character of this attack on things Victorian and its eventual impact, some observations about socialism are in order. Not that the critics were necessarily socialists: some were, and some were not. But the criticism was certainly grist for the mills of socialists, and they managed somehow to identify themselves with all of it. Socialism was a product of the nineteenth century, and it remains stuck in the grooves of the nineteenth century. More, it is the *hybrid* product of two contradictory strains in nineteenth century thought. It is a hybrid because it is infertile and unproductive (having always to borrow from freedom such innovations as it adopts). It is the product of abstract rationalism, on the one hand, and romanticism, on the other. To put it another way, socialism is the stubborn mule sired by the donkey, abstract rationisism, bred to the flighty mare, romanticism. Like the mule, socialism has some of the worse traits of its forebears: it is as unimaginative as the donkey and as irrational as the horse.

Nonetheless, socialism has an almost irresistible attraction to a certain turn of mind. It attracts because of its criticism and rejection of the way things are, and its promises of the way things will be when they have been reconstructed. Socialism appeals particularly to those who are alienated from and thus do not feel a part of the society in which they live. Its greatest attraction is for intellectuals, particularly those of a literary and artistic bent. It is probable that, in earlier times, most such men found some religious vocation. But in the eighteenth century, they began to be more numerous as laymen. Since that time, they appear to have increased greatly in number and influence.

Much of the initial criticism of Victorian society came from literary romantics, from poets, from architects, from essayists, from novelists, and from dilettanti who dabbled in all these things. They not only justified their alienation from society but also gloried in it. To be aliented from society was a badge of distinction to many romantics; it was a sign of superiority. Society was vulgar, insensitive, unaesthetically inclined, materialistic, practical and almost wholly unattractive. Moreover, society has a way of imposing its standards, however subtly, upon all within its orbit. Many romantics had subsumed libertarian ideas into their outlook and would think of themselves as liberals; but they went beyond seeking freedom from governmental restraint; they also sought freedom from the prescriptions of society. They tended toward anarchy. But some romantic intellectuals went even further, seeking not only to be free from social prescription but at the same time trying to prescribe for society. When they sought to do this by governmental action, they usually became socialists of some sort.

There was a great range and variety to the criticism of Victorian England, from the criticism of flaws to the wholesale condemnation of the social order. Charles Dickens was one who highlighted many of the flaws in his numerous novels. He satirized "poor law institution, Chancery, and judicial procedure in general, profiteering private

204

schools, and many other social ills of his times.... Having been a poor boy himself he had an instinctive and burning sympathy with the poor."[15] Nor should there be any doubt that he frequently has a reformist purpose in mind. "In all my writings," he said on one occasion, "I hope I have taken every available opportunity of showing the want of sanitary improvements in the neglected dwellings of the poor."[16] Even so, it is not clear that Dickens had much more in mind than that men should reform their ways, and that the poor should struggle to better themselves.

Thomas Carlyle was quite different from Dickens and a much deeper critic of his age. He saw the age as common and unheroic, and lacking in leaderhsip or traditons that made for greatness. One of his characters exclaims:

"Thus, too, does an observant eye discern everywhere that saddest spectacle: The Poor perishing, like neglected, foundered Draught-Cattle, of Hunger and Over-work; the Rich still more wretchedly of Idleness, Satiety, and Over-growth. The Highest in rank, at length, without honour from the Lowest; scarely, with a little mouth-honour, as from tavern-waiters who expect to put in the bill. Once-sacred Symbols fluttering as empty Pageants, whereof men grudge even the expense; a World becoming dismantled: in one word, the Church fallen speechless, from obesity and apoplexy; the State shrucken into a Police-Office, straitened to get its pay!"[17]

Of Carlyle's impact, an historian says: "By the strength of his convictions and the extraordinary language in which he clothed them, he caused many Englishmen to share his dissatisfaction with the materialism of the age and to give more thought to moral and social issues."[18]

Matthew Arnold was a much clearer case of the rejecter of Victorian England. He satirized and held up to scorn the Englishman's fascination with machinery, his worship of wealth, and his vaunted liberty to do as he pleased. The middle class, he said, were *Philistines*. "For *Philistine* gives the notion of something particularly stiff-necked and perverse in the resistance to light and its children; and therein it specially suits our middle class, who not only do not pursue sweetness and light, but who even prefer to them that sort of machinery of business, chapels, tea-meeting, and addresses from Mr. Murphy [Mr. Murphy was depicted as boorishly intolerant of Roman Catholics], which makes up the dismal and illiberal life on which I have so often touched."[19] The English aristocracy he calls the Barbarians. In a passage dripping with satire, Arnold describes some of the salient features of this class:

205

The Barbarians, to whom we all owe so much, and who reinvigorated and renewed our worn-out Europe, had, as is well known, eminent merits.... The Barbarians brought with them that staunch individualism, as the modern phrase is, and that passion for doing as one likes.... The Barbarians, again, had the passion for field-sports; and they have handed it on to our aristocratic class, who of this passion too, as of the passion for asserting one's personal liberty, are the great natural stronghold....[20]

He would classify as Philistines, too, all that portion of the working class which either by its ambitions seeks to be a part of the middle class or by organizing in labor unions hopes to occupy the place of dominance held by the middle class.

But that vast portion, lastly, of the working class which, raw and half-developed, has long lain half-hidden amidst its poverty and squalor, and is now issuing from its hiding-place to assert an Englishman's heaven-born privilege of doing as he likes, and is beginning to perplex us by marching where it likes, meeting where it likes, bawling what it likes, breaking what it likes, — to this vast residuum we may with great propriety give the name of *Populace.*[21]

What was the point of all this, and much more besides? What was the point of describing England as divided into *Barbarians, Philistines,* and *Populace?* Matthew Arnold was saying that Victorian England lacked true culture and was tending toward anarchy — to the loss of cohesion, to disintegration. England would be saved, if at all, he taught, by turning to the State.

Thus, in our eyes, the very framework and exterior order of the State, whoever may administer the State, is sacred; and culture is the most resolute enemy of anarchy, because of the great hopes and designs for the State which culture teaches us to nourish. But as, believing in right reason, and having faith in the progress of humanity towards perfection, and ever labouring for this end, we grow to have clearer sight of the ideas of right reason, and of the elements and helps of perfection, and come gradually to fill the framework of the State with them, to fashion its internal composition and all its laws and institutions conformably to them, and to make the State more and more the expression, as we say, of our best self, which is not manifold, and vulgar, and unstable, and contentious, and ever-varying, but one, and noble, and secure, and peaceful, and the same for all mankind....[22]

Arnold is a near perfect example of the confused joining of abstract rationalism and romanticism to reach a conclusion with deep inner contradictions. He abstracted society so as to arrive at disintegration in his description, a disintegration which his very analysis produced. Then,

206

he turned off his analytical powers, such as they were, when he looked at the state, and made it an object of romantic adoration. He was, of course, following the path already trod by many German romantics and by the spiritual godfather of all romantics, Jean Jacques Rousseau.

The final step from the rejection and denunciation of the Victorian Way can be illustrated by reference to John Ruskin. Ruskin disliked machinery, repetitive tasks, mass produced articles, laissez-faire, competition, the law of supply and demand, and just about everything associated with Victorian England. He longed, mainly, to see medieval society restored, or, at least, medieval craftmanship, and things of that sort. He described his ideal society in this way:

I have already stated that no machines moved by artificial power are to be used on the estates of the society; wind, water, and animal force are to be the only motive powers employed, and there is to be as little trade or importation as possible; the utmost simplicity of life, and restriction of possession, being combined with the highest attainable refinement of temper and thought. Everything that the members of any household can sufficiently make for themselves, they are so to make, however clumsily; but the carpenter and smith, trained to perfectest work in wood and iron, are to be employed on the parts of houses and implements in which finish is essential to strength. The ploughshare and spade must be made by the smith, and the roof and floors by a carpenter; but the boys of the house must be able to make either a horseshoe, or a table.[23]

Ruskin could, of course, be precise and analytical, as in his discourses on political economy, but when he visualized the society to supplant the present one, he became a full-fledged romantic. That he became a socialist, of some variety, will appear from the following. "The first duty of a state," he said, "is to see that every child born therein shall be well housed, clothed, fed and educated, till it attains years of discretion." To accomplish this, "the government must have an authority over the people of which we do not so much as dream."[24]

Of course, the above only touches the surface of the critiques, attacks, denunciations, and rejection of the Victorian Way. Many other people and works would have to be examined to get to its full flavor, and many other facets of the attack examined. For eventually everything Victorian became suspect: the architecture, the furniture, the morals, the productive system, the government, and so on. The debunking of things Victorian reached its peak in the 1920's, following the publication of Lytton Strachey's *Eminent Victorians* (1918) and *Queen Victoria* (1921). In the wake of this rejection, D. H. Lawrence said:

207

Now, although perhaps nobody knew it, it was ugliness which really betrayed the spirit of man in the nineteenth century. The great crime which the moneyed classes and promoters of industry committed in the palmy Victorian days was the condemning of the workers to ugliness, ugliness, ugliness: meanness and formless and ugly surroundings, ugly ideas, ugly religion, ugly hope, ugly love, ugly clothes, ugly furniture, ugly houses, ugly relationship between workers and employers. [25]

The English people, then, did not simply forget the principles and practices which had made England great. They were turned against them. The attack upon the Victorian Way was kept up until the very thought of it began to be distasteful, at least to anyone of literary or artistic awareness. Those who had defended it and expounded its principles became suspect also. The rejection of existing society was but a prelude, of course, to a vision of a new society to supplant it. Such visions were most effectively pushed by socialists. To that part of the story we may now turn.

16
The Fabian Trust
to Socialism

THE FABIAN SOCIETY was organized January 4, 1884. Its organization resulted in the split-up of a group that had formed the year before and would be called "The Fellowship of the New Life." There were probably nine members of the Fabian Society at the outset.[1] This was the motto adopted by the Society:

For the right moment you must wait, as Fabius did most patiently, when warring against Hannibal, though many censured his delays; but when the time comes you must strike hard, as Fabius did, or your waiting will be in vain and fruitless.

The significance of the Fabian Society is not immediately apparent. It was only one among numerous collectivist and socialist organizations at its inception. At a conference held in 1886 fifty-four such societies had representatives, and the Marxist Social Democratic Federation was not even in attendance. There were such organizations as the Socialist League, the Socialist Union, the Guild of St. Matthew, the Anarchist Group of Freedom, the Land Restoration Leagues, the Land Nationalization Society, and the National Secular Society.[2] Not only was the Fabian Society only one small group among many other socialist groups at the beginning, but even after more than sixty years of existence (1947) it had only about 8,000 members.[3]

The importance of the Fabian Society did not arise from the number of its members. Instead, it became so influential because it attracted into its ranks men and women who were leaders or would become leaders in a variety of intellectual fields. Shortly after its founding, George Bernard Shaw, Sidney Webb, Graham Wallas, and Beatrice Potter (who married Webb) joined the Society. Over the years, many other prominent English intellectuals and politicians would belong. In the 1920's, for example, it numbered among its adherents those who were or would become prominent such as Clement Atlee, Stafford Cripps, R. H. Tawney, Michael Oakeshott, Ernest Barker, Rebecca West, C. E. M. Joad, Bertrand Russell, Malcolm Muggeridge, Harold Laski, and G. D. H. Cole.[4] Of equal, or greater, importance, the Fabians had an *idea,* and it was this idea which helped to draw so many intellectuals into their ranks. The idea can be succinctly stated: The Fabians linked reformism by government action with socialism, the latter to be achieved gradually by way of the former.

So stated, the idea may not now be very impressive; certainly, it may not strike us as original, unique, or anything but obvious. That is because we are more or less familiar with it, because it has become a part of that baggage of ideas we carry around with us. This was not the case in the 1880's and 1890's. Socialism and reformism were antithetical currents whose advocates were usually in dogmatic opposition to one another. To appreciate what they did, it will be helpful to go a little into the background of these antithetical dogmas.

Modern socialism was conceived in the midst of the French Revolution and was shaped within a few decades following the Napoleonic Wars. It was the work mainly of Frenchmen: of Saint-Simon, Charles Fourier, Pierre Joseph Proudhon, Auguste Comte, and Louis Blanc. Men from other nations also contributed: Karl Marx, Friedrich Engels, Robert Dale Owen, and William Godwin, among others. At the time of the founding of the Fabian Society, there were three main streams of socialism: communitarian, revolutionary, and anarchistic.

Many of the early socialists were communitarians. That is, they proposed to achieve socialism instantly, as it were, by living in communities separated from the rest of society. An example of such a community would be Robert Dale Owen's New Harmony community in America, but there were many other such experiments. In these communities, there would be no private property; all would share in useful work; all would receive from the goods produced and the services provided. These communities were quite often conceived as places where men having taken care of their brute needs could devote most of their energies to intellectural and esthetic fulfillment. They were conceived as voluntary efforts, and if they were to become universal it would be because of their success as a way of life.

There were also the revolutionary socialists, of whom Karl Marx was to become the most famous. Marx spoke of his as scientific socialism — denouncing others as utopians — but that facet of his work has been covered already. He envisioned — predicted or scientifically calculated, he might have said — a time in the future when the proletariat would rise up, cast off their chains, and destroy the bourgeois state and all its paraphernalia. Socialism would somehow replace it in that last great stage of history.

Anarchism was most famously propounded by William Godwin and Prince Peter Kropotkin. Its central notion was that the state was unnecessary, that formal government employing force was equally unnecessary, that if it were abolished, society would take over and manage its own affairs peacefully. Some anarchists went about attempting to destroy the state in the most direct fashion, i.e., by political assassination. This was generally intended as a terrorist tactic, to so terrorize those in government that they would abdicate and all others would be afraid to take on their jobs. Not all anarchists, of course, pursued their objective in such a forthright manner.

What gave these people title to be called socialist? What did they have in common that made them socialists? The point has long since been lost sight of largely, but it is this: they proposed that government or the state could be abolished and that society would wholly replace it by subsuming its functions. This doctrine might be clearer if it were referred to as societism rather than socialism. Generally speaking, early socialists abstracted from liberal doctrine the idea that the state, or government, existed to protect property. (Liberals did not, of course, hold that this was the *only*, or even the underlying, reason for the existence of government.) Property — individualist, private property — then, was the occasion for the state with its oppression, wars, and dislocative impact upon society. Abolish private property, and the state would no longer have any function. Or, abolish the state, and there would no longer be any private property.

There was, then, a deep hatred of and animus against the state by most socialists. The communitarian would abandon the state to its own devices. so far as possible. The revolutionists would assault it directly, and for Marx it would wither away. The anarchists would make it impossible. This attitude prevailed among many socialists down to the end of the nineteenth century, or beyond. (Indeed, it can be argued — conclusively, so far as semantics are concerned — that once they accepted the state and began to use it they ceased to be socialists.)

This was the state of socialism when the Fabians began to study it in the 1880's. Socialists were nowhere in power in any land, and it is difficult to see how they could have been, considering their animosity to government. Such communities as had been tried had been failures. Their revolutions had aborted, as, for example, that of the Paris Commune in 1848. Anarchists were widely recognized as a menace, and of interest generally to the police. Socialists were fragmented into numerous groups, their antipathy a product both of temperamental differences among their leaders and their penchant for nit picking over fine points of doctrine. Their doctrines had been repudiated by most men who had heard of them, the estimate of them ranging from thinking of them as downright silly to being profoundly dangerous. Their leaders were frequently *personae non gratae* in their native lands. The inevitability of the triumph of socialism had no direct evidence with which to sustain the faithful.

Yet, there was a great ferment of ideas at work in England, and elsewhere, in the last three decades of the nineteenth century. The Victorian Way was under attack, as has been shown. Men were losing confidence in the validity of ancient certainties. There was a depression in the 1870's, which became known as the Great Depression. Reports of poverty and suffering were beginning to make an impact. Neomercantilism and nationalism were gaining sway in many countries. New ideas were being applied in many fields. Reformers, reform ideas, and reform organizations abounded.

The early Fabians were socialists searching for a *modus operandi* by which to achieve their goal. This distinguished them from most other socialists; these had very definite ideas about how utopia would be achieved: by way of communities, following some great revolutionary upheaval, by political assassination, via labor organization, by a revival of peasantry, and so on. In like manner, reformers were usually wedded to a favorite panacea: inflation, a single tax on land, a redivision of the land, urban housing projects, settlement houses, and such like. The Fabians were not encumbered by any such fixed ideas as regards means (though some would eventually become attached to nationalization in this manner). It would be unjust to them to suggest that they were all willing to use any means for attaining socialism, but they were certainly open to the use of a great variety of means to the eventual socialization of England. They had no bias in favor of revolution, nor any in opposition to government. Ameliorative reform was quite acceptable, so long as it thrust England in the direction of socialism.

So it was that the Fabians acted as a kind of filter for the currents of ideas and movements sweeping about them, eclectically taking from whatever sources whichever ideas or programs suited their purposes. It would not be appropriate here to trace down all the sources of their ideas, but it will help to see what they did — and to see why that were eventually so successful — to note how they took from or flowed with certain currents that were already under way.

One of the elements of Fabianism, as has been noted, was reformism, the willingness to use government power to make changes of a limited nature. The stage had been set for this by the liberals in the course of the nineteenth century. They had given reform a good name generally and had shown how, when it is applied in a limited manner, it can be made to work. The main impetus of liberal reforms, of course, had been to remove government restrictions, regulations, and prescriptions — to establish liberty — such as the lowering of tariffs, removing religious qualifications for officeholding, repeal of the navigation acts, repeal of wages legislation, freeing of the press, and so on.

But there was also a minor strain of interventionism in English liberal thought. This can be best approached by noting that there were two distinct currents that went into nineteenth century English liberalism. They were, respectively, the natural law philosophy and utilitarianism.

Those who adhered to the natural law philosophy — David Ricardo, for example — were not interventionists, at least not in the first half of the century. They believed in a naturally harmonious universe in which to intervene was but to bring about dislocations.

The utilitarians had a quite different foundation for their beliefs, though they frequently arrived at similar conclusions. They are usually characterized as philosophical radicals. The leading figures among utilitarians were Jeremy Bentham, James Mill and John Stuart Mill, in that chronological order. Bentham repudiated natural law, saying of those who had attempted to uphold it that they "take for their subject the pretended *law of nature;* an obscure phantom, which in the

213

imaginations of those who go in chase of it, points sometimes to *manners*, sometimes to laws; sometimes to what law *is*, and sometimes to what it ought to be."[5] In its place, he substituted happiness or utility as his standard of measurement for what ought to be done. This cut away any absolute measure or standard by which to judge what action should be taken. (Utilitarians inclined toward democracy, toward determination by the majority of what would conduce to the greatest happiness.) This opened the way for reform in many directions.

At any rate, Bentham and his followers were enthusiastic reformers. One historian notes that "Bentham had a genius for practical reform. From his tireless pen flowed a series of projects for the practical reform of everything: schools, prisons, courts, laws.... By sheer energy and perseverance, Bentham and his followers ... forced upon the public constant consideration of the question, 'What good is it? Can it be improved?'"[6] John Stuart Mill edged closer and closer toward some degree of some sort of socialism as he grew old, and was for a considerable while under the influence of Comte's thought.[7] The thrust of the utilitarians was toward the extension of the suffrage, educational oportunity for everyone, reform of the Constitution, reform of the laws, and so on. By the time of William Gladstone and the emergence of the Liberal party, these ideas were bearing fruit in proposals to restrict the sale of alcoholic beverages and the supplanting of church controlled education for some state variety.

The utilitarian influence or bearing on Fabianism was threefold, then. The utilitarians made reform respectable, and established a bent in that direction. The utilitarians championed political democracy (and Mill especially emphasized freedom of expression) which would be taken up by the Fabians. Thirdly, Fabians harked back to particular thinkers in support of some of their ideas. One writer says, "The derivation of Fabian ideas from the Liberal tradition has always been stressed by historians, and the Fabians themselves insisted on it, sprinkling their writings plentifully with footnotes and other references to John Stuart Mill, the contemporary Liberal economists and other respectable authors."[8]

But there was an important influence on the Fabians — or a current which they could use — from the natural law side of liberalism too. This may be a good place to note that any idea or philosophy can have some aspect of it abstracted so as to be used for quite different ends than its general tendency. This was what happened, at any rate, to an aspect of the natural law philosophy. A line of thought was developed in this way that led to the justification of a major government intervention. Several people traveled a similar route to this conclusion, but for reasons that will appear the American Henry George's thought may be used to exemplify this particular usage.

Henry George was in the line of natural law thought. More specifically, he was a latter-day Physiocrat. The Physiocrats had sought for a natural order for economy, and they had placed great emphasis upon land and agriculture. George started from these premises and arrived at the conclusion that rent on land, or some portion of it, is unearned by the landlord — is an "unearned increment" — is not rightfully his, and should be appropriated by the government to be used for the benefit of society, which is the original source of this rent. The Fabians were early acquainted with this doctrine, though they were more inclined to use Marx's phrase "surplus value" than George's "unearned increment." Even so, George's reformism by way of taxation was grist for their mill.

George's *Progress and Poverty* was published in 1879. He made speaking tours in England in 1882 and again in 1884. One writer goes as far as to say that "four-fifths of the socialist leaders of Great Britain in the 'eighties had passed through the school of Henry George."[9] Another historian declares that George's *Progress and Poverty* was the starting point for Fabian socialism.[10] Another says, more circumspectly: "His eloquent writing and lectures brought many young men of the 'eighties, including some Fabians, to think along lines which were to lead them to Socialism."[11] If any doubt of his influence remains, George Bernard Shaw's testimony should clinch the argument. "I am glad to say," Shaw wrote, "that I have never denied or belittled our debt to Henry George."[12]

The Conservative party prepared the way and helped to establish the tendency for reformism in England also. This was especially true of it under the leadership of Benjamin Disraeli. In his novels Disraeli displayed his interest in and concern for poverty. One writer says that "he believed that the conditions of the common man could be improved by government action. He was, indeed, a believer in the maxim that much should be done for the people but very little by the people."[13] In 1875, when Disraeli finally had an assured parliamentary majority behind him as Prime Minister, he began to press through a number of reform measuires. A Trade Union Act was passed, an Artisans' Dwellings Act, a Food and Drugs Act, and a Public Health Act.[14]

But of equal or greater importance than the Conservative championing of reformism, usually dubbed "Tory paternalism," was something which the Fabians must have imbibed from conservative philosophy. The *gradualist* approach to socialism is rooted in an abstraction from conservative sociology, whose progenitor was surely Edmund Burke. Implicitly, Burke tells us much about how society must be changed, to the extent that it can be successfully changed. Society is an organism, Burke held, and it cannot be changed or altered casually, or at will. Such changes as occur must not be offensive to the system as it is, should be in accord with it, and must be introduced slowly so as not to shock it. Now Fabians really had no objection to a socialist revolution, at least most did not, but they did not believe that this could be accomplished in England. Thus, their gradualist tactics at least accorded with a widespread English belief which owed much to conservative thought, however offensive what they introduced might actually be to the English system.

Another element that went into the Fabian view, a current which they could turn into their own stream, was the evolutionary theory of development. For several decades prior to the organization of the Society, the evolutionary conception of things had been gaining sway, particularly as a result of Hegel's philosophy of history, Charles Lyell's *Principles of Geology,* Herbert Spencer's *Social Statics,* and Charles Darwin's *Origin of the Species* and *Descent of Man.* Evolutionary theories were particularly important to utopians and socialists because they could be interpreted so as to give the impression that everything was changing, that nothing was fixed, and that all things were possible. This was another source and support, too, of the notion of making changes gradually. In view of the currency of these ideas, "it was only to be expected that the Fabians would avail themselves of these ideas to justify their programme. The extent to which they did so may be seen in several theoretical Tracts written for the Society at different times by Sidney Webb, and also in *Fabian Essays....*"[15]

Marxism was a major influence on the Fabians. In this case, however, the adoption of Marxist ideas did not give added impetus to the Fabian cause. On the contrary, they would be an impediment at this time. Hence, Fabians were disinclined to ascribe ideas to Marx or to credit him where credit was due. But the Fabians were socialists, and there is good reason to believe that their socialism was informed by Marxist ideas. The Marxist influence can be shown both by external and internal evidence. H. M. Hyndman, leader of the Social Democratic Federation in England, was greatly influenced by Marx.[16] He published two books at a crucial time which was largely cribbed from Marx's writings:

England for All (1881) and *Historical Basis of Socialism in England* (1883). A number of the early Fabians were deeply involved with the Social Democratic Federation. Not only that but also early reading lists for the Society indicate that several of Marx's works were available and presumably read. As one writer says, "The particular kind of Marxist works in currency amongst the Fabians had an effect on the development of their own theory...."[17] He notes that the *Fabian Essays* reveal "a number of elements taken over from Marxist theory. In addition to the emphasis on the role of the working-class in bringing Socialism into existence, the doctrines of the narrowing of the numbers of the capitalist class and the increasing misery of the working-class can both be found there...."[18] It is worth noting, too, that both George Bernard Shaw and Sidney Webb virtaully embraced Russian communism later in their lives.[19]

One other current present at the time greatly assisted the Fabians in the spread of socialism. It was utopianism. The great age of utopian literature, particularly the utopian novel, in English was from 1883 to 1912. Some seventy-four works appeared during this period.[20] According to one historian, the most influential of these works on British socialists were two books by Americans: Laurence Gronlund's *Co-operative Commonwealth* (1884) and Edward Bellamy's *Looking Backward* (1888). But the English also published important works of the genre: William Morris, *News from Nowhere* (1891), and Robert Blatchford, *Merrie England,* the latter selling over a million copies.[21] It is important to keep in mind, too, that utopian literature was frequently vague about how socialism was to be obtained but provided glowing pictures of the ideal society that would emerge. This helped greatly in popularizing socialist goals.

From these elements, however disparate and antagonistic they may have been at the time, the Fabians concocted a blend which has come to be known as Fabianism. They fatefully linked government action (reformism) with the thrust to socialism. By so doing, they provided a *modus operandi* for achieving their goals which became increasingly believable to many people. By riding certain currents that were underway, they began to achieve respectability for their doctrines. In contrast to America, "socialism" became a word to conjure with in England rather than a dirty word. This should be attributed mainly to the Fabians and their methods. Moreover, they linked gradualism and democracy to the movement toward socialism, thus making it that much more acceptable. The Fabians were not so much original in conceiving

217

any of the elements as they were successful fusionists and propagandists. It was by their efforts, more than others, that England was bent toward socialism.

17
The Fabian Program

THE MOVEMENT TOWARD socialism in England was guided, directed, and pressed by the Fabians. Of course, others had a hand in it: Marxists, cooperative commonwealthers, Christian socialists, land nationalizers, syndicalists, utopians, Liberals, and labor unions, to name a partial list. But the Fabians were central to the undertaking. From the mid-1880's, they pressed vigorously and along many lines for the socialization of England. Most of the big names in English socialism eventually either became Fabians or were closely associated with them. The Fabians moved most unerringly toward political power, provided additional impetus to every rising current, gave the movement its aura of intellectual respectability, and trained so many of the leaders who would move into the political sphere. An examination of the Fabian program, too, will show that the means employed in the movement toward socialism in England were generally those advocated by the Fabians. What follows is an outline of the Fabian program as it was set forth from the 1880's into the early twentieth century, mainly in the Fabian Tracts.

The goal of the Fabians was socialism. They never made any secret of this, and, indeed, on many occasions affirmed it. For example, Tract #7 proclaims that "The Fabian Society consists of Socialists." It goes on to explain what that means:

It therefore aims at the re-organization of Society by the emancipation of

219

Land and Industrial Capital from individual and class ownership, and the vesting of them in the community for the general benefit....

The Society accordingly works for the extinction of private property in Land and of the consequent individual appropriation, in the form of Rent, of the price paid for permission to use the earth, as well as for the advantages of superior soils and sites.

The Society, further, works for the transfer to the community of the administration of such industrial Capital as can conveniently be managed socially....

The Fabians proposed to achieve these ends by the use of governmental power. The matter is bluntly stated in Tract #70: "The Socialism advocated by the Fabian Society is State Socialism exclusively." More comprehensively, "Socialism, as understood by the Fabian Society, means the organization and conduct of the necessary industries of the country and the appropriation of all forms of economic rent of land and capital by the nation as a whole, through the most suitable public authorities, parochial, municipal, provincial, or central."

However, Fabians claimed to favor constitutional means of taking over the government in England and to be advocates of democracy. Sidney Webb claimed in Tract #70 that the "Fabian Society is perfectly constitutional in its attitude; and its methods are those usual in political life in England." Moreover:

The Fabian Society accepts the conditions imposed on it by human nature and by the national character and political circumstances of the English people....

Elsewhere, he affirmed that "all students of society who are abreast of their time, Socialists as well as Individualists, realize that important organic changes can only be ... democratic, and thus acceptable to a majority of the people, and prepared for in the minds of all...."[1] It should be clear, however, that considerable constitutional changes in the structure of English governmental power would have to be made before socialist programs could be made into law and that democracy in their hands would take on new connotations.

If George Bernard Shaw can be accepted as a spokesman for the Fabians, they believed in equality. In a speech before the National Liberal Club in 1913, he had this to say:

When I speak of The Case of Equality I mean human equality; and that, of course, can only mean one thing: it means equality of income. It means that if one person is to have half a crown, the other is to have two and sixpence. It means that precisely.... The fact is that you cannot equalize anything about human beings except their incomes....[2]

The chances are good, however, that Shaw was going beyond what the Fabian Society would have wanted to declare. Perhaps, some such equality was an ultimate goal, but, in practice, the Fabians only pressed toward it, as was their way, in gradual increments.

The favorite tactic of the Fabians for pressing England toward socialism was one they called "permeation." "In its most general sense, it meant that Fabians should join all organizations where useful Socialist work could be done, and influence them.... Taking a broad interpretation of the meaning of Socialism and having an optimistic belief in their powers of persuasion, the Fabians thought that most organizations would be willing to accept at least a grain or two of Socialism. It was mainly a matter of addressing them reasonably, with a strong emphasis on facts, diplomatically, with an eye to the amount of Socialism they were prepared to receive, and in a conciliatory spirit."[3] In the following, Shaw tells how they actually achieved "permeation" in 1888:

We urged our members to join the Liberal and Radical Associations of their districts, or, if they preferred it, the Conservative Associations. We told them to become members of the nearest Radical Club and Co-operative Store, and to get delegated to the Metropolitan Radical Federation and the Liberal and Radical Union if possible. On these bodies we made speeches and moved resolutions, or, better still, got the Parliamentary candidate for the constituency to move them, and secured reports and encouraging little articles for him in the *Star*. We permeated the party organizations and pulled all the wires we could lay our hands on with our utmost adroitness and energy; and we succeeded so far that in 1888 we gained the solid advantage of a Progressive majority, full of ideas that would never have come into their heads had not the Fabians put them there, on the first London County Council. (Tract #41).

It is not necessary, of course, to accept at face value all the claims of success of Fabians, for they were never modest in their claims, in order to see that this is how they intended to operate by "permeation."

In Tract #7, the Fabians described the activities which they were to pursue in the following way:

1. Meetings for the discussion of questions connected with socialism.
2. The further investigation of economic problems, and the collection of facts contributing to their elucidation.

221

3. The issue of publications containing information on social questions, and arguments relating to socialism.
4. The promotion of socialist lectures and debates in other societies and clubs.
5. The representation of the society in public conferences and discussions on social questions.

Actually, the Fabians engaged in a wide range of activities: holding their own meetings, issuing tracts, doing research, joining organizations, engaging in socio-political gatherings, using their individual talents in subtle ways to promote socialism, writing letters to editors, making speeches, and so on.

They cast their nets as wide as possible to draw in as many as possible of the wide range of people with beliefs amenable to some degree of socialist activity. While they usually rejected any particular panacea, as, for example, syndicalism and revolution, this did not mean that they rejected the people of these persuasions. The Fabians did not neglect to appeal to Christian socialists. Several of the Tracts are devoted to this subject. They attempt to show that there is a close affinity between socialism and Christianity and, indeed, that the attainment of socialism is a necessary framework for realizing the ideals of Christianity. The Reverend John Clifford conveys this character of the appeal in the following excerpts from Tract #78:

> Another sign of the closer kinship of Collectivism to the mind of Christ is *in the elevation and nobility it gives to the struggle for life.* Collectivism does not extinguish combat, but it lifts the struggle into the worthiest spheres, reduces it to a minimum in the lower and animal departments, and so leaves man free for the finer toils of intellect and heart; free "to seek first the Kingdom of God...."
> Again, Collectivism affords a better environment for the teachings of Jesus concerning wealth and the ideals of labor and brotherhood. If man is ... only "the expression of his environment," if, indeed, he is that in any degree, then it is an unspeakable gain to bring that environment into line with the teaching of Jesus Christ.

Nor were the Fabians above appealing to communists. In Tract #113, they published a lecture that had been delivered by William Morris in which he held that "between complete Socialism and Communism there is no difference whatever in my mind. Communism is in fact the completion of Socialism: when that ceases to be militant and becomes triumphant, it will be Communism."

The Fabians, then, tended to be all things to all men that they might win people to socialism. Nowhere is this clearer than in the particular programs they advocated. Here they appeared to be completely eclectic.

They had few biases against any type of program so long as it was in the general direction of socialism. Such eclecticism has come to be known as pragmatism in reformist circles, but this is only another instance of how socialists take words out of context and give them their own content. For the English Fabians have been no more pragmatic in testing the value of their programs against their ultimate results than have American reformers. They have only been pragmatic in the sense that they tested an approach by how successful it was in actually getting a program put into effect.

In any case, the Fabians advocated, from the first, a wide range of programs. They embraced government intervention and ameliorative reform, though these were, from their point of view, half-way measures at best. For example, a number of the Tracts are concerned with changes in and administration of the Poor Laws. The following argument, in Tract #54, is clearly melioristic:

The expense of relieving the poor, who are not wilfully improvident, is part of the ransom that Property has to pay to Labor; and it is a ransom which is not begged as a charity but demanded as an instalment of justice. With the growth of enlightenment and the spread of humane ideas amongst all classes, and consequently greater intelligence amongst the mass of voters in the use of their political power, we shall have better laws better administered. The worn-out, deserving worker will be maintained in self-respect in his old age; the temporarily disabled will be helped without pauperization....

Of a similar ameliorative character was the proposal for a national minimum wage law advanced in Tract #127. (Incidentally, the title of this Tract is "Socialism and Labor Policy," and it was published in 1906). The proposal reads, in part:

Of far greater urgency and importance is the need for a minimum wage by law.... Every worker in a civilized state must receive a wage high enough to give him the food, clothing and house-room necessary to physical health and efficiency....

The first step towards this end should be the determination of a real minimum of food, clothing and housing by an authority appointed by the government.... Then the government should be pressed to put its own house in order by the institution of a minimum in the public service throughout the kingdom. A Minimum Wages Bill should follow, bringing all sweated trades within the scope of the law, and punishing all employers who, after a certain date, pay less than the legal minimum....

The Fabians worked at many levels and addressed themselves to

223

many different audiences. Even the different Tracts were apparently aimed at people of widely varying degrees of receptivity to socialism. One might be addressed to something as unrevolutionary as the Poor Laws. On the other hand, the next might deal with the intricacies of socialist theory, while a third might be burdened down with statistics about conditions in laundries in England. The immediate thrust of the Fabians was to get the government involved in as many economic activities as possible. The long range aim, of course, was to achieve government ownership and control over the major means of production and distribution of goods and services. This goal could be painlessly achieved, or so they claimed. Tract #13 put the matter this way:

> The establishment of Socialism, when once the people are resolved upon it, is not so difficult as might be supposed. If a man wishes to work on his own account, the rent of his place of business, and the interest on the capital needed to start him, can be paid to the City Council of his district just as easily as to the private landlord and capitalist. Factories are already largely regulated by public inspectors, and can be conducted by the local authorities just as gas-works, water-works and tramways are now conducted by them in various towns. Railways and mines, instead of being left to private companies, can be carried on by a department under the central government, as the postal and telegraph services are carried on now. The Income Tax collector who to-day calls for a tax of a few pence in the pound on the income of the idle millionaire, can collect a tax of twenty shillings in the pound on every unearned income in the country if the State so orders....

This was the large plan, but each step had to be taken in its own time, and particular arguments were advanced for each one. A favorite mode of argument was to use analogy with some service government already performed to claim that another should be brought under the arm of government. For example, here is the argument for municipal milk supply in Tract #90:

> If we want good milk, let us establish our own dairy farms in the country and our milk stores in the city. Many of our large towns have spent enormous sums of money to provide their citizens with water: why should they not also provide them with milk? the arguments in favor of municipal water apply with greatest force to municipal milk....

In the early years, the Fabians directed much of their attention to getting local governments to take over enterprises. The Tracts called for "municipalization" much more frequently than for nationalization. Tract #91 called for municipal pawnshops. Tract #92 advocated

224

municipal slaughterhouses. Tract #94 advanced the notion of having municipal bakeries. There appears to have been no particular order of priorities, for municipal hospitals did not gain the limelight until Tract #95. Municipal steamboats got full attention in Tract #97. The argument for municipal slaughterhouses was similar to the others in many respects, so it may be presented in brief:

> Many of our private slaughterhouses are in so insanitary a condition that the meat is exposed to foul emanations from drains, decomposing blood, offal, etc. They may easily become a source of grave danger to the surrounding districts. In municipal slaughterhouses, on the other hand, the buildings are especially designed for their purpose; they are kept in good sanitary condition, and the meat is therefore not subject to deterioration....

The Fabian Society had earlier, in Tract #86, called for the municipalization of liquor traffic.

Provisions existed from 1890 onwards for municipalities to build houses for private occupancy, and the Fabians wished to accelerate this kind of activity. In Tract #76 they noted that the "provision of housing accommodation for the industrial classes has hitherto been left almost entirely in the hands of private enterprise, with the inevitable result that high rents are exacted for the privilege of occupying squalid dwellings whose very existence is a grave social danger." They give this advice: "In order to get the Acts utilized by the local sanitary authority, it is advisable to carefully collect facts relating to insanitary areas and dwellings, and thus to prove the necessity for municipal action. In large towns the work of demonstrating such need is only too easy."

Of course, the Fabians did not overlook a prominent role for the national government and for nationalizing. Local governments in England are, in their inception, creatures of Parliament, and their activities have been at one time or another authorized by that body. Thus, whatever body undertook socialization directly, its activities would be authorized and could be directed by Parliament. In Tract #108 the Fabians advocated "National Efficiency," and a "National Minimum" for working conditions, for housing, for standards of living, and for education.

To achieve this, they proposed the use of grants-in-aid, a device with which Americans have since become familiar. Their argument for the grant-in-aid is sufficiently revealing of the way they advanced an idea to be worth examining briefly. They described it as a middle way between centralization and local autonomy. "The middle way has, for half a

225

century, been found through that most advantageous of expedients, the grant in aid. We see this in its best form in the police grant." According to the Tract, local police were frequently ineffective, and poorer districts were not financially able to maintain efficient police. "A grant in aid of the cost of the local police force was offered to the justices and town councilors — at first one quarter, and now one half, of their actual expenditure on this service, however large this may be."

But for activities which were nationwide, the Fabians proposed nationalization. It is clear, too, that even where the activity was not truly nationwide, they were thinking of national planning for and control of it. For example, Tract #125 deals with the question of electricity and street transportation. The author(s) argues that the provision of these services efficiently extends beyond the bounds of any municipality. He proposes, then, that the country be divided into several provinces, in each of which there will be a provincial board empowered by Parliament to plan for these services. Nationalization, however, appears to be the ultimate aim. For they say:

The establishment of a system of provincial boards as here indicated does not exhaust the possibilities of coordination of area in connection with local government and the collective control of industry. In course of time it will be found possible to carrry the development a stage further, and from the Provincial Boards to elect National Boards, which would stand in the same relation to the Provinces as the Co-operative Wholesale Society does to the various societies which are its component parts. For instance, a national Board elected from the provincial Transit and Electricity Boards might be empowered to carry on the work of building rolling stock by direct employment in its own workshops for the whole of the publicly owned transit services of the country. It might also start factories for the manufacture of tramway rails and motor cars. It could undertake the work of constructing plants of all kinds for publicly owned electric light and power installations. Various local authorities build their own vans, carts, and wagons, and there is no reason why tramcars could not be built in a public workshop with equal ease....

The above has been quoted at length because it indicates how Fabians would move from local activity to regional control to nationalization to socialism.

Some nationalization was to be more directly undertaken, as they envisioned it. Tract #119 called for the direct nationalization of the railways and merchant marine. This would involve some kind of confiscation, as they foresaw. Of course, the owners should be compensated, but the Fabians proposed that the compensation should only constitute a payment of profits to shareholders, not the return of

226

their capital investment. In short, the capital would simply be expropriated. As for agriculture, Tract #123 says: "Our ultimate aim is to bring the whole of the land into national ownership...." Land would be acquired in much the same way as railroads and shipping. "The Committee would have power to acquire land compulsorily. If a fair rent had already been fixed, then the purchase would proceed on the lines of securing to the vendor his net income, that is, the rent.... If such a rent has not been fixed, then its ascertainment would form a preliminary to purchase."

Thus would England proceed step by step toward complete socialism. This involved no necessary order to action. Each step would draw the country inexorably toward the next, or toward others. Government ownership at any level of anything would prepare the English mentally for ownership at another level of something else. Government planning of one activity would make necessary the planning of associated activities. Since an economy is ultimately inextricably intertwined, it must all be eventually socialized to attain national integrity. The productivity and flexibility of private enterprise could be continued without what were for them the infelicities of private ownership, and all could be achieved without anyone being greatly hurt.

This was the Fabian blueprint for England. The Fabians were remarkably provincial. The rest of the world concerned them hardly at all in the early years. That England was the world's financier during the years in which they were constructing their pipe dream hardly concerned them. But they were probably as innocent of knowledge about international finance as they were of how to milk cows. Yet the English people were greatly attracted to these notions, and they were drawn into the political efforts by which the blueprints were supposed to result in a new edifice.

18

Reform Ideas Into Political Action

JUST WHEN GOVERNMENT intervention in England had been introduced on a scale sufficient to mark the turn from the liberal state to the interventionist welfare state is problematical and conjectural. There never was a time when there was not some government intervention, of course. Probably the high tide of liberty generally was from the late 1840's to the late 1860's, though the tendency had been in that direction for more than a century and a half preceding the mid-nineteenth century. Some measures smacking of the new intervention were passed in the 1830's and 1840's, even before the repeal of the last of the major mercantilist measures. And there should be no doubt that intervention gained headway once more from the 1860's onward.

Writing in 1884, Herbert Spencer perceived already the oppressive character of the trend:

Dictatorial measures, rapidly multiplied, have tended continually to narrow the liberties of individuals; and have done this in a double way. Regulations have been made in yearly-growing numbers, restraining the citizen in directions where his actions were previously unchecked, and compelling actions which previously he might perform or not as he liked; and at the same time heavier public burdens, chiefly local, have further restricted his freedom, by lessening

228

that portion of his earnings which he can spend as he pleases, and augmenting the portion taken from him to be spent as public agents please.[1]

Spencer gives such examples as the following: an act passed in 1860 providing for the inspection of gas works, establishing quality controls and controlling prices; an act of 1863 requiring compulsory vaccination in Scotland and Ireland; an act of 1866 regulating cattle sheds and allowing local authorities power to inspect sanitary conditions; the establishment in 1869 of a state telegraph system; an act of 1873 requiring merchant vessels to show the draught of the boat by a scale and making it necessary for ships to carry certain life-saving equipment. "Again, there is the Act which ... forbids the payment of wages to workmen at or within public-houses; there is another Factory and Workshops Act, commanding inspection of white lead works ... and of bakehouses, regulating times of employment in both, and prescribing in detail some constructions for the last, which are to be kept in a condition satisfactory to the inspectors."[2]

On the other hand, one historian holds that the fabric of English liberty had hardly been rent as late as 1914:

Until August 1914 a sensible, law-abiding Englishman could pass through life and hardly notice the existence of the state, beyond the post office and the policeman. He could live where he liked and as he liked. He had no official number or identity card. He could travel abroad or leave his country for ever without a passport or any sort of official permission. He could exchange his money for any other currency without restriction or limit. He could buy goods from any country in the world on the same terms as he bought goods at home.... An Englishman could enlist, if he chose, in the regular army, the navy, or the territorials. He could also ignore, if he chose, the demands of national defence. Substantial householders were occasionally called on for jury service. Otherwise, only those helped the state who wished to do so. The Englishman paid taxes on a modest scale....

Even so, he notes that the "tendency towards more state action was increasing."[3]

Actually, though, most historians are inclined to fix the date of the turning point toward government intervention and welfare state in the year 1906. Better still, that year may be taken as the consolidation of the turning, for the turn to a new direction had been building for a goodly number of years. Invervention had been increasing; both major parties had come to champion various sorts of intervention; the thrust to socialism was making an ever stronger impact. Within the next 15 years following 1906 major changes would be made — by legislative acts, within the constitution, by the concentration of power, and changes within party strength — which would set England firmly on its road toward socialism.

Nineteen hundred six was the signal year because of the results of the general election which was held. The Liberals came to power with 377 members in the House of Commons to only 157 for the Conservatives. In itself, the return of the Liberals to power would hardly have been remarkable, for they had many times controlled the government in the nineteenth century. But they were not the Liberals that had once held power. One historian described the change in this way: "Nineteenth-century liberalism ... did not win in 1906. In domestic affairs the real significance of the election is in its impetus to social democracy: the rising demand for better standards of living for the workingmen, for greater equality of opportunity, for limitations of economic privilege and for security against sickness, unemployment and old age."[4] Reformist ideas had made deep inroads into this old party. Of great importance, too, 53 Labour Party men were elected to the House, the first time that party had any representation to speak of. Moreover, their victory and subsequent activity indicates the way the Liberals were moving.

In 1903, Liberal and Labour representatives had worked out an agreement to concert their efforts against the common Conservative enemy.[5] In payment for this, for the next several years Labour members usually voted with the Liberals. In addition, as the result of the election of 1906 there were 83 Irish Nationalists in the House. "The Liberals had thus a majority of 84 over all the other parties combined, and on the natural assumption that they would for most purposes be supported by the Labour men and the Nationalists they could expect a majority of something like 400. There had never been anything like it before...."[6]

There followed a spate of legislation which began to turn England into a welfare state. In 1906, a Workmen's Compensation Act was passed, greatly extending the coverage of an earlier act. An Education Act was passed which provided for the provision of meals for needy school children. While the act only permitted such action, it did acknowledge the principle of government responsibility, a considerable breakthrough.[7] The Fabians had, of course, advanced the idea for such a measure.

Of somewhat different character — though generally reckoned to be of greater significance — was the passage of the Trade Disputes Act. This legislation was passed to alter the effects of the Taff Vale Decision made by the House of Lords in 1901. The Lords had held that a union was financially responsible for damages it had done by a strike against a railroad. The Liberal ministry introduced a measure in 1906 to deal with the matter. However, it was unsatisfactory to Labour members, and one of them submitted a simple measure which was then passed. It provided that labor unions were not financially responsible for damage occurring during strikes. It also authorized peaceful picketing, or, in effect, trespass.[8]

Further legislation was passed in 1908-1909 taking England toward the welfare state. Of considerable importance as a step was the Old Age Pensions Act. This act provided that everyone, with a few exceptions, who had an annual income of less than 21 pounds would receive a pension of five shillings per week at the age of seventy. Protective legislation was passed for workers in the coal mines, limiting the hours of work for adult male workers to 8 hours per day. Earlier legislation had regulated such employment for women and children, but this was the first for adult males. The Labor Exchange Act provided for employment offices to be set up over the country. Another act set up Trade Boards for certain of the so-called "sweated" industries. These gained the power to establish minimum wages for certain trades. This "established the revolutionary principle of fixing by law 'a decent wage' in industries not protected by unions."[9]

The National Insurance Act of 1911 was another major step. This was compulsory contributory health insurance for a large portion of the populace of England. It applied mainly to people remuneratively employed, and covered such things as medical treatment, hospital care, and compensation during incapacity. There was also attached to this act a provision for unemployment compensation.[10]

But before the passage of this last act, important constitutional changes had been initiated from the House of Commons. The House of Lords had been reduced to a virtual nonentity in the Parliament. What was involved was the destruction of the centuries-old balance of power in the English government. This action was preceded, however, by a long-term decline in the powers of the monarch. Before telling the story of the assault upon the House of Lords, then, it is in order to survey the power situation and call attention to the decline of monarchical powers.

Since the late seventeenth century, England had a precariously balanced system of power dispositions. The executive power was vested in the monarch, though it came increasingly to be exercised through Parliament. The legislative authority belonged to Parliament, with

231

much of the initiative located in the House of Commons because that body only could originate money bills. Even so, the negative power of the Lords was great, for that body could not only amend and veto bills but was also the highest court in the land. The independence of the courts was fully established in the latter part of the eighteenth century.

The powers of the constitutionally limited monarch reached their peak under George III (1760-1820). That stubborn ruler was able to bend Parliament to his will in the latter part of the eighteenth century by various expedients, not least of which was the buying of members by astute dispensation of privileges and incomes. Neither of the two dissolute monarchs who followed him for brief reigns — George IV (1820-1830) nor William IV (1830-1837) — were such as would build the power of the office or endear the people to the institution. Queen Victoria (1837-1901) did re-establish monarchy in the affections of the people and stamp the age with her name, but the power continued to slip away. By a series of acts the franchise wa extended to more and more of the populace, and the democratic ethos that came increasingly to prevail made it appear unseemly for hereditary authority to be exercised. One historian notes that between "1874 and 1914, while the person of the monarch may even have gained importance as a figure-head, it steadily lost power as a factor in government."[11]

Just how low monarchy had sunk can be illustrated by the following occurrence. The Liberals thought that it might be necessary to have the King appoint hundreds of new Lords in order to get a bill to reduce their power through that House. In any case, Prime Minister Asquith wanted to be able to use this possibility as a threat, so he approached the new king, George V, about the matter in secret in 1910. The exchange went something like this. Mr. Asquith asked:

> *If* he took the responsibility of advising another election and *if* he then retained his majority, would the King agree to create peers?
> The King ... asked if that was the advice which would have been tendered to his father. "Yes, sir," said Mr. Asquith, "and your father would have consented." So George V agreed that there seemed to be no alternative.[12]

The natural affinity of the monarch was with the House of Lords. It was largely an hereditary institution, and its members at one time or another resulted from his appointment. Yet so tenuous had the position become that the King dare not resist the request of the leader of the Commons, though that request be for an action that would lead to the diminution of the powers of the Lords.

By the early twentieth century, then, there remained only one major check on the power of Commons — the ancient House of Lords. To say that the Constitution checked Commons was litle more than to say that the Lords checked them, for without the Lords to interpret that tradition, the Constitution would become what Commons would make of it. Undoubtedly, too, power had been gravitating toward the Commons for a long time. Lord Salisbury resigned as Prime Minister in 1902, and he was the last Peer to head a government.[13]

However unideal some of its members might be as individuals, the ·House of Lords was in many respects an ideal body to check the Commons. It did not depend upon the populace for selection. On the other hand, it posed virtually no threat to the liberties of Englishmen, for it was unlikely to originate any legislation. But because of its independence it could serve to limit government to protect the traditional liberties of Englishmen.

There is considerable evidence that many of the Lords were intent on doing just that in the early twentieth century. Their overwhelming victory in 1906 had placed unprecedented power in the hands of Liberals in Commons. The opposition party was reduced to an ineffectual minority. There was, however, a potential counterbalance to overweening partisan action in the Lords. Though the Lords were not technically members of a political party, in their inclinations they lined up this way, according to one tabulation: 355 Conservatives, 88 Liberals, 124 Liberal Unionists (who had lately been inclined to vote with Conservatives):[14]

While the Lords did not prevent some reform measures from passing, they did tend to place restraints on the reformers. The Liberals in Commons found a number of their measures rejected by the Lords. An Education Bill was greatly altered in the hereditary House. That body rejected a Plural Voting Bill, and vetoed, in effect, a Licensing Bill aimed at curtailing the number of Public Houses.[15] And though historians have not generally made much of the fact in this context, the House of Lords ruled in 1909 that labor unions could not use compulsorily collected dues for political purposes.

The event which precipitated the crisis, however, was the Budget Bill of 1909. There are indications that the Liberals in Commons were ready to reduce the power of the Lords almost from the moment they came to power, but the budget affair gave them the occasion. Some of the provisions of the budget were startling enough.

Its unusual features were these: (1) sharp increases in death duties (inheritance taxes): for example, estates of £1,000,000 and over were to be taxed at about 25 per cent; (2) increases in income tax schedules which continued the distinction between earned and unearned income first made in 1907; on incomes of £5,000 or more there was to be an additional super-tax, an innovation; (3) land taxes, of which the most significant was a 20 per cent tax on the unearned increment in value when land changed hands; (4) higher levies on tobacco and spirits.[16]

The House of Lords rejected the budget by a vote of 350 against to 75 for.

This budget reads as if it might have been the result of a collaboration between Karl Marx of the time of *The Communist Manifesto* and Henry George of the somewhat later *Progress and Poverty*, with bemused Fabians peering over their shoulder. Actually, of course, it was the work of David Lloyd George. Lloyd George played such a significant role in these years in the centralization of power in the Commons, in its concentration in the Prime Minister, and in the demise of the Liberal Party that he deserves a little closer look. In 1909, he was a member of the House, a Liberal, and Chancellor of the Exchequer in the government of Asquith. He was of obscure Welsh parentage, and came to the fore in the late 1890's as a Welsh nationalist, radical, and outspoken critic of the Conservatives.

Lloyd George was indeed influenced by Henry George,[17] had obviously adopted some of his central terminology, and would off and on devote himself to schemes for land reform for the rest of his political career. He was a socialist, too, in all but name. His budget was a "war budget," he said, a budget for a war on poverty; as a result of which he hoped that poverty would become "as remote to the people of this country as the wolves which once infested its forests."[18] One writer describes him in this way:

> If his convictions had been otherwise than emotional, he would have been a Socialist by this time. . . . He was less a Liberal than a Welshman on the loose. He wanted the poor to inherit the earth, particularly if it was the earth of rich English landlords. . . .[19]

Whether chosen for the spot or not, he was to spearhead the movement to destroy the older British order and set the stage for full-fledged socialism.

Following the rejection of the budget in 1909, the movement to reduce the powers of the Lords accelerated. It did not reach its fruition, however, until two elections had been held, and a new monarch had come to the throne. The House of Lords was shorn of most of its powers by the Parliament Act of 1911. It provided that, in the case of money bills, if they are not passed without amendment by the upper house within one month, they become law without the assent of that body. In the case of most other bills, if they are passed by the House of Commons once in each of three successive sessions, they can become law if the Lords refuse their assent.[20] The Lords could now delay legislation temporarily, but they could no longer prevent its passage. All governmental power was now centered in the House of Commons. The forms by which power had been balanced were outwardly preserved in the institutions of monarchy and an upper house, but the content was gone from them.

The concentration of executive power in the hands of the Prime Minister occurred during World War I. The man who did it was, once again, David Lloyd George. H. H. Asquith had formed a coalition government in 1915, with the Liberals preponderating in it. But he gave way in 1916 to new leadership headed by Lloyd George. The latter proceeded as quickly as possible to concentrate effective power in his own hands. One historian described the development this way: "Lloyd George's accession to power in December 1916 was more than a change of government. It was a revolution British-style. The party magnates and the whips had been defied. The backbenchers and the newspapers combined in a sort of unconscious plebiscite and made Lloyd George dictator for the duration of the war."[21]

The traditional cabinet was subordinated, its members losing most of their historic independence. Most of the governmental functions were directed by a "war cabinet" made up of five members who were chosen primarily to execute the will of Lloyd George. "Lloyd George's war cabinet was a committee of public safety, exercising supreme command under his direction.... The holders of the other great historic offices merely received their marching orders."[22]

In effect, the government took over the direction of many facets of the lives of Englishmen during World War I. Military conscription was instituted; the merchant marine was appropriated; the mines were taken over. The whole paraphernalia of controls, with which peoples have become familiar in wartime, were introduced: price controls, rent controls, rationing, allocation of materials, manipulation of the money supply, confiscatory taxation, and so on. Some British historians call this development "war socialism." The phrase is apt, for socialism is the generic term to describe the large role that government assumed in the lives of the people during the war.

It is a commonplace of historical generalization that this development was born of wartime expediency. This judgment should not be casually accepted. Undoubtedly, socialists have discovered grist for their mills in the methods employed during wars. But have they not also helped to shape those methods? There is no doubt that England was being bent toward socialism before the war came. Lloyd George was full of plans for accomplishing what should certainly be called socialistic, at the least. Given the occasion of the war, he would think in such terms to deal with it. So would many another.

An inkling of the nonexpedient character of much compulsion may be gained from the matter of military conscription. A Military Service Act was passed in January 1916 introducing such conscription. Yet one historian points out: "The army had more men than it could equip, and voluntary recruitment would more than fill the gap, at any rate until the end of 1916. Auckland Geddes, who was in the best position to know, later pronounced this verdict: 'The imposition of military conscription added litle if anything to the effective sum of our war efforts.'"[23] David Lloyd George wanted it, and much of the country had apparently come to favor such compulsion.

One other major development needs to be told here: the decline of the Liberal Party and the rise of the Labour Party. The election of 1922 foreshadowed the downfall of the Liberals. The Conservatives won with 347 members elected; the Labourites came in second with 142; the Liberals were a poor third with 117, and these were divided about equally between followers of Asquith and Lloyd George. The Liberals gained a few members in the election of 1923, but they were still the third party. A new election in 1924 returned only 42 Liberals, and a one-time major party had fallen from the national councils.

It can be argued that the Liberal Party was on the way out, in any case. The party had been increasingly abandoning the historic principles of liberalism. In the nineteenth century, the Liberals had championed free trade and generally worked for the removal of governmental restrictions by which liberty might be extended. By the twentieth century, they were turning more and more to reforms which restricted liberty. As ameliorative reformers, they were doing little more and not much different from what the Conservatives would do. The Labourites, on the other hand, preempted the position at the forefront of the movement for more radical change.

Even so, David Lloyd George played a major role in the division and destruction of his party. He undermined its leadership at the outset of World War I. He formed a coalition government which relied mainly on the Conservative opposition. He gave short shrift to what remained of the historic liberal principles in the conduct of the war effort. In 1918, he fostered an election which was aimed at continuing his personal leadership of a coalition rather than the victory of his party, and he succeeded. The Liberal Party was then divided between followers of Asquith and himself. Probably, Lloyd George did not intend these results, but his actions contributed much to them.

There was no longer a major party in England devoted to the protection and extension of liberty. The Conservatives were trimmers in such matters, as they had ever been.

The rise of the Labour Party parallels that of the decline of the Liberal Party. One is reminded of the limerick of the lady and the tiger. Labour had become a factor in English politics largely by the tacit aid of Liberals. When the Liberal majority dwindled in 1910, the Liberals governed with the support of Labour. The latter had provided support for reducing the Lords. During the war years, Labour Party leaders had served in the coalition government, most prominently under David Lloyd George. (It is interesting to note, once again, the role of Lloyd George. He wooed Labour members astutely to bring them into the government. "He promised state control of the mines and of shipping, and the introduction of an effective system of food rationing."[24] "War socialism" was perhaps politically "expedient.") The Liberal Lady had ridden the Labour Tiger for a number of years. But at the end of the ride, the Lady was inside.

Even while it was being ridden, however, the Labour Party could and did occasionally get a quid pro quo. Most notably did it do so in the Trade Union Act of 1913. A few years before, as has been noted, a decision was rendered making it illegal for union funds to be used for political purposes. These funds were, of course, the potential life blood of the party. The Trade Union Act permitted the union funds to be used for party purposes. It required that they be kept separate from other funds so that union members who did not wish to contribute to the political fund could refuse to do so by making a written statement to that effect. Obviously, they would have been much more effectively deterred in gaining such funds if union members had to sign an authorization for them to be so used. But the Labour Party overrode such objections in the Commons.[25] Thereafter, the Labour Party had an assured source of income.

In the early years, the Labour Party was not clearly a socialist party. A considerable portion of the men who represented it in Parliament were trade union men advancing what they conceived to be the interest of trade unions. The party drew its members from the trade unions and from socialist societies, the former providing most of the numbers. It was transformed into a thoroughgoing socialist party at the end of World War I, at about the time that it separated clearly from the Liberals.

A new constitution for the party was adopted in 1918, and a general statement of policy soon followed it. These were the work of the Fabian Sidney Webb primarily who, according to his wife, had become "the intellectual leader of the Labour Party" by this time.[26] The constitution opened the way for those not associated with the societies or trade union members to become members of the party. More importantly, it committed the party to socialism. It read, in part:

> To secure for the producers by hand and brain the full fruits of their industry, and the most equitable distribution thereof that may be possible, upon the basis of the common ownership of the means of production and the best obtainable system of popular administration and control of each industry or service.[27]

Shortly thereafter, a statement of Labour's aims was set forth in *Labour and the New Social Order*, the work again of Sidney Webb. It called for the establishment of a general national minimum, for the political control of industry, for heavy taxes, and a more general appropriation of private wealth for the general populace. One writer describes its importance in this way:

> *Labour and the New Social Order* was a significant document. Its socialist objective clearly distinguished the new party from its older rivals.... The Fabian gradualism of the program and the reliance upon parliamentary democracy enabled Labour to win support where its new Communist competitor failed dismally. It outlined the policies to which Labour has consistently adhered.[28]

In 1924, Ramsay MacDonald, a Labourite, became Prime Minister of England. Socialism was not yet in power—his ministry lasted only months, but that one of its spokesmen had risen so high was surely a portent of things to come.

Within fifteen years or so, great changes had occurred in England. In 1906, England still afforded a good example of the liberal state with limited government, protections of private property, and extensive liberties for the inhabitants. After 1906, England made lengthy strides toward the welfare state, had its constitution altered so that power was centered in the House of Commons, experienced "war socialism" and the concentration of power in the hands of the Prime Minister, witnessed the decline of the Liberal Party, and the transformation of the Labour party into a socialist one. Nor would the effects of all this be long in making themselves felt.

19
The English Quandary

THE IDEA that now has the world in its grip introduced factors into the political, economic, and social equation of life with which people were hardly prepared to deal in the years between World War I and World War II. It was not that socialism had arrived so suddenly on the scene. It was rather that it came in so many different guises and produced such a variety of disorders. Its basic character was everywhere concealed behind a cover of good intentions. It advanced under guise of being at the forefront of progress. It was, instead, a retrogressive thrust to power, to such power as has rarely been conceived.

In England, the gradualist approach tended to conceal the thrust to power behind the facade of traditions and institutions. It should be clear, however, that the political institutions by which power had been constrained, balanced, and limited had mostly become nullities. The monarch reigned but did not rule. The Lords sat but could do little to alter the course of affairs. All power rested in the House of Commons where it could potentially be directed by a ministry chosen by the dominant party. The old political balance between Liberals and Conservatives was gone. The instrumentalities for dictatorship lay ready to hand, and it must speak well for the strength of a tradition bred into men that none reached out and grasped them.

A reluctant electorate stood in the way, too. The Liberals had abandoned most of their principles, turned to economic intervention, and tilted toward gradualism. Their following melted away. The Conservatives depended upon and tentatively defended a system that remained largely as a collection of relics, albeit relics which still retained great public appeal. For the Conservatives were the only political party in England able to command a majority in the Commons during the interwar years. But they were increasingly reluctant to govern, preferring to join with others to going it alone. The instinct may have been sound even when the effort was misguided. The Conservatives were not sufficiently committed to any principles to give coherent direction to a government. Prudence is no doubt a virtue, but it is not a principle. As for the Labourites, they were held at arm's length from power by a reluctant electorate.

The English quandry in the interwar years was the result of political indecision, international instability, declining world trade, and the toying with economic nationalism which could only harm the specialized English. Nineteenth century liberalism had left a sorry bequest to England, as well as the rest of the world. In their heyday liberals had championed and secured many prized liberties. But by the twentieth century they had succeeded in cutting away most of the supports to these (thanks to the utilitarians particularly). About all they had left to bequeath to the twentieth century was an overweening enthusiasm for universal suffrage and democracy. Their thrust was toward unlimited democracy. They provided the setting for democratic, or gradualist, socialism, and its advocates found a fertile field in which to appeal to the unbridled appetites of an undisciplined populace by offering to use the power of government to satisfy its wants.

The British did not buy socialism outright between the wars. But they had come sufficiently under its spell that the economy was badly hampered, no clear direction was followed, and British influence and position in the world declined precipitately. Gradualism tends to produce political paralysis. It tends to undermine existing institutions and practices, to throw doubt on all the received wisdom, and to make all pursuit of self-interest appear corrupt. All who refuse to accept the socialist answers find mental blockades thrown in the way to action. Those who attempted to govern England were caught in the cross currents of an ideological conflict whose dimensions they were unprepared to grasp. The government tacked to and fro as the country's prestige, power, and wealth declined.

England's decline occurred also within the framework of the disintegration of the general European order. A little of that needs to be recalled here.

241

"To think," Kaiser Wilhelm lamented at the outbreak of World War I, "that George and Nicky should have played me false! If my grandmother had been alive she would never have allowed it."[1] "George" was George V of England, and "Nicky" was Nicholas II of Russia. "Grandmother" was Queen Victoria of England. She was not only the Kaiser's grandmother but also Czar Nicholas' grandmother by marriage. Moreover, it was not simply a felicitous phrase to refer to her as "Grandmother of Europe."[2] In view of the heavy tomes since written on the "causes" of World War I, historians are inclined to rate the Kaiser's remark as highly naive. Yet, it should not be casually dismissed. Grandmother Victoria might not have prevented World War I, most likely could not have. But monarchy had provided balance and continuity for nations and empires between the Congress of Vienna and World War I — that century of peace. It had come generally to be limited monarchy in which the monarchs' powers for abuse were shorn but in which sufficient power was retained to counterbalance legislatures. Moreover, the intertwining of royal families by kinship and marriage did tend to make for good relations among the countries of Europe. The spirit of nationalism had distinguished peoples from peoples, but they were still linked to one another in royal families.

The disintegration of the European order was twofold during or after World War I. On the one hand, monarchy was abandoned by major countries: Germany and Russia most notably. Secondly, the empires of Central and Eastern Europe were broken up: German, Austro-Hungarian, Russian, and Ottoman. In their place, new nations were brought into being and old ones revived: Poland, Czechoslovakia, Yugoslavia, Latvia, Lithuania, and so forth. New as well as old nations were highly nationalistic, jealous of one another, and no longer generally linked with one another by royal families, though some monarchs were retained or restored.

The disintegration was both signaled and fostered by attempts of each country to become economically self-sufficient — by economic nationalism or neo-mercantilism, whatever term may be preferred. One history gives an example of this for one group of countries:

As an expression of their sovereignty and independence each of the states in Danubian Europe erected its own tariff system.... In general the tariffs ascended in this order: Austria, Czechoslovakia, Yugoslavia, Hungary, Bulgaria, and Rumania.... Recourse was also made to quota and licensing systems.

It adds: "The small states of Central Europe cannot be censured for trying to create a rounded national economy when the whole world was doing the same thing."[3]

In many respects, this economic nationalism was a continuation and extension to new states of developments which were becoming general in the last decades of the nineteenth century. Country after country had erected tariff barriers: the United States, Germany, and so forth. These had set the stage for the new surge to get colonies and dominate territories in various places on the globe. The roots of World War I can be found in this expansionism which grew out of protectionism. England grasped for colonies while holding out against the protectionist measures.

This new mercantilism differed significantly in the animus behind it from the mercantilism of the sixteenth, seventeenth, and eighteenth centuries. It was spurred by the trend toward socialism and the welfare state. Countries found it expedient to erect "trade curtains" to protect themselves from the world market in order to control and regulate domestic economies. Black and Helmreich point up the connection in their discussion of the bills of rights in the new constitutions of the Danubian governments in the 1920's: "The government must assure the right to work; the health of the citizens, particularly the laboring man, must be safeguarded; the aged must be cared for; the family protected, etc. To implement all these 'rights' the government would of necessity have to provide a far-reaching social service program, regulate trade and industry, and become in truth the very nurturer of the whole population...."[4] England held out longer than other nations against the interior logic, or illogic, of the requirements of the welfare state, but, as we shall see, eventually succumbed.

The League of Nations was supposed to bring about and maintain order and peace during the interwar years. It did not do so; indeed, it could not do so. That organization was to promote international cooperation and provide collective security. Yet nation was pitted against nation economically; manipulated currencies made movement of goods and peoples from one land to another increasingly difficult; ideology and action severed the natural bonds of one people with another. Nations cannot use the power of their governments against one another in trade and collaborate to maintain peace politically. They cannot establish national socialism, on the one hand, and international collective action, on the other. The notion that if the United States had joined the League matters would have turned out differently pays too high a compliment to the colossus of the New World. The vaunted

243

inventiveness of Americans would not have sufficed to overcome the interior contradictions of disintegrating Europe.

At any rate, the old order in Europe was not replaced by a new order in the interwar years. Instead, disorder spread, became more violent, and threatened the peace of the world. Governments made that variety of internal war upon their own populations which is implicit in socialist ideology and attempted to forge a new unity by preaching class and race hatred. Governmental power was totalized, first in the Soviet Union, then in other lands. Power was concentrated in the hands of dictators or would-be dictators in land after land — in the hands of Stalin, Mussolini, Hitler, Marshall Pilsudski, Salazar, and so forth — in the absence of the old monarchical and aristocratic restraints and under the guise of the thrust toward socialism. Dictators consolidated their power by turning to aggression in the 1930's. Word of new horrors began to spread, suggested by such phrases as concentration camps, Siberia, secret police, dossiers, travel permit, shot in the back of the neck, Gestapo, liquidation of kulaks, and so forth. Intellectuals in France, Great Britain, and the United States — themselves bent toward socialism — disavowed the misbegotten step-children of socialism known as Italian fascism and German nazism, but were generally unrepentant in the face of Soviet purges and the Nazi-Soviet Pact.

Such was the setting of England's decline.

That decline is most readily measurable in foreign trade and economic production. In some areas, the decline was relative; in others, it was absolute. The United Kingdom's relative share of world trade — exports and imports — is indicated by these figures: in 1840, it was 32 per cent; 1913, 17 per cent; 1938, 13 per cent.[5] More important, British imports accounted for an increasing proportion of the trade, while exports decreased.[6] The United Kingdom's portion of world manufacturing production was 31.8 per cent in 1870; 14 per cent in 1913; and 9.2 per cent in the 1936-1938 period.[7]

Britain's decline was most notable in the older basic industries, those industries which the British had dominated in the nineteenth century: coal, iron and steel, shipbuilding, shipping, cotton goods, and so forth. The decline in coal mined was absolute. A record 287 million tons were mined in 1913; in the 1920's, annual production averaged about 253 million tons.[8] A decreasing proportion of this was sold in foreign trade.[9] "Until 1937, pig-iron production declined steadily from its absolute peak of 10¼ million tons in 1913."[10] In general, iron and steel production fell during the interwar years until it began to rise in the late

244

1930's. What happened to the cotton goods industry is probably most important, for it had accounted for a large portion of exports in the nineteenth century. Piece goods production fell from a little over 8 billion square yards in 1912 to 3½ billion square yards in 1930 to only a little over 3 billion yards in 1938. Exports of piece goods declined even more drastically: from nearly 7 billion square yards in 1912 to less than 1½ billion square yards in 1938.[11] British shipbuilding fell off badly between the wars.

From 1920 onwards the tonnage under construction fell, though the years 1927-30 were relatively good years, British launchings then running at about 75% of the level of 1911-13. In the slump, with millions of tons of shipping laid up, the building of new tonnage virtually came to a standstill: in 1933 the launchings from British yards fell to 7% of the pre-war figure. Throughout the early 1930's a large part of the industry was idle....[12]

Some new industries did grow and develop during the interwar years, such as electrical goods, automobiles, aircraft, silk and rayon goods, and chemical products,[13] but these did not alter the fact of the general decline.

British agriculture did not fare well during the period either. There were just over 11 million acres in cultivation in 1914 (in England and Wales). It had fallen to 9,833,000 acres in 1930. Acreage under wheat in 1931 dropped to the lowest point ever recorded. There were some increases in production in some categories, but the English were producing far less than they consumed of agricultural products.[14] A flight from the land was characteristic of these years: "employment in agriculture and forestry in the United Kingdom fell from an average of 1,004,000 in 1920-22 to an average of 735,000 in 1927-28.... Workers left the industry at the rate of 10,000 a year, and the exodus of young men was particularly marked...."[15]

Many historians attribute the commercial and industrial decline of England to the protectionist policies of other nations, to other countries finally catching up to an earlier lead England had gained, and to the failure of the British to modernize. Undoubtedly, the protectionist policies of other countries made trade more difficult for the British. The latter two points, however, require explanations rather than constituting them. In truth, the British were mainly responsible for their commercial decline. The reasons for that decline are not far to seek. England had risen as a great industrial and commercial nation when the energies of men had been freed, when restrictions upon land were removed or

245

reduced, when special privileges were struck down, when liberty and property were secured for individuals, and when they were motivated by belief to constructive achievement.

England's decline followed the onset of government intervention on a scale that could not be fully compensated for. That intervention began to take effect in the early years of the twentieth century, was temporarily vastly expanded during World War I, and in the interwar years began to mount once more. The thrust toward intervention came from Fabian socialists and other reformers, was spearheaded by the Labour Party in Parliament, and gained sway during every major cabinet administration from 1906 onward. High taxation made the accumulation of capital a forbidding task; regulation made new investments in many areas unenticing; labor unions introduced inflexibilities into the economy; and Britain became less and less competitive around the world. The determination of interventionists to regulate and control was inconsistent with free trade and the gold standard; one or the other had to go, and it was freedom that went. There is not space here to tell the story in detail, but enough must be told to show how the decline followed from the intervention.

Following World War I, there was a considerable attempt at reconversion and restoration of the old order. "During 1919 the controls of trade and shipping were allowed to end. Rationing of food and most price controls ended by 1920.... Factories and stores of 'war surplus' goods were sold off. The Government made every show of its conviction ... that Governments ought to get out of business...."[16] This last sentence exaggerates somewhat, but it does indicate one tendency. The budget was balanced once again, and the inflation halted. Trade with the rest of the world was virtually freed. In 1925, Winston Churchill, as Chancellor of the Exchequer, was able to restore the gold standard. Most of this had been accomplished under governments headed by David Lloyd George, Bonar Law, and Stanley Baldwin, the latter two being Conservative Prime Ministers.

These measures did not succeed fully in reviving England for two reasons mainly. In the first place, the reconversion was not that thorough; much intervention was continued, and more came. One historian notes that during the war "departments, bureaux, committees, controllers were created and piled on top of each other...." After the war, "though the flood subsided, government never returned to its old channel."[17] Signs of increasing government appeared in the establishment of a Ministry of Labour in 1916, a Ministry of Health in 1919, a

Department of Scientific and Industrial Research in 1916, a Forestry Commission in 1919, and a Medical Research Council in 1920.[18] Railroad consolidation was prescribed after the war; coal mines were greatly regulated; high taxes were imposed; and some tariffs were continued. Two new welfare acts were passed shortly after the war. "The Housing and Town Planning Act of July 1919 ... provided for government subsidies through local authorities." An unemployment insurance act was passed in 1920. "Nearly twelve million workers, including eight million not previously insured were brought within the scope of the act...."[19] This last was to become very shortly a great burden on English taxpayers.

The other great obstacle to the revival of England in the 1920's was the labor unions. These had grown greatly during World War I, and they now had a powerful political arm in the Labour Party. Labor unions find it very difficult to survive deflation. They depend for their following to a considerable extent upon frequent increases in wages. This can only be accomplished generally by increases in the money supply or reductions in employment. When the government began balancing the budget and later returned to the gold standard, labor unions resisted any cut in wages vigorously. There were widespread strikes, this activity coming to a head with the General Strike of 1926 (an event significantly preceded by the return to the gold standard). The government came to the aid of miners by subsidizing them and prescribing the conditions that should prevail. More generally, however, those union workers with jobs continued to get high monetary wages. They did so at the expense of other workers, for unemployment became endemic in England in the 1920's, and was a fixture throughout the interwar years. By June of 1922, the registered unemployed had reached 1½ millions. The government came to the rescue, and began its subsidization of unemployment on a large scale. The government, "by a series of Acts in 1921 and 1922 ... extended the period during which benefits could be drawn ..., altered the rates of benefit, and increased the contributions."[20] One of the major reasons for economic decline in England during the interwar years was that a considerable portion of the people were not working. The labor unions produced the situation, and the government sustained it.

Unemployment was highest in the old staple industries, and remained high during these years. These were the industries, of course, where unionization had its great impact. A further reason for decline can be seen in wages and productivity. British wages were generally higher than in other lands.[21] On the other hand, productivity did not

247

keep pace. In coal mining, for example, other countries in Europe were greatly increasing the output per manshift; England had only small gains. "By 1936, the peak year in every country, Britain's output per manshift was 14 per cent above that of 1927, whereas the increase in the Ruhr mines was 81 per cent, in the Polish mines 54 per cent, in the Dutch mines 118 per cent."[22] Small wonder that Britain could not maintain its trade position.

Government intervention and labor union obstruction prevented the revival of the economy in the 1920's. With the coming of the depression of the 1930's, the government abandoned the feeble effort it had made to restore the policies which had made England great. The great symbols of these, the gold standard and free trade, were given up: the gold standard in 1931; protective tariffs and imperial preference were inaugurated in 1932. The pound sterling was no longer good as gold, and England was no longer the trading Mecca of the world.

It has been suggested that England backed into socialism in the interwar years. But this was not always the case. In the 1920's under a Conservative government there was a straightforward movement in that direction in two instances. Radio was taken over by the government as the British Broadcasting Corporation. A Central Electricity Board was created, and it was empowered to make wholesale distribution of electricity. In retrospect, though, it does look as if the stage was set for socialism by the backdoor. The government appeared to do its best to wreck free enterprise by abolishing competition in many areas in the 1930's. Cartelization was authorized and fostered in several industries, notably coal mining, iron and steel, and shipbuilding.

The government fostered combinations, collaborations, and price setting, similar to what was undertaken under the N.R.A. in the United States. What was involved is suggested by this description: "The Government looked for the benefits of monopoly, tempered by planning in the national interest. Accordingly, the British Iron and Steel Federation was formed in April 1934.... In 1935-36 it took over the price-fixing functions of earlier sectional associations, and it negotiated with foreign cartels to impose quantitative restrictions on imports. ..."[23] Nationalization was only a step away after this.

If anything, the intervention in agriculture was more massive than that in other areas in the 1930's. England had already, in the 1920's, attempted to establish sugar beet growing by giving subsidies (what were called bounties generally under the older mercantilism). In the 1930's protectionist policies for agricultural products were followed, and attempts at cartelization, of a sort, were made. Potato Marketing Boards, Milk Marketing Boards, Bacon and Pig Marketing Boards were set up to do such things as control production and prices. One historian describes the inconsistency in this way: "Viewed in the broadest possible perspective, the world was suffering from a surfeit of food, and Britain, the world's chief food market, reacted to this glut by closing her frontiers to imports and encouraging her farmers to add to the world output by expanding their high-cost production."[24] At any rate, the vaunted independent Englishman was independent no more; he was caught in the toils of government power by the promises of government favors.

There was a revival of the British economy in the middle and late 1930's. It did not, however, signalize the recovery to full health of the patient. Instead, it was only an instance of that deceivingly healthful flush that patients sometimes develop just before they succumb.

England declined in many other ways than the economic in the interwar years. British influence and power were waning in the world at large. At the Washington Naval Conference, and then more completely at the London Naval Conference, Britain abandoned its naval pre-eminence. The United States was accorded equality, and the Japanese acquired a leading role in the Pacific. These indicated the decline of power and of the will to be the strongest.

The waning of British influence was more subtle and probably much more significant. In the nineteenth century, British political forms and institutions had been the models for much of the world. In the interwar years, this ceased to be the case. Intellectuals began to cast admiring glances toward the Soviet Union: to its social planning, to one-party government, to the dictatorship instituted there. Italian fascism had its admirers, too, as Mussolini consolidated his power in the mid-twenties. (At least, some said, the trains run on time in Italy.)

But to look at it this way is probably to approach the matter wrong-end-to. What was there to admire and imitate about British institutions any longer? What were they? How convinced of their probity were the British themselves? Power had already been centralized in the House of Commons and concentrated in the cabinet. The balance of powers now remained largely in relics which were forms without substance. Political parties represented about all that was left of the means of balancing power. But these, too, lost vitality during the years under consideration.

The only party that managed to get a clear majority in the interwar years was the Conservative Party. But its leadership was usually reluctant to govern. Labour got a plurality in the election of 1929, and Ramsay MacDonald, the Labourite, formed a government. It fell in 1931, and MacDonald led the movement for a National goverment. There was an overwhelming vote for candidates pledged to the National government. Actually, Conservatives elected 472 members to the House of Commons, a preponderant majority itself. Nonetheless, Ramsay MacDonald served as Prime Minister for a National government from 1931 to 1935, followed by two Conservatives, Stanley Baldwin and Neville Chamberlain, to 1940. This was surely the peacetime nadir of party responsibility in modern British history. Without effective party responsibility for what was done, there was little check left upon government. In short, England turned to its own variety of "one-party" government in this period — a pale imitation of what was occurring in the dictatorships.

Britain was withdrawing from the world, retreating from competition behind tariff barriers, going off the gold standard, pulling in to the hoped-for safety of empire. Other nations were becoming aggressively expansive: Japan, Italy, Germany, and the Soviet Union. Nobody did anything of real consequence when Japan invaded Manchuria in the early 1930's. Britain and France agreed not to intervene significantly when Mussolini's forces invaded Ethiopia in 1935. This would throw Mussolini into the arms of Hitler, it was feared, and Britain clung to the relics of a balance of power policy which, in fact, at this point meant a withdrawal of influence. When Spain became a battleground between communists, on the one hand, and fascists — assisted by Germany and Italy — on the other, no British weight was used to prevent the intervention. Indeed, as Germany rearmed, as the Rhineland was remilitarized, as international treaties were flagrantly violated, Britain acquiesced piecemeal in virtually every measure.

The depth of the bankruptcy of British foreign policy was reached at the Munich Conference in 1938. Prior to this conference, Chamberlain had made hurried trips to meet and treat with Hitler, pleading with the arrogant dictator to moderate his claims. At Munich, Hitler refused to allow Czech representatives to be present at the meeting of himself, Mussolini, Daladier (for France), and Chamberlain. Yet the men present agreed to the cession of Czechoslovak territory (the Sudetenland) to Germany. But if the Czechs had been present, they could have been outvoted; such are the possibilities of democratic collective agreements. Chamberlain returned to England exultant; the Munich agreement had, he proclaimed, secured "peace in our time." And the crowds cheered!

That men are fallible beings is undoubtedly true. They fall short of their ideals; they do not invariably hue to the line of principle; they compromise quite often where moral questions are involved. Yet there are tides in the affairs of men, and it is not simply individual fallibility involved in these affairs. Chamberlain had not simply varied from principle; in the best of times men do this. He was confused, and his confusion was the reflex of that of a large portion of the English people. The decline of England was preceded and accompanied by moral and religious decline. It is one thing to violate the known and agreed upon principles of morality; it is quite another not to know what these principles are, to be torn between conflicting views, or to be uncertain as to the existence of verities. It was the latter which afflicted the English, as well as people elsewhere.

One historian describes the decline of religion in the interwar years in this way:

> More broadly, religious faith was losing its strength. Not only did church-going universally decline. The dogmas of revealed religion — the Incarnation and the Resurrection — were fully accepted only by a small minority. Our Lord Jesus Christ became, even for many avowed Christians, merely the supreme example of a good man. This was as great a happening as any in English history since the conversion of the Anglo-Saxons to Christianity....[25]

Another points out that by the 1930's the number of communicants in the Church of England only barely exceeded that of Roman Catholics. The well-to-do still availed themselves of the rites of the church. "But no more than socially; and Puritanism languished except in a few Dissenting congregations, and among the elderly."[26]

For several decades, the erosion of belief in verities had proceeded apace or accelerated. Intellectuals had swung over to relativism. Morals, people were taught, are relative to time and place, are matters of customs and mores. Moral absolutes were for Englishmen reflexes of Puritanism and Victorianism, hence, old-hat, out-moded, and increasingly despised. Rationality had been undercut by new currents of irrationality.

There was a close relation between these developments and the movement toward socialism. Socialists could not advance their dogmas in a framework of individual responsibility. The virtues of industry, thrift, clean living, and careful husbandry must be undermined. Traditional morality abjured violence, enjoined respect for property, taught that men should not steal but be content with the fruits of their own labor. Covetousness was enjoined by Holy Writ. These had to be, and were, denigrated for socialism to make its gains.

The point is this: When Chamberlain confronted Hitler, he brought no high moral position from England with which to oppose the Führer. The gradualist movement toward socialism in England had acclimated the English to methods analogous to those of Hitler, if not in so brutal a guise. The British had come to accept labor union violence as a legitimate means to achieve their ends. They had been familiarized with increasing use of government force against the population to regulate trade, to confiscate wealth, to provide funds for idle men. What was right was what the majority voted for, according to an underlying ethos. If the majority voted for programs which took the profits of corporations, that was not theft; it was only social justice. If the House of Lords stood in the way of this thrust for power, it should be shorn of its effective veto. There was no high ground in all of this from which to counter Hitler's moves. Moreover, the British people did not want adventures; they wanted peace.

It must not be thought that socialists believed consistently in the protection of minorities. Which minorities? Not the Lords. Not the farmers. Not factory owners. Not the unemployed (and their right to work in struck plants). Not of women, for the labor unions had worked diligently to drive women from their employment after World War I. The Czechs were, after all, only another minority. Why should their selfish wishes stand in the way of the great goal of world peace?

It is not my point, of course, that the British were more responsible than others for these international events, or that they acted more ignobly. They did eventually stand and fight, and they did so sturdily and even heroically. In the dark days of 1940-41, they stood alone against the Axis might which bestrode the continent of Europe. Winston Churchill's promises to "wage war, by sea, land, and air" until victory was achieved rallied his people behind him. The point, rather, is that England's decline was of its own making, that the decay of morality underlay this decline, that the British abandoned ancient principles and vitiated their system, that government intervention produced the decline, and that waning influence abroad was a logical consequence of the loss of certainty at home. Nor was war anything more than a temporary interruption of the British on their road leading toward oblivion.

20
Socialism in Power

IN JULY, 1945, an election was held throughout the United Kingdom. The war was over in Europe, but fighting still continued in the Pacific. Despite the fact that a National Government, headed by the Conservative, Winston Churchill, had been successful in prosecuting the war, the decision was made to have a partisan election. To the consternation of almost everyone, the Labour Party won overwhelmingly, returning 393 members to the House of Commons to 189 for the Conservatives and 58 for all other parties. For the first time in history the Labour Party came to power with a clear-cut majority. Twice before, the party had formed ministries, but each time they had ruled with Liberal support. This time they had as clear a mandate to govern according to their ideas as they were likely to get. Socialism had come to power. In its election manifesto for 1945, the Labour Party proclaimed that it was "a socialist party and proud of it."[1]

In several respects, the times had been propitious for the socialists to make their move. Clement Attlee, the Labour Party leader, must have realized this, for he had pressed for an early dissolution of the government and a new election.

The times were right, in the first place, because the English people had become accustomed to collective efforts during the war. They were acclimated to vast undertakings by government — to large-scale evacuations, to massive mobilizations of armed forces and their deployment around the world, to collective responses to air raids and the attendant blackouts, to concentration on war production, and so forth. One writer says, "All this produced a revolution in British economic life, until in the end direction and control turned Great Britain into a country more fully socialist than anything achieved by the conscious planners of Soviet Russia."[2] At any rate, they were psychologically prepared for the continuation of such undertakings in peacetime.

Moreover, during the war the government had either taken or promised measures moving in the direction of socialism. The most famous of the tacit promises was the one contained in the Beveridge Report, made public in 1942. It was comprehensive in what it called for:

It covered all the known causes of the "giant" Want, by providing for unemployment benefit, sickness benefit, disability benefit, workmen's compensation, old age, widows' and orphans' pensions and benefits, funeral grants, and maternity benefits. In addition to these financial provisions, the Report was also based on the assumption that a comprehensive health and rehabilitation service was to be established, its full resources available to all....[3]

"Its popular appeal was immense, 250,000 copies of the full report and 350,000 of an official abridgment being sold within a few months...."[4] The thrust toward socialism during the war was, to a considerable extent, bipartisan. The Beveridge Report was authorized by the government, which was predominantly Conservative. Moreover, Anthony Eden, speaking for the Conservative Party, had this to say in the House of Commons, December 2, 1944:

We have set our hands to a great social reform programme ... and even though there be an interruption it is the intention of each one of us who are members of the Government to carry that programme through. I have no doubt that ... if a Labour Government were returned, that Government would put through what was outstanding in this programme. And I can say, on behalf of the Prime Minister that we, as members of the Conservative Party, would give them support in putting through that programme....[5]

Both major parties, then, had done their part to prepare the people for great changes after the war.

The times were right, too, because the long-term trend toward greater and greater government intervention and control was well established. Since the early twentieth century, the government had become more and more involved in the economy: by minimum wages, by the dole, by "insurance programs," by heavy taxation, by monetary manipulation, by ownership of certain undertakings, by control and regulation. The minds of the people were set toward intervention: by the activities of the Fabians, by the Left Book Club, by the very popular Keynesian economics, and by the tendency of most of the literary cadre to write favorably toward it. Few in positions of leadership or authority were apparently able to think in other than socialistic terms. Conservatives sometimes held back against more radical measures, but they were hardly inclined to oppose the general trend.

One other condition made it relatively easy for the socialists at the end of the war: wartime controls were still in effect, and could be continued with less resistance than if they were introduced for the first time.

On the other hand, whichever party came to power after the war could expect some rough going. This was especially true for the Labour Party, for socialists tend to take on responsibility for all economic effort, or at any rate to claim credit for any achievements. To take on the British economy — or lack of one — at the end of the war was not an enviable task. There had been considerable physical damage in Great Britain during the war. An estimated £1,500,000,000 damage had been done to factories, railways, and docks. Some 4,000,000 houses had been either destroyed or damaged.[6] Eighteen million tons of shipping were lost, and only two-thirds of this replaced in the course of the war.[7] According to one writer, "A large part of her industrial equipment was desperately in need of replacement, for instead of spending, as she would normally have done over five years, £1,000,000,000 to maintain and renew plants and factories in the civilian industries, she had spent this money on munitions of war."[8]

The most serious difficulty confronting the British at the end of the war was in the realm of foreign trade. They had come to depend on imports for much that they consumed. "Nearly three-quarters of all the food she ate came from abroad, 55 per cent of her meat, 75 per cent of her wheat, 85 per cent of her butter, all of her tea, cocoa, and coffee, three-quarters of her sugar. Every year more than 20,000,000 tons of imported food had to be brought across the seas and unloaded at her docks."[9]

What made this situation pressing was that the British had long since ceased to balance these imports with goods exported. The difference was increasingly made up in recent decades by income from foreign investments, services such as shipping and insurance, and payments in gold. At the end of the war, Britain was deeply in debt abroad, most of the gold supply depleted, much of foreign investments sold to defray the expenses of the war. Moreover, Britain had for the two decades preceding the war been losing out to competitors in those things for export where she had traditionally dominated.

In addition, the British as victors in the war had heavy military obligations. They undertook to occupy a zone in dismembered Germany. They had heavy commitments in other parts of the world also, and were very soon confronted with volatile situations in areas to which their hegemony had long extended.

Even so, the leadership of the Labour Party plunged into socialization with a will, even with apparent alacrity. For more than a decade they had been committed to such a course if and when they came to power. And there was no counterbalancing power now to hinder them in their surge. A working majority of the House of Commons was all they needed. The Conservative Party was supine. The House of Lords was powerless to do more than delay or make helpful amendments. The monarchy was reduced to a symbolic role in affairs. Indeed, it was the King who announced to Parliament the course it was to pursue. He said, in part: "My Government will take up with energy the tasks of reconverting industry from the purposes of war to those of peace, of expanding our export trade and of securing by suitable control or by an extension of public ownership that our industries and services shall make their maximum contribution to the national well-being."[10] Such power as there was in the United Kingdom rested in the hands of a socialist ministry.

There were three main facets to the domestic socialization program in England: (1) the completion of the welfare state, (2) the nationalization of certain key industries, and (3) control over those portions of the economy which remain technically in private hands.

The welfare aspect of socialization has probably received more attention generally than any other, though it is not clear that socialists would consider it most important. In any case, a full-fledged welfare state was established by several acts shortly after Labour came to power. Indeed, one act was passed in 1944 which should be mentioned. It was the Education Act. This act raised the school-leaving age to fifteen, provided "free" secondary education for all children, and set up a system of separating at the age of eleven those pupils to go to preparatory schools and those to attend terminal schools.[11]

The two most dramatic welfarist acts, however, were passed in 1946

256

under the Labourites: National Insurance Act and National Health Service Act. The National Insurance Act provided protection against various vicissitudes to that large portion of the public which had not been so protected as yet. It covered "every person who on or after the appointed day, being over school-leaving age and under pensionable age, is in Great Britain and fulfills such conditions as may be prescribed as to residence in Great Britain...."[12] These would then be eligible for unemployment benefits, sickness benefits, maternity benefits, and so on and on. The expenses were to be defrayed by employer, employee, and taxpayer (government) "contributions." The National Health Service Act was much more controversial. Many physicians opposed it. Even so, it was passed, and eventually went into effect in 1948. The act provided for free medical and dental services for eveyone, and for those who provided the services to be paid by the government. It was intended as a comprehensive plan for looking after the health of those living in England and Wales.

Welfarist in nature also was the massive house building program undertaken under Aneurin Bevan, Labourite Minister of Health. The program tended toward nationalization of housing also, for it encouraged the building of rental housing and discouraged building for private ownership. It "was decided that the major part of the permanent building programme should be carried out through the local authorities, who would employ builders under contract to build houses to rent and who would be given financial aid by the Government in order that ... the houses when constructed could be let on the basis of need at fairly low standard rents." To discourage private building, "builders were to be allowed to build for sale or under contract to private purchasers only to a restricted degree and only after a license had been secured from the local authority."[13]

Nationalization was undertaken with considerable vigor. The broad categories of industries nationalized were banking, power and light, transport, and iron and steel. The first nationalization was authorized by the Bank of England Act passed in 1946; the last major one was authorized by the Iron and Steel Act of 1949. A fairly typical nationalization measure was the Coal Industry Nationalization Act passed in 1946 to go into effect January 1, 1947. "The act provided for a National Coal Board appointed by the minister of fuel and power and consisting of nine representatives of various functions within the industry (such as finance, technology, labor, marketing), who were to operate all coal mines subject to the general supervision of the ministry.

257

The public corporation replaced more than eight hundred private companies, which surrendered their assets for a compensation...."[14] The way had been prepared for further consolidation and eventual nationalization of most of these industries by the cartelization that had taken place in the 1930's by government sponsorship.

It was not simply a matter of chance that these particular industries were selected for nationalization. Socialists may not know how to plan an economy to achieve their ends. The record would indicate that they do not. And British socialists had, in effect, organized irresponsibility on a large scale in these industries, for they had placed them under the control of boards whose members had much authority but few responsibilities — responsibilities to stockholders, responsibilities to operate efficiently, even responsibilities to Parliament. Even so, British socialists demonstrated that they knew where the main arteries of a modern economy are. They meant to bring these directly into the hands of government agencies, and did.

Before spelling out the import of nationalization and indicating the extent of much more extensive controls, it will be helpful to review briefly the vision which the socialists had in mind. One of the men who participated in the early stages of this broad effort described it as a test and an experiment. He said, in part:

Here at last a practical test of two vast and so far unproven assumptions is taking place. The first is that a planned socialist system is economically more efficient than a private-enterprise capitalist system; the second is that within democratic socialist planning the individual can be given broader social justice, greater security, and more complete freedom than under capitalism.[15]

To make this test, planning has to reach through to every ligament of an economy. The above writer's description suggests the extent of such planning:

The central planning organization, for example, is required to estimate the total number of men and women available for employment, the amount of essential raw materials such as coal, steel, and timber likely to be available from all sources, the total national production of goods possible in the current situation, and how this productive effort should be divided between home consumption, exports, and capital investment.

Having made this analysis, the Planning Board assesses industrial priorities in the light of it; decides what proportion of the total working population is needed for national security in the defence services, what proportion in the public and administrative services, how many in trade, industry and agriculture in order to reach the production targets set, and what general division of

258

manpower there ought to be between export and home production, and between the productive and distributive trades. A similar assessment of the correct distribution of basic raw materials between various types of users is also required....[16]

In short, the determination of what was to be done in the economic realm was to be taken out of the market and made by government officials. To accomplish this — if it could be done — it would be necessary to have full control of key industries. The key industries of a modern economy are, undoubtedly, banking, power and light, transport, and iron and steel. No modern enterprise can operate effectively without the use of one or more, and usually all, of these goods and services. Power is essential; capital is required (not necessarily borrowed money, but money, and central monetary authorities can either maintain the money supply or destroy it); transport must be had; and equipment and housing made in some part of iron and steel are practical necessities. The government which, in effect, possesses these essential goods and services can dictate to virtually all other undertakings.

Of course, British socialists did not content themselves with nationalization. Additionally, a vast network of controls, subsidies, priorities, prescriptions, proscriptions, and regulations were extended over the remainder of industry and agriculture. It will have to suffice here to call attention to some of these.

One of the most dramatic examples of compulsion can be examined in the regulation of the location of industry. The compulsion was provided for by a Distribution of Industry Act, and Town and Country Planning Act, and procedures adopted by the Board of Trade. The main impetus was to have new industries located in areas where labor was most abundantly available — to move factories to the workers. The Distribution of Industry Act aided by making loans, by giving financial assistance to companies that would open factories in desired areas, and by the use of tax monies to build factories for lease. This, in itself, was largely an effort by the government to influence the location of industry. But stronger weapons were at hand. In order to build a new factory, it was necessary to get a license from the Board of Trade. The Board of Trade could, in effect, veto a plan to build a factory anywhere. This was bolstered by the powers exercised under the Town and Country Planning Act: not only were new towns planned but also building activity was directed.[17]

Economic activity of every sort was minutely regulated. Wanted "production was encouraged; luxury production was limited. Licenses were required to export raw materials and any manufactured articles... needed at home. Domestic consumption was regulated by rationing, subsidies and price controls.... New industrial enterprises seeking capital had to be approved by a government committee...." There was much more, of course: "paper control was directed by the manager of a large paper manufacturing concern; matches were controlled by an official of the largest manufacturer...." Moreover, "Treasury budgets were drafted with a view to controlling investment.... For foreign travel, limitations, changed from time to time, were placed on the amount of cash which could be taken from the United Kingdom."[18] The bureaucrats made ubiquitous attempts to control everything.

As for agriculture, it was decided not to nationalize the land but to regulate and control activity in this area. The Ministry of Food was authorized to buy agricultural produce and became, in effect, the sole market in which farmers were to sell. As the only buyer and seller, it proceeded to set prices to the farmers, on the one hand, and to the consumers, on the other. In general, the Ministry paid high prices for products wanted and sold them at a loss, the aim being not profit but to encourage the kind of production and consumption wanted. Agriculture was controlled "by a range of other measures, such as the giving of acreage grants for particular crops, financial aid for improvements, loans to agricultural workers to become farmers on their own account, and the establishing of pools of labour and machinery upon which individual farmers can call during sowing and harvesting seasons. There is also power to give directions to farmers to plough up land and grow particular crops."[19]

Finally, a large portion of the income of Englishmen was "nationalized" by way of taxation. Taxes were excruciatingly high under the Labour government. An economic historian indicates that the government took 37.7 per cent of the value of the gross national product from the people in 1946.[20] The income tax was confiscatory. "Here is a story which shows it: a big American business which had decided to pay the head of its English subsidiary a salary of 20,000 dollars (£5,000) was informed that, owing to the Income Tax, the recipient would in fact touch half only. Not to be put off, the American business asked how much it would need to pay its servant to ensure him £5,000 net. The answer came back — £50,000, the figure which will, after taxation, leave £5,093 10s. 0 d."[21]

Two things should be immediately apparent. The first is that

260

socialism had made the English people dependent upon government. They were made dependent for food, for markets, for education, for health services, for licenses, for loans, for subsidies, for jobs (it became necessary to belong to a labor union to work in unionized employments), for maternity benefits, for funeral subsidies, for unemployment benefits, for disability payments, for building payments, for the amount that could be taken abroad, for priorities for buying, for authorizations to sell, for houses in which to live (in the case of numerous renters), for broadcasting facilities, and so on. Such dependence has not customarily been known as freedom; the generic term for it is bondage.

Secondly, British economic activity was strait-jacketed by government ownership, control, and regulation. Such overall bureaucratic direction greatly reduced the number of minds to cope with economic tasks and the number of ways that may be used to deal with them. When enterprise is free, when men receive the rewards of their labor, every man may use his initiative, ingenuity, and energy to grapple with the economic problem of scarcity. But under state dictation men are not permitted to exert their energies as they see best. If they perform at all, they are to perform as they are directed, with whatever will they muster for the effort. Under socialism, the English people were told what to produce, where to produce it, where to sell it, where they could buy, and when if at all to undertake it. Bureaucrats were free to plan; the people were free to obey.

The economic situation of England was precarious enough in 1945, as has been pointed out. The English people had a big job ahead of them to recover from the effects of the war and to regain their position in the world. It was task enough to challenge the initiative, ingenuity, and energy of the whole people. Unfortunately, they decided to strait-jacket a large portion of the population and to depend upon bureaucrats. It was as if a drowning man should encumber himself with balls and chains fastened to one arm and both legs, leaving himself only one arm with which to swim. In such circumstances, England's fall was precipitate.

261

The Failure of Socialism

SOCIALISM FAILED in England. True, the times were not propitious for it to succeed. They never are. Both revolutionary and evolutionary socialism have common traits as well as a common end. They turn the power of government upon their own people, and by so doing inhibit, restrain, and prevent the people from effectively accomplishing their tasks. This is a prescription for failure, and the evidence drawn from history supports the conclusion which can be arrived at by reason. The cause and effects stand out clearly in English history.

Such power and force as the British government had was turned on the British people. No matter that a majority of the electorate had voted for the Labour Party in 1945, they had, in effect, voted for the government to unleash its power on them. Socialists in power, as has been shown, continued and extended the watime controls, appropriated property, regulated, restricted, and harassed the British people as those people tried to come to grips with the difficulties that confronted them.

How this power was employed at its nether reaches is illustrated by the following examples from the latter part of the 1940's:

The Ministry of Food prosecuted a greengrocer for selling a few extra pounds of potatoes, while admitting that they were frostbitten and would be thrown away at once. The Ministry clamped down on a farmer's wife who served the Ministry snooper with Devonshire cream for his tea. A shopkeeper was fined £5 for selling home-made sweets that contained his own ration of sugar. Ludicrous penalties were imposed on farmers who had not kept strictly to the letter of licenses to slaughter pigs; in one case, the permitted building was used, the authorized butcher employed, but the job had to be done the day before it was permitted; in another case the butcher and the timing coincided, but the pig met its end in the wrong building....[1]

These homely examples may tell more than volumes of theory of the true nature of the socialist onslaught.

In short order, the socialists were able virtually to wreck what remained of a once vigorous and healthy economy. Economy had suffered greatly from the interventions of the interwar years. It was hampered even more drastically by wartime restrictions. But the measures of the Labour government were such as to make economic behavior very difficult to follow.

The wreckage was wrought by nationalization, controls, regulations, high taxes, restrictions, and compulsory services. There was a concerted effort to plan for and control virtually all economic activity in the land. The initiative for action was taken from the people and vested in a bureaucracy. Where industries were actually taken over, they were placed under the authority of boards which were perforce irresponsible, for the usual checks and restrictions (such as the necessity to make a profit) were removed. In short, the bureaucracy was let loose and the people were bound up. To put it another way, much of the great ability and energy of the British people was turned from productive purposes to wrestling with the bureaucracy.

By examining in detail, it would be possible to show all sorts of reasons for the failure of the socialists. However, in such brief scope as this it will be more appropriate to take two of the reasons and explain them. These two are central, but surely not the only ones. One is somewhat peculiar to England; the other is a universal fallacy in socialism. Let us take the broadest one first.

Socialists have periodically claimed, at least since the publication of *The Communist Manifesto* in 1848, that the problem of production has been solved. Indeed, they have waxed wroth over the dangers of overproduction, of glut, and of affluence. They have gone so far as to claim that capitalist countries have to have war in order to get rid of the excess production. The problem, they have said again and again, is one of distribution. Moreover, English socialists have been devoted to the idea of as near equal distribution of goods and service as is possible (or "practical"). If they were right in believing that the problem was one of distribution and not of production, they were probably also right in

263

believing that government could solve the problem.

At any rate, the Labour government undertook redistribution with a right good will. They levied highly graduated income taxes, taxed luxury goods at high rates, controlled prices of food, clothing, and shelter, and rationed many items in particularly short supply. Not only that, but they provided free medical services, provided pensions, and otherwise aided those with little or no income. They distributed and they distributed.

Yet, a strange thing — at least to them — occurred: the more they redistributed, the less they had to distribute. Not only did such shortages as they had known during the war continue, but others cropped up as well. One writer points out, "By 1948, rations had fallen well below the wartime average. In one week, the average man's allowance was thirteen ounces of meat, one and a half ounces of cheese, six ounces of butter and margarine, one ounce of cooking fat, eight ounces of sugar, two pints of milk, and one egg."[2] Even bread, which had *not* been rationed during the war, was rationed beginning in 1946. The government had first attempted to fool the English people into buying less bread by reducing the amount in a loaf. When that did not work, they turned to rationing.[3] Housing, clothing, food, fuel — everything, it seemed — was in short supply.

The situation became perilous in the winter of 1946-47. It was, undoubtedly, a bitterly cold winter, accompanied by unusual large snowfalls. Ordinarly, the winters in England are mild, protected as the island is by the water and the prevailing currents and winds. Not so, this time; the full fury of winter settled upon the land. The effect was near catastrophe, even when reduced to dry textbook language: "...in February the coal stocks which were already low could not be replenished because of transport difficulties.... For several days much of the industry of the country had to close down; almost two million people were temporarily unemployed; and domestic use of electricity was forbidden during normal working hours."[4] In the midst of all this deprivation, the Labour Party continued on its ideological way, "doggedly pushing their complex nationalization Bills through Parliament whilst wrathful Tories attacked them for paying too little attention to food and fuel, and for employing three times as many civil servants as miners."[5]

It will be worthwhile to pause in the account briefly to consider why a cold winter should cause such distress. We should all be familiar enough by now with the fact that socialist countries seem to be ever and again victims of freakish weather, and such like. Assuming that the rains fall

264

on the just and the unjust alike, there is no need to conclude that these are simply a result of Divine disfavor. On the contrary, a rational explanation is ready to hand. Socialist restrictions make it virtually impossible to adjust with the needed speed to unusual circumstances. In the market, the rise of prices signals distress, and the opportunity for profit induces men to concentrate their energies at the point of greatest demand. But in England prices could not rise, for they were controlled. Transport could not be shifted readily to carrying coal, because it was controlled. The coal miners did not respond to the challenge, for they were enjoying the political perquisites they had won by nationalization. In short, national planning is for an ever-normal situation based on averages which have never exactly occurred and can hardly be expected to in the future. The very unexpectedness of the unusual makes planning for it a contradiction in terms. When men are free, their energies may be turned readily to relieving distress; when they are restricted, they use up much of their energies in complaints against the powers that be.

At any rate, the socialists in power discovered very quickly that the problem of production had not been solved. In England, as elsewhere, socialists have been confronted with mounting problems of production. By the summer of 1947 the British government was making no secret of the problem. "'We're up against it,' intoned the Government posters, £400,000 worth of them, all over the country: 'We Work or Want.'"[6] There is little evidence that socialists have learned the source of what must be to them the paradoxical development of mounting problems of production when they follow their policies of distribution. If they did, of course, they might give up socialism. The fact is that when production is separated from distribution to any considerable extent the incentives to produce are reduced. When this is accompanied by numerous restrictions which hamper men in their productive efforts, goods and services will be in ever shorter supply.

The other major reason for the dire impact of socialism and interventionist measures on England was closely related to the historical economic development of that country. Throughout the modern era the British have been a seafaring and trading people. In the nineteenth century, they accepted the prescription of Adam Smith, in large, specializing in what they did well, depending much on foreign trade, and importing much of what they consumed. The great prosperity which they enjoyed testified to the efficacy of this approach to economy. But from World War I on, interventionist measures made it

265

increasingly difficult for the British to compete in foreign trade. Union wages, the subsidizing of the idle, high taxes, the progressive disjoining of production from distribution made it more and more difficult to sell goods abroad. Domestic inflation and the appropriation of foreign investments reduced Britain's position as financier in the world.

Then the Labour Party came to power in 1945. They were quickly faced with mounting deficits in foreign trade — beginning to be referred to by then as a "dollar shortage." The "dollar shortage" was, of course, a result of governmental policy. The government was trying to distribute what it did not have in hand to pass out. It inflated the currency, supported higher wages, increased services provided without charge, subsidized basic goods, fixed prices below what they would have been in the market, and then tried to supplement the goods and services available from abroad without giving a *quid pro quo* for these. "Dollar shortage" is a convenient shorthand term for the notion that the United States ought to subsidize Britain.

How the contradictions worked out in practice have been described by Bertrand de Jouvenel. "The incomes of British private citizens, taken as a whole, were, in 1945, seventy-five per cent above the 1938 level. But it was far from the case that there was on offer to buyers a seventy-five per cent increase of goods and services!..." On the contrary, "the actual position in 1945 was that a seventy-five per cent increase in incomes was matched by a fourteen per cent diminution in consumable goods and services...."[7]

In the free market, this disparity would have been closed by rising prices. But the government did not allow this to take place. Instead, it maintained price controls and rationing. In consequence, prices remained comparatively low for such things as food, clothing, such shelter as could be had, and electricity. The British people were able to spend a much smaller percentage of their incomes for such necessities, compared, say, with Americans. As a result, "British purchasing power ...overflows wherever it can. Expenditure on drink rose to 238 per cent of what it had been before the war, on tobacco to 340 per cent."[8] Much of this income was spent on goods that were imported, such as tobacco.

Since government action had produced the conditions in which such ironic results occurred, the logical course would have been to change the policies: stop the inflation, end the rationing, remove the price controls, and so forth. To have done so, of course, might have entailed the admission of error by politicians, a general phenomenon without precedent in popularly elected governments. It would certainly have meant the abandonment of much of the surge toward socialism.

Instead of admitting it was to blame, the government turned more of its force on the British people. The government acted as if the people were to blame. They should not spend the money in the way they did. They should not buy so much that could otherwise be sold to foreigners, nor consume so much that had to be bought from abroad. One writer describes the increased use of force in this way:

Whilst appeals for higher production rang in their ears, the public found, in Dalton's autumn budget of 1947, cigarettes rising ... in price "in a deliberate drive to cut smoking by a quarter." "And smoke your cigarettes to the butts," said the Chancellor, "it may even be good for your health." American films stopped arriving in Britain when a seventy-five per cent import duty was imposed, and cinemas began to empty. Timber and petrol imports were cut, so newspapers shrank back to four pages and the basic petrol ration was abolished, although anyone living more than two miles from public transport could draw a supplementary allowance. Foreign travel was suspended and public dinners dwindled into silence. Clothing coupons were cut, and there seemed to be less food than there had ever been since the beginning of the war. It became a criminal offense to switch a fire on during the summer months.[9]

These measures were accompanied by efforts to increase production. "Much of the wartime direction of manpower was revived.... Under the Control of Engagements Order, which went into effect in October [1947], new employment could be secured only through the exchanges. Applicants would be advised to go into priority industries and under some circumstances would be directed to do so.... In November an order required registration of all the unemployed and those in trades considered non-essential — football pools, amusements arcades, night clubs, and the like. By these measures it was hoped to draw into industry a million additional workers."[10]

Even this combination of Draconian measures did not close the "dollar gap." As a matter of fact, once independent Britons had gone hat in hand to the United States asking for a large extension of credit, the delegation having been headed by Lord John Maynard Keynes. They were granted 3¾ billions of dollars which was supposed to last for several years. Actually, however, the deficit was so great in 1947 that the amount of credit available could hardly cover it. In 1948, Britain was granted nearly one billion additional dollars under the Marshall Plan. Americans were led to believe at the outset that aid to Britain was for the purpose of enabling that country to recover from the war. Yet, it should be clear that for the several years following World War II the

British were not simply having difficulty recovering from the war. Matters grew much worse after a couple of years of socialism than they had been during the war. The British were caught in the toils of their own government, at the behest of a majority of the electorate. They were struggling with might and main against the disabling impact of socialism. The United States was not helping Britain recover from the war; it was subsidizing socialism. By subsidizing socialism, the United States government helped the Labour government to survive a few years, while concealing from the British people, as well as from other peoples of the world, the full extent of the debacle.

Socialism in England did not simply wreck the economy; the efforts which had these results had other and undesirable side effects. Among these was a widespread demoralization and corruption of some portion of the populace. The British have long enjoyed a high repute for obedience to the law. They have usually been exemplary citizens in contrast with the peoples of some continental countries, where evasion of the law is so common as to be nearly universal. Socialism changed things in Brtiain, or let loose something in the British character that had been more restrained theretofore. In 1937, there had been only 266,265 indictable offenses; the number had jumped to 522,684 by 1948. "In 1951, cases of violence against the person, which had soared steadily since the war, were two and a half times more than in 1938, and criminals, it seemed, were three times more viley sexual."[11] Another writer describes the development in this way, saying that since 1945 the "public have increasingly devoted themselves to the evasion of the law and to operations upon the black markets. Contempt for authority has increased; class consciousness has become more acute; cynicism regarding corruption in public life more prevalent; personal and class irresponsibility more in evidence; gambling practices more widespread."[12]

However elegantly the rationale for socialism may be expressed, it does not succeed for long in obscuring its true nature from at least some portion of the citizenry. Socialism is a plan for the use of force, for confiscation, for taking from some to give to others, for disturbing or changing the character of relations among people. When people find themselves thwarted by deprivation and restrictions attendant upon such programs, they turn to the very methods government has more subtly been using: theft and violence.

The English electorate signaled their own belief in the failure of socialism by turning the Labour Party out of power in 1951. The Conservatives returned to power from 1951 to 1964. They restored a modicum of domestic tranquillity to the United Kingdom. There was even talk once again of British affluence. The value of the pound was stabilized on the world market in this interim between two socialist governments. The iron and steel industries were denationalized. Controls were already being relaxed in certain areas before the return of the Conservatives, and they were much more generally removed thereafter. As rationing ended, so did the shortages it had produced.

The return of Labour to power in 1964 under the guidance of Harold Wilson was the signal for new troubles and an accentuation of old ones. The pound has, of course, declined in value, and while it still could, the United States was called upon to shore up the currency. The will to nationalize was not very strong, but the tentacles of gradualist socialism are still firmly fastened on the country.

Indeed, it may well be that the British experience, plus that of communist and other countries, has convinced many evolutionary socialists that government ownership of the means of production is not necessary or even desirable for the attainment of their ends. So far as the economy is concerned, it may be sufficient that government have firm control over production and distribution. That is certainly the most general tendency of the movement. To examine this type of gradualism, we turn now to Sweden and then the United States. Sweden offers an opportunity also to focus upon gradualism within a monarchical and traditional frame; while the United States provides an example of the republican case. More important, perhaps, both countries provide evidence of what may be a shift in gradualism toward the emphasis upon the transformation of man and society.

(It is too early, of course, even to hazard a guess as to what the results of the general elections of 1979 presage for Britain. It may mean no more than that the electorate are weary of the directionless backing and filling of the Labourites. Or, it could indicate that the British, who had earlier largely abandoned nationalization, or further nationalization, are preparing to abandon socialism entire. If Britain should break the grip of the Idea, liberal intellectualism would no longer have a secure base. That would be a portentous event!)

Book V

Social Democracy in Sweden

The Matrix of Tradition and Gradualism

TO THE NORTH, Sweden extends into the Arctic circle. In the summer, that portion of the country is in the land of the midnight sun. In winter, there is darkness at noon. Even as far south as Stockholm the sun does not ascend very high in the midst of winter. Such light as it gives for a short time is more like twilight than daylight. Indeed, it is appropriate to think of Sweden as a Twilight Zone.

Physically, Sweden lies very near to the twilight zone between Soviet Communism and the Europe that yet enjoys considerable freedom. Its northern boundary is not far from that of the Soviet Union. Its southern boundary is across the Baltic Sea from East Germany. Socially, Sweden is in the twilight zone between tradition and the compulsion of socialism. Economically, Sweden is in the twilight zone between private enterprise and the controlled economy. Internationally, Sweden has long been neutral, a twilight zone inhabited by nations which refuse to take sides. Gradualism, or evolutionary socialism, is a twilight zone, and Sweden has for a good many years been the reputed showpiece of that ideology.

There are several good reasons for selecting Sweden as one of the exemplars of evolutionary socialism. The most obvious reason is in some ways the least convincing: namely, Sweden's reputation as a socialist country. This, it turns out, is largely press agentry. There should be no doubt that the idea that has the world in its grip has a firm grasp on Sweden; but Sweden is not socialist by conventional definitions, an important point to which we will return. Nevertheless, Sweden has had some forty years under the political leadership of Social Democrats, a party that is professedly socialist and has its roots in Marxism. Nowhere is the welfare state aspect of the idea more firmly imbedded.

Another reason for selecting Sweden is the place that tradition still formally holds in the country. Evolutionary socialism is everywhere national socialism (which is to say that it occurs within the framework of nations and partakes of the character of each particular nation), but even so there are two distinct political settings in which it has taken place: monarchies and republics. Sweden is a monarchy. As such, it belongs to a configuration of nations, largely on the periphery of Europe, such as Denmark, Norway, the Netherlands, and England, which have thus far survived the thrust to republicanism which had its onset in Europe with the French Revolution. At any rate, Sweden has a monarch, an established church, and an hereditary nobility.

Such things are, of course, anathema to socialists. Every good socialist is *ipso facto* a republican, an anti-monarchist, an opponent of the religious establishment, and despises all signs of inequality — in theory, anyway. In practice, it has not worked quite that way. Evolutionary socialism had made some of its deepest inroads in lands with hereditary monarchs. Gradualism has proceeded most smoothly and with the least disturbance in these lands.

There is a reason for this. In republics, men are theoretically equal before the law, and they do not relish or readily accept the intrusions in their affairs that come with gradualism. To put it another way, republicans are generally anti-authoritarian, and socialists are bent on using the political authority to accomplish their ends.

By contrast, monarchs are the very symbols of authoritarianism. People living under them have been conditioned to accept the imposition of authority by those who rule. Socialists may not be comfortable bedfellows with kings, but the exercise of arbitrary power is made easier for them when they have the royal authority behind them. Tradition, too, accommodates change, even those changes made by evolutionary socialism which destroy tradition at its roots. For these reasons, it is important to examine gradualism against a monarchical background.

274

There is yet another reason for selecting Sweden. Sweden is an industrialized country with a relatively high standard of living. As such things go, it is a prosperous country. When choosing examples, it is better to take from what are reckoned to be the best than to take the worst.

It should be clear already that there are important differences between revolutionary and evolutionary socialism. But it may be helpful to highlight some of them. Revolutionary socialism is brutal, tyrannical, destructive, and dictatorial. Its most conspicuous fruits are totalitarianism and total war. The "law school" of revolutionary socialism is the concentration camp, as has been pointed out. Citizens in such countries are only by some degrees removed from slavery. Gradualism, in a country such as Sweden, is clearly an improvement over such conditions. It is, however, only a shift from darkness into the twilight.

Revolutionary and evolutionary socialists are brothers under the skin. To put it in the terms of this work, communists, Nazis, and gradualists are ideological brothers. All of them derive their spring from the same central idea. That is, they aim to concert all energies toward common goals, to root out and destroy all cultural supports to the individual's pursuit of his own self-interest, and use government power to impose their programs. They differ as to methods, not as to goals.

There are two major differences between revolutionary and evolutionary socialism, along with subsidiary ones. One major difference is that evolutionary socialists are pragmatic rather than dogmatic. That is, they are pragmatic as to method though they may be equally dogmatic with revolutionary socialists as to goals. When they are being pragmatic, they may, for example, prefer the control of industry over ownership. In like manner, they may abondon one sort of approach in favor of another without any sense of betraying their goals. One way to say it is that they do not know exactly how socialism will be achieved, or when, but they believe that they are headed in the right direction so long as more and more control over affairs is being collectivized.

Another major difference between gradualists and revolutionaries is that gradualists propose to achieve their ends democratically. They advocate and generally hold free elections, advance near universal suffrage, and permit a variety of candidates to enter the races for office. There is, however, a fundamental contradiction in their position. The implicit theory on which they operate holds that by the process of voting and election the government becomes the voice and arm of society. Society is, so to speak, politicized and empowered. (Rousseau's theory of the "general will" is the best known and probably most thorough exposition of this notion. It is set forth in *The Social Contract.)*

In fact, however, modern democracies operate by the rule of majorities and pluralities. Even if we assume that the output from voting machines could somehow be the will of society — a notion which puts considerable strain on the imagination — society is divided by democratic elections. Nor can it be otherwise if there are to be choices of candidates and positions.

Whatever the virtues of majoritarian rule, unity is not one of them. Yet it is essential to the idea that has the world in its grip that government should act to concert all efforts for the common good. If society is divided as to what constitutes the common good, this can be but a forcing of some people's notions of the common good on others. Hitler's plebiscites and Soviet Communism's one-party slates are much more nearly consistent with the idea. It is fundamentally inconsistent to suppose that real choices can be made politically, that society can be politicized, and that there can be general accord on actions taken. If society could be politicized it would be polarized by every election.

Gradualists attempt to paper over this contradiction. Their programs are what "the people" want, they are given to saying. Theirs are "social reforms," they declare, implying somehow that they arise from society. Too, they attempt to narrow the gap between parties by having them all support similar ideas and policies. To the extent that they can get agreement that whatever is at issue is a legitimate concern of government, they tend to succeed in this. To the extent that they are able to keep the issue in the frame of how much and when, rather than whether, they tend to succeed also. These tactics tend both to obscure the real divisions among a people and enable gradualists to advance toward their goal step by step.

Gradualists generally preserve the *procedural* protections of civil liberties. Thus far, this is a critical difference between evolutionary and revolutionary socialism. Procedures tend only to be a facade for revolutionaries, something to be ignored if they get in the way of the desired line of action. Procedural protections have generally enabled citizens in lands where gradualism holds sway to enjoy a considerable variety of civil liberties. But procedures are just that — established ways for government to act — not anything substantial.

There is no place in socialist ideology for liberties to be natural rights;

276

their only theoretical justification is utilitarian. Utility is a slippery concept at best, and where the common good is arbiter of utility, utility is whatever those who have the power to determine it say it is. There are two other supports to civil liberty: tradition (which includes constitutions) and private property. Since gradualists are devoted to eroding away tradition and private property, the more they succeed the more precarious will be civil liberties.

Be all that as it may, there are important differences between revolutionary and evolutionary socialism. The differences become blurred in many countries of what is called the Third World. But in the constitutional democracies of Western Europe and America the differences are thus far clear and distinct. The tyranny of communism is on a different scale and order from anything yet occurring in these lands. Gradualists operate within the framework of laws, however attenuated these may become, to achieve their ends. They do not usually crush groups; rather, they empower them within a framework of controls. It is the individual, then, who usually feels the weight of their force. He is isolated if he does not belong to some group. He is powerless, or nearly so, if he cannot conjure up some popular support. If he does not yield voluntarily to the weight of numbers, he will most likely be punished by the state. The individual's last line of defense is his property, but that is increasingly circumscribed as gradualism advances.

So it is in Sweden and in other lands where gradualism holds sway.

Even so, Sweden is not a socialist country by conventional definition. By the usual definition, socialism prevails when the government owns the means of production and distribution of goods. This is hardly the case in Sweden. Most of the productive enterprises in Sweden are privately owned. A London newspaper said, "Sweden has proportionately more private enterprise than any other country in west Europe."[1] The usual figures cited run something like this: about 7 per cent of the enterprises are state owned; 4 per cent cooperatively owned; and the remainder privately owned. The state is deeply involved in iron mining, the railways, the airlines, atomic energy, making of alcoholic beverages, and such like. Most of the rest of manufacturing is privately owned.[2] It is important to understand this when we come to discuss the sources of Swedish prosperity.

The notion that Sweden is socialist, in the conventional sense, is made up partly of assumption and partly of astute publicity. Until very recently, the Social Democrats have headed the governments in Sweden since the 1930's. The Social Democratic Party originated as a Marxist party, shifted toward gradualism, but continued to claim to be socialist. The long years of rule gave the impression, which Social Democrats found more advantage to claiming than denying, that Sweden was socialist.

Many Americans got their notions about Sweden from a little book by Marquis Childs. It is called *Sweden: The Middle Way,* was first published in 1936, and has appeared in several editions and a good many printings. Childs hailed Sweden as the exemplar of the middle way between communism and fascism. The "wave of the future" which Childs thought he beheld in Sweden was collectivism largely by way of cooperatives. However, Sweden did not develop along the lines that Childs foresaw in the mid-1930's. Cooperatives never gained much of a foothold in manufacturing and related enterprises, though they were somewhat more successful in merchandising. However mistaken his prophecy, Childs helped to spread the notion of a socialist Sweden.

If the Social Democrats had been bent on nationalizing Swedish industry, which some no doubt were, they never gained the kind of majorities that would have given them a free hand. Usually, they had only a plurality and had to govern along with some other party. They could ordinarily command only a slight majority in the *Riksdag* for much less controversial undertakings than the wholesale nationalizing of industries. But it is by no means clear that they would have gone that route had their support been much more substantial.

In any case, Swedish prosperity can hardly be attributed to socialism as it is usually defined. Moreover, it is greatly to be doubted that socialism, however it may be defined or extended in meaning, plays any significant role in that prosperity. There are other and more cogent reasons which provide a sufficient explanation for that.

Sweden has some important natural resources and advantages of location. Perhaps the most impressive natural resource is the huge reserve of some of the finest iron ore in the world. Much of Sweden is forested, and lumbering, paper, and pulp are major industries. Streams in the north with their origins in the mountains provide the basis for numerous hydroelectric dams. Although Sweden lies north of the United States in latitude the climate is much milder than might be supposed, particularly in the south, owing to warming by the Gulf Stream. Hence, farming flourishes in southern Sweden. For the same reason, ports are generally open year round on the Baltic. Shipping and shipbuilding are major industries in Sweden.

What Sweden lacks, above all, are deposits of coal, oil, and gas. These must be imported, and Swedish industry and prosperity depend upon foreign trade. Indeed, Sweden is one of the major trading nations in the world. Fine Swedish steel has long enjoyed an international reputation, and Swedes compete on the world market in some of the most advanced products of modern technology. It may well be that the Swedes are addicted to modernity as much as or more than any other people in the world.

Sweden has enjoyed and benefited from over 160 years of being at peace at home and abroad. The country has not gone to war since the end of the Napoleonic wars. The Swedes have been in our era if not the most peaceful people at least among the most neutral. Their energy and vitality have not been sapped by war, and their cities and countryside have not been destroyed by an invader. True, the Swedes maintain a considerable military establishment, and their troops have gone forth in recent times on call from the United Nations, but Sweden continues to enjoy the benefits of peace.

The Swedes have been a remarkably homogenous people ethnically and religiously. This may have contributed little to their prosperity in recent times, but it has probably made it much easier to remain at peace. Minorities, when they are very numerous, sometimes — ofttimes — make for internal discord, and if they are recently from other lands they may well promote involvement in wars.

At any rate, the Swedes are very nearly separated from the mainland of continental Europe by the sea, joined by land only to Norway and Finland, and have not been troubled for a long while by invasions or propulsive migrations of other peoples. Until the twentieth century, the flow of Swedes was outward rather than of other peoples toward them. The Vikings pressed downward upon Europe in the Middle Ages, and many of them settled there. Even as late as the latter part of the nineteenth century, there was a massive Swedish migration to the United States. By contrast, other peoples have not been drawn to Sweden. Before the twentieth century, the people were generally poor, and the climate is such that only Eskimos, Finns, and some Norweigians would find it an improvement.

As to religion, most Swedes are technically Lutherans, as their forebears have been for centuries. There is only a scattering of Jews and Roman Catholics among them, and the "free" Protestant churches have drawn but a few into their fold. Motorcycle riders are more numerous than any of these minorities, are probably more influential, and are certainly more likely to disturb the peace.

279

Resources, location, peace, and other such conditions are but potentialities, however. What makes the difference is the use of resources, the taking advantage of location, and the following of productive peaceful pursuits. Location and relative weakness may have contributed to Sweden's neutrality, but the peace achieved has been the result of a more positive concept than that. It has been the concept of a world drawn together in trade, in intellectual interchange, free movement of people, and living in mutual tolerance of one another. The Swedes appear to have grasped more clearly than most that their prosperity and well-being was dependent on a far-flung trade which worked best in times of peace.

More than anything else, it was the triumph of liberalism in nineteenth century Sweden which loosed the energies of the people who began to change the potentialities of their condition into the actuality of productivity and prosperity. The foundations of Swedish prosperity were laid in a series of developments which took place between 1750 and the third quarter of the nineteenth century.

The first major development was the break-up of the medieval pattern of farming. This occurred by two related developments: the enclosure of land into consolidated holdings, and the acquiring of more and more land privately owned as small and medium-sized farms. Swedish tenants had customarily tended several small strips of land spread out over an estate. The consolidation of holdings began in the latter part of the eighteenth century and continued apace in the nineteenth century. As a result, there was considerable increase in agricultural production.

Another major development was the freeing of trade. Sweden was, in the Age of Mercantilism (seventeenth and eighteenth centuries most notably and disastrously), under the sway of mercantile practices. The Swedish government levied tariffs on exports and imports, granted monopolies, subsidized production, and restricted domestic trade. These restrictions may well have peaked just after the Napoleonic wars when hundreds of items were placed on a forbidden list. The results were disastrous.

By the 1820's a countertrend was getting under way, and by 1860 trade was substantially free so far as the Swedes were concerned. Accompanying the establishment of free-trade was the freeing of enterprise generally from the fetters of mercantilism. Free trade is often thought of as an absence of or very low tariffs. This, however, is only its most obvious surface feature. What is more deeply involved is the

280

opening of the way for whoever will to offer his custom in the market-place. At its outermost reaches, it is free enterprise.

When enterprise was substantially freed, there was a rapid growth in industrial and agricultural production. These developments are well described by a historian of Sweden:

Previously, most of Sweden's iron had been exported, but during the last decades of the nineteenth century, a rising proportion of it was used to feed her own industries.... While factories and work shops were widely scattered, the town of Eskilstuna became the "Sheffield" of Sweden. And Norrköping became her Manchester for this and Boras ... were the leading textile centres of the country. Expansion here was not so dramatic, but twice as much cotton was spun in 1900 as in 1870. In addition to these key enterprises, a host of other forms of manufacture either, like the chemical, electrical and cement industries, appeared for the first time, or were greatly expanded during the period.

... In 1860 farming methods were fundamentally little different from what they had been in the seventeenth century. The following decades, however, brought a great transformation. Iron ploughs and harrows began to be widely used, and harvesters and other mechanical devices were rapidly adopted. The use of chemical fertilizers and the improvement of seed by selection raised the productivity of land already under cultivation, while many marshes were drained and wasteland made fertile.... In dairying, the use of the mechanical cream separator, invented by the Swede Gustaf de Laval in 1878, greatly increased the output of butter, which again became one of Sweden's major exports....[3]

These were the conditions within which the Swedes became much more productive and relatively prosperous. No sooner, however, did they substantially increase their productivity than did the gleam of redistribution appear in the eyes of their politicians. The justification of both redistribution and control over production was found in socialist ideology. The Social Democrats, carriers of revisionist Marxism, have been the main proponents of this ideology in twentieth century Sweden, but they have been aided and abetted in their endeavors quite often by the members of other political parties. They have made great headway in putting many of these ideas into practice.

Before getting into that, however, one point needs to be re-emphasized and a new one made. The point that needs to be re-emphasized is that most industry in Sweden has remained in private hands. Thus, private enterprise (not to be confused here with free enterprise) is the basic source of such prosperity as the Swedes enjoy. The new point is that the economic system which prevails in Sweden might best be described as Welfare State Capitalism.

Some little explanation of the phrase — Welfare State Capitalism — may be helpful. There are those who use the word "capitalism" in a laudatory sense, and they are apt to equate it with the free market and free enterprise. Socialists usually use the term invidiously. Even so, capitalism is a socialist concept; Karl Marx popularized it. Those who think to pre-empt the term and give it a favorable connotation might do well to reconsider.

"Ism" smacks of ideology; and ideology smacks of some scheme to use the power of government. However that may be, capital*ism* denotes a preference for or bias in favor of capital expenditure or investment. Socialists use the term to connote a system in which private capital and capitalists are accorded special privileges. The connotative uses of capitalism have entered into the rhetoric which those of all persuasions employ, and there is little likelihood that will change in the foreseeable future; but it is important here that the word be used with as much analytical precision as can be attained.

All peoples use capital, i.e., make capital investments. The savage who has an instrument to remove the husk of a coconut is a user of capital. The primitive who saved seed and used an implement to furrow the soil was a capitalist. Every economic system is, in this sense, capitalistic in that capital is employed to increase production. The only possible difference is in how the capital is provided. There are two basic ways of doing this. One is for individuals to save and invest voluntarily. The other is for the government to take the money from individuals — to confiscate it, that is — and for the investment decisions to be made by those who rule. When the first system prevails it is sometimes called private capitalism. When the second prevails it can be called state capitalism. Such a system is generally employed in the Soviet Union, for example.

Variations and combinations of these two basic systems are possible. The most common combination has been joint financing of projects by private investors and money raised in some fashion by government. Another variation is for government to promote saving and capital investment by tax policies. Sweden has used both these methods, but predominately it has provided tax advantages in order to foster capital formation and investment.

One way this is done is by the Investment Funds. These were first authorized by law in 1938, and the enactment has since been amended several times. "The current position is that by law, every company is permitted to set aside 40 per cent of its profits before tax in any year to an investment fund. There are, however, restrictions attached to this concession. Forty-six per cent of this money must be deposited interest free in a blocked account in the Central Bank of Sweden and can only be spent on authorization either by the Crown or by the Labour Market Board for specific projects concerned with investment — the only exception is that after five years a company can spend up to 30 per cent of the money set aside without authority from the Board provided this is on a capital project."[4] Since taxes on profits of corporations are high, on the average about 54 per cent when those of the central and regional governments are combined, there is considerable incentive to place money in the Investment Funds.

The other major device for promoting investment is the depreciation policy of the government. All capital expenditure from the Investment Funds must be fully depreciated within twelve months of the outlay. All other capital expenditures must be depreciated fully within five years, either in equal installments or on a pre-arranged scale. The result: "There is pressure on the companies to maintain a steady stream of investment with a major installation at least every five years, both to obtain the depreciation tax allowance and to even after-tax profits."[5]

It would help in clarifying our thinking if the word capitalism were reserved for use to refer to those systems in which the compulsive power of the state is used to form capital and direct its investment or to instances of it. Why? Because in a free economy there is no preference for or bias in favor of capital expenditure. Nor is it at all clear why there should be preference for capital expenditure over any other in public policy. It may appear that in view of all the benefits that accrue from capital a bias in favor of it might be in order. But appearances can be deceiving, and they are in this case. It happens that capital expenditure can be wasteful and counterproductive. No benefit would presumably result from expenditure to produce a product which no one wanted. Such expense would be a waste of scarce resources.

There will undoubtedly be instances of malinvestment in a free economy, for there is no certainty that any investment will pay off. But there is a sure way to achieve wasteful and counterproductive capital expenditure. It is to separate the ultimate investor from the responsibility and benefits of careful management as occurs in state capitalism, or to make capital expenditures profitable by tax breaks and depreciation allowances. (In a free economy, taxes would fall only on individuals, not on fictitious entities such as corporation and companies. Hence, there would be no occasion for depreciation allowances and some portion of the present crop of Certified Public Accountants.) It would be descriptive to refer to such systems as capital*ism* and capital*istic,* and they could have whatever onus anyone wished to attach to them. They would describe a preference for or bias in favor of capital expenditure.

Since current usage is generally either rhetorical or propagandic, it is necessary to add qualifiers in order to make them as nearly as may be descriptive. The terms private capitalism and state capitalism may be reasonably precise. I here add the phrase, Welfare State Capitalism, by which I understand government policies, such as those in Sweden, aimed at promoting capital expenditure in support of the welfare state. A Swede put it this way, "The state keeps the cow fat in order to increase the amount of milk it can get from it." That is, of course, only a felicitously phrased half-truth. There is evidence that the "cow" is bloated rather than healthily fat in some industries, such as shipbuilding, for instance; and there are critical shortages, such as in housing, due to misallocation of funds. It is well to keep in mind, too, that Sweden's tax policies are aimed not only at fueling the welfare state but also at bringing industry under centralized planning.

Even so, the main point here is that Sweden does not have socialism as that word is understood. The government may be gradually killing the goose that lays the golden eggs, but to date it has put maximum pressure on the goose to lay more eggs. So much has been told to make it clear that the sources of such prosperity as Sweden enjoys are in private industry.

Yet Sweden is deeply under the sway of the idea that has the world in its grip. And that idea can be identified with socialism usually. To understand how this can be, it is necessary to expand our understanding of socialism. The heart of socialist doctrine is the idea of purging the individual of his pursuit of self-interest. The main line of attack is on the inherited culture and tradition — on the family, the church, education, morality, and society itself. In place of these will come government power. That is what has been happening in Sweden.

On the face of it, tradition is honored and preserved in Sweden. This is largely an illusion. Sweden has a monarch, but he does not rule. He sits in at the formal cabinet meetings for the perfunctory presentation of matters that have already been decided, but he may only enliven proceedings by remarks, not by participating in the decisions. Sweden has an established church with beautiful buildings lavishly furnished, but few people attend except at Christmas and Easter. Sweden's industry is largely privately owned, but the independence of investors has been eroded away. Sweden has an elected legislature, but the fount of decisions is usually the advice of experts. What remains of tradition has perhaps more importance than the restored hull of a medieval Viking ship which has been raised from the bottom of the sea to be put on display in one of the cities, but not much more. Tradition has been eviscerated in favor of gradualism.

The story of how this has taken place needs now to be told.

23
The Paternal State

ONE OF THE most curious notions of our era is that of the paternal state. Not that it lacks antecedents; it even has a history, of sorts, going back into the dim past of which there is little record. Nor is it curious because we ordinarily refer to it as the paternal state, for we do not. Ordinarily, it is called the welfare state, or, by some of its proponents, the social service state. It is a notion only in the sense, then, that it is the idea which underlies the practices we have come to associate with something that is called the welfare state.

The welfare state notion does not strike most people as odd or curious, so far as we can tell. Clearly, if politicians can run for office and get elected on the basis that they will provide a great variety of goodies, the idea is widely accepted. That it should be so accepted, however, does not mean that it lacks curiosity; it is rather testimony to the fact that when an idea becomes sufficiently familiar, no matter how peculiar it is, it can become a part of the perspective from which we see things. Then it will seem strange that at other times and places people did not see or do it that way.

The paternal state notion is curious, in the first place, because it misconstrues the character of the state. The state is not something that can be likened to a father. It does not beget, as a father has done. Nor is it a provider, as the father is supposed to be. The state, or government, is begotten, but is itself sterile, sexless, and forever barren. It has no means of its own and is incapable of producing any. It is, so to speak, an abstraction. Whatever the state bestows, it must first take from those who have produced it. Unlike a real life father, it cannot look after us; we must first look after it.

In the second place, the paternal state is a curious notion when viewed in the light of most of history. Those who have governed have usually been the possessors of such ostentatious wealth as was abroad in the land. They have usually been in possession of the finest residences, the best clothes, the most servants, the finest conveyances, and whatever happen to be the going trappings of office. Far from being material benefactors of the people, they have usually been beneficiaries of an unwilling largess from the people. They have entangled their peoples in dynastic wars, taken their substance in order to realize the personal ambitions of rulers, and all too often played havoc with the lives and goods of the people. Far from being father-like — seeking the good of their children — they have all too often been robber-like and jailor-like. It is greatly to be doubted that the notion of the paternal state would ever have arisen from an empirical study of history.

Even so, government, or the state, may have arisen on analogy with paternity or as the paternal state. Historians have been generally of the view that government may have come into being as rule over the extended family. The organization is usually referred to as the clan. The clan was ruled over by the oldest male, or the male from whom all traced their lineage. If the orientation was maternal, or if allowance was made for maternal rule, the ruler might be the oldest female. The bounds of the state would be the lands claimed by the clan. Such an arrangement would, no doubt, be a paternal state. Nor would its character change greatly if it were enlarged to include several clans and these should be ruled by a council of elders. Family ties, at least within clans, would make it still fundamentally paternal. Undoubtedly, the task fell upon the elders of providing for and looking after those in their care.

The rudiments of this idea can be discerned in hereditary monarchy and similar arrangements. The king was not literally the father of his people, of course, but he could be thought of in that way. Some monarchs have been described as "father," or "little father." The council of elders might survive, too, under various names. (The Witan was some such council in England, for instance, as is the surviving House of Lords.) The Roman Catholic Church uses language drawn from paternity to describe many of its clergy. The hereditary feature of monarchy must derive from the paternal concept. While we may doubt

287

that the paternal state could rightfully be applied to monarchies, it does trace its roots to the same idea.

What is curious here, however, is that socialists should produce and champion a paternal state. Virtually every idea in it has been anathema to socialists. They have ever been ideologically opposed to monarchy. They have been, in all instances, convinced and committed republicans. The paternal state is a conservative idea. Modern socialism stems from the time of the French Revolution, when the emphasis was upon individual rights, when family, tradition, and the whole paraphernalia from the past were in question. Custom and age were losing veneration. Mechanical concepts were replacing ancient ties of flesh and blood.

Moreover, conservatives have played a role in advancing the paternal or welfare state. Disraeli in England, a leading conservative of the latter part of the nineteenth century, took a hand in introducing welfare measures. Even more impressively, Otto von Bismarck, a reputed conservative and Germany's leading political figure of the latter part of the nineteenth century, brought welfarism to Germany. As one history says, "Between 1884 and 1889 gigantic welfare schemes, the first of their kind in the modern world, provided health, accident, and disability insurance, pensions for widows, orphans, and the aged, giving workers greater security and better living conditions."[1] It is not uncommon to read that conservatives enacted welfare measures in Sweden.

However, writers often ascribe this penchant for welfare legislation in conservatives to untoward motives. Bismarck, it is sometimes said, was end-playing the socialists. He may have been, of course, but we have no way of being certain of his motives. In any case, conservatives are as entitled to a presumption in favor of the purity of their motives as anyone else. And for politicians to seek advantage through their acts only appears strange to those who can imagine large numbers of self-less people, something that is possible in the imagination but unlikely in the real world. In short, if conservatives have, with some consistency, advanced welfarism the answer should be sought in conservatism, not in something they share with everyone else.

And there is an explanation within conservatism. One of the facets of conservatism is paternalism. The role of the father as head of the household is an ancient and venerated practice. In an extended fashion, the role of the elders within the community as providers and carers for those in need is of long establishment. That those-who-have should aid those-who-have-not is one of the deepest springs of conservatism. Thus are the bonds of community knit together and the common humanity of those within it confirmed. Conservatives in power in a state have a tendency to devise and support the paternal state.

This may be somewhat confusing to many of those who think of themselves as conservatives in the United States. Many thoughtful American conservatives are not in the least sympathetic with governmental paternalism (though there are those who are). Indeed, it can be argued that to be conservative in America is to be opposed to governmental paternalism. There is a historical explanation for this. A strenuous effort was made at the founding of the United State to delimit paternalism. The doctrine of limits pervades our constitutional arrangements. Whatever arrangements a father wished to make for his household were left to him. Associations of men were in like manner left to their devices to form communities and do within them what they would, so long as in so doing they avoided doing some civil or criminal injury. Such arrangements required, of course, that the force of government be denied to any and all in effecting their ends.

It is commonly said that there is a separation of church and state in the United States. The matter runs even deeper than this. Though it is nowhere formally stated, there is a separation of parenthood and the state. At the founding of the United States the individual was released from the tutelage of the state, so to speak. A profound distinction was made between what is the affair of individuals and what are affairs of state. That is the essence of constitutionalism in America. To defend those arrangements became political conservatism in America. Paternalism may have been augmented in America, but it was a paternalism divorced from politics.

European conservatism has a different flavor to it. The separation between parentage and the state that occured in America did not occur generally in Europe. An American and a European conservative may share similar values, but the import of these values is altered by differences of perspective. The dangers of the state were not so obvious to European conservatives as to Americans. Indeed, those who hold and wield power are unlikely to be impressed with the danger of it, for men do not ordinarily consider themselves dangerous. The paternal stance is, after all, ego flattering, and European conservatives kept it within the makeup of their perspective.

It is not my point, however, that the animus to the creation of the welfare state came from conservatives. That is about as likely as that sow's ears come from silk purses. Socialism provided the yeast for the welfare state; the people provided the dough; and conservatism provided its intricate patterns. To put it another way, the paternal or welfare state is the end product, thus far, of socialist equalitarian prescriptions when they have been winnowed through the overlay of conservatism in society. The distributive thrust is socialist; the shifting bubbles are populist; and the paternalism is conservative.

As if all this were not irony enough, this strange blend is often referred to as liberalism, not only by American writers but by those in other parts of the world as well. Historic liberalism was not in the least paternal. Its main thrust in the nineteenth century was to limit government, to free the individual, to permit trade without let or hindrance, to expand the suffrage and popular government. The equality that animated liberals was one that held that no man having reached seniority ought to be under the tutelage of another. In the quest for this condition, liberals relied rather heavily on extending the vote and establishing or maintaining popular government. Now, however, we have the paternal state which is widely proclaimed as liberal. Proponents of the welfare state have gone far toward co-opting the available intellectual positions.

The topic at hand, of course, is Sweden and the paternal state. Since Sweden does not proclaim itself to be a paternal state, and since the phrase is by no means generally employed, some proof of the proposition is in order.

What is a paternal state? It is, in brief, a state which takes over and performs the functions of a father, or those of the dominant parent. Since some may have forgotten the role of the father and the grounds for it, it may be helpful to recall it. It is on the father's physical initiative that the act is begun by which conception takes place. Since the male's physical condition is unaltered by the ensuing pregnancy and since, in any case, he is larger and stronger, it is his responsibility and function to provide for the female and the unborn infant during the period of pregnancy. It is his task, of course, to make provision for the delivery of the child.

A newborn infant is helpless, or very nearly so, having only the ability to breathe and the capacity to take nourishment. In this situation, the main task of the father is to protect infant and mother and provide food, clothing, and shelter. Since the human child does not become large or strong or sufficiently well developed to look after himself for several years after birth, both parents perform assorted functions for him. They not only provide for his basic material needs but also such medical care as he requires, for instruction (education) in their culture, for his moral

290

indoctrination, and for such training as may fit him for becoming an adult.

To the father particularly belongs the instruction and training of a son, and to the mother that of a daughter, assisted as they may be by the surrounding community. As the child grows toward manhood, he takes on more and more the role of the adult and becomes less and less dependent on his parents. As the parents grow old and lose their powers the time arrives for the child to attend them in their declining years.

In practice, of course, it does not always happen that way. The father can terminate the relationship at any stage that he will. Nor does it necessarily occur that mother and offspring will perform in the way described. Hence, there have usually been cultural prescriptions, religious sanctions, and, mayhap, legal enactments to insure the performance of these roles. The roles are themselves founded in nature, but the support of them is cultural.

"Paternal" is descriptive of and derives from the normal role of the father during the formative years of the child. A paternal state is one which assumes or imitates this role. Sweden was one of the first and may be thought of as the model of the paternal state. Until a more thoroughgoing one is devised, Sweden *is* the paternal state.

A qualification is in order. Human fathers have not been entirely replaced in Sweden. But a major shift of the functions of paternity from the father to the state has taken place.

To wit. There may be a gleam in the prospective mother's eye before conception ever takes place, a gleam aroused by the hope of reward. At the birth of an infant, the state steps forth and awards the mother over one thousand kronor (the Swedish monetary unit). Sometimes, a human father who was especially pleased has bestowed gifts on the new mother. The paternal state in Sweden has removed the element of chance; it is established by law and as sure as taxes.

As incubation begins, the state stands by to perform vital paternal functions. There are "free" maternity clinics for expectant mothers and their unborn children, and Papa State will pay three-fourths of the cost of dental care. Should custom or remote location lead to the use of a midwife, the state will pay the fee. If the expectant mother needs transport at her appointed time, the paternal state will pay for the cost of the taxi, even if the infant should be born therein. Should they be so fortunate as to make it to the hospital, the service there is "free." If the new mother has been renumeratively employed, she need have no anxiety about her job. The state has established that she may have up to

291

a total of six months leave which may be taken in any combination of prior to, during, and after the birth of the child.

There is one fly in all this ointment, however; in multiple births, the mother receives only one-half the award (only some 500 kronor) for each child above one.[2]

Having taken such pains thus far, it is hardly to be expected that the paternal state will abandon mother and child at the hospital. It will, of course, supplement the cost of housing for mother and child and, should the human father deign to live with them, for him as well. Should the mother be a "single parent," i.e., in a situation in which no wedding has preceded the birth, the state offers special attention and care. The state has caused to be built and set aside for their special use apartments for unmarried mothers. (As yet, no "swinging single" apartments have been built for unwed fathers.) There is also a category known as a "one-parent family," in which the parent may be either male or female, and the state offers aid to them in their undertaking.

Naturally, the paternal state provides support for each child regardless of the parental status of those with whom he dwells. The allowance to the mother for each child is 900 kronor per year. This particular payment ceases at the age of sixteen. In addition, if one of his parents dies, the child receives a "pension" of 1,300 kronor. If both parents should die, the amount is increased to 1,820 kronor. These payments stop at the age of sixteen also. Especially needy families can apply for and get additional supplements for each child. Mothers who grow weary of attending children can apply to the paternal state for a holiday grant. The grant pays not only for travel to and fro but also for the costs while at the rest home. Of course, there is industrial insurance to protect workers from injury or disease when they are at their employment (paid for by the employer as required by the state), but compensation takes into account the value of housework lost as a result of being harmed on the outside job.

The paternal state has not neglected to provide day nurseries for small children, although such facilities are said to be in short supply. There are nurseries where children may be placed for the day. There are also afternoon homes for children in school who can come to them after school and be looked after and fed while the mother is at work.

It should come as no surprise that the paternal state in Sweden provides for the formal education of the children. Of course, the schools are "free," as are schoolbooks, dental care, and such psychological attention as the child may require. College and university students are assisted by various loans and grants. Nor is there any need for parents to concern themelves about the character or quality of education, for that has been determined by the state. Of late, there have even been two sorts of school in the land, one of which was intially somewhat experimental.

Children are sometimes sick and afflicted in Sweden as elsewhere, as are also adults. All treatment in Swedish hospitals and clinics is "free." If, however, a physician is called to the home, he must be paid by the patient who can then turn in the receipt and get a refund of about three-fourths of the amount of the bill. Taxis to and from hospitals must also be paid on the spot, but the cost can be reclaimed by the presentation of the receipt.

Once the child has grown up and is ready to marry, or at least set up housekeeping on his own, the fatherly state is on hand to make the transition easier. The state does not quite provide a dowry; it is rather more like a combination of loans and aids. There are housing loans available, and the state will come forth with up to 15 per cent of the collateral value of the house. In some circumstances, a rent subsidy may be forthcoming if that path is followed rather than purchase. A home-furnishing loan can be obtained from the state also, with a maximum of 5,000 kronor to those in the greatest need.

Just as natural parents are relieved of much of the responsibility for their children, so does the paternal state relieve children of the necessity for caring for their parents in old age. An elaborate system of old age pensions is established. "The idea is to provide every wage-earner, on retirement, with a substantial pension directly related to — in practice about two-thirds of — his or her earnings in his or her prime. There are upper and lower limits to qualifying incomes, that part of the income lying outside these lines not counting for the calculation of supplementary pension. The eligible sum is termed the *pension-bearing* income, and it is a percentage of this amount.... which is payable by the employer in premiums. Self-employed persons must pay their own."[3] If an old person is not living in suitable accomodations, he can apply for housing in blocks set aside for old people. If, because of some debility, he should need occasional assistance this can be provided in his home. If he is no longer able to look after himself, he can go into an old people's home or into hospitals for the chronically ill.

Now here is an anomaly. It might be supposed that with much of the burden of the child bearing and rearing removed from natural parents there would be a great baby boom. Moreover, an additional thrust in this direction has been provided by removing every stigma from bearing

293

children out of wedlock (if one may employ so dated a term). But it has not turned out that way. As one writer says, "Sweden is extraordinary in its low birth rate and low rate of population increase."[4] As a matter of fact, the lump sum payment to the mother on the birth of a child was devised many years ago with the specific purpose of spurring an increase in births. To no avail. For some time now, Sweden has been encouraging immigrants to come in to augment the declining work force.

Cause and effect in human action is more complex than we may think. It takes place within a context much broader than man's simple legislation and piddling interventions. There is a law in physics that "For every action there is an equal and *opposite* reaction." (Italics added.) The working of the law may be illustrated in this fashion. When someone fires a gun there will be a kick from it. The kick from the gun is the equal and opposite reaction to the action of the bullet being fired from the gun. Reverberations (or repetitions) of action and reaction continue until the stock of the gun is still and the bullet has come to rest. The implications of this law are far-reaching, and we are justified in supposing that they extend to all happenings on this planet.

What will be the equal and opposite reaction to the action of a paternal state conferring benefits on some portion of the population? No answer can be made to such a question in the abstract. One might as well ask how strong a kick a hunter will receive from firing a gun. The recoil of a weapon is, of course, in direct proportion to the size of the explosion which propels the bullet from the gun. The size of the explosion is determined by the amount of the charge in the shell. There is no meaningful limit to the potential variations in the charge.

On the other hand, the expression of the recoil depends upon the materials used and the design of the gun. In some guns, the recoil comes out in the rise of the barrel. In others, it is felt in the stock of the weapon. In some, there is no perceptible kick, owing to weight distribution in the gun. There are even what are called "recoilless" weapons, by which we understand not that the law of compensation has been abridged but that the equal and opposite reaction has been so cushioned and dispersed that it can no longer be detected. All this is by way of saying that the character of the equal and opposite reaction is determined by the variables of the context within which the action occurs. It is, so to speak, a conditioned effect.

It is, then, the conditions in Sweden that determine the reaction to the actions of the welfare state. By many outward appearances Sweden is still a traditional land. There is the monarch, the royal family, the established church, and a government with roots deep into the past. Long observed festivals are reenacted, and folk songs and dances are performed as of yore. Much of the legislation which has brought forth the paternal state has a conservative cast to it. It is conservative to encourage young people to go out on their own and have their own housing. It is even more conservative to encourage marriage and the founding of families. The nurture and caring for children and seeing that they are housed, fed, clothed, and educated has about it a conservative aroma. That people should be looked after in their old age is of similar vintage.

The sound is not to be taken for the substance, however. Sweeden is a profoundly different land from what it was at the beginning of this century. A traditional overlay survives; but beneath it, surrounding it, and now overwhelming it, is something quite different. Sweden is under the sway of the idea that has the world in its grip. Those who think of Sweden in terms only of a modified socialism with certain economic policies have not begun to grasp the extent of the change.

The great change has come in the rooting out of the moral, spiritual, and cultural foundations of the society. The established church is still there; old churches still stand sometimes and many new ones have been built. But attendance is exceedingly slim. Individuals are in the church registers, but such a status requires nothing by way of religious observance, and little is done. Marriages often take place in churches but the frequent divorces saw the bonds of ties in civil surroundings. A new "morality" has arisen, a morality without foundation in transcendent sanctions. Gradualism has slowly devoured what formerly existed and replaced it with something else.

A major tenet of the idea that has the world in its grip is that government shall concert all efforts and bring about a collective unity. The power over affairs is shifted from individuals and families inwardly directed by custom, tradition, and morality to a state driven by goals proclaimed for the future. The acquisition of this power comes by way of the promises which add up to a paternal state.

What human motives are engaged from the populace in this shift of power to the state? Freud said that man wishes to return to the womb. Whether this is so or not, the present writer cannot profess to know. But it is clearly the case that there are aspects of childhood to which we would like to return if we have left or to retain if we are still there. Perhaps the most prominent one is freedom from responsibility. The child, the small child anyhow, ever has his material needs provided by someone else: he is suckled, diapered, warmed, and watched over by others. As he grows a little older he can arise at will, play until he is tired at whatever amuses him, and rest until he has recuperated. His is a life without the nuisance of responsibility and bounded only by the aggravations there may be in the exercise of external authority over him.

The paternal state grows on the tacit premise of restoring and maintaining an irresponsibility which has its roots in the childhood experience, then. It shifts the burdens of the adult to the state and, in hope, provides a perpetual childhood for the citizenry.

Within this framework it can be seen why the equal and opposite reactions to the actions of the paternal state are not what might be supposed. Why, when the paternal state has relieved so many of the burdens of parents and even provided rewards, is there not a baby boom in Sweden? Because — to put it in its simplest terms — the state has not relieved *all* the burdens, and that is the underlying promise and the expectation which its actions arouse.

Because expectant mothers grow large and unwieldy, have "morning" sickness, and their feet and legs are apt to swell on them. Because an infant is still brought forth in pain and suffering, even if the "free" taxi makes it to the "free" hospital. Because children still require a great deal of attention, however much assistance the state may provide. Because the bearing of children has its ultimate meaning within the framework of extended family, community, and moral and spiritual overtones. Because beaming grandparents are the human reward for a newborn child. Because the gathering of friends and relatives to inspect and "ooh" and "ah" over the infant is a normal incentive. Because Divine injunction supports replenishing the earth with children. Because the normal consequence of aroused sexual passion is conception.

Because socialists in devising the paternal state have tampered with and cut away the framework of bearing and nurturing of children and the purpose of the family. Because the idea of a perpetual child-like carefree existence would require that there be no children for whom to care. Because contraceptives and abortions are in accord with this idea rather than the bearing of children. Because the paternal state substitutes a cold and impersonal mechanism for the warmth that arises from the freedom and responsibility of normal human action. Because for every action there is an equal and opposite reaction, though the opposite reaction is the appropriate reaction to the action.

Because, in the final analysis, the paternal state is an anomaly. It is of the same character as the notion that there can be a rifle without recoil. The paternal state is a notion born of and promoted by hiding the consequences as the recoilless rifle is an appearance achieved by design and materials. The state is an abstraction. Unlike a human father it neither toils nor spins. All that the state hands out as benefits must first be taken from those who labor. It is time now to look at the carefully concealed other side of reality hidden by socialist rhetoric.

24
Tightening the Screws

THE LOSS OF liberty is quite often subtle under evolutionary socialism. So also is the loss of private property, or control over it. Under revolutionary socialism only the purblind can fail to grasp the assault on property and the onset of confinements of the population. The brutality of the attack is too blunt and persistent to escape detection by any except those who resolutely will ignore it. By contrast, evolutionary socialism is intruded in such a way, particularly under long-established parliamentary governments, that its restraints, confinements, and erosions of the ground of liberty and property are not so readily seen.

This is so in part because as the paternal state takes shape the focus is upon benefits to be conferred rather than the price to be paid, both monetary and in individual rights. There is a broader reason than this, however. It is that the population, or a considerable portion of it, has been induced in advance of the measures to accept certain underlying ideas which make the intrusions appear plausible and, perhaps, even inevitable.

One of the leading ideas is that of the desirability of distributive equality. This is joined, of course, with the notion that all should work together in collective harmony for the general good. When these ideas are linked to the belief that government is the instrument by which this should be achieved the way has been prepared for the introduction step by step of socialism.

The mechanism by which evolutionary socialism has been advanced is democracy. Herein lies a paradox. As popular control over government has increased the control by people over their own lives and affairs has declined. The paradox is more apparent than real. That anyone should find it strange that people's control over their lives declines as their participation in government increases is the result of one of the most impressive selling jobs in all of history. In the latter part of the nineteenth and in the twentieth century a tremendous selling of democracy took place. Democracy was advanced as the great cure for the ills of the world: if all peoples of the world would only adopt and practice it, a worldwide prosperity, harmony, and peace would ensue. The massive bloodletting which is now known as World War I was even described as a war to make the world safe for democracy. Democracy would then, it was claimed, make the world safe from wars.

These ideas gained plausibility from the fact that the development of democracy occurred more or less simultaneously with other developments in the nineteenth century. Such causal connection as the spread of democracy had with these other developments was almost certainly accidental, but it did not appear so at the time. The other nineteenth-century developments to which I allude were constitutionalism, the establishment of individual liberty, the casting off of feudal restrictions and the securing of private property, and the tendency to negotiate agreements among nations rather than going to war to settle disputes. Under these conditions trade expanded greatly, industries developed on an unprecedented scale, population increased dramatically, and prosperity began to become more general than ever before. It was under these conditions that Sweden became an industrial and prosperous country, as noted earlier.

In retrospect, there appears to be little enough reason to connect these developments with the spread of democracy. True, these developments occurred first generally in countries which had representative or popular government, that is, in Western Europe and America. And, there was undoubtedly a temporal connection between representative government and the other developments. It was this. The thrust to remove feudal and mercantile restrictions, to extend liberty, and to restrain and limit government was generally expressed through parliaments (legislatures, congresses, or whatever they might be called). This was especially so of the elective branches of parliaments. As a result of this, representative government began to be though : of as the champion of liberty.

The connection was temporal, as I have said. For the historical moment, as it were, representative governments curtailed the power of kings and limited government. The foundation of liberty was in constitutionalism which was itself based on the natural law philosophy. The practical defense of liberty lay in the separation of powers within government, a separation that would have the tendency to restrain and limit government. Popular or representative government can, at best, only reflect the prevailing mood among the populace, whatever that may be. If that mood is libertarian, representative government may act upon it; if it is totalitarian, representative government can do little more than be its agent.

Even so, the thrust toward democracy got a tremendous boost from this temporal, and temporary, connection. Champions of democracy pressed to have governments more and more representative, to extend the franchise ever more broadly, and to having all political decisions made on the basis of popular support. The practical effect of this was to concentrate all power in the legislatures and to negate the restraints upon government that rested upon a separation of powers. In limited monarchies, such as Sweden and England, the monarch became more and more limited, as did the hereditary nobility generally, and the representative portions of parliaments triumphed.

The champions of democracy ignored the fundamental nature of democracy, a wealth of historical experience with it, and a two-thousand-year-old reasoned argument against it. They made it an unquestioned good and a thing to be desired above all else.

Whatever the merits of representative government, they do not extend to a thoroughgoing democracy. It is an ancient insight that democracy is mob rule. True, the mob-rule feature is moderated so long as the populace acts through representatives; but representation is an inhibition on democracy, not a part of its essential character. It was Greek democracy which sentenced Socrates to exile or death. It was the mob which shouted to Pontius Pilate that Christ should be crucified. It was the Roman mobs who turned their fickle support from one conquering general to another that aided and abetted the horrors of the Roman Empire. "Democratic" New England was the most intolerant locale in the American colonies.

Democratic socialism has attempted to legitimize a modified mob rule. It has done so by attributing to democracy virtues it does not possess and ignoring its implicit vices. If democracy were not modified by representation and rules which hold it in check it would be tyrannical.

As it is, it is a compelled conformity, a conformity which takes away individual liberty and intrudes upon private property.

It is ironic that so many intellectuals should have championed social democracy (or democratic socialism or collectivized democracy, whatever describes it best). Modern intellectuals developed an early distaste for social conformity. Ralph Waldo Emerson said that society is at war with every one of its members. His meaning was that society is trying to settle us into a groove — make us conform — that is contrary to what each of us as an individual would wish to be. Society became and remains the villain for many intellectuals. It operates upon the basis of tradition and bids those within its ranks, so to speak, to conform or suffer rebuke, ostracism, or whatever punishments are within its power. And conformity has been the *bete noire* of intellectuals.

Yet many of the same intellectuals who have condemned conformity to society have been vigorous promoters of democracy, even democratic socialism. They have promoted a compelled conformity by the use of government power over the conformity induced by influence of society. They avoided the onus of this by attributing goodness to democracy and claiming to identify society with government by way of democracy. If conformity were the evil, it might be supposed that compulsory conformity would be worse than elective conformity.

Actually, most intellectuals are no more opposed to conformity than are the generality of people. Each of us harbors in his breast the desire to have others conform to his will. What has troubled most intellectuals has not been conformity but rather kinds of conformity to which they are opposed and over which they have no control. Conformity to society, its norms and prescriptions, has been, in their view, irrational and backward. By their lights, they would substitute for conformity to tradition a conformity to reason, a reason that by their conceit they are uniquely equipped to divulge. The idea that has the world in its grip is a vision of just such a conformity.

The role of democracy in this needs also to be grasped. The theory of democracy holds that democratic government would actuate the will of the people. If this were the case, it is difficult to see how government action would be brought under the control of intellectuals. What is more likely, however, is that there is no such thing as a "will of the people." True, majorities can often be obtained either for men, or on one side or another of issues, especially if there is only one choice to be made. But the getting of a majority depends on how the issues are stated and the personal appeal of candidates. In short, the statement of issues and the formulation of the candidate's opinions are crucial. These are pressure points for manipulating decisions in democracies. They are the points occupied by intellectuals. Democracy, then, is the means by which intellectuals would exercise control over and produce the kinds of conformity they desire.

It has been made to appear that, by voting, the individual increases his control over his affairs. This is only the case, however, if he successfully votes to reduce government involvement in his affairs. If he votes to increase government action, as he does if he votes for the programs of gradualist socialism, he votes to diminish his own control over his life and affairs. He may be induced to do this by the promise of benefits, benefits which will free him from many of his individual responsibilities. But when he does this he is only voting himself greater responsibility for others and less control over how it will be exercised.

Sweden is one of the most democratic countries in the world. Not only is there universal suffrage but also a great variety of consultative and mediative mechanisms by and through which people may express themselves. There is even an official known as an Ombudsman who has the power to penetrate and hold the bureaucracy to account. No group, at least organized group, is apt to be ignored when some decision is made which would affect its interests. Collective decisions are a la mode in Sweden, and the Swedes have applied their passion for orderliness to see that as little as possible is done without consulting the collectivity. All of which is just another way of saying that the Swedes have lost much of their individual liberty and control over their lives and property. The screws on the individual which make him conform to the collective will are continually being tightened.

One of the most obvious ways in which Swedes individually have lost much of their control over their affairs is by way of taxation. On the average, Swedish workers work over forty hours per week. According to reports, they work hard when they work; and pay in much of industry is on a piece work basis, which is certainly conducive to productivity. Local and national income taxes take away about a third of their pay on the average. Taxes rise sharply on those with higher incomes and go to as much as 71 per cent. The well-to-do also pay a "wealth" tax on top of the regular income, but there is, mercifully, a ceiling of 80 per cent on the combined national and local taxes on income.

A general sales tax of 10 per cent on the cost of items bought prevails. In addition, unusually high taxes are levied on gasoline, liquor, beer, cigarettes, and chocolates, among other things. Technically, the pension fund is financed by employer contributions. In fact, of course, this payment is a wage cost and is a reduction of employee wages or employer income or both. This last aside, however, it is not uncommon for a workman to lose 50 per cent of his pay to direct taxes. Then there is the ubiquitous and invisible tax gatherer — inflation — and Swedes have been hard hit by it as have most other peoples. Of course corporation profits are taxed, taxed, that is, if they are not placed in an investment fund, taxed at a rate of up to about 53 per cent of combined national and local levies.

It should be clear that the individual loses personal control over all his money taken by taxation, whether direct or indirect. According to social democratic theory, the control over that portion lost by the individual passes over to the collectivity. The matter is not so simple, however, for so long as there is a choice people are by no means united as to how or whether the money should be taken and spent. For example, in the late 1950's, a major controversy developed in Sweden over the proposal by the Social Democrats for a supplementary pension program. Following a national election in which the program was a major issue, the legislature passed the measure by a vote of 115 to 114. This was surely not the expression of a collective will but the imposition of a measure on the whole populace by the narrowest of majorities.

Probably the best known infelicity of Social Democratic Sweden is its housing shortage. It is a good example, too, of how the Swedes have lost effective control over their affairs and are thwarted in their aims by government policy. There are two aspects to the housing shortage. One is that there is a shortage of housing in places where it is wanted. The other is that the dwellings available are remarkably small. The majority of city dwellers live in apartments, and these generally run to 2½ rooms each. One-fourth of urban dwellings have but one to two rooms.

Both kinds of shortage are a result of government practice and policy. Rent controls over many years have kept rents below what they would be in a free market. Hence, private builders have seen little advantage to be gained from building places for rent. A remoter reason for the shortage of houses has been the rapid industrialization in the twentieth century. As a result more than 75 per cent of Swedes now live in towns and cities. There is reason to believe that this industrialization and urbanization has been accelerated by government policy which favors capital expenditure.

It looks, too, as if the government were deliberately going about creating a housing shortage. Much urban housing has been demolished, under the claim that slums were being cleared away, but a goodly amount of this housing was quite habitable and much more commodious than the housing built to replace it. In any case, government determines what housing is provided. As one writer says, "The government and local authorities erect a third of all new dwellings, and almost all housing projects are backed by government loans. It is the government that decides on the number of housing starts each year, enforces building standards, and subsidizes pensioners and low-income families to about 25 per cent of their rent."[1]

It is a result of government policy that apartments are so small. One aim of this policy is egalitarian, to see that every Swede has a "quality" dwelling. To put it another way, if everyone cannot have a large house, then no one should have one. But the matter goes deeper than that. The government has, after painstaking calculation and consideration, decided what sort of housing people need. It has decided what size and what components a kitchen should have. It has decided that central heat, double glazed windows, and garbage disposal chutes are needed rather than more space for rooms. It has set the kind of limitations on what is to be included so as to make it expensive to build very small accommodations. Large families are almost unthinkable in the postage-stamp houses, and Swedes must long for summer when they can get out of the stifling atmosphere of their houses into the open spaces.

Sweden is in a squeeze from the make-up of the population, and no relief is in sight. The basic problem is that a larger and larger percentage of the population is reaching retirement age. The low birth rate is not replenishing the population. In consequence, a smaller and smaller work force is having to carry the burden of feeding and caring for that portion of the population that is retired. The increase of productivity per worker might make it possible to continue for a while, but it should be noted that this could only be accomplished by denying to the workers any benefits from the increased productivity.

Moreover, if earlier analysis is correct, government policies already encourage much wasteful capital spending, spending which may indeed increase the productivity of workmen but which requires much more work to replace the equipment being retired. About the only area in which the Swedes could move to enhance their productivity would be to use all the time that goes into social planning, consultation, negotiation, and other such acitivities for productive purposes. But if they were to do so it would be to abandon democratic socialism.

The Swedes have invested a great deal of intelligence, ingenuity, and determination into making their variety of socialism work. Of this, there should be no doubt. They have done so under as near optimum conditions as are likely to be found on this planet. They have avoided participation in wars that would have cost so much and returned so little of a material character. They had a homogenous population which should be ideal for collectivism. They have benefited much from international peace. They have avoided internal revolution, or anything approaching it. They have modernized with great vigor, taken advantage of specialization of labor, and promoted capital accumulation and investment with a will.

The result of this effort and ingenuity is this: The Swedes have probably come as close to creating a materialistic and mechanical system as it would be possible to do. Does it work? It works as well, and as ill, as a materialistic and mechanical system is likely to do. It works to inhibit the able and adventuresome and to reward the less talented and least venturesome. It works to produce a modernistic sameness which may have sweep to it as viewed from a distance but is stifling from inside. Office space is determined by the amount reckoned to be enough to keep the worker from being overcome by claustrophobia. It works to stifle every grain of idealism that ever was raised by socialism.

The Swedes are a proud and stubborn people. They have labored for a lifetime to establish their variety of socialism and to make it work. If they are aware of the loss of liberty, they are not given to admitting it, or that they miss it. If loss of control over their property troubles them, they do not make much over it. Businessmen are acclimated to the manipulations by which it is often possible to operate in a thoroughly politicized economy.

Is the natural progression of gradualist socialism toward tyranny? One way to answer this question is to say that from its outset it is in one sense tyrannical. It is tyrannical in that it makes the individual conform to the majority or collective will. It is tyrannical in that it forces the individual into the mold of experts, social planners, and the lowest common denominator of the popular will. It forces the individual to deny himself and to bow to the will of others. It forces the individual into a life of continual compromise, compromise between the way he would do something and what the law requires, compromises between what he wants done and what others who have managed to get behind them the power of government want done.

The tendency of democratic socialism is to make the individual deny himself in all those ways in which he is unique, different, or peculiar. It

305

may be the worst tyranny of all, for it denies the individual conscience, denies it by not allowing it room for operation in the ordinary warp and woof of life. To be forced to yield to the collective will in the ordinary decisions of life is to deny to the individual a significant portion of his humanity.

The shift from living under the social influence of tradition to living under the compulsions of collectivism may occur so gradually that the individual is hardly aware of it. It is a crucial part of the theory and practice of gradualism that this should be so. This has been especially the case in a country like Sweden where the outworks of tradition have been preserved while their inwards have been eroded away. The church still stands, of course, but it stands for very little. The home has not been outlawed, but many of its functions have been subsumed by the state.

The moral and spiritual dimensions of life have been severed from their roots in social democratic Sweden. This has not been done by outlawing them; Swedes have substantive religious freedom and may spend about as much time as they will contemplating the domain of the spirit. It is rather that an order of priorities has been established — priorities that are material in character — which leaves little room for the development of moral and spiritual beings.

Some of the most sensitive Swedes have given expression to the otherwise stifled longing for a spirituality to life. Dag Hammarskjold lived an outward life that conformed well to social democratic prescriptions, suppressing, it may be, his deep spirituality. "It was only after his death that it was revealed how much ... the quietly competent, serenely self-confident diplomat, was really a mystic who had worked out a personal philosophy about the idea of life as a sacrifice." His posthumously published diary, *Markings*, which became an international best seller, was, by his own account, "a sort of 'white book' on my deliberations with myself — and God."[2] He left no doubt of what he lacked and longed for when he said, "I ask the impossible that life shall have a meaning. I fight the impossible that life shall have a meaning."[3]

Ingmar Bergman is surely the best known of Swedish film makers. He enjoys an international reputation. But there is a dark and morbid character to his films, depressingly so, it is fair to say. Bergman chooses to bare the souls of his characters, and to have them troubled with the ancient problems, such as those of good and evil. Bergman has attributed these preoccupations to the fact that he grew up as the son of a minister.

"When one is born and reared in the home of a minister," Bergman has said, "one has a chance at an early age to catch a glimpse behind the scenes of life and death. Father conducts a funeral, father officiates at a wedding, father performs a baptism, acts as a mediator, writes a sermon. The devil became an early acquaintance, and in the way of a child, it was necessary to render him concrete...."[4]

Probably it was Bergman's childhood background that acquainted him with his themes, but his near obsession with them as an adult almost certainly stems from the spiritually deprived character of Swedish life.

In any case, he has given us a hint in his account of his youth of what social democratic Sweden has very nearly smothered. Birth, baptism, marriage, and death, these are great events of life which ancient religious ritual celebrated in their spiritual dimensions. It is most difficult to know God for those who have not known a human father in all his dimensions. It is difficult to know love for those who have not experienced the sacrificing love of a mother. It is difficult to separate the sacred from the profane for those who have not actively participated in the communion of a religious congregation. It is difficult to know concern and care if one has not witnessed it evinced in the help extended from neighbor to neighbor. It is difficult to develop morally if one is denied individual choices and saved from responsibility for such as he makes. It is these things that the paternal state eviscerates or deactivates.

The paternal state tends to mechanize and diffuse basic human relationships. It is doubtful that the baptism of a newborn infant can compete with a check from the state awarded to the mother. Marriage is an inessential relationship to the Swedish state, for if there is no registered father of the child the state will make special provision to take care of it. The paternal state becomes a kind of surrogate father of all children. So far as the state can do so, it removes the element of sacrifice, if not love, from motherhood. Neighborhood and community lose meaning by being nationalized and administered by a bureaucracy. State appropriated money replaces compassion and concern. Morality and spirituality survive in a virtual vacuum; their functions have been taken over by the omnipresent state.

Socialism diffuses concern so broadly, so far from the natural relationships of kinship and proximity as in neighborhoods, that the benefits the state hands out take on the abstract character of rights rather than being suffused with warm human concern. Care for aged parents may indeed be a burden for children, but it is not less so for being nationalized. It is only that when it is nationalized it is bereft of such meaning as it had. The birth of every child is a cost to the taxpayer.

307

The retirement of any person is a burden to the working population. All this without benefit of being warmed by a baby's smile or recalling the tender moments of childhood with one's own parents. It is cold, mechanical and devoid of any but the relics of humanity.

But let us return to the question of tyranny. Will gradualist socialism proceed to other and more easily recognized forms of tyranny? Although there is little enough historical evidence on which to base a conclusion, there is reason to believe that it may, though how it will come is still a matter of contingency. One way it may come is by way of the onset of barbarism to which socialism tends. Liberty, in practice, depends upon an underlying respect for the rights and private realm of others. It is just this that collectivized democracy is contiually assaulting. Barbarity is a logical result of the dehumanized relationships discussed above.

Care in equal measure for all the people of a nation posits a godlike concern which is beyond most mortals. When parents cease to care for their own children, and children for their aged parents, they do not extend that displaced concern to all children and to all aged parents. Much more plausibly, they are not much concerned about any children or old people. The trend toward barbarity is already apparent in loss of concern for unborn babies and in the shunting of old people into special "homes." Neither life, liberty, nor property are apt to be much protected when concern and respect are sufficiently and widely lost.

There is another way in which democratic socialism may prepare the way for a broader tyranny. Social democrats know how to deal in a variety of ways with recalcitrant individuals. They can arrest them, levy penalties against them, deny them favors, send them to prison, or even put them in mental institutions. But they have only one approved way of dealing with groups or collectives, whether these be nations, labor unions, youth organizations, or retirees. That approved way is negotiation. The gradualist state does not negotiate with individuals. It makes them conform or suppresses them. But groups are not to be suppressed; concessions are to be made to them, and they are to be brought somehow into amiable accord with other collectives.

Sweden is the example, par excellence, of this penchant of socialism to negotiate peace among groups. The country enjoys an unusual amount of labor peace. Despite the fact that unionization is widespread, and that employers are organized as well, strikes are rare. (All these organizations are so closely regulated, however, that there should be doubt as to the extent to which they are free.) In international relations, the Swedes have both promoted international negotiations and maintained a posture of neutrality. Swedish diplomats have long been famous for serving as mediators.

Revolutionary socialism, particularly communism, poses a continual threat to evolutionary socialism. While communists do sometimes negotiate, their methods in general are not such as are conducive to mediation. Far from professing to mediate differences among classes, they seek to suppress most classes. They accept warfare among classes as the norm until such time as all "exploiting" classes are put down. Moreover, revolutionary socialists stand ready at all times to build upon the inevitable frustrations of evolutionary socialism.

It has been noted already that idealism can hardly survive socialism. The reason for this is that once socialism is in power it bogs down in compromises and in the continual pressures of groups for economic advantage. Revolution holds out the prospect of a quite different scenario, of an end to the struggle, of a final victory of the righteous, and of an eventual perfect justice. The social democratic bent to mediate and negotiate among groups unfits it for dealing with revolutionaries. It does not will to suppress them, and given this weakness the time arrives, or may arrive, when it cannot.

In any case, the love of liberty is a diffuse thing. There is much evidence to support the view that people are as readily enamored of freedom from responsibility as they are of individual liberty joined to personal responsibility. They can be and have been enticed to support measures which reduce everyman's liberty by collectivizing responsibility. That way lies tyranny, of one sort or another, perhaps all sorts.

Sweden represents but one variety of evolutionary socialism. It is time now to examine another, one much nearer home.

Book VI

The United States: Republican Gradualism

25

A Republic and Gradualism

IF SAYING SO made it so the United States would today be the stronghold of capitalism and the citadel of free enterprise. Many intellectuals who deplore this state of affairs nonetheless proclaim it to be so. The notion crops up frequently in writings about America by Europeans. There are even Americans who say they favor free enterprise and who declare that the United States is the prime example of it in the world. They may be right in their judgment, but if they are it should give more than a little pause as to the state of freedom of enterprise in the world.

There should be no doubt that the United States was long considered as and was in fact a land of opportunity. Immigrants poured into America from other lands in increasing numbers after the first third of the nineteenth century. They came, in part at least, because they hoped for and often found greater opportunity than in the lands from which they came. There are still opportunities in the United States today. Many of the oppressed peoples from around the world still try to gain entry to this country. They are oppressed as a result of the idea that has the world in its grip. But they must surely discover when they arrive here that the idea has its grip on the vaunted land of opportunity as well as on other lands.

How free is enterprise in the United States? No one has, to my knowledge, devised a means for making the kind of measurements which would give a precise answer to the question. Computers have now been made that can provide swift, almost instantaneous, answers to all sorts of questions, but the most sophisticated computer would be unable to tell us how free enterprise is. This is the case mainly because there is no way to quantify the obstacles that government puts in the way of enterprise, but there is also no way to take into account the ways human ingenuity will discover for overcoming or getting around these obstacles. Even so, the question can be answered with sufficient exactitude to show that enterprise is being stifled, choked, throttled, limited, and restrained in America, and that there is a well established trend in this direction. And government restriction is in some way a limitation on enterprise, and restrictions abound today.

Perhaps the best way to test how free enterprise is in America would be to survey the obstacles that stand in the way of someone contemplating going into business today. No brief survey can hope to cover all the obstacles; indeed, they may now be so numerous that a lifetime would be too short to learn them. Some of the obstacles are of such complexity that anyone contemplating going into business in a particular locale would need expert legal advice from those familiar with the local situation. But a survey of the obstacles can show the character of many of the limitations and the trend toward increasing them.

The first need of anyone going into business will almost certainly be some capital reserves, since virtually all undertakings require capital of greater or lesser amount. To get capital it is usually necessary either to save it oneself, borrow it from others, or get them to invest in the enterprise. The greatest obstacle to individual saving today is inflation, and inflation is a direct consequence of government monopoly of the money supply and continual increase of it. Inflation discourages saving; it even introduces doubt as to the merits of it. Inflation reduces the value of money saved because as the money supply is increased prices rise. This means that the saver could have bought more with the money at the time that he first received it than he could at a later date, if the inflation continues over a long period of time. Inflation has been almost continual in the United States since the early 1930's and shows no signs of abatement.

The graduated income tax is another deterrent to capital accumulation. Not only does the United States government have such a tax but so also do most states. The more one makes the larger proportion of it is taken by governments. Proponents of the graduated income tax often talk about it is as if it were a means of taking from the "haves." It is better understood in its most devastating effects as taking from those who are "getting," for the "haves" can sometimes avoid it entirely. At any rate, progressive taxation limits and obstructs enterprise by making it difficult to accumulate investment capital.

Social Security payments are another inhibiting tax on those who would save to start an enterprise, and this tax has mounted precipitously in recent years. Social Security payments might be conceived as a system of forced saving, but they hardly qualify as savings at all. All that is paid into it is forfeited by the individual, forfeited as far as any control over it is concerned. He cannot draw the money out in order to make investments. He cannot use it to take advantage of greater opportunities as they come along. In short, so far as saving for starting an enterprise is concerned, Social Security payments are just so much money lost to taxation.

Borrowing offers hardly more freedom from obstruction by government than does saving for the would-be enterpriser. Banks are the most readily available sources of loans, but they are also probably the most severely regulated undertakings in America today. National banks are chartered by the United States government, and state banks by the states, thus limiting the number and variety of such institutions.

The federal government regulates the activities of all national banks and all those which are members of the Federal Deposit Insurance Corporation, which is to say virtually all of them. State laws regulate all banks within their bounds as to such matters as branch banking and interest rates. Most states have usury laws which place limits on the percentage of interest to be charged. This latter restriction is particularly obstructive to new enterprisers, for all enterprises are risky and new ones especially so. Banks are loath to take such risks when they can charge maximum interest on insured and government guaranteed loans. Moreover, state and federal regulations discourage or prohibit certain types of long-term loans, and government comptrollers look carefully at the type of collateral pledged to secure loans.

Then, too, federal, state, and local governments are competitors with private individuals for the money that is available for lending, and they enjoy some decided advantages in this competition. The federal government requires and/or encourages the banks to have some proportion of their investments in government securities. Municipal bond proceeds are exempt from federal taxes. Banks are much more

315

likely to be able to help a new enterpriser by discounting any paper he holds from his customers than they are to put money directly into the enterprise.

The frustrated enterpriser may look hopefully toward incorporation and the selling of shares in his projected business. But he will discover quickly enough that if he decides to go "public" with his offering governments have erected obstacles here as well. The Securities and Exchange Commission keeps a wary eye on stock offerings, and the more recently set up consumer protection agencies may be no less alert to what he is doing. The SEC is more than a little dubious as to the validity of any claims that might be made about the future prospects of the business. Should the shareholders lose for one reason or another, the new enterpriser may find himself the object of civil, or criminal, suits by various government agencies.

People somehow manage sometimes to overcome the great variety of obstacles in the way of it and get together sufficient capital to go into business. But in trying to decide what business to go into they encounter another impressive array of obstacles. In contemplating the possibilities, anyone will discover, if he did not know already, that many sorts of enterprise are very nearly or entirely closed to him. The coining or issuing of money has been a monopoly of the United States government for so long that hardly anyone would conceive of it as a potential field for enterprise.

The other most general monopoly of the United States government of a possible business undertaking is that over the carrying of mail, especially first class mail. In earlier times, even with the government occupying the dominant position, there were many opportunities for entrepreneurs to engage in mail transport and even, sometimes, delivery. Star routes, as they were called, were serviced by individuals and private companies; trains, boats, and busses transported mail. Now, most of those opportunities have been foreclosed. The United States Postal Service maintains its own fleet of trucks; and privately owned airlines are the only remaining private domestic transporters of mail of any consequence.

There are other monopolies by the federal government, but they are not so extensive in scope. There is the monopoly of merchandising on military posts by the Post Exchanges. There is the monopoly of the generating and sale of electricity in some regions such as the Tennessee Valley.

The Panama Canal Zone has long been the most thoroughgoing

316

monopoly of the United States government. "Private parties are not allowed to own any land in the Zone and private businesses do not operate there. Therefore, the many other businesses in the Zone other than the Panama Canal are maintained and operated by the Panama Canal Company. These businesses include a steamship line between New York and the Isthmus of Panama; a railroad across the Isthmus, the cargo docks and piers and harbor terminal facilities on the Isthmus; a coaling plant for ships; an oil-handling plant; commissary stores . . .; a printing plant; restaurants, theaters, bowling alleys," and so forth.[1] If Communists do take over the Canal Zone they will find their basic work has already been done.

The federal government now virtually monopolizes intercity rail passenger transport by way of Amtrak and is extending its sway into freight hauling by way of Conrail.

State governments have also established various monopolies. The most dramatic of these may well be that over the sale of liquor and certain other alcoholic beverages. About one-third of the states have a monopoly of the sale of at least some of the alcoholic beverages. Where there are state liquor stores, those who are considering going into some legal business must put this area of potential opportunity out of mind. But even where states do not own and operate the stores, there are usually strenuous restrictions upon entry into such undertakings.

Although neither the federal nor state governments monopolize the manufacture of spiritous liquors, their laws and prohibitions are such that in effect they secure a monopoly to a select few domestic and foreign manufacturers. During much of American history no single undertaking, besides farming, had so many entrepreneurs as distilling, and many farmers supplemented their income with the product from their stills. These distillers have now become an endangered species as a result of decades of relentless search for and pursuit of them by "Revenuers."

The state of New York has long maintained a system of barge canals 525 miles in length, which it operates at public expense, charging no tolls. The Commonwealth of Massachusetts, since 1918, has operated the transit system of Boston and neighboring cities and towns. Harbor facilities at ocean ports — wharves, docks, warehouses and the like — are usually owned by state governments. At New Orleans a State Board of Port Commissioners, formed in 1896, operates grain elevators, coffee terminals, banana conveyors, cranes, derricks, a belt line railway, a canal, and a free trade zone. . . . [2]

Local governments generally have several monopolies which exclude private enterprise. Municipalities frequently monopolize trash and garbage collection, water distribution, sale of electricity, distribution of natural gas, and bus or other street and subway systems. At one time, virtually all local transportation systems were privately owned and operated, but price and service restrictions became such a handicap that cities took them over.

Indeed, the whole field of transportation is now very nearly closed to enterprisers. Railroading was so regulated by the Interstate Commerce Commission that it ceased to be a growth business. Nowadays, a would-be enterpriser would be as likely to think of building a railroad as he would to go into manufacturing buggies. City transport is not a viable opportunity, and it is being made less so by massive government grants for the building of rail systems. It is possible to go into trucking, but the obstacles to doing so are such that only the most intrepid enterpriser would venture into the field. Taxis are so regulated in most cities, and the privilege of operating one so restricted that opportunity in this field is limited. Entry into the air transport business is hampered by the Civil Aeronautics Board, and it sometimes takes years for established carriers to get authorization to provide new service to some city or locale.

The field of education has never been a particularly good arena for private enterprisers, and it is generally becoming less so today. Laws requiring school attendance for young people have taken that facet of education out of the realm of economic goods, that plus the fact that "free" public schools are provided. Such private schools and colleges as exist are usually subsidized by gifts and tax-free contributions, hence making it difficult for anyone to enter the field in the hope of profit. On the fringes of education, e.g., teaching various skills such as auto repairing or barbering, there used to be considerable opportunity for enterprisers to found and operate schools. These are being hard pressed today, however, by vocational courses in the public high schools and by the vocational emphasis in many government funded trade schools and community colleges. Governments are well on their way to monopolizing education by using their taxing powers to exclude competitors.

Many hospitals were once privately owned and operated, but such hospitals are rare today. The Hill-Burton Act brought large doses of federal money to hospital building and gave encouragement to government owned and operated hospitals. It would be exceedingly difficult today to raise the capital necessary to provide the expensive equipment necessary to compete with government owned hospitals.

Governments at all levels are vigorous competitors in providing

318

recreation facilities. This is particularly true for parks, zoos, golf courses, swimming pools, lakes, and waterways. Many buildings in which recreation activities take place — e.g., auditoriums, ball parks, civic centers — are now being built with tax funds. Not only does the prospective enterpriser find his potential savings taken away in taxes to support such undertakings but also his entry into such enterprises made difficult by government competition.

The federal government is in the research and information business in a big way. The Government Printing Office is enormous, and keeps busy printing numerous pamphlets, making available research reports, publishing agricultural treatises, and providing information for businesmen. A United States Senator pointed out a while back that the Commerce Department gathers around 100,000 research and development reports each year, and that the government spends approximately $10 billion each year on research.[3] Although governments have not preempted the information field, they have made great inroads into it.

There are, of course, enterprises that can be started in which there is little direct competition from government, but there are obstacles to be overcome in going into any of these. A minimum requirement in almost any locale is to get a license. Beyond that, many undertakings require a charter or franchise from some one or more governments. Many kinds of undertaking have special training or knowledge or moral requirements. For example, barbers may have had to have spent a specified length of time in training in a state recognized school, nurses to have undergone a particular regimen, teachers to have taken certain education courses in order to be certified, real estate salesmen to have passed a written examination, plumbers to have served an apprenticeship, saloon-keepers to have conformed to certain moral standards, and so on. Lawyers usually have to pass the bar examination in the states in which they wish to practice.

It may be instructive in getting some idea of how far this goes to look at this partial list, in one state, of those agencies charged with overseeing certain undertakings: State Board of Accountancy, State Board for Examination, Qualification and Registration of Architects, Commission for Auctioneers, State Board of Examiners for Speech Pathology and Audiology, State Board of Barbers, Board of Chiropractic Examiners, State Board of Cosmetology, State Board of Dentistry, State Board of Electrical Contractors, State Board of Engineers and Land Surveyors, State Board of Registration for Foresters, State Board of Funeral Service, State Board of Registration for Professional Geologists,

State Board of Hearing Aid Dealers and Dispensers, Board of Landscape Architects, Board of Physical Therapy, State Board of Private Detective and Private Security Agencies, State Board of Examiners for Sanitarians, Commission of Structural Pest Control, Board for Registration of Used Car Dealers, State Board of Registration for Used Motor Vehicle Parts Dealers, Motor Vehicle Dismantlers, and Motor Vehicle Rebuilders. The list is not complete by any means, but the point perhaps emerges.

Anyone going into business has to have some place from which to operate, i.e., land, buildings, or offices. If he needs land, he will find himself in competition — though that hardly seems to be the right word — with federal, state, and local governments for the dwindling supply of land. Governments were once the great sellers of land in America, but they have now reversed the field and become major buyers — perhaps "condemners" would be more descriptive — for military installations, for parks and forests, for highways, for urban renewal projects, for hospitals, for lakes and dams, for schools, and so forth. As one writer puts it, the federal government "is the biggest landlord on earth, aside from the communist countries."[4]

Of course, the land and building will have to be selected with care if one is going into business. There are increasing restrictions on land use in the United States. Zoning laws have been around since the 1920's, though they get ever stricter, and they are now being supplemented with land use laws in many states for rural areas. But lately the United States government has gone into comprehensive land use control, or very nearly that, under the auspices of the Environmental Protection Agency. The government has asserted its sovereignty over land use to protect water, air, endangered species, and what have you. Anyone thinking in terms of operating a factory or manufacturing establishment must undertake the difficult task of assuring state and federal agencies, by way of surveys and tests, the he will not significantly harm the environment within which he locates.

Although the above are only a partial listing of the obstacles which a would-be enterpriser must overcome, let us suppose now that our enterpriser has managed to set himself up in business. However improbable it may seem, however much of at least a minor miracle it surely is, some men are actually able to begin new enterprises in the United States. They manage to accumulate the saving necessary despite the inflationary thrust, the progressive income taxes and the burden of Social Security, or manage to borrow the money despite restrictions that make this difficult, or even succeed in selling stock in a corporation so as

320

not to arouse the ire of the SEC. They select an undertaking that is not monopolized by government or that government competition has not effectively foreclosed. They get franchised, certified, licensed, authorized, permitted, qualified or whatever, find some land on which to locate in which their kind of undertaking is allowed, and satisfy the authorities that they will live in harmony with the environment.

Such an enterpriser is by no means out of the woods, however, simply because he has managed to open his doors for business. Indeed, it would be more correct to say that many of his troubles have just begun. The man who enters business discovers rather soon, if he did not know it already, that he has a Senior Partner — government. More precisely, he has a committee of Senior Partners, composed of federal, state, county, and, depending upon the locale, township and municipal authorities. These Partners may have thrown any number of obstacles in the way of his going into business in the first place; they may be in competition with him; they may have made low interest loans to his competitors or even granted them special privileges which he does not enjoy. They will rarely have invested anything in the business themselves. Yet once he opens his doors these Partners join the firm, so to speak.

In the first place, the Senior Partners require the businessman to be a tax collector. If he sells to consumers, he will generally be expected to collect federal excise taxes and state and local sales taxes. If he employs other people he will be expected to withhold federal and probably state and local income taxes from their wages. Under most conditions, he must collect the workers' Social Security taxes by way of payroll deductions. Some cities have employment taxes which he may have to collect.

No matter how small his business may be, the Senior Partners will require that the businessman keep extensive and precise records of his various transactions. He will need records, of course, of the taxes he has collected from others, and records for his own income and Social Security taxes.

The Senior Partners are not particularly mollified by getting the first fruits from any income and having the businessman collect taxes for them. They take an active role in determining how the business should be run. If he sells to consumers, various federal and state consumer agencies may take the side of his customers against him and haul him into court on their behalf or because he has not complied with one or more of the multitude of laws governing these relationships. In like manner, the Senior Partners stand ready to intrude in a great variety of

321

ways on behalf of his employees against the businessman employer. They have, of course, generally specified that he cannot employ those who have not attained a certain age. They prescribe minimum wages, maximum hours, time and a half for overtime, and have long been solicitous of female employees.

Of late, federal and state governments have exerted themselves to see that employers do not discriminate in hiring because of race, sex, age, color, religion, or country of national origin, among other things. In order to prove that he does not do so, an employer is often bidden to take Affirmative Action to assure that he has the proper "mix" of minorities amongst his workers and be diligent in promoting such of these as he has assembled to the better positions he has available.

If his employees should decide to organize themselves into a labor union, the National Labor Relations Board has laid down all sorts of rules to which the businessman employer must comply. Should he be judged to have failed to comply he may well find himself saddled with back wages to pay and employees on his payroll whom he would prefer to do without.

The Senior Partners concern themselves, too, with the safety and health of the businessman's employees. To that end, OSHA, a federal agency, promulgates all sorts of rules and standards for safeguarding the health of employees. Should an employer fail to comply with these standards he is subject to potentially heavy penalties.

Particular industries are subject to their own kinds of regulation. For example, the powers of the Federal Power Commission over producers and sellers of electric power show the extent to which the interference of a Senior Partner may go. It exercises the following powers:

> Prescribes and enforces a uniform system of accounts for privately owned public utilities engaged in the transmission, or sale or wholesale of electric power in interstate commerce; determines the original cost and accrued depreciation of facilities for the generation and transmission of such energy; investigates and regulates the rates, charges and services for such energy; passes upon application of such utilities for authority to issue securities, to dispose of, merge or consolidate facilities, to interconnect facilities, or to acquire securities of other public utilities; passes upon applications of persons seeking authority to hold interlocking positions; evaluates applications for and, when in the public interest, issues permits for the construction, operation, maintenance or connection of facilities at the borders of the United States for the exportation or importation of electric energy; passes upon applications for authority to export electric energy for the United States.[5]

The Senior Partners are also potential customers of the businessman.

322

The federal government is today the largest purchaser of goods and services in the country. When it is joined by states and local governments, the role of government as purchaser is an immense one indeed. Needless to say, these governments extend additional authority over anyone from whom they buy goods or services. A seller does not just offer his custom in the market to government; government uses the leverage of a buyer to further control the businessman's business.

The above only scratches the surface of government intervention in the economy today, but perhaps enough has been told to warrant a conclusion. Enterprise is not free in the United States today. It is hampered, obstructed, restrained, constrained, restricted, limited, compelled, and otherwise confined by a multitude of regulations, requirements, and government competition. And there is a well established tendency to increase the intervention more and more over the years. Occasional "deregulation" is overmatched by restrictions introduced from other directions. For example, farm crops are not controlled as much now as they were twenty years ago, but land use restrictions are being introduced into rural areas.

Thirty or forty years ago there was considerable debate over whether the United States should have a planned economy or not. The issue was not resolved by the debate, but it has been largely resolved in practice by step by step intrusions into the economy. By government's regulatory powers, control over the money supply and hence over credit and banking, over education, over the communications industries, over transportation, over labor, over the environment, and so forth, planning is widely established today. In most of the United States today, no structure can be erected without permits, inspections, compliance with set-back ordinances, zoning laws, and other such restrictions. Government subsidies to cities and regions determine the character and direction of developments in those areas.

A broader conclusion is warranted, too. The United States is under the sway of the idea that has the world in its grip. Whatever the merits or demerits of any or all of the government interventions discussed, one assumption underlies and powers them all: namely, individuals and voluntary associations of men cannot be trusted to provide for themselves and others by pursuing their own self-interest. They must be directed and controlled in their activities by an interest that is outside of and above them as individuals. Self-interest of individuals must be contained, restrained, and redirected — ultimately rooted out — and for it must be substituted what is supposedly in the common interest. The instrument for imposing this common interest is government. That is the idea.

Under the sway of the idea, government has asserted its power into virtually every area of American life. Government has grown mighty and the individual weak and limited. How did this state of affairs come about? It is certainly a reversal of the idea on which these United States were founded. The United States was founded as a republic. Both the United States and the state governments operate under the auspices of written constitutions. The idea that informed these constitutions was that governments should be limited in order that individuals might be freed — freed to pursue their own interests in order to fulfill themselves as best they could and according to their own lights.

It is, of course, the end of government that those within its jurisdiction shall be protected in their life, liberty, and property from harmful intrusions by others. To that end, governments were empowered to legislate, to use force, and to resolve disputes which threatened the peace in order that men might go about their affairs undisturbed by malefactors.

But beyond the granting of powers believed necessary to maintain governments which could keep the peace, put down domestic insurrection, and repel foreign invaders, the main efforts of the constitutions were to limit the governments they authorized. It was for this purpose that bills of rights were incorporated in them. It was to this end that the powers of government were separated into three branches. The listing of powers granted was supposed to constitute an inherent limit upon government. Even the dispersion of power into federal and state jurisdictions was thought to act to limit the exercise of power. If this was not the aim and purpose of the United States Constitution then those who successfully argued for its adoption were themselves either deceived or engaged in deceiving others.

Among the opponents of ratification of the Constitution of 1787 (the United States Constitution), not one could be found who did so because the government lacked power. On the contrary, it was the fear that it would become powerful and oppressive that animated them. A goodly number of men in that day took the time and made the effort to study the history of governments. One conclusion stood out among all the others that they drew: All governments tend to become oppressive. Few would have dared to rise in the conventions in those days, amidst the displays of historical erudition, to proclaim that men vested with the power of government have been so transformed that they could be trusted with determining what is for the well-being of those in their jurisdiction. On the contrary, it was settled opinion that those who govern will pursue power to the detriment of the well-being of their fellows if they are not deflected from the course. Limited constitutional government offered the best means they could conceive for delaying, if not ultimately preventing, the appearance of the oppressive tendency of government.

How, then, did this reversal take place? How were many of the confines on government removed and did government begin to confine the individual more and more? A portion of the answer is not difficult to find. It came about gradually, and step by step. Probably, none envisioned that when national banks were given a monopoly of the issue of bank notes in the 1860's by placing a prohibitive tax on state bank notes that in the 1960's virtually all concrete limitations on the money supply would be removed and that such powers as remained over the money supply would be under the control of the federal government. Yet the stage was being set for this course of events, not with malice aforethought but by a process of accretion of power.

Another point can be asserted here; it has been written about and documented elsewhere, and the present theme precludes discussion of it in detail. The point is this, Americans, or a significant portion of them, came under the sway of the Idea that has the world in its grip.[6] That is, they came to believe that when individuals pursue their self-interest it is detrimental to the general welfare, that the supports to the individual should be removed and the individual confined, and that government was the proper instrument to perform these undertakings. Although the idea generally goes by the name of socialism, most Americans never consciously became socialists and, of those who did, few avowed it. The attack upon the American system and the intrusion of government was done piecemeal. Yet when the development is viewed whole, it makes sense only in terms of the prevalence of the socialist idea.

It is important, however, to delve somewhat into the methods by which government power has been concentrated and unloosed. The dispersion of power by which these United States began had to be overcome and evaded. How this was accomplished needs now to be told.

325

26
The Concentration of Power

POLITICS, IT HAS been said, is the art of compromise. But compromise is not the object of politics; it is only a method. The end of politics is to gain and maintain control over the instruments of power over people. Politics is, then, the art of the struggle for power, any kind of power, but above all the power residing in government. There are other ways of gaining political power, of course. The most common way, historically, has been to inherit it. Another way has been by conquest. The *coup d'etat* has also been used, but this usually involves some combination of the methods mentioned earlier. But in modern day democracies, the approved way of gaining and maintaining power is by politics. That is certainly the case in the United States.

The primary task of those who wished to introduce socialism in the United States was to get control of political power. There were a considerable variety of such socialists in the latter part of the nineteenth century. There were anarchists, syndicalists, Marxists, nationalists, unionists, and other sorts of socialists. They made what political splash they made, at the outset, with inflationist schemes of one sort or another. In the early twentieth century, the Socialist Party, under the leadership of Eugene Debs, emerged and gained considerable following as a minor party until the end of World War I. It continued to exist thereafter but ceased to grow. Indeed, it went into a decline from which it has never recovered. The Communist Party, under the leadership of William Z. Foster and others, had even less political success.

But even before the 1920's many of those who were inclined toward socialism had concluded that they could not attain power in America by professing to be socialists. Most Americans simply would not buy the package of socialism when it was wrapped in that way. The best way to move toward socialism would be by way of the established political parties and by gaining footholds in governmental and other institutions. There was no need to call particular programs socialistic and to describe their adoption as a movement toward socialism. In fact, it would be counterproductive to do so. Much better to advance them as cures for particular problems and as made necessary by changing conditions. The Fabians in England had pointed the way, and the American socialists modified their tactics to fit their own conditions.

The movement toward socialism in the United States has been surreptitious, even sneaky, and infiltrative in character. Even so, it has not been directed by some master plan conceived by some planner, or planners. Nor has it been advanced, by and large, by a conspiracy. It would be easier to understand if there were a master plan and a well-organized conspiracy. But the evidence does not warrant the drawing of any such conclusion. A conspiracy is, after all, an agreement between two or more people to do something illegal. Whereas, the distinctive feature of gradualist socialism is that it will achieve its goals legally. (Communists have, of course, often engaged in illegal acts, been under the control of foreign powers, and been parts of conspiracies. However, communism is an adjacent movement to the main thrust toward socialism in America and has never been in control of it.)

Moreover, the movement toward socialism is not done by a plan in the United States. It is not a plan but a method. There is an objective: It is to gain control of political power and transform America. The method is to employ those means which, at any given time, give the greatest promise of producing the desired results. This method is called pragmatism, and its practitioners pride themselves on their lack of commitment to any overall plan or strategy. Pragmatists feel their way toward their objective, thrusting through at weak spots and turning aside when resistance becomes so great as to threaten failure.

Though the goal of the gradualist socialist movement in America is power — political power — it is not, as such, a political movement. It is, at bottom, an intellectual movement, a movement aimed at controlling what men think, or at the least establishing a subtle authority over what men say. Those who persist in thinking of it as a political movement will ever have difficulty in grasping how it could maintain a coherent direction without a master plan and planners. Once it is understood as a set of ideas, an ideology, this difficulty disappears. The coherent direction derives from the ideology.

Anyone who is to any extent under the sway of the ideology can perceive which proposals for the use of government power are most in keeping with it. Those who do not subscribe to the ideology are disciplined by denying them the advantages that stem from adherence to the prevailing ideology. It requires no conspiracy to carry out the punishment or ostracism; it does require the concurrence of true believers in the ideology. In addition to the concurrence of true believers, the thrust toward socialism is accomplished in America by the desire of many to be in keeping with what they believe to be intellectual fashion or their fear of flouting it.

A great deal more could be said on this head, but only so much need be said as will put at naught the notion that what follows is an account of action by an organized conspiracy. Viewed in retrospect, the thrust toward socialism in America — or, for that matter, in the world — may appear to follow a pattern, a pattern such as events have when they are planned and directed by some body of men. This pattern arises from two sources: one, there is a direction, of sorts, to the course of development; two, the historian organizes them for the telling so that the events have a greater coherence than they had in reality. At any rate, what follows is an effort to explain how the thrust toward socialism gained momentum and power over the American people.

The United States government was deliberately designed to thwart the efforts of any one man or group of men from gaining any continuing control over it. To that end, the powers of the federal government were separated into three branches, as were those of the states. Further, the powers of government were dispersed by granting certain powers to the general government and reserving others to the states. In addition, some powers have been specifically denied to the general government and others to the states. Some of the other safeguards against the concentration of power were: staggering the terms of Senators so that only one-third of the Senate is to be elected at any one time, having Congressmen elected for two-year terms and the President for four, and providing for an appointed judiciary. The states have generally dispersed their powers by having them exercised by municipalities,

328

counties, and other local governments. All these arrangements tended both to prevent the concentration of power and its use by any faction for its own purposes.

Anyone conversant with developments in government in the twentieth century knows that these obstacles to concentrating power and its regular use by a faction — a faction under the sway of the idea that has the world in its grip — have been largely overcome or circumvented. How it has come about does, however, need to be explained. It has not come about, not to any significant extent, by amendments to the United States Constitution. The separation of powers among the branches still formally exists. The reserve of powers to the states has been only slightly altered by amendment. The constitutional protections of life, liberty, and property can still be found stated in the cadences of eighteenth-century rhetoric. But much of the substance has been drained away while the forms still stand.

In the broadest terms, here is what has happened. Power in the United States is today concentrated where it is least subject to popular control and most amenable to manipulation by intellectuals and intellectual fashion. More specifically, it is concentrated in the executive branch, the courts, and the bureaucracy. Preceding and accompanying this has been the concentration of power in the federal government. The federal government is the most amenable of governments to ideological influence brought to bear by the press, national magazines, television, book publishers, and other media of communication. In a similar fashion, the executive branch, the courts, and the bureaucracy are readily swayed by these ideological influences.

Vast political power is exercised today by those in the federal government over whom there is little or no popular control. This state of affairs came about gradually over the better part of a century. Indeed, in the case of the Federal courts the potential was there from the beginning. Federal judges were always appointed by the President subject to the approval of the Senate. Their tenure in office is for life or during good behavior. But the "good behavior" requirement early became largely a dead letter because of the failure of Congress to persist with impeachments. Thus, the courts have ever had but a tangential relation to popular control.

This was by design, of course. The idea was that the judiciary should be independent, independent of politics so as to make their determinations according to law. This was a noble concept and was reasonably workable so long as judges believed themselves to be bound

329

by the Constitution, by precedent, and by reason. But a subtle change began to occur in the latter part of the nineteenth century. Legal realism, as it is sometimes called, began to replace the concept of fixed and immutable laws. What was the law began to be thought of as something that was changing, relative, and subject to continual mutation. This set the stage for a judiciary that was not only independent of politics but independent also of the received law. To an amazing extent, the Supreme Court became a law unto itself, upsetting and ignoring precedent and ruling by pronouncements which were considered binding upon the lower courts.

Popular control over the bureaucracy declined as Civil Service reform made headway. The idea of having a body of civil servants who would be professionals free from the shifting political tides had broad appeal in the latter part of the nineteenth century. It got much impetus from the fact that President James A. Garfield was assassinated by a disappointed job seeker. Thereafter, a tenured civil service began to be created. Over the years, more and more employees came under it.

Having a tenured civil service did not matter so much as long as the sway and activities of the federal government were limited. But in the twentieth century, as the federal government intervened in more and more matters and began to touch and control the lives of Americans in an ever greater variety of ways, the effect of having an independent and tenured civil service became something else again. So far as the bureaucracy was the government, they were controlling the lives of people but were themselves subject to very little popular (political?) control.

Another significant development in cutting government loose from popular control and concentrating power was in the authorization of independent commissions. The Interstate Commerce Commission was the first of these bodies. It was created in 1887 and given limited powers over the railroads but has since had its powers greatly augmented and extended over other forms of transportation. It has since been joined by a goodly number of other such organizations, among them the Federal Reserve Board, the Federal Power Commission, the Civil Aeronautics Board, and others.

Only a tenuous control over these organizations is maintained by the elective branches of the government. They are authorized by Congress, their members approved by the Senate after nomination by the President, and after that they proceed more or less on their own. Generally, they combine in single bodies powers of government that were separated by the United States Constitution. That is, they legislate — create a body of administrative law by their decisions; execute — carry into effect their rulings; and adjudicate — hold hearings and make decisions which often have the effect of law.

Not only do these independent commissions concentrate powers within the federal government but they also have tended to claim large new powers for the federal government. By way of them, the federal government exercises extensive powers over transportation, electricity, money and banking, basic fuels, and labor relations. Nowadays, by way of their sway over energy and the environment, the federal government reaches through to the most basic undertakings of Americans.

The growth of power vested in a bureaucracy was long paralleled by and even was an augmentation of presidential power. Presidential power began to dominate the other branches during the administrations of Theodore Roosevelt and Woodrow Wilson. It became preeminent during the three terms plus a fraction of another of Franklin D. Roosevelt. These Presidents proceeded to dominate the legislative branches by setting forth programs — described respectively as the Square Deal, New Freedom, and New Deal — which they undertook to push through Congress. Once these programs were enacted into legislation, the executive branch was usually given many new powers and more extensive ones.

After the death of Franklin Roosevelt, three Democratic Presidents — Truman, Kennedy, and Johnson — attempted to advance similar broad programs under the rubrics of the Fair Deal, the New Frontier, and the Great Society. Truman, however, faced increasing opposition to his programs, and Kennedy was assassinated before he managed to translate much of his program into legislation. (In fact, until the media transformed Kennedy into a folk hero following his assassination, he had made little mark on government.) In the wake of Kennedy's assassination, President Johnson was able to get a multitude of laws passed, though there have been no prophets to proclaim that the Great Society emerged from it. But before he had served out the term to which he was elected on his own Johnson had become so unpopular, at least among radical elements, that he grew fearful of making public appearances and declined to run again.

It is now possible to conclude that following World War II the tide began to turn against presidential power. Democratic Presidents, the main architects of the surge of presidential power, were repeatedly drawn into actions which placed them at odds with some of the most

331

vocal of their constituents in the intellectual community. As Woodrow Wilson had written long before he came to the presidency, the major constitutional opening for the increase of presidential power is in foreign affairs. Nor can it be doubted that Presidents reached the peak of their hold on power during wars.

After World War II, the United States was confronted with expansive communist powers, became embroiled in a Cold War with them, and there were two hot wars, Korea and Vietnam. Anti-communism, however, was not popular with many Democrats, and particularly not with intellectuals. Moreover, those Americans who were anti-communists were hardly inclined to support Presidents who conducted lukewarm and increasingly limited wars in Korea and Vietnam. In consequence, Presidents were unable to rally many members of their own party behind them and alienated much of the rest of the populace by their conduct of the wars.

There have been many indications that the tide has begun to run against presidential power. There was, of course, a Constitutional amendment, the 22nd, ratified in 1951, limiting Presidents to two terms. There have been congressional efforts to restrain Presidents in foreign engagements. There were the weakened positions of both Truman and Johnson in their last years as President. There was the forced resignation of Vice-President Agnew and the even more dramatic resignation of President Nixon under the threat of imminent impeachment. The attacks on the FBI and CIA, and subsequent limitations placed on them, have had the effect of limiting the President. Moreover, President Carter was the first Democrat elected to the office in the twentieth century who did not run on the basis of some program name such as New Deal, Fair Deal, or the like. Nor has Carter thus far succeeded in getting much of his proposed legislation through Congress.

None of this should be interpreted to mean that there has been any lessening in the trend toward concentration of power in the general government. On the contrary, that has gone on at an accelerated pace even as presidential power was being restrained. While Johnson was being made virtually impotent by critics of the Vietnamese War, the Department of Health, Education and Welfare was expanding its powers into more and more fields. Even as Nixon was approaching disgrace, the Environmental Protection Agency and OSHA were extending their reach into every nook and cranny of America. Vast grants made from the federal government to states and cities during

Nixon's presidency concentrated decision-making power in Washington and continued the process of making state and local governments administrative arms of the federal government.

Rather, the relative decline in presidential power should be interpreted as a further decrease in popular control over this vast government with its concentration of power. The executive branch, i.e., the bureaucracy, increases in power as the powers of the Chief Executive decline. The Congress, historically the branch over which there has been the most direct popular control, does not, and cannot, exercise effective control over the bureaucracy and the independent commissions. Congress has failed for several decades now to restrain the judiciary, though there are ways it could do so. Presidents exercise only the most tenuous control over the bureaucracy.

The determinative role of bureaucracy is well described in this story which appeared in the *Atlanta Constitution,* March 26, 1978:

Almost nobody has heard of Joe Sherman, a $47,500-a-year federal civil servant. He commutes quietly to Washington every morning from a modest brick home in suburban Alexandria, Va. His work is seldom noticed by the press or the public.

But Joe Sherman may have an enormous impact on the everyday lives of Americans for years, even generations, to come....

Sherman and his staff at the Department of Housing and Urban Development are devising energy standards for building construction that are likely to alter the appearance, shape, or inner workings of every office building, hospital, school, factory, and private home in the United States after February 1981.

The process is much like that by which thousands of other small but important decisions are made throughout the government. The decisions influence the type of food that people eat, the clothes they wear, the kinds of loans they get, the construction of the cars they drive. The process is usually followed very closely by the specialists with a financial and a professional stake, but the public mostly learns little until it comes time to pay the bill, use the product and learn to live — and maybe suffer — with the results....

This is the story of how one law is being carried out. It began in 1976 when Congress passed the Energy Conservation Act. A little-noticed provision, heavily influenced by lobbyists for architects, ordered the administration to draw up "performance standards for new residential and commercial buildings which are designed to achieve the maximum practical improvements in energy efficiency and increases in the uses of nondepletable sources of energy."

Congress often leaves laws vague like that and allows the bureaucracy to work out the details. It is people like Joe Sherman who must figure out just what Congress meant by "maximum practical."

The standards, which are expected to be incorporated into building codes all over the country, will for the first time require that all buildings be designed to meet an "energy budget" — that is, they should be built to operate without using more than a specific amount of energy per square foot of space, depending on the purpose of the building and the climate where it is situated.

The vast accretion of governmental power involved in this should not go unnoticed, either.

The Department of Health, Education and Welfare may be most correctly conceived as a sort of independent kingdom or fiefdom set up within the bounds of the United States and being charged with or assuming authority over some of the most sensitive areas of American life. When it was founded during Eisenhower's presidency it brought together a hodge-podge of bureaus which theretofore had modest pretensions. Its activities and sway burgeoned with the spurt of legislation during the first two years of the Johnson administration. Congress and Presidents might have conducted diplomatic relations with it during most of its lifetime if they could have discovered who, if anyone, was in charge of it.

If the bureaucracy, the independent commissions, and courts — the organs of the concentrated power of the federal government — are not under the effective control of the elected representatives of the American people, who does control them? One way to answer the question is to say that nobody does. And that answer is correct so far as it goes. The President does have some little residual power over them; the Congress does have potential power; and pressure groups do sometimes modify their actions. But nobody controls or directs them in the ordinary conduct of their doings. Yet it would be incorrect to suppose that each bureaucrat or commissioner or judge simply decides his course of action, letting his conscience be his guide, and doing as he will. It may sometimes happen, but it is not characteristic.

As indicated earlier, the bureaucracy, the commissions, and the courts are ruled, by and large, by intellectual fashion. It is not usually called fashion; more commonly it has been thought of as the *zeitgeist,* spirit of the times, intellectual milieu, or reigning ideology. These latter terms and phrases may be more precise or comprehensive, but "fashion" captures better the way in which the ideas work on individuals and groups.

Intellectual fashion changes even as do fashions in women's clothes. One year it is environmentalism, another consumerism, another the eradication of poverty, another the menace of big business, another investigative journalism aimed at purifying politics, and so on. These intellectual fashions appear, decline, virtually disappear, and recur

334

much as do fashions in men's jackets, say. Just as padded shoulders in jackets become fashionable, then not, then again, so do fashions in prevailing ideas; the abolition of poverty was prominent in the 1890's, 1930's, and 1960's. The purification of politics was a major theme in the early twentieth century and then again in the 1970's.

Intellectual fashion is determined in much the same manner as fashions in clothes. Just as there are leading clothes designers, so there are leaders in setting forth what becomes intellectual fashion. For intellectual fashion, there have been such thinkers as John Kenneth Galbraith, Ralph Nader, Michael Harrington, and the like. Just as among clothes designers, there is competition for whose notions will prevail among intellectuals. And just as in clothes design, the more radical ideas are for the *Haute Coterie*. Beneath these, those who conform to the fashion do so in less drastic and, hence, more popular formulations.

Underlying and supporting this shifting intellectual fashion is an ideology which does not change. Ideology informs the continuing thrust to change, providing its direction and substance. What is in fashion at the moment is the leading wedge of the drive toward transformation. American intellectuals and politicians generally pride themselves on their pragmatism, but they are pragmatic only in changing emphases with the fashions.

Control over American government and increasingly over the lives of Americans is exercised by intellectual fashion and the underlying ideology. It is thus that the United States has been brought under the sway of the idea that has the world in its grip. This was made possible by the concentration of power in the central government and its further concentration in those areas of government most remote from popular control. More and more people vote, but they have less and less control over the government and their own affairs and lives.

The greater the concentration of power the more readily can it be manipulated by intellectual fashion under the subtle control of ideology. It is easier to influence one man than several, to influence the President, say, than the nine justices of the Supreme Court. In like manner, the Supreme Court may be more readily influenced than can 100 Senators, and the Senate more readily than the House of Representatives. It should be equally clear that one general government can be swayed more easily than can fifty state governments.

Influence may not be the right word; what often develops may be more correctly understood as pressure. Leaders of intellectual fashion

335

exert pressure on government, exert pressure until they get action quite often. Some examples may make the process clearer. In the 1960's, Ralph Nader wrote a book entitled *Unsafe at Any Speed.* He charged that American auto makers were turning out unsafe cars, failing to incorporate features that would save lives, and thus making auto travel precarious. In consequence of his charges a campaign to change all this emerged, laws were passed, and in the course of time various safety devices became mandatory for all automobiles. The impetus from this and similar works provoked two much broader campaigns: consumerism in general and safety requirements by governments in general. Hence, a Federal Office of Consumer Affairs was authorized, and most states followed suit with their own offices or bureaus. Also, the federal government set up an Occupational Safety and Health Administration (OSHA) which began to promulgate thousands of rules and restrictions affecting the safety of workers. As for the governmental intrusion into the automobile business, a newspaper reports that more vehicles were recalled because of defects in 1977 than were sold in that year.

Some years back, the late Rachel Carson came out with a book entitled *Silent Spring.* This was the intellectual opening for the environmentalist campaign which got underway in the late 1960's. Environmentalism swiftly became *the* fashionable cause, horror stories spread of how we were destroying the environment with chemicals, threatening the oxygen supply, making the air poisonous to breathe, the water hazardous to drink, and making our surroundings desolate. Protective legislation was, of course, forthcoming, and a new branch of the bureaucracy was created to see to the well-being of the environment.

Where does this pressure come from? It comes from those who deal in one way or another with ideas, with opinion making and the spread of ideas, those in the grip of the idea of transforming man and his universe. They are mostly intellectuals, or have intellectual pretensions: they are professors, students, teachers in general, journalists, writers, preachers, publicists, and what have you. How do they exert the pressure? They do so by the holding of key positions in the media of communication and by their success in purveying the approved attitudes. Mere Presidents must be continually wary of them, lest a thoughtless word will ruin their chances for re-election. Generals who voice unapproved attitudes are likely to be hounded out of the service, denied promotions, or buried in some administrative office in the Pentagon. Judges who hope for promotion must take care that they have never harbored opinions, or at least spoken or acted upon them, which will bring them to the unfavorable attention of media spokesmen.

There are numerous examples of what horrendous things can happen to those who provoke the wrath of media spokesmen, but no more dramatic one has yet occurred than that of the resignation of President Nixon in the wake of Watergate charges and revelations.

Ordinarily, however, the power of intellectual fashion directed by those under the sway of the idea that has the world in its grip is not demonstrated by the destruction of men in high places. It evinces itself, rather, in the day-to-day pressures on politicians and others to take approved positions and advance their enactments. It makes certain courses of action unthinkable and those that are approved largely unquestioned. It is a subtle and effective tyranny over thought. The concentrated power of government is wielded by those who dare not oppose this intellectual fashion. There are enough victims strewn along the wayside to serve as cautionary examples for those who consider any other course.

The power of government is wielded both directly and indirectly. We are all aware, more or less, of how control over our lives is wielded directly. It may be instructive, then, to examine into one of the prominent indirect ways government wields power.

27

Business as an Instrument of Political Power

BRIDLES FOR HORSES are equipped with blinkers. They are flaps on both sides of the horse's head at the level of the eye. Horses are skittish animals, and the purpose of the blinkers is to shut off peripheral vision so that the horse will not atttend to or be startled by something seen out of the corner of the eye.

Modern man is provided with blinkers, too. These are intellectual blinkers provided by the prevailing ideology. Under the sway of the idea that has the world in its grip, intellectuals blinker or blind us by determining what are the issues and in what terms they are to be discussed. Our intellectual vision is narrowed to take in only what we are supposed to see. True, there are those who persist in seeing more than is prescribed, but they are usually denied any forum from which to dramatize their viewpoint.

The prevailing ideology holds that "business," defined as an interest group, is in a continuing opposition to government intervention and regulation. The antecedents of this notion are in ideology. Marxist ideology proclaimed that a class struggle was in progress. The main antagonists in this struggle were the capitalist class and the proletariat

338

class. Gradualists have watered down this doctrine considerably, softened it at the edges, and made it less pronounced. But as they have instituted their reforms and regulations in the United States, they have clung to a subtle variation of the class struggle notion that capitalists are the enemy. On this view, businessmen favor *laissez faire* and oppose government intervention, while government intervenes on behalf of "the people" to hold obstreperous businessmen in line. These are the terms in which the issues must be discussed, if intellectual fashion is to be observed.

The Marxist notion that capitalists constitute a class vigorously defending their interests against all challengers is about as valid as would be the notion that all females eligible for marriage constitute a class pursuing the common aim of marriage. The fact is that eligible females are in competition with one another for the available swains, if matrimony is their object. In their own way, businessmen are in competition with one another. They compete for customers, for materials, for workers, and for whatever they conceive would be advantageous to them. True, some businessmen oppose regulation as a matter of principle; and a goodly number oppose regulations when it is expedient to do so. It is also the case that businessmen are more apt to denounce regulation than are, say, journalists or teachers — regulation of business, that is.

Be that as it may, it is a grotesque distortion of what is happening to look at the matter this way. There is every reason to believe that businessmen spend vastly more ingenuity, energy, and money to get regulations construed so as to be able to live with or take advantage of them than they do in opposition to intervention. If this were the issue, however, there would be room for it as an issue in the framework of the prevailing ideology. There has been much discussion over the years about how the regulated manipulate the regulators. Those favoring government restraint of business have deplored it, while those more favorably disposed toward the needs of business activity have been more charitably inclined toward something they consider inevitable in any case.

But what is happening most prominently is of a different order. The grip of the Idea is being fastened on America by using business as an instrument of political power. Much of the force of government power reaches the individual today indirectly by way of his employer and the other business and financial institutions with which he is involved.

Some of this instrumentation of business by government for its own ends is well known and needs only to be alluded to in order to be accepted. Businesses collect most of the taxes from individuals and pay them into local, state, and federal treasuries. This has already been discussed in connection with restrictions on enterprise, but it needs further elaboration in the context of government use of business to extend political power. Employers collect most income taxes, both state and Federal, by withholding them from salaries. They also collect Social Security taxes in the same way. Stores and other retail outlets collect sales taxes. On budget type mortgages, the mortgage company collects one-twelfth of the projected real estate taxes by way of the regular monthly payment. Telephone, electric, and gas companies add whatever taxes there may be upon their services to their bills, and when the bills are paid, the tax amounts are set aside to be paid into governments. Service stations collect the taxes on gasoline, tires, and other automobile accessories. There are also a considerable variety of hidden taxes on businesses which are generally passed on in the price of the product. The most extensive of these, though it is not usually referred to as "hidden," is the tax on corporations.

Businesses collect these taxes, of course, because they are required by law to do so and would be subject to punishment if they did not. The collection of them, the keeping of records, and the other costs associated with it, are generally a cost of doing business. The consumer pays these costs as well, though it is only fair to observe that he would no doubt pay them, and they would probably be higher, if government collected the taxes directly.

However that might be, it should be clear that government has empowered businesses to perform the bulk of one of its most disagreeable functions — the collection of taxes. This does not mean that people usually blame businesses for the taxes, though they are apt to blame them for high prices when, in fact, much of the price is attributable to taxes. The main impact of this use of business by government is somewhat more subtle. When business collects the taxes the individual loses his ability to contest paying them. He can only prevent income taxes from being withheld by quitting his job. He can only refuse to pay the sales taxes by declining to buy what he wants. The normal route for taking a case to court is denied him because of the difficulty in refusing to pay. The individual's economy is intertwined with the power of government over him.

Business becomes an instrument of government, too, as the main executor of the government's labor and employment policies. The individual is the pawn in the midst of the complex rules by which

340

government activates its policies through business. Whether he can get a job at all, whether he will have to join a labor union, how long he will work for how much, among other things, are determined by government policy.

Wages and hours legislation has been around for forty years now. Government prescribed minimum wages determine practically whether a person may be employed or not. If a person is unskilled, handicapped, or slow, he may not be sufficiently productive to be employed for a job because of the mandatory wage. The inexperienced are at a particular disadvantage, because a prospective employer has no way of knowing how long it will take or even whether an applicant may become productive enough both to earn the minimum wage and repay the expense of training him.

Union wages and other rules and restrictions are often an extension of government policy over business. The National Labor Relations Board, an arm of the federal government, establishes the framework, though it may not be known, sometimes, in advance of a ruling, within which company-union relations are to be carried on. Once a company recognizes a union, it tends to become an instrument of union policy — collecting dues, hiring through a union hall, requiring union membership of those it employs, maintaining seniority rules, and paying a union wage. The individual is at the mercy of the NLRB, the labor union, and the company when they act in concert.

Fair employment practices, as they are called, and Affirmative Action are prescribed by the federal and many state governments. Thus, the hiring and promotion practices of business become an instrument of government policy. To avoid litigation or government penalties many firms undertake joint ventures with minority owned companies, establish what are in effect quota systems in hiring and promotion, and conduct searches for minority personnel to fill vacancies. To the extent that political prescription is substituted for business judgment, a business becomes an instrument of political power.

Many of the regulations, restrictions, and restraints under which we live are imposed by way of business. For example, automobile safety equipment and emission controls come by way of requirements on auto makers. Safety belts, shoulder harnesses, interior design, structural strength, and so on, have made their appearance not from customer demand but by way of legislation. Buzzers, filters, and an assortment of other devices are attached to the vehicles by government fiat. An individual who wishes to have his vehicle divested of any of this impedimenta must either do it himself or find a wayward mechanic to do it for him.

Most of the housing available to us has its quality and character determined by building companies and financial institutions acting as instruments of government. Most of the financing of homes comes from privately owned institutions. However, their lending policies are heavily influenced and widely determined by government policy. VA and FHA guarantees undergird a considerable portion of the loans made to individuals. Although the money comes from private sources, VA and FHA lay down standards for and determine much about the houses so financed. Many savings and loan associations are federally chartered and make their loans in terms of these government charters. Builders impose, as it were, the numerous requirements of local, state, and federal government on buyers, such things as zoning restrictions, setback ordinances, distances of buildings from property lines, structural standards, sanitation and electrical prescriptions, the paving of streets, and so on and on. Real estate agents, if their services are to be used, impose the rules governing them upon their customers.

Examples could be multiplied of businesses as instruments of government, but perhaps enough has been told to establish the point. Virtually every business in America (if there is an exception, it has escaped my notice) acts as an arm of government in one way or another and to a greater or lesser extent. While the evidence to substantiate much of this must be familiar to most of us, the implications and results of it may not be so readily apparent.

The matter is more complex than the above would indicate. The examples thus far could be interpreted as being simply a case of government imposing rules upon business which they in turn, however reluctantly, impose on their customers. Undoubtedly, that is the way it is often enough. But that is hardly the whole story. *Government and business are so intricately intertwined today that many businesses have taken on the character of governments.* I would like to back into an explanation of the how and why of this development with a simple story.

Some years back I lived in a state which had a tax, imposed annually, on checking accounts in banks. This tax came to my attention one day when I was going over my monthly bank statement. There was a deduction from my account to pay this tax. This struck me as highly impertinent behavior by the bank. My understanding of the agreement I had with the bank was that when the spirit moved me I would deposit money with them. Then, when, as, and if I decided to do so I could order all or some portion of it to be paid out by writing checks on the account. They were trustees, so to speak, of such money as I deposited with them and were only to disburse it on my order. It seemed to me they had violated that trust by paying out my money without my knowledge or consent.

With that understanding in mind, I placed a call to the highhanded bank in question. (I am now older and wiser and therefore know in advance the futility of such calls, although I still make them sometimes just to prove that I am alive.) When I had finally been connected with someone sufficiently high up in the bank to deal with so exalted a question, I made inquiries about their behavior. I was assured that the bank had acted in accord with state law, something I had never for a moment doubted. But, I asked, has the law been challenged? He did not know, as best I can recall, nor, so far as I could make out, care.

My thought was that this manner of taking my money was in violation of the Fourteenth Amendment to the United States Constitution, which prohibits states from taking the property of their citizens without due process of law. Moreover, it seemed to me that the bank had strong incentives to challenge such a law. After all, the bank wanted deposits from customers, and one of the best arguments for using their services was the security they provided for your money. It happened, too, that the bank was ideally situated to challenge this law, for it could do so by refusing to pay the tax, an option not available to me. In addition, the bank probably had a prestigious law firm on retainer to protect its interests, since this particular bank was one of a large chain spread over the state, there being no law in that state to prohibit branch banking.

My reasoning was not so much faulty as incomplete. True, banks have the incentive to reassure and protect their depositors. But I was ignoring something so basic as that the state government was probably one of the largest depositors in the bank. Indeed, the likelihood is so great as to amount to virtual certainty that the tax money taken from mine and other accounts did not even leave the bank; it was just shifted to the state's account. That, however, might not have been determinative if it were all that was involved.

I was ignoring the more trenchant fact that banks are creatures of government, that their very existence by charter depends upon government, that their privileges arise from the state, and that banks can be harassed, audited, have their charters revoked, or be closed down.

That being the case, banks are about as likely to take on an adversary relationship to the state over some paltry tax as an unemployed spinster is to sue her parents with whom she lives over the lack of variety in her breakfast. Besides, the tax could hardly harm this chain of banks if all other banks in the states had to collect it too. Laws applied to a whole industry become merely a condition of doing business.

Is this an indictment of business? No, it is a description of what is happening in America as the concentrated power of government tightens its grip on people. The idea that has the world in its grip only permits what is called private business to exist on sufferance. It can exist only to the extent that it serves the ends of the idea as determined by those who control or manipulate government. Businessmen know that as a rule they cannot even survive, much less prosper, if they adopt an adversary relationship with government. Both politicians and businessmen sometimes speak as if they were adversaries. No great harm results. The ideological view of the relationship is affirmed, and each is given an opportunity to vent his spleen. But beneath the surface something quite different is going on.

Business and government are intricately intertwined. Businesses generally depend upon government for charters, for licenses, for contracts, for subsidies, for guarantees of foreign investments, for favors for their particular industry, and so on, and on. Business serves government in the ways that are specified, becomes an instrument of government, in order to continue to function and, hopefully, make a profit. Airlines seeking new routes, continued payment for carrying the mail, and favorable rates are not about to contest the regulations on smoking that they apply to their passengers. Home builders hoping for some new government subsidy program to enable them to sell more houses have the incentive to work with rather than oppose government. Public utility firms seeking higher rates can hardly afford to object to being tax collectors. Whether unwillingly or not, business acts as a partner with government in imposing political power on Americans.

You cannot play with fire without getting burned, of course. The more closely business becomes intertwined with government, the more like government it becomes. The object of politics is power. The aim of business is profit. The method of business is attraction and persuasion. The method of government is force. As business becomes politicized, it does not forgo its aim of making profits. What it does do is begin to seek to use the force of government to increase its profits. Power and profit are linked together as government and business become intertwined.

This development may best be illustrated by an example. In the 1970's a gasoline shortage occurred. It was a shortage engineered by politicians, of that there should be no doubt. The governments of several major oil producing countries declared an embargo and proceeded, thereafter, to raise the price of oil drastically. The shortage evaporated and was no more, though prices of gasoline were much higher than before. Nonetheless, American politicians proclaimed that we were in the midst of an incipient energy crisis. What the politicians had discovered was something known to economists for at least two hundred years, and to most other folks considerably longer, namely, that the sources of energy are *scarce*. Indeed, it is the very *scarcity* of fuel that makes it costly at all. We shall not, of course, run out of energy — not, that is, until the sun grows cold or this planet is wrenched away from its favorable location to the sun — but different sources may have to be tapped to get it.

Nonetheless, having misconstrued permanent scarcity as incipient and worsening shortage, some politicians went into their "sky is falling" routine, made a national problem out of it, and began to bring forth programs to solve it. Not surprisingly, these programs involved various sorts of government intervention. What may have been surprising, however, was the way in which fuel suppliers joined into this hue and cry. Full-page advertisements began to appear in newspapers, ads paid for by oil companies, electric power and gas companies, and such like, urging the conservation of energy and describing the efforts they were making to deal with the shortage. Power and gas companies began to include tips on conservation of energy in the envelopes containing their bills. Business instrumented itself swiftly to political policy.

For years, electric companies had urged their customers to use more and more electricity. They had extolled the virtues of electric appliances over all others. Moreover, they had encouraged greater use by giving customers lower rates as the amount used increased. Indeed, there did not appear to be anything odd about this earlier behavior. It was what advertising was for, to encourage use of a product. It was in keeping with what is economic. There are economies of scale in production. In the case of electricity, this means that when the investment in machinery has been made, the more that is produced with it, the less it costs to produce each unit. In order to sell this electricity, the company would promote greater use by reducing the rate as more was used.

And then, overnight, as it were, electric power companies stopped advertising their product and began propagandizing for conservation, adopting the same line as the government. Utility commissions began to approve what are called "inverted rate structures." What these rate structures do is penalize heavy users of electricity, by charging higher rates for greater amounts of electricity. The model for this rate structure must have been the graduated income tax.

Why would a power company stand still for such a rate structure? After all, it still got the advantage of economies of scale whether there was an energy shortage or not. Moreover, it costs little, if any, more to get the electricity to a home using 1500 kilowatts per month, say, than one using 500. The meter has to be read only once each month regardless of how much electricity is used. It costs as much to bill the user for 500 as for 5000 kilowatts, and the same expenses attend processing either account.

There are two answers which help to explain this otherwise strange power company behavior. One is that the power company was serving the source of its monopoly — government. The other is that the company was being well served, at least temporarily, by the utility commission. Undoubtedly, a power company could be greatly enriched if it could enjoy economies of scale and charge even more for this electricity than that bought by small-scale users.

Most likely, such a policy would, in the long run, be harmful to the power company, for profits would surely dwindle as use declined. But in the short run — before those who had all-electric homes could convert to other power sources, before alternative sources of power have been developed, before people changed their life styles to reduce the consumption of electricity — the companies should reap a windfall of profits.

Of course, high profits would bring them to the unfavorable attention of utility commissions who had approved the rates in the first place. Except that some power companies have already been foresighted enough to forecast a need for a vast amount of capital to increase production to meet demand. It apparently does not matter that the demand they are forecasting is based upon a projection of increases in the past, increases which took place when the use of electricity was being vigorously advanced by advertising and lower rates for heavy users. What the present policies will lead to is uncertain. Meanwhile, the intertwining of government and business has produced some strange uneconomic policies.

The final stage of business as an instrument of government will almost certainly be that business will be transformed into government, or be so much like it that we will have a distinction without a difference. The most basic distinction between business and government is this: Business serves; government commands. That distinction has been breaking down for years. One way it has broken down is that government has provided many services itself; education, parks, electric power, mail delivery, garbage collection, and so forth. The other way is that many businesses have been granted monopolies and special privileges so that they become more like governments than businesses.

Government regulation of business is almost always advanced as a way of restraining or inhibiting business. But it does not necessarily work that way. Government regulation limits and restrains business in serving customers. If a business is only permitted to stay open during certain hours, that limits its service to those hours. If rates are regulated, this may appear to limit the businessman, but it also limits the way in which he can serve. But most importantly, as the businessman is more closely regulated he shifts from serving to enforcing the conditions under which he will serve. He comes to resemble the policeman more than a businessman.

Public utilities are apt to be as inflexible in enforcing their rules as any government. The telephone installer will not install the telephone unless the householder is at home. The utilities will not begin service, ordinarily, until the person wishing to be served has made his way to their offices, put up a deposit, provided whatever information they require, and otherwise satisfied them that he is responsible. Hospitals are notoriously rule-ridden places, and many a nurse appears to be a frustrated prison matron. (It should be noted in this connection that hospitals are generally heavily subsidized by government and are coming under ever more strenuous regulation and controls.)

Every organization must have internal discipline over its employees, of course. What is at issue here is the shift of business from service to compulsion. It is, no doubt, a natural tendency of those who live under rules to shift the weight of the rules from themselves toward those whom they are supposed to serve. There is a corrective to that in the open market under competition. The customer does not like to be ordered around, and he goes elsewhere. He gives his business to those who wish to serve him rather than command him. Any rules that he perceives that apply to him had best be kept to the minimum and be unobtrusive.

When government steps in, that changes. So long as the rule applies to all in the industry, competition is no longer a factor in whatever is involved. The business no longer has to serve in that particular way; it needs only to do whatever the law requires. When rates are regulated, the business need no longer compete in that way. If some of the rates are not particularly profitable, those in the industry will discourage that particular custom, providing only the bare minimum of service that the law allows. Indeed, the burden of obtaining the service is often shifted to the customer. For example, when long-term interest rates for home buyers have been set below the market rate, the borrower usually has had to pay for the loan by what are called "points" and other advance charges. In addition to that, the conditions to be met in order to obtain the loan are usually quite exacting. Long waits for loan approval are common. The lender is not gladly serving; he is emphasizing the commanding position he occupies.

Evolutionary socialism advances gradually and step by step in America. The inroads are usually made under the guise of controlling, regulating, and taxing business and the sources of capital. On the surface, this does indeed occur. But beneath the surface government and business become intertwined. Business becomes an instrument of government, willing or not. Business becomes politicized. Business begins to serve its master, government, instead of or in addition to the consumer. Business begins, unwittingly perhaps, to adopt the posture of compulsion rather than of service.

According to the lore of our time there is a public sector and a private sector in the economy. But where is the private sector? Does it consist of privately owned companies such as those of the auto makers? What is private about mandatory seat belts and shoulder harness? What is private about mandatory emission controls? What is private about being forced by government to recall millions of automobiles annually to replace parts? What is private about having to pay union wages and submit to union requirements reinforced by the National Labor Relations Board? Rather than referring to this as the private sector, it would be accurate to refer to it as the politicized sector of the economy. But which "sector" is not? Some are more, some are less, but all are being politicized.

The deeper significance of this development needs to be clearly understood. To understand it, it is necessary to see it in terms of the appropriate theory. Much has been written about the impact of intervention in terms of economic theory. This is enlightening and informative. But when business becomes an instrument of government, economics becomes secondary, for the framework and the determinative

348

element is no longer economic. It is political, and political theory must provide the framework from which it is to be understood.

Political theory has to do with how effectively to govern and how government may be restrained and limited. The greatest work on political theory in the United States was *The Federalist*. It was written as an exposition and defense of the Constitution of the United States and, more specifically, to urge its ratification. The great principles set forth there are those of constitutionalism, of representative government, of the dispersion of power in a federal system, of the separation of powers into three branches — all of which they argued would provide an energetic and strong but limited government.

The reason for limiting government was clear to the Founders of these United States. Government is dangerous. It differs from other organizations in that it has the power and authority to use sanctions. In a word, it is empowered legally to use force. Unlimited government means unlimited use of force. In practice it means that all institutions and organizations are permeated by force. The end result is tyranny.

No better prescription for tyranny could be written than to make business an instrument of government. Every businessman and every employee of businessmen becomes a servant of government. Every consumer, each one of us, is at the mercy of politicized business. The usual argument against intervention is that it is harmful economic restraint of goods and services business can and would provide. There is a more telling argument. It is that government control over business is inevitably government control over consumers, and the instrument of that control is business.

28

The Thrust to Transformation

THE OCCASION WAS a civilized one, very nearly formal, and certainly decorous. Military personnel in their dress uniforms presented the colors. The well dressed audience, many of the women in full-length evening dresses, stood for the singing of the "Star Spangled Banner." A multi-coursed dinner was served by male waiters, well trained in those flourishes which add to the decor of an occasion. A goodly number of prominent people were present, and the main speaker was the lieutenant-governor of the state. The audience was well mannered, polite, and conscious of doing the right thing by applauding at all the places where it seemed to be indicated. Civility was an unannounced guest of honor at the occasion.

For a brief span of time in the midst of the proceedings, two men entered the room. Their attire was only a slight improvement over that of ranch hands returning from a long cattle drive. One of the men wore a cap which remained on his head for the whole time they were there. One man was a photographer, and the other was his lighting assistant. They went about their picture taking with no apparent regard for the audience or participants, standing between some of the audience and the dais, moving about at will, shining bright lights here and there, and making it difficult for all others there at the high point of the proceedings.

Undoubtedly, the photographers were invited to come to take pictures. Undoubtedly, too, they were going about doing so in the most direct way. My point, however, is that they were an alien element in our midst. Their attire and manner would have been little different if they had been photographing hogs wallowing in their mire. Our manners, our customs, and our purposes could hardly have concerned them less if they were invaders from Mars.

My larger point is this. There is an alien force in our midst, a force (or pervasive influence) which is alien to our manners, customs, traditions, morality, and institutions. We are all familiar with it in its most obtrusive form, that of the newsman or reporter. We have all seen such reporters, at least on television, crowding about some person, pushing for attention, shoving microphones in his face, blinding him with flashbulbs, and insistently demanding answers to questions which are none of their business. It is a good analogy to think of them as wolves, baying at some prey they have surrounded, preparing to strip his garments away and render him helpless before them.

Reporters are, however, only the most colorful of a much more extensive alien element. It holds sway in a whole vast industry, or, more precisely, a congeries of industries. In its lesser dimension, it is often referred to as the communications industry, the opinion industry, or, simply, the media. In its broader dimensions, however, it embraces much more: the entertainment industry, the information and education industry, and a vast assortment of other businesses which lie on the periphery of these. It includes records, tapes, books, magazines, movies, radio, television, newspapers, much of live entertainment, schools, a portion of organized religion, the world of fashion — clothing, hair styling, adornment — and so on. In terms of its thrust, it should be called the "Transformation Industry."

If it be considered a single industry, it is a huge industry, and much of it is highly profitable. The publishing industry alone is so vast and profitable that large corporations have bought old houses in order to diversify and become more profitable. The ownership of a television station is the nearest thing there is to a franchise to print money in the United States. Although the Life-style or Transformation Industry includes activities that are generally not profitmakers, such as schools, those who work in them are often well rewarded.

Despite the size, sway, and profitability of much of this industry, a strange and apparently contradictory development has been taking place over the last decade. As business in general has been ever more closely regulated and controlled, as much of business has been turned into an instrument of government, the Lifestyle or Transformation Industry has been breaking loose from such regulations and controls over it as there have been. An ever wider arena of freedom from either social or political control for those in this industry is being carved out. The tendency is for the Lifestyle Industry neither to be controlled by government nor to be an instrument of government. Its thrust is rather toward the control and use of government and to assume for itself the role of society.

Much of the great tradition of liberty in the United States has been pre-empted by the Transformation Industry and instrumented for its specialized purposes. The industry relies mainly on the First Amendment to the Constitution to expand the boundaries of its uncontrolled activities. The Amendment reads, in part: "Congress shall make no law ... abridging the freedom of speech or of the press...." It has long since been stretched far beyond the meaning which could be deduced from its language to include all governments and is widely used to inhibit any criticism of things spoken or written. The battle cries of "censorship" and "academic freedom" are employed to deter any control over the press and schools.

Freedom, it has been said, is like a seamless cloth. Those who point this out have been most often inclined to argue that you cannot have freedom of speech, press, religion, and political activity without the corresponding freedoms entailed in private property, trade, enterprise, and managing your own affairs. The theory supporting this view is well established, and much historical evidence can be adduced which tends to prove it. But there is another aspect of this principle which is not usually noticed. It is that partial liberty tends to degenerate into license.

When does liberty become license? Or, when does the exercise of liberty become licentious? One way to answer the question is to say that liberty becomes license when its exercise intrudes upon the realm of other people and becomes abusive. Another way is to note that liberty tends to become license when it is cut loose from that to which in its proper exercise it is responsible. The principle can be stated more directly: Unrestrained liberty tends to become license. Partial liberty, enjoyed by some portion of the populace only, that is unrestrained not only becomes licentious but tyrannical. Freedom without responsibility is indistinguishable from tyranny.

Those who claim that everything must be regulated are correct. (The fact that we have come to identify regulation with something that government does in our day should not mislead us on this point.) The

352

principle may be most readily grasped by a mechanical illustration of it. Every automobile is equipped with a generator or alternator and battery. The battery is for storing electricity, and the generator is for replenishing the supply. However, the electricity cannot go directly from the generator to the battery. Between the two is a voltage regulator, a device which keeps the voltage entering the battery within a tolerable range and prevents the battery from being overcharged and destroyed. All transmitted electricity requires similar regulation.

In a like manner the amount of fuel going into an engine must be regulated. The driver of an automobile regulates the fuel by depressing or releasing pressure on the accelerator. It is impractical, however, to regulate the amount of fuel going into all engines this way. For example, power mowers need more or less fuel depending on the height, thickness and toughness of the grass that is being cut. Lawn mowers are equipped with governors to provide regulation in ordinary circumstances. Without them, lawn mower engines would either be continually stalled or run dangerously fast most of the time.

Price is regulated in the free market by supply and demand. The demand is kept within the confines of supply by variations in the price. Price is held down and supply is kept up by competition. It happens, too, that so far as the quality of material goods and physical services is concerned, better quality generally sells for a higher price and poorer quality at a lower price, other things being equal. (With fruit and vegetables, the time of year or season must be taken into account, of course. High quality tomatoes are usually less expensive in summer than are the poorest quality in winter.)

But the laws of economics are almost entirely ineffective in regulating quality by price in the intellectual and spiritual realm. It costs no more to reproduce the words in the Bible than it does those in the most scabrous pornographic novel. Once the recording has been made, it costs no more to make copies of Mozart's harmonic symphonies on records or tapes than it does of the outrageous noise of the Sex Pistols. Supply, demand, and competition still regulate price, but the market has no device for registering spiritual or intellectual quality.

The market, as the late Ludwig von Mises was fond of pointing out, is democratic in tendency. It tends to provide the greatest number of goods to the greatest number of people. It responds to the most widespread and urgent demands. The market, as such, has no values, no standards, no morality, except such as are fed into it by buyers and sellers. The market is, let us face it, a potential monster, catering to the most debased

353

taste, the most depraved yearnings, and ready to provide the perverted with the means for practicing their perversion.

There is, normally, a corrective to and inhibitor of this monstrous potentiality of the market. Normally, the free market does not exist and function alone and in splendid isolation; it is an integral aspect of freedom and responsibility within the society generally. The free market is part of the seamless cloth of the free society.

The market may be democratic, but society is, by nature, aristocratic. The market, as such, may be value free, but society is value laden, ever sifting in a timeless way the wheat from the chaff. The market is a mechanism of society. Society is the normal regulator of the market, insisting upon quality as well as quantity, inhibiting what may be bought and sold there, bringing standards, values, taste, judgment, and morality to bear on what takes place there.

This brings us to what has happened and what is happening in the United States. There should be no doubt that the fabric of liberty is torn. There is not a free market in general. The market is hampered, restrained, controlled, planned, and intervened in by government. Meanwhile, a limited aspect of the market, that which offers fare for the soul and mind, is being given ever freer rein. It is not possible to buy an automobile without seat belts, but every sort of depravity is luridly described in books and magazines readily available. Diabetics may not be able to buy substitutes for sugar, but there is none so depraved that his tastes are not freely pandered to in the market.

More, society cannot effectively maintain its taboos today. It cannot bring to bear a discriminatory taste, judgment, the weight of custom and tradition, and morality upon what is sold in the market. Its prescriptive powers have been largely deactivated. Society is wounded and crippled where it is not entirely disabled. The regulator has been removed from that portion of the market that is free.

How this has come about is too large a story to tell in all its detail. It is much too complex to do more than call attention to the outlines of the process here. One thing should be clear: It has come about largely as a result of government intervention in and inhibition of society. Society wields its influence and maintains its prescriptions by a great variety of customs, institutions, traditions, and organizations. The most basic institution of society is the family. The basic tasks of the family are the nurture and upbringing of children, the provision for those in their midst who are unable to take care of themselves, and the looking after aged relatives. To accomplish these tasks, authority must be exercised, and divisions of responsibility must be maintained.

354

Government has now assumed much of the role of the family. Compulsory school attendance and government prescription of what must be taught relieves parents of much of their responsibility for the children and authority over their upbringing. Welfare and Social Security payments eroded dependence upon the family. When dependence is gone much authority is lost as well. The tendency of government intervention has been to reduce the family to an affectional unit, to remove much of its disciplinary authority, and to make it no stronger than the fickle ties of affection.

The authority of employers has been drastically reduced by government intervention. Every government prescription of wages, of hours, of working conditions, and of employer-employee relations reduces the authority of the employer.

A spirit of litigation afflicts Americans today. Patients are suing physicians, students suing teachers, employees suing employers, wives suing husbands, women suing men, blacks suing whites — even children suing parents. What this signifies, when it becomes rampant, is the breakdown of society, the substitution of force for persuasion, and the intrusion of government into every nook and cranny of life. It is a state of covert civil war superintended largely by federal judges. Those who bring suits may not realize it, but every suit invites, even requires, that the force of government be brought to bear to bring the parties into line.

What has all this, and much else of similar character, to do with the largely uninhibited onslaught of the Transformation Industry upon us? It has everything to do with it. Society enforces its prescriptions mainly by approval or disapproval of acts. Public decorum, morality, and civility is maintained because the individual seeks the approval of others around him. In a similar fashion, good taste and high standards depend upon the desire people have for the good opinion of others. It seems natural to many of us to wish to be in good standing with those with whom we come in contact. But for the generality it needs to be reinforced by exigent social ties. One seeks the good will of an employer, above all, to keep a job. Children obey parents, in the final analysis, because their livelihood depends on them. Men have a care to their language, observe the taboos, behave themselves not only because they wish to be well thought of but also because their well-being in general depends upon it. When these finanacial and familial supports are cut away, social prescriptions lose their bite.

The stage has been set, then, for the transformation of society. The social regulator which links freedom to responsibility has been

355

disconnected. Business, in general, is ever more severely controlled and regulated. The Transformation Industry, by contrast, is enlarging its arena for freedom of action divorced from responsibility for the consequences. The media has assumed much of the prescriptive authority once exercised by society. It proclaims, often subtly, approved attitudes, rewarding those who conform and ignoring or punishing those who do not. Generals cower before the lash of enraged media-men, resign their positions, and retire to obscurity. But the media is not society; it is, instead, one of the alien elements thrusting toward social transformation.

The Transformation Industry is alien to American society in so far as and to the extent that it is bent upon transforming it. Some qualification is in order here. There is nothing inherent in journalism, in book publishing, in music making, or any other of these undertakings that would bend them toward transformation of society. Magazines may as readily defend as attack the existing social order. Education is, by nature, a conservative process whose main purpose has usually been imbuing the young with their culture and heritage. Undoubtedly, too, there are magazines and schools that have as no part of their purpose obstructing or transforming the social order. Almost any newspaper will have a considerable variety of material in it, much of which will have little or nothing to do with social transformations. Some television programs may lovingly portray aspects of our culture and heritage.

Be that as it may, for a considerable while now a major thrust of the media, education, the information industries, and entertainment has been toward social transformation. Intellectual fashion has prescribed social transformation as a desirable goal. The Idea that has the world in its grip has held sway in the United States as elsewhere. Intellectuals bent on transforming have often pictured and thought of themselves as being an embattled minority. That is a misconstruction of the actual situation. They are a majority, or at least determine much of the course of things, in the intellectual realm. But they are alien to the society and, as such, do occupy a potentially precarious position. The fact that they are continually attacking and undermining the received social arrangements makes them aliens.

To grasp what has been happening it will be helpful to get in mind as clearly as can be what a society is. A society begins to be formed when two or more people begin to interact on a regular basis. What we speak of as society emerges from the modes that are tacitly agreed upon and accepted for interacting with one another. The society consists of those

356

who accept these modes of behavior. The modes consist of manners, morals, conventions, customs, taboos, and traditions. Amongst civilized peoples, social prescriptions not only facilitate intercourse but tend to protect individuals in the enjoyment and use of what is theirs. (Those prescriptions that are amenable to it are often formalized as law.)

Man was made for society, wise men have said, and there is no end to the advantages which follow from social cooperation. Indeed, the advantages of association and cooperation are so obvious and great that societies will continue to be formed so long as there are people. Social arrangements exist for the purpose of enabling people the better to enrich themselves by interacting with one another.

However, there is a nether side to the relations between people. All interaction between people is potentially abrasive, fraught with dangers of abuse of some persons by others, and sets the stage for every harmful act that can occur. Society exists for the specific purpose of providing means for keeping relations among people smooth. The more intimate the relations among people the more potentially dangerous the situation.

Taboos take shape especially to govern and restrain intimate relations. Since sexual relations are the most intimate of all relations, it is not surprising that taboos often are strenuously applied in this area. There is, for example, a near universal taboo against incest — a taboo which serves not only to abate the dangers of inbreeding but to protect the close family unit from the conflicts that would arise within it from sexual rivalries.

Social conventions tend to change with the passage of time. Sometimes, society gets religion, so to speak, professes very high standards, and is purified somewhat of its dross of accretions over the years. Social prescriptions change to deal with new conditions and new opportunities and dangers. Positive law often arises from social prescription, as well it should, but law is frequently too gross, precise, and inflexible for the complex and shifting shades of social prescription. But social change must be gradual, otherwise it is disruptive and confusing, thus failing to facilitate interaction or to protect individuals within it. A certain comfort within and accord with the rules of society is essential to the working of society.

Socialists regard the received social arrangements as a major detriment to their undertakings. Revolutionaries require that they be destroyed. Evolutionary socialists attempt to change them gradually by law so as to merge government with society. At any rate, both agree that the whole complex of distinctions which society maintains must be broken down before man can be collectivized, communized, or socialized. The received institutions, customs, and traditions provide a protective shield for the individual, a shield which must be broken before he can be melded into a mass.

The most drastic experiments with forced collectivization did not occur in Stalin's attempt to collectivize agriculture. They occured in Soviet forced labor camps and in Nazi concentration camps. They were alluded to earlier in this work. They involved especially the uninhibited use of obscenities, profanity, and inducing the individual to violate various taboos. Alexander Dolgun, an American who spent years in Soviet prisons and labor camps, tells how when he was first put in prison he was subjected to a physical examination by a woman doctor who gave special attention to his private parts. This surely was not accidental, for it fit the general pattern of trying to break him down by removing the normal expectation of observing the social mores.

The most dramatic thrust of the Transformation Industry in recent years has been to break down or through the social prescriptions that have to do with the use of language and sex. Rampant public expression of obscenities became commonplace in the 1960's. Novelists began to lard their works with just about every vulgar expression imaginable. Underground newspapers printed the theretofore unprintable. Magazines, even some of general circulation, began to do likewise. Even more profound in its impact was the use of obscenities in the speech of characters in movies. After all, reading is usually a private undertaking. But movies have public showings as a rule, and are usually made for that purpose. Nowadays, profanity and obscenities are regular fare in movies designated PG (meaning acceptable for the admission of children but parental guidance suggested).

Many sexual taboos have been ignored and violated with impunity. The most intmate matters are now publicly discussed, written about, and portrayed in picture magazines and movies. Many restrictions are still observed in family newspapers, television, and radio, but they are being broken down there as well. Explicit descriptions of sexual intercourse were only available in brown covers to discreet patrons a generation ago. What was not then conceived as properly printable is now shown in technicolor on wide screens in movies. If present trends continue, in a few years the family can gather round to watch vivid portrayals of bestiality, necrophilia, and incest, with some orgies thrown in, on their home television sets. Such fare is already available on closed circuit television in hotels and motels.

Decorum is the condition of peaceful public assembly. Good manners are the clothes the civilization wears. By the clothes we wear we signify our respect for the sensibilities of others as well as our own dignity. Propriety in the use of language preserves the communion involved in communication. Custom, tradition, and morality are not merely the ornaments, they are the lineaments of society.

My point is this. What occurred as concentrated dosage in Soviet prisons and forced labor camps and Nazi concentration camps is now being done in a much less concentrated manner on a national scale by the Lifestyle or Transformation Industry. The defenses of life, liberty, and property are being removed by the hammer blows on our sensibilities. The right to life depends upon the prohibitions against murder. Sensibility for others is the foundation of the taboo against murder. There are religious sanctions against murder, but the acceptance, observance, and appreciation of these depends upon sensibility as well. Obscenity, vulgarity, and depravity publicly displayed are indications of a profound loss of respect for man. Liberty for such a man is no more than opening the gate and turning the beast out to forage at will. Such a man is no more worthy of property than would be a jackal.

The Transformation Industry is bent toward collectivizing us. It is stripping away from us our civility, our decorum, our good manners, our taboos, our customs, our traditions, and our individuality. Man must be reduced to be collectivized, his language reduced to guttery curses, his body reduced to its respective and undistinctive parts, and his culture to its meanest remains.

The process may be observed most directly by attending a Disco. What made dancing civilized is almost entirely missing: the breaks from song to song, the dance patterns changing with the number, the couples dancing together. The music, or noise, is continuous at the Disco; colored lights flash in psychedelic fashion; the music is devoid of almost anything except blare and beat; and couples are not easy to discern. It is an orgy of dancing. It is, at once, each individual alone and the whole a collective mass driven to a frenzy directed by the disk jockey.

It is easy enough to believe that many of those in the Transformation Industry know not what they do. Since much of the industry is highly profitable, there is reason to suppose that many of those engaged in the business are not doing anything much but making money, at least so far as they are concerned. There is money to be made in pandering to man's baser desires, nor is there anything new about it. It is also true, however, that it is not necessary for those under the sway of an idea to know it.

There is a kind of demonic urge to the egalitarianism implicit in the idea that has the world in its grip. Women must be the same as men, children the same as adults, all races the same, and each no higher than the others.

And, to prove it, we must all be disrobed. Here is a parable for our time, a parable that is factual, if the columnist, Bob Greene, who reported it, be accepted (Atlanta *Constitution*, May 19, 1978, p. 7-B). It seems that a photographer has put together a collection of his photographs which he calls "Dallas Nude." Charles R. Collum, the photographer, says that he took three and a half years on the project.

"My idea," he says, "was to show the city through its nude people. Dallas had the reputation of an uptight, conservative, banker-religious-middle-of-the-Bible-Belt city. I think that reputation was wrong. My pictures show Dallas as being happy, innocent, exuberant, full of freedom." He accomplished this by photographing people from all walks of life — librarians, dental assistants, optometrists, nurses, bank tellers, and so on — in the nude. "The soul of a city," Mr. Collum is quoted as saying, "is in its people. And people without their clothes on are more expressive than people who are dressed."

Mr. Collum is so impressed with what he has done with, or to, Dallas, that he is eager to do the same for other towns and cities in the United States. Indeed, he has in mind an even more ambitious project, Greene reports, and has approached the State Department about it:

I want to go to Russia and do "Moscow Nude." We were brought up to think that the Communists were bad people, were our enemies. But on a one-to-one level, I think the Russians are just as warm and wonderful as the people of Dallas. I think that "Dallas Nude" and "Moscow Nude" would go great together. Together, their message would be "Peace on Earth, good will toward men."

Why would such a notion strike anyone as plausible? Indeed, where would anyone get such an idea? Actually, the antecedents of Mr. Collum's idea are not difficult to trace. They are the progeny of Jean Jacques Rousseau, the spiritual godfather of our age. Strip away the cultural raiment, and man will emerge as a Noble Savage, Rousseau informed us. Man in the nude will be his natural, good self. This idea has worn a groove into the mind of an era. It is not necessary to read Rousseau to discover it; it is enough to breathe the fumes that emanate from the intellectual climate. The idea that has the world in its grip holds that man is naturally good but that he is deformed by his culture. Divest him of his culture, and the goodness will shine forth.

360

The Transformation Industry is under the sway of this idea. This is the demonic urge which impels its assault upon society, culture, manners, mores, and civility. There are quite an assortment of ways to go about it. A George Bernard Shaw comedy could go about it with style and verve. Nudity is a relatively innocent approach. The more powerful weapons are profanity, obscenity, vulgarity, and the vivid depiction of perversions. The record thus far shows that when the protective cover of culture has been removed, we are exposed to the more drastic forms of political power. It is a crucial part of the process of collectivization.

29
A Bemused People

THERE IS A public service advertisement that appears on television from time to time. One scenario has everyone in it moving around in wheel chairs except one person who walks about normally. Everything is arranged for the convenience of people in wheel chairs, which poses dangers and inconveniences for anyone afoot. In the other scenario, everyone is blind except one person. He opens a book but sees no words in it. He asks if there are any books with words in them in the library. They assure him that the books they are using have words in them. Since the person who can see cannot read in Braille, the others assume he cannot read.

The point of the advertisement is, in part at least, to arouse sympathy and understanding for the handicapped. So far as that is its purpose, there is nothing exceptional about it. To sympathize with and have concern for the less fortunate is in keeping with the highest concept of charity. Moreover, to put oneself in the place of others, by way of the imagination, is laudable.

However, the method used to do this in the advertisement is questionable. The method entails a *reversal of the norms*. The handicapped, because of their implicit normality, have changed from being subjects worthy of sympathy and concern into threats to those who have been normal. What is convenient to their condition becomes the way things are to be arranged. This emerges as a threat because the

362

people who have been handicaped show no sympathy or understanding for erstwhile normal people.

The transformation that has been going on in the United States proceeds by reversing normality. In effect, new norms are created, and the old established norms are abandoned. This change is impelled by the idea that has the world in its grip. Just as in the above scenario, what was normal becomes exceptional and unusual, or, at least, not distinctively normal. What was formerly rare or unusual takes its place among the expected and normal.

The process by which this transformation occurs should be familiar, for the pattern has been established by constant repetition and by expansive application into more and more areas. The change is advanced by relativistic arguments. In its bluntest formulation the argument goes something like this. What is normal? Who can say what is normal? At the ordinary level of discourse, these are unanswerable questions. They are difficult to answer, in the first place, because we are unprepared to defend our concepts of normality. We may be convinced that we know what is normal, but proof is quite another matter.

There is good reason for this. Inquisitive children usually learn at a fairly early age that questioning the norms is a fruitless and unrewarding undertaking. Far from being commended for being brilliant, they are apt to be maligned for their stupidity. After all, what kinds of questions can be raised about norms? Why do we walk on our feet instead of our hands? Why do we drive on the right instead of the left? Why do women have babies and men have hair on their chests? In most cases, no satisfactory answers can be given. Hence, children are discouraged from raising such questions. The best answer we can make in many cases is simply, "That is just the way things are." And what we are apt to think after saying it a few times is: "If you weren't so stupid, you would have figured it out for yourself."

There is yet another reason for our usual inability to make an apology for our norms. One of the primary concerns of society is to maintain the norms. All social function depends upon norms and their general acceptance. Take them away, or abandon them, and society disintegrates. All acts lose their meaning, and everything is unexpected and strange. To debate the validity of norms is to debate the validity of society. That is, of necessity, a debate for which there are no rules, and one which society cannot tolerate. Society's business is to discover, preserve, and maintain the norms, not to challenge them.

That is not to say that norms are not well grounded. On the contrary,

363

many of them are grounded in nature. Where that is not the case — where they arose as custom, for example — they have been instilled by nurture and have become second nature by usage and veneration. Our very social existence is grounded in norms. Their reason for being, if there is no other reason, is the smooth functioning of society. It is a sound instinct that resists discarding a norm because we do not perceive its reason for being, for experience teaches that if we probe deep enough we may discover reasons we did not even suspect.

None of this is acceptable to socialists, of course. The received norms stand athwart the path which both revolutionary and evolutionary socialism must tread. Socialism requires that all efforts be concerted toward the achievement of human felicity on this earth. The great strength of the idea that has the world in its grip lies in that very conception. Its weakness lies in the conception, too, as well as elsewhere. The irony of it is that the achievement of human felicity, so far as is practicable, *is* a social norm. More, the purpose of society is to provide the framework for achieving such felicity as is possible for man.

But society does not define human felicity. That is left, in the main, to individual decision. In the same manner, individuals are left to a great variety of devices and means for achieving their own ends. this is anathema to socialists. They would transform society from a framework into the determinant of the content of felicity and the means by which it would be achieved. The individual would be confined and society politicized. Social norms would become whatever appeared to be useful in controlling the individual and politicizing society. Norms have to become what is decreed as normal by the political power. Gradualists, however, have no absolute power as yet. In the United States, the communications industry has made forceful strides in determining what is normal.

The first stages of socialism are concerned mainly with breaking down the distinctions on which the norms are based. The breakdown of the norms proceeds along two lines. One is intellectual, and the mode is relativism. The tendency of relativism is to discredit all norms. Norms are, according to this line, simply matters of opinion. The authority for them becomes either majority opinion or simply whatever is done by large numbers of people. Normality in America has become indistinquishable from the average, or better still, the lowest common denominator of behavior. The logic of such an approach is that if norms are relative there are no norms. There is only what happens to prevail at the moment.

The other line is to pose continual challenges to the established norms. Journalism is particularly well suited to this undertaking. There is an old saw to the effect that if a dog bites a man that is not news, but if a man bites a dog that is news. That is a way of saying that journalists focus on the odd, strange, curious, different, and unusual. But when journalism becomes pervasive, as it bids to do in America today, it becomes a continual assault on the norms. This is especially the case when the odd, strange, and curious are not portrayed as unusual but as commonplace and normal. It happens over and over again that radicals are interviewed in such a way as to make them appear normal.

The technique by which this is done is easy enough to discern. Let us suppose that an advocate of communal living arrangements is being interviewed. The act is cleaned up for television, for instance. There is no obscenity or profanity. The interviewee is likely to be well enough dressed, be clean, well brushed, and reasonably neat. The impression prevails that he is different in one respect only — that is, that he believes the "nuclear family" is outmoded and new and extended families are emerging. New norms are taking shape before our eyes, as it were, painlessly and with no apparent wrench to a whole body of belief and practice. The odd, strange, and curious — the shifting and unsettled relationships in some sort of communal arrangement — are presented as an emerging norm.

Why is this assault on the norms made necessary by the idea that has the world in its grip? The reason is not difficult to grasp. There is one norm that must be wiped out if the idea is to prevail. It is the norm that individuals can, do, and will pursue their self-interest as they perceive it, ordinarily and generally. The pursuit of self-interest is the apple of discord in the socialist visionary Garden of Eden. It is the unpardonable sin, the source of man's fall, and the continuing obstacle to harmony and beatitude on this planet. So long as it remains normal, the vision of socialism is only a will-of-the-wisp.

On the face of it, the socialist problem would be easy enough to solve. All that would have to be done would be to get people to abandon the individual pursuit of self-interest and devote themselves to the common good. Isolate self-interest, pillory it, make it unacceptable, and people will abandon it. There have been attempts to do this, of course. But the solution is not that easy. Self-interest is not a norm existing in splendid isolation from all other norms. Instead, it is intertwined in the warp and woof of the whole fabric of the received normality. Socialists have generally understood this well enough and have grasped at least some of

365

the dimensions of the problem confronting them.

The whole system of private property buttresses and supports — even rewards — the pursuit of self-interest by individuals. Free enterprise invites individuals to prosper by laboring to advance themselves. The norm that a man should receive the fruits of his labor places a premium on the pursuit of self-interest. The family is an enclave of self-interest or at least limited interest seeking. Members of the family are bidden to look after the family interest primarily. The institution of private property is so developed and conceived that it is tied up with the limited family interest — with inheritance, with wills, with shares for members of the family, and so on.

Even religion has been generally entangled with individual self-interest. (Indeed, Marx believed that organized religion was at the apex of the whole structure of capitalism.) The individual is bidden to take care of his interest in eternal beatitude in the hereafter by getting right with his Maker. The Hope of Heaven is, after all, a Hope primarily for individual salvation.

On the socialist view, then, the received norms are honeycombed with supports for and enticements to the individual to pursue his own self-interest. The pursuit of self-interest is a norm, as they see it, because the whole fabric of normality makes it appear to be so. In order to cut away the pursuit of self-interest, the whole structure of normality must be replaced. Those under the sway of the idea differ about means and, perhaps, about how drastic the surgery must be, but they basically agree over the problems presented by the received norms.

There have been two major thrusts of socialism in the United States in the twentieth century, with many more smaller and interrelated developments. The first thrust evinced itself primarily as a political movement aimed at bringing about economic changes. This political thrust has gained momentum several times, but it was most successful in making headway in the 1930's. Roosevelt's New Deal succeeded in passing legislation which seriously altered the framework of economic normality and morality.

The use of government power to redistribute the wealth was established as a principle during the decade of the 1930's. The Social Security enactment turned out to be the centerpiece of the distributionist legislation. By means of it money was taxed from earners and distributed after retirement to those who had paid into it. It was, and is, redistributionist because benefits do not depend upon amount paid in; they are determined by Congress according to formulas which have been revised over the years.

366

Redistribution was also the operative principle in many other New Deal programs. The farm subsidy programs redistributed wealth. The government put its weight behind labor unions, and hence the use of coercion by unions to get higher wages and shorter hours. Subsidized houses and government supported loans were also redistributionist in character. The graduated income tax which, along with Social Security, undergirds redistribution, had already been used, but it was much extended under the New Deal.

New distributionist programs have been enacted over the years. The most notable, and notorious, have been the welfare programs. Less well publicized, but more ubiquitous, are the numerous subsidies to everything from airports to local police to school lunch programs. The Federal hand is not only in every pocket but the Federal handout is extended in every direction.

That government power should be used to control and direct the economy was also established as a principle in the 1930's. Manipulation of the money supply was one of the earliest and main instruments of this control. Another major instrument is government spending and it is linked with taxation to direct economic action. Government has so long concerned itself with employment and unemployment that for most people it must appear as legitimate a government function as is the apprehending and punishing of criminals. All these ways of controlling and directing the economy have been steadily expanded and extended since that time.

The other major thrust to socialism came in the 1960's and has continued apace since. Although it, too, is political, the primary aim is not so much economic as social. This thrust is toward social transformation. It emerges as an effort to overturn the established norms as a means of changing the existing order. Legislation is mainly a framework only for this transformation.

Every norm is grist for the mill in this transformation. Indeed, it is not clear, in general, that overturning one norm is more important than another. Since all norms support the existing order, they must all be overturned or transformed. It hardly matters whether what is involved is sex, marriage, the family, the role and position of the husband, education, military authority, the authority of the President, ownership and control over property, or whatever. Every norm overturned weakens the authority of all norms.

In this sense, priority for destruction of norms may best be given to those most deeply entrenched. It is from this angle that the assault on sexual norms may be understood. Sexual norms have been long

367

established, and would appear to be most difficult to alter. Indeed, many of the sexual norms are rooted in nature, and some of the most fundamental inequalities are sex related. It is reasonable to suppose that if the sexual norms could be destroyed, all other norms might fall in their wake.

The attack on sexual norms has been blatant in recent years. Male dominance and authority have been under consistent assault. The norm has been that the male is dominant in male-female relationships — that his opinion is deferred to, his decision final, and that he is the fiscally responsible partner in the household. This norm is supported by custom and tradition, and has been supported by religious authority. A portion, at least, of this norm has a natural basis. Normally, men are taller, heavier, and stronger than women. Women are the childbearers by nature, and many of the skills and abilities which they have developed have been related to that role. The nuclear family, as monogamous marriage has been lately dubbed, is founded in the nature of parental responsibility, and the desirable conditions of child bearing. The norms are threatened by what is called female liberation.

Aggressive homosexuality threatens the whole concept of normality. If homosexuality is "normal" there are no norms in sexual relationships. The male dominance takes on only a symbolic, and entirely relative, significance. Parental responsibility has no foundation in homosexuality. The distinction between male and female is obliterated. Normal is cut loose from its foundation in nature. The whole framework of norms entailed in marriage, the family, property inheritance, loses its meaning when homosexuality is accepted as normal.

The reversal of the norms has a devastating impact on society. Norms are to society what the fixed points of a compass are to navigation. It can be argued that norms are relative, that some of them are even arbitrary, which they may be. In a similar fashion, it can be argued that the directions on a compass are relative, as indeed they are in some senses. But it is absolutely essential to agree upon and accept them else charts become worthless, and no definite course can be plotted to go from one place to another. The functioning of society is equally dependent upon agreement upon and acceptance of a set of norms. Norms are the foundation of privileges, positions and functions within a society. When they are overturned, a chaos of relationships results. No one can any longer be sure what function he is to perform, or who has the right or authority to make any decision or perform any act.

Every body must have a head. Every household must have a head.

Every undertaking involving two or more people must have someone who is in charge. Constructive activity depends upon each person knowing what he is to do. When the norms are overturned, constructive activity declines and debates and contests over authority ensue. Force tends to replace voluntary cooperation, and the strongest or most determined assert what is often enough entirely arbitrary authority.

That is what is happening in large in the United States. The norms may not have been overturned in many instances, but they have been so seriously questioned that their validity is in doubt, and there is no longer universal agreement upon and acceptance of them. Those who insist upon traditional male-female roles are denounced as "male chauvinist pigs." Those who are affronted by open homosexuality are accused of being intolerant. Those who exercise firmly the authority of their positions are charged with being dictatorial. Students would determine the content of their courses and formally evaluate their teachers. Prison inmates attempt to organize politically in order to run the prisons. Unions negotiate and enforce work rules.

What a man may do with and on his property is in such doubt that experts must be called upon to set matters right. The courts are burdened down with litigation as civil suits burgeon. Court cases are increasing in length and complexity, and no decision ever seems final as appeal follows upon appeal from whatever decision has been rendered. Interminable hearings precede all sorts of undertakings. Debates and contests over who has the right and authority to do what supersede the constructive activity by which it might be accomplished.

The American people are bemused. The word has two rather distinct meanings. It means "confused, muddled, stupefied" and it means "lost in thought" or "preoccupied." Americans have every reason to be confused. They have been repeatedly confronted and affronted by scandalous behavior that has gone unreproached. They have witnessed in a span of little more than a decade the breakdown of social restraints as in the case of the public use of profanity and obscenities. They have seen the breakdown of the proprieties as they apply to female behavior. On the day before four students were shot down by the National Guard at Kent State, teen-age girls roamed the campus making lascivious invitations to the guardsmen, shouting unprintable obscenities at them, and otherwise behaving like tramps. People have witnessed the loosening of all sorts of restraints and have felt powerless to do anything about it. The symbols of political authority — the military and the police — have been defied with impunity and subjected to verbal and physical assault. Why would not people be confused?

And, whether lost in thought or not, the American people have been preoccupied. Better, they have increasingly occupied themselves with their own affairs and closed their eyes to what is going on with society. It is understandable that they should. The disintegration of society means that the individual can no longer rely on support in bringing reproach and discredit on those who flout the norms and proclaim their disdain for social prescription. The disintegration of society means, too, that the individual had best look to his own protection and well-being. But it also means that force will be brought to bear in more and more areas of life. The breakdown of authority is not the prelude to liberation, it is rather the precondition of the restoration of some sort of authority by the exercise of force.

Today, that force evinces itself as government intruding ever more deeply into our lives. It manifests itself as the loss of control over our own affairs to those who hold the reins of political power. The New Deal type intervention has continued apace in conjunction with the assault on the norms. But in those areas where society is impotent, government is just about equally impotent. Thus, the authority of government declines even as society disintegrates.

The idea that has the world in its grip would replace the pursuit of self-interest by a pursuit of the common good. There is no evidence that this has resulted as yet. True, politicians and spokesmen in the communications industry speak a rhetoric of the common good. But the most obvious development thus far has been the disintegration of society and the decay of civilized behavior — the very instruments of the promotion of the common good. There is much verbal evidence that the American people have lost confidence in government as an instrument of the general welfare and for the promotion of the common good. But in their bemused state, they do not readily grasp or believe in an effective alternative.

Of course, the United States does not exist in a vacuum. The hold of the idea upon America is an integral part of its hold on the people and governments of the world. It is appropriate now to turn to an examination of it in that perspective.

Book VII

The Cold War

30

Revolutionary versus Evolutionary Socialism

THE UNITED STATES emerged from World War II as the pre-eminent military power in the world. That pre-eminence was symbolized by the development of the atomic bomb, two of which were dropped on Japanese cities inducing that country to surrender. The great world powers of the inter-war years had either been crushed or were very nearly impotent. Germany had been as absolutely defeated as possible. About all that remained to make the devastation complete would have been to sow the bombed-out cities with salt. Japan saved a shred of honor by being permitted to keep its emperor. The weakness of France had been decisively demonstrated by the Nazi conquest. Only the swaggering and boasting of Mussolini had made Italy appear to be a great power. Britain emerged victorious in the war but was shortly reduced to minor power potential by the nationalizing zeal of the Labour Party, China faced, as it had, incipient civil war and was hardly in position to play the role of a major power.

The Soviet Union, too, emerged victorious in World War II. How that empire would rank as a military power is still a controverted question. The devastation wrought by the German armed forced on that country had been great. Stalin had so disrupted agriculture with his efforts at collectivization that production was far from adequate for the population. Forced industrialization had succeeded only in getting produced what the political powers considered most urgent. But the Soviet Union had something beyond ordinary military powers; its leaders had the will and know-how to use terror. Terror was used both in the subjection of the peoples of Eastern Europe and probably more extensively than ever the peoples within the Soviet Union. The combination of military power, terror, and deception made the Soviet Union a major power in effect.

At any rate, most of the powers that had been were no longer major powers. Western Europe was largely a power vacuum, as was the Far East. This had repercussions in many other parts of the world, for the former great powers had carved much of the rest of the world into spheres of interest and colonies. Many of these colonies broke away or were turned loose to fend for themselves. The British Empire hardly deserved the name any longer after a few years of Labour rule.

The United Nations was supposed to fill this power vacuum, or at least, to stand guard while old nations recovered and new nations took shape and emerged. It did not work out that way. Such authority as the United Nations had was vested in the Security Council. The permanent members had a veto power over any action, and the Soviet Union began quickly using this power to forestall unwanted action. This was especially disruptive because, as it turned out, the major threat to the peace was the Soviet Union and the international communist movement it spawned. Wherever they could, Soviet leaders fomented civil war to advance Communist Party takeovers anywhere the opportunity occurred.

The world was not as clearly in the grip of an idea at the end of World War II as it has since become. The defeat of Nazism and Fascism discredited those particular varieties of revolutionary socialism. West Germany and Japan were not only freed from the control of totalitarian regimes but also given great impetus by the occupying forces to adopt institutions more in accord with freedom. It is true that the United Kingdom went headlong toward socialism for the few years after the war and that India's leaders were under the spell of socialism, but the course of many countries was unusually uncertain. The United States bent away somewhat from the collectivist path of the 1930's — not for long, no doubt, but enough to illustrate the possibilities.

Television had not yet taken hold as the shaper, molder, and decider of opinions. The sway of the intellectuals was still largely dependent upon the influence they could wield upon politicians. College education had not become so common a possession, and it is perhaps the single most important way that intellectuals fasten their ideas upon people. Intellectuals were still marginal in many lands, and the lines between ideologies rather more clearly drawn than in a later day. Many people still lived mainly by custom, tradition, and within the framework of family and religion, a much larger percentage, at any rate, than would so live thirty years later. It is difficult to grasp how drastic the changes have been, facilitated by technology and guided increasingly by ideologies.

It will be helpful to keep this in mind as we explore the impact of the Cold War. There was a time, as least for Americans, when the Cold War appeared to be simple enough and readily understood. The world was divided in two, or so we were told. One world was communist, and the other was free. The two worlds were engaged in an ongoing conflict which was not out-and-out war, but was not peaceful either. (The conflict was also often described as between communism and democracy.) The United Nations became the verbal battleground of this conflict, and nations were aligned there with one side or the other. Bench marks in the conflict were such events as Churchill's "Iron Curtain Speech" at Fulton, Missouri, military aid to Greece and Turkey, the revelations of Soviet atomic spies, the fall of China to the Communists, the North Atlantic Treaty Organization, and the Korean War, among others.

What was once clear and distinct, however, has since become fuzzy and indistinct. What was called a Third World emerged in the late 1950's and in the 1960's, aligned with neither side. The Soviet Union and Communist China became embroiled in their own ideological conflict. Revisionist historians began to reinterpret the Cold War. The more radical of these declared that the conflict was all a product of American hysteria, that communism had not so much fomented it as been victimized by it. Communism, in this view, was a bugaboo invented by Americans so far as its aggressiveness and threat to world peace was concerned.

While such revisionist history is sorely out of touch with reality, it may at least open the way to revision that is needed. The nature of the conflict has indeed been misconstrued, perhaps not so much as it was originally represented to be but as it turned out. The tyrannical character of communism has rarely, if ever, been exaggerated. Nor would it be easy to overstate the imperial aims of Soviet Communism. An international conspiracy has existed as long as the Soviet Union, and there are several of them now. That this movement has engaged in

375

subversion, espionage, and terrorism is well-established fact. Whether it has posed an immediate threat to the United States, or what the nature of the threat was and is, may be open to debate, although there is no conclusive answer available.

Most of the misconstruction of the Cold War, however, has been over the nature, character, and tendency of the opposition. That the opposition has been between communism, on the one hand, and freedom, on the other, is certainly doubtful. This is not to question that there are many who are opposed to communism or that there are those who stand for freedom. It is rather to question that they have generally been in control of or directed the actual conflict. The actual events of the Cold War come into much clearer focus when we conceive of it as conflict between revolutionary and evolutionary socialism. This takes into account the actual tendencies in the so-called Free World as well as the thrust of developments within the Cold War.

There are undoubtedly many angles from which communism may be opposed. Indeed, they may be as numerous as have been the abuses of power and atrocitites of communist rulers. Some have opposed communism because the rulers do not permit freedom of speech and of the press and suppress dissenters. Others, because there is no freedom of religion but rather religious persecution. Some find it objectionable that there is no freedom of migration, and they are apt to see the Berlin Wall as the symbol of what they oppose. The slave labor camps have been more than many people can stomach. There are even those who find most deplorable the prohibition of jazz and experimentation with the arts in general. The ubiquitous bureaucracy has its articulate opponents. There are those who focus mainly on the economic wrongs of communism: the confiscation of private property, the state planning, and the absence of the free market.

But all opposition to communism that amounts to anything can be reduced to two headings. One is what will here be called Metaphysical Opposition to Communism, and the other Tactical Opposition to Communism. These can be employed in such a way as to subsume virtually every level and kind of opposition.

The use of the term "metaphysical" may appear to be a poor choice of words, It is certainly the case that in the last century or so many have used the term as if it were synonymous with mystical, superstitious, something vague and imaginary, or evanescent. These are, however, misuses of a most valuable word for which there is no ready replacement. Metaphysics is the study of and refers to that underlying order in the universe which gives form and regularity to things and relationships. It is the source of natural law and normality in beings. If it is mystical it is so only in the sense that our sensual knowledge of this realm is indirect. Metaphysics is actually the foundation of precise knowledge. Without it, we are left only with a poor substitute — statistics — whose precision is achieved only by distortion.

It may be objected, however, either that my phrase does not take into account religious opposition to communism or that what I am really referring to when I call it metaphysical is religious. An explanation of the meaning of Metaphysical Oppositon to Communism should make it clear that neither of these objections is valid. I mean that the oppositon of communism is based upon fixed and immovable positions, on the belief that communism cannot and will not work, that it can only be tyrannical and destructive. Why? Because it requires the transformation of human nature, something that is fixed and immutable. Because it requires the abridgement of the natural order of things, something that has not occurred and so far as we know cannot and will not occur. Because it requires that individuals no longer pursue their self-interest, that they abandon what is essential to their survival. In brief, these things constitute the metaphysical opposition to communism.

It should be clear that this is not a religious opposition to communism. It is a philosophic or, mayhap, scientific opposition. True, there is religious opposition to communism, and for good and sufficient reason. Communism is atheistic and committed to wiping out all independent theism. But when the religious opposition is examined carefully it will be discovered that so far as it is a fixed and immovable position it is based on a metaphysic-like position, namely, that God is the same yesterday, today, and tomorrow, that He has implanted in us our immutable human nature, and that He has ordained an order for things and for men. Take away the conception of God as Creater and man as Creature, with all that is implicit in this, and the religious opposition to communism tends to melt away. In short, the firmness of the religious opposition to communism has a metaphysiclike base. For any who might have difficulty accepting the above formulation, let me put the matter another way: Metaphysics provides sufficient grounds for an unaltering opposition to communism.

It still may be objected, however, that there are those who are apparently immovably opposed to communism who know naught of metaphysics. This is an objection, fortunately, which involves only semantics. For example, there are those who oppose communism on the grounds that it is contrary to human nature. This position, and others like it (the economic arguments, for instance), are metaphysically founded, whether those who use them are aware of it or not. Ignorance of philosophic terminology does not alter in the least the philosophic base of a position.

Even so, it may be useful to broaden somewhat those that might be included among the metaphysical opponents of communism. There is a sense in which all who are inalterably committed to an opposition to communism — as, for example, those who would maintain that if it would work they still would not want it, for whatever reasons — are metaphysical opponents. It is permissible to use the word in this way, for by so doing we embrace all metaphysiclike positions, i.e., all that are firm, hard, rocklike, and underlyingly immovable.

Tactical Opposition to Communism is of a quite different order. It is opposition to communism on the ground that one or more or many of its tactics or methods are wrong. (Those who oppose it on metaphysical grounds might be expected to find the tactics objectionable also, and they usually do. They may even make arguments against communism in terms of methods, but that is not the final ground of their opposition.) The position amounts to this: If communists would "clean up their act," they would be acceptable. If they would grant free speech, not persecute religion, provide due process of law, permit migration, allow opposing political parties, abolish slave labor camps, and so on, they would no longer be objectionable.

When they oppose communism, evolutionary or gradualist or democratic socialists are by the necessity of their position tactical opponents. Twentieth century liberals (who vary in the extent to which they are socialists) are also generally tactical opponents of communism when they oppose it. Communism-in-power has been a source of great embarrassment to other socialists. Indeed, it has been an embarrassment or much worse, to many communists as well. The violence, the terror, and the drastic action have raised doubts as to the validity of the socialist enterprise.

It is worthwhile to note that most vociferous opposition of socialist intellectuals is class-like. They object most strenuously — indeed, many reserve their objections — to the persecution of intellectuals. Thus, Stalin's most heinous crime for many of them was the Purge of the late 1930's. Millions of peasants and Kulaks could be persecuted and die with never a whimper from Western intellectuals. But when a few thousand intellectuals came under the gun, many

378

socialist intellectuals began to question Soviet Communism. The same play is still being enacted today, though the scene has changed. A few intellectual dissidents in the Soviet Union can bring the glare of publicity to bear on their persecutors, thanks to Western intellectuals, but the other persecution goes largely unnoticed.

However that may be, socialist opponents of communism have usually had to try to balance themselves on a razor's edge. On the one hand, they have opposed communism. In its own way some of this opposition has been real enough. That is, evolutionary socialists do believe, often enough, that the revolutionary way is the wrong way, that drastic measures are harmful and unnecessary. Moreover, they may be as opposed to Soviet or Chinese or Cuban Communist expansion as anyone else. In fact, evolutionary socialists, may go to war against communists, albeit reluctantly and limitedly.

But the anti-communism of gradualists must always be restrained. It must stop short of being or becoming Metaphysical Opposition to Communism. If it should become metaphysical in character it would be tantamount to a repudiation of socialism. Another way to say it is to formulate it this way: Opposition to communism must not trace communist practice to the socialist idea — to the idea that has the world in its grip. Deplorable communist practice must be ascribed to an excess of revolutionary zeal, to evil men, such as Stalin (once he had passed from the scene), to persecution of communists and inhibition of their legitimate aims by others. It has been a most difficult task for evolutionary socialists to oppose communism, one that has frequently been made necessary by the communists but unpalatable at best. If communism would just become another political party, the difficulty would vanish, for evolutionary socialists could oppose it without any danger of the opposition becoming metaphysical. But that can only happen where communists have not come to power or have not consolidated their power.

One way that evolutionary socialists (which generally includes liberals in the United States) maintain their balance on the razor's edge is to focus their efforts on opposing anti-communism. Technically, they oppose communism, but this position can be made largely harmless by rigorous attention to the methods by which communism is to be opposed. The method that is generally proscribed in the United States and Western Europe is what goes by the name of McCarthyism (which takes its name from the late Senator Joseph McCarthy of Wisconsin). One dictionary defines McCarthyism as "1. public accusation of

379

disloyalty, esp. of pro-Communist activity, in many instances unsupported by proof or based on slight, doubtful or irrelevant evidence. 2. unfairness in investigative technique. 3. persistent search for and exposure of disloyalty...." Indeed, "McCarthyism" is the unpardonable sin in the American liberal ranking of evils. It ranks alongside if not above "Red Scares" and "witch hunts" for communists.

Tactical Opposition to Communism turns into tactical oppositon to anti-communism. The threat of communism is transmuted into the threat of anti-communism. This is an easy shift for evolutionary socialists to make, indeed, a shift difficult to avoid. The reason is that opposition to anti-communism has a metaphical base or, if anyone prefers, an anti-metaphysical base. All socialism is premised on the possibility of transforming human nature. Metaphysics is the level at which this is found to be impossible. Hence, revolutionary and evolutionary socialists are at one at the metaphysical, or anti-metaphysical level. They are irreconcilably opposed to metaphysical anti-communism.

I do not deduce this from the phenomenon of "McCarthyism," of course. It is deduced, so far as it is deduced, from the philosophical, or ideological, premises of socialism. But there is a great body of evidence which is explained by and supports this conclusion. When "McCarthyism" or a "Red Scare" is underway these occupy the center stage of tactical opposition. But once they have abated, then virtually any tactic by which communism might be opposed comes under fire. In the final analysis, all metaphysical or "hard core" opposition to communism is intolerable to socialists, though tactical opposition is permitted except by "hard core" communists.

The depth of this division has not been generally admitted, if it has been understood. There are many practical reasons for not dramatizing or for not recognizing it. Evolutionary socialists cling to or at least profess many of the common values which derive from Western Civilization, such as representative government (which they tend to telescope into democracy), religious toleration, free speech and press, free elections, and so on. By their very evolutionary method they attempt to avoid arousing a metaphysical opposition to themselves. Anti-communists, too, have hoped to enlist them in a common cause against communism. Some anti-communists have portrayed social reformers and liberals as dupes of communists, as taken in by them. (Indeed, this was the general view of the matter as held by anti-communists in the 1950's.) They may have been, indeed may be, but if

380

the above analysis is correct the affinity between them is not something skin deep as such a construction implied.

In any case, it is what has happened when common cause against communism has been made by metaphysical opponents and tactical opponents. The contest has been called the Cold War. The main contest has been between the United States and its allies on the one hand and the Soviet Union and its allies and satellites on the other. Communist China was formally excluded from the Cold War most of the time but was nonetheless a subordinate part of it. The contest was carried on in many ways — by diplomacy, by propaganda, by subversion and espionage, and in actual wars — but the examination of it here will be restricted to three levels: war, foreign aid, and espionage.

If the preceding analysis is correct, it is unlikely that evolutionary socialists and metaphsical anti-communists could make common cause against communism. They cannot effectively wage war, either hot or cold, against communism. They cannot, that is, if evolutionary socialists are to maintain their balance on the razor's edge. To wage war effectively the enemy must be clearly identified, support for the war must be mustered, and force brought to bear sufficient to overcome the enemy. It is not possible to do this from a razor's edge; it requires a broad base rather than a tenuous position.

It may well be that the animus behind the Cold War came from metaphysical anti-communism. The provocation came from the communists, of course. But the Cold War strategy was largely shaped by Democratic Presidents. Between 1933 and 1969 there was only one Republican President — Eisenhower. Nixon worked vigorously to defuse the Cold War, so he was not an architect of it, not as President anyway. The main outlines of the Cold War were shaped by President Truman. Eisenhower and Dulles continued it, as did Kennedy and Johnson.

It is significant in the context that Democrats were the main strategists. The Democratic Party has been by far the more deeply infected of the two major parties by evolutionary socialism. Liberal intellectuals have had their greatest influence within the Democratic Party, though they have exercised considerable influence on Republicans as well. The domestic programs of the Democrats since 1913 have been in the direction of centralizing power in the federal government, manipulating the money supply, regulating and controlling business, managing the economy and redistributing the wealth. True, they have only limitedly pushed for government ownership and have taken the

381

route of control instead. But that has come increasingly to be the method of evolutionary socialism for the past several decades.

Democrats have tended to get the United States embroiled and entangled in international affairs in the twentieth century. Beyond that, they have tended to get us into wars. There is no particular mystery as to how this should be explained. Democrats have been enamored with the use of government power. Whatever they have been confronted with, they have inclined to the view that the solution lay in the exercise of political power. In international relations, this tends to lead to war or to involvement in whatever conflicts are taking place.

Twice during the Cold War, the United States became extensively involved in an armed conflict: first in Korea and then in Vietnam. President Truman gave the order which brought Americans into combat in Korea. President Kennedy got the United States armed forces increasingly embroiled in Vietnam, and President Johnson made the war primarily an American responsibility.

The main point here is the kind of wars these became, not whether American involvement was justified or who was to blame for them. In both cases, they were what came to be called limited wars. Under General Douglas MacArthur's command, American forces, along with such allies as they had, mainly South Koreans, were close to overrunning and defeating the North Korean army. At that juncture the Communist Chinese intervened with massive ground forces. MacArthur proposed the bombings of the Chinese access, but he was refused permission to do so. When he persisted by criticizing the policy behind the scenes, he was relieved of his command. The war zone was restricted to Korea, and the war was eventually ended without a decision having been reached.

In Vietnam, no American military commander attempted to win the war by invading North Vietnam. Even the bombing of North Vietnam was restricted, and major ports were not shelled by sea. The justification of the conflict, where any was given, was so narrow and subtle, with infinite attention given to subtle niceties, that Americans were confused and baffled by the whole affair.

After MacArthur's dismissal, no grand strategy was devised to achieve victory at arms. None was ever inaugurated in Vietnam. The justification offered was that the war might be vastly expanded by any aggressive action. Actually, this might have been a sound argument for never becoming involved in the conflicts at all. After all, it was certainly possible to foresee that China might intervene in Korea. North

Vietnamese intervention in South Vietnam was a fact, and Chinese or Russian intervention a distinct possibility from the outset. What the enemy might do is hardly ever a foregone conclusion.

The deliberate limitation of these wars needs a better explanation than those that were offered. The framework has been supplied for a better explanation. It is this. Evolutionary socialism must prevent, even at very high cost, the opposition to communism from becoming metaphysical. Any all-out war — any war to be fought through to victory — will become metaphysic-like because of the ideological character of the conflict. Once the general opposition to communism becomes metaphysical, all of socialism is likely to be indicted. Undoubtedly, the motives that inhibited American leaders were complex. What persuaded any one of them to the limited war concept cannot, of course, be known. But that an extensive apology for limited warfare was prepared and disseminated by American intellectuals, aided and abetted by their counterparts in other lands, cannot be doubted. That these same intellectuals have bent their energies over the years to forestall the arising of an articulate metaphysical anti-communism can be demonstrated *ad nauseam*.

Intellectuals have worked diligently over the years to turn the Cold War into an internecine conflict between revolutionary and evolutionary socialism. A concerted effort was made to do that in Vietnam. They kept up a continual clamor over the alleged undemocratic character of the government of South Vietnam. Similar, though not as vociferous, charges were leveled at the South Korean government. That many South Vietnamese continued to pursue their individual self-interest economically was considered shameful by these intellectuals. Efforts were made to turn the American army into a combination of Red Cross and Little Sisters of the Poor. They were set to the task of rebuilding Vietnamese villages, tending the sick, and feeding the hungry. Only if evolutionary socialism (usually described as democracy) could demonstrate its superiority to the claims of communism (revolutionary socialism) would the American involvement be justified, presumably.

My purpose in discussing these matters is to describe the role that the Cold War has played in spreading the idea and fastening its grip upon the world. The initiative belongs to international communism. Communist lands are generally closed to foreigners except on a limited and supervised basis. Massive efforts have been made over the years to shield the rest of the world from the reality of communism. In effect, the attempt has been made to have communism known only as an ideal system. This ideal is spread around the world by whatever propaganda outlets communist powers have. The reality in other lands is measured against the communist ideal, to its detriment, as a rule.

Evolutionary socialists tend to take these criticisms seriously as, in a sense, they must. They are, after all, of a competing brand of socialism and must constantly demonstrate the superiority of their way. Hence, communist pressure is turned into a necessity for pushing socialist measures by the other camp. In short, anti-communism becomes pro-socialism at the hands of evolutionary socialists.

This was nowhere better illustrated than in the foreign aid programs. When the foreign aid programs got under way under President Truman they were billed as an effort to stop or contain Soviet expansion. As such, military aid had top priority. Very soon, other kinds of aid became increasingly important. It became, in the course of time, a major international device for propping up socialist regimes in many lands. Actually, the above chronology is not quite correct. Some foreign aid programs propped up floundering socialist regimes from the beginning. In England, the Labour Government was in deep trouble by 1947, within two years of its installation, and was appealing, with success, to Washington for aid. The European Recovery Program was from the outset a venture in promoting collective efforts among nations. But foreign aid must be given closer examination later on.

The points here are rather general ones. They are:

(1) That the Cold War, whatever its origins, was turned into a contest between evolutionary and revolutionary socialism.

(2) The conflict between these two varieties of socialism is over means not ends.

(3) To prevent their common end from becoming apparent, as well as the probability that they would not ultimately differ much from one another, the whole attention must be focused upon methods.

(4) The common cause between Metaphysical Opponents of Communism and Tactical Opponents could not and did not survive the trial by fire. Truman's conduct of the Korean War disenchanted those who deeply opposed communism. Foreign aid was subjected to withering criticism over the years by both sides. American intelligence and security agencies have now been subjected to such exposure and curtailment that it is doubtful they can perform any function successfully.

(5) In the conflict between evolutionary and revolutionary socialism, evolutionary socialists advance their own variety of socialism.

384

(6) Communists are thus enabled by their criticism to push toward more and more socialist policies in the world. In brief, the Cold War provided the occasion for the spreading of socialist ideas, even though it was supposed to contain communism.

This is the general framework from which the Cold War is to be viewed. It serves as a transition, too, from the more detailed examination of the application of the idea in a few countries to its general spread to countries around the world. It has been spread both by international communism and from country to country as socialism, liberalism, the welfare state, social democracy, or whatever. First, we will deal with the spread of communism.

31

The Spread
of Communism

THE IDEA THAT has the world in its grip is not as it is billed or the way it is made to appear by those who favor it. It is not fundamentally an economic idea or theory, though that is the guise that it often assumed from the outset. It is not basically a political theory, although it often appears to be, and there is considerable temptation for those who oppose it to treat it in that way. Instead, it is in essence a power theory or idea, a mode for attaining and exercising power. *All its claims and promises are,* in the final analysis, *but justifications for holding and exercising power.* That is not to say that the attainment or exercise of power is the motive of those who suscribe to or advance the Idea. It may or may not be, but that is irrelevant. Rather, the attainment and exercise of power are the unavoidable consequences of the triumph of the Idea. Power unlimited is the destination of the victorious Idea.

The power motif is implicit in the formulation of the Idea that is being used here. There are three parts of the formula:

(1) To achieve human felicity on this earth by concerting all efforts toward its realization.

(2) To root out, discredit, and discard all aspects of culture which cannot otherwise be altered to divest them of any role in inducing or supporting the individual's pursuit of his own self-interest.

386

(3) Government is the instrument to be used to concert all efforts behind the realization of human felicity and the necessary destruction or alteration of culture.

It is, of course, the use of government which makes this a power theory. But that only becomes clear by further examination of the Idea.

The Idea that has the world in its grip is not an economic idea. Some of the best economic minds of our era have gone to great lengths to expose the fallacies of Karl Marx. On a lesser scale, some thorough economists have examined in detail, and found wanting, the work of John Maynard Keynes. They did so for good reason, no doubt, because the economic thought of these men was having great impact in the world of affairs.

Despite the fact that Marx engaged in a goodly amount of economic analysis, or economiclike analysis, he was not grappling with the problem of economics. The problem of economics is scarcity, and Marx denied the validity of the problem, at least in the context within which he wrote. He and Engels wrote these words, in *The Communist Manifesto:* "In these crises there breaks out an epidemic that, in all earlier epochs, would have seemed an absurdity — the epidemic of over-production.... And why? Because there is too much civilization, too much means of subsistence, too much industry, too much commerce."[1]

No more did Keynes perceive the problem as being one of scarcity, at least not scarcity of consumer goods. So far as there was a problem it was a problem of insufficient money with which to fuel demand. Hence, his involved and intricate analysis in support of inflation.

John Kenneth Galbraith, an American Keynesian, of sorts, denied the validity of the problem of scarcity in advanced countries. He put his position bluntly: "Given a sufficiency of demand, the responding production of goods in the modern economy is almost completely reliable. We have seen in the early chapters of this essay why men once had reason to regard the economic system as a meager and perilous thing. And we have seen how these ideas have persisted after the problem of production was conquered."[2]

The point is this. The formulators and advocates of the idea that has the world in its grip changed what had once been conceived as an economic problem into a power problem. The problem of production had been solved, they alleged; what remained was a problem of distribution. To solve this problem required the use of political power.

It might be supposed, then, that the idea with which we are dealing is a political theory. It is not. Marx had no political theory at all, certainly not one worthy of the name. He had a power theory to explain what government had been in the past. It had been a means for particular classes to wield power over the masses. When the revolution had broken the power of the classes and there remained only the one class — which is to say no class — the state would wither away.

Talk of rule by an elite or dictatorship of the proletariat does not constitute a political theory. In any case, this was to be only a transitional phase before the state withered away; no theory had to be constructed for how the power would be wielded. Lenin and Stalin (and Mao) enthroned the state, apparently perpetually, but their political theory can be reduced to a sentence. Power in the hands of an elite is exercised for the working classes; it requires no restraint so long as it is wielded for the masses. But this, too, is a power theory, not a political theory.

Gradualists, evolutionary socialists, social democrats, twentieth century liberals, or whatever they should be called, often appear to have a political theory. On closer examination, however, it turns out that what they have are the residues of earlier political theories and a political faith. By the nature of their methods, gradualists must give at least lip service to the residue of political beliefs in their countries. If they live in a land that has a monarch, they must profess their loyalty to him. If there is a separation of powers, they may give lip service to this arrangement. But they will be observed always to be working to remove these as obstacles to the exercise of power. Monarchs are reduced to ceremonial nonentities. The separation of powers is evaded by the creation of instruments which bypass the principle, or those powers which obstruct are made of little or no effect.

What gradualists have, in the final analysis, is a political faith. Their faith is in an ideologized democracy, which is best called social democracy, though Americans are not much used to the phrase. To be more specific, their faith is in democracy which entails much more than simply the process by which those who are to govern are chosen. It involves also what the ends of the government shall be. Only that government is democratic, according to their faith, which is moving toward distributive or substantive equality. While they ostensibly favor popular or democratic government, only that government which is socialistic in tendency is truly democratic. Otherwise, it has come to power on too narrow a base or has succeeded in misleading "the people" (by corruptly acquiring campaign funds from wealthy patrons, for example). Therefore, it does not legitimately hold power.

This is a power theory, not a political theory. The means by which those who govern are to be selected has been so entangled with the ends for which government is to act that they have become indistinguishable. The will of "the people" has been determined in advance of any election; it is none other than what has been ideologically pre-determined is for the good of the people, i.e., further redistribution of the wealth, greater direction by government of the life of the people, and more restraints on all independent elements working in any other direction. If an election should turn out differently, it must be because the will of "the people" has somehow been thwarted. Such a theory is a program for the acquisition and exercise of power.

It is doubtful that there can be effective political competition with the idea that has the world in its grip. (The full import of this must await discussion at another point.) If it were a political idea among other political ideas this would not be the case. But it is not. It is a power idea wedded to a seductive and most attractive vision. Political competition gets turned into a contest for power to realize the vision by different varieties of means. It becomes a contest over who could use the power most effectively to realize the vision.

In lands where gradualism holds sway, all political parties tend to be drawn into the contest to administer the programs by which a country is drawn into the maws of socialism. Who can best exercise the power by which the people are controlled is the issue. In communist lands, there is only one political party; hence, the issue becomes a contest between individuals as to who shall exercise the power.

Power, however, within the framework of the Idea, is only a means. It is not the quest for power that makes it so difficult, if not impossible, to compete politically with those advancing the Idea. All politics is a contest over who shall exercise power. It is the promises that make competition so difficult. How does one compete with the idea that all things shall be made right, that justice, peace, prosperity, and felicity shall follow upon their policies? And — and this is the clincher — those who have wronged us from time immemorial shall have their property and wealth taken from them and divided among us.

Gradualists attempt to will out of sight the power by which this is to be accomplished. They do so by trying to hide from us, and perhaps from themselves, the use of force by mesmerizing us into believing that when it is done democratically significant force is not involved. The communists are much blunter. They revel in power but identify it with the people. Theirs is a kind of mesmerism, too, for the personal character of the exercise of power is hidden behind a variety of facades, the most important being that of ideology.

But even the explicit promises do not convey the sweep of the vision

389

that stems from the idea that has the world in its grip. The sweep may not be readily apparent from the opening phrase characterizing the idea, namely: To achieve human felicity on this earth by concerting all efforts toward its realization. Yet it is there, however implicit, and it entails a vision the like of which has rarely, if ever before, been conceived by mortal man. True, the vision of world conquest is not new to our era; it has even been very nearly accomplished within the limited framework of earlier times. But this vision is in significant ways different from and much more than the vision of an Alexander the Great or Julius Caesar.

It may be best approached by conceiving it as the vision which Jesus rejected when He underwent the temptations prior to His ministry. According to Matthew, following His baptism Jesus went into the wilderness. He fasted for forty days. Then, He underwent a series of temptations. The culminating temptation is the one that concerns us here:

> Again, the devil taketh him up into an exceeding high mountain, and sheweth him all the kingdoms of the world, and the glory of them;
> And saith unto him, All these things will I give thee, if thou wilt fall down and worship me.
> Then saith Jesus unto him, Get thee hence, Satan: for it is written, Thou shalt worship the Lord thy God, and him only shalt thou serve. [3]

The conventional interpretation would be that Jesus was tempted to become an earthly ruler, an emperor over all the earth. But it was surely more than that. Given the circumstances, it does not seem likely that to be an earthly ruler would have been much of a temptation. And we are to believe that Jesus was tempted, was drawn toward the idea. His mood could hardly have been such that being an emperor as such things are understood would have appealed to Him. He had spent forty days in fasting, in contemplation and preparation for fulfilling His mission. How He was to proceed was surely a live question. The temptation was to use power to accomplish His mission, not the mission of kings and emperors, but His mission.

His mission was to draw all men unto Him, a holy, divine, and good mission. Would it not be appropriate to use power — the great force residing in government of an empire — to accomplish His purpose? Why not use the glory of all the kingdoms of the world to draw all men into loving fellowship with one another and union with God? There was a catch, of course. First, He would have to fall down and worship

Satan, which is to say, He would have to worship and serve power and force, even as it must be served by those who would use it. Jesus answered him, "Get thee hence, Satan; for it is written, Thou shalt worship the Lord thy God, and him only shalt thou serve." Those who will may learn somewhat of God from that.

The vision which Jesus rejected has been revived in our time. Like the vision which Jesus rejected it is not simply a vision of a world empire or even of world conquest. We misunderstand it when we read it into the framework of ancient empires, or modern ones either. Momentous changes have occurred in the world since the times of such empires, and since the time when Jesus was tempted. The most obvious of these are the great changes in transportation and communication.

Not only is the whole world now known, but its furthest reaches are available within a few hours by jet airplane, and within moments by radio, telephone, and by television signals transmitted by satellites. A vast array of inventions has made available a technology such as has never before been available to man. There have been developments in thought, too, which have changed the complexion of things. Of particular importance are those in psychology, sociology, and economics. Men once conceived of ruling empires; today it is possible to conceive of total control over the peoples of the world.

What can be, and has been, conceived is a vision of all the instruments of the world brought under a single power, or concert of powers, of all the possibilities known for organizing men to be centrally controlled. That is the end toward which all who embrace the idea that has the world in its grip are driven. Communists press toward that goal bluntly, crudely, and, from the outset, oppressively. Gradualists move toward it circumspectly, with great outward show of benevolence, and pragmatically. The instruments are there, and the struggle to grasp and control them, and through them all men, is well advanced.

Communism was once only an idea. In its Marxian formulation, it was only one idea amongst a goodly number of other socialist notions. But a momentous event occurred in the fall of 1917. The communist idea was joined to power in Russia. The power which Jesus rejected was seized and embraced by Lenin and his fellow Bolsheviks. At that juncture, communism ceased to be an idea only, or even mainly, and became a reality. Those who persist in thinking of communism as an idea will find difficulty in grasping this point. Those who think in this way are inclined to ponder such questions as these. Is Soviet Communism true Marxism? In what ways did Lenin, or Stalin, or Krushchev alter

391

Marxism? When will the Soviet system pass from socialism to communism?

They are idle questions, of course. They have the same practical import as the question of how many angels can dance on the point of a pin. Lenin put the matter bluntly: "Soviet power plus electricity is communism." It might be better to put it this way, since people get hung up on his reference to electricity in the equation: At this stage in history, Soviet power is communism. Communism is whatever those in power in the Kremlin, or Peking, or Havana, or wherever, determine that it is. Those who do not live in those lands are free, of course, to discuss such questions as those above; those who do live in them have no such happy options. Communism is what the powers that be say it is. But such discussions do not alter the reality which is proclaimed as communism.

My meaning might be clearer if put this way. Prior to November of 1917 communism was only a fantasy. When the Bolsheviks seized power, the fantasy became a reality. A change, big with future portent, occurred. The fantasy produced a new reality, the reality of communism in power. Communism in power became, for all practical purposes, communism. If Soviet power is communism, the reverse is also the case, and it may be phrased this way: Communism is power. Not yet the only power in the world, but the intention becomes clear when we understand that the aim is for communism to become all power, and the only power. The idea is the driving force toward total power, but it is not something distinct from the power, not in Marxian terms; it has become power.

Power is central to communist thought and action. "The scientific concept of dictatorship," Lenin said, "means neither more nor less than unlimited power resting directly on force, not limited by anything, nor restrained by any laws or any absolute rules."[4] "When the idea enters the mind of the masses," Marx said, "it becomes a power."[5]

From the outset, it was the aim of Soviet Communist leaders to extend this power over the world. Lenin declared that "the existence of the Soviet republic side by side with imperialist states for a long time is unthinkable. One or the other must triumph in the end. And before that end supervenes, a series of frightful collisions between the Soviet republic and the bourgeois states will be inevitable."[6] Stalin said, "The victory of socialism in one country is not an end in itself, it must be looked upon as a support, as a means for hastening the proletarian victory in every other land. For the victory of the revolution in one country ... is likewise the beginning and the continuation of the world revolution."[7] In an even more famous statement, Khrushchev blustered, "Our firm conviction is that sooner or later capitalism will give way to socialism. No one can halt man's forward movement, just as no one man can prevent day from following night.... Whether you like it or not, history is on our side. We will bury you."[8]

Although the entry of Red China has brought about some differences in the communist camp, the Central Committee affirmed its commitment to the overall aim in these words:

> The Chinese Communists firmly believe that the Marxist-Leninists, the proletariat, and the revolutionary people everywhere will unite more closely, overcome all difficulties and obstacles, and win still greater victories in the struggle against imperialism and for world peace and in the fight for the revolutionary cause of the people of the world and the cause of international communism.[9]

The spread of communism around the world is one of the most remarkable, if not *the* most remarkable, developments of the twentieth century. Communism has now spread into every country in the world. I do not mean simply that communist ideas have been spread in every country in the world. That is obviously the case. There is surely not a major library in the world that does not have some books or compendiums of the teachings of Marx, Lenin, Mao, or others. It would hardly be possible to teach a course on twentieth century history without summaries of and probably quotations from various communists, and the same goes with greater or lesser validity for philosophy, economics, political science, and sociology. Nor is it simply the case that educated people must be in some degree acquainted with communism. It is also the case that amongst those who are illiterate, or barely literate, there must be few who have not picked up and embraced some of the communist doctrines.

Ideas know no boundaries, and there is enough within Marxism that is universal to assure us that almost everyone holds or has encountered at least some of the notions that have place in the ideology. In any case, twentieth century transportation and communication make it almost inevitable that all sorts of things are spread around the world, quite often with great rapidity.

Something much beyond the spread of ideas has taken place. Communist power has spread around the world and into every country in the world. That is what is remarkable. The Bolshevik seizure of power in Russia was the prelude to the extending of the tentacles of that power into every land in the world. The meaning and import of this is not readily grasped. Our modern notions of diplomacy, of national sovereignty, of international relations, and of political theory provide no categories with which to conceive it. Even the conception that communist power extends itself by a conspiracy to take over the government is much too confined and narrow a concept. For when I say that communist power has already spread into every land, I mean to convey the understanding that it is already there and operating, not that it may some day overturn the government. The presence of communist power in every land has already reduced national sovereignty and is contesting over the monopoly of that power.

The manner of the spread of communist power may be best explained by the description of the power mechanism of the Soviet Union. It is true that today there is a communist power independent of the Soviet Union — Red China — but the Soviet Union has much the longer history and has served as the model for all communist exercise of power. (Indeed, the ideological struggle between the two has been highlighted by differences over Stalinist tactics, championed by the Chinese, and downgraded by the Russians.)

Soviet power is exercised by and concentrated in the secret police. The secret-police have been called by many names over the years — CHEKA, GPU, NKVD, MGB, and KGB — but their role has remained constant since the beginning. Today, the KGB is supplemented by the GRU, which is the military branch of the secret police. John Barron has described the role of the KGB this way:

In everything it does, within the Soviet Union and without, the KGB thinks of itself as being the "Sword and Shield of the Party," and this is probably its best single definition. For the KGB serves not so much the Soviet state as the Communist Party and, more particularly, the small coterie of men who control the Party. It is the sword by which Party rulers enforce their will, the shield that protects them from opposition. The characteristics of the KGB which distinguish it from other clandestine organizations, past and present, all derive from the inordinate dependency of the Party oligarchy on the force and protection it provides. Because preservation of their power depends so on the KGB, the Soviet leaders have vested it with resources, responsibilities, and authority never before concentrated in a single organization.[10]

The secret police serve not only as the arm of Soviet power within Russia but also around the world. They are present in all countries of the world, always undercover, on embassy staffs, in legations, or engaging in any number of other operations. The gathering of intelligence from foreign countries is one of their major activities, of course. But beyond that, they use whatever means are available and necessary to enforce the will of the Kremlin on all who fall under the sway of communism. They are the invisible mechanism of communist power.

The visible mechanism of communist power in any land is the communist party. Its presence in any country is the sign that the revolution has begun. Its task is to proclaim the revolution, to arouse discontent, to draw into its fold adherents who can be trained and disciplined, and, when the time comes, to provide the personnel for taking over the power of government. Although much party activity is undercover, and party membership is usually kept secret, the party is itself a cover. It is a cover for the foreign character of the communist intrusion. It provides what appearance there can be that communism is a native movement. Yet these communist parties have generally been captive parties, instruments of foreign powers who controlled them. Elizabeth Bentley, who was for several years a communist espionage agent in the United States, says that Earl Browder, then head of the American Communist Party, was fearful before and but a figurehead for the Soviet powers.[11]

The size of a communist party is not usually a crucial factor. No party anywhere has ever come close to including a majority of the electorate. Nor would such a large, unwieldy, and undisciplined party be considered desirable. Not politics but power is the object of communism. Leverage is the principle on which communists gain and occupy power. If a majority were to vote for a communist candidate or for a party slate, leverage would be gained by a small minority, usually within the party.

In any case, conditions are supposed to provide the setting for communists to come to power, not numbers. To Marx, the conditions were supposed to be provided when capitalism had reached a certain stage. For Lenin, and his successors, the conditions were right at any time when a government became sufficiently irresolute, weak, or divided and confused in its counsels. Any number of things can produce such conditions: military defeat, military conquest, civil war, political elections, terrorized officials, and so on. It is at this juncture that the resolute and disciplined party plays the decisive role at the forefront of revolution.

In the countries of eastern Europe the conditions for a communist take-over were right by way of military defeat and the presence of the Red Army after World War II. Soviet leaders had carefully nurtured the communist parties of these nations during the war, had even provided a place of exile for them in the Soviet Union. Although there were variations from land to land, Hugh Seton-Watson says that in general the take-over went through three stages:

In the first phase government was by a genuine coalition of parties of left and left centre. The coalitions in all cases included communist and socialist parties....

In the second phase government was by bogus coalition. Several parties still nominally shared power and possessed independent organizations: but their leaders were in fact chosen not by them but by the communist leaders, and the policies of the coalitions were determined by the communists....

In the third phase the bogus coalitions were transformed into what the communists like to call a "monolithic block." The communist leaders not only laid down the lines of policy, but centrally controlled the organisation and discipline of the non-communist groups that were still left in the governments. Socialist parties were forced to "fuse" with communist parties. No more political oppostion was tolerated in parliament, press or public meeting.[12]

How this power was seized is particularly instructive:

Already in the first phase ... the communist seized certain key positions. The most important of these was the Ministry of Interior, which controlled the police.... The Ministry of Justice, controlling the formal justice machinery, was considered less important, but was held by communists in certain cases. Control of broadcasting was seized at an early date. Great efforts were made to control and to create youth and women's organisations. In industry, communists were placed in key positions in the management of nationalised factories and in trade unions.[13]

These were, Seton-Watson says, the "Levers of Power."

Sometimes within the secret police, sometimes within the parties, but always the strength and power of communist organizations are what are called the "cadres." The term "cadre" is taken from military usage, where it refers to those who are assigned the task of indoctrinating, training, and disciplining military forces. They are the dedicated communists, those who have been most thoroughly molded, trained to absolute obedience to the powers over them.

"The ideal type of the Communist," Frank Meyer said, "is a man in whom all individual, emotional, and unconscious elements have been reduced to a minimum and subjected to the control of an iron will, informed by a supple intellect. That intellect is totally at the service of a single and compelling idea, made incarnate in the Communist Party: the concept of History as an inexorable god whose ways are revealed 'scientifically' through the doctrine and method of Marxism-Leninism,"[14]

396

The "cadres" consist of all those who have been most thoroughly molded into this pattern. It is the cadre, not the formal party, Meyer pointed out, that is competent to the task that Stalin assigned the party, namely, "the only organization capable of centralizing the leadership of the struggle of the proletariat, thus transforming each and every non-Party organization of the working class into an auxiliary body and transmission belt linking the Party with the class."[15]

These, then, are the main instruments for applying power. Applying power on what? In answering this question we come to the heart of communism as power. So far as communism is a power theory, it is a theory of the exercise of power by a tiny minority over the whole of peoples. How is it done? It is done by occupying pivotal positions in organizations. It is important to understand that any organization will do for the purpose, any organization that has people under its control in any way: police, armies, churches, corporations, businesses, clubs, political parties, governmental units or whatever. Those who think of "communist front" organizations as only facades mistake the principle. They may be facades and covers so far as the ultimate purpose is concerned. But they are as important to communism as they would be if they revealed their purpose completely, for they are instruments of the revolution in process.

The spread of communism proceeds, then, by the creation, penetration, and infiltration of organizations. Otto Kuusinen, one of Stalin's men, described a part of the process this way in 1926, "We must create a whole solar system of organizations and smaller committees around the Communist Party so to speak, smaller organizations working actually under the influence of our party...."[16] Willi Muenzenberg, considered somewhat of a theoretical genius on communist movement by way of organization, declared: "We must penetrate every conceivable milieu, get hold of artists and professors, make use of cinemas and theatres, and spread abroad the doctrine that Russia is prepared to sacrifice everything to keep the world at peace. We must join these clubs ourselves...."[17] The eventual aim can be deduced: it is either to destroy or to control all organizations within a society. It is only when there is no longer an independent organization, or an independent person, that the triumph of communism is complete.

An analogy may help in grasping the mode of the spread of communism. From where I sit, I can see across the road to a field covered with Kudzu. Not so many years ago most of the area covered by Kudzu was a cultivated field. I do not know how the Kudzu got started there.

397

How it got started in this part of the country is not a mystery, however. It was deliberately set out. If memory serves, it was recommended by agricultural experts as a means of stopping soil erosion. (The government may even have provided the seedlings without charge, or for a nominal price.) It does stop soil erosion in those areas to which it spreads, but it does much more than that.

Kudzu is a vine, for the information of those unacquainted with this ubiquitous plant. It is a perennial on which large leaves grow in season. Indeed, Kudzu is a pretty enough plant, such a vine as an innocent person might set out to provide shade over an arbor. But it has a monstrous trait. It spreads. And spreads. And spreads. It can only be stopped from spreading by uprooting it, although it will not directly cross a well traveled road. And it chokes out all plant life over which it spreads. The cover of leaves is so thick during the season that plants depending on the sun to carry out photosynthesis, which is to say all non-parasitic plants, must succumb. Even large trees in its path must eventually be overcome by it. No independent plant life can co-exist with it.

Being across from it on a well traveled road is no protection, however. Kudzu produces seeds which can be blown across the road by the wind. That must have happened already to my neighbor, for some sturdy vines have taken root there. If it is not nipped in the bud, so to speak, it will spread over that land, and from thence to wherever it can, covering and crushing out all plant life as it goes. Kudzu is a power plant, as it were, and moves relentlessly to become the only power.

Communism is analogous to Kudzu in its spread over the world. But communism is not a plant; it is an idea. It is idea joined to power. It is spread not by the wind but by terror. That aspect of it needs now to be examined.

Terrorizing Many Lands

THE SPREAD OF communism around the world is preceded and accompanied by the spread of terror. Even that way of saying it does not put it as directly as it can be stated. The spread of communism *is* the spread of terror.

Terror is not incidental to communism; it is essential and organic. Indeed, terror is the *modus operandi* of revolutionary socialism. Those who will to believe in the possibilities of the revolution of our age hope that it is incidental. Apologists for communism — and they are legion — attempt to make it appear incidental. Terror was justified, they will say, because of the terror of the regime against which it was used. The terror of a communist regime arises from the history of brutal governments which have beset particular peoples in their past. Terror is made necessary by the recalcitrance of the opposition. Tales of the terror are either fabricated or greatly exaggerated by those who hate the new regime. (This, they said, of the White Russians, of the Nationalist Chinese, of Cuban emigrants, and so on.) But, above all apologists for communism make the terror appear incidental by treating it as isolated incidents rather than the pattern of behavior that emerges when it is surveyed whole.

They are assisted in this by communist regimes. Communism is Janus-faced — two-faced — as was suggested earlier in this work. One face may well be called the Ceremonial Face, the carefully conceived and made-up face presented to the world. It is the face that bespeaks regular government, democratic elections, government-provided free schools, free medical care, subsidized culture, and so on. It is the face presented by carefully engineered tours for foreign visitors. It is the face of parliaments, written constitutions, cultural achievements, housing projects, prosperous collective farms, of orderly crowds, and contented people. It is the face of justice sought and on the way to being attained, the face which draws recruits from among intellectuals around the world. All these things comprise the facade of communism.

The other face is concealed, or partially concealed, most of the time. It is the Face of Terror, a terror which outruns the imagination in conceiving it and before which many prefer to avert their eyes. Whittaker Chambers suggested that it is a terror the like of which the world had never experienced.

> Other ages have known a terror equal to, or a little more than equal to, their powers to endure it.... Other ages have known a frightfulness equal to their imagination in inflicting or enduring it. Ours is the first age in which the havoc that men wreak on men has outrun the imagination, which can no longer cope with the plain reality and turns away, helpless, exhausted, and incredulous....

> Ours is the first age in history in which duly constituted governments, duly recognized by others calling themselves civilized, practise the extermination of their own people by millions, as a matter of calculated policy. Within [our] lifetime..., the Soviet government...exterminated so many of its people that it did not dare publish the census figures.... The same government decreed, because its peasants were hiding their grain, that they should be starved to death. So they were, from three to six million of them.[1]

That, however, was but one of the cores of the terror stalking the earth.

Terror, I say, is essential to communism. It is essential both to the gaining and exercising of power by communists. Communism is a power theory, and undergirding that power is terror. It is not simply that communism entails rule by a tiny minority. All rule, excepting that in a direct democracy, perhaps, is rule over the majority by a minority. But communism lacks accepted sanctions for its rule. Its basic theory denies validity to government and thereby any sanction for the exercise of its authority or use of force. Its thrust to transformation pits it against the populace at large; they could only sanction it by willing their own destruction. Its sanction is only that it rules, and it rules by terror.

It may be feasible to divide the terror that stalks the earth in the wake of the spread of communism into four stages. It may be, that is, because

400

our knowledge of communism in action is still fragmentary. Much communist activity is clandestine and secret. As yet, no entrenched communist power has fallen so that its secrets might have come into the hands of a conqueror. (Such as did so many of those of the Nazis, for example.) Thus, we rely on the reports of defectors, immigrants, counter-espionage, revelations (such as those made by Khrushchev about Stalin's rule), deductions from official pronouncements and documents, and surmise, for our knowledge of the inner workings and plans of communists.

The evidence certainly points to the fact that much of the terror is planned and coordinated. Yet there are gaps in our knowledge as to whether or not it is done according to some overall plan. Moreover, there is often no way to determine which acts of terror associated with the international spread of communism are a part of a plan and which are the result of local initiative, which are by communists and which not, or whether the motives of those who commit the acts are the same as those who order or approve of them. In short, if there is a "science" of communist terrorism, it has not become public knowledge.

Even so, a pattern of terror can be discerned from the history of communism. That it was a universal pattern did not begin to become clear until the 1950's and 1960's. Prior to World War II communism-in-power had occurred only in the Soviet Union. The Communist International, the instrument for the spread of communism, was controlled by the Kremlin leaders. Hence, the pattern was the Soviet pattern, not necessarily the communist pattern. But with the emergence of other communist powers, the pattern has been much the same, pointing toward the conclusion that it is a communist pattern. This does not mean that the use of terror falls into a rigid and unvarying configuration. On the contrary, all sorts of variations occur in it. It is rather that if it be assumed that terror is organic to communism, that it serves certain broad and general purposes, then the general pattern is discernible.

At any rate, there is a discernible pattern of at least four stages of the terror. They frequently overlap one another, and excepting for the second stage there is no predicting in advance how or when they will occur.

The first stage of terror may well be called The Disordering Terror. It encompasses all that terror which precedes the seizure of power by the communists. It may last for months, for years, for decades, or for as long as it takes to bring communism to power in a given land.

It is disordering because the general object — as distinct from the particular object of any act — is to create the conditions of disorder which will be favorable for communists to seize power. Marx taught that the conditions would be right for revolution when capitalism had reached the stage of development in which the lot of workers became intolerable. It followed that revolution would come first in what were then the most advanced countries. Lenin altered this doctrine by demonstrating that the conditions were right for revolution when disorder had proceeded to the disintegrating point. Hitler's seizure of power demonstrated the same point, as did that of Mussolini. Communism spreads by bringing about conditions of disorder. Terror is the most direct means of producing confusion, arousing fear and distrust, and challenging the ruling government.

Specific dramatic examples may best illustrate this stage of the terror. Take the case of Vietnam. The Republic of Vietnam (South Vietnam) was organized as an independent country in 1954. There were communists in South Vietnam, of course, as there were throughout Indochina. At first, they went underground, but they soon began to be heard of by assassinations and became known as the Viet Cong (Vietnamese Communists). "Between 1957 and 1959 the Viet Cong killed sixty-five village chiefs who had tried to resist Communist pressures." In 1959 radio Hanoi (the voice of the Communist government in North Vietnam) proclaimed the desirability of destroying the Diem regime in South Vietnam. In 1960, the National Liberation Front was orgnized at the instance of the Communist party of North Vietnam. In "1960 and 1961 village officials, schoolteachers, and health workers were being murdered by the thousands. In 1960, through harassment, plus the murder of teachers and sabotage of buildings, the Viet Cong succeeded in closing two hundred primary schools n South Vietnam, interrupting the education of more than twenty-five thousand students. And this is when the terror was just beginning to explode with full force, warning of the horrors to come."[2]

There is not space here to detail the story of the terror that eventually engulfed South Vietnam and sent shocks outward into much of the rest of the world. Those who will to do so may at least know the outcome of it. South Vietnam is now in the grip of a communist regime, as is much of the rest of Indochina. Terror prepared the way.

An even more dramatic use of terror occured in Angola. From March 14-16, 1961, the northern portion of that large Portuguese colony was ravaged by Bakonga tribesmen from within Angola aided by their

402

kinsmen from the Congo. These concerted assaults were organized in cold blood by Holden Roberto, among others, and fomented by Algerian, Soviet, and Chinese Communists. They were carried out, with a ferocity that can hardly be imagined, by drunken and drugged savages. All the inhabitants of whole villages — men, women, children, black and white — were murdered, the women repeatedly raped, even infants in cribs dismembered, and many people disemboweled. At one village where there was a sawmill, the victims, both dead and alive, were lashed to boards and run through the saw lengthwise.

Most of the tales by eyewitnesses are too full of horrible things to repeat. Here, however, is a snippet from what happened in the village of Fazenda:

Then the turn came for the women and the children. The beasts made no color discrimination. They slaughtered white, mulatto and Negro alike. They would throw the smaller children high into the air, let them drop on the soil to break their bones and then ... would play a brutal game of football with the bodies of those dying children, while the poor mothers screamed like crazy in the hands of the beasts. I didn't believe that anything so evil could exist in the world.[3]

The object of this concerted terrorism was to paralyze the will of the Portuguese and drive them from Angola. Had it succeeded then, it would have brought into power men under the sway of communism.

It would be a mistake, however, to conclude from these two dramatic examples that the Disordering Terror is usually concerted or concentrated so as to accomplish such comprehensive objects. More commonly, the terror which precedes communist take-overs is sporadic, isolated and episodic, rises to a crescendo and subsides, getting nowhere as far as can be determined at the time. Even that it is going to lead to a communist take-over is a matter of communist faith until it happens. Its immediate object may be much more restricted than that, and frequently is.

Some of the terror may not be planned or directed by communists. Yet, whether it is or not, it becomes grist for the mills of communists. There are at least two general ways this may come about. One of these is where apparently free-lance acts of terrorism become a part of the disordering atmosphere which communists can utilize for their purposes. An example would be the terrorist acts by anarchists in the last decades of Czarist Russia. There were many such terrorist acts, usually the assassination or attempted assassination of government

403

officials. Most of these were not coordinated or directed so far as is known. But they helped to create the atmosphere of fear and paralysis which enabled the Bolsheviks to bring off a revolution.

A more familiar case, one much closer home both in place and time, was what we may call the terrorizing of Presidents of the United States from 1963 to 1973. It began with the assassination of President Kennedy in 1963 and subsided with the withdrawal of American forces from Vietnam. It encompassed the assassinations of John F. and Robert Kennedy, Martin Luther King, the wounding and crippling of George Wallace, and, as an eiplogue, the two assassination attempts on President Ford.

So far as we know none of this maiming or killing was directed by any communist or revolutionary organization. True, the assassins of the Kennedy brothers were Marxists or communists of some stripe. But no evidence has been forthcoming that they were ordered to assassinate anyone. Indeed, the only assassin, or would-be assassin, with an ongoing revlutionary organzational connection was the would-be assassin of President Ford, a member of the Manson "Family." It is relevant to point out, however, that revolutionary socialism creates a framework both for organizational terror and for individual acts of terror. The preaching of class hatred and allegations of injustice arouse individuals to act on their own and inspire the formation of "free-lance" terrorist organizations such as the Manson "Family" and the Symbionese Liberation Army.

At any rate, there was a framework for the terrorizing of Presidents provided by the spread of communism. The American participation in the Vietnam War was the most obvious part of the framework. More broadly, there was the spread of communism into southeast Asia, Latin America, and Africa. This, plus the fact that the United States was providing just about the only opposition by any outside nation to the spread of communism.

The Cultural Revolution in Communist China during these years was also an important part of the context. That revolution spread especially to Germany, France, and the United States, where it was the model for the Youth Rebellion. The Youth Rebellion was not only inspirited by Mao's Cultural Revolution spearheaded by students but also by "mind expanding" drugs, psychedelic lights, hard rock music, sexual promiscuity, and hippie lifestyles. Simultaneous with these developments was widespread rioting in the cities, mainly by blacks.

A great many people were terrorized during the turbulent sixties. At the gentler level, there was the terror felt by older people as young

404

people began to crop up in revolutionary clothing, the men sporting Castro-like beards, and girls shedding their femininity by wearing field jackets and dungarees. The sudden change was too swift to be digested; it had the odor of revolution about it, something much more than just a fad. Parents of youth were filled with dread that their children were taking drugs, their daughters might run away from home, their lifestyles cut them off from their elders.

As demonstrations became the order of the day, many people were harassed and intimidated by them. Riots in numerous cities brought terror to shopkeepers, peaceful citizens, and policemen. Indeed, policemen along with anyone who represented authority were especial targets for terrorization. Deans of colleges, an especially benign breed inhabiting academia, were singled out for a while by their student charges to bear the brunt of terroristic acts.

What brought all these things into focus as a disordering terror in the service of the spread of communism, so far as they were, was the effort to secure American withdrawal from Vietnam. It was this, too, that led to the terrorizing of Presidents. There is no mystery about why that should have been the case. American involvement in Vietnam was an undeclared war. A succession of Presidents — Kennedy, Johnson, and Nixon — took the initiative in dispatching American armed forces and conducting the war. Johnson took the initiative in the heaviest commitment of American forces, and for the last three years of his presidency he became virtually the whole focus of discontent with the war.

Johnson was terrorized. He was subjected to such vituperation as to surpass anything that had happened before. Demonstrators descended upon Washington periodically, picketing the White House, screaming epithets, carrying Viet Cong flags, quoting Mao, emulating Castro, proclaiming their affection for Ho Chi Minh, and yelling unprintable obscenties. Some civil rights leaders joined in the clamor against the war in Vietnam. Following the triumph of Eugene McCarthy — a "dove" on Vietnam, as those who wanted to wind down the war and withdraw were called — in the New Hampshire primary, President Johnson announced that he would not be a candidate for re-election. After the assassination of Senator Kennedy, the President was increasingly cautious about making public appearances. When the forces opposed to Vietnam descended upon the Democratic Convention in Chicago, Johnson declined even to attend a birthday party given in his honor. A President had been terrorized.

The pressure was kept up during the early Nixon years. It would

405

mount to a crescendo following the bombing of Cambodia. How far Nixon yielded to the terrorization is uncertain. At any rate, the siege of disordering terror achieved this much. American forces were withdrawn from Vietnam. Communists came to power there and in surrounding countries. It was a settled mood in many quarters that there should be no more Vietnams. The role of the ROTC in colleges and universities was greatly reduced as a result of student pressures. The draft was suspended. Communist guerrillas continued their incursions in Africa and Latin America, and as this is being written are threatening Rhodesia, Nicaragua, and Iran, among other countries. The revolution did not follow upon that disordering terror in the United States, though communism spread elsewhere, but the softening up succeeded here.

The other kind of terror that is not entirely planned by communists but is utilized by them for spreading their ideology is terror they have provoked. Provoked terror from the other side is most useful for propaganda purposes and the swaying of public opinion. It creates confusion in people's minds, making it difficult to decide who is right and who is wrong. The man who became known to the world as Joseph Stalin enunciated the principle, or a part of it, after he had helped to stage a mass demonstration in 1901. In the course of the demonstration, the demonstrators were fired upon by the police. Stalin drew these conclusions: "The whips play on the backs of all, irrespective of sex, age, and even class. Thereby the whip lash is rendering us a great service, for it is hastening the revolutionizing of the 'curious onlookers.' It is being transformed from an instrument for taming into an instrument for rousing the people.... Every militant who falls in the struggle or is torn out of our ranks arouses hundreds of new fighters."[4]

Stalin described the technique as one to gain new recruits for the cause, but as it has developed it is much more than that. It enables communism to spread from behind a cloud cover of being on the side of the angels. It enables the makers of terror and consistent users of terror to point the accusing finger at their opponents, to describe the regime which opposes them as corrupt and oppressive. The development of television and satellite transmission brings the evidence of repression into the homes around the world while the provocative acts have either already taken place or are concealed.

Examples are so numerous that they can only be alluded to. In the 1930's, Edgar Snow described the Kuomintang of Chiang Kai-shek as corrupt and oppressive. He told stories in the *Saturday Evening Post* of such things as the burying of peasants alive by minions of the regime. In the 1950's, Americans, and others, were treated to tales of the cruel tortures in Batista's prisons in Cuba. More recently, there have been stories of terror by the Greek Colonels and the Argentine Generals. The Buddhists who burned themselves alive — who terrorized themselves, so to speak — were the *cause celebre* which brought down Diem in Vietnam.

There is ample, even overwhelming evidence that much of the violence used against communists and other revolutionaries is deliberately provoked.[5] The reverse terror which communists find most useful is some incident which can be magnified, dramatized and can become the symbol of the repression of a regime. "Bloody Sunday" became such an incident in Czarist Russia. The event occurred in St. Petersburg in 1905 when demonstrators marched on and massed before the Winter Palace. The throng ignored commands to turn back and the firing of blanks, so the soldiers fired into their ranks, killing some of the demonstrators. Here was the dramatic incident which could be recalled over and over again for purposes of undermining the government.

The happenings at Kent State University in the spring of 1970 provide an example of the reverse terror tactic. There is space here only to give a bare outline of what occurred. Prior to the events that have become known as "Kent State," a radicalization of much of the student body had taken place. The Students for Democratic Society was the organization most directly responsible. The local chapter was provided with additional revolutionary fervor from time to time by "regional travelers," adults trying to spark activity in the locals. Among the regional travelers to Kent State were Bernadine Dohrn, Terry Robbins, and Mark Rudd. Miss Dohrn professed to be a revolutionary communist, and Terry Robbins was known as "V.I.," the initials used by Lenin.[6]

On May 1, 1970, public announcement was made concerning a series of bombings by the United States Air Force of the access route to South Vietnam used by the Communists. This was made the occasion for student eruptions on a goodly number of campuses. Saturday, May 2, became the target day for action at Kent State. The ROTC building was burned; thugs with clubs beat off those who tried to put out the fire; and an atmosphere of terror prevailed as other buildings were threatened. The National Guard was sent in to restore order. The Guardsmen were subjected to a continual torrent of verbal abuse. A grand jury declared that "the verbal abuse directed at the Guardsmen by the students during the period in question represented a level of obscenity and vulgarity

407

which we have never before witnessed. The epithets directed at the Guardsmen and members of their families by male and female rioters alike would have been unbelievable had they not been confirmed by the testimony from every quarter. . . ."[7]

The Guardsmen were confused and frustrated — terrorized — after a weekend of such psychological warfare. On that fateful Monday, as the Guardsmen began a retreat to regroup there was a large throng of rioters on their right flank. A contingent of Guardsmen turned back, pointed their rifles toward the throng, and began to fire. Four students were killed.

The revolutionaries had their event now. Hundreds of colleges and universities were closed down. A moment of reverse terror had taken place, one which could be made into a battle cry, one which could be turned into a symbol for an alleged repressive society. The symbolic fire ignited there soon subsided, but there are still smoldering coals which are fanned from time to time in the hope of kindling a flame.

The thrust of the disordering terror is toward civil war. Indeed, the disordering terror becomes regularized when sustained guerilla warfare is underway. Guerilla warfare is terrorism leading directly toward the seizure of power. Since his death, Ché Guevara has been the symbol of this mode of operation as it has caught on in various places around the world.

The other stages of the terror can only be described in brief here. While it is important to know that they occur, they belong to the story of the consolidation of revolution rather than directly to its spread. They do help to confirm the fact that undergirding communist power is a prolonged and permanent terror. Of course, once communists have seized power they not only monopolize it but the terror as well.

The second stage of the terror is The Terror of Suppression. This is the terror which accompanies and follows upon the seizure of power. Although there is no timetable, so far we know, it has usually lasted as long as two to three years. In the Soviet Union, its dates were 1918-1921, those that are usually given for the civil war. In Hungary, it was approximately 1945-1948. In Cuba, it occurred mainly within a couple of years of Castro's seizure of power.

This terror has a specific purpose. It is to bring all power into the hands of the communists. Communists do not usually get all power directly. They usually share power with a coalition, such as other revolutionary parties, labor union leaders, peasant and other farmer organizations, and military leaders who are more or less under their sway. Moreover, the organizations through which society normally operates — business firms, churches, fraternal associations, schools, the media of ccommunication, local governments, and so on — may be independent organizations on which hold over the central government has no immediate impact. Beyond these, there is the matter of the bulk of property being in private hands. All other political parties must be suppressed, all organs of force brought under the communists, social organizations made subservient to communist rulers, and property seized. Terror is essential for a minority to accomplish such a coup.

Such political parties as are permitted for a time are terrorized by the police whom the communists control. Any parties that remain are then fused with the communist party. The leaders are generally disposed of in one way or another. For example, "The Roumanian socialist party had always been very small and weak; it won some importance in 1945 only because it was less disliked by the Roumanian workers than was the communist party. But communist pressure, reinforced by Soviet military power, quickly brought it to heel. At a congress held in March 1946 the party split, the opponents of the communists forming a separate party which had but a short life. In November 1947 'fusion' took place."[8] Which is to say that only the Communist Party remained.

Other organizations survive only to the extent that they are useful to communism and can be controlled by the communists. The old leaders are subjected to such terror as may be necessary to drive them out or subordinate them. In doing this, as well as seizing private property, communists use to good effect the greedy and avaricious have-nots among the populace. Castro's regime in Cuba illustrated how this may be done shortly after the seizure of power. Castro organized militia units to take over organizations and to bully those within them into submission. Paul Bethel says that "Almost without exception ... the militia units ... came from the bowels of ... society. The least productive and the least capable were to be found there. ... "

Dressed in militia uniforms, authority dangling from the holsters on their hips, hotel bus boys, garbage collectors, taxi drivers and office clerks found that they could intimidate their superiors and receive the support of the revolutionary regime. ... As organization progressed, instructions began to flow through the ranks, instruction which had no other aim than to bring the whole of Cuban society under the control of government. ...

Local labor unions began to lose their hold on laborers as militiamen usurped both power and position. Union officials were intimidated, harassed, and threatened outright. ...

More than one business leader was jolted when a group of militiamen-employees walked unannounced into his office and flatly told him how to conduct his business. . . .[9]

This was but a prelude, of course, to the taking over of private property. Quite often this has been accomplished in a moblike atmosphere as renters seize the places where they live, as employees seize factories, and as peasants seize the land.

The third stage may be called the Transformation Terror. This is in many ways a continuation of the Terror of Suppression, but it is often enough sufficiently separate from it to constitute a separate stage. It is probable that many Russians in the 1920's and Chinese in the 1950's believed that the worst of the terror was behind them. They had undergone the Terror of Suppression. But worse lay ahead — the Terror of Transformation. This is the stage of the totalizing of power, the wiping out of the last relics of independence, the purging of the old revolutionaries, the taking of lands and factories from peasants and workers, if that has not already taken place, and the molding of the population to the will of the rulers. Terror may be reckoned to be as essential to these tasks as to the others. This was the period of the Stalinist terror in Russia.

Its transformation character may be best illustrated by the Cultural Revolution which took place in Communist China in the mid-1960's. This revolution was promulgated and let loose by the communist leaders. It was a purge, not only within the Party but in the society at large. The instrument used for the purge was students — young peole in high school and college. Its purpose was to discredit and shake from power the bureaucracy which exercised authority in China. In terms of communist ideology the bureaucracy had become corrupt and reactionary. In fact, one suspects, power had become to some degree dispersed in China. It is a natural tendency for authority to become dispersed, for those who exercise power, however acquired, to begin to do so as a matter of right. Indeed, some of the harshness of dictatorship is often reduced by the dispersal of authority. At any rate, the government sponsored a rampage by students against authority, and those who had exercised power, as well as the general populace, were terrorized for several years.

The first to be terrorized generally were school administrators and instructors. Many of these were brought before students to be judged. They were accused of being corrupt reactionaries. They were humiliated, tortured, often enough stomped and beaten, made to

410

confess and recant, and stripped of their authority. From the schools, the revolution expanded out into factory and field. Students battled with the police and, at times, even took on the army. Civil war raged, instigated by the top leaders of China.

Mao Tse-tung and Chou En-lai had shown much greater imagination in unleashing terror than had Stalin. To set the young to terrorizing their elders must surely be the ultimate betrayal of a people by the government.

So far as can now be determined, the fourth stage, the Permanent Terror, may be the final stage. When the populace has been terrorized into submission the terror subsides. There may, of course, be new outbreaks of terror, and the possibility of these is surely a part of the permanent terror. But the outward terror is generally greatly reduced. It can be more subtle, be psychological more often than physical, become a permanent war on the spirit of man. Terror becomes an enduring threat, an intimidating force which permeates life.

In its deepest dimensions, the terror arises from the use of force unredeemed by love. The Reverend Richard Wurmbrand tells this story. It occurred somewhere behind the Iron Curtain, in what country I do not know. Mr. Wurmbrand was no longer permitted to have the forum of a pulpit or any other formal setting for his preaching. So he went about quietly, taking the Gospel to such individuals as would hear it.

One day he fell into conversation with an army officer on the street. They talked for a bit, and Mr. Wurmbrand invited the officer to his home. When they had sat down, Mr. Wurmbrand related to him the story of the life of Jesus, and of his death on the cross, in a simple and direct manner. When he had finished, the officer's eyes filled with tears and he wept unashamedly. In explanation, he said something to this effect: "I did not know that there was such a man. I did not know that there was such love."

No doubt, the army officer knew much of hate. He had during his lifetime been subjected to a constant barrage of propaganda aimed at arousing his hatred for the class enemy. No doubt, he knew something of the brutalizing use of force by the regime over him. He must have witnessed the jockeying for power and privilege. Surely, he had experienced sexual appetite, and there must have been those along the way for whom he had affection. What a relief it must have been to find himself warmed by a transcendent love, a love that had in it no element of calculation, a love that expressed itself through sacrifice, a love that

411

somehow had reached across the ages from a carpenter in Galilee to touch an army officer in Eastern Europe!

The ultimate terror is the pervasive use of force in an atmosphere of hate. This is the permanent terror of communism.

33
The Spread of Gradualism

GRADUALISM IS A power theory, too, as communism is. That is, it is a theory for the gaining and exercising of power. It is a theory of gaining power by the use of the force of government to redistribute the wealth and establish substantive equality. It is a theory of holding and exercising power by continually promising more and more benefits and ever extending the sway of government.

Gradualism does not, of course, ordinarily adopt the guise of a power theory. Indeed, we are enjoined from recognizing it as a power theory by a prevailing intellectual temper which disdains theory. It operates under the guise of benevolence. In countries where socialism is an acceptable goal, it claims that goal and purports to be doing what is good for society. Where socialism is not generally recognized as a good, gradualism claims to be acting pragmatically for the common good.

Yet, gradualism is a power theory; socialism is a power theory; and pragmatism is a power theory. It is only by grasping it as a power theory that we can understand its character, its mode of operation, and the manner of its success. This may become clear when we look at the matter this way. Socialism is a failure in every respect, save one. It fails in its tacit promise to lead us toward utopia. It fails to provide a bounty of goods. It fails to distribute wealth either justly or equally. It fails to

413

fulfill its promises. In one respect only does it succeed. It succeeds in gaining, holding, and exercising power. It succeeds, by its very success, in transforming all political parties which contend with it into facsimiles of itself.

Ideas have consequences which follow from the essence of the idea. Theories produce results in accord with the theory, whether the theory is explicitly stated or not. The one tangible result of socialism is power, power concentrated and extensively employed. It may well be that most of those who embrace socialism are not aware that they are embracing a power theory. Certainly, most of those who vote for the measures of gradualist socialism are not informed that they are placing vast power in the hands of those over them. Yet that is what they do. Because power is the fruit of gradualism, its necessary antecedent is a power theory. The theory is here stated as the belief in the use of government to transform society.

Gradualism differs from communism in practice in this way. Communism is spread and its grip fastened upon a people by the use of terror. Gradualism, by contrast, fastens its grip upon a people by providing unearned benefits to some or all of the people at the expense of some or all of the people. Virtually the whole appeal of this notion is that those who receive the benefits are either not taxed to pay for them, or taxed much less than the sum of benefits received. The graduated income tax and corporation taxes are essential to bolstering this belief. (If wealthy stockholders and corporations did not exist, gradualists would have to invent them. Indeed, in those countries where they do not exist, governments convey benefits derived from them by way of foreign loans and other sorts of aids.)

There is an even more clever device for hiding the taxation by which wealth is acquired to pay for the unearned benefits. It is inflation, i.e., the increasing of the money supply by the government. Gradualist governments everywhere use this covert means of raising money. It is, of course, a form of taxation, for the value of the money thus raised is taken from the money which people hold or have owed to them. The effect is experienced as rising prices.

In gradualist countries, which is to say, in effect, in all non-communist countries, a continual struggle goes on between groups to get the largest share of unearned benefits and to pay the smallest portion of the costs. It is a struggle in which the apparent winners are often the biggest losers, for the benefits carry a price tag. Those who receive them pay by loss of independence. Those who rule thus increase their power over the

414

people. The power thus gained by government is used to shape the populace according to its will.

Gradualist socialism is a power theory, too, in that its eventual aim is to have all force in the world monopolized by a single government. No such aim is generally avowed, of course, but it is nonetheless the tacit logic of the position. The idea that has the world in its grip requires the eventual concerting of *all* human effort to achieve felicity on earth. Moreover, the position sometimes gets explicit, albeit tentative, statement. Here is such a statement in the mysticized evolutionary language of Teilhard de Chardin. He leads into it by way of the discussion of the future necessity of applying eugenics to individuals. Then, he says:

> Eugenics applied to individuals leads to eugenics applied to society.... Points involved are: the distribution of the resources of the globe; the control of the trek towards unpopulated areas; the optimum use of the power set free by mechanisation; the physiology of nations and races; geo-economy, geo-politics, geo-demography; the organisation of research developing into a reasoned organisation of the earth. Whether we like it or not, all the signs and all our needs converge in the same direction. We need and are irrestibly being led to create, by means of and beyond all physics, all biology and all psychology, *a science of human energetics.*[1]

If we strip away the prophetic mysticism in which his thought is cast, Chardin is saying that what is needed is a science of concerting human energy, and one is emerging. Government is, of course, the approved instrument for accomplishing the concerting of human energy.

Arthur M. Schlesinger, Jr., put the case for world government more prosaically a few years back:

> Yet world government, in a sense, cannot emerge too soon; for the people of the world cannot long afford to expend their energies in squabbling with each other. The human race may shortly be confronted by an entirely new range of problems — problems of naked subsistence whose solution will require the combined efforts of all people if the race is to survive.... The results of industrialization and introduction of public health standards in Asia, for example, may well be calamitous, unless they are accompanied by vigorous birth-control policies and by expanded programs of land care and conservation.[2]

The time was not yet right for it, however, he pointed out. "When Russia loosens the totalitarian grip, then the noble dream of world government will begin to make some contact with reality.... In the meantime, we had better do what we can to foster community where we can, through regional federations and through the United Nations...."[3] Schlesinger was stating the gradualist position in contrast with that of the enthusiasts for immediate world government.

Effective world government can only emerge, then, on this view, when all the nations of the earth have come under the sway of democratic socialism. If this gradualist vision be thought of as a timetable — a term that is only apt if it be understood as a figure of speech — the stages of progression are roughly these. First, socialism must come to power within nations. When several nations which have common bonds are socialized, they can form regional unions. Eventually, these can be linked together in a world government. Before that can happen, however, all cultural, religious, racial, and social differences from people to people and nation to nation will have to be blurred or obliterated. In short, the very transformation and homogenization toward which socialism tends must have taken place.

But the process does not occur in timetable fashion. It goes on simultaneously at many different levels. It proceeds at any time and place when collective decision making and action is substituted for individual decision and acting. Thus, the United Nations Organization, which is already in existence, might eventually become the world government. But whether it does or not, the yielding to it of any power of decision and action is a step in the direction of world government within the socialist eschatology. But so is the decision of some local government to fluoridate the water supply, for that, too, is a step toward total collectivization. My point is that the process may go on simultaneously at many different levels, that gradualists have no precise blueprint or plan, but that they understand themselves to be proceeding toward the goal wherever decisions are being collectively made that were formerly made by individuals.

The spread of gradualism proceeds, then, by the spread of the collectivizing of decision making and action. Gradualism is a power theory, a theory for eventually consolidating all power in a single world government, but it does not necessarily proceed by the direct exercise of power. And it certainly does not rely on terror for its spread. Its chosen instrument is democracy, although there is no necessary aversion to autocratic methods so long as there is a general framework of democracy. In the world today the spread of gradualism is a concomitant of the spread of democracy.

Anyone who undertakes to tell the story of the spread of gradualism around the world in the mid-twentieth century has set himself a

416

formidable, if not impossible, task. The task does not simply arise because the world is a large and diverse complex of nations, though it is. The problem is more fundamental than that. It arises from the very nature of gradualist or evolutionary socialism. The very idea is that the movement toward socialism must be by gradual, and often imperceptible, steps. Usually, gradualists operate within the received framework of institutions.

Often enough, those who advance gradualist measures do not proclaim themselves as socialists. Journalists usually confuse the issues. Headlines do not announce that a gradualist regime has come to power in some land. (If they did, it would probably mean that some communist had seized the government.) The world of scholarship provides no greater aid. There are no textbooks on the spread of gradualism in the world. Such references as are usually made by writers to such matters are apt to describe a regime as "moderate" or "left wing" or "right wing," terms which may provide a better indication of the predilections of the classifier than about the tendency of the government.

In truth, the spread of gradualism is largely unreported, though it is surely one of the most significant developments of the twentieth century. If gradualism were a fact, I think it would have been reported. But it is not a fact; it is a theory. It is a theory that if you begin at one point with certain sorts of measures and advance them relentlessly and successfully, you will eventually end up at your destination. Gradualism is also a tendency, a movement, a direction, and an ideology. As a tendency, when it is recognized, a great many facts may be accounted for by it. More, it is surreptitious movement, operating under cover of other names quite often, and moving toward its eventual goal slowly and by indirection.

The problem of the historian in dealing with gradualism may be illustrated by analogy with describing a man on a journey whose destination is uncertain. Let us suppose that the man begins his journey at Dallas, Texas. Amongst friends and those with whom he is comfortable he has often talked of going to New York City to settle there. He has even discussed on several occasions the ways and means of getting there. For purposes of the analogy, we will equate New York City with socialism. But when he sets out from Dallas, he buys a ticket to go only to Longview. From Longview, he travels to Texarkana, thence to Little Rock, then on to Memphis, then, unaccountably, to Muscogee, Oklahoma. From Muscogee, he proceeds to Birmingham, and then north once again to Chattanooga.

417

Let us interrupt his journey at Chattanooga, with the observation that he has only got that far to date. Is he going to New York? From the information available to us, we do not know. There is some evidence that he might be. There is a pattern to his travels, thus far, if the tacking to and fro is discounted, which could eventually get him to New York. He could, however, travel next to Atlanta instead, and wind up in Miami. The only substantial clue we have is that he had talked as if he were going to New York.

There are, however, some pieces of missing information. We have not been told in what sort of vehicle he is traveling, nor do we yet know how its intermediate destinations are determined. Let us say, somewhat playfully, that he is traveling by a sail-driven wind-propelled prairie schooner. Its intermediate directions are determined by two variables, each more or less independent of the other, and neither of which is predictable in advance. One factor is that the passengers vote before they set out from a city, and the majority decide which city they will go to next. The other factor is that they may be driven off course, even to different destinations, by strong wind currents. There is another factor, however, which makes their eventual arrival in the vicinity of New York fairly certain, if they stay on the journey long enough. The prevailing winds in the United States blow in an easterly direction. Indeed, those from the southwest, Dallas, for example, blow in a northeasterly direction, i.e., toward New York.

With this information, the analogy becomes very nearly a paradigm. The traveler is the nations of the world. The vehicle is democracy. The course is gradualism. The prevailing winds are the intellectual climate, driving toward the eventual destination of socialism. The tacking to and fro is occasioned by the shifting currents of popular opinion.

This provides us an analytical tool, of sorts, with which to discern the mode, methods, and extent of the spread of gradualism. The spread of democracy in the twentieth century is more or less coextensive with the spread of gradualism. On the face of it, there is no reason why this should be true. Political democracy could be, perhaps should be, ideologically neutral. It may have been at one time, but it is not in the twentieth century. Democracy is now ideologically loaded and bent toward collectivism. What makes this so is the intellectual climate.

A major change in what is called democracy — more properly, representative government — occurred in the late nineteenth and early twentieth century. Democracy emerged in modern times as a means of controlling government, of limiting and restraining those who govern.

418

Representative government was earliest and firmest established in England following the Glorious Revolution. Its most prominent task was to control and limit the exercise of power by the monarch. The control over the purse — over revenues — was reckoned to be the most crucial power for exercising that control. That was the reason for vesting the authority for initiating appropriations in the United States House of Representatives — the most democratic branch of the Congress — to keep the power over the purse nearest to the people.

The major change referred to above occurred when the emphasis shifted from the people controlling government to the government controlling the people. What occurred, let me reiterate, was a shift in *emphasis,* not some absolute change. There never was a time, of course, when government did not exercise some control over the people. Moreover, as long as people vote in contested elections, they exercise some control over government. It is a matter of degree and emphasis.

Anyone who will study in depth English history in the seventeenth century will surely discover that much of the great effort going on was to discover means of controlling government. In like manner, the documents of the American Revolution are replete with evidence of concern for limiting and restraining government. Placing basic powers in the elective legislatures was one of the important devices by which the founders hoped to accomplish this.

In like manner, it should be clear that governments in more recent times have shifted toward more and more control over the people. That is not the way those who favor the controls describe them, of course. They talk of planning economies, of controlling business, of controlling prices and wages, of providing social security, of setting standards for this or that or the other, and so on. But they are always using power upon and controlling people, and not just some of the people either, but all of them. As has been shown in this work, the control over business is a means for reaching through to and controlling all who work for or trade with it. Compulsory school attendance, compulsory retirement "contributions," building codes, "check off" payment of labor union dues, tax payments to subsidize undertakings, fair employment practices acts, and so on, are people control.

The "have-nots," the "have-littles," the "ne'er-do-wells," the uneducated, the old, the young, minorities, industrial workers, tenant farmers, working mothers — whatever disfurnished classification that can be conceived — are essential to gradualist socialism. Their condition provides the grist for the program mills of gradualism. The emphasis

419

shifted from controlling people in conjunction with the thrust toward universal suffrage. The tie between democracy and gradualism was knotted with this development. The enfranchisement of those who hope to gain by weight of numbers what they had not achieved by their efforts is the basic political, or power, technique of gradualism.

But the impetus toward socialism does not arise from those who can in one way or another be described as disfurnished. They could no more provide the continuous impetus for such a movement than they could effectively direct the development of great corporations. Nor does the impetus come from politicians primarily, though politicians do much of the work of arousing the populace and the enactment of programs.

The impetus toward socialism comes from what Russell Kirk refers to as the "clerisy," or what are more commonly called intellectuals. "Clerisy" may be the better term, however, for it suggests the pseudo-clerical character of the undertaking. The impetus toward socialism is provided by secular clergymen, so to speak, by those who have taken up the mission of transforming man and society by the use of force. The natural habitat of these secular clergymen is the modern college and university. But they are almost equally at home amongst the regular clergy, as journalists, as writers, and in any one of the hundreds of intellectual pursuits. Whatever their vocation, their avocation is transformation. They are the makers and purveyors of intellectual fashion, or, more pointedly, they make gradualist socialism fashionable under whatever guises it adopts at the moment. They create and spread the intellectual climate which propels us toward socialism.

Gradualist socialism advances under many guises, but there is one that is very nearly constant in the world today. It is democracy. "Democracy" is the code word for gradualist socialism. The situation is somewhat confused, however, because communists also use it as a code word. Thus, it is not always immediately clear when we are informed by the great news media of the world that democracy has triumphed somewhere or other whether communism or gradualism has come to power. But it does usually eventually get straightened out. If one-party rule is tyrannically imposed, and if close relations with one or more of the great communist powers are established, a country will likely be recognized as communistic, not "democratic." (There is yet another element in the confusion — the Third World. That will have to be discussed in its own place, however.)

The spread of gradualism, then, can be very nearly equated with the spread of democracy. There are other ways of saying much the same thing. In those countries of the world in which the influence of the

United States and Western Europe is predominant, gradualist socialism is generally well established. More bluntly, it is that portion of the world tied either directly or indirectly to the inflationary spiral of the dollar. However, this last formulation better describes the predicament of much of gradualism than it does the extent of the sway.

At any rate, the geopolitics of the West has been deeply intertwined with gradualism since World War II. Much of the Western influence on the rest of the world had been wielded by way of colonies prior to World War II. Every major (world?) European war since the beginning of the eighteenth century had embroiled colonies and entailed reshuffling of colonial possessions. World War II marked a major break with the past. Theretofore, colonies had been sought mainly, though not exclusively, in order to gain dominant trading positions in other parts of the world. The diminution of military power in Western Europe in the course of the war, plus ideological pressure, resulted in the release of colonial possessions, many of them within a decade after the war. With the release of colonial possessions went also the loss of European hegemony in many parts of the world.

The quest for favorable trading positions, and the conflicts that were engendered by it, was transformed into an ideological conflict. The general name for that conflict, of course, has been the Cold War. The expansive pressure of communism provoked resistance to it which was centered in the United States. Whatever the interest of those who opposed communism, this conflict became mainly a contest between revolutionary and evolutionary socialism, as I pointed out earlier.

The answer to communism, many claimed, was democracy. Hence, much of the influence of the West and a considerable amount of the wealth and know-how of the United States was put into establishing and bolstering democratic regimes which, according to theory, might be able to defend themselves from communism and maintain their own independence. The result was the spread of democratic socialism where it was successful. Where it failed, which was in most places, it set the stage for some nationalistic and autocratic socialist regime.

It is certainly simplistic and probably untrue to explain the failure of these regimes on the grounds that the people are unprepared for democracy. If by being "prepared" for democracy is meant the willingness and readiness of peoples to go to the polls and vote themselves a share of the wealth, most peoples of the world are probably well prepared. The problem lies elsewhere. They don't have the wealth to distribute!

Democratic, or evolutionary, or gradualist, socialism is a product of

421

industrially and agriculturally advanced nations. It succeeds in holding power only in these nations, if it is not massively aided from other sources. There is no mystery about why this is so. Democratic socialism is a parasite on the back of capitalism. It is a theory of gaining and exercising power by controlling and distributing the wealth produced by tools, techniques, and sophisticated business organizations. It can succeed, so far as it succeeds, only in such countries as Sweden, the United States, England, Canada, Japan, and Germany — in those countries in which capital has already been employed so as to produce great wealth. It can only hold power elsewhere by massive transfusions of wealth from those nations in which capital was earlier sufficiently free and the incentives were there for producing wealth.

After World War II, many of the peoples of the world came to the West asking for bread and we gave them stones instead. More specifically, they came to the colleges and universities of Europe and America seeking to learn the sources of our wealth and prosperity. We gave them instead the power theories of democracy laced with pallid socialism.

True, they sometimes learned how to operate our machines, but they learned little of how they are to be acquired and less about how they may be effectively used. From our histories they learned of the horrors of the industrial revolution, how businessmen were rapacious and greedy, and what great evils attended the growth of great corporations. In economics they learned macro-economics, which is, in effect, distribution-ist economics. They went back to their native lands well instructed about how to distribute wealth but largely ignorant of how to produce it. Or worse, they had been indoctrinated against the most effective means of achieving prosperity.

Even so, the spread of gradualism around the world has been impressive indeed. From tiny beginnings in the minds of a few men, mainly in England and Germany, it is now firmly established in every advanced industrial country in the world. It was once said that the sun never set on the British Empire. It is equally true today that the sun never sets on gradualism. Of course, gradualism has spread to every non-communist country in Europe, to the United States, to Japan, to Australia, to Canada, to New Zealand, to the Philippines, to South Korea, and so on. It has also spread to many countries in Latin America, Africa, and Oceania.

Indeed, there is hardly a petty dictator in the world who cannot point with pride to the accoutrements of gradualism he has introduced in his country: medical clinics, free schools, subsidized housing, land reclamation and redistribution programs, minimum wages, empowered trade unions, and so forth. Few countries in the world are so backward that they cannot boast a parliament, the emblem of democracy, which has not busied itself in the not too distant past in confiscating foreign assets in order to redistribute them according to such lights as it has. In short, the outward forms of democracy and the inward thrust of gradualism have been introduced in states around the world.

Westernization evinces itself in our time as the spread of gradualism around the world. The technology which resulted from invention, saving, investment, efficient management of great enterprises which were concentrations of capital has been used to give universal sway to intellectual fashion. More specifically, intellectuals can now utilize high-speed planes, fast automobiles, telephones, television, and radio to see to it that intellectual fashion prevails.

Intellectual fashion prescribes the collectivization of decision making and action. It prescribes a collectivized democracy within each land, one whose government shows its good faith by passing socialist measures. It requires that governments negotiate and come to terms with all radical and socialistically inclined groups within their borders. Intellectual fashion proclaims the desirability of free speech and a free press in all lands, but does not require it in order to extend respectability to communist regimes. Intellectual fashion not only prescribes the collectivizing of decisions within countries but also in international relations. Intellectual fashion is gradualist, and gradualists no more want independent nations than they want independent individuals. They want nations to negotiate with one another, to form regional associations with one another, and to act collectively in all matters. A nation today, particularly a non-communist nation, which makes a unilateral decision, i.e., acts on its own in its own interest, may expect to be denounced and to be subject to every sort of pressure that the makers of intellectual fashion can mount.

The United States intervention in Vietnam is a case in point. Communists and gradualists united in condemning this action, communists for obvious reasons and gradualists mainly because the action was unilateral. (In Korea, gradualists had been hoist by their own collectivist petard, for the United States intervention there was approved by a United Nations Resolution.) Rhodesia has suffered the calumny of the intellectual community for several years for the determination of its government to go it alone. Israel confounded intellectual fashion by making successful war against the Arabs on its own, confounded, I say, for the Western intellectual community, at least much of it, had long had its sympathies bound up with the fate of Israel and for a while the juices of collectivism had to be held in abeyance. But they were only in abeyance — after all, gradualists are gradualists, not insisters that everything be done at once — for it now appears that Israel has finally been brought to the negotiation table, and eventually the collectivist mode may regain its sway in that corner of the world.

Gradualists have a goal. It is to socialize the whole world and bring it under one all-embracing government. They have a faith, too. It is that they are moving toward that goal, however slowly and gradually, whenever any decision is made collectively. Indeed, it sometimes appears that the manner of the making of the decison is more important that the decision reached, and that may well be the case for any particular decision. John Dewey put the premises of the faith this way. You cannot separate means from ends, for the means that you employ will eventually determine the ends you will achieve.

Gradualists believe, then, that so long as more and more decisions are being collectively made they are moving toward their goal. That accounts for their commitment to democracy, for by their understanding it is a means of collectivizing decision making. That accounts for the pressures they continually mount to have decisions by nations negotiated, mediated, and made collectively.

In large, then, gradualism was spread within an intellectual atmosphere arising from Western intelligentsia and propagated as intellectual fashion. This fashion is expressed as a pressure to collectivization. It is advanced as democracy. Within the Cold War framework it was supposed to be democracy versus communism. The welfare, goverment planning, and distributionist schemes were advanced both as an antidote to communism and as substantive requirements of democracy. The programs of gradualism, however, were devised in the advanced industrial and agricultural countries of the West where the technology for producing wealth already existed. Industrially backward countries frequently had little wealth to distribute, and gradualist measures could have little attraction. Therefore, the spread of gradualism had to be subsidized. For that part of the story, it will be necessary to examine the foreign aid programs.

424

34
Foreign Aid

THE UNITED STATES became the center from which the Idea that has the world in its grip, in its evolutionary socialist, gradualist, or democratic socialist formulations, was spread after World War II. The main device for spreading the collectivist practices associated with the idea was foreign aid. Foreign aid was extended by way of grants and loans from the United States government to governments of other lands around the world. It consisted mainly of military aid, commodities and other economic aid, and technical assistance.

Perhaps it does not go without saying now that those who devised, promoted, voted for, and carried out foreign aid activities for the United States did not avow the aim of spreading socialism. On the contrary, it was promoted primarily as a means of containing communism and secondarily as a means of establishing stability and peace by promoting security and prosperity. Moreover, there was much talk of advancing and supporting individual liberty and free enterprise around the world. For example, the "Benton amendment" to the Mutual Security Act of 1951 contained these admonitions:

It is hereby declared to be the policy of the Congress that this Act shall be administered in such a way as (1) to eliminate the barriers to, and provide the incentives for, a steadily increased participation of free private enterprise in developing the resources of foreign countries consistent with the policies of this Act, (2) to the extent that it is feasible and does not interfere with the achievement of the purposes set forth in this Act, to discourage cartel and monopolistic business practices prevailing in certain countries receiving aid under this Act which result in restricting production and increasing prices, and to encourage where suitable competition and productivity. . . .[1]

While this was less than a clarion call for free enterprise, it did state that as a part of the aim. That the aim was to defend and establish freedom was stated often and in a variety of ways. Secretary of State George C. Marshall, who articulated the Marshall Plan of foreign aid for Europe, declared before the Senate Committee on Foreign Relations that its high purpose was "the establishment of enduring peace and the maintenance of true freedom for the individual."[2] The Economic Cooperation Act of 1948, which was passed by Congress to put the Marshall Plan in effect, included these assertions of purpose:

The restoration or maintenance in European countries of principles of individual liberty, free institutions, and genuine independence rests largely upon the establishment of sound economic conditions, stable international economic relationships and the achievement by the countries of Europe of a healthy economy independent of extra-ordinary outside assistance. The accomplishment of these objectives calls for a plan of European recovery ... based upon a strong production effort, the expansion of foreign trade, the creation and maintenance of internal financial stability, and the development of economic cooperation, including all steps possible to establish and maintain equitable rates of exchange and to bring about the progressive elimination of trade barriers.[3]

At their inception, and for several years thereafter, these programs had widespread bipartisan support in the United States. One historian suggests that this was achieved by the appeal to a broad spectrum of ideas and beliefs:

The relative ease with which Truman got the substance of this European Recovery Program (E.R.P.) through an economy-minded Republican Congress can be easily explained. The administration had done unusually careful and thorough spadework. Sensing the conservative temper of the country, it made business leaders partners in the venture. The success of E.R.P. in Congress was assured when the three most powerful national pressure groups were persuaded that their constituents, as well as the United States, stood to gain from the proposal. The business group (represented by the National Association of Manufactuers) hesitated to bolster the socialist economies among the sixteen nations. The N.A.M. realized, however, that European recovery would foster American foreign trade and might possibly uproot the seed beds of Communism in France and Italy. Moreover, Truman's liaison officers promised that E.R.P. would be run according to "sound business principles," and that it would help counteract the trend toward socialism. . . . E.R.P. was headed by the president of the Studebaker Corporation, Paul G. Hoffman, who pleased the industrial bigwigs by advertising abroad the merits of the American system of free enterprise.

The all important agricultural associations were also enthused by the prospect of increased foreign outlets for farm products, as were the A.F.L. and C.I.O. . . . The support of the country's most influential lobbies was secured before Congress began its debates.[4]

Whatever the aims and intents of those who supported these programs, however, the thrust of them was collectivist. The desire to forestall the spread of communism was probably quite sincere, so far as it went. The desire to contribute to European recovery and, more broadly, to the stabilization of countries in various parts of the world may have been equally sincere. There is evidence, too, that some of the initial animus, at least, of American involvement was directed toward the freeing of trade and enterprise. The best examples of this were in West Germany and in Japan where Americans were most deeply involved. The shadow of Woodrow Wilson still hung over America at the end of World War II, a shadow cast by Wilson's peculiar combination of nineteenth century liberalism, with its emphasis upon free trade and open markets, with twentieth century liberalism, with its collectivist bias.

But a fuller explanation of a collectivist thrust behind a facade of promoting individual liberty and free enterprise requires that we call to mind how gradualism works. Gradualism proceeds by advancing programs which have their meaning within socialism but are advanced only to deal with particular exigent situations. It is English Fabianism writ large, so to speak. The gradualist, too, utilizes, so far as possible, familiar ideas and works within the framework of established institutions, even when he aims at their eventual overturn. Gradualism proceeds by altering the content of ideas and the character of institutions. The collectivist premises are often kept out of sight but are made to inform such acceptable ideas as international cooperation, mutual security, and multi-lateral agreements. Familiar terms are subtly informed by collectivist premises.

How this works may be made clearer by examples. New Dealers worked to lower tariffs in the 1930's by what were called "reciprocal trade agreements." The lowering of tariffs had been correctly identified with the movement toward free trade. But reciprocity brought a new ingredient to the undertaking, and one which, on closer examination, is quite confusing. "Reciprocal" implies that a quid pro quo has been given. But in a reciprocal trade agreement who gives the "quid" and who gets the "quo"? It is not at all clear when looked at as a matter of economics.

The problem arises because neither nation benefits from a protective tariff. Revenue aside, the peoples of both countries are harmed. So far as the protective tariff succeeds in its object, they are denied goods they might have had at more favorable prices than they can obtain. It is even questionable whether in the long run those interests that are supposed to benefit from the protection, industrial workers, for example, do benefit. But whether they do or not, it has been demonstrated conclusively, and many times, that the general populace of a country does not gain from a protective tariff. That being the case, and assuming that government is supposed to be the agent of the general populace, no reciprocal agreement to lower tariffs is necessary, and none is possible in a meaningful sense. In short, the people of the country in which the tariff is lowered are the most direct beneficiaries of the action. It is in their interest for the tariff to be lowered, whether the tariff of any other country is lowered or not. In a similar fashion, it is in the interest of other countries to lower their tariffs.

Reciprocal trade agreements do not make sense within the theory and framework of a free market. They are a collectivist device. Socialist theory justifies them, and they are in accord with the Idea that has the world in its grip. We can understand both reciprocal trade agreements and foreign aid within the framework of that Idea. At the heart of the Idea is the notion of getting rid of the pursuit of self-interest. According to mercantile interventionist theory, the protective tariff benefited the country which imposed it by helping to establish a favorable balance of trade. Therefore, according to this theory, the national interest was advanced by the protective tariff. By a reciprocal trade agreement, then, two or more nations would mutually agree to sacrifice their national interests for their common welfare and benefit. It was equally important, too, that governments act in concert with one another in the movement toward collectivism.

Socialism provided the framework for the foreign aid idea. By foreign aid, a nation sacrifices its interest for the common welfare of all the nations involved. Although there is an egalitarian animus behind foreign aid, it is quite possible that the most important push was to get nations acting in concert for their supposed common good.

Socialism is nationalistic. Virtually every species of socialism is national socialism. The late Ludwig von Mises explained the reason this way:

> Intervention aims at state control of market conditions. As the sovereignty of the national state is limited to the territory subject to its supremacy and has no jurisdiction outside its boundaries, it considers all kinds of international economic relations as serious obstacles to its policy. The ultimate goal of its foreign trade policy is economic self-sufficiency....
>
> The striving after economic self-sufficiency is even more violent in the case of socialist governments. In a socialist community production for domestic consumption is no longer directed by the tastes and wishes of the consumers. The central board of production management provides for the domestic consumer according to its own ideas of what serves him best.... But it is different with production for export.... The socialist government is sovereign in purveying to the domestic consumers, but in its foreign-trade relations it encounters the sovereignty of the foreign consumer. On foreign markets it has to compete with other producers....[5]

In short, in order to control the domestic economy, and have it subject to no outside influences, socialism tends to try to have a self-contained economy.

The market is anathema to socialism, the Idea that has the world in its grip. Socialists inveigh against capitalism and capitalists. But they are not the true enemy. Capitalists can be, and regularly are, bought: they can be controlled, manipulated, even used as instruments of government. They are paper tigers, easy to abuse in slogans but hardly formidable opponents of socialism generally. The free market is another matter. It epitomizes what must be crushed if the idea is to triumph. In the free market, the pursuit of self-interest reigns supreme. There, the sellers display their wares as attractively as possible, hoping to get the best price possible for them. There buyers are dominated by one thought: to get the best merchandise for the lowest price. The market must be abolished. Or, it must be altered so drastically that self-interest no longer holds sway.

The massive revolutionary thrust in this century has been aimed at somehow abolishing or decisively altering the character of the market. Entailed in this effort is the determined and tenacious attempt to transform man and society, for men make markets, and the market is a salient feature of society. In theory, nothing should be easier than to abolish the market. All that is necessary is to abolish *all* private property. Then, since men will lack all means with which to trade, all trade will cease — all legal trade anyway. Any government that would

429

go so far, however, would almost certainly be committing suicide. By abolishing private property and the market, it would not only remove the positive means that induce men to produce but a goodly portion of the negatives ones (e.g., fear of punishment) as well. The most common and widely used means by which governments punish malefactors in our day is imprisonment. But imprisonment would involve no significant change in status for a people who could have no private property or engage in trade.

The parallel between the socialist premises and imprisonment is striking. The main impact of imprisonment is felt in the virtual abolition of private property and the drastic restriction of the market. The aim of imprisonment is presumably to punish by detention. But the effect would be the same if the aim were to abolish the market. It is true that socialism has never threatened to cut off all non-pecuniary exchanges, but to the extent that it limits the market, it reduces the opportunity for these as well.

Even tolalitarian socialist regimes have stopped short of abolishing all private property in their assault on the market, however. Indeed, it is probably beyond the power of government to extinguish all private property. Property is antecedent to government, having a factual basis in production and possession. The nearest thing we know to the aboliton of private property occurred in the Nazi concentration camps and the Soviet labor camps, but even there men clung to the residues of possessions as property.

Be that as it may, socialists — that is, all those under the sway of the Idea that has the world in its grip — everywhere carry on a virtually unremitting effort to limit, restrain, and control the market. Every effort to do so, however, tends to isolate each socialist state from every other nation. Efforts to control the money supply hamper foreign exchange. Efforts to control wages, usually to raise them, makes trade with other nations difficult. In short, socialist experiments tend to cut nations off from one another and to pit them against one another. This was dramatically demonstrated by the Iron Curtain around the Soviet Union and the Bamboo Curtain around China. The isolation of gradualist nations is not so dramatic, but the tendency is at work there as well.

The problem can be phrased this way: How can a nation's economy be managed when the economy is subject to the world market? The answer, of course, is that it cannot be. In their efforts to manage economies between World War I and World War II, nations almost everywhere erected barriers against world trade. This national socialism followed its logical course most fully in Nazi Germany and Fascist Italy. It followed an equally logical course as imperial socialism in the Soviet Union, although there it did not reach fruition until 1948, when all of Eastern Europe had fallen under Soviet domination. To the extent that a country is cut off from the world market it loses the advantages of international division of labor and specialization. It is cut off from many of the best sources of materials and better markets for it products. The most logical course then becomes to expand the area over which it has control. Indeed, the logic is world conquest.

After World War II national socialism was in disrepute. That does not mean that it has not been practiced — Red China being the most horrendous example — but that it was not avowed as a purpose. Two varieties of international socialism emerged as dominant. One of these is international communism, which, after the war, was centered in Moscow. The other, unnamed but nonetheless present as impetus, is international democratic socialism, or gradualism. Its center was in Washington. The contest between them was the Cold War. The Soviet Union sought to remove its isolation by expanding the communist system. (It could be argued that this represented no change in Soviet policy, since it had been trying to do so since 1918. Perhaps, though, there was a shift toward the emphasis of fostering communism instead of simply extending Soviet power.)

The precise role of the United States in these developments needs a little further explanation before it becomes clear. Neither the United States nor other nations were opposed to foreign trade as such. The opposition of socialists is to the market, not to trade. To put it another way, if trade could be conducted as part of the managed economy, could be collectivized, and carried on so as to advance democratic socialism, it would be entirely acceptable. In short, if trade could come under the auspices of government instead of being carried on between peoples in the market it would lose its onerous character.

It is quite possible that no one conceived the matter in just this way, and it is certain that those who advanced the American programs did not publicly state the case for them in this fashion. In any case, socialists have not been inclined to acknowledge that barriers to trade arise from socialist practice, if they were aware of it. (Quite often, they don't even admit they are socialists — especially in the United States.) So far as Nazi Germany and Fascist Italy were concerned, those were "right wing" movements, according to other socialists. Of course, it is no secret

431

that countries following collectivist practices have difficulties in foreign trade. But they are not ascribed to socialism. They are ascribed to dollar shortages (American printing presses have finally eased or removed that one!), to trade imbalances, to the devastation of wars, to cold winters, to droughts, to industrial backwardness or underdevelopment, to colonial exploitation, or to a hundred and one other conditions.

Even so, the problem was there, and it was real, whether it could be openly faced or not. Namely, how could socialism be an international movement? How could nations open up to one another in mutual benefit rather than each be cut off from the other in isolation and mutual anatgonism? How could Soviet socialism be undercut, contained, and perhaps tamed by gradualist socialism? Although there is no reason to suppose that American intellectuals were wrestling with these problems formulated in this way just after World War II, they were wrestling with problems stemming from them.

An American plan for dealing with these problems began to emerge in 1947. There had been an earlier American plan — the United Nations — but it was thwarted by Soviet obduracy plus a lack of determination by other nations. It was first expressed in the Truman Doctrine in connection with aid to Greece and Turkey. President Truman said, in part:

> The seeds of totalitarian regimes are nurtured by misery and want. They spread and grow in the evil soil of poverty and strife. They reach their full growth when the hope of people for a better life has died. We must keep that hope alive.
> The free peoples of the world look to us for support in maintaining their freedoms. If we falter in our leadership, we may endanger the peace of the world — and we shall surely endanger the welfare of our own nation.[6]

It was, however, Secretary of State George C. Marshall who gave much more definitive form to the plan. In a speech at Harvard University, delivered on June 5, 1947, he set forth some ideas which were quickly dubbed the "Marshall Plan" and became the foundations of an American plan. Two key points emerged from the address. The first was Marshall's statement of purpose: "Our policy is directed not against any country or doctrine but against hunger, poverty, desperation, and chaos. Its purpose should be the revival of a working economy in the world...."[7] The other was the method. Secretary Marshall took care to emphasize that the initiative in devising the particulars of the plan must come from European nations. "It would be neither fitting nor efficacious," he said, "for this Government to undertake to draw up unilaterally a program designed to place Europe on its feet economically. This is the business of the Europeans. The initiative, I think, must come from Europe. The role of this country should consist of friendly aid in the drafting of a European program and of later support of such a program so far as it may be practical for us to do so. The program should be a joint one, agreed to by a number, if not all, European nations."[8]

If Marshall's program was anti-communist, it was surreptitiously so. Communist countries were invited to the initial conference, and Czechoslovakia accepted. The Soviet Union intervened, and none of the countries in its orbit particpated.

When the Marshall Plan (officially, the European Recovery Program) was put into effect heavy emphasis was placed upon the "joint effort" and "economic cooperation." Truman described the plan this way: "This was our proposal, that the countries of Europe agree on a cooperative plan in order to utilize the full productive resources of the continent, supported by whatever material assistance we could render to make the plan successful."[9] The participating countries made a formal pledge "to organize together the means by which common resources can be developed in partnership...."[10] The thrust of the programs as activated was to promote economic union of European countries.[11] The main outcome was the Common Market.

The Marshall Plan was a major breakthrough for gradualist socialism. Theretofore, the interventionist measure associated with gradualism had tended to raise barriers between nations. The Marshall Plan attempted to lower the barriers within a region of the world while promoting collectivism on a broader scale. The Marshall Plan was socialistic, in the first place, because it entailed American aid to European countries. Tens of billions of the wealth of Americans were transferred to Europe, a clear cut case of redistribution of wealth. More, the program promoted collective action by participating countries. Moreover, it enabled countries to continue their domestic socialist programs by negotiating arrangements with other countries that would leave them undisturbed. The question of whether or not the United States should promote free enterprise by the European Recovery Program was resolved in this way by a committee:

Aid from this country should not be conditioned on the methods used to reach these goals, so long as they are consistent with basic democratic principles.... While this committee firmly believes that the American system of free

433

enterprise is the best method of obtaining high productivity, it does not believe that any foreign-aid program should be used as a means of requiring other countries to adopt it.[12]

It would have been surprising if the committee had determined otherwise, since the United States was extending aid to the Labour government of England which was busily nationalizing industries before the Marshall Plan got under way.

Despite its extensive scope, the Marshall Plan was a limited program, limited to Europe and to a few years of helping these countries recover from the ravages of war. However, President Truman was not long in extending a vision of American help to the whole world. Following his re-election in 1948 he announced what he called the Point Four Program. He explained the program this way:

Point Four was aimed at enabling millions of people in underdeveloped areas to raise themselves from the level of colonialism to self-support and ultimate prosperity. All of the reports which I had received from such areas of the world indicated that a great many people were still living in an age almost a thousand years behind the times. In many places this was the result of long exploitation for the benefit of foreign countries.... This was the curse of colonialism....

In this country we had both the capital and the technical "know-how." I did not see how we could follow any other course but to put these two great assets to work in the underdeveloped areas in order to help them elevate their own standards of living and thus move in the direction of world-wide prospertiy and peace....[13]

The following are examples, cited by Truman, of programs undertaken under the auspices of Point Four:

A monetary, fiscal, and banking system was introduced in Saudi Arabia. Schools of medicine, public health, and nursing were set up in several countries. A 75,000-acre irrigation project in the Artibonite Valley of Haiti got under way. A great multi-purpose hydroelectric plant was constructed in the Mexican state of Michoacan. Irrigation projects in Jordan were started to create 120,000 acres of arable land providing homes and six-and-a-quarter-acre tract for 21,000 families consisting of 105,000 individuals.[14]

Very soon after its inception, indeed, in some places from the beginning, foreign aid was of two kinds: economic aid and military aid. The whole became a vast effort to arm and assist in feeding peoples around the world. Within a decade after World War II, American influence was extended to virtually the whole of the non-communist world. A political scientist imaginatively described the American "presence" this way:

The extent and depth of American commitments in the postwar world were staggering. In the decade after the war Americans took the lead in the United Nations and American soil became the site of the world's "capital." Americans ruled alien peoples in Germany, Austria, Italy, Trieste, Japan, and Korea; and American generals, like Roman generals of old, became world famous as proconsuls. Peacetime "entangling alliances" were made with Europeans, with Asiatics, and with countries as far away as Austrialia and New Zealand. American spheres of influence arose in Greece, Turkey, and Saudi Arabia, and extended in circular half-moon fashion through the Japanese islands, the Ryukus, Formosa, the Philippines, the Carolines, and the Marshalls. The internal politics not only of Latin American countries but also of European, African, and Asiatic countries turned on American policy.

The following are net figures for foreign aid from the United States for the years 1945-1965. The total for economic and military aid was slightly over $100 billion. Economic aid to Western Europe amounted to $23.8 billion, military aid, $16.2 billion. To the Near East and south Asia, $15.4 billion in economic aid, $6 billion in military aid. To the Far East and Pacific, $14.5 billion in economic aid, $12 billion in military aid. In the Western Hemisphere, $5.6 billion economic aid; $1 billion in military aid.[15]

Our concern here is primarily with how this expansion of wealth and influence contributed to the spread of gradualism. The ostensible purpose of the aid was to spread and buttress democracy and build the sort of regimes that would resist communism "Democracy," as ealier noted, was a code word for democratic socialism, at least as used by many intellectuals. In practice, this meant that where American aid went the prevalent American notions of the role of government went also. Here is an example of the development of an argument for this in an ECA report to Congress:

> No modern self-governing state — and especially no state with a democratic form of government — can maintain itself and develop its potential unless it performs a minimum of public services in the fields of health, agriculture, education, transport, power and communications, industry and overall planning. The countries of southeast Asia ... are acutely deficient in these public services.... The initial step in any program ... must therefore be the organization and maintenance of adequate, self-sustaining public services.[16]

Another report was even blunter, declaring that we must assist in the "creation of social and economic conditions and institutions under which the people feel that their basic needs and aspirations are being satisfied by their own free and independent governments."[17] In short, the foreign aid programs aimed to strengthen governments by helping them to provide for the needs of their citizens.

In the broadest sense, what animated the foreign aid programs can be described as follows. The most basic appeal of socialism is the promise of redistributing the wealth. However, industrially undeveloped countries had very little wealth either to distribute or redistribute. (The same had been true, to a much lesser extent, of war ravaged countries.) Nor did they have modern weaponry with which to consolidate their own power over the populace or to defend themselves from foreign invaders. The United States intervened by providing wealth, or a modicum of it, for governments in these countries to distribute and weaponry to build up military establishments. But the aim was not to make these countries permanently dependent on largess from the United States. Direct aid in goods and materials was supposed to be a stop-gap measure. The aim was to develop these countries so that they would no longer require such aid. This was affirmed over and over again in public statements, and there is little reason to doubt the sincerity of such intentions. One may surmise that if a country could learn the techniques and develop industries they could then engage in their own redistribution programs.

But if each country in the world became self-sufficient, the world would presumably be caught up in the inner contradictions of socialism, namely, each country isolated from every other. There is, of course, no danger that countries will become self-sufficient. The tacit premise of socialism is that all the goods will be more or less equally available to all the people of the world. That is hardly a project that could be accomplished once and for all, if it could ever even be momentarily accomplished. Droughts, floods, hurricanes, tornadoes, discoveries of rich mineral deposits, inventions, and what have you would be continually unbalancing the division.

The foggy dream which impels gradualists is not of some final resolution in which socialism will have been achieved but of an enduring effort to shift the world's goods to where they are wanted. They will have the mechanism for the activity when some international body has been empowered to take from the haves and provide for the have-nots everywhere in the world. Pending that, the task is for wealthy and "enlightened" nations to provide for those who have less. A kind of brotherhood of all nations is supposed to emerge from all this, nations which no longer advance the self-interest of their own people but are exclusively concerned will the well being of all mankind.

In the real world that did not come to pass. As soon as the Arabs had the technology for producing oil within their bounds they took it over

436

and jacked up the price of oil. They utilized their regional association to form a giant oil cartel. Military aid has all too often turned into military rule within recipient countries. American aid was often a handy device for keeping a particular party in power. But, above all, the amount of foreign aid never kept up with the dreams and expectations of the people to whom it was extended. Underdeveloped countries remained underdeveloped countries for the most part, their foreign aid spent for showy demonstration. True, the foreign aid programs spread the virus of socialism. They helped to fasten on most of the peoples of the world the notion that they should look to their governments to take care of them. But it was never enough — it could not be — to produce what it promised.

In consequence, by the 1960's many countries were leaving the American orbit. For the most part, they were not going into the Soviet orbit, not headlong anyway. They declared themselves unwilling to be participants in the Cold War, and many of them were clearly not sold on the superiority of gradualism. That was for Western nations who had already developed their technology. They would have to find another way. It is time now to discuss the development of this "Third World."

35
The Third World

THE NEAT DIVISION of the world into two camps began to lose what validity it had in the mid-1950's. This did not initially signal any lessening of tension between the United States and the Soviet Union. Indeed, the division began to lose its sharpness at just that juncture when American foreign policy was most adamant under the leadership of John Foster Dulles. Nor was there any lessening of the American effort to form regional alliances and support them in various parts of the world. Nonetheless, it is now about as clear as it can be in a world muddled by rhetoric which quite often has little discernible connection with reality that the Cold War peaked in the middle of that decade. The two-world concept began to lose it cogency.

Some revisionist historians now claim that the division of the world, and expecially the Cold War, was an American device. For example, a recent textbook declares that "the United States having invented the bogey of the international Communist conspiracy, and then by its own policies having turned that fantasy into fact, now became frightened out of its wits by it."[1] The United States did not, of course, invent the Communist conspiracy. On the contrary, American political leaders did their best for years to ignore the evidence for it, admitting it, to the extent they ever did, after revelations made denial impracticable. In point of fact, it was communists who divided the world in two. From the time of the formation of the Communist International, they held to a view that the world was critically divided. Their writers have long referred to it as a division between socialist and capitalist nations. Soviet writers have kept to this terminology over the years.

At any rate, a congeries of events occurred in the 1950's which made the bipolar — one pole in Moscow and the other in Washington — world-view less and less applicable. With the driving of the Nationalist Chinese from the mainland, Red Chinese leaders consolidated their rule and began to develop a sphere of Communist influence outside the Soviet sphere. It was the Chinese who intervened in the Korean War, not the Russians. Washington's credibility as the defender against communism may have waned as a result of the acceptance of the Korean standoff. It definitely did when the United States did not intervene on behalf of the uprising in Hungary. European unity was severely strained by the failure of the United States to support Britain in the Suez crisis.

But a much better indication of the break-up of the bipolar world was the emergence of what has been called the Third World. The term began to come into currency around 1955.[2] The term was given body, of sorts, by the Bandung Conference held during the same year. Representatives of twenty-nine Asian and African nations met in Bandung, Indonesia. "Communist and proto-Communists vied with anti-Communists in denouncing Western colonialism..., in lauding the high purposes of the UN, and in asserting that recourse to arms in national self-defense was wholly justifiable. In a notable demonstration of solidarity, at least in sentiment, the delegates promised to steer clear of East-West quarrels, if that could be achieved. Speaking for Red China, Chou En-lai ... uttered sentiments calculated to soothe apprehension that Peking nurtured aggressive designs upon neighbors...."[3] For a brief period it looked as if the Third World might become a definite entity, but it did not. It has remained largely a concept with whatever content one wished to ascribed to it, although it usually refers to Asian, African, and sometimes Latin American nations.

France has not figured to any extent in this account thus far. Although the omission can be explained by the necessity of keeping the presentation within some sort of bounds, it is nonetheless an unfortunate one. French thinkers have had considerable impact on and many of them have been clearly under the sway of the Idea that has the world in its grip. Although France has declined precipitately as a world power in this century, Frenchman have often been at the forefront of cultural developments. Indeed, France — perhaps Paris would be more accurate — has been the spiritual home of the *avant garde* in literature

439

and the arts. And that is a way of saying that much of the cultural transformation of this era has had its inception in France and has spread outward from that center. The significance of this is more easily perceived when it is understood that cultural alteration both prepares the way for the victory of the Idea and is the main object of those under the sway of the Idea.

A strong case can be made that ideology is the natural mode of French thought. Modern intellectual history provides ample evidence to support such a thesis. John Calvin tended to ideologize Christianity. Rene Descartes provided an ideology for modern science, although Francis Bacon's formula is better known. The Marquis de Sade brought forth an ideology of sadism, which furnished the kinky motif of modern revolutions.[4] Jean Jacques Rousseau constructed an ideology of democratism, and provided as well the seminal work for undergirding educationism. The fundaments of socialism first appeared in the works of an obscure Frenchman by the name of Morelly.[5] Communist thought had its French forebears, but it was, of course, Karl Marx who gave it the formulation which has now swept over much of the world. Perhaps for that reason French intellectuals have been less than satisfied with the Marxist dogmas even when they have been enamored of them. They must somehow be twisted into a Gallic framework, as witness Jean Paul Sartre's existentialism and Teilhard de Chardin's evolutionism.

Be that as it may, the Third World concept may be French in it origin. Sartre may have been the first to use the term.[6] Moreover, in the last years of the Fourth Republic, the French referred to the "center" complex of socialist parties as a "Third Force," a phrase sufficiently similar to have given rise to the other. Two components of the Third World concept are national independence and ideological eclecticism. Both components involved "nonalignment," nonalignment with either the Soviet or American camp and nonalignment with either ideology. Charles de Gaulle took the lead both in trying to revive French influence and in having France follow an independent course in foreign affairs. He was particularly concerned to shake off dependence on the United States. To that end, he promoted the development of nuclear weapons by France, and downgraded French participation in NATO. He favored, however, a continental force of European powers, which he referred to as a "Third Force."[7] By boldly following this course France set an example for Third World nations.

De Gaulle was ideologically eclectic, too. Although he was a nationalist more than anything else, he presided over a government that was more or less socialist in its animus. (None other would have been acceptable to the generality of Frenchmen.) But the strain of ideological eclecticism runs deeper than that in post-World War II French thought. There were rumblings amongst French thinkers of the decline or end of ideology. The kind of eclecticism that this portended had much earlier been formulated by Americans as pragmatism, or instrumentalism. The French semi-Marxist, Jean Paul Sartre, provided a different gloss for it in his exposition of existentialism. Sartre denied the validity of Marxian materialism. It is a species of essentialism, and since existence precedes essence, there are no such preconditioning essences. Nor is the emergence of socialism, or communism, written in the historical stars, so to speak. If emerge it does, it will be because men made it emerge and, if they do so, they must do it in terms of the situation that they find themselves in. There is no order and no particular set of circumstances which will bring it forth. Sartre stated it this way:

The revolutionary considers that he *builds* socialism, and since he has shaken off and overthrown all legal rights, he recoginzes its existence only in so far as the revolutionary class invents, wills and builds it .... It does not lie at the end of the road, life a boundary-mark; it is *the* scheme formulated by humanity. It will be what men make it; it is the outcome of the soberness with which the revolutionary envisages his action....

Thus the philosoply of revolution, transcending both idealist thinking which is bourgeois and the myth of materialism which suited the oppressed masses for a while, claims to be the philosophy of *man* in the general sense.[8]

It may appear that Sartre had opted for evolutionary, or gradualist, socialism, but by his language he denies this. He claims to be a revolutionary, which would separate him from that persuasion. He was claiming, too, to be the proponent of another way, as "third way," to socialism. Of necessity, it would be ideologiclly eclectic, for it would be a building of socialism within given situations. Some such notions went into the Third World concept.

Another prime influence on the Third World concept was India and its leader Jawaharlal Nehru. Nehru was educated in England, and while there he imbibed deeply of socialist doctrine. During the period of his indoctrination British socialists were committed to government ownership (nationalization) of all major industries. The debacle of English nationization did not turn Nehru against socialism, but it did sway him toward a more eclectic course. In any case, India was hardly in a position to follow Western models of gradualism. Nehru embarked on a course of neutrality in relations with East and West. As one history describes his position: "Much impressed though he was by Soviet economic achievements, Nehru stood forth as the most influential non-Communist voice in Asia.... Without equivocation, he declared that Marxism was an outmoded nineteenth-century creed, incapable of solving the vexing problems of India.... Nehru only tepidly fought communism outside of his homeland, and adopted the middle way of neutralism, on nonalignment, in the secular struggle between the communist bloc and ... the West."[9]

But whatever its origins, and whatever influences may have helped to shape the Third World concept, it was nonetheless grist for the mills of communism from the outset. It could be, and was, fitted into the communist dogma of imperialism. Lenin had leaned heavily on the imperialist dogma, both to justify the revolution in Russia and as the basis of a predicted forthcoming world-wide revolution. He also reinterpreted the Marxist vision of the future in terms of imperialism. Marx's prediction, according to Lenin, had been thwarted by the development of Western imperialism, and capitalism had been temporarily saved from the onslaught of a disinherited proletariat. Here is a summary statement of Lenin's position:

> Lenin's explanation for the loss of revolutionary enthusiasm among the Western workers was simple — they were no longer exploited. More accurately, an important section of the workers, the most skilled and intelligent, were no longer exploited and had become bourgeoisified. This section of the workers and the financiers joined together to exploit the backward nations of the world: the financiers thus replaced class exploitation with the exploitation of other countries. The industrial nations will never therefore be revolutionized until the backward nations are freed from the colonial powers. Beginning with Lenin, then, the focus of the Communist Revolution shifts to Asia, Africa and Latin America....
>
> The Leninist *tour de force* saved Marxian revolutionism. The class struggle then became an international struggle between two camps: on the one side the exploited, non-industrialized nations ...; on the other side the industrialized nations of the West...."[10]

The Stalinist strategy, however, did not follow this pattern with any consistency. Stalin concentrated on developing communism in one country, the Soviet Union, on fostering the development of Moscow dominated parties in all others countries, and eventually the use of the Red Army to fasten communism on Eastern Europe. Communists always carried on a verbal assault against Western imperialism, of course, but it was only after Stalin's death, and in a new context, that

Lenin's theory emerged to undergird a full-fledged strategy.

When so many colonies either broke away or were cut loose from colonial powers after World War II, the stage appeared to be set for communist expansion. Indeed, the Cominform became quite industrious in fostering guerilla warfare and other forms of incipient revolution. Things did not, however, go according to communist plan. As has already been noted, the United States intervened to take up much of the slack occasioned by the withdawal of former colonial powers, began to offer economic and military aid, and to form regional alliances around the world. The Cold War developed. The golden opportunity for communist expansion was being lost, in the main.

There was yet another problem for communism, a problem of how to appraoch these newly freed colonies. The militantly aggressive tactics of the Stalinist period were hardly calculated to win friends and influence people in these former colonies. These were the "exploited" people. To foster parties under the control of Moscow and designed to stir up revolts against their own government, however newly formed, would surely alienate these peoples. (That is not to say that the Soviet Communists were above doing all these things, but it was an ineffectual tactic and hardly a posture to be avowed.)

The Third World concept provided a convenient solution to these problems, too "convenient," one suspects, not to have been at least partially devised by the communists.

A new line about former colonies was advanced. The old colonialism was being replaced by a new colonialism, referred to as "neo-colonialism." As Thomas Molnar pointed out, "Circles which promote the slogan of 'neo-colonialism' insist, of course, that the big companies (in French Africa, in the Copper Belt, for example) exploit their host countries just as much as before independence. In fact, it is alleged that exploitation has been stepped up because there is an increasing demand for minerals by industrialized countries, and also because the companies' freedom of action in decolonized territories is no longer checked as it was in the days of an Administration representing a strong overseas government."[11] According to this view, only the communist countries, which had no private businesses, could bring about real decolonization.

In keeping with all this a new Soviet strategy took shape. One writer describes it this way:

The basic Soviet view of the less developed countries changed radically from

443

that held in the period 1948-1953.... The U.S.S.R. came to believe that in the short term, at least, countries might exist which because of their own convictions and interests chose to be aligned with neither the West nor the Communist camp.

Concomitant with the basic shift in Soviet foreign policy outlined above was the increased reliance on economic means of influencing the less developed countries. A sweeping economic offensive in the third world emerged after 1953 in the form of numerous trade and economic aid agreements....[12]

Another ascribes the change to Soviet Cold War strategy:

In the 1950's, the third-world strategy was attached to the so-called process of decolonization, and non-Communist ... regimes were enlisted in a general posture of neutralism which, while it was not particularly helpful to Communist expansion, was immensely harmful, to the strategic position and moral prestige of the West.[13]

A Soviet writer, writing in the late 1960's, made the following claims for the extent of foreign aid by the Soviet Union:

The Soviet Union began to establish extensive economic ties with Afro-Asian countries in the mid-1950's. Alongside the growing volume of ordinary export-import trade, an important role was played by technical and economic cooperation based on inter-government agreements. By 1956, such agreements had been signed with Afghanistan and India alone, where today the USSR is giving economic and technical assistance to 29 Afro-Asian countries.[14]

The granting of aid was of great symbolic ideological significance for the Soviet Union. I noted earlier that underdeveloped countries could not readily follow the gradualist model of industrialized countries. They have neither the technology to produce it nor great wealth to redistribute. The way of the West to socialism could hardly be appropriate to their circumstances. By contrast, Soviet Communists claimed that Russia had been an underdeveloped country and that communism had provided the way for its development. Foreign aid, particularly the provision of factories, constituted the best sort of proof they could offer. A scholar summed up the position this way: "The emergence of the Soviet Union as a major economic power and an additional source of capital has enabled it to present itself to the developing countries as an alternate economic model: a former economically backward country which had attained an impressively rapid rate of economic growth in a relatively short period of time." The "Soviet Union has pressed its claim that only a centrally planned and

444

controlled economy ... can provide the desired social and economic development."[15]

This Soviet aid was not, however, carried out in the simple context of the Cold War conflict between East and West. It was also a part of the mounting rivalry between the Soviet Union and Communist China. Each of these countries was contesting for dominance of communist parties in many countries, and for leadership of the communist movement in general. The Soviet shift to economic assistance occurred at about the same time that the Chinese began tentatively to offer assistance. A recent book gives a brief history of that aid in these words. "Peking has been in the aid business since 1953 ..., and to date has aided more than fifty-five countries on five continents.... China's economic aid program had increased many times in size and scope since 1953.... Recent aid promises offer further evidence. In 1970 Chinese aid nearly matched its total official aid to non-Communist countries up to that time and amounted to nearly sixty-five per cent of the total Communist bloc aid to underdeveloped countries...."[16] Among the countries China had extended aid to were Cambodia, Burma, Nepal, Laos, Ghana, Algeria, Kenya, Nigeria, Chile, and Peru.

The purpose of Chinese aid is suggested in this argument by a French Marxist: "There is really no way out for the people of the Third World in this context [imperialism and exploitation]. It is not a question whether socialism is attractive to their rulers or leading thinkers.... It is simply a matter of accepting the evidence; there *is* no other possible solution; like it or not, for them China is the great example."[17]

The Chinese credentials were advanced as being impeccable for the leadership of the Third World, in contrast, say, to those of Russia. Russia had been an independent nation (more properly, empire) before the Bolshevik Revolution, and had been little subject to "imperialistic exploitation." By contrast, China had been carved into spheres of influence in the late nineteenth century and had been the playground of "imperial" powers until the Communist takeover. Incidentally, the militant nationalism of Chinese Communists was palpable to foreigners who happened to get detained in China during the period of Chinese isolation (from 1950's into the 1970's).

Moreover, there were ugly racial overtones enunciated in the Chinese thrust to leadership of the Third World. The Russians were excluded from the Bandung Conference on the grounds that they were white.[18] The explicitness of this racism has been pointed up by Boris Meissner. He says:

445

The violence of the collision between Russian and Chinese nationalism is partly a result of racial components which lend the struggle of the two powers certain atavistic features. The Russians fear that the Chinese might succeed in playing off the various races within the communist camp against one another, thus splitting world communism into white and colored wings, with the latter having numerical predominance. Peking makes use of Communist front orgainzations such as the World Peace Council and the World Federation of Trade Unions, as well as Chinese-oriented bodies such as the Afro-Asian Solidarity Conference, as forums where they attack the policies of the Soviet hegemonial power and play off the colored peoples against the whites.[19]

Given the Communist interpretation of Western "imperial exploitation" and the hypersensitivity to race in the world since World War II, the racist connotations were virtually unavoidable. Most of the peoples in subject colonies in the twentieth century have been "colored." If colonies were devices for exploiting these people, then they were devices for exploiting the "colored races." Indeed, the Third World concept was shot through with these racial overtones. Although it has never been so explicit as absolutely to exclude countries with a preponderance of white people, such as some Latin American countries, that has nevertheless been its tendency.

Even though the Communists have tried to take full advantage of the Third World concept, it would be a mistake to view it simple as a plot to foster communist expansion. The greatest advantages, at least initially, accrued to the politicians and dictators of the Third World. Not only did communists subscribe to the notion that Western imperialism had been a system of exploitation of subject peoples but so did most Western intellectuals.[20] This gave Third World politicians ready made enemies — "Western imperialists" — something most useful to politicians, especially when the enemies are not constituents. They could appeal for the unity of their peoples against these outsiders. It also provided an explanation and an excuse for their economic backwardness. They were not to blame for their condition; they had been overcome by superior technology and exploited by Westerners.

The Third World concept was useful in many other ways to those countries which could use it. It enabled them to play off East against West. Most of these countries accepted aid from Washington, from Moscow, from Peking, or from whatever source they could get it. Since they were nonaligned, the aid they received entailed few, if any, responsibilities. Indeed, the Third World concept was, and is, an irresponsible concept. The Third World countries are not, according to the concept, responsible for the conditions which prevail there, and they

446

accept little or no responsibility for what goes on in the world. If, or, better still, when, since it is usually only a matter of time, they confiscate the private property of foreign investors, or foreigners in general, the concept justified that, too. After all, the foreigners had only been there to exploit them.

In short, the Third World concept is a most useful ploy for politicians and dictators in many parts of the world. They can shake their fists at the great world powers. They can hold out their hands for aid, threaten one side that if they do not give aid they will get it from the other, and offer little or nothing in return. Numerous small nations claim the full fruits of sovereignty, take their places among the great powers in the United Nations, work in concert with other small nations to extort concessions, and do not even pay their dues. The concept provides an apology for two-faced behavior, beggary, thievery, extortion, and irresponsibility.

But our main concern here is with the place of the Third World concept in the fame of the Idea that has the world in its grip. It is, of course, part and parcel of that Idea. It fits in most particularly as a part of the pressure for redistribution of the wealth from the haves to the have-nots, as the phrase has it, among the nations. Since the redistribution is from nation to nation, or, as in the case of the confiscation of foreign holdings, from private sources to national states, it is very much a socialist idea. Its nationalism is a means of concerting efforts within the nation behind the programs that are advanced and the oppressions they entail.

The Third World concept covertly implies, when it is not explicitly stated, that there is a third way to socialism. There is a nonideological way to socialism, an eclectic way. In short, there is a way to socialism that does not entail the dogmas either of revolutionary or evolutionary socialism. It is not a matter for wonder that anyone setting out for socialism in the last couple of decades should hanker for such a possibility. After all, Stalin had managed to thoroughly soil whatever of the Marxist dogmas had gone into Leninism-Stalinism. He had to some degree succeeded in hiding the full degradation of communist rule from the world during his reign. But he was not long dead before he was being publicly denounced by Soviet Communists. By the late 1950's, if not before, only the purblind could deny that Soviet communism was terrorism, tyranny, bureaucratic oppression, and a failure from whatever angle it could be examined save one — it did succeed in fastening totalitarian rule on the Russian and Eastern European

447

peoples. The dogmas of Marxism as they had been strained through the Soviet mesh had about as much appeal as stale bread laced with poison.

The most cherished dogma of Fabian socialism — nationalization — had proved a disaster for the English. Hitlerism had cast a pall over national socialism, at least in its racist formulation. The pale socialism of continental Europe smacked of everlasting compromises, compromises in which an increasing portion of the wealth of the citizenry was drawn into the maw of government machines, in which private industry was shackled by regulation, and in which the money in hand was declining in value because of inflation. The United States was neither much better nor much worse, and few enough recognized it as a road to socialism. In any case, gradualist socialism offered few prospects for the politicians of the Third World. They did not have the wealth to distribute, nor the patience and time to acquire it.

The Third World concept is a fraud. There is no third way to socialism. In fact, there is no way to achieve the vision of socialism, hence all socialisms are frauds, but let that go. One way is by terror and violence — that is revolutionary socialism. The other is to buy votes with the promise of goods taken from certain segments of the populace by subtle uses of force — that is democratic socialism. True, there are many possible combinations of terror and violence with populism, but Hitler had used most of them before many of the Third World dictators had reached their majority. About all that the Third World has contributed to the mix is an apologia for extorting alms from other governments.

The Third World concept is, however, fearsome testimony to the firmness of the grip the Idea now has on the world and to the decline in clear thought that has accompanied the process. More nations have been born since World War II than existed before that catastrophe. They were brought forth with proud claims of independence and bouyant cries of freedom. Yet one by one they have been dragged down the dreary by-path marked as the third way to the Valhalla of socialism, if it has been marked at all. The roll call of these nations is too long to make here; the sordid account of their petty rulers would take up too much space, their oppressions too dreary to make good newspaper fare. Even the recognition of ideologies, much less the construction of a passable one, surpasses their skill.

The Third World concept did not signify the end of ideology; it more nearly signified the reduction of ideology to obscenity. The barbarization and degradation which attends socialism produced its pale

448

reflection in the Third World. For a brief span of time, concentrated in the mid-1960's, the Third World concept captured the imagination, perhaps even the idealism, of a good many people. The Third World concept promised redemption, redemption not only for the Third World, but for the whole world.[21] There was a way other than the way of life of Europe, America, or the Soviet Union. Virtue resided in the former oppressed peoples of the world, in Africans, in Chinese, in Indians, in American Indians, and so forth. Western technology was an affliction of the world. We must go in sack cloth and ashes to learn from the gurus of the Third World the secret of life. So many young people exhorted us.

There was something exceedingly strange about all this. The young people who heralded this new dispensation in Europe and America foreswore ideology, yet carried banners proclaiming the virture of Mao Tse-tung, Ho Chi Minh, and Ché Guevera, prime ideologues, if any there were. They claimed reaches of tolerance for themselves never before conceived, but were intolerant of all disagreement. There may have been a modicum of thought which preceded their emergence as enthusiasts, but it was drowned out by their obscenities once they were underway. It is not too much to say, then, that in the hands of its youthful proponents, the Third World concept became obscenity.

Although the Third World concept no longer glitters with bright promise — indeed, it never got very far off the ground — it nonetheless had considerable impact. It sometimes served as a cover for communist regimes to be established. But, equally important, it introduced a deal of confusion into the world. Ideological lines were blurred. The theretofore clear distinction between communist and non-communist was now much harder to make. The world was not divided into two; it was divided into many. A softening process had taken place, perhaps a softening up for further stages of the development of the Idea that has the world in its grip. It contributed much to a further lessening of confidence in Western Civilization, or what remained of it. It helped to prepare the way for a different scenario, which may be no more substantial than was the Third World.

36
Coexistence, Détente, and Convergence

WHEN THE COLD WAR was at it height, it was sometimes suggested that there was a parallel between it and the religious wars of the sixteenth and seventeenth centuries. The idea behind this analogy was supposedly to put the Cold War in perspective. Those who pushed the analogy were saying, in effect, "Look, don't get so excited about this conflict. Our forebears went through just such a conflict. There was a time when men were so heated up about religious differences that they fought grisly wars with one another about them. And what do we, with the advantage of historical perspective, think of the merit of these differences? Do we think them worth fighting about? Hardly!"

There are some interesting parallels between the earlier religious wars and those of this century, more interesting even than those who have advanced the analogy have pointed out. The earlier conflicts were between Christians, people of the same basic faith. The ideological conflicts of this century are between socialists, mainly — people of the same faith. In both conflicts considerable attention was and is paid to doctrinal differences, and differences in practice have occasioned acrimony. Moreover, socialists have been as inclined toward sectarian squabbles over dogma as Christians ever were.

There is yet another parallel. Both the earlier religious wars and the twentieth century conflicts were and are contests over political power, but since this parallel is crucial, the discussion of it should wait for a bit.

Reasoning by analogy has its pitfalls, however. Where complex phenomena are involved, as in these conflicts, it is important to attend both to similarities and to differences. It is even more important to distinguish between superficial similarities which may be accidental and critical differences which may be essential. Nor is any valid historical perspective to be gained by ignoring critical differences.

It is true that Christians are generally at peace with one another today. It is also true that sectarian differences which once were battle cries hardly excite a murmer. A certain amount of convergence has even taken place amongst some Christians, but it is also the case that where some union takes place, those who oppose the union often form their own denominations. The important point to get at, however, is to understand why Christians are generally at peace with one another. It is not, as secularists may suppose, that differences in doctrine no longer matter, or that there has been a decline in religion and religious fervor. It may be the case that dogmas were more important, say, in the course of the Protestant Reformation. But this is surely only a matter of degree and is by no means universal. As to a decline in religion, there has been such a decline among intellectuals in the last century, accompanied by an impact on the intellectual climate, but this does not of itself signify a decline in religious belief but rather an intellectual narrowing of its import.

In any case, religious enthusiasm has waxed and waned several times in the period since religious differences among Christain were the occasion of any widespread conflict. This suggests to me that the degree of relilgous belief is not the key to an explanation of martial conflict over religion.

Religious differences only become an occasion for warfare when religion is linked to political power. To put it another way, conflict arises over the attempt of those who hold political power to force their beliefs on others who differ with them. Or it can arise when there is a contest between those who have differing religious persuasions over who shall exercise the power in matters of religion. The Protestant Reformation, and the Catholic Counter-Reformation, spawned wars because state and church were intertwined and because only one religion could be, or was, established. The power contest contributed much to sharply defined dogmatic positions and thus to the proliferation of denominations. (The more sharply drawn doctrinal positions are, the

451

less the likelihood of general agreement. But doctrines must be sharply defined if adherence to them is to be enforced by law.) The way to religious peace is to deny to any religion the power to force its doctrines on others or to establish its religion over them. This idea is found in the doctrine of the separation of church and state.

The matter runs deeper than this, however. There is a critical and essential difference between Christianity and modern socialism. At bottom, Christianity is not a power theory. As was earlier affirmed, socialism — whether revolutionary or evolutionary — is a power theory. But let us consider the case of Christianity first. It has already been pointed out that when Jesus went into the wilderness and was tempted that he rejected the vision of an earthly kingdom or empire. That is, He rejected the use of force to attain His ends. He did so again, in another way, just before His trial and crucifixion. When Judas betrayed Jesus and the crowd laid hands on Him, this event occurred:

And behold, one of them which were with Jesus stretched out his hand, and drew his sword, and struck a servant of the high priest's, and smote off his ear.
Then said Jesus unto him, Put up again thy sword into his place: for all they that take the sword shall perish by the sword. [Matthew 26:51-52.]

It should be made clear, however, that these remarks were made in connection with the attainment of Jesus' ends. He goes on to say that He could have legions of angels to defend him, if He would but ask. "but how then shall the scriptures be fulfilled, and thus it must be." (Matthew 26:54).

Christianity is not a power theory. Jesus rejected the use of force to achieve His purposes. The methods He employed were concern, love, healing, sacrifice, attraction, and persuasion. Those who would follow Him, He bade to take up, *not* their swords, but the *cross* (i.e., the way of sacrifice). What Jesus seeks cannot be attained by force. Men cannot be made to believe. They cannot be forced to have a change in which they comprehend the superior reality of spirit. The sword is an instrument of death, not of life, and He said that He came to bring life.

None of this is said to deny the obvious, namely, that many of those who have professed to be His followers have taken up the sword with the avowed purpose of defending or advancing Christianity. They have often enough intertwined religion with government. They have established churches by law. They have used the force of government to attempt to compel many things that were said to be in keeping with Christianity. But they have not done so with the authority of Jesus; they have done so because they were impatient, because they were weak, because they were wilfull, because they substituted their wills for the will of Him they claimed to follow. They have even beset one another in violent and destructive wars. The carnage of the religious wars, and especially of the Thirty Years' War, was great. They took up the sword, and many perished by it. That prophecy was fulfilled, not for the first time and, sadly enough, not for the last, for it has lately come to pass once again in Ireland.

Christianity does not require the use of force. On the contrary, Christianity cannot be advanced by force. We have it on good authority that if God willed to use force He could call forth such force as none could resist Him. But He does it not, for it is foreign to His nature and to His purpose. He wills peace, harmony, love, and that men should be at one with Him. These ends *cannot* be attained by force. To put it philosophically, in essence Christianity is not a power thoery. When this guise has been forced upon it, it has been accidental and attributable to the weakness of men.

Socialism *is* a power theory. In essence, it is nothing but a power theory. Its affinity for the state is as near absolute as anything can be in this world. The further it goes toward its goal the more absolute its reliance on the state. None of this is accidental. It follows inexorably from the professed goal and from the complex of hatreds which animate it. The moment socialists abandon the state as the instrument for the achievement of their purposes they cease to be socialists, and socialism is no more.

Socialist thinkers did not, we may believe, consciously set out to contrive a scheme to bring about such a state of affairs. Many of them did not even embrace the state willingly, and most have professed reluctance. For Marx, the state was to be a temporary expedient, something to be used temporarily until its purpose had been achieved and it could wither away. Gradualists have labored mightily to hide the mailed fist of the state behind the velvet glove of democracy.

What socialists contrived, whether they sought to do so or not, was a religion, or a substitute for religion. It was a religion of man, and it was a manmade religion. The appeal of the idea that has the world in its grip is fundamentally religious. It has within it elements derived from traditional religions, but in it they become earthbound and temporally oriented. The promise of the idea is that all things shall be made right here on earth and that man shall be finally liberated. The tacit promise is of an end to all restraint and hence of an end to government and the

453

use of force upon people. Man's inhumanity to man, a favorite phrase of those enlivened by the Idea, will cease.

That the application of this Idea with the avowed purpose of fulfilling the promises leads to statism, to terror, to violence, to the ubiquitous use of the force of the state has been the burden of this work to show. But why should it do so? Indeed, why must it do so? Because of the premises which underlie socialism. Society is rended and sundered by a fundamental disharmony. The disharmony results from man's pursuit of his own self-interest, socialists claim. This, they say, turns man against man, defeats the common good, results in pervasive injustices, and is the occasion for the use of force. The received social institutions support and reinforce the pursuit of self-interest. The disharmony is thereby istitutionalized.

In theory, a religion of humanity could change all this. There are, here and there, devotees of such a faith. And socialists in general subscribe to its tenets. But the Idea that has the world in its grip is not the religion of humanity. Its religion is statism. The reasons for this may not be apparent, but they can be surmised. There are two main ones, I think.

The first of these is the inadequacy of the religion of humanity as a religion. It is a pallid thing. It is the worship of an abstraction which can never be personified. That is, man in the abstract, or humanity in the abstract, can be an object of veneration only so long as it does not entail actual men. Actual men have faults, something which most of us discover sooner or later, and are therefore not fit subjects for worship. A religion with wide appeal must have both personification and some sort of transcendance, or, at least, unquestioned purity. Abstraction is not transcendance, and actual men lack purity.

The other need of socialism as a religion was a means or instrument for altering social institutions and trnasforming man. By their focus on man and this world, they denied a transcendant being, thereby requiring that their instrument be immanent. The dimensions of the problem made the choice of the state as the instrument inevitable. Only something with power over the whole could conceivably achieve the alterations and transformations involved.

State is the crucial term here. Socialists are not much given to making the distinction, and they are quite unlikely to proclaim themselves as state worshippers, but there is a crucial distinction between the state and government. The worship of government is attended by the same difficulty as the worship of humanity. The difficulty is that actual governments have flaws, or rather the men who man them do. The state is an abstraction; it is pure; it can even be an ideal. Power vested in the state cannot be misplaced, for it is the natural repository of all power over a given territory. Sovereignty, absolute sovereignty, is its prerogative, its reason for being. The state, in socialist underlying conception, is the rightful instrument of "the people," and so far as it acts for the people, whatever power is exercised is legitimate. (Communists sometimes say "proletariat" rather than "people," but for them the proletariat is the people.) A constant struggle goes on to bring the government up to the level of the state, i.e., to make it a perfect instrument of the people. What prevents it from being so is the persistence of "the class enemy," as communists put it, or of conservatives, reactionaries, business interests, or "the vested interests," in gradualist countries. "Fascism," which is the socialist conceptual personification of all the evil forces, is ever lurking around the corner ready to seize and misuse the power of the state.

When the class enemy has finally been eradicated, when the last fascist has been rounded up, when the vested interests are at last divested of their power and influence, then government can be raised to the level of the state. The people will be identical with government, and government and state will merge. When this state of affairs comes about, the use of force will be a redundancy. There could be no occasion for the use of force, for the will of the governors could be no different from the will of the people. Communists have usually declared that this state of affairs will shortly come about. Gradualists foresee a much more extended struggle, with no culmination now in sight. In any case, it is a struggle for power, for the monopolization of all power by the people.

This is the mystic vision of socialism. So far as it is a religion, it is a religion of state worship. And that turns out to be a worship of power. The whole world is caught in the vise-like grip of an Idea which propels it toward the struggle toward power. The Idea promises beatitude; it leads to destruction, to tyranny, to murder, to rapine, to suicide. The Idea requires the subordination of the individual to the state. This requirement is no less than the death of the ego or the end of the individual self. It is possible to commit suicide, of course, without going through the whole vast process of lengthy evolution, massive revolution, the creation of a vast state mechanism, and so on. The Jones cult showed the way in the horrifying mass suicide-murder at Jonestown, Guayana, in late 1978. Self-immolation, the tacit goal of socialism, can be achieved directly by individuals, cults, and small groups. But that is a "cop out," so to speak, for it must be done on a world wide scale.

What has all this to do with coexistence, with détente, and with

455

convergence? It has everything to do with them. Can East and West coexist? Can peace be attained by a policy of détente? Will communism and gradualist socialism eventually converge? There is no way to answer these questions definitively, of course, for they entail events and developments that have not yet taken place and may never. There is a way to understand, however, what is involved in peaceful coexistence, détente, and convergence. It is through understanding the idea that impels the developments. Trying to make heads or tails of these events with historical data in the absence of the ideological framework is akin to trying to put the pieces of a puzzle together without a picture of the completed puzzle before you. Explanations shift with changing leaders and changing policies, and no clear pattern emerges. The Chinese and Russians squabble over the meaning of coexistence. Soviet leaders hint at the possibility of convergence. Is détente anything more than the one step backward of the old Stalinist formula of two steps forward and one step back?

All these things begin to come into focus when we perceive that socialism is a power theory. Communism is a theory of coming to power and extending and holding it by way of revolution. Evolutionary socialism is a theory of coming to power and extending it gradually by means that only subtly alter the received framework. Coexistence, détente, and the possibility of convergence are *tactics* in the struggle for power. Peaceful coexistence and détente are communist tactics for moderating the conflict and allowing time and room for further communist expansion to take place. Convergence is not an avowed policy of the communists, and it cannot be so long as and to the extent they are wedded to the idea of the necessity of revolution. Convergence is the dream, however, of many Western intellectuals. Every accord between East and West arouses hope that convergence is coming. It may well be a Communist tactic to keep that hope alive.

Socialism is not merely a power theory; it is a power theory animated by a mystic religion. It has a world vision. That vision is of the whole world under a single power, of every organization and every individual subordinated to that power. Only then, it is believed, can the vision of socialism become an actuality. So long as there is one independent power in the world, the peace, i.e., socialism, is threatened. I understand this to mean that coexistence can never be more than a temporary policy. In like manner, détente can never be more than a temporary policy. Thus far, history bears this out. Coexistence and détente are largely illusions of Western intellectuals and the governments under their sway.

456

Can communism not change? It depends upon what is meant. If it is a question of tactics, there is no doubt that communism can, has, and does change. Communist tactics differ considerably from one country to another. Chinese and Cuban communism belong to the same genus, but they are quite different national species. Moreover, the tactics change greatly from time to time and under different leaders in the same country. Many of Stalin's tactics differed greatly from those of Lenin, and Khrushchev disavowed many of Stalin's tactics. Stalin fostered militant antifascist tactics in the Comintern for most of the 1930's, then entered into a pact with the Nazis. Communists have sometimes formed political parties, or semblances of them, and had candidates run for office in lands where they were not in power. At other times, they have refused to run for office on the grounds that such elections were a bourgeois trap. Tactics are but accidents, philosophically speaking, something to be changed according to the circumstances.

But could communism not change in essence? Those who believe in this possibility have not fronted what is involved. What is communism in essence? Communism is power, to restate the position. It is power wedded to a mystic vision of world dominion. Or, mysticism or not, it is power thrusting to the monopoly of all power in the world. Any essential change within communism would necessarily entail yielding up the monopoly of power which has been substantially attained wherever a Communist system prevails. If one-party rule were relinquished so that two or more real parties could compete, the monopoly of power would be gone. Freedom of speech and freedom of the press entail public debate in which appeals by those who differ are directed toward the populace. They would inevitably divide the populace and undercut the monopoly of power. The same goes for freedom of religion and any significant amount of private property.

Communist systems have that toward which all socialism tends, namely, a monopoly of power. Why would Communists give it up? Better still, what would happen if they did? Communism without a monopoly of power is only a fantasy. It is like an electrical appliance without electricity; it is inoperative. Communism without a monopoly of power is not communism. It would be as if the revolution had not occurred. Communism without a monopoly of power would be, at most, another variety of evolutionary socialism. But evolving toward what? Evolving toward the monopoly of all power, something which Communists had already attained in their own countries.

There is another reason why communism cannot change, or perhaps it is only the logical extension of the reasons given above. *All socialism is braced to communism!* The Idea that has the world in its grip finds its culmination in communism, in the monopoly of all power in the state. All socialist roads lead to Moscow, to Peking, to Havana, or to wherever a Communist regime is established. Socialist intellectuals are drawn to these centers as surely as a moth is drawn to a flame. Much of the intellectual history of the twentieth century, or at least the history of intellectuals, could be written about these pilgrimages to the New Rome. It is not knowledge that draws them there, nor exactly the quest for it. It is a feeling, a feeling that they will find there the concrete reality toward which they yearn. Whether they do so depends upon the degree to which they cooperate with their hosts by succumbing to the illusions presented for their edification.

If communism should fall — that is, lose power everywhere — the whole structure of socialism must crumble with it. It would happen because there would no longer be a concrete reality to sustain socialism. Socialists would discover that they were leaning into thin air. The measures of gradualists would be proposals to be treated on their own merits, for they would have no vision behind them. Remove the religious mystic vision from socialism, and its proposals become transparent crackpot schemes. Communism has often enough been an embarrassment to Western socialists, of course. Communists even commit the unpardonable sin sometimes, persecution of intellectuals. But it is the embarrassment which children feel about the behavior of their parents. Remove the parents, and the family disintegrates. Remove the Communist parents of socialism and the family of socialism will disintegrate. Socialism was only a fantasy until World War I. It took on flesh and blood with the Bolshevik Revolution. With the Nazi revolution it took place in yet another guise. With the defeat of the Nazis and their Fascist allies, revolutionary socialism survived only in its communist manifestation, and it is in that manifestation of it that we may know it best today.

Braces work both ways, however. To say that evolutionary socialism is braced to communism is but another way of describing the dependence of communism on the non-communist world. The dependence of evolutionary socialism on communism is largely spiritual. It is the religious ingredient — the vision of a forward-marching, triumphant world socialism riding the wave of History — in communism that is necessary to sustain evolutionary socialism and propel it onward. By contrast, the dependence of communism upon the non-communist world is political and economic. Politically, the non-

458

communist world provides the stamp of legitimacy to the communist powers. By treating them as regular governments: by according diplomatic recognition, by making treaties and agreements, by carrying on various sorts of intercourse, non-communist powers say, in effect, to the captive peoples in communist countries, "Yours is a legitimate government. It rightfully imposes its will upon you, for it is entitled to all the prerogatives of a government." More, by recognizing the legitimacy of the regimes, it tends to countenance whatever communist governments do to their people as being their business since such matters involve internal affairs.

Communism is a vastly counterproductive system economically. Its primary aim of exercising power and extending that power over the peoples of the world makes it a counterproductive system. It is not that the rulers of communist countries would not like to have economic production and efficiency; it is rather that the repression entailed in the communist effort makes it impossible to achieve. The freedom to innovate is largely taken away, and the rewards for producing are arbitrary and insufficient to spur production. Hence, the relics of freedom in the non-communist world provide invaluable aid to communism. Communists depend largely on the non-communist world for inventions, for technological innovations, and for the fruits of scientific progress. Grain shipments from the West have helped much in staving off famine in communist countries in recent years. Communist rulers lust after Western machinery as a lecher does a comely maiden. Take away the West, and the retrogressive character of communist economies would be even more transparent.

These braces should be conceived as temporary, however. When a building is completed the temporary braces are removed. Communist dependence on the West is always conceived as an expedient matter by communists. In like manner, the dependence of Western intellectuals upon communism is necessary only so long as socialism has not been achieved at home. In short, the mutual dependence is temporary when viewed from either perspective.

The greatest threat to peace at the present time, such peace as there may be, is aggressive, belligerent, and expansive communism. Gradualist socialist countries do not pose any great threat at this time. They are most likely to disturb the peace by resisting the spread of communism. But the prospect of that has lessened in recent years. The United States does not appear to have the will to resist communist expansion now. Indeed, resistance was always hemmed in by such subtle niceties that it was always far from effective. So far as other highly developed industrial nations are concerned, their will to resist communism has never been strong.

That evolutionary socialists are just naturally peace loving people, or that they are not power bent, does not follow. It is rather that each gradualist socialist country has a domestic power problem. Communists usually solve their domestic power problem shortly after coming to power. They concentrate all power, subdue all organizations, and imprison or kill such opponents of the regime as can be discovered or imagined. Ordinarily, it takes only a few years to do this. Then, the Communist thrust for power shifts outward upon the world. Gradualists, by contrast, are unwilling or unable to grasp all power over the domestic population. (They would cease to be gradualists if they did.) Thus, their power struggle continues domestically; they do not have to look outward in their quest for additional power. Gaining and consolidating power over their own people remains a problem large enough to occupy most of their attention.

The United States has been a partial exception to this rule. The presidential system of government, with the president in charge of the conduct of foreign affairs and in command of the armed forces offers power incentives for foreign involvements. That is, presidential power tends to increase as foreign affairs become more important. This provides the basis for an outward thrust to American power. However, intellectuals and the media, both domestic and foreign, appear finally to have convinced our presidents that they are not to extend their powers by way of resistance to communism. There is a way, however, to get their accolades; it is to reach accords with communist countries. Presidents Nixon, Ford, and Carter appear to have learned this lesson well. Congress has cooperated by circumscribing the presidential instruments for resisting communism: the military, the FBI, and the CIA.

It is conceivable that there could be convergence between East and West. Evolutionary and revolutionary socialism have common goals — the concerting of all human effort, the removing of all centers of opposition to it, and the use of collectivist means. They both sanction, in practice, the vesting of the state with increasing power. It is plausible to suppose that as the West becomes more and more statist, if indeed it does, it would merge with the East.

Convergence is, however, a dream, and a hope only of Western intellectuals and the politicians under their sway. There is no hard evidence that communists would converge with gradualists. A deeper look suggests how unlikely this is. Total power can be joined to partial power only by either totalizing all power or reducing the total power. Thus far, all the historical evidence that can be brought to bear on the question leads to the conclusion that convergence with communism is submission to communism. That is what happened in Poland, in Hungary, in Czechoslovakia, in Bulgaria, in East Germany, in Vietnam, in Cambodia, and so on. Any survival of contending parties as communists move to take power is only temporary.

In any case, it is not possible at present to converge with communism, per se. Communism is now divided. There are communist powers independent of one another. If convergence with communism were possible it would only be possible to converge with one or another communist nation or empire.

Indeed, the Cold War appears to have taken a turn. As this is being written, a submerged conflict has been taking place over Cambodia, a conflict between the Soviet Union which supports the Vietnamese invaders, and Red China which has been supporting another Cambodian government. The more pertinent question now seems to be not whether East and West can coexist or will converge but whether independent Communist powers can coexist with one another or not, and whether they can converge or not.

We cannot know what will actually happen in this newer contest, of course. What we do know is that the Idea that has the world in its grip is a mystic vision of the eventual concentration of all power into one world power. Communism is the most virulent embodiment of the Idea. The existence of more than one revolutionary socialist power is more intolerable to communism than the existence of a West that has not been assimilated. The expansion of communism has taken on a new dimension and a new urgency. It is impelled by the quest for communist allies in the struggle over which will be the power center of communism. Terror and violence, the established communist tactic, will probably be stepped up, as one center of communism attempts to overawe and intimidate the other.

The religious wars of the sixteenth and seventeenth centuries suggest an even more fearful prospect. The religious wars that erupted between Protestant and Catholic lands had been preceded by a more desultory religious war, a centuries-long conflict between Christian Europe and Islam. Although the parallel is not exact, this conflict can be likened to that between evolutionary and revolutionary socialism. The contest

461

between communist powers has the potentiality of a full-fledged religious war, such as the Thirty Years' War in Europe. No war can equal the fury of that between peoples of the same faith divided against one another. If history repeats itself, the world may be in for a horrendous and catyclysmic conflict. Be that as it may, it is to the conquest of the individual that has already occurred or is taking place that we must turn. The world conflicts of socialism are but a reflex on a grand scale of the determination imbedded in the idea to crush all independence.

Book VIII

The Individual

37
Victim of the Idea

There's only one general feeling at Westminster [the British Parliament]. That independence must be stamped out at all costs.... The policymakers in all three parties are in complete agreement on that.[1]

THE THRUST OF the Idea that has the world in its grip is to take away the independence of the individual. This thrust inheres in the Idea as it is formulated here as well as in the socialist way of looking at conditions which were supposed to be remedied. The formulation of the Idea being used here is that the aim is to concert all human efforts for the common good. The only direct way to achieve this aim is to make the individual into a cog in a vast machine, to make the efforts of each individual coordinate with those of the whole human race. Such a coordination is only possible when individual independence no longer exists or is no longer capable of action.

The animus of the idea runs deeper than this. It is, as has been stated before, to root out the penchant of the individual to pursue his own self-interest. It is a religious, or, at least, quasi-religious, aim at bottom. In the socialist view, man's oroginal sin is the pursuit of self-interest. It is, they think, the source of all the ills in the world. That is not quite how Jean Jacques Rousseau, the godfather of socialism, put it. (This is not to say that Rousseau was a socialist, but he set forth some of the basic

465

conceptions which went into it.) He claimed that man was basically good and had been corrupted by his institutions. Critics of Rousseau have pointed out that there is a logical fallacy in his reasoning. How, they ask, could man who is basically good, build bad institutions?

Whatever the case may have been with Rousseau, there is an unstated premise in socialism. The premise can be elaborated this way. Man has potentialities for both good and evil. One of his potentialities is for the pursuit of self-interest without regard to the general good. Institutions were devised, such as those protecting private property, which support and license the pursuit of self-interest. These institutions deform man, socialists claim, and Marx held that man would only finally be freed when the individual no longer pursued his own good but rather that of all. The harmony that would result would be a great release from the tension produced by contentions born of each seeking his own.

All efforts to eradicate man's pursuit of self-interest have been to no avail. The greater the effort to erase it, the more determinedly do men pursue their self-interest as they conceive it. There is abundant evidence that even when the most drastic efforts have been made to remove the opportunity for the pursuit of self-interest, in slave labor or concentration camps, for example, men continue to do so, even if it is to the detriment of fellow prisoners. When man is bereft of all else — wealth, family, position, religion, and the amenities of society — he pursues self-interest as long as any will remains in him.

There is reason for this. The denial of the right to pursue self-interest is the denial of the right to life. Our very survival hinges regularly on a lively interest in self. From the most primitive savage to the most urbane civilized man this has been true. Nor could it be otherwise. Each individual needs to be aware of and take the necessary steps to avoid the dangers that threaten him. He must either see to his bodily needs or it must be done for him. He must be constantly wary of things about him that can do him harm: fire which can burn him, water in which he may drown, high places from which he may fall, objects that may fall on him, and a thousand and one other dangers. He must be on the lookout for ways to provision himself and be on guard lest his provisions be taken from him.

None of this is meant to imply that the individual is alone in his effort to survive, though he may sometimes in some ways be. Ordinarily, though, he may have help from others and render assistance in return. Society is founded upon mutual exchange and aid. It is rather to affirm that the individual pursuit of self-interest is as deeply imbedded in his

466

nature as the will to survive, and necessarily so. There is no need to suppose that it is man's only motive, or always his predominant one. Socialists to the contrary notwithstanding the opposite motive from that of the pursuit of self-interest is not the pursuit of the common good; it is the pursuit of self-destruction.

Socialism does not succeed, then, in eradicating the individual's penchant for pursuing his self-interest. It can, at most, induce him to conceal it by making hypocritical claims about the motives behind his acts. Socialism does not do what it cannot do; it does instead what it can. It does not root out self-interest; instead, it reduces and places formidable obstacles in the way of individual independence. In contrast to the pursuit of self-interest, individual independence is not a trait stemming from the nature of things; it is acquired. The assault upon independence is the way to making the individual a cog in a giant wheel which socialists call society.

Socialists use two devices mainly both to take away and undermine the independence of the individual and to instrument him as a cog in their wheel. They are *organization* and *numbers*. The most basic organization used is government, but all organizations are utilized to the extent that they can be. The secret police in Russia are referred to as "the organs." This is most appropriate nomenclature for them. They represent organization in its most completely diabolical embodiment. They are a secret society, in effect, empowered by the rulers to use whatever means are necessary upon the populace to bring it to heel. Communists use all organizations to this end, some more directly than others, but all of them in some way. Gradualists tend to interpenetrate all organizations and to make them instruments of government power.

Socialists attempt to reduce the individual to a number, to encompass him within a framework of one among many, and to use the weight of numbers to bring him into line. Communists sometimes refer to this as the "dictatorship of the proletariat." Gradualists refer to it as democracy. (Communists do also, particularly for international consumption, but they use other terms as well, as already indicated.) However, there are so many facets to this reduction of the individual to a number that it will have a separate discussion later.

Independence is essential to individual freedom and responsibility. Freedom without the independence to choose and act is a contradiction in terms, a notion without content. In like manner, the individual cannot logically be held responsible for acts not freely and independently done, nor can he assume his responsibilities without a measure of

467

independence. As a practical matter, freedom consists of the right of the individual to dispose of his own energies, employ his faculties, use his own resources — that is manage his own affairs — for his own good and constructive purposes. Responsibility entails both attending to those obligations which arise from his situation and taking the consequences of his acts. Socialism victimizes the individual by its continuing assault upon his independence. Tacitly, socialism promises freedom without responsibility; in fact, it takes away the means — individual independence — for exercising either.

Most of us are, I suspect, ambivalent in our attitude toward individual independence. If we concede that it is a virtue, it is one more complacently contemplated in the abstract than endured in the flesh. That child has an independent streak in him, we say, and it is not apt to be intended as a compliment to the parents. The independence of others sets unwanted bounds and limits to our control over them. We are apt to be aggravated, if not outright frustrated, if these limits to our control are flaunted.

A case can be made that self-centeredness is the Original Sin, but my candidate is the desire to control others. In any case, it happens that what we may condemn as self-centeredness is largely benign until the self reaches out to take what belongs to someone else or extend its control over them. The desire to control others has some foundation in the necessities of family and social life. Parents must exercise control over their children. Teachers, acting *in loco parentis,* must do so as well. All social activity presupposes some degree of order which sometimes requires control. It could be said, then, the necessity for some restraint and control arises from man's social condition. It is in order to accept it and, when necessary, to employ it. It may be that this engenders in us a desire to exercise control over others. Whatever the case, it is a common human failing which, when recognized as such, may be tolerable.

That is not how the matter stands in socialism. Socialism authorizes, licenses, and gives the stamp of legitimacy to this bent to control others. It bids men to form collectives and use force to bend others to their will. It is virtuous so to do; it is democratic. The bent to control others becomes a virus of the will. The prospect which socialism holds out is dominion over man, to finally have his despised independence obliterated and to have him subservient to organization. The appeal of socialism is to the worst that is in us, the desire to control others and make them subservient to our will. Socialist ideology does not, of course, focus upon these methods; it is an extended apology for the necessity for collective action.

468

Our main task here, however, is to grasp how the individual is being controlled and victimized by organizations, how these undercut his independence. There are difficulties in the way of doing this fairly, however. Socialists neither invented the desire to control nor the use of organizations to control people. Organizations have been used in many ways throughout history to sap the independence of individuals and control them. To all appearances, the seeking of salvation through organization is by no means an exclusively socialist trait. Socialists are the modern champions of government as the means to cure our ills, but the Idea that has the world in its grip is broader than that. It is the notion of concerting all human efforts, an idea which finds its most explicit expression in socialism but has the world more firmly in its grip by way of the veneration of organization. It is my belief that we can only loosen the grip of the idea when we are ready to put organizations, all organizations, in their place. After all, if organizations are the way, then logic does lie with socialism, for that doctrine follows the premise to its logical conclusion. In order to grasp the impact of organization it is important to understand how organization, as such, tends to confine the individual and sap his independence. That is not to say that organizations should be, or could be, dispensed with but rather contained and limited.

Modern ideological contentions have confused the issue almost beyond hope of unscrambling it. Socialists have focused their attention on business organizations and have ascribed great ills to business activities. Opponents of socialism have focused their attention largely upon the dangers of government and its threat to liberty. Both have tended to ignore, in their polemics, a crucial congruity between industrial organization and governmental organization. Namely, they have ignored how both these have the effect of undermining the independence of the individual. Socialists have sometimes seen well enough how business did this, indeed, have exaggeratd it. Opponents of socialism have shown how government intervention and government ownership undercut the individual. But neither side has cut through this to the point where the centrality of organization was exposed.

What I am getting at is this. The congruity between industrial organization and socialism has hardly been noticed, and when it has, it has been stuffed into ideological bags which conceal its significance. This has kept from us the possibility of a much better understanding both of socialism and the business motif. It has sometimes been noticed that businessmen do not oppose socialism very vigorously. We are all beguiled by Marx, of course, who portrayed the capitalist as the deadly

469

enemy of socialism. And here and there and from time to time a businessman surfaces who gives substance to the Marxist notion. Undoubtedly, the generality of businessmen are put off by socialist rhetoric; their feelings may even be hurt that their motives should be so misconstrued. Nor are socialists taken with the rhetoric of businessmen, as a general proposition. But the enmity never seems to go much beyond the rhetoric so far as businessmen are concerned. If businessmen have ever anywhere risen up in determined opposition to socialism, it has escaped the attention of the present writer.

There are many possible explanations for this. It may be in error to conceive of businessmen as a class. While they may have common interests, they are usually in competition with one another both for workers and for customers. Then, too, they are businessmen, not politicians or warriors. Where gradualist socialism is concerned, they often conclude that the smart thing to do is not to contend with government but rather get such advantages as can be had from working with it. Businessmen can often be bought by government largess, and are. Like the rest of us they are no better than they ought to be.

But then there are the congruities between "business" and socialism. Four, at least, come to mind. First, modern industrial organization and socialism arose more or less simultaneously in the nineteenth century. This might be thought to be accidental were it not for the other congruities. Second, the factory system became the model for economic organization, to socialist thinkers. This point will be more fully made below. Third, the entrepreneur paved the way for the conception of concerting all effort by organization. So far as his vision extended to nations and the world, he conceived of the idea of concerting all efforts under one head, at least in his line of business. Fourthly, as business production grew, the entrepreneur tended to become utopian. This utopian bent is nowhere better viewed than in contemporary advertising where the euphoria that will supposedly result from using products can have no other locus than in utopia. It is my contention, then, that industrialization provided significant modes, models, and visions for socialism. Socialism is, to put it metaphorically, the errant child of what Marx called capitalism. The businssman is unlikely to be greatly appalled by the loss of individual independence entailed in socialism, for he was about the business of reducing that independence long before socialists ever came to power.

To see how this happened it will be helpful to review a little of the history of the rise of the factory system. The factory system probably had forerunners in mines and mills, but it took definite and distinct form in the textile industry in England in the late eighteenth and early nineteenth centuries. From there it spread to other countries.

The crucial thing that happened was the concentration of production in central locations, in factories. Theretofore, most textile manufacturing had gone on in homes, and if it was done for sale, it was mostly handled in what was called the "putting out" system. "Factors" put out raw materials to workers in their homes, and the yarn or other products were then picked up from time to time. The workers were what we would call self-employed, providing their own simple equipment and housing (capital), doing the work themselves, and being paid on the basis of the quantity they produced. A critical change occurred when production was moved into factories.

Why production was moved into factories is not difficult to explain. There was a series of inventions — the spinning jenny, the "mule," and an assortment of other devices. Not only was much of this equipment larger and more expensive than earlier equipment but what was even more crucial, much of it required a source of power, other than the worker, to turn it. Falling water provided the power for early textile factories, and it was the development of this power source which made the concentration of work in factories necessary.

Much has been written about the harshness of conditions in these early factories, of small children chained to machines working from dawn to dusk, of pallid faces rarely touched by the sun, of girls for whom the flower of youth was nipped in the bud by unremitting toil, of young-old men bent to the shapes required for tending the machines. There may be some exaggeration in some accounts, but surely the descriptions are substantially correct. It is in point, too, to pause to pay tribute to reformers and socialists who, seeing such conditions, were appalled by them. Their hearts were in the right place even when their heads were screwed on wrong. The man who can harden his heart, lift his skirts, and pass by unconcerned is exceedingly short on compassion for fellow human beings.

The factory system was a retrogressive development. The failure to recognize this — though some early socialists did — has wrought havoc in the world ever since. It was a retrogressive development because those who went into it could no longer manage their own affairs in their work. It was retrogressive because there was a dramatic loss of independence in their work for those who went into it. It was retrogressive because capital was used much more extensively

471

thereafter to control men as well as things. It was retrogressive because it subjected men to the exigencies of machines, which is another way of saying that it made labor subject to capital. It was retrogressive because, far from utilizing the full potentialities of a man, it utilized only that portion which could make the operation of equipment efficient. It was retrogressive, above all, because it fastened upon the world the notion that progress is attained by the ever tighter organization of men. The veneration of organization has now become well nigh universal.

The factory system was retrogressive because it ran counter to the great liberating movement which had been going on in England and, to a lesser extent, elsewhere for a considerable while. In agriculture, great headway had been made in separating ownership of property from control over people. Serfdom, which tied the peasant to the soil and made service to the owner of the estate obligatory, had been abolished. Before long, indeed, serfdom and slavery would be abolished in all lands where Western and Christian influence was strong. New arrangements had been devised for farming land which left the tenant increasingly on his own to manage his own work affairs; the only thing he owed the landlord was a portion of the product.

In the light of this development, the factory system was a portentious step backward in human arrangements. It fatefully linked the ownership of capital to control over workers. The factory system organized the workers. (We are accustomed to describing labor unions as "organized labor", but we see here that labor was first organized and controlled by the factory managers.) It prescribed when they would come to work, how long they would work, what tasks they would perform, how the tasks were to be performed, and, in the early stages of the factory system, tended to extend the control over the worker to his whole life. Villages were built around the factories, and workers were often required to live in these houses. In any case, there was usually little or no alternative housing available. There was often a company store, company police , and company surveillance of the morals of the worker.

Some utilitarians have declared that work is a disutility. That proposition should not go unchallenged. Let it be granted that there are ardors connected with work which we would prefer oftimes to avoid. Grant, too, that there are often conditions surrounding the work which make it unpleasant. But work itself is not a disutility; that is a conclusion drawn from the pleasure-pain principle, not from life. Through work we not only provide for ourselves and our own but also realize ourselves, fulfill our potentials, have much of our vital kinship with other men,

472

and become fully useful and meaningful human beings. It is in work, whether we call it that or not, that we develop our intellects, solve problems, take on the challenges that life holds. To regard work as merely onerous is to reduce man to a mere sensual creature which there is bountiful evidence that he is not.

It may well be that the factory system makes work a disutility, or very nearly so. But it does so mainly by reducing man to a virtual disutility. The factory system divests work of all but its most rudimentary meaning, the providing of a livelihood. It reduces man's connection to his work to the wage he receives. The wage is the price paid to submit himself to the requirements of a machine as decided by the owners. What is wanted is not the full services of a man — his intellect, his ingenuity, the full range of his skills, his best efforts according to his best judgment — but only his time and such effort as may be required to tend machines.

The factory system was a great success, or so it appeared. Goods poured forth from it in such quantity as had never before been seen. Nor was it long before these goods were being sought and enjoyed by people from every walk of life. To what should this success be attributed? This was, and is, a question of great importance, one which needs the most careful pondering and analysis. Was it the factory system itself? That, I think, is what most people have thought, when they have thought about it. Indeed, men have been enflamed in the modern world with what could be accomplished by organizing and controlling men. We cannot grasp the Idea that has the world in its grip until we grasp that. The factory system is the model for the notion that by integrating the undertaking and regimenting men in organizations great wonders can be accomplished.

It is a chimera. The factory system was a historical accident. The initial inventions were made at a time when falling water was the only considerable power system available. Thus, places for housing the machines had to be built adjacent to the water supply. But there was something else of great moment. The principle of separating the ownership of property from control over people was incompletely realized. Servants were then being widely employed for wages. Farm workers were also sometimes hired for wages. Indentured servitude was still common. It was a widespread practice for fathers to hire out their children or even to sell them into indentured servitude. The early factories used children and women mostly. Given the attitudes of the time about the subordinate position of children and women, it would have been strange if the factory masters had done other than asserted control over them.

In any case, the great increase in production was not due to the factory system but to the use of machines and power from falling water or, in time, steam engines. The organization of workers is inessential to production. The work force does not need integration ordinarily; only the product requires some steps in its making, shipping, and sale. Not only is it wasteful to manage and organize workers, as well as being an insult to them, it is counterproductive to harness them in a system which prohibits them using their full energies and abilities. Leonard Read has often made the point that the great weakness of communism is that it utilizes only the intelligence of one or a few men rather than that of the generality of men. The point is well taken, but it applies to the factory system also, and, beyond that, to organizations in general. The fact that men have consented to work does not alter the fact that it employs them in ways so as to deny their potentialities, is thus wasteful, and probably counterproductive.

The ownership of property — capital, equipment, buildings, or whatever — does not by nature confer any right to control men. It is his business, we say however, and he can run it as he pleases. So it may be, but no man is another man's business, nor is it desirable that one should be under another man's control. If it is desirable that each man be independent, so far as may be, that he manage his own affairs as best he can, that he come and go at his own bequest and dispose of his time as he will (understanding, of course, that he has needs and wants which will induce him to be productive), it follows that organizations and systems for the control of men are generally abominations. There are much better ways to accomplish work than through organization, as that is generally understood, and when I come to it I have some thoughts about them. There is some history to get out of the way first. My main point here is that the factory system arose in a particular historical setting in which the subjugation of the generality of men was taken for granted.

The factory system did provoke the wrath of men. Indeed, the history of the nineteenth century is laced with uprisings, revolts, strikes, ideologies, movements, and what not aimed at doing something about it. The Luddites went about it in the most direct way. They proposed to solve the whole problem by breaking up the machines. If man was to be tied to the machine, there was a certain logic in breaking the machine. The machine was blameless, of course, and, besides, it greatly augmented man's productive capacities. Some early socialists, too,

474

blamed the machines. Robert Dale Owen, himself a factory owner, wanted to dispense with all sorts of mechanical devices. Reformers set about the business of regulating the factories, thus ameliorating some of their effects, perhaps, but leaving the basic problem intact. Labor unions were organized, and they lashed out at businesses in various ways.

It was at this juncture that Karl Marx entered upon the scene. Marx claimed that the problem lay in the private ownership of capital, a view that he shared with many other socialists. By a grotesque distortion of classical economics, he demonstrated that the worker was being cheated out of his fair share of the product of labor. Indeed, Marx downgraded capital to the point that it was an insignificant factor in production. What counted, and should be rewarded, was labor. This misconstrued the whole matter, opened up endless hassles over the question of what labor should be paid, as if the matter could be objectively determined, and almost completely ignored the central question of organizational control of man. Marx proposed to solve the whole problem by collective ownership and control over production and distribution. In practice, this means government ownership or control.

Marx did something else, without which he would have been just another socialist, despite his polemical skill. He did not reject the factory system or view it as a retrogressive development. He saw it, instead, as a harbinger of a bright tomorrow, as the beginning of the wave of a great and glorious future. Once the workers had seized the factories and were running them, all the problems of the world would be solved. The state would wither away, and men would live with one another in peace and harmony.

Communism is the nineteenth century factory system writ large. It is the factory taken over by the state and bureaucrats substituted for owners and managers. It is the mill village confiscated by the state and housing become a prerogative of those who serve and please the government. It is the company store become a state store and the state's script substituted for company scrip. It is the fence that one sur-rounded the factory now expanded to surround the state and keep the inhabitants in. It is the organizational control of the workers universalized with no alternative employers or way out. It is the company spies as secret police now the instruments of a totalitarian state with full-fledged force at their disposal. It is the carrying out to its ultimate conclusion of the notion that man's propriety can be achieved by integrating him into the organization and using him as a cog in a giant wheel.

475

In highly industrialized countries, where gradualist socialism has made great inroads, a multiplicity of organizations struggle for control over the individual. The main struggle, albeit a muted one usually, is between business organization and government. Much of the business effort evinces itself as competition, since business exists in thousands of different organizations. There is little reason to suppose that the businessman, as such, is animated by a collectivist bias. On the contrary, he may despise collectivism. His animus, as a businessman, is to fit the worker into what he reckons to be the requirements of his organization, to establish the dependency of the worker upon him, and to make him a pliant instrument of the managers. He spends a great deal of money and time, too, in trying to lure customers by way of advertising to persuade them that what they want is what he can most effectively produce, or what he does produce. The thrust of this latter is to serve the common taste, not that of any individual, but that which the largest number will accept as approximating their preferences. In this, the business effort has some kinship with collectivist democracy. My main point, however, is the animation of business to fit the individual into a mold suitable for its purposes. Competition tends to restrain this tendency and might have turned business into much more fruitful paths, in view of the inherent wastefulness, contentions, and inefficiency of attempting to control people had government not intervened. (We should not rule out, however, the strength of the desire to control people, particularly when it is construed as a virtue or necessity.)

The struggle between private business and government is not over the necessity, desirability, and even virtuousness of controlling individual man and establishing his dependency on them. On that point, they share a common animus. The struggle is over which shall control him. On the face of it, they appear to be unevenly matched. Government has a monopoly of the use of force. Business uses mainly the appeal of employment — the paycheck — and such appeal as resides in or people can be induced to believe its product or service has. Gradualist socialism intertwines and confuses these. It uses government to empower businesses, to enable them to become pseudogovernments in certain respects. (Some of this occurred long before socialism had emerged as a full-blown ideology, so it could be said that socialists only stepped up the process.) It does so by way of franchises, licenses, subsidies, government contracts, guaranteed loans, requirements which effectively exclude competitors, subsidizing consumers of particular businesses, granting general privileges such as those involved in incorporation and fractional-reserve banking, and even manipulating the money supply to aid certain undertakings, such as housing, for example.

There is, in this activity, the rudiments of what for want of a better term may be called a conservative dream. It is the dream of a "fruitful union" between business and government, of the two linked together and "looking after" the people. Government uses its power to enable business to attain its ends. The result, of course, would be to place the individual at the mercy of both. Any who doubt this should consider the present energy crisis in that light.

The empowering of business, however, is not the aim of socialism. It is only an expedient; the "carrot" side of the "carrot and stick" policy. Gradualism does further confuse the roles of business and government by having the government take on the task of providing certain goods and services. By so doing, it attempts to change the outward appearance of government from being an instrument for the use of force to an organization which serves as business does. Some of these, such as building roads and highways, often make partners of business and government. Others may introduce struggle into the equation, as when government begins to supply electrical power, for example.

Socialists do not view private business as a partner of government. It is a contestant with government for control over the individual. Business must be subdued on the way to subduing all individuals. Even when the two are in alliance — when government is empowering business and business is acting in numerous ways as an instrument of government — it is an uneasy alliance. Government is apt at any time to lash out with antitrust attacks, empower labor unions to go on the rampage, and is always bent toward increasing regulatory control over business. Government attempts to intrude itself between employer and employees and between businessmen and their customers. So far as the covert struggle is ever joined between business and government, it is usually over such matters.

Some years back, John Kenneth Galbraith advanced what was called the theory of countervailing power. He claimed that big government, big business, and big labor (labor unions) each tended to limit and contain one another. The result was a sort of healthy tension, a kind of Newtonian force of gravity which held each in its orbit and made the whole work well. Undoubtedly there is sometimes tension among these powers. It may be, too, that so long as all three exist in their own right all power is not concentrated in one. But the individual is only a pawn in this equation; he can lose his independence just as well to three as to one, and the tension aids him not a whit in retaining it. And the individual who has lost his independence, or never had it, is the victim.

It is in order now to examine more particularly the ways in which the individual is subdued.

38
The Subjugation of the Individual

THERE IS UNDOUBTEDLY an egalitarian animus behind the Idea that has
the world in its grip. The matter cuts much deeper, however than may
be generally supposed. It entails a continuing assault on individuality
itself. Everything that distinguishes one individual from another, all
differences in personality, any uniqueness, any peculiarity, any rough
edges, anything that would hinder or disrupt his serving as a cog in the
wheel must be sublimated, subordinated, or obliterated. He must be
denied so that he may serve "the people," "the masses," the
organization, the machine, and, in the final analysis, his masters, the
rulers of state or empire. The individual must be reduced to the status of
representative of some element within the organization or collective.
For all practical purposes, he must no longer be an independent being.

The individual must be reduced to a number, not a number with
which to calculate, but a meaningless number.

The late Ludwig von Mises made a telling economic criticism when
he demonstrated that in a pure socialist system economic calculation
would be impossible.[1] Mises did not, however, carry the insight to its full
implications. The Idea that has the world in its grip tends to banish all
calculation and, with it, all thought. It does so by denying the import of
the individual. All calculation begins with the individual, the unit, as

479

does all thought. The attempt to make the collective or organization into a unit, the one and only unit, renders calculation superfluous and impossible. The coordination and collectivization of all humans makes of thought a disruption not to be tolerated.

Socialism cannot, of course, reach such a point, so it is more valuable to look at the tendency and direction as the effort is made to reduce the individual to a nullity. It will help to start with names and numbers.

An individual is known by his name. That name has about it something of a magical quality for the person to whom it is applied, especially his given name. It has been said that the most pleasing sound to a person is that of his name. There is good reason for this. A person's name stands for his personality, for his individuality, his uniqueness, his differences, all he has done and become. He who loves and respects himself must in some fashion love his name, even when he does not like it as a name when considered objectively. Religious ceremonies sometimes give public sanction to the sacramental quality of the name. In Christianity, this is often done by coupling naming with baptism. An individual's status as a distinct being is conferred upon him socially by his name.

Numbers, too, have meaning. They have a culturally prescribed, fixed, and precise meaning. They are devices for calculation, for conveying magnitude, and for keeping quantitative records. The size of a given number is determined both by how many numbers there are and in what order they appear. The zero is invaluable in calculation, for with it numbers can be rounded off and extended indefinitely. It has this peculiarity, however, that if it is not preceded by some ordinal number it expresses nullity.

What has all this to do with the subjugation of the individual? It provides us the framework for perceiving how the reduction of the individual to a nullity is proceeding symbolically. The reduction is real; the symbols are a way of seeing it.

The assigning of numbers to persons has much greater significance than we ordinarily suppose. So far as I know, ours is the only age in which it has been done. It is of moment, too, that this began to be done in the wake of the widespread use of machines, the spread of the factory system motif into business organization, and the growth of collectivism. In the United States, numbers were probably given to individuals first when they were assigned to prisoners. Certainly, that was the most ostentatious use of a number for a person. The number is prominently displayed in photographs which people ordinarily see on wanted posters. The assigning of a number may have some slight residual use for purposes of identification, but that is not its significance. It is the stamp of the state on the prisoner, the modern equivalent of branding. It is the emblem signifying that he is no longer his own man but belongs to the state. A prisoner is stripped at the outset of much of that which sets him apart as an individual: his possessions, his clothing, his standing in the community, and many of his legal rights. The number is the seal of his new status.

Alexsander Solzhenitsyn, with his special insight and sensitivity, has suggested more of the import of assigning numbers to prisoners. He says that they did not get around to giving political prisoners numbers until late in the Stalinist era, long after it had been common practice in some "civilized" countries. Here is an abbreviation of his account:

> Then again, they quite blatantly borrowed from the Nazis a practice which had proved valuable to them — the substitution of a number for the prisoner's name, his "I," his human individuality, so that the difference between one man and another was a digit more or less in an otherwise identical row of figures....
>
> Warders were orderd to address prisoners by their numbers only, and ignore and forget their names. It would have been pretty unpleasant if they could have kept it up — but they couldn't....
>
> In work rolls, too, it was the rule to write numbers before names. Why before and not instead of names? They were afraid to give up names altogether! However you look at it, a name is a reliable handle, a man is pegged to his name forever, whereas a number is blown away at a puff. If only the numbers were branded or picked out on the man himself, that would be something! But they never got around to it... [2]

It has not been much noticed, but to give a name to anything is most apt to foster attachment to it. In fact, it attributes personality and, perhaps, an immortal soul to it. When I was a boy growing up on a small farm, we named some of the domestic animals: milk cows, sometimes their calves, horses and mules. Names did help to identify them, but there was more to it than that. We did not name hogs. There was a good reason for this. Hogs were grown for meat, and when they were fat we would have to kill them. This would be much more readily accomplished if we had not named them, had not attended carefully to their differences, and had not, by implication, attributed a soul to them.

Numbers are quite often essential to the legal identification of mass-produced items. This tells us something about mass production as well as about numbers. Tens of thousands of automobiles are turned out which are, for all prctical purposes, almost exactly alike. Quite often the only certain way to distinguish one from another so as to lay certain claim to it is by the manufacturer's serial number. The number enables the owner to assert his claim over the vehicle. There is a great difference between applying a number to a mass produced item and to a person. The number distinguishes such items from others like it. But when a number is assigned to an individual, far from adding to his distinguishing features, it tends to make him much more like others of his kind.

Americans more generally, other than prisoners that is, were assigned numbers for the first time as members of the armed forces. These numbers may have sometimes been helpful in making positive identification. The mangling of bodies in modern war is sometimes such that little may remain for identification except, it's hoped, "dog tags." And, it is true that the information provided by first name, middle initial, and last name may not be sufficient. For example, there may have been several hundred "John D. Smith's." It cannot be gainsaid, however, that the military had broader purposes which the serial number symbolizes. The military wanted only those aspects of the individual which could be fitted into the organization and be used for its ends. The military sought uniformity, obedience, and conformity. The individual must become a cog in a larger wheel. "The unit," in the argot of the armed forces, is the outfit, not the individual. Hence the question, "What unit do you belong to?" It is a nonsensical question which seems to make sense when the aim is to make the many as one. Numbers are much better for this purpose than names, but soldiers have both.

The generality of Americans got numbers for the first time, however, in the 1930s, when to have a Social Security number became a requirement for employment. The explanation at the time was that the number would identify one's "contribution" into the Social Security "fund." So it does, but it has long since been upgraded to serve other purposes: a taxpayer identification number, and who knows what else? The push is on to make this number identical with everything about the individual.

The bent to assign numbers is of a piece with the Idea that has the world in its grip. It is an attempt to reduce the individual to those proportions whereby the organization can deal with him with the least effort. It is, at the computer level, an effort to reduce him to holes punched in a card which can then be transferred to a magnetic tape. They are power or control devices, too, devices by which the customer is made to serve the company in his own interest. The use of computers in billing, and such like, is supposed to be time saving and efficient. For whom? They may save time for the company, for aught I know, but they are not time savers for the customer. If he writes numbers on checks and on return envelopes, as he is often admonished to do, that takes time.

Often the way in which the customer is made to spend his time and energy is subtly accomplished. Here is an example. In a recent Sunday supplement to the newspaper there was an article with some such intriguing title as "How to get Even with the Computer." It turned out upon examination, however, to deal mostly with all the things the customer was supposed to do to help make computers work. There was a list of things one might do to try to get an error corrected. By my casual estimate, to do all the things on the list might take from one to two days. All of which would be unpaid service to the company! I once billed a mortgage company for $100 for straightening out an error they had made. This elicited a letter from an executive in the company in which he explained that the error was mine because I had boloxed up the works by exercising my option to change my insurance. I did what any good libertarian recommends you should do in such circumstances — I stopped trading with them. More specifically, I stopped making the mortgage payments. Happily, the house sold before they foreclosed.

It is not always easy or inexpensive to withdraw your custom from some organization which is causing you difficulties. Take life insurance, for example; as one grows older it becomes more and more expensive to buy. Therefore, there is considerable incentive for hanging on to those policies which were bought when one was younger. This happened to me. For some reason, or unreason, I failed to receive my bill for the annual premium on what is for me a substantial life insurance policy. After waiting for a while to give it additional time to come, I wrote asking that the statement be sent. In due course, the statement arrived, but it was accompanied by a form letter which declared that my policy had lapsed because my payment had not been made within the grace period permitted. If I sent the check immediately I might be reinstated; or they might do such untoward things to me as have me take a physical examination before the policy would be reinstated. It seemed to me that if the policy had lapsed it was through no fault of mine. But think how much time might have been spent in correspondence before I contacted a human being! I could sue for reinstatement, of course, but that would be expensive and the result uncertain. Better to send the check off immediately and trust that the machine had been programmed to accept it with a minimum of resistance.

There are those who claim that the solution to all such problems, indeed, virtually all problems, is government regulation. They could only be further wrong by proposing government ownership. Government regulation to aid the individual would be like unto pouring water on a drowning man. When government and business become intertwined what had formerly been aggravations and occasional involuntary servitude to assorted companies takes on sinister overtones. Here is an example from my experience. It is an extension of the foretold encounter with the mortgage company. I changed my insurance because when my old policy expired my independent insurance agent issued a new policy on a different firm. He billed the mortgage company, was paid, and, perhaps as an afterthought, sent me the policy. (Actually, he said that the law permitted him either to notify me that time was running out on the policy or to issue a new policy. No matter that my contract with the mortgage company permitted me to choose the insuror with the consent of the mortgagee. Once government enters the picture, contractual relations become secondary.)

Upon examining the policy, I noticed that the premium was some $60 per year higher than before. Whereupon I made inquiries and discovered that I could get the same coverage for about $75 less from another company. I called the mortgage company, asked them to cancel the other policy, and, if they would, notify the independent insurance agency and retrieve the money. They said they would, but they did not. They did, however, pay for the policy I had ordered as well. In consequence, there was a shortage in my escrow account at the end of the year. Naturally, I was only able to ferret all this out by the most diligent efforts, spending much of my time talking to people too low in the pecking order to deal with such high and noble matters.

By the time I had uncovered all this I had begun to wax wroth at my independent insurance agent. After all, he was the villain of the piece; he was the one who had taken my money without my knowledge or consent. Determined not to let the sun set on my anger, as Scripture enjoins, I sallied forth to find my insurance agent. Surely he would be eager to make restitution since he had made himself liable to be seized by the sheriff and incarcerated for breaking the law. He wasn't, not eager anyway. After we had exchanged assorted pleasantries, he did say that he would get my money back but that it would take some time to recover it. I let him know that in my opinion he had already had the money too long, that his procedures were his affair, not mine, and that I would prefer to take the money with me. After that, the conversation deteriorated and, sad to say, things were said that were better left unthought, let alone spoken.

Now government regulation enters into the story more fully. The state I lived in had a law making liability insurance compulsory for vehicles operated on public roads. This law subtly alters the role of the insurance agent and even more the attitude of insuring companies. They still have to sell insurance, for there are competing companies, but they can be much haughtier about it than before. They can often adopt the posture that they are conferring a boon by letting you have the insurance. At any rate, I had my automobile liability insurance with the same agent who had tried to work the scam of shifting homeowner policies on me. It did occur to me that perhaps I ought to change that insurance, but since the premium would soon be due, I waited. That was a mistake, for apparently the agent acted with revenge as the motive. In any case, one day a notice arrived in the mail from the insuring company advising that they would not renew my insurance when the present policy expired. Why? The notice did not say. It did say that, in accordance with the *law*, upon receipt of a written request they would divulge the reason within 30 or 45 days, or something like that. I picked up the telephone and called the man whose name was printed on the form. He claimed not to know the reason but assured me that if I would make written request he would find it out and let me know. But why would my request by telephone not serve? After all, I had been a good customer for several years, paying my premiums on time, and never making a claim. Because, he said, that was what the law required. No, I said gently, the law required that he make answer if I made a written request, but he was surely free to give me the reason without it. Even so, he insisted on sticking to the letter of the law. I asked him for the name of his superior. He had none, he said. If I wanted to know, I would just have to make a written request. I did not want to know that bad.

The story does not end there, however. In due time, I received another notice, this one from the state highway department. It said that since my insurance had been *cancelled,* it was required that I notify the department within fifteen days of my new insuror and the policy number. That was no immediate problem — I had already applied for and paid the premium on new insurance — but there was something potentially ominous in the note. The policy had not been *cancelled;* the company had only announced its intention *not to renew* it, and that when I had no intention of renewing with them. It might be bad for me in the future for the highway department to have in its records that the

485

policy had been cancelled. I had better call and get the record straightened out. Probably they had just made a mistake which could be easily corrected. No, they had not made a mistake, the lady who answered the phone said. The law held that cancellation and nonrenewal were the same thing. But surely, I asked, the legislature had not bestirred itself to deal with such minute matters. I was right about that, she admitted, the filling in of details had been left to the department, and its decision had the force of law. At that point I tried to explain to my unwilling auditor that there is such a thing as the English language, that there are even dictionaries, and that *cancel* and *not renew* are not the same things. Nor, to my mind, did the state have the authority to do other than use the language as it had been before there was such a state. That was more than she could bear; she hung up. Having been excommunicated by the highway department, I replied in kind. I excommunicated them. I threw their notice into the trash can. Having since removed myself and all my possessions from that state, I feel moderately secure. But, then, one never knows nowadays. Perhaps some machine not having been given its prescribed diet of an answer within 15 days is just waiting to call forth from its memory bank the whole sordid story of my misdeeds for the delectation of others who will finally bring me to heel.

My interpretation of these events is that I had struck a nerve running directly to the spirit and animus of an age, an age bent on reducing the individual to the proportions of a number that will fit into a machine and whose task it is to straighten out anything that may get garbled in the machine. These organizations had once had me in my proper place. I had been assigned numbers, had the correct holes punched in my cards, and been given my place on magnetic tapes. I had even been a good little number at one time, making my payments regularly and even sending along the proper card without bending, spindling, mutilating, adding extra holes, or tearing it. That is not to say that I stood out, that I was especially loved or appreciated; after all, I was only doing what a number was supposed to do.

Then something happened. The number came to life, so to speak. The holes took on flesh and blood, and the tape when demagnitized gave birth to a full-fledged individual human being. This man behaved in ways that numbers are never supposed to do: he made choices, insisted on being paid for correcting the errors of others, refused to concern himself with the rules and regulations of organizations, and even denied to the state the rightful power of determining the meaning of words. Such behavior could not be tolerated, of course. There were two possibilities for dealing with it. One was to reduce me once again to a number on a good little card once again. My impression is that the mortgage company tried to do that for several months, sporadically and unsuccessfully. The insurance agent did not make that mistake, perhaps because he had seen me in person and tested my mettle. In any case, his actions suggest that he knew I was not such stuff as good little numbers are made of; I did not fit nicely into the pidgeonholes of organizations. He did not want my card in his bin; I had to be discarded; I had to be folded, bent, spindled, mutilated, and torn, or whatever he could activate the state to do to me.

"It is not enough to love mankind," a former inmate of the Soviet labor camps wrote Solzhenitsyn, "it is necessary also to be able to stand people." There spoke a man who bore on his body the scars from the application of the Idea that has the world in its grip. Jonathan Swift smelled this age acoming when he had Gulliver witness the loathsomeness of man by living among the Yahoos. To be able to "stand people" often does require more than a little of the grace of God. The Idea that has us in its grip provides a way of dealing with all this. "The people," in the abstract, are lovely and loved; it is only concrete individual human beings that are loathsome. The solution is obvious: reduce the individual to an abstraction. Fit him into an organization, and reduce him to a number. If he persists in emerging as a full scale individual human being, punish him by whatever means are available until he sees the light.

The assigning of numbers is not only an assault upon personality but also upon "personalty," i.e., property. To see this more clearly, we must look again at naming and assigning numbers. Naming is a prerogative of ownership, possession, or trusteeship. This had not occurred to me until a few years ago. My children had adopted a stray dog and named her "Trixie." However, the children who lived across the street refused to call her by that name, insisting that they had seen her first and that she answered to another one. Ostensibly, it was not a dispute over ownership, since it was settled that we were feeding and caring for the animal. The refusal of these children to accept the name we had given the dog aggravated my children, which it was probably supposed to do. Having thought the matter out, I explained to my children that the name we had given the dog was indeed her "name." She was, after all, *our* dog.

The assigning of a number is likewise a device for asserting a claim, ownership, or control over property, or personalty. It is a subtle device, quite often, for asserting that what was yours is now mine or under my control. Let us take as an example, first, a common and apparently innocent number: the number assigned to one's checking account at the bank. Ostensibly, the number stands for the claim of the customer against the bank for moneys he has deposited there. So it does, of course, but there is much more involved than immediately meets the eye. A process of abstracting occurs when a deposit is made in a bank, a process for which a number is the perfect symbol and instrument, though much of this was done before numbers were used, but not so effectively. The physical money turned over to the teller is reduced to a claim; it ceases to belong to the customer when it is joined to the common stock. The customer has not only yielded up ownership of particular pieces of money but also the control over and management of that money so long as it remains on deposit.

Government empowers banks to do highly interesting things with deposits. *Fractional reserve* describes most of them, but banks also enjoy some other subsidiary privileges. Functionally, the bank acquires ownership prerogatives over the money. It does this by placing the money received from the depositor into its "reserve." While the depositor may correctly think of the money as being in reserve against the time he needs it, the bank is empowered to use that reserve as if it belonged to the bank. More, the bank is required to keep a certain amount in reserve against deposits, 10 per cent let us say, though there are differences, such as between national and state banks. Functionally, this means something much more than it appears to mean. It means that if a depositor deposits $100, on the basis of that the bank can make a loan of $1,000, i.e., create a deposit of $1,000, though nothing was actually deposited but a promise to pay. In short, the bank is empowered to create money out of the void, as it were.

Actually, something quite different from what appears to have happened has taken place. Banks can be and are a medium through which paper moeny can be created by government to fulfill such transactions. But they cannot increase the worth of the money deposited one whit. What is being described is the process of inflation, increasing the money supply. If there were only the one set of transactions set forth above, what would have happened is this. The $100 that had been deposited in the bank would only be worth $10 — that is, would only purchase what $10 would have purchased when the deposit was made — and the borrower's $1,000 would be worth only what $100 would have bought before the transaction.

488

Actually, a single transaction can only have a very small impact upon the money supply and, hence, upon prices. Moreover, a deposit can only have any discernible impact as it becomes a part of a trend. Banks have many depositors and loans. If one deposits $100, another may withdraw a like amount simultaneously. In which case, no change will have occurred in the bank's reserve. It is only as a bank's reserve is increased — for the reserve is an average only for some short period of time — that the money supply can be increased by creating deposits. The other variable is the possibility of reducing the reserve requirement. Hence, the process of inflation may be gradual, and may even require stimulation from other sources than bank deposits, if it is to continue.

Nonetheless, the potentiality of fractional reserve banking is just as it is described in my simple example. And it works that way, except as withdrawals match deposits. It should be clear that theft is entailed in fractional reserve banking. The theft evinces itself in the declining value of money. Every depositor is an accessory to the theft; every borrower is a receiver of stolen goods. The punishment for the theft falls upon the whole population of the country, and there is no way for the individual to evade the punishment short of ceasing to use money, have property, and earn income. The legal-tender laws close the door to any effective means for evading the consequences of the fractional reserve system. One can cease to participate in the theft by ceasing to do business with banks, but the consequences will still be visited upon him.

The user of banks believes that he is managing his affairs in every reasonable respect when he keeps a careful record of his deposits and withdrawals and makes his payments on time. He does not understand that he has hold of only the tip of his affairs, that by depositing money or getting a loan he sets into motion a process which is very much his affair, but he knows not of it. The bank, the FDIC, the Federal Reserve, the banking commissioners, take over the control of a crucial portion of his affairs. The number of his account is the symbol of the shift of the control over his property to others. Organizations take over, and the individual is subjugated. Inflation is the name of that by which he is subjugated.

The Social Security number, as it was originally used, is an even more clear-cut case of a shift in ownership and control being signified with a number. Moneys paid into Social Security no longer belong to the individual who paid them in. He no longer has any claim on the funds; they are forfeit to the government. The only claim he has is to such benefits as Congress may decide at any time to allot to those falling in the category to which his payments — which can be discovered by the use of the number — and his condition entitle him. The only management, control, and possession he will ever have over any of this, as matters stand, is over such benefit payments as he may be allowed to receive.

When the Social Security number became a Taxpayer Identification number a more subtle development occurred. The government began to use a number to assert its control as well as potential ownership of all our property and possessions. It is used mainly as a means of ferreting out income, but it stands for much more. The Internal Revenue Service considers only so much of an individual's income as his as he can show does not belong to the government. This position was established by requiring proof from the individual that he is entitled to exemptions. Ingmar Bergman left Sweden after the government insisted that he pay taxes which he claimed amounted to 139 per cent of his income. His decision was reached after these events. He

was called out of a rehearsal by government investigators, who hauled him away for questioning, confiscated his passport and accused him of evading $120,000 in income taxes. Bergman protested his innocence, but even after the criminal charges against him were dropped, Swedish officials continued to dun him for the back taxes they insisted he owed. Bergman went to pieces; he stopped work, suffered a nervous breakdown and contemplated suicide. Then..., having snapped out of the depression, the 58-year old director announced he was leaving his homeland for good.

Not before declaring, however, "I am leaving my fortune in Sweden at the disposal of the National Tax Board."[3] The extent of government's claims is not usually made so clear, because most gradualist governments do not deal so harshly with taxpayers as Sweden did Bergman. In any case, the Taxpayer Identification number (nee Social Security number) is the symbol of that claim in the United States.

There is more to taxpaying and identification numbers than that, however. The tax policies of government intrude upon how the individual manages if he would keep what he thought was his. Some kinds of expenditures are encouraged by government, others not. For example, contributions to charitable organizations — to *organizations,* let it be noted, not to individuals — are exempt from taxation up to a point, as are many sorts of state and local taxes, but not taxes on alcoholic beverages. Thus, while the individual may be managing his affairs tangentially quite often, he is being guided and directed in this by tax policy. To put it another way, the individual is permitted to manage his affairs at will only if he is willing to give up a considerable portion of the means by which he might manage his affairs.

The subjugation of the individual is usually accomplished directly in Communist countries. His property is taken from him. There are no media through which he may express himself except those under governmental control. If he would work, he must do so as directed by the bureaucracy and whatever controls the group with which he works may exercise. Managing his affairs is usually reduced to finding food, clothing, shelter, and some sort of transport he can afford. There are no banking or savings institutions not under government control, so that wherever he turns his management is circumscribed by the state.

Evolutionary socialism moves much more slowly and gradually to divest the individual of his independence and control over his affairs. The gradualist thrust is toward the managed economy, and beyond that to turn all wealth and property to "socially useful" purposes. The "managing" of the economy is supposedly done by governmental control of the money supply, over transportation, over energy, over wages, over foreign trade, over the stock market, over housing, and in a hundred and one other ways. The ideal is that the individual be under the control of some organization or set of organizations. If he is in the employ of some corporation or company, the income tax can be confiscated (deducted) before he receives his wages, as well as Social Security and any payments his employer must make to the unemployment compensation fund. Statistics, which are the key to the "management" of the economy, are much more readily compiled for people who are in organizations and institutions. Governments encourage and support organizations such as labor unions, professional organizations, and cooperatives by special privileges. Although it is not an absolute rule, gradualists increasingly seem to prefer to exercise their control over individuals — put the squeeze on — indirectly through "private" organizations rather than directly.

There was a time when it could be said of a man not blessed with great wealth or high income that he had a "competence." The term meant, literally, that he was competent to manage his affairs for the foreseeable future, that he had sufficient income and property to take care of himself and his family. The term has fallen into disuse, for obvious reasons. The ravages of inflation, confiscatory taxation, and dependence on shifting government policy have tended to make everyman insecure. For example, many people discover that when they reach retirement age and have paid off their houses, they can no longer afford them because of high property taxes. Competence is now possible only for those who have such wealth that they can afford batteries of lawyers, tax accountants, investment counselors, large political contributions — and they are increasingly threatened.

The subjugation of the individual has been accomplished by reducing him to a number. More specifically, it has been done by reducing him to an anonymous number, an integer of a statistic. This is called voting or, more broadly, the democratic process. Democratic socialism turns voting into a kind of self-immolation by which the individual yields up his independence and control over his own affairs by casting a ballot, being reduced to an anonymous number, and becoming a statistic. Man's potential weight in both his own affairs and public affairs is reduced to a scratch on a ballot or, more appropriately, the flip of a switch in a voting machine. In the framework of the Idea that has the world in its grip the only issue that can arise is over what means shall be used to concert all efforts to promote the general well being. Not only does the individual reduce himself to a number by voting but also to a statistic in favor of one method of being concerted as opposed to another, if any issue at all can be discerned. The man who wishes to manage his own affairs is unlikely to find that among the available options.

Actually, voting for candidates may be a reasonably satisfactory means of determining *who* shall govern, so long as the demonstrably corrupt and unlettered are excluded. It is hardly a satisfactory means of determining *what* government shall do, which gradualism continually intrudes into the process. That is a constitutional question requiring for its answer not man reduced to a number but present in the full weight of his being as an individual. Socialism turns voting into the quest for the holy grail. It turns the mundane business of selecting who shall govern into the choosing of religious leaders. A modicum of meaning remains, for it does matter, at least marginally, who governs, and to have to stand for election does restrain politicians. Power can never be absolute so long as choices among candidates are available to the electorate. But for those who do not accept the religious vision of socialism, voting is largely counterproductive.

Power is never complete until it is arbitrary. Control over people is never as great as it might be until it is by whim. So long as anything is fixed, certain, or immutable, so long as there is any standard or rule to which to appeal, so long as a reason or explanation has to be given, power is that far restrained. The animus of our age is not only to reduce the individual to a number but also to make that number flexible and ultimately meaningless. Man must finally be reduced to zero in order to be fully integrated with organization.

It may help to illustrate this tendency to return again to the world of computer numbers. A strange thing began to happen to computer

492

numbers a few years back. When they were first assigned, they usually consisted of a recognizable sort of number. Let us say, for example, that my number on my mortgage payment cards was 14530. Then, unaccountably and without explanation, it became 014530. Probably, I might never have paid any attention to this were it not for the fact that in making some payments the payer is exhorted to write his number on the check and on the envelope. That raised the question in my mind of whether or not I should write down the zero as well. That brought up an even more intriguing question: What is the effect of prefacing a number with a zero? Does it add anything or take anything away from the number which follows? If it does not — and although mathematics is not my forté, I could perform no calculations in which it did — why would it be there? I felt both foolish and aggravated, foolish at writing down pointless zeros, and aggravated at the atrocity being committed on our mathematical language. It was an abuse of numbers in a serious context, and that struck me as intolerable. (Some numbers were preceded by more than one zero, as if it were possible to double or triple pointlessness.)

My inquiries netted me this answer, for what it is worth. It seems that the computer can be more effectively utilized if the numbers fed into it have the same number of digits (for particular categories, one imagines). At the time my mortgage number was assigned, let us say, all mortgage numbers from that company have five digits. Now, however, the company had issued so many mortgages that another digit had to be added. To make them all the same, zeros were placed before the old numbers. Conceivably this made the task of programming the computer easier.

It might have been supposed that when man and his particular affairs had been reduced to a number to be introduced into a machine for the purposes of an organization that the ultimate reduction had been made. Not so. A number, with a fixed number of digits, poses limitations on the machine or its programmer. The number must be flexible, else it is not perfectly manipulable. The zero is the perfect symbol for the ultimate reduction.

The Idea which has the world in its grip impels us toward meaninglessness. It impels us toward acts that have no discernible purpose for the individual. So long as acts are purposeful, there are guidelines and standards that are exterior to the acts; the individual is not perfectly concerted, and power over him is not complete. So long as the individual is acting for purposes that are in any way indentifiable as

493

his own, he is somewhere short of being concerted. Prisoners are sometimes put to performing apparently meaningless tasks. For example, they may be made to dig holes and fill them in again. This is done to show the prisoner he is nothing and that the power over him is absolute. Slave labor camps are necessary to communism because somewhere and somehow the idea must be realized. But the whole population could not be put into slave labor camps, not at one time anyway. There would be no one to guard the prisoners.

Communists have found a way, however, to accomplish the same purpose by less drastic means. It is called voting, the democratic process, or participating in elections. Elections in the Soviet Union, for example, are meaningless affairs, so far the the participants are concerned. A party slate has been nomimated by the leaders, and it will be elected. It does not matter whether one hundred, one thousand, or one million vote: the result will be the same. Even so, a great effort is made to get out the vote. Pressure is brought on people to go from door to door urging people to vote. Why? For one thing, as earlier noted, there is the facade of democracy, which has propaganda uses. But it serves a highly important interior purpose as well. The individual is not only reduced to a number which can be rendered as a statistic but also to a meaningless number and statistic. The power of the rulers over the populace is demonstrated. The more who vote, the more complete the demonstration of power.

The subjugation of the individual descends to degradation by voting under communism.

39
The Restoration of the Individual

IN THE MIDST of doing this work, I received a long distance call from a
gentleman. He said that he had been asked to talk to a civic group and
that he wanted to talk about the recognition of Red China and what had
been done to Taiwan. He did not say, but in the course of the rather long
conversation it became fairly clear that what he wanted to do was focus
on whether trade with China would be profitable or not. I came to this
conclusion because I kept bringing up communist tyranny, nationalism,
and the horrendous regime in Cambodia supported by Chinese
Communists, and even the treatment of missionaries in China. He was
most polite, and listened, with apparent interest, to all I had to say. But
he kept coming back to the question of profits. After stabbing around
for what turned out to be inconclusive answers, I hit upon one that
satisfied me. I quoted Scripture: "For what does it profit a man if he gain
the whole world and lose his own soul?" He let that pass without
comment.

What my caller might have told me, had it occurred to him, and if he
had wanted to make his point by way of a little exaggeration, would have
gone something like this: "Look, I have been asked to speak to a

gathering of pagans in a nearby town. They are, for the most part, businessmen, and one of their idols is profit. If I could show them that trade with China would be unprofitable, I could get their attention. Perhaps they are not pagans entire; some of them still worship on occasion at the shrine of the great God Jehovah, but I want to reach them at the level of what they have in common — the belief in and desire for profits." I could no more prove that it is not possible to profit at the expense of others than that a man may not pick fruit from a tree he has not planted. If there is extensive trade with China there will undoubtedly be profits. I have no doubt that there is much to be said in favor of profits, but they provide no answer for grave questions.

Some years back, I received a call from a young man who asked me to speak to a group of students. What he wanted me to do was to restrict myself to economic matters, if I would, he said. Specifically, he wanted me to leave God out of it, though he must have put it more circumspectly than that. It seems that his group was composed of what he called "Thomists and Randians," and the religious issue would surely sunder them. I sent my condolences but declined the invitation.

One suspects that the young man supposes that God is like a domestic pet, a cat, say, which one trots out to show cat fanciers, but when guests arrive who are allergic to cats is put away out of sight until they leave. It is not that way at all. God is not an addendum to economics; He is not scrollwork around the edges. Without God, the belief in economics is idolatry. Without God, the quest for profits is idolatrous. Without God, efficiency is an idol. God is my premise and my conclusion. The first words of Genesis put the matter clearly: "In the beginning, God...." And as the Book of Revelation moves to its conclusion, there are these words: "I am Alpha and Omega, the beginning and the end, the first and the last." This is no god to be trotted out for god fanciers. He is *God,* the ground of all being. How could I speak and leave God out?

The matter can perhaps be stated more palatably in a different way. It is neither possible nor desirable to discuss economics without discussing man. But once man is entered into the equation, we need to know what he is and what he is about. Is man a stomach to be filled? Is he a being to be used for the ends of others as they will? Is he a creature to be ground to the dimensions that can efficiently fit to the requirements of a machine? Is he an object? Is he a thing? Is he a number? Is it his destiny to be fitted to the efficient requirements of vast organizations? Is he made up of fragments which are to be separated one from the other and used as others will? Or is he something much more than and different

496

from all these. Is man valuable, and if so, from what does this value stem?

These questions, I maintain, are at bottom religious. They must be answered, either implicitly or explicitly, before any meaningful discussion of economics can be had. And they are! Man is incurably religious, even if some men are able somehow to reduce their gods to arid assumptions. There is no such live questions as this: Will you serve some god? The questions is always this: Which god will you serve? Freidrich Nietzsche had no sooner proclaimed that god is dead than he proposed man as god. It is ever so, though men may sometimes be unaware of their assumptions. A man will either serve the well-nigh universal and usually secret god — self — or he will serve a god or gods outside of and beyond self. (He may, and frequently does, pay tribute to the prevailing public gods while secretly worshiping and serving the god of self.) In general today, the choice of those who would worship something beyond the self is between *the* God and an assortment of gods who go by such name as the team, the group, the people, the proletariat, the organization, the state, or the leader. (Interestingly, modern man is ever forgetting to worship the organization as he should and having to be chastised for worshiping the leader.) This species of religion we may denominate paganism because of the low order of what is worshiped.

Value is the crucial concept of economics, and it is at this point that we may bring religion to bear on economics. The god that is worshiped determines value. If the self is god, then the individual decides and determines value. If some sort of organization is god, then the organization determines value. God determines value if He is at the center of worship.

Now it may be possible to worship the self — a rare person might do it consistently — and the self might elect the most exquisite values. But a catalog of these would not be a general economics; it would be some sort of autobiography. The thrust to make the self-worshiper's values prevail — become the base of economics — is the thrust toward dictatorship. Self-worship is a terribly confining concept; the only acceptable contact with others is control over them in order to put them at the service of self. It may be argued, indeed, is argued, that the enlightened self should will a society in which others are free and whose rights are perfectly respected. Unfortunatly, it is not in the least a requirement of self-worship that one be enlightened in order to practice it. Hitler was the logic of self-worship; interventionist economics is its instrument.

497

The paganism entailed in the worship of the organization, the people, numbers, or society, has produced an economics. In this economics, value is determined by organization and numbers. While there are several schools of economics, for purposes of discussing the economics of organization and numbers, I shall refer to the basic premise of most of these as utilitarianism. What is often referred to as classical economics — and now neoclassical economics as well — is mainly utilitarian economics. Its basic premise is social utility, which is often expressed by the phrase, "the greatest good for the greatest number." This is the touchstone of its measure of value.

Utilitarian economics, as it has been modified and refined, has made a quite adequate description of modern economic behavior, and in the hands of its masters, often brilliant ones. This is achieved for two reasons. First, it incorporates some of the enduring principles of economics into its system. On the basis of these, it is able in dealing with facts to discount the impact of government intervention and to show that many untoward effects are attributable to government and not economic behavior. Secondly, however, its adequacy stems from the fact that it was advanced concurrenly with the rise of the factory system and the spread of democracy. This tends to obscure the fact that it is an extended apology for the use of organization and numbers for the efficient use of machines. No other possibilities are contemplated in it.

Utilitarian economics leaves God out of account and, *ipso facto,* leaves man out. Specifically, utilitarian economics reduces man to only certain of his aspects, to those aspects that can be incorporated in the system of economics being espoused. It reduces him to his aspects as saver, investor, entrepreneur, worker, and consumer. It leaves out of account man as a whole human being with all his potential for humanity. By making work a disutility, it makes of the necessity for workers in practice a disutility. Man the consumer is not even fully taken into account; it is only some sort of averages that are catered to.

Perhaps this leaving of man the individual out of account can be most directly illustrated from the Austrian School of economics. What they did to the concept of value is most instructive. Values are subjective, they say. They are a matter of individual preference, of taste, as it were, and as everyone knows there is no accounting for taste. If there is to be an economic science, the late Ludwig von Mises declared, it must be value free. To make it value free, man must be rigorously excluded from it. Professor Mises did not draw this last conclusion, of course; I did.

He made what appears to be a valiant effort to include man in his system, going so far as to entitle his major opus *Human Action*. He posited a rational and volitional man and described economics as a science of man acting. Economics belongs to the category of praxeology, that is, it deals with the means by which men achieve their purposes, not with the ends. But surely, it must be objected, ends or values are as much a part of economic behavior as means. Man is concerned with the means primarily as they get him to his ends. What Professor Mises' presentation conjures up in my mind is an economics which could be likened to a road map that shows all the roads but has no names of towns and cities along the way.

There is, of course, no such economics. General systems of economics are, as a rule, value laden, and there should be no doubt that utilitarian economics is. What is denied entry into this economics is not value but the *value of man*. "The greatest good for the greatest number" is a value or, more precisely, a value judgment. It assumes the desirability of that end. "Consumer sovereignty" entails a value judgment if it assumes that this is desirable. Values can no more be excluded from economics than hydrogen can be excluded from water. It is possible, of course, to isolate hydrogen, but when it is done you have not water but hydrogen and oxygen. In like manner, it may be possible to separate means from ends, but what you have when you have done it is praxeology, not economics.

Utilitarian economics sanctions the reduction of man to a number (either as a member of the greatest number or the lesser number, whatever an individual's lot may be). Thereby, it sanctions an efficiency tied to the most efficient use of machines. It justifies the use of capital to control men so as to use machines in ways they judge to be most efficient. It does this by ignoring and excluding from consideration the *value of man*. It makes the potentialities of machines the thing to be realized, not the potentialities of man. It does not exclude values from economics; it excludes man in the fullness of his being. Man's reason is not something exhausted when he has made a choice, of a job, say, it is then on but the threshold of its potentialities.

Socialism is a jerry-built structure nailed haphazardly to the back of utilitarian economics. Utilitarian economics tacitly sanctions the control over man by organization, numbers, and tools. Socialism, because it misconstrues the problem, works to tighten vastly the control over man, both by making the management of man universal and by using the power of government to accomplish this end. All this results from an erroneous view of man.

The contemporary mind is in thrall to the belief that the individual is only a *part,* not a complete whole. It sees him as ineffective and incomplete until he has been integrated into a larger whole. I cannot overemphasize the fact that this is a religious conception at its roots. Man has devised wholes, or attributed to wholes, a greater-than-man quality, and by joining him to these wholes it is supposed that man's powers are to be greatly augmented. It is a way of looking at man that dwarfs him and makes organizations appear important and overwhelming. This way of looking at things is very nearly an inevitable consequence of assessing man without God.

Man without God is indeed a puny creature. He is a fragile creature, born of woman in labor, who flourishes for a fleeting moment of maturity, and is no more. He is dependent upon others in infancy, at least, and probably in old age. Even the smallest accident can wipe him out, should some vital organ be severed from him or irreparably injured. He is vulnerable, usually readily intimidated, and it is not difficult for him to feel his helplessness when confronted by organization and numbers. Viewing himself so, he seeks comfort in the warm smell of the herd, as H. L. Mencken said. The collective answer appears to be the only answer, for collectivism is the logic of man without God, even of man with an uncertain grasp upon God.

Make no mistake about it, if force rules, man's only hope is to seek safety in numbers and find his security somewhere as an appendage of some organization. Man without God is inclined to learn from experience that force rules; there is so much evidence to that effect. There is a saying that the whole is greater than the sum of its parts. (This is a variation on the mathematical axiom that the whole is *equal* to the sum of its parts.) There is one sense in which this is true for men conceived as parts. If force is the arbiter, then an organizational whole is greater than the sum of its parts (individual men). A collective whole (an organization) is much more effective in intimidating, coercing, restraining, and exerting force than are the same number of individuals in their separate capacities. A small army can conquer a large populace which has no organized army. Indeed, a few bandits, organized under the control of a leader and prepared to use force, can intimidate and terrorize a community. A labor union can stop production in a factory or even in a whole industry. The principle upon which this is true needs to be stated bluntly so that it can be clearly understood. It is this: An organizational whole is greater than the sum of its parts in its *destructive* potential.

The principle has a most important corollary. It is this: An

500

organizational whole is *less* than the sum of its parts in its *constructive* potential. It is the belief to the contrary that undergirds collectivism. The Idea that has the world in its grip holds that if all efforts could be concerted the positive results would be of a magnitude incomparably greater than those of individuals acting independently from one another. Every person who believes in organizational control over individuals for any constructive undertaking believes this, though he may not take the idea to its ultimate logical conclusion. The logical conclusion of the idea is, of course, world socialism.

The validity of the principle — that the organizational whole is less than the sum of its individual human parts in constructive potential — has been dramatically illustrated in the Soviet Union. Virtually all of the land in the Soviet Union is in the hands of the state and is organized either in large state or collective farms. But the farming people have been allowed from time to time to have their own small plots, the produce of which they as individuals could keep and sell. The difference between the produce from these tiny plots and the giant farms was summarized this way several years ago by Eugene Lyons:

According to the government's own figures ..., private plots with a mere 3 per cent of the nation's sown acreage accounted for 30 per cent of the gross harvest, other than grains; 40 per cent of all cattle-breeding; 60 per cent of the country's potato crops, 40 per cent of all vegetables and milk; 68 per cent of all meat products. Their fruit yields ... are double those of state orchards for equivalent areas, its potato harvest per hectare two-thirds higher than on collective farms. Even in grain, which is a very minor element in the private sector, it produces one-third more per sown unit than an average socialized farm.[1]

The reason for these dramatic differences can be readily explained. When an individual is working on his own plot, managing his own affairs, and receiving the fruits of his labor, the effort can engage the full potential of the individual. It engages his intelligence, his ingenuity, his knowledge, his skills, and his full attention. An organization cannot do this. An organization subjects the individual to the will and determination of another, does not engage him fully because he is neither free to manage the undertaking nor responsible for the results. This is true of all organizations, of private corporations as well as government-owned ones, of charitable undertakings as well as those for private profit, of factories as well as farms, and of colleges as well as coal mines. The tighter the control the more ineffective the organization for productive purposes, of course. The inefficiency is mostly hidden in highly industrialized countries by a vast overcapitalization. To put it another way — a way that most businessmen will readily grasp — the ineffectiveness of workers is largely concealed in many industries by the use of ever more efficient machines. But we are much too deeply thus far under the sway of the notion of the efficiency of organization to attribute it to that. (Behind the scenes, men groan about the laziness, stupidity, ineptness, and irresponsibility of workers, never guessing that organization, numbers, and machines are used to bend them in that direction.)

The attachment to organization has been built up by a vast selling job, and great effort has been put into "perfecting organizations" in our era. Some years back, William H. Whyte wrote a book called *The Organization Man.* He focused entirely on private organizations, mostly businesses, but so far as it goes, his point is well taken. He maintained that in the United States an ideology of the group had been shaped. He described it this way:

> Its major propositions are three: a belief in the group as a source of creativity; a belief in "belongingness" as the ultimate need of the individual; and a belief in the application of science to achieve the belongingness.[2]

Much of the book is devoted to describing the ways in which the individual is supposed to be fitted into and made loyal to the organization. It might be more appropriate here to characterize what he was describing as the idolization of the organization. If he had included government and the state in his analysis, the full significance of all this might have been exposed.

What has happened, then, is that the organization has been made into an idol, beside and without which the individual is as nothing. Only as a member of a collective does the individual have a chance. It is as a cog in a machine that man makes what impact he can. The machine is surely immensely greater than its individual parts, even when it is not greater than their sum. Can this be gainsaid?

Now we come to the nub of the matter. Organizations are not as they have been conceived. Man is not as he has been portrayed. In a deep and abiding sense, this world is ever engaged in a giant conspiracy to conceal the truth about man and to overawe him with organizations. (To which numbers and machines have been added in our era.) Organizations are derivative. They derive every ounce of their human energy from individual men. They derive all their initiative, all their force, all their

502

direction from individual men. Whatever purposes they have are derived from individual men. Organizations cannot think, imagine, will, or act; only individuals can do these things. Organizations are not superior to man; they are creatures of man. In the final analysis, this world is not ruled by force but by love.

There is a whole that is greater than the sum of its parts. It is individual man. Far from being a mere cog, a zero, an object or thing of use, individual man is valuable beyond compare. Far from being loathsome, detestable, something to be rid of if we can, he is lovely because he is loved. He is a living, breathing being with a soul, mind, and body. Each child that is born is a miracle, and every full-grown person potent with possibilities beyond our dreams. Organizations are but gossamer; man is the substance.

Strive as he will, natural man cannot devise an answer which can penetrate the demeaning spirit now besetting man. The idols of socialism cannot be laid with the idols of capitalism. The low religions of statism and collectivism do not yield ground to un-religion. The only effective answer to low religions is a high and noble religion. The only way to avoid the worship of numerous idols is to worship the one God. The only way to transcend the subjectivity of values and the relativity of all knowledge is to go to the source of value and knowledge. If this world is all there is, force does indeed rule, and some sort of collectivism is the appropriate answer.

There is good news for any and all who will hear it. It is electrifying news. It is not news addressed to any group, team, class, race, or organization; it is news for individuals alone. It is news beside which *Das Kapital* is a mishmash of history laced with hatred. It is news beside which *Mein Kampf* is the distorted assertions of an egomaniac. It is of something which we would not dare hope for did we not know it already. It is news which confirms, vivifies, animates, and restores man. The primary source of this news is the Bible. It is vouched for by the death and resurrection of its bearer. Its truth is confirmed by the testimony of the saints down through the ages. If it come not from God, then whence came it? Surely, it is not of this world.

The good news, first, is not that man is the origin of values but something much more: he *is* a value. He is valuable because God places a high value upon him. Contemplate the words of Jesus:

"Are not two sparrows sold for a farthing? and one of them shall not fall to the ground without your Father.

503

"But the very hairs of your head are numbered.

"Fear ye not therefore, ye are of more value than many sparrows."³

And again:

And, behold, there was a man which had his hand withered. And they asked him saying, "Is it lawful to heal on the sabbath days?..."

And he said unto them, "What man shall there be among you, that shall have sheep, and if it fall into a pit on the sabbath day, will he not lay hold on it, and lift it out?

"How much then is a man better than a sheep? Wherefore it is lawful to do well on the sabbath days."⁴

There is more, however; these verses tell us that man is valuable, but they do not suggest the extent. The greatness of his value is indicated in the following verse. Jesus said,

"For God so loved the world that he gave his only begotten Son, that whosoever believeth in him should not perish, but have everlasting life."⁵

This tells us much more besides. It tells us that man is immortal, that he is a creature chosen for eternity. The "whosoever" in the sentence tells us that only individual human beings may have that promise of immortality. The magnitude of man compared to organizations begins to appear. All organizations are but temporary things, destined it may be to flourish for a time and then be no more. The record of history is replete with instances of kingdoms, nations, empires, cities, and all sorts of organizations which once were and are no more. They lasted only so long as they were sustained by individuals; then they disappeared, things dependent finally upon the memory of men. Man, by contrast, has a future of which this life is only the beginning.

There is a way to test the quality of a religion. It is in that to which it appeals. Does it appeal to the baser motives? Or does it appeal to the highest and best? Socialism is a mean, low, and vulgar religion, and it is as a religion that it finally stands or falls. It appeals to greed, to avarice, to popularity with the crowd, to the desire to get something for nothing, to envy, to jealousy, to class hatred, to the lust for power, to the lowest common denominator, to the will to be free of responsibility, to the urge to destroy, and to the longing to crush that with which one disagrees. The mainspring of socialism is the fear of individual man and a loathing for him as he is. Socialism incarnates force, and worships the state as the embodiment of it.

504

By contrast, Christianity appeals to the highest and noblest in man. The God revealed by Jesus Christ does not use force and power upon men in this world. God is love, we are told; He woos man by sacrifice, by coming in lowly guise, having naught of the things of this world by which to awe man. He comes not as an earthly conqueror with force, terror, and violence to destroy men but in boundless love to redeem them. The virtues He commends are higher than any man can conceive. But let them speak for themselves. First, from the Sermon on the Mount:

"Blessed are the poor in spirit: for theirs is the kingdom of heaven.

"Blessed are they that mourn: for they shall be comforted.

"Blessed are the meek: for they shall inherit the earth.

"Blessed are they which do hunger and thirst after righteousness: for they shall be filled.

"Blessed are the merciful; for they shall obtain mercy.

"Blessed are the pure in heart: for they shall see God.

"Blessed are the peacemakers: for they shall be called the children of God.

"Blessed are they which are persecuted for righteousness sake: for theirs is the kingdom of heaven."[6]

What should stand out in all of this is that there is nothing commended to which any should take offense.

There is a marvelous congruity permeating the New Testament in the virtues commended. Here is an example from the writings of Paul the Apostle:

Let love be without dissimulation. Abhor that which is evil; cleave to that which is good.

Be kindly affectioned one to another with brotherly love; in honour preferring one another.

Not slothful in business; fervent in spirit; serving the Lord;

Rejoicing in hope; patient in tribulation; continuing instant in prayer;

Distributing to the necessity of the saints; given to hospitality.

Bless them which persecute you; bless, and curse not.

Be of the same mind one toward another. Mind not high things, but condescend to men of low estate. Be not wise in your own conceits.

Recompense to no man evil for evil. Provide things honest in the sight of all men.

If it be possible, as much as lieth in you, live peaceably with all men.

Dearly beloved, avenge not yourselves, but rather give place unto wrath: for it is written, Vengeance is mine; I will repay, saith the Lord.

Therefore, if thine enemy hunger, feed him; if he thirst, give him drink: for in so doing thou shalt heap coals of fire on his head.

Be not overcome of evil, but overcome evil with good.[7]

The Apostle Peter summarized the great virtues this way:

and beside this, giving all diligence, add to your faith virtue; and to virtue knowledge;
and to knowledge temperance; and to temperance patience; and to patience godliness;
and to godliness brotherly kindness; and to brotherly kindness charity.

And from Paul again:

Finally, brethren, whatsoever things are true, whatsoever things are just, whatsoever things are pure, whatsoever things are lovely, whatsoever things are of good report; if there be any virtue, and if there be any praise, think on these things.[9]

Jesus Christ was God Incarnate; He was the Word made flesh. He came to reveal God's ways to men. The beauty of what He taught and was has brought forth singular words of praise. He has been described as the Lily of the Valley, the Rose of Sharon, the Pearl Beyond Price, and in Isaiah, as prophecy: "For unto us a child is born, unto us a son is given: and the government shall be upon his shoulder: and his name shall be called Wonderful, Counsellor, the mighty God, the everlasting Father, the Prince of Peace."[10]

This aspect of him has tended to shield us from understanding an equally important truth: Jesus Christ was man incarnate. He revealed to men their full potentialities and possibilities; He lived and taught — was the embodiment of — not a religion, as we understand such things, but a way of life. He showed that the individual person is of great and momentous account. He restored man the individual to his central place in all of creation. The way of the world is wrong, He said; it is the way of death. The way of the world is to use force, coercion, to attempt to control men to the purposes of others, to use them. There is another way: the way of love, of service, of persuasion, of influence, of kindliness, of giving, and of becoming. It is the way of life.

Ancient pagans believed that man was a plaything of the gods. Modern pagans believe that he is an instrument of the organization to be intimidated by numbers. "Enlightened" Greeks and Romans believed that man is either a comic or tragic figure. Contemporary intellectuals incline to view man as a sensual being, caught in the grip of passions and desires which rend him.

Man without God is indeed capable of every debasement that can be imagined. He is comic or tragic as you will, a creature of the senses, a

506

plaything, an instrument, an object, a belly, a power monger, or whatever. If proof were needed, this century offers enough for all time. Without God, values are subjective; no judgment can be made. Man is a buffoon; and television offers continuous programs which prove it. Without God, reason is a blunt instrument, for there is no truth. Without God, there are no rights; there are only such perquisites as those who occupy the leverage points over the exercise of power permit. Without God, life is a situation comedy, and the idols provide the canned laughter at man's antics. Without God, life is a tragedy for those who aspire to something better. Without God, individual man is but a dot in the scheme of things, and those who control the organizations work out the puzzle by drawing lines from "dot to dot."

With God, the perspective changes dramatically. Individual man acquires leverage with which to deal with the world. The basis of that leverage is reason and right. Individual man can think; no group or organization can do that. If there is a God, there is truth, for He knows it. If a tree falls, and no man hear it, it still makes a sound, for God hears it. Man's special means for discerning truth is reason. Reason provides truth before which organizations, numbers, and machines must bow, else they proclaim their own futility.

The other lever is right. The individual in the right, and secure in the knowledge of right, is formidable. The most fundamental right of the individual is his right to his property. That right is affirmed over and over in Scripture. "Thou shalt not steal" is an ancient commandment, as is "Thou shalt not covet." The Apostle Paul put the most basic principle this way:

Let him that stole steal no more: but rather let him labour, working with his hands the thing which is good.... [12]

Since all other rights stem from or depend upon the right to property, all just rights of the individual have transcendant support.

Jesus demonstrated what an individual man can be and do; in this, He was man incarnate. The bare details of His life indicate that this was what He demonstrated. Of the things of the world, He had none of any consequence. He was born in a stable, in a trough from which the animals ate. His parents were people of low estate. He must have had very little of formal education or training. Legend has it that when He reached an age to work and provide for Himself, He learned and practiced the trade of carpentry. No organization ever set its seal of approval upon Him. He lamented the fact that He was without honor even in His own community. He had for support only twelve men; they were such as He gathered about Him in His wanderings, and of uncertain loyalty. He became what we would call an itinerant preacher, traveling here and there, speaking to such as would hear Him.

True, there were some who heard Him gladly. There were even those who said that He spoke with such authority as no man ever had before. But the rich young man turned away from Him sorrowfully, and people of prestige, if they came at all, came in secret, as Nicodemus did. In all those things which a man is supposed to have in order to make an impact, He had none. Organizations and men of authority suspected Him of sedition. The Sanhedrin condemned Him and turned Him over to the civil authorities of Rome to be tried. He was condemned by a throng of accusers and, though Pontius Pilate, the judge for Rome, found no fault in Him, He was condemned to be crucified to please the crowd. At the last, the authorities offered to release Him, or such as the crowd might choose. They chose a notorious thief instead.

Why were the Jewish rulers so fearful of this man? Why did the pillars of Rome tremble in His presence? Why was the crowd so determined to see Him put to death? We are not told. Yet we know. He had flung no challenges, broken no laws, formed no revolutionary party. He was innocence personified. But He had taught a way of life which undermined the way of the world, a way so superior to the way of the world that no comparison is possible. Organizations had to show their power; numbers (the throngs) had to intimidate, else they must yield; force must be triumphant. If might did not silence Him, it would give tacit approval to right, the very means by which it is constrained and limited.

But force was not triumphant. He rose again from the dead; many witnesses testified to the fact. Nor did putting Him to death put an end to His teachings. God used even this great wrong to bring about good, as He had purposed. Jesus had said, "And I, if I be lifted up from the earth [crucified], will draw all men unto me."[12] And so it has been. The good news has been told from one end of the earth to the other. Where once there were only twelve disciples, and they not firmly planted, there have since been millions moved to follow Him. True, many wrongs have been done in the name of Christ, but everyone of them was without warrant. Unable to stifle the message, the world has often enough done the next best thing: adopted it and adapted it to its own purposes, even to the use of force for supposedly good and constructive purposes. These actions have done much damage to the name Christian, but to those who will hear the message, it still shines through undimmed. To those who

508

would take it to their hearts and study it with understanding there has been given the gift of a new birth of the spirit. Everywhere that the message of love, sacrifice, and concern has gone in the world it has gentled hearts, produced works of charity, freed slaves, buttressed responsibility, and begun its work of liberation. All this has come about, "not by might, nor by power, but by my spirit, saith the Lord of Hosts."[13] It is a testament to the influence of example and to the potentiality of man — with God.

Individual man without God is very little. Man with God is in another dimension; he is man as he may be. Lest it be thought that what Jesus did does not tell us anything of the possibilities of men generally, Jesus made it clear that it does:

"Verily, verily, I say unto you, He that believeth in me, the works that I do shall he do also; and greater works than these shall he do; because I go unto my Father."[14]

Man the individual begins to come into focus with all his potentialities. "Ye are the salt of the earth," Jesus said. "Ye are the light of the world."[15]

Moreover,

"Ask, and it shall be given you; seek, and ye shall find; knock, and it shall be opened to you.
"For everyone that asketh receiveth; and he that seeketh findeth; and to him that knocketh it shall be opened."[16]

What emerges from this is a vision of a man who can stand against the might of this world. How can this be? Paul says that to do so one should "Put on the whole armour of God."

For we wrestle not against flesh and blood, but against principalities, against powers, against the rulers of the darkness of this world, against spiritual wickedness in high places.
Wherefore take unto you the whole armour of God, that ye may be able to withstand in the evil day, and having done all, to stand.
Stand, therefore, having your loins girt about with truth, and having on the breastplate of righteousness;
And your feet shod with the preparation of the gospel of peace;
Above all, taking the shield of faith ... ;
And take the helmet of salvation and the sword of the Spirit, which is the word of God.... [17]

Men who are thus prepared can stand. They have stood in the past, and they may stand again in the future.

Man is not a number, a thing, a vote, an extension of some system, an instrument of an organization, a cog in a wheel, a machine tender, a being who finds his meaning in some collective. He is touched by the Divine, a creature worthy to put in their places principalities, powers, rulers of darkness, and the wicked in high places. Each individual is a potential whole greater than the sum of his parts. Organizations and numbers have only such strength as he enables them to derive from his flesh and blood. God has placed a value on man; none may reduce that value with impunity.

40
Establishing Individual Responsibility

As THIS CONCLUDING chapter is being written there is a hint of spring in the air. The ice has melted away, and the weather has turned mild. A gentle rain has fallen, preparing the earth for a new season. A moment ago, I heard a bird chirping outside. The sap has begun to rise in the trees; the matted down grass blades look here and there as if they might be changing color from brown toward green; flowers not yet ready to bloom are nonetheless pushing gently upward toward the sun. In a few weeks, if I mistake not, tiny green leaves will be thrusting forth from the branches of trees, flowers will be blooming, and people will be emerging joyfully from their winter cocoon. The earth which lately looked so glum will be suddenly supplied, as it were, with new raiment in an ever recurring annual cycle.

Experience teaches, however, that however hopefully we anticipate the coming of spring we should be wary as well. Spring will not be likely to arrive without a great struggle in the atmosphere. The warm winds blowing up from the south collide time and again with the cold winds from the north as winter gives ground grudgingly to spring. These collisions often spawn thunderstorms, heavy rains, floods, high winds, and even tornadoes, the most locally devastating of all natural phenomena. The best things in life are not free; there is always a price to

511

pay. Stormy weather is the price we pay for spring.

But then, on the heels of these things there comes a very special moment — a few hours, a day, or, when we are lucky, several days — for all who will attend it. A time when the sun shines brightly, when the last bit of chill has gone from the air, when the wind has finally blown itself out and a near stillness is upon the earth. The fragrance of flowers fills the air, the birds are singing, and animals are at play. It is a time for sitting or lying under a tree, for suspending the never ending struggle, for drousing if that should occur, or just for peaceful contemplation. At such moments, a man may be as near to peace and a sense of harmony with nature as he gets, a nature against which he has so often struggled. He may feel himself at the threshold of some great truth. Perhaps he is. It is a time for reading and pondering these words of Jesus:

"And why take ye thought for raiment? Consider the lilies of the field, how they grow; they toil not, neither do they spin:

"And yet I say unto you, That even Solomon in all his glory was not arrayed like one of these.

"Wherefore, if God so clothe the grass of the field, which to-day is, and tomorrow is cast into the oven, shall he not much more clothe you, O ye of little faith?

"Therefore take no thought, saying, What shall we eat? or, What shall we drink? or, Wherewithal shall we be clothed? . . .

But seek ye first the kingdom of God, and his righteousness; and all these things shall be added unto you."[1]

Of course, these passages are not to be interpreted literally. No one is supposed to conclude that because lilies neither toil nor spin that man need not do so either. Clearly, that is not the case. Nor are we literally to stop giving some thought to what we will eat, drink, or wear tomorrow. If we did so, the cupboard might well be bare. Although the outward subject of these passages is faith, they also contain a lesson in economics. It is a lesson in economics with man as a value because God values him. A part of the message I glean from the quotations can be stated in this way. Do not engage in vain struggles to accomplish what cannot be done. (The immediate preceding verse reads, " 'Which of you by taking thought can add one cubit unto his stature?' ") Get yourself in accord with the nature of things. Let your efforts follow a natural course. Be right, first, and what is good and desirable will then follow from your efforts.

A simple story about economy of effort may illustrate the point. One of my older brothers explained to me how he goes about splitting logs.

512

"I don't go out and start flailing away at a log," he said. "First, I look the log over carefully, searching for clues as to which way the grain runs. If there are any cracks in the log already, they are apt to show where it will split most readily." Then, and only then, does he use the ax. A log from the right kind of tree splits easily when you go with the grain; it is virtually impossible to split it against the grain. The best way, sometimes the only way, is also the easiest way. That is the first principle of economics, from which all other principles follow. But it has an antecedent principle from which it must never be separated. It is the first principle for all of human action. Namely, *the best way is the right way for man.*

The Idea that has the world in its grip is propelling us in what is profoundly the wrong direction. It has led to multiple disasters, and we are apparently headed for catastrophe under its sway. A massive effort against the grain is going on. It is an effort to transform man, to reduce him to those aspects that are "socially useful," to integrate him into massive systems, and to subjugate him. In the effort, the attempt is being made to use collectives to intimidate him, and to transform society into an instrument of force. There is an effort to use government for ends for which it is neither suited nor effective.

All this misdirected effort has produced a vast and continuous struggle. It is not a struggle between capitalism and socialism. That Marxist canard should be laid once and for all. Socialism has subsumed capitalism, by and large, and uses it for socialist purposes. Indeed, capitalism and socialism are not foes. By capital*ism,* I understand an ideology, outlook, or set of policies that gives precedence in the economic equation of land, labor, and capital to capital, i.e., tools, machines, and the devices used in production. It devalues man and overvalues productive equipment. Private capital evinces itself as capital*ism* by using ownership to extend control over the worker so as to get the most efficient use of machines, and the use of advertising to persuade the consumer that what the machines produce is what he wants. It is true that Marx and other socialists attacked what they called capitalism, but as it turned out, what they were opposing was not capitalism but the private ownership or control of capital. Whether they intended to attack the whole structure of capitalism or not and that somehow got lost in the shuffle need not concern us here. The fact is that the more nearly socialist a country is the more capitalistic it is, i.e., the greater the emphasis upon capital. Communism turns the mechanism of the state to the accumulation of capital by confiscation and taxation. The Russians have even made movies which focused on Machine Tractor Stations. These were supposed to be a great triumph of communism, but they were in fact an indication of the weight Communists give to capital. Government intervention in gradualist countries frequently gives added weight to capital, even when that is not the stated purpose. For example, the New Deal crop restrictions and allotments for money crops gave added weight to capital (for fertilizer, improved seeds, and machinery) and made human labor much less a factor in production. In consequence, small farmers had to leave their farms in great numbers, and large farmers often got wealthy on subsidies and other price support devices.[2] Businessmen in gradualist countries generally use what leverage they have to get government to make favorable provision for capital accumulation and investment. Sweden may well be the most capitalistic of gradualist socialist countries because of government provisions encouraging capital investment. Governments themselves also make huge capital investments in gradualist countries.

The struggle is not between capitalism and socialism, then, although socialism does make greater or lesser inroads on private ownership of capital or on property generally. There is an overt struggle that goes on in gradualist countries. It is among groups, collectives, and organizations for leverage in the exercise of power. It manifests itself in confrontations, strikes, protest marches, boycotts, and a hundred and one other intimidatory methods. When revolutionary socialism enters the picture this struggle is characterized by the employment of terror and violence as well. This struggle can have devastating consequences within localities and even countries.

But this is not the main struggle going on in the world. A vast struggle is going on provoked by the massive effort to transform man and fit him to the purposes of huge organizations. It is a covert struggle. It is ordinarily so well concealed that no report of it is made in the newspapers. It is the struggle of individual man to survive and retain some shreds of his dignity as he is engulfed by huge organizations (and some not so large) in their efforts to use and control him. In what ways he conducts the struggle is often known only to the individual man, for he would be subject to penalties if it were known. The struggle evinces itself as malingering, as carelessness, as unconcern, as extra trips to the water cooler, as inefficiency, and often as nothing short of sabotage at work. One wonders how many workers have said something like this to themselves: "By God, that efficiency expert not even dry behind the ears

514

can't come in here and tell me how to do my job! I'll show him. Oh, I'll do it his way, all right, but I'll do it so poorly that production will actually fall off." During Stalin's reign in the Soviet Union, the secret police were always discovering "conspiracies" to sabotage industrial production. Probably, there were no conspiracies. What was happening was the silent resistance of individual men against being dragooned into work by a massive state. The result was shoddy goods, unfilled quotas, and work that never got done.

But this resistance is by no means confined to industrial workers; it infects every walk of life and every sort of activity. It is done by teachers who never teach but assign continual seat work to children to keep them quiet and busy. It occurs in management as men resist the hold of the organization, putting in their time, but to little effect. It occurs in other areas than the world of work. It appears as theft from chain stores, as concealment of income from government, as the dire attempt by individuals to cling to some of what is theirs by how they spend and use their money, and by every sort of evasive action that can be imagined. The customer who cannot get served or the citizen trying to work his way through the bureaucratic maze of government complains of slovenly clerks and bureaucrats. He is unlikely to attribute the behavior to its root cause: the irresponsibility which is inextricably a part of organizational approaches.

I recently overheard a conversation at a nearby table in a sparsely filled restaurant. A man who looked as if he might be nearing retirement was saying something like this: "I am going to have to quit my job. I can't stand the pressure any more. They make me responsible for getting people to do all this work, but I don't have the authority that should go with the job." What the man thought he was complaining about is usually described as "responsibility without authority." People in the lower and middle ranks of management often make this complaint, believing, I think, that there is somewhere a power to get things done that is being denied to them by the top management. It may be, of course, that an individual foreman is being denied some power, such as the power to hire and fire, which might be of some assistance to him, but that is not the basic problem. He is looking for something in the organization structure that does not inhere in it, namely, the power to make men work constructively. Organizations work quite well so long as we focus on the managerial level and ignore the purpose for which they supposedly exist. That is, the men at the top can put the pressure on and turn the screws on those lower down in the scale. They can give them ulcers and heart attacks. But at just the point where this power should be felt most strongly, at the level of getting people to do effective constructive work, it loses its motive force. Work is not something to be accomplished by regimentation; it is something best done when the whole man is engaged in it.

I incline to the view that Western Civilization is either dead or is nearing the end of a phase it entered about two hundred years ago. It entered its death throes in World War I and expired in World War II. War, however, was a consequence, not the cause. We have very nearly perfected the techniques of making machines; we have lost the art of developing men. Man is not a defective machine which, if we could only get him reworked and fitted into an organization, could perform wonders. He is an immortal soul with a mind and body, meant to grow, unfold, and blossom, even as do "the lilies of the field." His value is not a price to be determined in the marketplace; God has set a value upon him. Above all, he is meant to become a responsible person, and we are bent on keeping him a perpetual child. For example, "the whole underlying notion of our social security system is that the average man is improvident, that he does not think about tomorrow, that he is incapable of taking care of himself and his savings, that he has to be treated like a child. *This is largely true,* but the answer is not to treat the person as a child forever, but to educate the overgrown child, to teach him to stand on his own feet."[3] This failure to develop the constructive potential in man has left a void into which force has rushed. Wars are, of course, the most dramatic instances of the thrust of this force.

We stand on the threshold today of the universalizing of force around the world. Gradualist socialism pushes us in that direction by the intrusion of government into more and more areas. It may be of even greater consequence that the barbarism of revolutionary socialism is not only at the gate but already within the compound. If force should be universalized, it may turn out that gradualist socialism was a Trojan Horse, preparing the way for the triumph of communism by disseminating the idea of concerting all efforts and by sapping the West's inner strength and will to resist. The technological means for the universalizing of force are now available. From the wreck of Western Civilization we have preserved the technology of destruction. Organization and techniques have been developed for the universalizing of force. If this should happen, it would probably mean the final conquest of man.

There are other possibilities, however. It may turn out that the violent storms of the twentieth century were the portents of a coming

516

springtime for mankind. Make no mistake about this though: Mankind stands today in God's Court of Equity. He who would succeed in a court of equity must come to it with clean hands. And ours are dirty. We are deeply entrenched in the belief in our way instead of God's Way. If force should be universalized the way of the world will have triumphed, and destruction will be complete. Before that would be complete, we have God's promise that He will intervene — and time will be no more. Since our hands are dirty, we must come into God's Court of Equity as supplicants, and confess that we have treated His beloved creature — man — with contempt, that we have sought to control, coerce, and intimidate him, that we have subordinated him to machines with our organizations, that we have abused the trust with our governments by employing their force in illegitimate ways for our own devices, that we have treated his most precious creature as a thing.

It is essential at this juncture that we not protest our innocence or proclaim our righteousness. God knows the hearts of men. He knows that when we professed our love of freedom we were concealing our flight from responsibility. He does not want to hear of the bounty of goods capitalists produced with their machines; He is searching for the man who gave water to the thirsty, food to the hungry, visited the sick, comforted the bereaved, and who went into the prisons to visit the outcasts. Foreign aid from nations is as bitter as gall to his taste; He prefers the widow's mite to all the wealth that was ever amassed by taxation. He knows the venality and thirst for power of socialists; He knows the greed and hardheartedness of capitalists. Somewhere, He has kept a record of all the tears that have fallen from the eyes of small children when their plastic toys — junk — broke, bright baubles displayed by greedy merchants to induce children to importune their parents to buy them, but which broke as soon as they were out of their wrappers. He knows the consummate irresponsibility of collectivism by which each is supposed to help all but in which every man gets what he can for himself. He knows the irresponsibility of the corporate structure and the evils of inflation fueled by a banking system hidden behind its marble facade of rectitude. He has heard the ghost written lies of politicians, listened to the honeyed promises of communist hangmen, seen the gradualists hide their thrust to socialism under cover of dealing with some contemporary expediency, heard the blast of government propaganda, and winced at the distortions, lies, and half-truths of advertising. God knows every confidence man that has plagued his creatures in this century in which deceit has become a way of life. God's sorrow must be overwhelming. We should weep for Him even as we plead for ourselves.

There is hope for man yet before time is caught up in eternity and God wipes away all tears. God may have a purpose for man on this earth that has not yet been realized. One thing is certain, man has not yet realized his full potentiality. There is beautiful music not yet composed, poetry not yet written, truth not yet discovered, clothes not yet designed, houses not yet built, craftsmanship not yet developed, fields not yet plowed, trees not yet planted, eye and body pleasing goods not yet produced. There are babies unyet born whose fathers may look upon them and know in their hearts that God still performs miracles. There is righteousness in man that has not yet unfolded. His potentialities for doing good, for loving kindness, for serving those for whom he cares, for overcoming evil with good, have hardly been touched. The apparent dead end looming ahead may conceal a passageway to a new beginning.

There is a hint of spring in the air, a hint not only of the arrival of a new season in the year but also of a new cycle in history, a new era in mankind's story. We stand too close to events to discern the shape they are assuming, but there are signs already of what may be.

But before getting to that let us say what must not be. We are surely *not* on the verge of a new surge of collectivism. The world is weary of socialism; the dead end toward which it leads should be apparent to all who examine it. It will not be a return to nineteenth century liberalism, that pallid offspring of the French Revolution which has done already what good it could do. It will not be a return to laissez-faire capitalism. And thank God. That was a theory for leaving the capitalist free to do what he pleased, and leaving the rest of us free to do what *he* pleased also. In any case, capitalism has now been largely swallowed up in socialism and is inextricably a part of the disease which afflicts us. Nor will it be a return to theocracy. True religion does not need the force of government to support it, and false ones should not have that power at their disposal. Nor is it my expectation that the generality of men will be converted to Christianity. I do hope that there will be enough to serve as that yeast, a little of which will cause the whole loaf to rise.

The hint of springtime for mankind is not of a recurrence of something that has been before. Jesus Christ broke the cycle of eternal recurrences which was the tale of history before His Incarnation. He intertwined the City of God with the city of man so as to give to earth a purpose beyond itself. He planted an idea which may yet bring forth such fruit as this world has never seen. Man's despair is God's

518

opportunity, and having witnessed the horrendous consequences of our devices we may be ready to try better ones.

Some of the signs that can be perceived already are these. Men appear to be losing what confidence they have ever reposed in politicians. It is near dead certainty that however much a president may talk of economy and balancing the budget during the first two or three years of his term he will do an about face and flood the country with fiat money as the time for his election approaches. The loss of confidence in politicians is prelude to a loss of faith that government can solve our problems. Many young people are almost unbelievably cynical about organizations and are ready to believe that just about everything is a "rip-off." These would not be hopeful developments in and of themselves were they not the preparing of the ground for something else.

Men are beginning to relearn an old truth: "If you want something done right, do it yourself." Specialization is breaking down. Many a person is learning to repair and service his automobile, do his own carpentry, make objects of art and use, do his plumbing, work with electricity, sew, and do a hundred and one other useful tasks. Men are subtly working to get control of their affairs back into their own hands. They are considering individual devices for providing electricity for their homes. In a thousand uncharted ways they are seeking to disentangle themselves from organizations and collectives. Associational and congregational churches are growing by leaps and bounds while what may be called the organizational churches are declining and disintegrating. The stock market is stuck in what appears to be a rut, a pattern of short rises and deeper drops. This may be a sign that the corporation is slowly dying.

We have turned to organizations for succor only to discover that they are battening on our own flesh and blood. That is so because all organizations are like government, which is their model; they give only what we have first put into them. They give much less than we could have given because we put only a small part of ourselves into the organizational effort. Nor can it be otherwise, for control from the top downward insures that what will be accomplished will be restricted largely to what can be determined and directed from above. The illusion of the effectiveness of large organizations is created by the immense outlay for and concentration of capital.

The fundamental flaw in collectives and organizations is their ingrained and irreversible *irresponsibility*. As soon as control is exerted over people — whether by private businesses, charitable organizations,

519

labor unions, or governments — they tend to believe they are no longer responsible for what they do. Make a complaint to someone in an organization and the most likely response will be: "Look, I just work here." Who has not heard it? What the person is saying is that he is not responsible for what the organization does, though he may be helping to do it. You can yammer at people until you are blue in the face about how they are in fact partly responsible but it is like trying to split logs against the grain. They know that if they do not personally control what is being done they are not responsible for it.

Leonard Read points out how people do not feel any sense of wrongdoing when they benefit from the wrongdoing of government:

Now take note of a startling fact. Those who wouldn't personally steal a dollar from anyone will favor the government stealing for them [by way of taxation] and with no sense of sin or guilt.... I wouldn't steal your horse but it's all right if someone else does the stealing for me!"[4]

It is hardly different where government is not directly involved. People who would not take a dollar bill from you and tear it in half will nonetheless continue to make deposits in and borrow money from banks which have the effect of reducing the value of your money. I pointed out in an earlier chapter how depositors and borrowers fuel inflation. My guess is that of those who may have read and been convinced of the validity of this analysis there may not have been one person who stopped using the banks. I did not expect that they would, nor have I done so myself.

There is a reason for all this. There is no such thing as collective, organizational, or corporate responsibility. All responsibility is individual and personal. It is pagan idolatry to attribute the kind of reality to collectives or organizations in which they could act or be responsible. Men make such silly statements as that they are speaking for an organization. This is impossible, for organizations have no thoughts which can be expressed. There is no collective guilt, for no collective has anything with which to register guilt. The individual can be responsible for collective action only if he has instigated it. Even then, the lines of responsibility are blurred. In any case, only individuals can be held responsible and punished. All wrongdoing is either by an individual or a conspiracy among several.

Individual responsibility is the key that will unlock the door leading out of the maze in which we are caught.

The establishment of individual responsibility entails reducing things to a man-sized level so that responsible individuals can be identified and held responsible. It means reducing things to the level that the individual can manage his affairs. It means reducing them to the level that the individual person is the beginning and the end of what happens. It means putting the one essential organization — government — firmly in its place and making all other organizations only occasional adjuncts of the individual. It means rigorously removing all government support from or control of organizations.

In logic, freedom is antecedent to responsibility. That is, an act must be freely done for the individual to be fully responsible for it. In time — i.e., in history, in the life of a person, in the development of a nation — responsibility is antecedent to freedom. In bringing up a child, he should be allowed only such freedom as he has demonstrated he can responsibly use. We are not free in order to be responsible; we are responsible in order to be free.

An attempt to establish liberty, however, goes against the grain. Most of the efforts to establish liberty in our era have foundered sooner or later, and most of them sooner rather than later. This occurs because individual liberty is not a primary social concern. It is primarily a concern of the individual, and each individual, so far as he may be concerned with it, is concerned with it only as it touches him. I do not mean that there are not benefits to others which arise from liberty but rather that they tend to be either obscure or so remote that they do not ordinarily engage the attention of the individual. In fact, people are much more apt to be interested in doing as they please and having other people do what they want them to than they are in any refined concept of liberty. Nor is liberty much of a concern to government. It is always an uphill battle to get government to make room for individual liberty. That is because individual liberty is a negative value for government; it involves the restraining and limiting of government.

By contrast, the establishing of individual responsibility goes with the grain of both society and legitimate government. Men are behaving most naturally in society when they are holding individuals responsible. Social judgments have to do mainly with standards of behavior, performance, and construction. Even gossip, the least attractive of society's activities, is a device which makes known generally immoral and other sorts of behavior that are not in accord with social norms. Men under the sway of the Idea that has the world in its grip have made a tremendous assault on the norms of society and tried to set at naught the normal function of society. The effect of these efforts, so far as they

521

have been successful, is not to transform society but to disintegrate it. We will either have society enforcing its norms or force in its place, and we are getting more and more force. My point, however, is that no particular effort has to be made to get society to perform its appointed role of holding individuals responsible; that is what it does in myriad ways when it is free.

Government can only act upon individuals, and when it is performing the function for which it is suited, it acts upon individuals to hold them responsible for wrongdoing. Government acts by intimidation, coercion, and the use of force. These are the necessary and appropriate methods for apprehending and punishing wrongdoers. It is necessary and proper, too, that a government have a monopoly of the use of force within its jurisdiction. Organization is essential and proper to government; it is the right means for coercive action. (Obviously, governments normally carry on relations with other governments and sometimes engage in conflicts with them. In such cases, they deal with aggregates of people, but not very effectively.)

The most difficult task of government is to locate, isolate and prove that particular individuals have been guilty of wrongdoing. The conditions that make it possible for individuals to control and manage their affairs are the ones that make it easiest for government to do its business, namely, hold individuals responsible for wrongdoing. Organizations which disperse and conceal responsibility are anathema to the proper function of governments. Labor unions and corporations, for example, make it quite difficult, and often very nearly impossible, for government to do its work effectively. It goes with the grain of government not to support, recognize, or permit the existence of organizations which vie with it to control individuals or provide a framework within which their wrongdoing can be concealed. The simpler the situation, the more readily can government do its work.

Governments everywhere pose two great problems today. (The problems are not new, but they have been intensified by the religious fervor of socialism.) The first is to restrict government to those functions for which the use of coercion is appropriate and effective. It follows from what has been said and shown in these pages that government is not an instrument to be used for constructive purposes, both because it is an organization and because it uses force. Force may be rightfully and properly used only as retaliation against individuals, nations, and groups who have been found guilty of wrongdoing or must be apprehended so that a determination of whether or not they are can be made. The limitation of government is best done by constitutions, and the world today is in a constitutional crisis.

The other great problem has hardly been faced anywhere in the world. It is this: The holding of individuals within government responsible for exceeding the authority of the constitution or otherwise violating it. The United States Constitution may have been the best and wisest ever drawn. Certainly, it gained for itself much greater respect and veneration than have most constitutions. Yet it includes no explicit provisions for holding individuals responsible for constitutional violations. Government is an organization and, as such, offers numerous possibilities for concealment of responsibility. It needs, therefore, carefully spelled out constitutional safeguards against violators. For example, legislators who vote for a measure which exceeds constitutional authority ought to be removable from office by court action instituted by citizens. Such penalties would induce those who act with the power of government to attend most carefully to the limits upon them.

The other great task today is to remove the handles by which individuals are controlled. The handles in the United States and many other countries are organizations, many of them private or semiprivate. It is by way of these that governments attempt to control the economy and exercise power over individuals. It is large organizations which provided the notion of integrating the economy and concerting all efforts. It was the limited liability corporation which paved the way for much of the irresponsibility rampant today. (By way of stock ownership, one may own property but be relieved of all responsibility for its management.) The way out is to make the individual fully responsible for his affairs, indeed, in general, to allow him no means of having affairs which he cannot personally manage.

The great task before us is one of *disorganization,* the disorganization of industry, the disorganization of education, the disorganization of entertainment, the disorganization of medicine, the disorganization of banking, and so on and on. This can be accomplished mainly by removing government privileges, subsidies, and operations from all constructive activities. Remove the privilege of limited liability from the corporation, and the corporation will disintegrate. Remove the fractional reserve privilege from banking, and if banks survive, they will cease to be an engine of inflation. Make every individual fully responsible at law for any uses to which his property is put, and the attractiveness of hiring other people will tend to evaporate.

When looked at from the angle of freedom many things would appear to be permissible and desirable which when looked at from the angle of responsibility become illicit and inefficient. There is nothing in the theory of liberty which would limit one from hiring as many people as he could and setting them to whatever tasks he sees fit (supposing the undertaking to be legal). It is illicit because ownership gets separated from responsibility. It is inefficient because the hired worker is unlikely to be fully engaged in his task. Freedom and responsibility must always be kept in tandem.

It may be objected that what is being proposed amounts to throwing the baby out with the bath. On the contrary, the whole focus is upon the baby, i.e., man the individual. Man today is caught in the tentacles of great organizations. The thirst for the capital which makes it appear that these organizations are effective is impoverishing us all. It is precisely the baby, i.e., man, that these proposals would place at the center of affairs. Tools are meant to be adjuncts of man, not man an adjunct of machines. Ownership confers control over property, not over men. Undoubtedly, economics takes on a different aspect when man is at the center of things. There is no longer a national economy or world economy. Indeed, there is no longer an economy of any organization, except for the one "organization" which is superior to all others — man. When man is in control of his affairs and doing his own work, labor ceases to be an expense; it becomes an asset to be used as fully as possible. The emphasis shifts from quantity to quality, for it is quality that labor can add to a product.

But how will all the things that we want be produced? O ye of little faith! I suppose that it is just those things that we want most that would get produced. When the individual is managing his own affairs he will study to produce what will most readily sell, not spend so much energy selling what is easiest to produce. Those who have an excess of capital beyond their own needs may spend their energy organizing things instead of people. But, in truth, I have no notion what different sorts of ways free and responsible men might devise to get things done. I only know that it is the easy way. I know that it is the right way. Today, a vast effort is being made to do things against the grain. Man supposes that by taking thought he can concert all human effort and produce a great bounty. Not only is this great effort monstrously wasteful and counterproductive, but it is also oppressive and destructive.

It is not for man to give thought to coordinating economies or concerting all human effort. There is an "invisible hand" that will take care of this for free and responsible individuals. All the thought in the world will not add one cubit to its effectivenessness. "Consider the lilies of the field, how they grow; they toil not, neither do they spin. And yet I say unto you, That even Solomon in all his glory was not arrayed like one of these."

It is for man to study only to do what is right. "But seek ye first the kingdom of God, and his righteousness; and all these things shall be added unto you."

Let it be so.

Notes

Chapter 1

[1]Hedrick Smith, *The Russians* (New York: Quadrangle, 1976), pp. 9-10.

[2]*Ibid.*, p. 255.

[3]Thomas Carlyle, *Sartor Resartus* (New York: E. P. Dutton, 1908), p. 46.

[4]Robert K. Massie, *Nicholas and Alexandra* (New York: Dell, 1967), p. 515.

Chapter 2

[1]Bertram D. Wolfe, *Marxism* (New York: Dial, 1965), p. 361.

[2]Karl Marx and Friedrich Engels, *Selected Works* (New York: International Publishers, 1968), p. 204.

[3]*Ibid.*, p. 207.

[4]*Ibid.*, p. 209.

[5]*Ibid.*, p. 212.

[6]*Ibid.*, p. 208.

[7]This is not to belittle the achievement of the Austrian School in their effort to refute Marx. Their achievement, however, is accomplished by denying the validity of Marx's concept of value. That is to say, their refutation depends on abandoning his framework.

[8]Wolfe, *op. cit.*, p. 369.

[9]Quoted in Thomas Molnar, *The Decline of the Intellectual* (New York: Meridian, 1961), p. 90.

[10]Marx wrote a goodly amount of verse in his youth, and even retained an interest in poetry after he became a revolutionary. See David McLellan, *Karl Marx: His Life and Thought* (New York: Harper & Row, 1973), pp. 20-25, 103-104. Engels was said to have been something of a poet, too.

[11]Z. A. Jordan, ed., *Karl Marx: Economy, Class and Society* (New York: Scribner's, 1971), pp. 126-27.

[12]*Ibid.,* p. 299.

[13]*Ibid.,* p. 283.

[14]*Ibid.,* p. 292.

[15]Quoted in McLellan, *op. cit.,* p. 118.

[16]*Ibid.,* p. 119.

[17]Jordan, *op. cit.,* p. 301.

[18]See Wolfe, *op. cit.,* p. 198.

[19]Jordan, *op. cit.,* p. 292.

[20]*Ibid.,* p. 294.

Chapter 3

[1]Quoted in Thomas Molnar, *The Decline of the Intellectual* (Cleveland: World Publishing Co., 1961), p. 81.

[2]Harry W. Laidler, *History of Socialism* (New York: Thomas Y. Crowell, 1968), pp. 220-21.

[3]Eugen Weber, ed. *The Western Tradition* (Boston: D.C. Heath, 1959), p. 663.

[4]Laidler, *op. cit.,* p. 212.

[5]Quoted in Peter Gay, *The Dilemma of Democratic Socialism* (New York: Collier, 1962), pp. 147-48.

[6]Weber, *op. cit.,* pp. 664-65.

[7]Gay, *op. cit.,* pp. 251-52.

[8]Laidler, *op. cit.,* p. 199.

Chapter 4

[1]Donald W. Treadgold, *Twentieth Century Russia* (Chicago: Rand McNally, 1964, 2nd edition), pp. 33-34.

[2]Erwin Oberländer, "The Role of the Political Parties," in Oberländer, *et. al., Russia Enters the Twentieth Century* (New York: Schocken Books, 1971), p. 61.

Chapter 5

[1]Robert V. Daniels, *Red October* (New York: Charles Scribner's Sons, 1967), p. 196.

[2]See Donald W. Treadgold, *Twentieth Century Russia* (Chicago: Rand McNally, 1964, 2nd ed.), p. 157.

[3]*Ibid*, p. 158.

[4]Robert Payne, *The Life and Death of Lenin* (New York: Simon and Schuster, 1964), p. 431.

[5]*Ibid*, p. 433.

[6]See Daniels, *op. cit.*, p. 40.

[7]Quoted in *ibid.*, p. 71.

[8]*Ibid.*, p. 157.

[9]Alfred G. Meyer, *Leninism* (New York: Praeger, 1957), p. 35.

[10]*Ibid*, pp. 69-70.

[11]*Ibid.*, pp. 32-33.

[12]Payne, *op. cit.*, p. 414.

[13]*Ibid*, p. 482.

[14]Meyer, *op. cit.*, p. 99.

[15]*Ibid*, p. 96.

[16]Payne, *op. cit.*, pp. 480-81.

[17]J.P. Netti, *The Soviet Achievement* (New York: Harcourt, Brace & World, 1967), p. 64.

[18]Treadgold, *op. cit.*, p. 156.

[19]Quoted in Edward H. Carr, *Socialism in One Country,* I (New York: Macmillan, 1958), p. 31.

[20]*Ibid*, p. 29.

[21]*Ibid.*, p. 38.

Chapter 6

[1]Leopold Tyrmand, *Notebooks of a Dilettante* (New York: Macmillan, 1970), pp. 85-87.

[2]Arthur J. May, *Europe Since 1939* (New York: Holt, Rinehart and Winston, 1966), p. 193.

[3]Alfred G. Meyer, *The Soviet Political System* (New York: Random House, 1965), p. 199.

[4]Merle Fainsod *How Russia is Ruled* (Cambridge: Harvard University Press, 1963), p. 353.

[5]*Ibid,* p. 367.

[6]*Ibid,* pp. 384-85.

[7]Oleg Penkovskiy, *The Penkovskiy Papers* (Garden City, N.Y.: Doubleday, 1965), p. 66.

[8]Hedrick Smith, *The Russians* (New York: Quadrangle, 1976), p. 436.

[9]Robert G. Kaiser, *Russia* (New York: Atheneum, 1976), p. 105.

[10]*Ibid,* p. 106.

[11]*Hearing,* House Committee on Un-American Activities. August 10, 1967 (Washington: U.S. Government Printing Office, 1967), p. 535.

[12]Kaiser, *op. cit.,* p. 105.

[13]Leopold Tyrmand. *The Rosa Luxemburg Contraceptive Cooperative* (New York: Macmillan, 1972), p. 80.

[14]*Ibid,* pp. 82-83.

[15]Kaiser, *op. cit.,* p. 176.

[16]Smith, *op. cit.,* p. 204.

[17]Kaiser, *op. cit.,* pp. 177-78.

Chapter 7

[1]Eugene Lyons, *Worker's Paradise Lost* (New York: Twin Circle, 1967), pp. 137-38.

[2]*Ibid,* p. 148.

[3]Alexander Dolgun with Patrick Watson. *Alexander Dolgun's Story: An American in the Gulag* (New York: Ballantine, 1976), p. 446.

[4]Robert Conquest, *The Great Terror* (Toronto: Macmillan, 1968), pp. 140-41.

[5]Roy A. Medvedev, *Let History Judge: The Origins and Consequences of Stalinism* (New York: Alfred A. Knopf, 1971), p. 269.

[6]Conquest, *op. cit.,* pp. 167-68.

[7]*Ibid,* p. 311.

[8]Isaac Don Levine, *Plain Talk* (New Rochelle: Arlington House, 1976), p. 263.

[9]*Ibid,* p. 266.

[10]*Ibid,* p. 273.

[11]*Ibid,* pp. 289-90.

[12]Alexsandr I. Solzhenitsyn, *The Gulag Archipelago Two* (New York: Harper & Row, 1975), p. 171.

Chapter 8

[1]Zhores A. Medvedev and Roy A. Medvedev, *A Question of Madness* (New York: Alfred A. Knopf, 1971), pp. 183-84.

[2]David Granick, "Plant Managers and Their Overseers," in Joseph L. Nogee, *Man, State, and Society in the Soviet Union* (New York: Praeger, 1972), p. 198.

[3]John Gunther, *Inside Russia Today* (New York: Harper & Row, 1962, rev. ed.), p. 76.

[4]Hedrick Smith, *The Russians* (New York: Quadrangle, 1976), p. 104.

[5]Leona and Jerrold Schechter, *et al., An American Family in Moscow* (Boston: Little, Brown and Co., 1975), p. 104.

[6]Smith, *op. cit.,* p. 104.

[7]Schechter and Schechter, *op. cit.,* pp. 235-36.

[8]*Ibid,* p. 372.

[9]Smith, *op. cit.,* p. 288.

[10]*Ibid,* p. 292.

Chapter 9

[1]Clarence B. Carson, *The Flight from Reality* (Irvington, N.Y., FEE: 1969), p. 302.

[2]Arnold J. Heidenheimer, *The Government of Germany* (New York: Thomas Y. Crowell, 1971, 3rd ed.), p. 4.

[3]R. R. Palmer and Joel Colton, *A History of the Modern World* (New York: Alfred A. Knopf, 1968, rev. ed.), pp. 759-60.

[4]Erich Eyck, *A History of the Weimar Republic,* II (Cambridge: Harvard University Press, 1963), p. 164.

[5]Robert Payne, *The Life and Death of Adolf Hitler* (New York: Praeger, 1973), p. 151.

[6]*Ibid,* pp. 161-62.

[7]See S. William Halperin, *Germany Tried Democracy* (New York: W. W. Norton, 1946), pp. 285-86.

Chapter 10

[1]Eliot B. Wheaton, *Prelude to Calamity: The Nazi Revolution* 1933-35 (Garden City, N.Y.: Doubleday, 1968), pp. 202-203.

[2]Adolf Hitler, *Mein Kampf,* trans. Ralph Manheim (Boston: Houghton Mifflin, 1943), p. 453.

[3]*Ibid,* p. 472.

[4]*Ibid,* p. 448.

[5]*Ibid,* p. 604.

[6]*Ibid,* p. 405.

[7]*Ibid,* pp. 577-78.

[8]*Ibid,* p. 581.

[9]Wheaton, *op. cit.,* p. 97.

Chapter 11

[1]Alan Bullock, *Hitler: A Study in Tyranny* (New York: Harper & Row, 1962, rev. ed.), p. 257.

[2]See Eliot B. Wheaton, *Prelude to Calamity: The Nazi Revolution, 1933-35* (New York: Doubleday, 1968), pp. 230-43.

[3]William L. Shirer, *The Rise and Fall of the Third Reich* (New York: Simon and Schuster, 1960), p. 194.

[4]*Ibid.*

[5]Bullock, *op. cit.,* p. 264.

[6]Wheaton, *op. cit.,* p. 436.

[7]Heinz Hohne, *The Order of the Death's Head,* Richard Barry, trans. (New York: Coward-McCann, 1969), p. 85.

[8]*Ibid,* p. 86.

[9]Bullock, *op. cit.,* pp. 274-75.

[10]Wheaton, *op. cit.,* p. 288.

[11]*Ibid,* p. 303.

[12]Shirer, *op. cit.,* p. 235.

[13]*Ibid,* p. 239.

[14]*Ibid,* p. 222.

[15]Bullock, *op. cit.,* p. 308.

[16]Bruno Bettelheim, *The Informed Heart: Autonomy in a Mass Age* (Glencoe, Illinois: The Free Press, 1960), p. 124.

[17]See *ibid,* pp. 133-34.

[18]*Ibid,* p. 136.

[19]*Ibid,* p. 171.

Chapter 12

[1]Albert Speer, *Inside the Third Reich,* trans. by Richard and Clara Winston (New York: Avon Books, 1970), p. 181.

[2]Nikita Khrushchev, *Khrushchev Remembers*, trans. and ed. by Strobe Talbott (New York: Bantam, 1970), p. 614.

[3]*Ibid*, p. 279.

[4]Speer, *op. cit.*, pp. 137.

[5]Khrushchev, *op. cit.*, pp. 320-21.

[6]*Ibid*, p. 648.

[7]Speer, *op. cit.*, p. 175.

[8]Vladimir Yurasov, *Parallax*, trans. by Tatiana Balkoff Drowne (New York: W. W. Norton, 1966), p. 124.

[9]Alan Bullock, *Hitler, A Study in Tyranny* (New York: Harper & Row, 1962, rev. ed.), p. 402.

[10]*Ibid*, p. 401.

[11]*Ibid*, p. 405.

[12]Richard Grunberger, *The 12-Year Reich* (New York: Holt, Rinehart and Winston, 1971), p. 331.

[13]See *ibid*, p. 395.

[14]*Ibid*, pp. 456, 461.

[15]*Ibid*, p. 163.

[16]Leopold Tyrmand, *The Rosa Luxemburg Contraceptives Cooperative* (New York: Macmillan, 1972), p. 165.

[17]Grunberger, *op. cit.*, p. 340.

Chapter 13

[1]See John Toland, *The Last 100 Days* (New York: Random House, 1966), pp. 130-49.

[2]Peter Calvocoressi and Guy Wint, *Total War: The Story of World War II* (New York: Pantheon Books, 1972), p. 267.

[3]David Irving, *Hitler's War* (New York: Viking Press, 1977), p. 363.

[4]Toland, *op. cit.*, p. 9.

[5]Calvocoressi and Wint, *op. cit*, p. 212.

[6]Irving, *op. cit.*, pp. 403-404.

[7]Hugh Seton-Watson, *From Lenin to Malenkov* (New York: Frederick A. Praeger, 1953), p. 74.

[8]*Ibid*.

[9]*Encyclopaedia Britannica* XXIII (1955), 793R.

[10]Arthur J. May, *Europe Since 1939* (New York: Holt, Rinehart and Winston, 1966), p. 76.

[11]Calvocoressi and Wint, *op. cit.,* pp. 476-77.

[12]May, *op. cit.,* p. 97.

Chapter 15

[1]Quoted in Walter E. Houghton, *The Victorian Frame of Mind, 1830-1870* (New Haven: Yale University Press, 1967), p. 39.

[2]David Thomson, *England in the Nineteenth Century* (Baltimore: Penguin Books, 1950), p. 103.

[3]Thomas B. Macaulay, *Miscellaneous Essays and Poems,* I (Philadelphia: Porter and Coates, 1879), p. 475.

[4]Quoted in Thomson, *op. cit.,* p. 104.

[5]Quoted in Houghton, *op. cit.,* p. 39.

[6]Macaulay, *op. cit.,* p. 769.

[7]W. E. H. Lecky, *History of Rationalism in Europe,* II (London: Longmans, Green, and Co., 1904, originally pub. 1865), p. 351.

[8]*Ibid,* p. 356.

[9]*Ibid,* p. 367.

[10]Quoted in Thomson, *op. cit.,* pp. 102-103.

[11]Quoted in Asa Briggs, *The Age of Improvement* (London: Longmans, Green, and Co., 1859), p. 464.

[12]Charles Kingsley, *Sermons for the Times* (London: Macmillan, 1899), first pub. by Macmillan in 1863), pp. 195-196. This is the same Charles Kingsley who, along with F. D. Maurice, was an early Christian socialist. This description of him, however, may be misleading. Not only does the above quotation not indicate any socialist sentiments, such as we have come to recognize them, but there is good reason to believe that he was a pre-statist socialist. "He looked rather to the extension of the co-operative principle and to sanitary reform for the amelioration of the condition of the people than to any radical political change." *Encyclopedia Britannica* (Chicago, 1955), XIII, 399.

[13]Herbert Spencer, *Social Statics* (New York: Appleton, 1865), p. 334.

[14]Samuel Smiles, *Thrift* (Chicago: Belfords, Clarke and Co., 1879), pp. 20-21.

[15]Thomson, *op. cit.,* pp. 113-14.

[16]Quoted in G. D. Klingopulos, "The Literary Scene," *From Dickens to Hardy,* Boris Ford, ed. (Baltimore: Penguin Books, 1958), p. 70.

[17]Thomas Carlyle, *Sartor Resartus* (New York: Dutton, 1908), pp. 174-75.

[18]W. E. Lunt, *History of England* (New York: Harper, 1957, 4th ed.), p. 752.

[19]Matthew Arnold, *Culture and Anarchy,* R. H. Super, ed. (Ann Arbor: University of Michigan Press, 1965), p. 146.

[20]*Ibid.,* pp. 140-41.

[21]*Ibid.,* p. 143.

[22]*Ibid.,* pp. 223-24.

[23]John Ruskin, *Ruskin's Views of Social Justice,* James Fuchs, ed. (New York: Vanguard Press, 1926), pp. 29-30.

[24]Briggs, *op. cit.,* p. 473.

[25]Klingopulos, *op. cit.,* p. 14.

Chapter 16

[1]Margaret Cole, *The Story of Fabian Socialism* (Stanford: Stanford University Press, 1961), pp. 3-5.

[2]A. M. McBriar, *Fabian Socialism and English Politics* (London: Cambridge University Press, 1962), p. 23.

[3]Cole, *op. cit.,* p. 273.

[4]Sister M. Margaret Patricia McCarran, *Fabianism in the Political Life of Britain* (Chicago: Heritage Foundation, 1954, 2nd ed.), pp. 41-45.

[5]Quoted in John Bowle, *Politics and Opinion in the Nineteenth Century* (New York: Oxford University Press, A Gallaxy Book, 1964), p. 66.

[6]Roland N. Stromberg, *European Intellectual History Since 1789* (New York: Appelton-Century-Crofts, 1968), p. 53.

[7]*Ibid.,* pp. 72-73.

[8]McBriar, *op. cit.,* p. 8.

[9]M. Beer, *A History of British Socialism,* II (London: George Allen and Unwin, 1953), 245.

[10]R. C. K. Ensor, *England: 1870-1914* (London: Oxford University Press, 1936), p. 334.

[11]McBriar, *op. cit,* p. 30.

[12]Anne Freemantle, *This Little Band of Prophets* (New York: Macmillan, 1960), p. 34.

[13]Salo W. Baron, "George Bandes and Lord Beaconsfield" in George Bandes, *Lord Beaconsfield* (New York: Crowell, 1966), p. vii.

[14]Ensor, *op. cit.,* p. 35-36.

[15]McBriar, *op. cit.,* pp. 60-61.

[16]Beer, *op. cit.,* pp. 67-69.

[17]McBriar, *op. cit.,* p. 11.

[18]*Ibid.,* p. 62.

[19]*Ibid.,* p. 92; C. Northcote Parkinson, *Left Luggage* (Boston: Houghton-Mifflin, 1967), p. 94.

[20]Glenn Negley and J. Max Patrick, *The Quest for Utopia* (New York: Henry Schuman, 1952), pp. 19-22.

[21]Ensor, *op. cit.,* p. 334.

Chapter 17

[1]J. Salwyn Schapiro, ed., *Movements of Social Dissent in Modern Europe* (Princeton: D. Van Nostrand, 1962), p. 161.

[2]James Fuchs, ed., *The Socialism of Shaw* (New York: Vanguard Press, 1926), p. 49.

[3]A. M. McBriar, *Fabian Socialism and English Politics* (Cambridge: Cambridge University Press, 1962), pp. 95-96.

Chapter 18

[1]*Herbert Spencer, The Man Versus the State,* Albert Jay Nock, intro. (Caldwell, Idaho: Caxton, 1940), p. xii.

[2]*Ibid.,* pp. 10-14.

[3]A. J. P. Taylor, *English History: 1914-1945* (New York: Oxford University Press, 1965), p. 1.

[4]Alfred E. Havighurst, *Twentieth Century Britain* (New York: Harper and Row, 1962, 2nd ed.), p. 85.

[5]*Ibid.,* p. 83.

[6]D. C. Somerwell, *British Politics Since 1900* (London: Andrew Dakens, 1953, rev. ed.), p. 55.

[7]Carl F. Brand, *The British Labor Party* (Stanford: Stanford University Press, 1964), pp. 20-21.

[8]Stephen B. Baxter, ed., *Basic Documents of English History* (Boston: Houghton Mifflin, 1968), pp. 250-51.

[9]Havighurst, *op. cit.,* pp. 99-100.

[10]See Baxter, *op. cit.,* pp. 257-58.

[11]R. C. K. Ensor, *England: 1870-1914* (Oxford: Oxford University Press, 1936), p. 31.

[12]George Dangerfield, *The Strange Death of Liberal England* (New York: Capricorn Books, 1961), p. 40.

[13]Havighurst, *op. cit.,* p. 69.

[14]*Ibid.,* p. 94.

[15]See Dangerfield, *op. cit.,* pp. 14-15.

[16]Havighurst, *op. cit.,* p. 102.

[17]See Carlton J. H. Hayes, *Contemporary Europe Since 1870* (New York: Macmillan, 1958, rev. ed.), p. 319.

[18]Quoted in *Encyclopaedia Britannica,* XIV (1955), 251.

[19]Dangerfield, *op. cit.,* pp. 18-19.

[20]See Baxter, *op. cit.,* pp. 256-57.

[21]Taylor, *op. cit.,* p. 73.

[22]*Ibid,* pp. 74-75.

[23]*Ibid.,* p. 53.

[24]Henry Pelling, *A Short History of the Labour Party* (London: Macmillan, 1961), p. 39.

[25]See *ibid.,* p. 28.

[26]*Ibid.,* p. 42.

[27]Quoted in *ibid.,* p. 44.

[28]Brand, *op. cit.,* pp. 56-57.

Chapter 19

[1]Walter L. Arnstein, *Britain: Yesterday and Today* (Boston: D. C. Heath, 1966), p. 237.

[2]See *ibid.,* pp. 372-73 for a simplified chart of the relationship of Queen Victoria to the other monarchs in Europe.

[3]C. E. Black and E. C. Helmreich. *Twentieth Century Europe* (New York: Alfred A. Knopf, 1960), pp. 293-94.

[4]*Ibid.,* p. 291.

[5]Shepard B. Clough, *European Economic History* (New York: McGraw-Hill, 1968, 2nd ed.), p. 419.

[6]See Charles Loch Mowat, *Britain Between the Wars* (Chicago: University of Chicago Press, 1955), p. 262.

[7]Clough, *op. cit.,* p. 397.

[8]Loch Mowat, *op. cit.,* p. 276.

[9]Sidney Pollard, *The Development of the British Economy: 1914-1950* (London: Edward Arnold, 1962), pp. 110-11.

[10]*Ibid.,* p. 114.

[11]*Ibid.,* p. 121.

[12]*Ibid.*, p. 117.

[13]*Ibid.*, p. 98.

[14]Loch Mowat, *op. cit.*, pp. 250-53.

[15]Pollard, *op. cit.*, p. 142.

[16]David Thomson, *England in the Twentieth Century* (Baltimore: Penguin Books, 1965), p. 67.

[17]Loch Mowat, *op. cit.*, pp. 13-14.

[18]*Ibid.*, p. 15.

[19]Alfred F. Havighurst, *Twentieth Century Britain* (New York: Harper and Row, 1962, 2nd ed.), p. 171.

[20]Loch Mowat, *op. cit.*, p. 127.

[21]*Ibid.*, p. 268.

[22]*Ibid.*, p. 276.

[23]Pollard, *op. cit.*, p. 116.

[24]*Ibid.*, p. 141.

[25]A. J. P. Taylor, *English History: 1914-1945* (New York: Oxford University Press, 1965), p. 168.

[26]Robert Graves and Alan Hodge, *The Long Week-End* (New York: Norton, 1963), p. 113.

Chapter 20

[1]Keith Hutchison, *The Decline and Fall of British Capitalism* (London: Jonathan Cape, 1951), p. 291.

[2]A. J. P. Taylor, *English History: 1914-1945* (New York: Oxford University Press, 1965), p. 507.

[3]Sidney Pollard, *The Development of the British Economy: 1914-1950* (London: Edward Arnold, 1962), pp. 348-49.

[4]*Ibid.*, p. 350.

[5]Hutchison, *op. cit.*, p. 285.

[6]Francis Williams, *Socialist Britain* (New York: Viking Press, 1949), p. 13.

[7]David Thomson, *England in the Twentieth Century* (Baltimore: Penguin Books, 1965), p. 202.

[8]Williams, *op. cit.*, p. 13.

[9]*Ibid.*, p. 11.

[10]Alfred F. Havighurst, *Twentieth-Century Britain* (New York: Harper and Row, 1962, 2nd ed.), p. 369.

[11]See Stephen B. Baxter, ed., *Basic Documents of English History* (Boston: Houghton Mifflin, 1968), p. 281-82.

[12]*Ibid.*, p. 288.

[13]Williams, *op. cit.*, p. 127.

[14]Havighurst, *op. cit.*, p. 370.

[15]Williams, *op. cit.*, p. 5.

[16]*Ibid.*, pp. 87-88.

[17]*Ibid.*, pp. 93-94.

[18]Havighurst, *op. cit.*, p. 384.

[19]Williams, *op. cit.*, p. 98.

[20]Pollard, *op. cit.*, p. 366.

[21]Bertrand de Jouvenel, *Problems of Socialist England*, J. F. Huntington, trans, (London: Batchworth Press, 1949), p. 206.

Chapter 21

[1]David Hughes, "The Spivs" in *Age of Austerity*, Michael Sissons and Philip French, eds. (Middlesex, England: Penguin, 1964), p. 99.

[2]Susan Cooper, "Snoek Piquante" in Sissons and French, *op, cit.*, p. 38.

[3]*Ibid.*, pp. 40-43.

[4]Henry Pelling, *Modern Britain.* (New York: Norton, 1960), p. 181.

[5]Cooper, *op. cit.*, p. 38.

[6]*Ibid.*, p. 52.

[7]Bertrand de Jouvenel, *Problems of Socialist England* (London: Batchworth Press, 1949), J. F. Huntington, trans., p. 107.

[8]*Ibid.*, p. 173.

[9]Cooper, *op. cit.*, p. 52.

[10]Alfred F. Havighurst, *Twentieth Century Britain* (New York: Harper and Row, 1962, 2nd ed.), p. 402.

[11]Hughes, *op. cit.*, p. 502.

[12]John Jewkes, *The New Ordeal by Planning* (New York: St. Martin's Press, 1968), p. 204.

Chapter 22

[1]Quoted in Donald S. Connery, *The Scandinavians* (New York: Simon and Schuster, 1966), p. 66.

[2]Paul B. Austin, *The Swedes: How They Live and Work* (New York: Praeger, 1970), pp. 89-90.

[3]Stewart Oakley, *A Short History of Sweden* (New York: Praeger, 1966), pp. 208-209.

[4]H.G. Jones, *Planning and Productivity in Sweden* (Totowa, N.J.: Bowman and Littlefield, 1976), pp. 22-23.

[5]*Ibid.*, p. 31.

Chapter 23

[1]Eugen Weber, *A Modern History of Europe* (New York: W. W. Norton, 1971), p. 813.

[2]These figures were taken from Paul B. Austin, *The Swedes* (New York: Praeger, 1970) and should be considered as illustrative rather than final, since the amounts do change from time to time.

[3]*Ibid*, pp. 84-85.

[4]Donald S. Connery, *The Scandinavians* (New York: Simon and Schuster, 1966), p. 392.

Chapter 24

[1]Donald S. Connery, *The Scandinavians* (New York: Simon and Schuster, 1966), p. 296.

[2]*Ibid.*, p. 290.

[3]*Ibid.*

[4]*Ibid.*, p. 436.

Chapter 25

[1]Harold Koontz and Richard W. Gable, *Public Control of Economic Enterprise* (New York: McGraw Hill, 1956), pp. 684-85.

[2]Clair Wilcox, *Public Policies Toward Business* (Homewood, Illinois: Richard D. Irwin, 1960), pp. 805-06.

[3]William Proxmire, *Can Small Business Survive?* (Chicago: Henry Regnery, 1964), pp. 99-101.

[4]Koontz and Gable, *op cit.*, p. 695.

⁵Cornelius P. Cotter, *Government and Private Enterprise* (New York: Holt, Rinehart and Winston, 1960), pp. 227-28.

⁶The present writer has discussed this in detail in *The Fateful Turn* (Irvington, New York: Foundation for Economic Education, 1963) and *The Flight from Reality* (Irvington, New York: Foundation for Economic Education, 1969).

Chapter 31

¹Eugen Weber, *The Western Tradition* (Boston: D.C. Heath, 1959), p. 609.

²John K. Galbraith, *The Affluent Society* (Boston: Houghton Mifflin, 1958), pp. 319-20.

³Matthew 3:8-10 (KJV).

⁴John Barron, *KGB: The Secret Work of Soviet Secret Agents* (New York: Bantam, 1974), p. 2.

⁵Frank S. Meyer, *The Moulding of Communists* in *Omnibus* Volume 3 (New Rochelle, N.Y.: Conservative Book Club, copyright Harcourt, Brace and Co., 1961), p. 25.

⁶Quoted in M. Stanton Evans, *The Politics of Surrender* (New York: Devin-Adair, 1966), p. 26.

⁷*Ibid.*

⁸*Ibid.*, p. 27.

⁹John W. Lewis, ed., *Major Doctrines of Communist China* (New York: Norton, 1964), p. 279.

¹⁰Barron, *op. cit.*, pp. 9-10.

¹¹See, for example, Elizabeth Bentley, *Out of Bondage* in *Omnibus* Volume 6 (New Rochelle, N.Y.: Conservative Book Club, copyright Devin-Adair, 1951), pp. 125-26.

¹²Hugh Seton-Watson, *From Lenin to Malenkov* (New York: Frederick A. Praeger, 1953), pp. 248-49.

¹³*Ibid.*, p. 255.

¹⁴Meyer, *op cit.*, p. 15.

¹⁵Quoted in *ibid.*, p. 14.

¹⁶Quoted in Eugene Lyons, *The Red Decade* (New Rochelle, N.Y.: Arlington House, 1970), p. 47.

¹⁷*Ibid.*, p. 48.

Chapter 32

¹Whittaker Chambers, *Cold Friday* (New York: Random House, 1964), pp. 149-50.

[2]Marguerite Higgins, *Our Vietnam Nightmare* (New York: Harper & Row, 1965), p. 14.

[3]Bernardo Teixeira, *The Fabric of Terror* (New York: Devin-Adair, 1965), p. 100.

[4]Eugene H. Methvin, *The Riot Makers* (New Rochelle, N.Y.: Arlington House, 1970), pp. 361-62.

[5]See *ibid.*, chs. XI-XIII.

[6]See James Michener, *Kent State* (Greenwich, Conn.: Fawcett, 1971), pp. 85-104.

[7]*Ibid.*, p. 222.

[8]Hugh Seton-Watson, *From Lenin to Malenkov* (New York: Frederick A. Praeger, 1953), p. 258.

[9]Paul Bethel, *The Losers* (New Rochelle, N.Y.: Arlington House, 1969), p. 125.

Chapter 33

[1]Franklin L. Baumer, ed., *Main Currents of Western Thought* (New York: Alfred A. Knopf, 1967), p. 736.

[2]Arthur M. Schlesinger, Jr., *The Vital Center* (Boston: Houghton Mifflin, 1962), p. 240.

[3]*Ibid.*, pp. 239-40.

Chapter 34

[1]Harry B. Price, *The Marshall Plan and Its Meaning* (Ithaca, N.Y.: Cornell University Press, 1955), p. 172.

[2]Robin W. Winks, ed., *The Marshall Plan and the American Economy* (New York: Henry Holt and Co., 1960), p. 15.

[3]*Ibid.*, p. 25.

[4]Selig Adler, *The Isolationist Impulse* (New York: The Free Press, 1957), p. 365.

[5]Ludwig von Mises, *Omnipotent Government* (New Rochelle, N.Y.: Arlington House, 1969), pp. 72-73.

[6]Hugh Ross, ed., *The Cold War: Containment and Its Critics* (Chicago: Rand McNally, 1963), p. 7.

[7]Winks, *op. cit.*, p. 14.

[8]*Ibid.*

[9]Harry S. Truman, *Memoirs*, II, *Years of Trial and Hope* (Garden City, N.Y.: Doubleday, 1956), p. 114.

[10]Price, *op. cit.*, p. 39.

[11]See *ibid.,* pp. 121-22.

[12]*Ibid.,* p. 44.

[13]Truman, *op. cit.,* p. 232.

[14]*Ibid.,* p. 237.

[15]Donald B. Cole, *Handbook of American History* (New York: Harcourt, Brace, & World, 1968), p. 287.

[16]Price, *op. cit.,* p. 205.

[17]*Ibid.,* pp. 205-06.

Chapter 35

[1]Forrest McDonald, Leslie E. Decker and Thomas P. Govan, *The Last Best Hope: A History of the United States* (Reading, Mass.: Addison Wesley, 1972), p. 950.

[2]See Ignacy Sachs, *The Discovery of the Third World* (Cambridge, Mass.: MIT Press, 1976), p. xi.

[3]Arthur J. May, *Europe Since 1939* (New York: Holt, Rinehart and Winston, 1966), p. 435.

[4]Erik von Kuehnelt-Leddihn, *Leftism* (New Rochelle, N.Y.: Arlington House, 1974), pp. 78-83.

[5]*Ibid.,* pp. 107-08.

[6]Sachs, *op. cit.,* p. xi.

[7]May, *op. cit., p. 368.*

[8]Franklin L. Baumer, ed., *Main Currents of Western Thought* (New York: Alfred A. Knopf, 1964), p. 712.

[9]May, *op. cit.,* p. 430.

[10]Leo Paul de Alvarez, "Imperialism: The Threat to Existence," *The Intercollegiate Review,* II (March-April, 1966), p. 312.

[11]Thomas Molnar, "Neo-Colonialism in Africa?" *Modern Age,* IX (Spring 1965), p. 178.

[12]Robert S. Walters, *American and Soviet Aid* (Pittsburgh: University of Pittsburgh Press, 1970), pp. 29-30.

[13]Joseph Schiebel, "Convergence or Confrontation?" *The Intercollegiate Review,* V (Winter, 1968-69), p. 110.

[14]I. Kapranov, "The USSR and Industrial Development of Newly Free States," in *Internationalism, National Liberation and Our Epoch* (Moscow: Novosti Press Agency, n.d.), p. 104.

[15]Leo Tansky, *U.S. and U.S.S.R. Aid to Developing Countries* (New York: Frederick A. Praeger, 1967), p. vi.

[16]John F. Cooper, *China's Foreign Aid* (Lexington, Mass.: D.C. Heath, 1976), p. 1.

[17]Pierre Jalee, *The Pillage of the Third World* (New York: Monthly Review Press, 1968), p. 110.

[18]William H. Chamberlin, "Communism in Disarray," *Modern Age,* IX (Spring 1965), p. 192.

[19]Boris Meissner, "World Communism: Decay or Differentiation," *Modern Age,* IX (Summer 1965), p. 244.

[20]See de Alvarez, *op. cit.,* p. 312.

[21]See Sachs, *The Discovery of the Third World, op. cit., passim,* especially the concluding chapter.

Chapter 37

[1]John Fowles, *Daniel Martin* (New York: New American Library, 1978), p. 336. This is spoken by a character in a novel and does not necessarily indicate the opinion of the author.

Chapter 38

[1]See Ludwig von Mises, *Socialism* (London: Jonathan Cape, 1951), pp. 135-37.

[2]*The Gulag Archipelago,* III (New York: Harper & Row, 1978), pp. 58-60.

[3]"Utopia's Dark Side," *Newsweek* (May 3, 1976), p. 38.

Chapter 39

[1]Eugene Lyons, *Workers' Paradise Lost* (New York: Twin Circle, 1967), p. 217.

[2]William H. Whyte, Jr., *The Organization Man* (Garden City, N.Y., Doubleday Anchor, 1957), p. 6.

[3]Matthew 10:29-31. (This and all quotations below are from the King James Version of the Bible.)

[4]Matthew 12:10-12.

[5]John 3:16.

[6]Matthew 5:3-10.

[7]Romans 12:9-21.

[8]II Peter 1:5-7.

[9]Philipians 4:8.

[10]Isaiah 9:6.

[11]Ephesians 4:28.

[12]John 12:32.

[13]Zechariah 4:6.

[14]John 14:12.

[15]Matthew 5:13, 14.

[16]Matthew 7:7-8.

[17]Ephesians 6:11-17.

Chapter 40

[1]Matthew 6:28-31, 33.

[2]See Clarence B. Carson, *The War on the Poor* (New Rochelle, N.Y.: Arlington House, 1969), pp. 107-11.

[3]Erik von Kuehnelt-Leddihn, *Leftism* (New Rochelle, N.Y.: Arlington House, 1974), p. 403.

[4]Leonard E. Read, *Notes from FEE* (March, 1979), p. 1.

Index

558

Social Security, 315, 320-21, 340, 355, 366-67, 482, 489-91, 516
Society, 67, 99, 104-9, 117, 151, 153, 160-61, 183-84, 201, 204, 206-8, 211, 215-17, 219-20, 269, 276, 284, 301, 352, 354-58, 361, 363-64, 368, 370, 408-9, 413-15, 420, 429, 454, 466-67, 497-98, 512, 521-22
Socrates, 300
Solon, 202
Solzhenitsyn, Alexsandr, 87, 93-95, 104, 150, 481, 487
Southey, Robert, 199
South Korea, 422
Soviet constitutions, 73-74
Soviet Peace Committee, 75
Soviet Union (Union of Soviet Socialist Republics), vii-viii, 5, 15, 37, 43, 58, 70-76, 79-80, 83-86, 96-97, 100, 102, 105, 106, 108-9, 114, 154-55, 157-58, 162-63, 165, 172-73, 175-78, 182, 187-88, 191-92, 244, 249, 250, 273, 282, 373-74, 375, 379, 381, 394, 396, 401, 408, 430, 431, 438, 442, 444-45, 449, 461, 494, 501, 515. See also Russia
Spain, 174, 178-79, 188
Spencer, Herbert, 200, 216, 228-29
Spengler, Oswald, 182
Speer, Albert, 157-58, 161
Square Deal, 331
SS, 144, 146, 149-50, 166, 169, 170, 174, 188-89, 191

Stalingrad, 178
Stalinism, 19
Stalin, Joseph, viii, 43-44, 46, 66, 72, 74, 84-85, 97-98, 109, 113, 115-16, 131, 155, 157-60, 173, 176-77, 182, 192, 244, 358, 373, 378-79, 388, 391-93, 397, 401, 406, 442, 447, 457, 515
Star of David, 146
State, 24-25, 27, 34, 36, 44, 61, 66-68, 75, 82-83, 85, 99-100, 104, 109, 117-18, 133, 141, 148, 150, 153, 163-64, 185, 190, 206-7, 211-12, 220, 224, 228-29, 238, 277, 284, 286-87, 289,93, 295-97, 306-8, 388, 435, 453, 454-55, 458, 475, 479, 481, 490, 497, 501-2, 504, 515
State Council for Religious Affairs (Soviet), 75
Statistics, 102, 184, 491-92, 494
Steel Act of 1949 (British), 257
Stockholm, 273
Stolypin, Piotr, 50
Storm Troopers (SA), 124, 128, 132, 136-38, 144, 145, 146, 149-50, 165
Stotski, Andrey A., 91
Strachey, Lytton, 207
Strasser, Gregor, 138
Students for a Democratic Society (SDS), 407
Sudetenland, 250
Suez Crisis, 439
Supreme Soviet, 71-72
Sweden, 177, 178, 188, 273-309, 422, 490, 514

561

Veterans Administration (VA), 342
Vanya, 93
Versailles, Treaty of, 120, 138, 149, 190
Victoria, Queen, 201, 207, 232, 242
Victorian, 198, 199, 201-3, 203-5, 206-8, 212, 251
Viet Cong, 402, 405
Vietnam (North), 402
Vietnam (South), 4, 332, 382-83, 402, 404-7, 423, 461
Vikings, 279, 285
Vyshinsky, Andrei, 91

Wagner, Richard, 182
Wales, 245, 257
Wallace, George, 404
Wallas, Graham, 210
War communism, 84
War on Poverty, 234
Warsaw, 191-92
Washington (D.C.), 333, 384, 405, 431, 439, 446
Washington Naval Conference, 249
Watergate, 7, 337
Weaver, Richard, 8
Webb, Beatrice Potter, 210
Webb, Sidney, 32, 36, 210, 216, 217, 220, 238
Weimar Republic, 120-22, 124-25, 127, 138
Welfare state, 228-29, 238, 243, 256-57, 274, 284, 288-89, 290, 385
Welfare state capitalism, 281-82, 284
Wels, Otto, 143

West Germany, 374, 427
West, Rebecca, 210
White Russians, 399
Whyte, William H., 502
Wilhelm I (Kaiser), 118
Wilhelm II (Kaiser), 4, 118, 119, 242
Wilkie, Wendell, 129
William IV (1830-1837), 232
Wilson, Harold, 269
Wilson, Woodrow, 171, 331, 332, 427
Winter Palace, 56-57, 407
Witan, 287
Witte, Sergei, 50
Wolfe, Bertram D., 19
Workmen's Compensation Act (British), 230
World government, 415-16
World War I, 4, 48, 49-51, 59, 68, 119-20, 121, 125, 171, 175, 235, 237-38, 240, 243, 246, 252, 265, 299, 326, 430, 458, 516
World War II, viii, 3, 91, 125, 154-55, 168-93, 240, 267, 331-32, 373-74, 395, 401, 421-22, 425, 427, 430, 432, 434, 441, 443, 446, 516
Wurmbrand, Richard, 75, 93, 411

Yakuts, 49
Yalta Conference, 192
Yugoslavia, 192, 242
Yurasov, Vladimir, 161-62
Yurovsky, 15

Zinoviev, Gregory, 114-15
Zionists, 114-15